TO

𝔓ast 𝔊reat 𝔈ncohonee

GEORGE W. LINDSAY

BALTIMORE, MD.

IN RECOGNITION OF HIS WORTH AS A MAN, HIS CONSCIENTIOUS
RESEARCH INTO THE HISTORY OF

THE IMPROVED ORDER OF RED MEN

AND HIS UNSWERVING LOYALTY AND DEVOTION TO OUR

BELOVED FRATERNITY

THIS HISTORY IS RESPECTFULLY AND FRATERNALLY

DEDICATED BY

THE PUBLISHERS

ADDITIONAL CONTRIBUTORS.

Thomas K. Donnalley, P. G. I.	Philadelphia, Pa.
Daniel M. Stevens, G. C. of R.	Camden, N. J.
J. P. Gardner, G. C. of R.	Boston, Mass.
John M. Hinkle, P. G. S.	Elmira, N. Y.
Thomas G. Harrison, G. C. of R.	Indianapolis, Ind.
Thomas J. Irwin, G. C. of R.	Martin's Ferry, O.
Henry A. Anthony, G. C. of R.	Baltimore, Md.
Jacob Emmel, G. C. of R.	Atlanta, Ga.
Ira T. Holt, G. C. of R.	Norfolk, Va.
J. W. Maher, G. C. of R.	San Francisco, Cal.
Edwin Hirst, P. G. S.	Wilmington, Del.
Thomas H. H. Messinger, Jr., G. C. of R.	Wilmington, Del.
John W. Hatstat, P. G. S.	Hartford, Ct.
Charles W. Skiff, G. C. of R.	Danbury, Ct.
Charles W. Howe, G. C. of R.	Rochester, N. H.
George H. Tandy, G. C. of R.	Freeport, Ill.
C. W. Foster, P. G. S.	Woodfords, Me.
A. B. McCown, G. C. of R.	Des Moines, Ia.
W. E. Davis, P. G. S.	Des Moines, Ia.
John B. Paterson, P. S.	Denver, Col.
Henry Klefus, G. C. of R.	Denver, Col.
John F. Clark, P. G. S.	Providence, R. I.
H. C. Ulrich, G. C. of R.	Lazearville, W. Va.
L. E. Hirst, P. G. S.	Grafton, W. Va.
Fred C. Temple, G. C. of R.	Grand Rapids, Mich.
J. H. E. Wiegant, G. C. of R.	Leavenworth, Kan.
H. M. Austin, G. C. of R.	Birmingham, Ala.
Will L. Scism, P. S.	Omaha, Neb.
George T. Walker, G. C. of R.	Glendale, S. C.
T. E. Price, G. C. of R. of Louisiana	New Lewisville, Ark.
James E. Dement, G. C. of R.	Washington, D. C.
Louis E. Kaltwasser, Great Sachem	St. Louis, Mo.
George W. Davis, G. C. of R.	Nashville, Tenn.
Robert E. Davis, G. C. of R.	Gainesville, Fla.
Robert J. Hanson, P. G. S.	Gainesville, Fla.
J. W. Mahood, G. C. of R.	Virginia City, Nev.
F. H. Saylor, G. C. of R.	Portland, Ore.
Thomas D. Tanner, P. G. S.	Easton, Pa.

ON THE TRAIL.

Official History of the Improved Order of Red Men

COMPILED UNDER AUTHORITY FROM THE

GREAT COUNCIL OF THE UNITED STATES

BY PAST GREAT INCOHONEES:

George W. Lindsay *of* MARYLAND

Charles C. Conley *of* PENNSYLVANIA

Charles H. Litchman *of* MASSACHUSETTS

EDITED BY

Charles H. Litchman

Past Great Incohonee

HERITAGE BOOKS
2012

HERITAGE BOOKS
AN IMPRINT OF HERITAGE BOOKS, INC.

Books, CDs, and more—Worldwide

For our listing of thousands of titles see our website
at
www.HeritageBooks.com

A Facsimile Reprint
Published 2012 by
HERITAGE BOOKS, INC.
Publishing Division
100 Railroad Ave. #104
Westminster, Maryland 21157

Copyright © 1893 Lee C. Hascall

— Publisher's Notice —
In reprints such as this, it is often not possible to remove blemishes from the original. We feel the contents of this book warrant its reissue despite these blemishes and hope you will agree and read it with pleasure.

International Standard Book Numbers
Paperbound: 978-0-7884-9500-7
Clothbound: 978-0-7884-9302-7

PREFACE.

To write history requires a love for the subject treated. Patriotism, love of country, a desire to preserve to posterity the annals of the past and the memory of noble deeds of a brave ancestry, have mainly inspired general historical work. None the less important and interesting to a fraternal organization is the collection in permanent form of the facts and traditions concerning its history. So well understood is this, that the best thought of every such organization has been called upon to place before the members thereof a record of the past that should be at once a pride and an inspiration; a pride of duty well done; an inspiration to greater achievements in the future.

With these thoughts in view, the Official History of the Improved Order of Red Men has been compiled, and is now offered to the fraternal consideration of the members of the Order. Full value and credit is due and cheerfully accorded to the work of that esteemed brother, now gone to join the Silent Majority, whose researches have entwined an interesting and valuable story around the theory that makes 1813 the date of the origin of our Order. Having at our command the originals of the documents upon which his work was based, there has been no hesitation in using such portions as were necessary to properly illustrate that part of the history of the Order herein treated as the second epoch in its chronology.

But the Great Council of the United States, after patient investigation and consideration of the researches of P. G. I. Lindsay, having decided that the traditions which gave inspiration to an organization, and the earlier movements that finally crystallized into active force, are justly to be considered parts of its history and necessary to truthfully trace its origin, this history has been compiled upon the theory that the Improved Order of Red Men had its origin in those patriotic associations existing prior to the American Revolution of 1776, and by whose influence freedom was secured to the Colonies, and our Republic launched among the nations of the earth.

These early societies turned to the uncultivated field of Red Men's mysteries for their ceremonies and so-called secret work, and in the sublimity and grandeur of the unsullied characteristics of the primitive race, then more plentiful around them, found inspiration for the mystical lore deemed necessary in their gatherings, and suitable for the concealment of identity inseparable from the dangerous work in which they were engaged to found a new nation.

This use of the forms and customs of the North American Indians as the basis of the ceremonies of these original organizations of 1771, of 1813, and of our Order, has compelled a study of their manners and peculiarities. No one can enter upon a study of the traditions and characteristics of the Indian race without coming under the spell of an enticing fascination, and becoming profoundly impressed with the noble traits of character possessed by the Aborigines of the American continent. The chapters of this book devoted to a sketch of their forms, manners, customs, and peculiarities are, to the writers, not the least of its attractions. No attempt has been made to give anything original in this direction. All available material has been long since exhausted, and each successive writer could be original only in the use of material gained from a common source. Due and appropriate credit has been given for the work of others, and the aim has been to show to the member of the Improved Order of Red Men who may read these pages, that in the origin, growth, and history of our Order are a strength of purpose, a beauty of conception, and an inspiration of character unexcelled by any fraternal organization.

PREFACE.

To those Great Chiefs of the United States and of the several State reservations, who have contributed the data necessary for a proper compilation of the work done in their respective localities, due acknowledgment and thanks are returned.

In submitting the result of our labors to the Order, we ask fraternal forbearance for any errors of omission or commission. Many, doubtless, could have done better than we with the material at hand. But no one could take up the work of compilation with more sincere love for the Order, with more genuine interest in its origin, history, and progress, or with a more abiding faith in its ultimate great prosperity.

The publishers have done everything in their power to make the book attractive and worthy the Order of which it is the history.

The illustrations are most valuable and interesting, many of them having been engraved at great expense from original drawings by well-known artists.

CONTENTS.

	PAGE
LIST OF ILLUSTRATIONS	9
INTRODUCTION	11

CHAPTER I.

Outline of Subject; Scope intended; How treated; Why written . . 17

CHAPTER II.

Primitive Red Men; The Race that welcomed the Pilgrims; Their Characteristics; Their Peculiar Forms and Customs; The League of the Iroquois 23

CHAPTER III.

Patriotic Societies at and prior to 1776; Their Motive; Their Need of Secrecy; Sons of Tammany in Maryland, Pennsylvania, and New York; Sons of Liberty in Massachusetts; Their Influence on the Formation and Conduct of the American Republic; Legend of Tammany 149

CHAPTER IV.

Societies of Red Men from 1812 to 1834; Their Management, Aims, and History 199

CHAPTER V.

Organization of the Improved Order of Red Men at Baltimore, Md.; Why this Name was selected; Those Instrumental in securing the Result 247

CHAPTER VI.

Organization of the Improved Order of Red Men at Baltimore — Another Version 270

CHAPTER VII.

The Great Council of the United States: its Origin, Powers, and Laws; Its Objects, Jurisdiction, and History from Organization. First Section, from 1847 to Council of 1880 281

CHAPTER VIII.

The Great Council of the United States: its Origin, Powers, and Laws; Its Objects, Jurisdiction, and History from Organization. Second Section, from 1881 to Date of Publication 303

CHAPTER IX.

State Great Councils; When and where instituted; Condition at Date of Publication 423

CHAPTER X.

Biographies of Prominent Members 449

CHAPTER XI.

Digest of the Decisions, Laws, Rulings, etc., of the Great Council of the United States, corrected to Date of Publication 475

CHAPTER XII.

Legislation, Constitutions, etc. 539

CHAPTER XIII.

Degree of Pocahontas; Origin, Purpose, and Growth 588

CHAPTER XIV.

Chieftains' League; Origin, Objects, and Present Condition . . . 595

CHAPTER XV.

The Degrees of the Order; The Theory of their Construction; The Lessons taught 605

CHAPTER XVI.

Nomenclature of the Order and Calendar 611

INDEX 619

LIST OF ILLUSTRATIONS.

On the Trail	Frontispiece
	PAGE
An Iroquois Warrior	Facing 32
Niagara Falls	" 44
An Iroquois Woman	" 74
Totems of the North American Indians	. 119
Robe of Mah-to-toh-pa, a Mandan Chief	. 130
Captured by the Braves	Facing 180
The Rain Maker	" 204
Call for a Meeting of the Society of Red Men	. 234
Return of the Hunters	Facing 244
Enlisting for the War Path	" 270
William G. Gorsuch, First Great Incohonee	" 282
Andrew J. Baker	" 314
Joseph Pyle	" 314
George W. Lindsay	" 314
Adam Smith	" 314
Badge of the Order	. 348
Flag of the Order	. 361
Morris H. Gorham	Facing 368
Charles H. Litchman	" 368
George B. Colflesh	" 368
William H. Hyronemus	" 368
Ralph S. Gregory	" 392
Charles C. Conley	" 392
Thomas J. Francis	" 392
Thomas K. Donnalley	" 392
Veteran Badge	. 421
Thomas E. Peckinpaugh, Great Incohonee	Facing 422
The Captive's Rescue	" 588
The Paleface Friend	" 594
Invoking the Great Spirit	" 604

INTRODUCTION.

THE wonderful progress and popularity of the Improved Order of Red Men have earned for it the prominent position it occupies among the social fraternities of the United States. There are many causes for its phenomenal increase in numbers and influence. The Order has intrinsic merit as a society which teaches and exemplifies the principles of friendship and brotherly helpfulness. Its precepts inspire all with the spirit of fraternal love and good fellowship, and with the divine idea of the brotherhood of man, and bring to the surface the generous impulses which tend to pleasant, harmonious relations among men. Its teachings refine their natures, ennoble their characters, and awaken their minds to highest aspirations. It especially appeals to the patriotic sentiments of the American citizen because of its origin, its traditions, and its ceremonies. We have been criticised in some instances because of our title, and the supposed barbarism of our ceremonials; but every true, intelligent Red Man takes great delight in the fact that we are the acknowledged conservators of the history, the customs, and the virtues of the original American people, — a people conceded by the early travellers and writers to have been intelligent, brave, and free, loyal in its friendships, generous in its hospitalities, and with many traits of character worthy of emulation by the civilized race. The Improved Order of Red Men is proud to perpetuate the memory of this, the noblest type of man in his natural state that has ever been discovered. Who will say that the civilization and the moral development of Montezuma and his people do not compare favorably with the brutality and greed of Cortez and his adventurers? Who will claim that the Pizarro and his followers excelled in any way the kind and hospitable Incas and their nation? In their knowledge of architecture, of the decorative arts, of the sciences, and in their agricultural and industrial skill, they had little or nothing to learn from their discoverers.

Not less wonderful than the Aztec of Central and South America was the North American Indian, the prototype of our organization. In addition to the complimentary descriptions of the early writers, we have the beautiful legends of the Aborigines which have descended to us to prove their courage, their intellectuality, their loyalty, their kindness of disposition, their moral worth, and their lofty conception of a Creator and Ruler of the universe. Through all the traditions of the Tribes and Nations there runs the belief in an ideal man, endowed by the Great Spirit with all the human attributes in perfection, who was to his people the highest type of physical strength and beauty, whose heart overflowed with love for his tribe and people, and whose knowledge and wisdom surpassed all others. He it was who taught them to love and help each other, to hunt, to fish, to fight, to plant, to build. He told them of the strength there was in unity. History records no coalition more wonderful than that of the Hodenosaunee, known to us as the League of the Iroquois. For centuries it stood unmoved and unbroken by any of the weakening internal or external influences, which have laid low so many of the mighty empires of the earth. It was not until long after the advent of the paleface invader that it fell asunder. It is said that the 13th successive Great Sachem was at its head when the white man first appeared. Hayowentha was the ideal man who came to them with Daganoweda in the beginning, who brought the nations together, gave them instruction and good advice, created their democratic form of government, which was a system of equality of rights with a common ownership of property. Honor was given to whom honor was due, and the brave and experienced, the true, the generous, and the wise only were given the posts of dignity and authority. He it was who smoked with them the calumet of peace, from which the smoke ascended to the Great Spirit, bearing their words of amity, and who gave them the sacred wampum belt, into which their vows of fealty and the compact of their union had been talked. It is a praiseworthy indication of their freedom from the meaner vices, that their code of laws had no reference to theft, because stealing was an unknown practice among them.

Their ideas of the Supreme Being compare favorably with those of the nations of greater pretensions. It is true the Indians had an evil spirit, the Mache Maneto, who was not much more than an incident, or exemplification of the ills which assail humanity; but their Kishe Maneto was a Good Spirit, indeed, not an implacable jealous God, dealing eternal punishments, but an altogether kind, merciful, generous Being, who filled the earth with corn and game, and brought death only as a means to translate the Red Man to eternal hunting grounds of peace, plenty, and perfect happiness. Thus it was a deserved compliment to the aboriginal people of this country that the earlier social and patriotic societies of America designated themselves and their purposes by use of Indian appellations. In the following pages the historian has traced the line of connection from these scattered associations to our present organization, and our brotherhood will therein find much to give it a laudable pride and pleasure in its aboriginal and patriotic ancestry.

In all the great suns through which the thread of our record runs, we have added to those thoughts, those aspirations, and those deeds which occupy the mind and give incentive to the action of Improved Red Men, until their hearts bear, deep stamped, the impress of our motto — "Freedom, Friendship, and Charity." Freedom, in honor of that race to whom the forests, the plains, the hills, and the valleys of this land were as free as the air to the eagle, and in memory of the early struggles to wrest these United States from dependency to foreign rule. Friendship, to commemorate the unswerving loyalty with which an Indian maintained a noble and unselfish affection for him to whom it was plighted, and which makes sweet and lasting the relations in which the members of our Order are united.

It is in the beautiful spirit of friendship that the Red Man holds the social and brotherly intercourse in our wigwams, which broaden his character, enlarge his heart, educate his faculties, give him amusement and recreation, and altogether help him to be a sober, upright, intelligent citizen, a better husband, father, son, or brother, and a man more qualified in every way to perform his duties and to enjoy the world. A man possessing the friendships formed in the Improved Order of Red Men with men who trust and believe in him, and in whom he believes and trusts, builds up a self-respect and a desire for the esteem of others which restrain him from many of the excesses into which he might otherwise be led. Thus we have Freedom and Friendship, ours by historical right, ours because we are the exponents of the virtues of a great departing race, ours because we are the lineal descendants of American patriots, and had our beginnings in the patriotic impulses that gave freedom to America, and ours, because, although we are a hundred and two score thousand, we are one, — one in object, one in name, and one in brotherhood.

We have also Charity, that charity —

> "which needs not be sought,
> Waits not for want to plead,
> But seeks the duty,
> Nay, prevents the need;"

and that charity which is love; which is expressed to a brother by the smiles of those who meet him around the brightly burning council fire; by the fraternal greeting in which he feels a responsive heart thrill in unison with the warm clasp of a brother's hand; by the sympathy which is pleased at his success, and which is grieved at his sorrows and disappointments. Such is the charity we seek to exemplify, in which the spirit of brotherly love and brotherly helpfulness go hand in hand, which cultivates the spirit of forbearance and good-fellowship, which tends to harmony.

The primary objects of our Order are to promote among men the exercise and practice of the true principles of benevolence and charity, the care and protection of the widows and orphans of its members, and the cultivation of friendly relations with those who have entered its circle. The democratic influences which attended its birth, the idea that all men are equal, are the tenets of the Order; and what a man is, not what he possesses, constitutes his claim for recognition among the brotherhood.

Friendship, fraternity, and hospitality are exemplified as cardinal virtues, and nowhere are hearts brought closer together than around the council fires of the Red Men. In sickness or distress a brother is visited, comforted, and assisted; and when the arrow of death has removed him from his trail on earth, he is buried by his brothers, who continue a watchful, protective care for his widow and orphans.

Our Order is a brotherhood of individuals whose personal characteristics are not sacrificed, but whose common interests are maintained and strengthened as the members harmonize around our council fires. We are proud of it for its past; we love it for what it is to us; and we hope much for its future. As the American citizen feels the patriotic blood tingle in his veins while reading the early pages of his country's history, so our hearts throb as we remember that the societies of Tamina and of Red Men were a part of that history; and every true Improved Red Man feels an added dignity and sense of responsibility because it is so. The virtues of the Aborigines are taught in the speaking books of the Society which is named for them, and are engraved on the trophies which hang in the wigwams where Red Men meet. When the Indian has disappeared forever from the hills and the valleys, the forest and the stream, then the paleface who occupies his wigwam, who owns the land where once he trailed, will look upon the skins and scalps which long before were brought home from the hunt or from the warpath, will take down the totem by which the primitive Red Man distinguished his friend from his foe, and from them teach object-lessons of the history of his county, and of Freedom, Friendship, and Charity to the coming young American.

There is and always will be much of sorrow and disappointment and death in this world; and inasmuch as the Improved Order of Red Men eases the burden of pain and brightens the pathway of life, it is a blessing and of value to man. We are entitled to its being and continuance as we are to the sunshine from the Great Spirit. May our Tribes multiply and increase, until the whole world shall feel the spell of our brotherhood, and may the seeds of fraternity we sow be ever watered by the divine showers of harmony to bring forth the flower of hope and the fruit of happiness.

Andrew H. Paton, *G.S.S.*, *G.C.U.S.*

CHAPTER I.

OUTLINE OF SUBJECT.

It is the intention that these pages shall gather in permanent form an authentic record of all available material bearing upon the origin, history, and objects of the Improved Order of Red Men; a record which shall inform members of matters now obscure, and those not members, of the beauties, excellencies, and peculiarities of a fraternity having a name which to them seems odd and grotesque.

From the traditions of the past will be given the evidence upon which is based our claim that the inspiration of the Order is the same that gave birth to the Republic. From existing records will be given such facts as show the evolution of the present magnificent fraternity of 130,000 members from the handful of self-sacrificing brothers, whose fidelity and patriotism fanned into flame the dying embers of the past epochs of the Order, and handed down to posterity the fraternity of to-day.

The compilation of this history has, of necessity, compelled an investigation into the history and peculiarities of that remarkable race which owned America only four hundred years ago, and upon whose customs the work of the Order is founded. Why this is done is stated at length in its proper place.

That there is a demand for the information here given, is apparent to all in any way active in the affairs of the Order. It has been manifested by correspondence, petition, and memorial to the Great Council of the United States, and in other ways.

At various times the Great Council of the United States has taken action by which to fix authoritatively the date of the organization of the Order. The elaborate research of Past Great Incohonee Morris H. Gorham, based upon documents recovered from the Society of Red Men, and now in the possession of the Great Council of the United States, sought to establish Fort Mifflin on the Delaware River, and a date approximating to the year 1813, as the place and time of the origin of our Order. Further research in another direction by Past Great Incohonee George W. Lindsay, of Maryland, collected testimony of sufficient strength to secure the subsequent endorsement of the Great Council of the United States, that the origin of the Order dated back even before 1813, and to the patriotic societies that existed prior to the American Revolution.

In collating the material upon which this history is based, it has been deemed fair to all interests concerned, as well as with a proper regard to historical fact, to consider the history of the Order as covering three epochs. First, that of tradition; second, that of supposition; and third, that of actual written record. It is true that the societies existing previous to the year 1813 made no use of the name of Red Men as a part of the title by which they were known. "Saint Tammany's Society" was a frequent appellation in the Middle and Southern States. In Boston an organization known as "Sons of Liberty" seems to have been organized with the same spirit, and to perform the same services, and the well-known fact will be recalled, that, on a certain important date, a party of men, "disguised as Indians," rushed down to the wharf by the water-side and pitched into Boston Harbor the tea which had been imported, but which the colonists refused to receive, and pay taxes upon. Undoubtedly these various societies had means of communication. Their purposes were identical, noble, and patriotic. The business in which they were engaged was extremely dangerous. If they succeeded they were heroes. If they failed they were traitors. Hence the necessity of some method of concealing their personal identity. Instinctively they turned to the Aboriginal race, then near neighbors, and on the manners and customs of that race founded the ritualistic work necessary for their purpose and for the concealment of their personal identity. It is a remarkable fact, which may be used to substantiate our claim that these earlier societies were followed in direct lineal descent by the Society of Red Men at Fort Mifflin and by the Improved Order of Red Men at Baltimore, that the customs and manners, and, indeed, some of the identical ceremonies, have descended in the ritualistic work of the Order. We have elsewhere given an account of that unfortunate race driven westward from the hunting-grounds and graves of their fathers and relatives, their lands devastated, their wigwams destroyed, and their very existence wiped off the face of the earth. As time passes and their history exists only in tradition, our Order will have historical value beyond even present estimation.

The first epoch in the history of the Order, then, will be covered by such references as seem necessary to be made to the Tammany Societies and other similar organizations existing previously to 1812.

The second epoch in the history of the Order will be fully covered by the records of the Society of Red Men that existed in Pennsylvania, branching out into the other States, from 1813 down to 1830.

The actual historical period, comprising the third epoch in the history, is given elsewhere in the extracts from the written record, from the organization of the Great Council of Maryland, followed by that of the Great Council of the United States, down to, and including, the council held at Atlanta, Ga., in September, 1892.

Among those who organized the Improved Order of Red Men in Baltimore, in 1835, was William Muirhead, who had been a member of the Society of Red Men, whose headquarters were at Philadelphia, Pa. A notable instance of membership, forming this connecting link between the Society of Red Men and the Improved Order of Red Men, may be mentioned in Past Great Incohonee Richard Marley. Richard Marley joined the Society of Red Men at Philadelphia, September 14, 1824. The records in our possession prove that the Order at that time was flourishing, and extending itself in various portions of the country. The meeting of Red Men which took place on the 13th of March, 1834, comprised members of prior but extinct tribes. Among them was an old Red Man, formerly of Philadelphia, who held the position of brigadier-general of the Society under Generalissimo Lappopetung, or Black Wampum, who gave warrant and authority to their proceedings. In every case of the adoption of a paleface into the Society of

Red Men, a new name was entered upon the record, by which the newly-made brother was known in the Society. On page 503, Vol. V., Record Great Council of the United States, are given the names of the brothers who organized the Great Council of Maryland, Society of Red Men, on the 20th day of the 5th moon in the season of blossoms in the year 1835, as well as the Indian titles by which they were designated on the records of the Society. If the early written record of the Society of Red Men was in existence and could be produced, we think it would show as complete a chain of connection between that Society and the societies of the revolutionary period as is shown between the Society of Red Men and its successor, the Improved Order of Red Men.

The following pages will give information concerning these earlier patriotic societies whose existence began about 1765, under the name of Sons of Liberty. A branch of this organization became the Saint Tamina Society of Annapolis, Md., in 1771. The Tamina Society, or Columbian Order of New York, was organized in 1789. Mention is made of these Tamina Societies at various times until the organizations of the Society of Red Men, which it is claimed took place at Fort Mifflin, on the Delaware, in 1813, and which certainly occurred previous to 1816. We know that members of this Society of Red Men, existing from 1816 to 1832, assisted at the organization or afterwards became members of the Improved Order of Red Men. From the fact that the Society of Red Men used the forms and customs of the Aborigines, and in many of their ceremonies were identical with the Saint Tamina Societies that preceded it, it does not require a vivid imagination to believe that those who organized the Society of Red Men were, or had been, of some Saint Tamina Society.

There will be found substantial ground for this assumption in the fact that Saint Tamina Day, which was celebrated on the 12th of May of each year, was observed by the army from the time of the Revolution down to just before the opening of the War of 1812, when, by order of the Secretary of War, the festival was forbidden among the troops. Saint Tamina was as popular among the citizens as among the soldiers, and the 12th of May was observed by them in like manner. One branch of this society, now existing in New York, was organized in 1789, by William Mooney, who had been a leader among the Sons of Liberty, and who was familiar with the usages of the earlier organizations, some of which were incorporated in the new organization.

A brief sketch of the organization of the Order in each reservation is necessarily included, and the date of institution of the first Tribe in each State, and of the kindling of the council fire of each State Great Council, forming a comprehensive, even though brief, history of the progress of the Order throughout the United States.

In many reservations several attempts were made to kindle council fires of the Order before success was attained, and by reason of this fact, much confusion exists as to the exact date of the institution of the Order therein. The present Great Chiefs, having nothing but the record of the latest organization to guide them, have placed the date of origin according to the information they possessed, while the records of the Great Council of the United States show an earlier origin. In all cases where this verification from the record of the Great Council of the United States can be made, we have given the date according to the record, even if it became necessary to change that stated by the Great Chiefs of any reservation.

For a long time the strength of the Order was confined to Maryland and Virginia. It was some years after the institution of the Order in these reservations before it had become firmly established in the reservation of Pennsylvania. It attained strength and power in many States where it does not now exist, and likewise strong and vigorous State Great Councils now hold control in reservations where the institution of the Order is of comparatively recent date.

Biographical sketches will be given of prominent members of the Order. It has been thought best to restrict these to biographies of the Past Great Incohonees, as to go beyond that would far exceed the space at our disposal. Surely all our members will be interested to know who have presided over the Great Council of the United States, and to learn something of their personality.

The two side Degrees which have been established as adjuncts to the Order will be fully treated and described. The Degree of Pocahontas has had a career of wonderful prosperity since its organization, and continues to grow in strength and popular favor in the Order. The Chieftains' League, with its attractive uniform of the Continental soldier, satisfies the desires of those who wish a uniformed branch of the Order. While the growth of the League has been slow, it has been sure, and its future progress and prosperity seem certain.

The laws by which a body is governed form the best index of the wisdom and tact of those who control it. In the chapter devoted to the Legislation of the Order will be given an outline of its interior government, and a complete copy of the latest revision of the Digest of Decisions issued by the Great Council of the United States. This chapter is a comprehensive epitome of the rules and regulations of the Order, and gives to the members in compact form a thorough knowledge of the laws by which they are governed.

The Degrees of our Order stand unique and original. Each is intended to teach a lesson illustrative of Indian life and Indian characteristics. It has been deemed proper, therefore, to present an indication of the theory upon which each Degree is founded, and to explain the lesson thereby taught.

The imagery and beauty of the Indian language, wherein every word was really a picture of the idea sought to be expressed, is alluded to in the chapter devoted to the nomenclature of the Order. Indelibly stamped upon the rivers and lakes and mountains of our land is the nomenclature of the Aborigines of the American continent, and long after every other trace of that wonderful people shall have passed from the face of the earth. the names of our mountains will be their monuments, and the musical designation of our lakes and rivers will perpetuate their memory for all coming time.

CHAPTER II.

PRIMITIVE RED MEN.

The annals of history show that in all cases where the ancient voyagers and discoverers touched upon the shores of America, North or South, they were met and welcomed by a race peaceful and hospitable at first to the new-comers, with characteristics and peculiarities differing from those of any people then known to the civilized world.

The name Indian was erroneously applied to this people, just as America was to the continent they inhabited.

The Indians have been called the Aborigines of America, although there is authority for the assertion that they themselves were the successors of at least one race, and perhaps two races, of people who possessed this continent and were driven from it by the Indians.

To trace the descent of a people when its records are traditions handed down from generation to generation, warped by individual prejudice, or perverted by malice and design, is manifestly a well-nigh hopeless task. We believe it is generally admitted that the claim of Asiatic origin for the North American Indian is based upon strong circumstantial evidence. The uniformity or agreement of the manners and customs of two nations is the most authentic monument of their original connection. This being so, there can be found many coincidences singularly indicative of the identity of origin of the Asiatic tribes and the North American Indians. Many customs, practised only by some nations in Asia, are distinctly traceable among the earliest inhabitants of the western continent, and a remarkable resemblance in language, religion, manners, habits, and customs, tends to establish their common origin.

It will not be expected that in the compilation of the material for this book any original addition can be made to the result of previous investigations of those who gave to the subject many years of study, and who had the advantage of personal contact with the people they described, or with the historians who preceded them. Generous requisition has been made upon the mass of material at hand, and due credit elsewhere given to the authors whose publications have been levied upon.

The various tribes of North America differed from each other in their individuality and characteristics, just as they all together, as a type, differed from the inhabitants of South America. But as far as history has been able to record, there was among them a similarity of ceremonies and customs which makes a description of the tribes inhabiting one part of the country typical of all. The history of the Five Nations, or League of the Iroquois, the most powerful confederation of Red Men found upon the continent, and existing down to the present day, is treated extensively in this chapter.

From a history of New England, of the year 1700, published in 1721, and from other sources, is gleaned the following account of the Indians of New England. It gives an admirable and interesting insight into the customs, ceremonies, and peculiarities which made the Red Men of the forest such strange beings in the thoughts and imaginations of the early settlers.

New England was inhabited by from twenty to thirty different nations at the advent of the Pilgrims, many of whose names are with us to-day in the nomenclature of the villages, cities, states, mountains, lakes, and rivers of that section. They are also perpetuated in the names of the tribes of our Order, which by its laws requires that each tribe shall be named after some Indian tribe or chief connected with the locality where it is instituted.

Among these nations was the Massachusetts, the largest of all and the most civilized, from which has come the name of the leading commonwealth of New England. Other nations whose names will be familiar when seen, were the Narragansetts, Pequots, Wampanoags, and the Maquas, otherwise known as Mohegans or Mohawks.

All accounts describe these nations as composed of people warlike and brave, who fought with the courage of despair against the encroachments of the new race whose advent in the decree of fate was to be followed by the extinction of the Aborigines whom they supplanted. The Maquas, or Mohawks, were one of the five nations originally comprising the League of the Iroquois. Their timely assistance turned the scale in favor of the English in the war with King Philip of the Wampanoags. Dr. Cotton Mather bore witness to their courage and valor, and records the fact that they controlled the country between the Hudson (which they called Mohegin) River, on the east, and the Mississippi, on the west.

The Indian of 1700 was described as of an olive complexion, flat nose, with black hair, cut short in front but allowed to grow long behind, and with a dress ornamented with feathers. They had no beards, but were generally tall and well developed in form. In summer they wore only a breech-clout made of leather. In winter they clothed themselves with deer skins, which were worn thrown around them like a mantle. Some of the tribes had breeches, leggins, and moccasins made of the same material, but in one piece. In winter they used snow-shoes, which were admirably adapted for travelling. They painted themselves with a variety of figures, which appeared ugly and misshapen to the palefaces, but had a significant meaning to the Red Men themselves. He was considered the bravest who had the most frightful forms pictured upon him, and he was thought thereby to inspire his opponents with terror. Their women wore earrings of copper or beads, and bracelets about their arms and chains about their legs. The men considered it beneath their dignity to labor, except on the hunt or upon the war-path, and the labor of taking care of the children, and managing the domestic affairs, fell upon the wives. The women planted, reaped, housed, and threshed their corn, built their wigwams, and waited upon the braves and warriors. The only employment of the men was hunting and fishing. When provision was low they went into the woods, fifty or one hundred in a band, with their bows and arrows, and brought in a fresh supply of food; or went out upon the rivers in their canoes to catch the fish with which they were abundantly supplied. Along the coast they regaled themselves with the different kinds of sea-fish, and with lobsters, clams, etc. They had a fashion of taking the lobsters in large bags at low water, also with a staff two or three yards long, made small, sharpened at one end, and with notches. When a lobster was seen crawling in the water about two fathoms deep, they impaled him with the staff and captured him. It was no uncommon thing for an Indian lad to capture twenty lobsters in this manner in a single hour. Bass, blue-fish, and sturgeon they struck with a sort of dart made of wood and sharpened with a fish-bone.

One author remarks that it is wonderful that during the many ages since the Indians first inhabited the country, no active spirit rose up among them to encourage arts and industry. They lived in a country full of copper and iron mines, and yet were never owners of as much as a knife until the English came among them. Indeed, their name for an Englishman was "Knife Man." The land was stocked with the best timber for shipping in the world, yet the only use to which they put it was to make canoes from the trunks by the use of fire or from the bark of the birch-tree. The canoe of bark was an ingenious affair, very light, but adapted to their uses. When they had burnt up the wood in the neighborhood of any place where they had pitched their wigwams, they pulled stakes and followed the wood, rather than bring the wood to their camp.

The Indian wigwam was made of young and tender trees, bent down like an arbor, covered on the top with bark and well-wrought mats made of rushes. The doors were about three feet high, one opening to the north and the other to the south, and when the wind shifted they closed up the door on one side with bark, and hung a deerskin or mat before the other. The chimneys were holes in the top of the wigwam, which were covered with mats in cold weather. All was warm and close in winter, for the houses were matted both outside and inside. Pots in which they cooked their food were strung upon poles attached to stakes driven in the ground. The beds were so many mats spread about the fire.

The ordinary food is spoken of as plain and simple, for when fishing and hunting failed they lived upon "Nokohick," which was a spoonful of parched meal with a spoonful of water, and on the strength obtained from this they would travel a whole day. Of course, the forest gave them an abundance of game, — deer, bears, and raccoons, but the moose seemed to be the most esteemed as a rarity. Flesh of the moose was prepared by the Indians, who dried it and kept it all the year round, not being acquainted with the use of salt until the English brought it among them. The skin of the moose made a very substantial garment, both for warmth and defence.

The health of the primitive Red Man previous to the advent of the white race seemed to be excellent, most of the diseases prevalent among the white men being unknown to them. The most fatal disease, apparently, among them was small-pox, a whole tribe being sometimes destroyed by this dread malady.

Aside from two or three nostrums, which they applied in certain cases, they had but two remedies for the sick, — the hot house, and the Powwow, or priest. The hot house was a little cave, about eight feet square, which was heated very hot, and in which they remained for about an hour. Upon coming out, they plunged into the adjacent river. This seems to have been a species of Turkish bath. If this did not cure, they sent for the Powwow, or priest, who came and performed his incantations and magical ceremonies to drive away the disease. Long practice undoubtedly gave the Powwow considerable skill in ordinary disease, and made it possible for him to judge if the disease was likely to prove fatal. If there was probability that the patient would recover, the Powwow told him that Hobbamocko sent the illness as a punishment for some offence, and that if he called upon him in his distress, relief would come. If the case was hopeless, he said to the patient that Kichtan was angry, and that all diseases inflicted by him were incurable.

Their manner of burying the dead was curious and interesting. A large hole was dug in the ground, across the bottom of which they laid a parcel of sticks; then wrapping the corpse in skins and mats, they laid it upon the sticks, and placed by its side all the treasures of the dead person; over this they raised a mound of earth. While this was being done, the friends of the deceased kept up a mournful screeching and howling. When the first English colonists were selecting a place for settlement, they discovered many of these Indian graves, one of which was opened. The outside covering was of boards, under which was a mat; next to that were bowls, trays, dishes, and then another mat, under which was a board finely painted and carved; then came another mat, under which were two bundles in which was discovered a large quantity of a very fine and perfectly red powder, with a strong, but not offensive, odor, and in this were the bones and skull of a man. Fine yellow hair was attached to the skull. There were also in the same bundle a knife, a needle, some iron implements, strings of beads, a bow and arrow, and other minor things.

The mourning for the dead continued for several days, night and morning, and all the friends of the deceased took part, in the southern parts of the country the women blackening their faces with a mixture prepared for that purpose. If the sick person happened to recover, there was always great joy, and when his friends came to congratulate him upon his recovery, they brought gifts to help make good the loss arising from his sickness.

Among New England Indians reverence of the aged was strictly observed. The young braves of the tribe relieved in every way the older warriors, even though the latter were strangers. No Indian, however old, was counted a man until he had signalized his bravery by some laudable act worthy of the approval of his tribe and nation.

The Indians divided their time by sleeps, moons, and winters. They seemed to have made some observation of the stars; and it is worthy of remark, that the constellation known among the palefaces as "The Bear" was called by the Indians "Paukunnawaw," which was the Indian name for bear. They had no written records by which to perpetuate the exploits of their ancestors, yet there is evidence of rude engravings upon rocks which apparently were intended to transmit to posterity some knowledge of important events of the past. They sought to supply this defect by digging deep holes in the ground in the place where any memorable act had been done; and he who understood the significance thereof could interpret its meaning, and learn the history of the circumstances it was intended to commemorate.

The Indians, of New England at least, believed not only in a plurality of gods who made and governed special nations of the world, but they elevated into Deity everything they imagined to be great, powerful, beneficial, or hurtful to mankind. For instance, they believed in a God of the Sun and a God of the Moon, etc. They believed fire to be a kind of god, inasmuch as it produced such remarkable effects, and they paid divine honors to thunder and lightning, which to them were very terrible. But let it be recorded that although the Indian acknowledged a great variety of inferior gods, yet he conceived and acknowledged one Almighty Being, who dwelt in the southwest regions of the heavens, and who was supreme above all the rest. This Almighty Being was called by various names, among which may be mentioned "Kichtan," "Kawtantowit," "Manitou." Among the Iroquois, "Ha-wen-ne-yu." They believed their supreme God to be a good being, and acknowledged their indebtedness to him for plenty on the chase, or victory on the war-path. They believed in the immortality of the soul, and a future state of existence. One legend stated that when good men died their souls went to Kichtan, where they met their friends, had splendid entertainments, and enjoyed all manner of pleasures. When wicked men died, they went, also, to Kichtan, and knocked at the door, but they received no answer but "Quachet," which meant "Go away," so they were doomed to wander about in restless discontent forever.

The Supreme Deity, Kichtan, they believed to be invisible even to their Powwows; but there was another power called by them "Hobbamocko," and by the English the devil, who appeared to the Powwows, as they themselves claimed, in different forms, sometimes as a man, then as a deer or eagle, but most commonly in the form of a snake. To him they applied in all difficult cases for the cure of disease, and the people stood in greater fear of him than of Kichtan himself. While the people were very anxious for the honor of a sight of this Hobbamocko, he never appeared only to the Powwows and the Paniese or counsellors of state; that is, to the men of intrigue and design whose business it was to keep the people in ignorance.

The Powwows referred to were the priests, so to speak, among the Indians, and by skilfully working upon their superstitions, they compelled obedience, respect, and even reverence as persons having familiar acquaintance with the Deity, and who by blessing or curse could make men happy or miserable in the happy hunting grounds. The Indians believed they could raise the devil and induce him to do whatever they desired unless Kichtan interposed. Dr. Cotton Mather in his letters relates many anecdotes of the incantations used by these Powwows to cure disease among the Indians. It seems if the patient died, the result was declared to be the inexorable decree of Kichtan; if the patient recovered, the Powwow claimed credit for his superior skill, and the virtue of his incantation. It is not surprising, that, under a theology like this, the Indians after a while thought more of appeasing the devil than they did of worshipping the Great Spirit.

It was customary among the Indians when children arrived at the age of discretion, whether male or female, to give them a new name, as women among civilized nations change their names at marriage. Again, when any remarkable exploit had been performed another new name was taken. A practice existed among nations of antiquity to add new titles to their names after any extraordinary performance; but to give up an old name entirely, and supplant it with a new one, was a custom peculiar to the Aborigines of America.

The government prevailing among the Indians is described as strictly a monarchy, the Sachem having absolute power even over the lives of his people. In all important matters a council of the sub-chiefs was summoned. Over this council the Sachem presided with great dignity, and after the decision of the chiefs and council had been made the orders of the Sachem were executed without hesitation. The Paniese were counsellors to the Sachem, and were selected from the wisest and most courageous of the tribe. They were consulted by the Sachem before war was declared, or any important business undertaken, and they seem to have been the Guard of Honor of the Sachem. They were held in high repute among the Indians, and could arrive at the distinction enjoyed only by a long course of training calculated to fit them for the duties they were to perform, and to prove their endurance and bravery. The Sachem seems to have collected tribute from the people, which was paid in the shape of skins, and such fruits or vegetables as were raised among them. Upon the Sachem fell the responsibility of upholding the proverbial hospitality of his nation, and the tribute referred to furnished the means for maintaining the obligations of his exalted position. In time of war, both person and estate being at the disposal of the Sachem, tribute was neither demanded nor expected.

That which served among them for money was called wampum, and was composed of strings of beads made from shells found upon the sea-coast. These beads were fashioned with instruments of stone, as they were unacquainted with the use of metal previous to the advent of the white race.

In the administration of justice the punishment inflicted was proportionate to the number of offences in each individual case. The punishment varied from a reprimand for the first offence to a beating on the naked back for the second, and a beating with a slitting of the nose for the third offence. The Sachem was the examiner, judge, and executioner. Murder was punished with death, the sentence being executed also by the Sachem. Should the criminal be absent at a long distance whence he could not be brought conveniently, the Sachem sent his own knife with which the execution should be performed. With this single exception the Indians would not receive punishment except directly from the hands of the Sachem. While enduring punishment no murmur of complaint was uttered, it being considered a more infamous thing than the offence itself for a person to cry out or flinch while being punished by the Sachem.

So absolute was the power of the Sachem over his people, that they could not understand the limited power entrusted to the Governors of the Colonies, and it is related that when one of them sought to make a treaty with Governor Mayhew of Martha's Vineyard, the Governor promising to grant a favor asked if the inhabitants consented, the Sachem responded: "Why do you recall your promise? What I promise or speak is always true; but you English Governors cannot be true, for you cannot make your words or intentions true; but mine are always true, for I make them true."

The bow and arrow were the chief weapons of the Indian; the skin of the beast gave him clothing, and its flesh, food. He had no learning or letters; he did not need them for hunting and fishing, which were his principal occupations. He was swift of foot and capable of enduring great fatigue and hardship. Personal courage gave him reputation among his people, and by this quality he was able to rise to positions of the highest trust and responsibility. He was ignorant of the nature of commerce, and when the Europeans first traded with him, he parted with things of greatest value for mere trifles. After a while he grew wiser, and realizing the value of the property the whites seemed so anxious to acquire, learned to drive as sharp a bargain as his paleface neighbor.

A description of the primitive Red Man will be incomplete without appropriate and full consideration of that wonderful confederation known to history as the League of the Iroquois. The people composing this League achieved for themselves a more remarkable civilized organization and acquired a higher degree of influence than any other race of Indian lineage except those of Mexico and Peru. For nearly two centuries after the advent of European colonists they maintained an unbroken organization, and, by the peculiar features of its federal system, maintained their independence, exhibiting wisdom in their civil institutions, sagacity in the administration of the League, and courage in its defence. The remnant of the League which exists to-day maintains the traditions of the past, and perpetuates the form of government by which every member was bound to every other by the tie of consanguinity. While the prestige and power of the League have passed away, the transition has been the result of the onward resistless march of so-called civilization, before which they were compelled to bow because powerless to avert what fate decreed them. The League was originally composed of five nations, — the Mohawks, Onondagas, Cayugas, Senecas, and Oneidas. In 1715 the Tuscaroras, having been expelled from North Carolina, turned to the North, and sought a home among the Iroquois. They were admitted into the League, and territory assigned to them for their future home. After this event the Iroquois became known among the English by the name of the "Six Nations." The origin and history of the League, previous to the discovery of America, are given to us only in the dim traditions of the past. The

AN IROQUOIS WARRIOR.

Indians had no written records, and preserved only such portions of their history as were handed down from generation to generation by their medicine men, or prophets, whom they designated "Keepers of the Faith." They were a branch of the Algonquin race, and the centre of the territory occupied by them was what now constitutes the State of New York. The project of a League originated with the Onondagas, among whom it was first suggested as a means to enable them more effectually to resist the attacks of surrounding nations. Traditions refer to the northern shore of Onondaga Lake as the place where the Iroquois chiefs assembled in general council to form the League.

After the formation of the League, the Iroquois rose rapidly in power and influence. They gained power by concentration of effort, and gradually assumed control of substantially the entire country east of the Mississippi River. In 1615 the Iroquois had grown into a populous and powerful confederacy, and had entered upon a career of conquest that, undoubtedly, but for the advent of the whites would have given them control eventually of the entire continent. This having been accomplished, the principles underlying the structure of the League would have been the source, doubtless, from which would have sprung by evolution a civilization at once remarkable and powerful.

Very soon after the arrival of the English, friendly relations were established with the Iroquois. A "covenant chain" was established between them which the Iroquois, with singular fidelity, reserved unbroken until the independence of the United States terminated the jurisdiction of the English over this country. In marked contrast was the action of the English and the French in their treatment of the Indians. The French thought to subjugate the Indian by intimidation and force, while the English used conciliation and forbearance. In those early days the rival colonies of France and England were nearly balanced, and the influence and power of the League of the Iroquois were sufficient to turn the scale in favor of the English. It is to this League that France must ascribe the final overthrow of her magnificent schemes to colonize in the northern part of America.

For nearly the whole century between 1600 and 1700, the Iroquois were engaged in almost perpetual warfare. They kept under subjection all other tribes and nations, which, feeble through lack of unity, fell easy prey to the strength and power of the League. The decline of the Iroquois commenced with their first intercourse with the Europeans. They were unable to cope with the firearms of the English, and they became degraded by the use of the "firewater" with which they were supplied by their paleface friends.

The "covenant chain," already referred to between the English and the Iroquois, led the greater portion of the members of the League to side with the English during the American Revolution. History records no more striking illustration of devotion to plighted word than the action of the League of the Iroquois in supporting the English, because the "covenant chain" bound them together in amity and trust. When peace came between Great Britain and the United States, the political existence of the League terminated. The jurisdiction of the United States extended over their territories, and from that time they became dependent nations, at the mercy of their conquerors, and recipients of their bounty. The manner in which they became dispossessed of some of the finest lands in America forms a chapter of human wickedness and human avarice over which no lover of humanity desires to linger. Fragments of the League now surviving still have their relationship and intercourse with each other, and cling to the forms and ceremonies of the ancient League. At stated intervals they assemble in council to raise up with their primitive forms a Sachem to fill a vacancy occasioned by death or deposition.

While the encroachments of the paleface nation have driven from their hunting-grounds the League of the Iroquois, they have left an indelible impression upon the geography and nomenclature of the original territory they inhabited which will endure for all coming time as a monument to their sagacity and intelligence. Great trails by which they communicated with different parts of their possessions were most judiciously selected, and after the country was surveyed, these trails were used for the public roads and turnpikes throughout New York. For centuries these old and wonderful trails had been trod by the Red Men. They reached from the Atlantic to the Mississippi, and from the northern lakes to the Gulf of Mexico, and were as familiar to the Iroquois as our own roads of travel have become to us.

The Iroquois called themselves Ho-de-no-sau-nee, which signifies the "people of the long house." They likened their confederacy to a long house having partitions and separate fires within each. The several nations were sheltered under a common roof. Among themselves they have never had any other name. Each of the nations composing the League had a name indicative of the location upon which it was established.

To the Iroquois, by common consent, has been assigned the highest position among the Indian races of the continent in the establishment of a league for the double purpose of acquiring strength and securing position. Their capacity for civil organization and their wisdom in legislation were favorably exhibited. The League contained orators and chiefs unrivalled for eloquence in council and bravery upon the warpath. Indeed the League of the Iroquois exhibited the highest development of the Indian ever reached by him in the hunter state.

In their own account of the origin of the League, the Iroquois invariably go back to a remote and uncertain period when the compact between the Five Nations was formed, its details and provisions settled and those laws and institutions established, under which, without essential change, they afterwards continued to flourish. Tradition has preserved the name of Da-ga-no-we-da as the founder of the League, and the first lawgiver of the Ho-de-no-sau-nee. As already stated, the northern shore of Ga-nun-ta-ah, or Onondaga Lake, was the place where the first council fire was kindled, around which the Chiefs and Wise Men of the several nations were gathered, and where, after a debate of many days, the League was established.

Great ingenuity was displayed in the system of government adopted. Fifty permanent Sachemships were created with appropriate names, and in these Sachems were vested the supreme powers of the Confederacy. The positions were made hereditary under limited and peculiar laws of descent. Their powers were joined and co-extensive with the League. Each Sachem was raised up and vested with his title by councils of all the

Sachems, with suitable forms and ceremonies, and until this ceremony was performed, no one could be a ruler. Thus the government of the Iroquois was an oligarchy. The Sachemships were divided among the nations, and upon death or deposition of a Sachem, the individual to succeed him was chosen from the nation to which that Sachemship belonged, and the name of the Sachemship held by his predecessor was conferred upon the new candidate. The several Sachems were the ruling body of their respective nations, exercising the same power over them, and in precisely the same manner, as, in connection with their colleagues, they exercised over the affairs of the League at large. The Sachems of each nation stood upon perfect equality in privileges, the influence of each being determined entirely by the talent of the individual. The title by which these Sachems were known as a class, intimated a check upon, rather than an enlargement of, their authority. It signified simply "counsellor of the people," a beautiful as well as an appropriate designation of a ruler. Besides these Sachemships, which were hereditary, there was an inferior class of rulers called chiefs. These chieftains were elected as a reward of merit. The title terminated with the life of the individual.

The powers and duties of the Sachems and Chiefs were entirely of a civil character, and confined by their organic laws to affairs of peace. No Sachem could go to war in his official capacity as a civil ruler. For that purpose he must lay aside his civil office for the time being, and take the warpath as a common warrior.

No religious functionaries were recognized in the League. There was, however, a class in each nation styled Ho-nun-de-unt, "Keepers of the Faith," who were regularly appointed to officiate at their festivals, and to take general supervision of their religious affairs.

There were two War Chieftains who took charge of affairs whenever the entire nation was engaged in general warfare.

Thus by the apparently intricate but simple form of government which they established, the councils of Sachems took charge of all matters pertaining to the public welfare. They exercised the executive, legislative, and judicial authority, so far as the same was not possessed by the people, although in many things their powers appear to have been advisory rather than executive. The Chiefs, at first counsellors between the Sachems and the people, increased in influence until they became rulers nearly equal to the Sachems themselves, thus widening and liberalizing the oligarchy. In all matters of war the power appears to have rested chiefly with the people, and its prosecution to have been left to private venture. If several bands united, they had as many generals as bands, who governed their proceedings by a council. Only, as in civil affairs, unanimity was necessary. The two supreme military Chieftains planned and generally managed the campaign.

The idea permeating the whole structure was that the government rested upon the public will, and not upon the arbitrary commands of the Chiefs. They desired to accomplish something more than a mere confederacy of Indian nations. It was rather a blending together of national sovereignty into one government. The League made the Ho-de-no-sau-nee one people, with one government, one system of constitutions, one executive will. The crowning feature of the League, as a political structure, was the perfect independence and individuality of the national sovereignties, in the midst of a central and embracing government, adequate to deal with all internal affairs, and powerful enough to conquer all other Indian nations with which it came in contact.

The plan adopted by the League, to weld into one political family the various nations composing it, was ingenious and effective. The Indian Tribe differed from the Athenian, Roman, and Jewish, although nearer in the result attained to the Jewish. In the Jewish Tribes the lineal descent is by the common father, while in the Tribes of the League of the Iroquois, the descent followed in all cases the female line. In each nation there were eight tribes, which were arranged in two divisions, the first of which included the Wolf, Bear, Beaver, and Turtle Tribes, and the second division included the Deer, Snipe, Heron, and Hawk Tribes. These names had an emblematical signification, the family name being the totem of that particular tribe. This division of the people of each nation into eight tribes became the means of effecting the most perfect union of separate nations ever devised by the wit of man. The effect was that each tribe was divided into five parts, one-fifth being placed in each of the Five Nations. Between these separate parts of each tribe there existed a tie of brotherhood which bound the nations closely together. This relationship was founded upon actual consanguinity. The Mohawk of the Wolf Tribe was actually the brother of the Seneca of the Wolf Tribe. Thus every member of any particular tribe, in whatever nation, was brother or sister to every other, as if children of the same mother. This relationship exists down to the present time, and furnishes the chief reason of the tenacity with which the fragments of the League cling together. Civil war was thus rendered impossible, as a collision would have turned each tribe against itself. The wisdom of this provision was proved by the fact that, during the long period through which the League gained and exercised such great power, it never encountered anarchy nor experienced any internal conflicts. Of the League, it has with great truth been said, that it was simple in its foundation upon family relationships, effective in the lasting vigor inherent in the ties of kindred, and perfect in its success. It achieved a permanent and harmonious union of the nations, and formed an enduring monument to that proud and progressive race which reared under its protection a widespread Indian sovereignty.

The laws on marriage restricted union to the two divisions of the tribes. Members of the Wolf, Bear, Beaver, and Turtle Tribes could not intermarry, but they could marry with the members of the Deer, Snipe, Heron, and Hawk Tribes. Although in process of time the rigor of this law was somewhat relaxed, the prohibition is yet religiously observed as applied to the individual tribe. They can now marry into any tribe but their own. Under these regulations the husband and wife were always of different tribes, and the children always followed the tribe of the mother. All titles, rights, and property were transmitted in the female line to the exclusion of the male. By these means the Sachemship assigned to any nation, or tribe of a nation, at the original organization of the League, could never pass out of that tribe. The certainty of purity of descent of their principal chiefs was secured by this infallible rule, as under it, it is absolutely certain that the ruling Sachem at the present day is of the same family or tribe by lineal descent with the first holder of the title.

Upon the decease of a Sachem, a tribal council assembled to determine upon his successor. The individual having been selected, a council was summoned by the nation, of all the Sachems of the League, and the new Sachem was raised up by such council, and invested with his office. With the power of tribes to select a Sachem was exercised an equal power of deposition. If by misconduct a Sachem lost the confidence and respect of his tribe, and became unworthy of authority, a tribal council at once deposed him, and having selected a successor, summoned a council of the League to perform the ceremony of investiture.

The rule prevailed in the League to assign to each Chief or Sachem a new name upon his assumption of official position. When an individual was raised up as a Sachem, his original name was laid aside, and that of the Sachemship itself assumed. In like manner, at the raising up of a Chief, a council of the nation which performed the ceremony gave the new Chief a new name, which, in some manner, referred to some striking peculiarity of the individual. The celebrated Red Jacket, renowned for his powers of eloquence, was given the title of Sa-go-ye-wat-ha, which signifies "Keeper Awake."

From what has already been stated in relation to the League of the Iroquois, it can be gathered that it was no ordinary sagacity that conceived such a wise and comprehensive scheme of organization. The confederacy was not formed for war, but it was the boast of the Iroquois that its great object was peace, and to break up the spirit of perpetual warfare which had wasted the Red Men from age to age. Thus they had the highest possible conception of human government. They sought to concentrate into one political fraternity the various Indian nations, and to prevent the injection of those elements of decay by which the nations of the earth, each in its turn, have been destroyed. Had the League of the Iroquois been left to work out its destiny, it is not too much to claim that it would eventually have ruled the entire continent, and founded a civilization equal, in time, to anything the history of the world has ever recorded.

Allusion has been made to the elective office of Chief, which was bestowed upon any member of the tribe, or nation, who, by military achievements or wisdom in the council, had proved himself worthy of distinction. Yet none of these Chiefs, however able or strong his individuality, could lift himself higher than to the title of Chief. The number of Sachems remained unchanged from the beginning, and the tenure of the office descended by inheritance in the tribe to which each was originally assigned. The Chiefs gained great power and influence; but the office of Sachem was surrounded by impassable barriers which could not be passed by those who were outside of the immediate family of the Sachem and the tribe in which the title was hereditary.

The Indian had a quick and enthusiastic appreciation of eloquence, and the chief, or warrior, with its magical power could lift himself as rapidly as he who gained renown upon the warpath. It may be said that the life of the Iroquois was either spent in the chase, on the warpath, or at the council fire. Nearly every transaction, whether social or political, originated or terminated in a council. The councils of the League were of three kinds : civil, mourning, and religious. The civil councils, Ho-de-os-seh, were confined to transacting business with foreign nations, and to regulating the internal administration of the Confederacy. The mourning councils, Hen-nun-do-nuh-seh, were summoned to raise up Sachems, to fill vacancies caused by death or deposition, and to ratify the investiture of such Chiefs as the nations had raised up as a reward for public service. The religious councils, Ga-e-we-yo-do Ho-de-os-hen-da-ko, were, as the name implies, devoted to religious observance.

The civil council, whose title signifies "devising together," could be convened by each nation under established regulations. A proposition having been submitted to one of the nations, the Sachems of that nation would first hold a council to determine if the matter were of sufficient importance to place before the general council of the League. If so determined, runners were sent to the nearest nation with a belt of wampum into which had been "talked" the fact that at a certain time and place, and for the purpose mentioned, a council of the League would be held. In obedience to the summons the Sachems and people assembled at the place of the council. Questions were reduced to propositions calling for an affirmative or a negative response, and were thus either adopted or rejected. The Sachems having assembled, the representative of the foreign nation was introduced. The council was opened by returning thanks to the Great Spirit for permitting them to meet together, and the envoy was informed that the council was ready to hear him open the business for which it was convened. Having stated his case, he retired, and the Sachems proceeded to deliberate and decide. Unanimity was the fundamental law. If this unanimity could not be reached, the whole matter was laid aside, and further action became at once impossible. The envoy was so informed, and the business of the council was terminated. A remarkable instance of this failure to agree was the action of the League at the beginning of the American Revolution. The Oneida Sachems firmly resisted the assumption of hostilities, and a quasi compromise was finally adopted which permitted each individual nation to act upon its own responsibility. The result was that part of the League assisted the British and the other part the Colonists.

The Hen-nun-do-nuh-seh signifies a mourning council, and was always called upon the occasion of raising up a Sachem, or confirming the investiture of such Chiefs as had been previously raised up by the nation. It embraces the two-fold object of lamenting the deceased and of establishing a successor in the Sachemship made vacant by death. To the nation which had lost a Sachem by death belonged the power to summon a council and to designate the day and place. Belts of wampum were sent out on such occasions, conveying the summons for the council, and announcing the place and time. In obedience to the summons the old and young from the remotest parts came to the place of the council. Runners were sent on in advance to announce the arrival of the approaching nation. On the day appointed, all preliminary arrangements having been perfected, the various nations were received with appropriate ceremony. A council fire was kindled, around which the Chiefs of the visiting nations walked, singing appropriate songs of mourning designed for the occasion. The pipe of peace was circulated, and speeches were exchanged between the parties. Then all advanced to the general council fire, where the principal ceremonies proceeded. Dignity and decorum, and great gravity and earnestness, marked these mourning councils. The lament was a tribute to the virtues and to the memory of the departed Sachem, a mourning scene in which not only the tribes and nations of the deceased, but the League itself participated. The ceremony of raising up a successor which followed was a succession of musical chants with choruses intermingled with speeches and responses. The whole ceremony was conducted with a spirit of silence and solemnity which invested it with singular interest.

A prominent part of the ceremonial consisted in the repetition of their ancient laws and usages, and exposition of the structure and principles of the League for the instruction of the inducted rulers. Among these injunctions was one that came down from the founder of the League, designed to impress upon their minds the necessity of union and harmony. In the figurative language of the Red Man, they were enjoined to plant a tree, with four roots branching severally to the north, south, east, and west. Beneath its shade the Sachems of the League must sit down together in perpetual unity, if they would preserve its stability, or secure the advantages it was calculated to bestow. If they did this, the power of the Ho-de-no-sau-nee would be planted as firmly as the oak, and the blasts of adverse fortune would rage against it in vain.

These laws were repeated from strings of wampum into which they had been "talked" at the time of their enactment. Only those familiar with the secret records could interpret them; but no importance was attached to a promise or assurance of a foreign power unless belts or strings of wampum had been given it in recollection. One of the original Sachems was constituted "Keeper of the Wampum," and was required to be versed in its interpretation. The original wampum of the Iroquois was made of spiral fresh-water shells, which were strung on deerskin strings, or sinews, and the strands braided into belts, or simply united into strings. Hubbard, in his narrative of the Indian history of New England, describes wampum in general as follows: —

"It is of two sorts, white and purple. The white is worked

out of the inside of the great conch into the form of a bee, and perforated to string on leather. The purple is worked out of the inside of the mussel shell. They are woven as broad as one's hand and about two feet long. These they call belts, and give and receive them at their treaties as the seals of their friendships."

The proceedings of the ceremony of investiture were closed with a presentation of the newly invested rulers to the people, under the names of their respective Sachemships, which from that day they were permitted to assume. Then followed feasting and dancing which continued sometimes for several days, the days being spent in athletic games, and the evenings in feasting and dancing. The council having been ended, and the spirit of festivity exhausted, the embers of the fire were raked together, and the several nations returned to their respective homes.

The third form of councils embraced their religious festivals and ceremonies, and will be more clearly understood by the description which follows of the various festivities, feasts, and dances.

History shows that man has ever sought to unravel the mystery of creation, and upon this impulse has been built whatever form of religion or worship the world has known. Instinctively man has turned to a higher power or influence made manifest in the elements around him, and whose grandeur he could appreciate, whose power he felt, and whose nature he vaguely comprehended. His mind grasped the idea that the source was beyond human control. Hence there arose in his mind the conception of an Omnipotent and Supreme Being by whose hand was controlled the destinies of himself and his people.

Thus it was with the League of the Iroquois, and it is claimed that while in their inferior spiritualities they fell infinitely below the splendid creation of ancient mythology, in the knowledge of the Supreme Being they rose above the highest conceptions of ancient philosophy. Indeed, ancient religions contained no such exalted conception as the Divine Being, worshipped by the entire red race under the appellation of the Great Spirit. Like the ancients, the Iroquois believed that the Great Spirit was born, and this belief prevailed among all the Indian nations upon the North American continent. They believed the Great Spirit to be their Creator, Ruler, and Preserver, and that he held supreme power. He created not only the animal and vegetable world, but also adapted the elements in the whole visible universe to the wants of man. They believed in the personal existence and constant superintending care of the Great Spirit, who was the God of the Indian alone, and who was believed to be self-existent and immortal. While they believed in the existence of the Great Spirit, Ha-wen-ne-yu, they also recognized the personal existence of an Evil Spirit, Ha-ne-go-ate-geh, the Evil-intended. According to their legends these were brothers, and both immortal. The Evil Spirit had creative power in a limited degree. The Great Spirit created man and all useful animals, while the Evil Spirit created all monsters, reptiles, and noxious plants. The Great Spirit created everything that was good and for the benefit of man, while the Evil Spirit created everything that was bad and injurious to him. They also recognized multitudes of inferior or subordinate spirits, but over them all, supreme in power, was the Great Spirit who could, if he chose to exercise the power, overcome all the subordinate spirits, including the Evil Spirit his brother. Thus He-no was the god of Thunder, who was declared to be partly human and partly of celestial origin, and who was addressed by the Iroquois as Grandfather. The legend of He-no is as follows:—

"A young maiden residing at Ga-u-gwa, a village above Niagara Falls, at the mouth of Cayuga creek, had been contracted to an old man of ugly manners and disagreeable person. As the marriage was hateful to her, and by the customs of the nation there was no escape, she resolved upon self-destruction. Launching a bark canoe into the Niagara, she seated herself within it, and, composing her mind for the frightful descent, directed it down the current. The rapid waters soon swept them over the falls, and the canoe was seen to fall into the abyss below, but the maiden had disappeared. Before she reached the waters underneath she was caught in a blanket by He-no and his two assistants and carried without injury to the home of the Thunderer behind the fall. Her beauty attracted one of the dependents of He-no who willingly joined them in marriage.

NIAGARA FALLS.

"For several years before this event, the people at Ga-u-gwa had been troubled with an annual pestilence, and the source of the scourge had baffled all conjecture. He-no, at the expiration of a year, revealed to her the cause and the remedy. He told her that a monstrous serpent dwelt under the village, and made his annual repast upon the bodies of the dead which were buried by its side. That to insure a bounteous feast, he went forth once a year and poisoned the waters of the Niagara, and also of the Cayuga creek, whereby the pestilence was created. The people were directed to move to the Buffalo creek. He also gave her careful directions touching the education of the child of which she was to become the mother. With these directions she departed on her mission.

"After the people had removed as directed, the great serpent, disappointed of his food, put his head above the ground to discover the reason, and found that the village was deserted. Having scented their trail, and discovered its course, he went forth into the lake and up the Buffalo creek in open search of his prey. While in this narrow channel, He-no discharged upon the monster a terrible thunderbolt which inflicted a mortal wound. The Senecas yet point to a place in the creek where the banks are semicircular either side, as the spot where the serpent after he was struck, turning to escape into the deep waters of the lake, shoved out the banks on either side. Before he succeeded in reaching the lake, the repeated attacks of the thunderbolt took effect, and the monster was slain.

"The huge body of the serpent floated down the stream, and lodged upon the verge of the cataract, stretching nearly across the river. A part of the body arched backwards near the northern shore in a semicircle. The raging waters, thus dammed up by the body, broke through the rocks behind; and thus the whole verge of the fall upon which the body rested was precipitated with it into the abyss beneath. In this manner, says the legend, was formed the Horse-Shoe fall.

"Before this event there was a passage behind the sheet from one shore to the other. This passageway was not only broken up, but the home of He-no was also destroyed in the general crash. Since then his habitation has been in the west.

"The child of the maiden grew up to boyhood, and was found

to possess the power of darting the lightning at his will. It had been the injunction of He-no that he should be reared in retirement, and not allowed to mingle in the strifes of men. On a certain occasion, having been beset by a playmate with great vehemence, he transfixed him with a thunderbolt. He-no immediately translated him to the clouds, and made him third assistant Thunderer."

The Iroquois had a beautiful myth in relation to three spirits which they called the Three Sisters; the Spirit of Corn, the Spirit of Beans, and the Spirit of Squashes. These plants were regarded as a special gift of the Great Spirit, and they believed that each was intrusted with a separate spirit for the benefit of the Indian. These spirits were supposed to have the forms of beautiful females, to be very fond of each other, and delight to dwell together. In the growing season they were thought to visit the fields and dwell among them. They were known under the name of He-o-ha-ko, "Our Life," or "Our Supporters." They are never mentioned separately. The legend supposed that originally the corn was of easy cultivation, yielded abundantly, and had a grain exceedingly rich with oil. The Evil Spirit, envious of this great gift of Ha-wen-ne-yu to man, went forth into the fields, and spread over it a universal blight. Since then it has been harder to cultivate, yields less abundantly, and lost its original richness. When the rustling wind waves the corn with a moaning sound, the pious Indian fancies that he hears the Spirit of the Corn, in her compassion for the red man, bemoaning with unavailing regrets her blighted fruitfulness.

Thus, in the mythology of the Iroquois, they surrounded themselves with innumerable spirits, to all of which they returned thanks as subordinates of Ha-wen-ne-yu under the general name of Ho-no-che-no-keh, signifying "the Invisible Aids," which included the whole spiritual world from He-no, the Thunderer, down to the Spirit of the Strawberry. At the religious festivals of the Iroquois, one invocation was, "Great Spirit, master of all things, visible and invisible; Great Spirit, master of other spirits, whether good or evil; command the good spirits to favor thy children; command the evil spirits to keep at a distance from them."

The Iroquois believed that tobacco was given them as a means of communication with the spirit world. The smoke of the burning weed ascending to Heaven carried with its incense their petitions to the Great Spirit, and rendered their acknowledgments acceptable for his blessings. By its instrumentality they believed that they would more easily reach the ear of the Great Spirit, and receive favorable responses to their petitions. The Iroquois believed firmly in the immortality of the soul, and looked forward to "the happy home beyond the setting sun" as a final resting-place after death. This was taught as a fundamental article of faith. They believed in probation and punishment after death.

Reverence for the aged, as elsewhere stated, was one of the precepts of the ancient faith of the Iroquois, and their religious teachers always inculcated the duty of protecting their aged parents as an invocation from the Great Spirit. Among the roving tribes of the wilderness, the old and helpless were frequently abandoned, and in some cases executed as an act of greater kindness than desertion. But the Iroquois, after the formation of the League, resided in permanent villages which afforded refuge for the aged. One of the prominent aims of the League was to join the people together by the family tie, thus creating among them the universal spirit of hospitality.

Respect for the dead was another element of their faith. There were various customs of burial, to which allusion has already been made in this chapter. Sometimes they buried them in the earth; at other times the body was exposed on bark scaffolds erected on poles, or secured on the limbs of trees. The religious system of the Iroquois taught that the journey from earth to heaven was of long duration. Originally it was supposed to be a year, and the period of mourning, for the departed, was fixed at that time. The spirit of the deceased was supposed to hover around the body for a season before it took its final departure. A beautiful custom prevailed in ancient times of capturing a bird, and freeing it over the grave, on the evening of the burial, to bear away the spirit to its heavenly rest. With the body of the deceased were deposited his bow and arrows, tobacco and pipe, and necessary food to nourish him during the journey from earth to the happy hunting-grounds. Included in their funeral ceremonies was a lamentation over the body addressed to the spirit, which they believed could hear them although unable to answer. The following is given as a specimen of these lamentations, being the address of an Iroquois mother over the body of her son before the body was borne away for burial:—

"My son, listen once more to the words of thy mother. Thou wert brought into life with her pains. Thou wert nourished with her life. She has attempted to be faithful in raising thee up. When thou wert young she loved thee as her life. Thy presence has been a source of great joy to her. Upon thee she depended for support and comfort in her declining days. She has ever expected to gain the end of the path of life before thee. But thou hast outstripped her, and gone before her. Our great and wise Creator has ordered it thus. By his will I am left to taste more of the miseries of this world. Thy friends and relatives have gathered about thy body to look upon thee for the last time. They mourn, as with one mind, thy departure from among us. We, too, have but a few days more, and our journey shall be ended. We part now, and you are conveyed from our sight; but we shall soon meet again, and shall again look upon each other. Then we shall part no more. Our Maker has called you to his home. Thither will we follow. Na-ho!"

Heaven was the abode of the Great Spirit, and the final home of the faithful, and they believed a road led down from heaven to every man's door, and along this road the soul ascended to heaven at death, until it reached its place in the happy hunting-grounds above. No evil could enter this peaceful home of innocence and purity. But among the Iroquois the idea of a hunting-ground was not prevalent as among the other Indian nations. Among the beliefs engrafted on the ancient faith, none is more worthy of notice than that relating to Washington, whose name among the Iroquois was Ho-no-da-ga-ne-ars, signifying "Town Destroyer." This legend we quote as follows:—

"According to their present belief, no white man ever reached the Indian heaven. Not having been created by the Great Spirit, no provision was made for him in their scheme of theology. He was excluded both from heaven, and from the place of punishment. But an exception was made in favor of Washington. Because of his justice and benevolence to the Indian, he stood pre-eminent above all other white men. When, by the peace of 1783, the Indians were abandoned by their English allies, and left to make their own terms with the American government, the Iroquois were more exposed to severe measures than the other tribes in their alliance. At this critical moment, Washington interfered in their behalf, as the protector of Indian rights, and the advocate of a policy towards them of the most enlightened justice and humanity. After his death, he was mourned by the Iroquois as a benefactor of their race, and his memory was cherished with reverence and affection. A belief was spread abroad among them that the Great Spirit had received him into a celestial residence upon the plains of heaven, the only white man whose noble deeds had entitled him to this heavenly favor. Just by the entrance of heaven is a walled enclosure, the ample grounds within which are laid out with avenues and shaded walks. Within is a spacious mansion, constructed in the fashion of a fort. Every object in nature, which could please a cultivated taste, had been gathered in this blooming Eden, to render it a delightful dwelling-place for the immortal Washington. The faithful Indian, as he enters heaven, passes this enclosure. He sees and recognizes the illustrious inmate, as he walks to and fro in quiet meditation. But no word ever passes his lips. Dressed in his uniform, and in a state of perfect felicity, he is destined to remain through eternity in the solitary enjoyment of the celestial residence prepared for him by the Great Spirit.

"Surely the piety and the gratitude of the Iroquois have, jointly, reared a monument to Washington above the skies, which is more expressive in its praise than the proudest recitals on the obelisk, and more imperishable in its duration than the syenite which holds up the record to the gaze of centuries."

The Iroquois had a systematic worship, consisting in the celebration of periodical festivals held at stated seasons of the year, and suggested by the changes in the seasons, ripening of the fruits, and the gathering of the harvests. There were six regular festivals or thanksgivings. These in regular order were the Maple festival, the Planting, the Strawberry, the

Green Corn, and the Harvest festivals; last, the New Year's festival, the great jubilee of the Iroquois, at which the White Dog was sacrificed. Each of these festivals referred to a particular plant, or season, at which it was celebrated.

While they had no priests, or preachers, as they are understood among palefaces, yet in each nation of the League there were certain persons selected to take charge of their religious festivals, and the general supervision of the worship. They were styled Ho-nun-de-ont, or "Keepers of the Faith," as the term literally signifies. The office was elective, and continued as long as the individual was faithful to his trust. It was their duty to designate the time for holding the periodical festivals, to make the necessary arrangements for celebration, and to conduct the ceremonies. Women, as well as men, were appointed, and in about equal numbers; and it was the special duty of the women who were keepers of the faith, to prepare the entertainment for the people who attended the festival.

At the various festivals the order of exercises seems to have included a thanksgiving address, smoking the pipe of peace, an invocation to the Great Spirit, and feasting and dancing. The festival usually lasted four days, and each day was used for its special feature in observance of the festival.

Among the ceremonies incident to the worship of the Iroquois, the most novel were those attending the New Year's jubilee. The prominent act in this festival was the burning of the White Dog. The festival lasted seven days, and the sacrifice of the White Dog was made on the fifth day of the festival. Preliminary to the festival, two of the Keepers of the Faith, disguised in deer skins, or buffalo robes, visited every house in the village, and summoned the people to the festival, in the name of the Great Spirit. A white dog was selected because white was the Iroquois emblem of purity and of faith. Around the neck of the dog was hung a string of white wampum, the pledge of their sincerity. On successive days of the festival feasting and dancing were engaged in. On the morning of the fifth day, soon after dawn, the White Dog was burned on an altar of wood erected by the keepers. The idea of the sacrifice seems to have been to send up the spirit of the dog as a messenger to the Great Spirit, to announce their continued fidelity to his services, and to convey to him their united thanks for the blessings of the year. The fidelity of the dog, the companion of the Indian as a hunter, was emblematical of their fidelity. No messenger more trusty could be found to bear their petitions to the Master of Life. The Iroquois believed that the Great Spirit made a covenant with their fathers, that when they should send up the spirit of a dog of spotless white, he would receive it as a pledge of their adherence to his worship, and his ears would thus be opened in a special manner to their petitions. The white wampum hung around the neck of the dog was a further emblem of their sincerity of purpose.

The burning of the dog was attended with many ceremonies. A fire was kindled upon the altar, a speech was made by one of the Keepers of the Faith, in which he referred to the antiquity of the festival and its importance and solemnity, and in which he enjoined upon all to direct their thoughts to the Great Spirit, and unite with the Keepers of the Faith in the ceremonies. A chant or song appropriate to the occasion was then sung, the people joining in chorus. A procession was then formed, the faith keeper preceding, followed by four others bearing the dog upon a kind of litter, behind which came the people in Indian file. After the dog had been laid upon the burning altar, and while it was being consumed, an invocation to the Great Spirit was made by the officiating Keeper of the Faith. Then followed the great thanksgiving address of the Iroquois. During the delivering of the address, the speaker threw leaves of tobacco into the fire, from time to time, that its incense might constantly ascend during the whole address. The following is given as the translation of this address of thanksgiving, and is an admirable specimen of Indian eloquence and imagery.

"Hail, Hail, Hail : Listen now, with an open ear, to the words of thy people, as they ascend to thy dwelling, in the smoke of our offering. Behold thy people here assembled. Behold, they have come up to celebrate anew the sacred rites thou hast given them. Look down upon us beneficently. Give us wisdom faithfully to execute thy commands.

"Continue to listen : The united voice of thy people continues to ascend to thee. Forbid, by thy wisdom, all things which shall tempt thy people to relinquish their ancient faith.

Give us power to celebrate at all times, with zeal and fidelity, the sacred ceremonies which thou hast given us.

"Continue to listen: Give to the keepers of the faith wisdom to execute properly thy commands. Give to our warriors and our mothers strength to perform the sacred ceremonies of thy institution. We thank thee that, in thy wisdom, thou hast given to us these commands. We thank thee that thou hast preserved them pure unto this day.

"Continue to listen: We thank thee that the lives of so many of thy children are spared to participate in the exercises of this occasion. Our minds are gladdened to be made partakers in the execution of thy commands.

"We return thanks to our mother, the earth, which sustains us. We thank thee that thou hast caused her to yield so plentifully of her fruits. Cause that, in the season coming, she may not withhold of her fulness and leave any to suffer from want.

"We return thanks to the rivers and streams which run their courses upon the bosom of our mother, the earth. We thank thee that thou hast supplied them with life for our comfort and support. Grant that this blessing may continue.

"We return thanks to all the herbs and plants of the earth. We thank thee that in thy goodness thou hast blessed them all, and given them strength to preserve our bodies healthy, and to cure us of the diseases inflicted upon us by evil spirits. We ask thee not to take from us these blessings.

"We return thanks to the Three Sisters. We thank thee that thou hast provided them as the main supporters of our lives. We thank thee for the abundant harvest gathered in during the past season. We ask that Our Supporters may never fail us, and cause our children to suffer from want.

"We return thanks to the bushes and trees which provide us with fruit. We thank thee that thou hast blessed them, and made them to produce for the good of thy creatures. We ask that they may not refuse to yield plentifully for our enjoyment.

"We return thanks to the winds which, moving, have banished all diseases. We thank thee that thou hast thus ordered. We ask the continuation of this great blessing.

"We return thanks to our grandfather, He-no. We thank thee that thou hast so wisely provided for our happiness and comfort in ordering the rain to descend upon the earth, giving us water and causing all plants to grow. We thank thee that thou hast given us He-no, our grandfather, to do thy will in the protection of thy people. We ask that this great blessing may be continued to us.

"We return thanks to the moon and stars which give us light when the sun has gone to his rest. We thank thee that thy wisdom has so kindly provided, that light is never wanting to us. Continue unto us this kindness.

"We return thanks to the sun, that he has looked upon the earth with a beneficent eye. We thank thee, that thou hast, in thy unbounded wisdom, commanded the sun to regulate the return of the seasons, to dispense heat and cold, and to watch over the comfort of thy people. Give unto us that wisdom which will guide us in the path of truth. Keep us from all evil ways, that the sun may never hide his face from us for shame, and leave us in darkness.

"We return thanks to the Ho-no-che-no-keh. We thank thee, that thou hast provided so many agencies for our good and happiness.

"Lastly, we return thanks to thee, our Creator and Ruler. In thee are embodied all things. We believe that thou canst do no evil; that thou doest all things for our good and happiness. Should thy people disobey thy commands deal not harshly with them; but be kind to us, as thou hast been to our fathers in times long gone by. Hearken unto our words as they have ascended, and may they be pleasing to thee our Creator, the Preserver and Ruler of all things visible and invisible. Na-ho!"

The sixth and the seventh days were observed in about the same manner as one of their ordinary religious days at which the thanksgiving address was introduced. These festivals were observed from generation to generation, from the foundation of the League down to the present time. They formed a striking illustration of the deep religious sentiment prevailing among the Iroquois, the fruits of which were peace, brotherly kindness, charity, hospitality, integrity, truth, and friendship among themselves, and reverence, thankfulness, and faith towards the Great Spirit.

The dance was a most important element among the Iroquois in the performance of their ceremonies, and was regarded as a thanksgiving ceremonial acceptable to the Great Spirit, and designed for their pleasure as well as for his worship. They had thirty-two distinct dances, of which twenty-six were claimed to be of their own invention. Each had a separate history and object, as well as a different degree of popular favor. Some were costume dances, and performed by a small and select band. Some were designed exclusively for females, others for warriors alone; but the greater part were open to both sexes. Many were used among the Iroquois exclusively, while others were in general use among the Indians from Maine to Oregon. The Feather and the War dances ranked first in estimation. Appropriate costumes were used, some idea of which may be gained from the illustrations given in this book of an Iroquois warrior and an Iroquois woman. Of the two dances mentioned, the War dance was the favorite. It was the mode of enlistment, and the dance which preceded the departure of a war party, and with which its return was celebrated. It was used at the raising up of Sachems, at the adoption of a captive, at the entertainment of a guest, and was the first dance taught to the young. The War dance was usually performed in the evening. The music was usually furnished by four singers, who accompanied themselves by beating time upon drums. The dance was chiefly upon the heel, which was raised and brought down with great quickness and force by muscular strength, to keep time with the beating of the drum, to make a resounding noise by the action, and, at the same time, to shake the knee-rattles, which contributed materially to the pomp and circumstance of the dance. In the War dance the attitudes were those of violent passions, and, consequently, were not graceful. At the same instant of time, in a group of dancers, one might be seen in the attitude of attack, another of defence; one in the act of drawing the bow, another striking with the war-club; some in the act of throwing the tomahawk, some of listening and watching an opportunity, and others of striking the foe. The War dance originated among the Sioux, and was adopted by the Iroquois at a remote period of time.

Next in favor and importance to the War dance was the great

Feather dance, sometimes called the Religious dance, because specially consecrated to the worship of the Great Spirit. Tradition stated that it was invented by To-do-da-ho at the formation of the League. It was performed by a selected band, ranging from fifteen to thirty, in full costume, and was chiefly used at their religious festivals. It is described as the most splendid, graceful, and remarkable in the whole collection, requiring greater powers of endurance, suppleness, and flexibility of person, and gracefulness of deportment than either of the others. The music was furnished by two singers, seated in the centre of the room, each having a turtle-shell rattle. The music was made by songs, the rattles being used to mark the time.

Each of the other dances used had a meaning and significance appropriate to the occasion upon which it was employed. One dance was peculiar, in that the Indian maiden selected her partner. The warrior never solicited the maiden to dance with him. Another dance worthy of mention was called O-ke-wa, the Dance for the Dead. It was danced by the women alone to plaintive and mournful music. This dance was had whenever a family which had lost a member called for it, which was usually about a year after the death.

As a matter of interest we give the following names of the various dances used by the Iroquois:—

1 O-sto-weh-go-wa	Great Father Dance.	For both sexes.
2 Ga-na-o-uh	Great Thanksgiving Dance.	"
3 Da-yun-da-nes-hunt-ha . . .	Dance with Joined Hands.	"
4 Ga-da-shote	Trotting Dance.	"
5 O-to-wa-ga-ka	North Dance.	"
6 Je-ha-ya	Antique Dance.	"
7 Ga-no-jit-ga-o	Taking the Kettle out.	"
8 Ga-so-wa-o-no	Fish Dance.	"
9 Os-ko-da-ta	Shaking the Bush.	"
10 Ga-no-ga-yo	Rattle Dance.	"
11 So-wek-o-an-no	Duck Dance.	"
12 Ja-ko-wa-o-an-no	Pigeon Dance.	"
13 Guk-sa-ga-ne-a	Grinding Dishes.	"
14 Ga-so-a	Knee Rattle Dance.	"
15 O-ke-wa	Dance for the Dead.	For Females.
16 O-as-ka-ne-a	Shuffle Dance.	"
17 Da-swa-da-ne-a	Tumbling Dance.	"

18	Ga-ne-a-seh-o	Turtle Dance.	For Females.
19	Un-da-da-o-at-ha	Initiation Dance for Girls.	"
20	Un-to-we-sus	Shuffle Dance.	"
21	Da-yo-da-sun-da-e-go	Dark Dance.	"
22	Wa-sa-seh	Sioux, or War Dance.	For Males.
23	Da-ge-ya-go-o-an-no	Buffalo Dance.	"
24	Ne-a-gwi-o-an-no	Bear Dance.	"
25	Wa-a-no-a.	Striking the Stick.	"
26	Ne-ho-sa-den-da	Squat Dance.	"
27	Ga-na-un-da-do	Scalp Dance.	"
28	Un-de-a-ne-suk-ta	Track Finding Dance.	"
29	Eh-nes-hen-do	Arm Shaking Dance.	"
30	Ga-go-sa	False Face Dance.	"
31	Ga-je-sa	False Face Dance.	"
32	Un-da-de-a-dus-shun-ne-at-ha .	Preparation Dance.	"

Beside their religious ceremonies, dances, and other festivals, the Iroquois had their national games in which they engaged with all possible zeal and enthusiasm. These contests were between nation and nation, village and village, or tribe and tribe, and not between individual champions. The prize was victory, and belonged not to the players, but to the party which they represented. They bet with each other freely on the result of the games, and it was not unusual for an Indian to gamble away every valuable article which he possessed, including his tomahawk, his medal, ornaments, and even his blanket. Prominent among these games was the ball game which easily led the others in popularity. Goals were erected at either end of the field in which the contest took place, the goals being about eighty rods apart. The contest between the players was to see which could carry the ball through the goal a given number of times. The game required great skill and endurance as well as physical courage. The other games, such as the game of Javelins, Deer Buttons, Snow-Snake game, Peach-Stone game, were used principally for gambling.

The Indian was also extremely proficient in archery. The Indian bow was usually three and one-half to four feet in length, and it required great muscular strength to draw the bow to its full extent. The arrow was about three feet in length and feathered at the small end with a twist which caused it to revolve in its flight, giving a motion similar to the twist in the rifle barrel. The arrow was pointed with flint, and was really a dangerous weapon in the hands of one proficient in its use.

The celebration of their games was carried on with enthusiasm that clearly attested their popularity, and proved that in the solitudes of the American wilderness, long before the advent of the white man, the Iroquois had enjoyed their surroundings, and were contented and happy with the forms and customs inherited from their ancestors.

In judging of the Indian character as portrayed by the League of the Iroquois, it should always be borne in mind that judgment should be based upon the influences which actuated them, and not upon standards founded upon our own experience as a civilized people. For a better understanding of these influences, a brief reference is appropriate to their social customs and their personal relations. They resided in permanent villages located on the banks of rivers and lakes, or in the vicinity of copious springs. The Ga-no-sote, or Bark house, was a simple structure erected by them in their villages, the dimensions being about twenty feet by fifteen, and from fifteen to twenty feet high. They were made with poles, and covered with bark, and fitted up with simple yet sufficient conveniences for the uses of the family.

The marriage relation among the Iroquois was peculiar. Affection was not considered, the affair being entirely a matter of convenience and physical necessity. The contract was not made between the parties to be married, but was usually adjusted by their mothers, and often after a conference among the leading and influential women and men of the tribes to which the parties respectively belonged. Disparity in age seems to have been no bar in the earlier history of the League, although in later days the ages of the couple more nearly approximated. The marriage ceremony was extremely simple. An announcement was made to the parties, and on the following day, the maiden was conducted by her mother, accompanied by a few female friends, to the home of her intended husband. She carried in her hand a few cakes of corn bread, which she presented, on entering the house, to her mother-in-law as an earnest of her usefulness and of her skill in the domestic arts. On receiving it, the mother of the young warrior returned a present of venison, or other fruit of the chase, to the mother of the bride as a proof of his ability to provide for his household. This exchange of presents ratified and concluded the contract which bound the new pair together in the marriage relation. Such a thing as love as understood among the palefaces was entirely unknown among the Iroquois. After marriage attachments naturally would spring up between the parties by association, habit, and mutual dependence. This was the result of the circumstances surrounding Indian habits and mode of life. The male sought the society of the male exclusively, and in the same manner the female sought the companionship of her own sex. The secret of this custom in part may be traced to the inequality of the sexes. The Indian regards woman as an inferior, and from force of habit and tradition, she accepted the position thus assigned her; this being remembered, the lack of association between the sexes is more easily understood.

Polygamy was forbidden among the Iroquois, and never became a practice. There was separation between husband and wife if they failed to agree, although every possible means was used by the mothers of the married pair to restore harmony before the final separation was permitted. It will be remembered that the husband and wife were never of the same tribe, and the children were of the tribe of their mother. The father had no right to the custody of the children, and after separation, he gave himself no further trouble concerning them. The Indian father seldom caressed his children, or manifested any solicitude for their welfare, until the sons reached manhood and were able to be his companions in the hunt or on the war-path. The care of the children during infancy and childhood was entrusted to the watchful affection of the mother alone.

The rights of property of both husband and wife continued distinct after marriage the same as before, each having the right of possession and of transfer of title. At the death of the husband, his property descended, not to his wife or children, unless in the presence of a witness he had so bequeathed them, but they were handed over to his nearest relatives in his own tribe as personal mementos of the deceased.

One of the strongest characteristics, and most attractive features of Indian society, was the spirit of hospitality by which it was pervaded, and a description of this crowning virtue, carried to a degree of universality by the Iroquois beyond that of any other people, is worthy of reproduction here, not only as an indication of the innate nobility of Indian character, but as an example worthy of imitation in the organization which seeks to perpetuate the memory of their forms and customs. Their houses were not only open to each other, at all hours of the day and of the night, but also to the wayfarer and to the stranger. Such entertainment as their means afforded was freely spread before him, with words of kindness and of welcome. The Indian had no regular meal after the morning repast, but he allayed his appetite whenever the occasion offered. The care of the appetite was left entirely with the women, as the Indian never asked for food. Whenever the husband returned, at any hour in the day, it was the duty and the custom of the wife to set food before him. If a neighbor, or a stranger, entered her dwelling, a dish of hominy, or whatever else she had prepared, was immediately placed before him, with an invitation to partake. It made no difference at what hour of the day, or how numerous the calls, this courtesy was extended to every comer, and was the first act of attention bestowed. This custom was universal, in fact, one of the laws of their social system; and a neglect on the part of the wife to observe it was regarded both as a breach of hospitality and as a personal affront. A neighbor, or a stranger, calling from house to house, through an Indian village, would be thus entertained at every dwelling he entered. If the appetite of the guest had thus been fully satisfied, he was yet bound in courtesy to taste of the dish presented, and to return the customary acknowledgment, Hi-ne-a-weh, "I thank you;" an omission to do either being esteemed a violation of the usages of life. A stranger would be thus entertained without charge as long as he was pleased to remain; and a relation was entitled to a home among any of his kindred while he was disposed to claim it. Under the operation of such a simple and universal law of hospitality, hunger and destitution were entirely unknown among them. This method of dealing with the human appetite strikes the mind as novel; but it was founded upon a principle of brotherhood and of social intercourse, not much unlike the common table of the Spartans. The abounding supplies of corn yielded, with light cultivation, by their fruitful fields, and the simple fare of the Indians, rendered the prevailing hospitality an inconsiderable burden. It rested chiefly upon the industry, and, therefore, upon the natural kindness, of the woman, who, by the cultivation of the maize and their other plants, and the gathering of the wild fruits, provided the principal part of their subsistence, for the warrior despised the toil of husbandry, and held all labor beneath him; but it was in exact accordance with the unparalleled generosity of the Indian character. He would surrender his dinner to feed the hungry, vacate his bed to refresh the weary, and give up his apparel to clothe the naked. No test of friendship was too severe, no sacrifice to repay a favor too great, no fidelity to an engagement too inflexible for the Indian character. With an innate knowledge of the freedom and dignity of man, he has exhibited the noblest virtues of the heart, and the kindest deeds of humanity.

A further illustration of these noble characteristics of the Iroquois is given in the following anecdote:—

"Canassatego, a distinguished Onondaga chief, who flourished about the middle of the last century, thus cuttingly contrasted the hospitality of the Iroquois with that of the whites, in a conversation with Conrad Weiser, an Indian interpreter. 'You know our practice. If a white man, in travelling through our country, enters one of our cabins, we all treat him as I do you. We dry him if he is wet, we warm him if he is cold, and give him meat and drink that he may allay his hunger and thirst; and we spread soft furs for him to rest and sleep on. We demand nothing in return; but if I go into a white man's house at Albany, and ask for victuals and drink, they say: "Where is your money?" And if I have none they say, "Get out, you Indian dog."'"

Crimes and offences were so infrequent among the Iroquois, that a criminal code was scarcely necessary. Offences were punished in proportion to their magnitude, as already described concerning the practices among the New England Indians. Adultery was punished by whipping; but the punishment was inflicted upon the woman alone, who was supposed to be the only offender. Murder was punished with death, but could be condoned. The murderer could be executed by the family of his victim whenever they found him, no matter what the lapse of time. But a present of white wampum, sent on the part of the murderer to the family of his victim, when accepted, forever obliterated and wiped out the memory of the transaction. This present of white wampum was not in the nature of a compensation for the life of the deceased, but was regarded as a regretful confession of the crime, with a petition for forgiveness. All the influence of the tribe to which the victim belonged was brought to bear upon his relations to secure the acceptance of the present of white wampum, and reconciliation was usually effected except in aggravated cases of premeditated murder. Theft was scarcely known among the Indians until after the advent of the white race. In striking contrast to their simplicity and innocence was the condition of affairs, the result of their intercourse with the whites, and with the introduction of "fire-water" among them by the traders. The use of liquor filled their villages with vagrancy, violence, and bloodshed ; it invaded the peace of the domestic fireside, stimulated the fiercest passions, introduced disease, contention, and strife, and it probably did more than any other single agency to secure the downfall and decay of the once powerful League of the Iroquois.

The love of truth was another marked trait of the Indian character. On all occasions, and in whatever peril, the Indian spoke the truth without fear and without hesitation. Their language was simple and direct, and did not admit of different shades of meaning and nice discriminations bordering upon actual prevarication. They adhered with unwavering fidelity to the faith of the treaties they made, and this fidelity furnishes one of the proudest monuments of their national integrity. Allusion has already been made to the "covenant chain" with the British, to which they remained faithful, until their entire country became forfeited by their fidelity. All their national compacts were "talked into" strings of wampum which were delivered to Ho-no-we-na-to, the Onondaga Sachem, the hereditary keeper of the wampum. The expression, "This belt preserves my words," was frequently used at the close of Indian speeches, as reference to this custom. Indian nations, after making a treaty, always exchanged wampum belts which were not only the ratification, but the memorandum of the compact.

Their manner of adoption of captives, and their form of enlistment for the war-path, are alluded to in another chapter of this book in describing the degrees of our Order.

Hunting was a passion with the Red Man. He pursued it not only for subsistence for himself and his family, but for the excitement and employment it afforded. In their pursuit of game, the Iroquois roamed the whole territory which they held under subjection, from the St. Lawrence on the north to the Ohio on the south. The great lakes, the rushing rivers, and the vast forests contained the game they sought, and which they regarded as the special gifts of the Great Spirit for the subsistence of their people.

About the year 1800 a new religious teacher appeared among the Iroquois, who claimed to have received a revelation from the Great Spirit, with a command to preach to the Iroquois the doctrines with which he had been intrusted. The new religion embodied all the precepts of the ancient faith, and recognized the ancient mode of worship, giving to it anew the sanction of the Great Spirit, and it also comprehended such new doctrines as came in to enlarge the primitive system without impairing the structure itself. The new religion became generally adopted as the prevailing faith of the Iroquois.

This religious teacher was Ga-ne-o-di-yo, or Handsome Lake, a Seneca Sachem of the highest class. He was born in 1735 of the Turtle tribe, and was a half-brother of Corn Planter. Upon his death Sose-ha-wa was appointed his successor. He was a grandson of Handsome Lake, and a nephew of the famous Redjacket.

At the mourning and religious councils of the League, held at intervals of a few years, it was customary to set apart portions of three or four days to listen to a discourse upon the new religion. At one of these mourning councils held in October, 1848, the discourse delivered by Sose-ha-wa was taken down, and the following is a translation of it: —

"The Mohawks, the Onondagas, the Senecas, and our children (the Oneidas, Cayugas, and Tuscaroras) have assembled here to-day to listen to the repetition of the will of the Great Spirit, as communicated to us from heaven through his servant, Ga-ne-o-di-yo.

"Chiefs, warriors, women, and children: We give you a cordial welcome. The sun has advanced far in his path, and I am warned that my time to instruct you is limited to the meridian sun. I must therefore hasten to perform my duty. Turn your minds to the Great Spirit, and listen with strict attention. Think seriously upon what I am about to speak. Reflect upon it well that it may benefit you and your children. I thank the Great Spirit that he has spared the lives of so many of you to be present on this occasion. I return thanks to him that my life is yet spared. The Great Spirit looked down from heaven upon the sufferings and the wanderings of his red children. He saw that they had greatly decreased and degenerated. He saw the ravages of the fire-water among them. He therefore raised up for them a sacred instructor, who, having lived and travelled among them for sixteen years, was called from his labors to enjoy eternal felicity with the Great Spirit in heaven. Be patient while I speak. I cannot at all times arrange and prepare my thoughts with the same precision. But I will relate what my memory bears.

"It was in the month of O-nike-ya (June) that Handsome Lake was yet sick. He had been ill four years. He was accustomed to tell us that he had resigned himself to the will of the Great Spirit. 'I nightly returned my thanks to the Great Spirit,' said he, 'as my eyes were gladdened at evening by the sight of the stars of heaven. I viewed the ornamented heavens at evening, through the opening in the roof of my lodge, with grateful feelings to my Creator. I had no assurance that I should at the next evening contemplate his works. For this reason my acknowledgments to him were more fervent and sincere. When night was gone, and the sun again shed his light upon the earth, I saw and acknowledged in the return of day, his continued goodness to me and to all mankind. At length, I began to have an inward conviction that my end was near. I resolved once more to exchange friendly words with my people, and I sent my daughter to summon my brothers Gy-ant-wa-ka (Cornplanter) and Ta-wan-ne-ars (Blacksnake).' She hastened to do his bidding, but before she had returned he had fallen into insensibility and apparent death. Ta-wan-ne-ars, upon returning to the lodge, hastened to his brother's couch, and discovered that portions of his body were yet warm. This happened at early day, before the morning dew had dried. When the sun had advanced half-way to the meridian, his heart began to beat, and he opened his eyes. Ta-wan-ne-ars asked him if he was in his right mind; but he answered not. At meridian he again opened his eyes, and the same question was repeated. He then answered, and said, 'A man spoke from without, and asked that some one might come forth. I looked, and saw some men standing without. I arose, and, as I attempted to step over the threshold of my door, I stumbled and should have fallen had they not caught me. They were three holy men who looked alike, and were dressed alike. The paint they wore seemed but one day old. Each held in his hand a shrub bearing different kinds of fruit. One of them, addressing me, said, "We have come to comfort and relieve you. Take of these berries and eat; they will restore you to health. We have been witnesses of your lengthened illness. We have seen with what resignation you have given yourself up to the Great Spirit. We have heard your daily return of thanks. He has heard them all. His ear has ever been open to hear. You were thankful for the return of night, when you could contemplate the beauties of heaven. You were accustomed to look upon the moon, as she coursed in her nightly paths. When there were no hopes to you that you would again behold these things, you willingly resigned yourself to the mind of the Great Spirit. This was right. Since the Great Spirit made the earth and put man upon it, we have been his constant servants to guard and protect his works. There are four of us. Some other time you will be permitted to see the other. The Great Spirit is pleased to know your patient resignation to his will. As a reward for your devotion, he has cured your sickness. Tell your people to assemble to-morrow, and at noon go in and speak to them."' After they had further revealed their intentions concerning him, they departed.

"At the time appointed Handsome Lake appeared at the council, and thus addressed the people upon the revelations which had been made to him: 'I have a message to deliver to you. The servants of the Great Spirit have told me that I should yet live upon the earth to become an instructor to my people. Since the creation of man, the Great Spirit has often raised up men to teach his children what they should do to please him; but they have been unfaithful to their trust. I hope I shall profit by their example. Your Creator has seen that you have transgressed greatly against his laws. He made man pure and good. He did not intend that he should sin. You commit a great sin in taking the fire-water. The Great Spirit says that you must abandon this enticing habit. Your ancestors have brought great misery and suffering upon you. They first took the fire-water of the white man, and entailed upon you its consequences. None of them have gone to heaven. The fire-water does not belong to you. It was made for the white man beyond the great waters. For the white man it is a medicine; but they, too, have violated the will of their Maker. The Great Spirit says that drunkenness is a great crime, and he forbids you to indulge in this evil habit. His command is to the old and young. The abandonment of its use will relieve much of your sufferings, and greatly increase the comfort and happiness of your children. The Great Spirit is grieved that so much crime and wickedness should defile the earth. There are many evils which he never intended should exist among his red children. The Great Spirit has, for many wise reasons, withheld from man the number of his days; but he has not left him without a guide, for he has pointed out to him the path in which he may safely tread the journey of life.

"'When the Great Spirit made man he also made woman. He instituted marriage, and enjoined upon them to love each other and be faithful. It is pleasing to him to see men and women obey his will. Your Creator abhors a deceiver and a hypocrite. By obeying his commands you will die an easy and a happy death. When the Great Spirit instituted marriage, he ordained to bless those who were faithful with children. Some women are unfruitful, and others become so by misfortune. Such have great opportunities to do much good. There are many orphans, and many poor children whom they can adopt as their own. If you tie up the clothes of an orphan child, the Great Spirit will notice it, and reward you for it. Should an orphan ever cross your path, be kind to him, and treat him with tenderness, for this is right. Parents must constantly teach their children morality, and a reverence for their Creator. Parents must also guard their children against improper marriages. They, having much experience, should select a suitable match for their child. When the parents of both parties have agreed, then bring the young pair together, and let them know what good their parents have designed for them. If, at any time, they so far disagree that they cannot possibly live contented and happy with each other, they may separate in mutual good feeling; and in this there is no wrong. When a child is born to a husband and wife, they must give great thanks to the Great Spirit, for it is his gift, and an evidence of his kindness. Let parents instruct their children in their duty to the Great Spirit, to their parents, and to their fellowmen. Children should obey their parents and guardians, and submit to them in all things. Disobedient children occasion great pain and misery. They wound their parents' feelings, and often drive them to desperation, causing them great distress, and final admission into the place of Evil Spirits. The marriage obligations should generate good to all who have assumed them. Let the married be faithful to each other, that when they die it may be in peace. Children should never permit their parents to suffer in their old age. Be kind to them and support them. The Great Spirit requires all children to love, revere, and obey their parents. To do this is highly pleasing to him. The happiness of parents is greatly increased by the affection and the attentions of their children. To abandon a wife, or children, is a great wrong, and produces many evils. It is wrong for a father- or mother-in-law to vex a son- or daughter-in-law; but they should use them as if they were their own children. It often happens that parents hold angry disputes over their infant child. This is also a great sin. The infant hears and comprehends the angry words of its parents. It feels bad and lonely. It can see for itself no happiness in prospect. It concludes to return to its Maker. It wants a happy home and dies. The parents then weep because their child has left them. You must put this evil practice from among you, if you would live happy.

"'The Great Spirit, when he made the earth, never intended that it should be made merchandise; but he willed that all his creatures should enjoy it equally. Your chiefs have violated and betrayed your trust by selling lands. Nothing is now left of our once large possessions, save a few small reservations. Chiefs, and aged men, you, as men, have no land to sell. You occupy and possess a tract in trust for your children. You should hold that trust sacred, lest your children are driven from their homes by your unsafe conduct. Whoever sells lands offends the Great Spirit, and must expect a great punishment after death.' "

Sose-ha-wa here suspended the narration of the discourse of Handsome Lake, and thus addressed the council:—

"Chiefs, Keepers of the Faith, warriors, women, and children: You all know that our religion teaches that the early day is dedicated to the Great Spirit, and that the late day is granted to the spirits of the dead. It is now meridian, and I must close. Preserve in your minds that which has been said. Accept my thanks for your kind and patient attention. It is meet that I should also return my thanks to the Great Spirit, that he has assisted me thus far in my feeble frame to instruct you. We ask you all to come up again to-morrow, at early day, to hear what further may be said. I have done."

The next morning, after the council had been opened in the usual manner, Sose-ha-wa thus continued:—

"Relatives, uncover now your heads, and listen. The day has thus far advanced, and again we are gathered around the council fire. I see around me the several nations of the Long House; this gives me great joy. I see also seated around me my counsellors (Keepers of the Faith), who have been regularly appointed, as is the custom of our religion. Greetings have been exchanged with each other. Thanks have been returned to Ga-ni-o-di-yo. Thanks also have been returned to our Creator by the council now assembled. At this moment the Great Spirit is looking upon this assembly. He hears our words, he knows our thoughts, and is always pleased to see us gathered together for good. The sun is now high, and soon it will reach the middle heavens. I must therefore make haste. Listen attentively and consider well what you shall hear. I return thanks to our Creator, that he has spared your lives through the dangers of darkness. I salute and return my thanks to the four Celestial beings, who have communicated what I am about to say to you. I return thanks to my grandfather (Handsome Lake), from whom you first heard what I am about to speak. We all feel his loss. We miss him at our councils. I now occupy his place before you, but I am conscious that I have not the power which he possessed.

"Counsellors, warriors, mothers, and children: Listen to good instruction. Consider it well. Lay it up in your minds, and forget it not. Our Creator, when he made us, designed that we should live by hunting. It sometimes happens that a man goes out for the hunt, leaving his wife with her friends. After a long absence, he returns, and finds that his wife has taken another husband. The Great Spirit says that this is a great sin, and must be put from among us.

"The four Messengers further said that it was wrong for a mother to punish a child with a rod. It is not right to punish much, and our Creator never intended that children should be punished with a whip, or be used with any violence. In punishing a refractory child, water only is necessary, and it is sufficient. Plunge them under. This is not wrong. Whenever a child promises to do better, the punishment must cease. It is wrong to continue it after promises of amendment are made. Thus they said.

"It is right and proper always to look upon the dead. Let your face be brought near to theirs, and then address them. Let the dead know that their absence is regretted by their friends, and that they grieve for their death. Let the dead know, too, how their surviving friends intend to live. Let them know whether they will so conduct themselves, that they will meet them again in the future world. The dead will hear and remember. Thus they said.

"Continue to listen while I proceed to relate what further they said: Our Creator made the earth. Upon it he placed man, and gave him certain rules of conduct. It pleased him also to give them many kinds of amusements. He also ordered that the earth should produce all that is good for man. So long as the earth remains, it will not cease to yield. Upon the surface of the ground berries of various kinds are produced. It is the will of the Great Spirit, that when they ripen, we should return our thanks to him, and have a public rejoicing for the continuance of these blessings. He made everything which we live upon, and requires us to be thankful at all times for the continuance of his favors. When Our Life (Corn, etc.) has again appeared, it is the will of the Great Spirit that we assemble for a general thanksgiving. It is his will also that the children be brought and made to participate in the Feather dance. Your feast must consist of the new production. It is proper at these times, should any present not have their names published, or if any changes have been made, to announce them then. The festival must continue four days. Thus they said. Upon the first day must be performed the Feather dance. This ceremony must take place in the early day, and cease at the middle day. In the same manner, upon the second day, is to be performed the Thanksgiving dance. On the third day, the Thanksgiving concert, Ah-do-weh, is to be introduced. The fourth day is set apart for the Peachstone game. All these ceremonies, instituted by our Creator, must be commenced at the early day, and cease at the middle day. At all these times we are required to return thanks to our Grandfather, He-no, and his assistants. To them is assigned the duty of watching over the earth, and all it produces for our good. The great Feather and Thanksgiving dances are the appropriate ceremonies and thanksgiving to the Ruler and Maker of all things. The Thanksgiving concert belongs appropriately to our grandfathers. In it we return thanks to them. During the performance of this ceremony, we are required also to give them the smoke of tobacco. Again we must at this time return thanks to our mother the earth, for she is our relative. We must also return thanks to Our Life and its Sisters. All these things are required to be done by the light of the sun. It must not be protracted until the sun has hid its face, and darkness surrounds all things.

"Continue to listen: We have a change of seasons. We have a season of cold. This is the hunting season. It is also one in which the people can amuse themselves. Upon the fifth day of the new moon, Nis-go-wuk-na (about February 1st), we are required to commence the annual jubilee of thanksgiving to our Creator. At this festival all can give evidence of their devotion to the will of the Great Spirit by participating in all its ceremonies.

"Continue to listen: The four Messengers of the Great Spirit have always watched over us, and have ever seen what was transpiring among men. At one time Handsome Lake was translated by them to the regions above. He looked down upon the earth, and saw a great assembly. Out of it came a man. His garments were torn, tattered, and filthy. His whole appearance indicated great misery and poverty. They asked him how this spectacle appeared to him. He replied that it was hard to look upon. They then told him that the man he saw was a drunkard; that he had taken the fire-water, and it had reduced him to poverty. Again he looked and saw a woman seated upon the ground. She was constantly engaged in gathering up and secreting about her person her worldly effects. They said, the woman you see is inhospitable. She is too selfish to spare anything, and will never leave her worldly goods. She can never pass from earth to heaven. Tell this to your people. Again he looked, and saw a man carrying in each hand large pieces of meat. He went about the assembly, giving to each a piece. This man, they said, is blessed, for he is hospitable and kind. He looked again, and saw streams of blood. They said, thus will the earth be if the fire-water is not put from among you. Brother will kill brother, and friend, friend. Again they told him to look towards the east. He obeyed, and, as far as his vision reached, he saw the increasing smoke of numberless distilleries arising and shutting out the light of the sun. It was a horrible spectacle to witness. They told him that here was manufactured the fire-water. Again he looked and saw a costly house made and furnished by the palefaces. It was a house of confinement, where were fetters, ropes, and whips. They said that those who persisted in the use of the fire-water would fall into this. Our Creator commands us to put this destructive vice far from us. Again he looked and saw various assemblages. Some of them were unwilling to listen to instruction. They were riotous, and took great pride in drinking the strong waters. He observed another group who were half inclined to hear, but the temptations to vice which surrounded them allured them back, and they also revelled in the fumes of the fire-water. He saw another assemblage which had met to hear instructions. This they said was pleasing to the Great Spirit. He loves those who will listen and obey. It has grieved him that his children are now divided by separate interests, and are pursuing so many paths. It pleases him to see his people live together in harmony and quiet. The firewater creates many dissensions and divisions among us. They said that the use of it would cause many to die unnatural deaths; many would be exposed to cold and freeze; many would be burned, and others will be drowned, while under the influence of the fire-water.

"Friends and relatives: All these things have often happened. How many of our people have been frozen to death, how many have been burned to death, how many have been drowned while under the influence of the strong waters. The punishments of those who use the fire-water commence while they are yet on the earth. Many are now thrown into houses of confinement by the palefaces. I repeat to you, the Ruler of us all requires us to unite and put this evil from among us. Some say that the use of the fire-water is not wrong, and that it is food. Let those who do not believe it wrong, make this experiment. Let all who use the fire-water assemble and organize into a council, and those who do not into another near them. A great difference will then be discovered. The council of drunkards will end in a riot and tumult, while the other will have harmony and quiet. It is hard to think of the great prevalence of this evil among us. Reform, and put it from among you. Many resolve to use the fire-water until near death, when they will repent. If they do this, nothing can save them from destruction, for then medicine can have no power. Thus they said.

"All men were made equal by the Great Spirit; but he has given to them a variety of gifts. To some a pretty face, to others an ugly one; to some a comely form, to others a deformed figure. Some are fortunate in collecting around them worldly goods. But you are all entitled to the same privileges, and therefore must put pride from among you. You are not your own makers, nor the builders of your own fortunes. All things are the gift of the Great Spirit, and to him must be returned thanks for their bestowal. He alone must be acknowledged as the giver. It has pleased him to make differences among men, but it is wrong for one man to exalt himself above another. Love each other, for you are all brothers and sisters of the same great family. The Great Spirit enjoins upon all to observe hospitality and kindness, especially to the needy and the helpless, for this is pleasing to him. If a stranger wanders about your abode, speak to him with kind words, be hospitable towards him, welcome him to your home, and forget not always to mention the Great Spirit. In the morning, give thanks to the Great Spirit for the return of day, and the light of the sun ; at night, renew your thanks to him, that his ruling power has preserved you from harm during the day, and that night has again come, in which you may rest your weary bodies.

"The four Messengers said further to Handsome Lake : 'Tell your people, and particularly the Keepers of the Faith, to be strong-minded and to adhere to the true faith. We fear the Evil-minded will go among them with temptations. He may introduce the fiddle. He may bring cards and leave them among you. The use of these are great sins. Let the people be on their guard, and the keepers of the watch be faithful and vigilant, that none of the evils may find their way among the people. Let the Keepers of the Faith preserve the law of moral conduct in all its purity. When meetings are to be held for instruction, and the people are preparing to go, the Evil-minded is then busy. He goes from one to another, whispering many temptations by which to keep them away. He will even follow persons into the door of the council and induce some, at that time, to bend their steps away. Many resist until they have entered, and then leave it. This habit, once indulged, obtains a fast hold, and the evil propensity increases with age. This is a great sin, and should be at once abandoned.' Thus they said.

"Speak evil of no one. If you can say no good of a person, then be silent. Let not your tongues betray you into evil. Let all be mindful of this ; for these are the words of our Creator.

"Let all strive to cultivate friendship with those who surround them. This is pleasing to the Great Spirit.

"Counsellors, warriors, women, and children : I shall now rest. I thank you all for your kind and patient attention. I thank the Great Spirit that he has spared the lives of so many of us to witness this day. I request you all to come up again to-morrow at early day. Let us all hope that, until we meet again, the Creator and Ruler of us all may be kind to us and preserve our lives. Na-ho."

The council, on the following day, was opened with a few short speeches from some of the chiefs, or Keepers of the Faith, returning thanks for the privileges of the occasion, as usual at councils; after which Sose-ha-wa, resuming his discourse, spoke as follows : —

"Friends and relatives, uncover now your heads : Continue to listen to my rehearsal of the sayings communicated to Handsome Lake by the four Messengers of the Great Spirit. We have met again around the council-fire. We have followed the ancient custom and greeted each other. This is right and highly pleasing to our Maker. He now looks down upon this assembly. He sees us all. He is informed of the cause of our gathering, and it is pleasing to him. Life is uncertain. While we live let us love each other. Let us sympathize always with the suffering and needy. Let us also always rejoice with those who are glad. This is now the third day, and my time for speaking to you is drawing to a close. It will be a long time before we meet again. Many moons and seasons will have passed before the sacred council-brand shall be again uncovered. Be watchful, therefore, and remember faithfully what you may now hear.

"In discoursing yesterday upon the duties of the Keepers of the Faith, I omitted some things important. The Great Spirit created this office. He designed that its duties should never end. There are some who are selected, and set apart by our Maker, to perform the duties of this office. It is, therefore, their duty to be faithful, and to be always watching. These duties they must ever perform during their lives. The faithful, when they leave this earth, will have a pleasant path to travel in. The same office exists in heaven, the home of our Creator. They will take the same place when they arrive there. There are dreadful penalties awaiting those Keepers of the Faith who resign their office without a cause. Thus they said.

"It was the original intention of our Maker that all our feast of thanksgiving should be seasoned with the flesh of wild animals; but we are surrounded by the palefaces, and, in a short time, the woods will be all removed. Then there will be no more game for the Indian to use in his feasts. The four Messengers said, in consequence of this, that we might use the flesh of domestic animals. This will not be wrong. The palefaces are pressing you upon every side. You must therefore live as they do. How far you can do so without sin, I will now tell you. You may grow cattle and build yourselves warm and comfortable dwelling-houses. This is not sin; and it is all that you can safely adopt of the customs of the palefaces. You cannot live as they do. Thus they said.

"Continue to listen: It has pleased our Creator to set apart, as our Life, the Three Sisters. For this special favor let us ever be thankful. When you have gathered in your harvest, let the people assemble and hold a general thanksgiving for so great a good. In this way you will show your obedience to the will and pleasure of your Creator. Thus they said.

"Many of you may be ignorant of the Spirit of Medicine. It watches over all constantly, and assists the needy whenever necessity requires. The Great Spirit designed that some men should possess the gift of skill in medicine. But he is pained to see a medicine man making exorbitant charges for attending the sick. Our Creator made for us tobacco. This plant must always be used in administering medicines. When a sick person recovers his health, he must return thanks to the Great Spirit by means of tobacco; for it is by his goodness that he is made well. He blesses the medicine; and the medicine man must receive as his reward whatever the gratitude of the restored may tender. This is right and proper. There are many who are unfortunate and cannot pay for attendance. It is sufficient for us to return thanks to the medicine man upon recovery. The remembrance that he has saved the life of a relative will be a sufficient reward.

"Listen further to what the Great Spirit has been pleased to communicate to us: He has made us, as a race, separate and distinct from the paleface. It is a great sin to intermarry and intermingle the blood of two races. Let none be guilty of this transgression.

"At one time the four Messengers said to Handsome Lake, lest the people should disbelieve you, and not repent and forsake their evil ways, we will now disclose to you the House of

AN IROQUOIS WOMAN.

Torment, the dwelling-place of the Evil-minded. Handsome Lake was particular in describing to us all that he witnessed, and the course which departed spirits were accustomed to take on leaving the earth. There was a road which led upwards. At a certain point it branched; one branch led straight forward to the Home of the Great Spirit, and the other turned aside to the House of Torment. At the place where the roads separated were stationed two keepers, one representing the Good, and the other the Evil Spirit. When a person reached the fork, if wicked, by a motion from the Evil keeper, he turned instinctively upon the road which led to the abode of the Evil-minded. But if virtuous and good, the other keeper directed him upon the straight road. The latter was not much travelled, while the former was so frequently trodden that no grass could grow in the pathway. It sometimes happened that the keepers had great difficulty in deciding which path the person should take, when the good and bad actions of the individual were nearly balanced. Those sent to the House of Torment, sometimes remained one day (which is there one of our years); some for a longer period. After they have atoned for their sins, they pass to heaven. But when they have committed either of the great sins (witchcraft, murder, and infanticide), they never pass to heaven, but are tormented forever. Having conducted Handsome Lake to this place, he saw a large and dark-colored mansion covered with soot, and beside it stood a lesser one. One of the four then held out his rod, and the top of the house moved up, until they could look down upon all that was within. He saw many rooms. The first object which met his eye was a haggard-looking man, his sunken eyes cast upon the ground, and his form half consumed by the torments he had undergone. This man was a drunkard. The Evil-minded then appeared, and called him by name. As the man obeyed his call, he dipped from a caldron a quantity of red-hot liquid and commanded him to drink it, as it was an article he loved. The man did as he was directed, and immediately from his mouth issued a stream of blaze. He cried in vain for help. The Tormenter then requested him to sing and make himself merry, as was his wont while on earth after drinking the fire-water. Let drunkards take warning from this. Others were then summoned. There came before him two persons who appeared to be husband and wife. He told them to exercise the privilege they were so fond of while on the earth. They immediately commenced a quarrel of words. They raged at each other with such violence that their tongues and eyes ran out so far they could neither see nor speak. This, said they, is the punishment of quarrelsome and disputing husbands and wives. Let such also take warning and live together in peace and harmony. Next he called up a woman who had been a witch. First he plunged her into a caldron of boiling liquid. In her cries of distress she begged the Evil-minded to give her some cooler place. He then immersed her in one containing liquid at the point of freezing. Her cries then were that she was too cold. This woman, said the four Messengers, shall always be tormented in this manner. He proceeded to mention the punishment which awaits all those who cruelly ill-treat their wives. The Evil-minded next called up a man who had been accustomed to beat his wife. Having led him up to the red-hot statue of a female, he directed him to do that which he was fond of while he was upon the earth. He obeyed and struck the figure. The sparks flew in every direction, and by the contact his arm was consumed. Such is the punishment, they said, awaiting those who ill-treat their wives. From this take seasonable warning. He looked again and saw a woman whose arms and hands were nothing but bones. She had sold fire-water to the Indians, and the flesh was eaten from her hands and arms. This, they said, would be the fate of rum-sellers. Again he looked and in one apartment he saw and recognized Ho-ne-ya-wus (Farmer's Brother), his former friend. He was engaged in removing a heap of sand, grain by grain, and although he labored continually, yet the heap of sand was not diminished. This, they said, was the punishment of those who sold land. Adjacent to the house of torment was a field of corn filled with weeds. He saw women in the act of cutting them down, but as fast as this was done they grew up again. This, they said, was the punishment of lazy women. It would be proper and right, had we time, to tell more of this place of torment. But my time is limited and I must pass to other things.

"The Creator made men dependent upon each other. He made them social beings; therefore, when your neighbor visits you, set food before him. If it be your next door neighbor, you must give him to eat. He will partake and thank you.

"Again they said : You must not steal. Should you want for anything necessary, you have only to tell your wants and they will be supplied. This is right. Let none ever steal anything. Children are often tempted to take things home which do not belong to them. Let parents instruct children in this rule.

"Many of our people live to a very old age. Your Creator says that your deportment towards them must be that of reverence and affection. They have seen and felt much of the misery and pain of earth. Be always kind to them when old and helpless. Wash their hands and face, and nurse them with care. This is the will of the Great Spirit.

"It has been the custom among us to mourn for the dead one year. This custom is wrong. As it causes the death of many children, it must be abandoned. Ten days mourn for the dead and not longer. When one dies, it is right and proper to make an address over the body, telling how much you loved the deceased. Great respect for the dead must be observed among us.

"At another time the four Messengers said to Handsome Lake, they would now show him the 'Destroyer of Villages'" (Washington), "of whom you have so frequently heard. Upon the road leading to heaven he could see a light, far away in the distance, moving to and fro. Its brightness far exceeded the brilliancy of the noonday sun. They told him the journey was as follows : First, they came to a cold spring, which was a resting place. From this point they proceeded into pleasant fairy grounds, which spread away in every direction. Soon they reached heaven. The light was dazzling. Berries of every description grew in vast abundance. Their size and quality was such that a single berry was more than sufficient to appease the appetite. A sweet fragrance perfumed the air. Fruits of every kind met the eye. The inmates of this celestial abode spent their time in amusement and repose. No evil could enter there. None in heaven ever transgressed again. Families were reunited and dwelt together in harmony. They possessed a bodily form, the senses, and the remembrances of the earthly life. But no white man ever entered heaven. Thus they said.

He looked and saw an inclosure upon a plain, just without the entrance of heaven. Within it was a fort. Here he saw the 'Destroyer of Villages,' walking to and fro within the inclosure. His countenance indicated a great and a good man. They said to Handsome Lake: 'The man you see is the only paleface who ever left the earth. He was kind to you, when, on the settlement of the great difficulty between the Americans and the Great Crown (Go-wek-go-wa), you were abandoned to the mercy of your enemies. The Crown told the great American, that as for his allies the Indians, he might kill them if he liked. The great American judged that this would be cruel and unjust. He believed they were made by the Great Spirit and were entitled to the enjoyment of life. He was kind to you, and extended over you his protection. For this reason, he has been allowed to leave the earth. But he is never permitted to go into the presence of the Great Spirit. Although alone, he is perfectly happy. All faithful Indians pass by him as they go to heaven. They see him and recognize him, but pass on in silence. No word ever passes his lips.'

"Friends and Relatives: It was by the influence of this great man, that we were spared as a people, and yet live. Had he not granted us his protection, where would we have been? Perished, all perished.

"The four Messengers further said to Handsome Lake, they were fearful that, unless the people repented, and obeyed his commands, the patience and forbearance of their Creator would be exhausted; that he would grow angry with them, and cause their increase to cease.

"Our Creator made light and darkness. He made the sun to heat and shine over the world. He made the moon, also, to shine by night, and to cool the world if the sun made it too hot by day. The keeper of the clouds, by direction of the Great Spirit, will then cease to act. The keeper of the springs and running brooks will cease to rule them for the good of man. The sun will cease to fulfil his office. Total darkness will then cover the earth. A great smoke will rise and spread over the face of the earth. Then will come out of it all monsters and poisonous animals created by the Evil-minded; and they, with the wicked upon the earth, will perish together.

"But before this dreadful time shall come, the Great Spirit will take home to himself all the good and faithful. They will lay themselves down to sleep, and from this sleep of death they will rise and go home to their Creator. Thus they said.

"I have now done. I close thus, that you may remember and understand the fate which awaits the earth, and the unfaithful and unbelieving. Our Creator looks down upon us. The four Beings from above see us. They witness with pleasure this assemblage and rejoice at the object for which it is gathered. It is now forty-eight years since we first began to listen to the renewed will of our Creator. I have been unable, during the time allotted to me, to rehearse all the sayings of Ga-ne-o-di-yo. I regret very much that you cannot hear them all.

"Councillors, warriors, women and children: I have done. I thank you all for your attendance, and for your kind and patient attention. May the Great Spirit, who rules all things, watch over and protect you from every harm and danger, while you travel the journey of life. May the Great Spirit bless you all, and bestow upon you life, health, peace, and prosperity; and may you, in turn, appreciate his great goodness. Na-ho."

The gifted author from whose wonderful description of the Iroquois the description presented in this chapter has been condensed concluded his description of the rise, progress, and decline of the League with the following mournful but truthful words:—

"The Iroquois were our predecessors in the sovereignty. Our country they once called their country; our rivers and lakes were their rivers and lakes; our hills and intervales were also theirs. Before us they enjoyed the beautiful scenery spread out between the Hudson and Niagara, in its wonderful diversity from the pleasing to the sublime. Before us were they invigorated by our climate, and were nourished by the bounties of the earth, the forest, and the stream. The tie by which we are thus connected carries with it the duty of doing justice to their memory by preserving their name and deeds, their customs and their institutions, lest they perish from remembrance. We cannot wish to tread ignorantly upon those extinguished council-fires, whose light in the days of aboriginal dominion was visible over half the continent.

"The political structures of our primitive inhabitants have, in general, proved exceedingly unsubstantial. Isolated nations, by some superiority of institutions, or casual advantage of location, sprang up with an energetic growth, and for a season spread their dominion far and wide. After a brief period of prosperity they were borne back by adverse fortune into their original obscurity; thus rendering these boundless territories the constant scene of human conflict, and of the rise and fall of Indian sovereignties. It was reserved for the Iroquois to rest themselves upon a more durable foundation, by the establishment of a League. This alliance between their nations they cemented by the imperishable bonds of tribal relationship. At the epoch of Saxon occupation, they were rapidly building up an empire which threatened the absorption or extermination of the whole Indian family east of the Mississippi. Their power had become sufficient to set at defiance all hostile invasions from contiguous nations; and the League itself, while it suffered no loss of numbers by emigrating bands, was endued with a capacity for indefinite expansion. At the periods of their separate discovery, the Aztecs on the south and the Iroquois in the north were the only Indian races upon the continent whose institutions promised, at maturity, to ripen into civilization. Such were the condition and prospect of this Indian League, when Hendrick Hudson, more than two centuries since (1609), sailed up the river which constituted their eastern boundary. This silent voyage of the navigator may be regarded as the opening event in the series which resulted in reversing the political prospect of the Ho-de-no-sau-nee, and in introducing into their Long House an invader more relentless in his purposes and more invincible in arms than the Red Man against whose assaults it had been erected.

"Their council-fires, so far as they are emblematical of civil jurisdiction, have long since been extinguished, their empire has terminated, and the shades of evening are now gathering thickly over the scattered and feeble remnants of this once powerful League. Race has yielded to race, the inevitable result of the contact of the civilized with the hunter life. Who shall relate with what pangs of regret they yielded up from river to river, and from lake to lake, this fair, broad domain of their fathers? The Iroquois will soon be lost, as a people, in that night of impenetrable darkness in which so many Indian races have been enshrouded. Already their country has been appropriated, their forests cleared, and their trails obliterated. The residue of this proud and gifted race, who still linger around their native seats, are destined to fade away until they become eradicated as an Indian stock. We shall, ere long, look backward to the Iroquois as a race blotted from existence; but to remember them as a people whose Sachems had no cities, whose religion had no temples, and whose government had no record."

All writers upon Indian history and Indian character have extolled the eloquence of the leading chiefs among them. It seems appropriate, therefore, to include in this account of the primitive Red Men some specimens of the beauty and imagery of the language used by these "untutored children of the forest."

One of the most noted Indians, at the close of the last and opening of the present century, was Sagoyewatha, called by the whites Red-jacket. He died January 20, 1830. In the year 1805, at a council held at Buffalo, N.Y., there were assembled many Seneca chiefs and warriors at the request of a missionary from Massachusetts, who explained that he had called them together to instruct them how to worship the Great Spirit, and not for the purpose of getting away their lands and money; that there was but one religion, and unless they embraced it, they could not be happy; that they had lived in darkness and great error all their lives; he wished if they had any objections to his religion they would state them; that he had visited some smaller tribes, who waited the decision of the present council before they would consent to receive him, as the Senecas were their older brothers. After the missionary had concluded, the Indians conferred together among themselves, after which an answer was made by Red-jacket as follows:—

"Friend and brother, it was the will of the Great Spirit that we should meet together this day. He orders all things, and he has given us a fine day for our council. He has taken his garment from before the sun, and caused it to shine with brightness upon us; our eyes are opened that we see clearly; our ears are unstopped that we have been able to hear distinctly the words that you have spoken; for all these favors we thank the Great Spirit, and him only.

"Brother, this council-fire was kindled by you; it was at your request that we came together at this time; we have listened with attention to what you have said; you requested us to speak our minds freely; this gives us great joy, for we now consider that we stand upright before you and can speak what we think; all have heard your voice, and all speak to you as one man; our minds are agreed.

"Brother, you say you want an answer to your talk before you leave this place. It is right you should have one, as you are a great distance from home, and we do not wish to detain you; but we will first look back a little, and tell you what our fathers have told us, and what we have heard from the white people.

"Brother, listen to what we say. There was a time when our forefathers owned this great island. Their seats extended from the rising to the setting sun. The Great Spirit had made it for the use of Indians. He had created the buffalo, the deer, and other animals for food. He made the bear and the beaver, and their skins served us for clothing. He had scattered them over the country, and taught us how to take them. He had caused the earth to produce corn for bread. All this he had done for his red children because he loved them. If we had any disputes about hunting-grounds, they were generally settled without the shedding of much blood; but an evil day came upon us; your forefathers crossed the great waters, and landed on this island. Their numbers were small; they found friends and not enemies; they told us they had fled from their own country for fear of wicked men, and came here to enjoy their religion. They asked for a small seat; we took pity on them, granted their request, and they sat down amongst us; we gave them corn and meat; they gave us poison in return. The white people had now found our country; tidings were carried back, and more came amongst us; yet we did not fear them; we took them to be friends; they called us brothers; we believed them, and gave them a larger seat. At length their numbers had greatly increased; they wanted more land; they wanted our country. Our eyes were opened, and our minds became uneasy.

Wars took place; Indians were hired to fight against Indians, and many of our people were destroyed. They also brought strong liquors among us; it was strong and powerful, and has slain thousands.

"Brother, our seats were once large, and yours were very small; you have now become a great people, and we have scarcely a place left to spread our blankets; you have got our country, but are not satisfied; you want to force your religion upon us.

"Brother, continue to listen. You say that you are sent to instruct us how to worship the Great Spirit agreeably to his mind, and if we do not take hold of the religion which you white people teach, we shall be unhappy hereafter. You say that you are right and we are lost. How do you know this to be true? We understand that your religion is written in a book; if it was intended for us as well as you, why has not the Great Spirit given it to us, and not only to us, but why did he not give to our forefathers the knowledge of that book, with the means of understanding it rightly? We only know what you tell us about it; how shall we know when to believe, being so often deceived by the white people?

"Brother, you say that there is but one way to worship and serve the Great Spirit. If there is but one religion, why do you white people differ so much about it? Why not all agree, as you can all read the book?

"Brother, we do not understand these things; we are told that your religion was given to your forefathers, and has been handed down from father to son. We also have a religion which was given to our forefathers, and has been handed down to us, their children. We worship that way. It teacheth us to be thankful for all the favors we receive; to love each other, and to be united; we never quarrel about religion.

"Brother, the Great Spirit has made us all; but he has made a great difference between his white and red children; he has given us a different complexion and different customs; to you he has given the arts; to these he has not opened our eyes; we know these things to be true. Since he has made so great a difference between us in other things, why may we not conclude that he has given us a different religion according to our understanding; the Great Spirit does right; he knows what is best for his children; we are satisfied.

"Brother, we do not wish to destroy your religion, or take it from you; we only want to enjoy our own.

"Brother, you say that you have not come to get our land or our money, but to enlighten our minds; I will now tell you that I have been at your meetings, and saw you collecting money from the meeting. I cannot tell what this money was intended for, but suppose it was for your minister, and if we should conform to your way of thinking, perhaps you may want some from us.

"Brother, we are told that you have been preaching to white people in this place; these people are our neighbors; we are acquainted with them; we will wait a little while and see what effect your preaching has upon them. If we find it does them good, makes them honest and less disposed to cheat Indians, we will then consider again what you have said.

"Brother, you have now heard our answer to your talk, and this is all we have to say at present. As we are going to part, we will come and take you by the hand, and hope the Great Spirit will protect you on your journey, and return you safe to your friends."

The chief and others then drew near the missionary to take him by the hand; but he would not receive them, and hastily rising from his seat, said, "that there was no fellowship between the religion of God and the works of the devil, and, therefore, could not join hands with them." Upon this being interpreted to them, "they smiled, and retired in a peaceable manner."

The Indians cannot well conceive how they have any participation in the guilt of the crucifixion, inasmuch as they do not believe themselves of the same religion as the whites, and there being no dispute but that the latter committed that act. Red-jacket once said to a clergyman who was importuning him upon the subject:—

"Brother, if you white men murdered the Son of the Great Spirit, we Indians had nothing to do with it, and it is none of our affair. If he had come among us, we would not have killed him; we would have treated him well. You must make amends for that crime yourselves."

PRIMITIVE RED MEN. 85

Another illustration is given in the following account of a trial of a chief who executed a woman for alleged witchcraft. The story is as follows: —

"In the spring of 1821, a man of Red-jacket's tribe fell into a languishment and died. His complaint was unknown, and some circumstances attended his illness which caused his friends to believe that he was bewitched. The woman that attended was fixed upon as the witch, and by the law, or custom, of the nation, she was doomed to suffer death. A chief by the name of Tom-jemmy, called by his own people Soo-nong-gise, executed the decree by cutting her throat. The Americans took up the matter, seized Tom-jemmy, and threw him into prison. Some time after, when his trial came on, Red-jacket appeared in court as an evidence. The counsel for the prisoner denied that the court had any jurisdiction over the case, and after it was carried through three terms, Soo-nong-gise was finally cleared. Red-jacket and the other witnesses testified that the woman was a witch, and that she had been tried, condemned, and executed in pursuance of their laws, which had been established from time immemorial, long before the English came into the country. The witch doctrine of the Senecas was much ridiculed by some of the Americans, to which Red-jacket thus aptly alludes in a speech which he made while upon the stand: —

"'What! do you denounce us as fools and bigots, because we still continue to believe that which you yourselves sedulously inculcated two centuries ago? Your divines have thundered this doctrine from the pulpit, your judges have pronounced it from the bench, your courts of justice have sanctioned it with the formalities of law, and you would now punish our unfortunate brother for adhering to the superstitions of his fathers! Go to Salem! Look at the records of your government, and you will find hundreds executed for the very crime which has called forth the sentence of condemnation upon this woman, and drawn down the arm of vengeance upon her. What have our brothers done more than the rulers of your people have done? And what crime has this man committed by executing, in a summary way, the laws of his country and the injunctions of his God?'"

Before Red-jacket was admitted to give evidence in the case, he was asked if he believed in future rewards and punishments, and the existence of God. With a piercing look into the face of his interrogator, and with no little indignation of expression, he replied: "Yes! much more than the white men, if we are to judge of their actions."

Upon the appearance of Red-jacket upon this occasion, one observes: "There is not, perhaps, in nature a more expressive eye than that of Red-jacket; when fired by indignation or revenge it is terrible, and when he chooses to display his unrivalled talent for irony, his keen, sarcastic glance is irresistible."

Red-jacket visited Philadelphia in 1792, at which time he was welcomed by the Governor of Pennsylvania, who delivered to him an address in behalf of the Commonwealth. Red-jacket made a speech in reply, which we here reproduce. "Onas" was the name the Indians gave William Penn, and which they continued to give to all subsequent governors of Philadelphia. This will explain the allusion in the following speech: —

"Brother Onas Governor, open unprejudiced ears to what we have to say. Some days since you addressed us, and what you said gave us great pleasure. This day the Great Spirit has allowed us to meet you again, in this council-chamber. We hope that your not receiving an immediate answer to your address will make no improper impression on your mind. We mention this lest you should suspect that your kind welcome and friendly address has not had a proper effect upon our hearts. We assure you it is far otherwise. In your address to us the other day, in this ancient council-chamber, where our forefathers have often conversed together, several things struck our attention very forcibly. When you told us this was the place in which our forefathers often met on peaceable terms, it gave us sensible pleasure, and more joy than we could express. Though we have no writings like you, yet we remember often to have heard of the friendship that existed between our fathers and yours. The picture to which you drew our attention" (a fine picture representing Penn's treaty with the Indians), "brought fresh to our minds the friendly conferences that used to be held between the former governors of Pennsylvania and our tribes, and showed the love which your forefathers had of peace, and the friendly disposition of our people. It is still our wish, as well as yours, to preserve peace between our tribes and you, and it would be well if the same spirit existed among the Indians to the westward, and through every part of the United States. You particularly expressed that you were well pleased to find that we differed in disposition from the Indians westward. Your disposition is that for which the ancient Onas Governors were remarkable. As you love peace, so do we also; and we wish it could be extended to the most distant part of this great country. We agreed in council this morning that the sentiments I have expressed should be communicated to you before the delegates of the Five Nations, and to tell you that your cordial welcome to this city, and the good sentiment contained in your address, have made a deep impression on our hearts, have given us great joy, and from the heart I tell you so. This is all I have to say."

Another famous Seneca chief was Ho-na-ya-wus, whose English name was Farmer's Brother. Throughout his whole life this chief seems to have been a peacemaker. He fought against the Colonists in the Revolution, but in the War of 1812 he fought with the United States forces. One of his most celebrated speeches was delivered in the Council at Genesee River in 1798, which after being interpreted was signed by the chiefs present and sent to the Legislature at New York. It was as follows:—

"Brothers, as you are once more assembled in council for the purpose of doing honor to yourselves and justice to your country, we, your brothers, the sachems, chiefs, and warriors of the Seneca nation, request you to open your ears and give attention to our voice and wishes. You will recollect the late contest between you and your father, the great king of England. This contest threw the inhabitants of this whole island into a great tumult and commotion, like a raging whirlwind which tears up the trees and tosses to and fro the leaves, so that no one knows from whence they come or where they will fall. This whirlwind was so directed by the Great Spirit above as to throw into our arms two of your infant children, Jasper Parish and Horatio Jones. We adopted them into our families and made them our children. We loved them and nourished them. They lived with us many years. At length the Great Spirit spoke to the whirlwind, and it was still. A clear and uninterrupted sky appeared. The path of peace was opened and the chain of friendship was once more made bright. Then these our adopted children left us to seek their relations; we wished them to remain among us and promised if they would return, and live in our country, to give each of them a seat of land for them and their children to sit down upon. They have returned and have for several years past been serviceable to us as interpreters. We still feel our hearts beat with affection for them, and now wish to fulfil the promise we made them, and reward them for their services. We have, therefore, made up our minds to give them a seat of two square miles of land lying on the outlets of Lake Erie, about three miles below Black Rock, beginning at the mouth of a creek known by the name of Scoyguquoydes Creek, running one mile from the River Niagara, up said creek, thence northerly as the river runs two miles, thence westerly one mile to the river, thence up the river, as the river runs, two miles, to the place of beginning, so as to contain two square miles. We have now made known to you our minds. We expect and earnestly request that you will permit our friends to receive this our gift, and will make the same good to them according to the laws and customs of your nation. Why should you hesitate to make our minds easy with regard to this our request? To you it is but a little thing; and have you not complied with the request and confirmed the gifts of our brothers, the Oneidas, the Onondagas, and Cayugas, to their interpreters? And shall we ask and not be heard? We send you this our speech, to which we expect your answer before the breaking up of our great council-fire."

It has with truth been said that there never flowed from the lips of a man more sublime metaphor than that made use of by this chief in the speech given above when alluding to the Revolutionary contest, "the Great Spirit spoke to the whirlwind, and it was still." This chief died before the close of the War of 1812, more than "eighty snows in years."

Another chief prominent among the Senecas was Gyantwaka, or Corn Planter. It will be remembered that the Six Nations, with the exception of the Oneidas, took part with England in the Revolution. At the end of that war the Indian nations were reduced to the alternative of giving up such of their country as the Colonists required, or of losing the whole of it.

In 1790 a most pathetic appeal was made to Congress for some amelioration of the condition of the Six Nations, which appeal was believed to be the production of Corn Planter and in which the following passage occurs:—

"Father, we will not conceal from you that the great God and not men has preserved the Corn-plant from the hands of his own nation. For they ask continually 'where is the land on which our children and their children after them are to lie down upon? You told us that the line drawn from Pennsylvania to Lake Ontario would mark it forever on the east, and the line running from Beaver Creek to Pennsylvania would mark it on the west, and we see it is not so; for, first one and then another come and take it away by order of that people which you tell us promised to secure it to us.' He is silent, for he has nothing to answer. When the sun goes down, he opens his heart before God, and earlier than the sun appears again upon the hills he gives thanks for his protection during the night. For he feels that among men become desperate by the injuries they sustain it is God only that can preserve him. He loves peace, and all he had in store he has given to those who have been robbed by your people, lest they should plunder the innocent to repay themselves. The whole season, which others have employed in providing for their families, he has spent in endeavors to preserve peace; and this moment his wife and children are lying on the ground and in want of food."

Corn Planter, accompanied by two other chiefs, subsequently came to Philadelphia, on which occasion the following communication was made to President Washington:—

"Father, the voice of the Seneca nations speaks to you, the great counsellor, in whose heart the wise men of all the thirteen fires" (thirteen United States) "have placed their wisdom. It may be very small in your ears, and we therefore entreat you to hearken with attention; for we are able to speak of things which are to us very great.

"When your army entered the country of the Six Nations, we called you the Town Destroyer; to this day, when your name is heard, our women look behind them and turn pale, and our children cling close to the necks of their mothers.

"When our chiefs returned from Fort Stanwix, and laid

before our council what had been done there, our nation was surprised to hear how great a country you had compelled them to give up to you, without your paying to us anything for it. Every one said that your hearts were yet swelled with resentment against us for what had happened during the war, but that one day you would consider it with more kindness. We asked each other, 'What have we done to deserve such severe chastisement?'

"Father, when you kindled your thirteen fires separately, the wise men assembled at them told us that you were all brothers, the children of one great father, who regarded the red people as his children. They called us brothers, and invited us to his protection. They told us that he resided beyond the great water where the sun first rises, and that he was a king whose power no people could resist, and that his goodness was as bright as the sun. What they said went to our hearts. We accepted the invitation and promised to obey him. What the Seneca nation promises they faithfully perform. When you refused obedience to that king, he commanded us to assist his beloved men in making you sober. In obeying him, we did no more than yourselves had led us to promise. We were deceived, but your people, teaching us to confide in that king, had helped to deceive us, and we now appeal to your breast. Is all the blame ours?

"Father, when we saw that we had been deceived, and heard the invitation that you gave us to draw near to the fire you had kindled, and talk with you concerning peace, we made haste towards it. You told us you could crush us to nothing, and you demanded from us a great country, as the price of that peace which you had offered to us; as if our want of strength had destroyed our rights. Our chiefs had felt your power and were unable to contend against you, and they therefore gave up that country. What they agreed to has bound our nation, but your anger against us must by this time be cooled, and although our strength is not increased, nor your power become less, we ask you to consider calmly: Were the terms dictated to us by your commissioners reasonable and just?"

After further alluding to the unjust treatment which they had received from the whites, the address continued:—

"Father, you have said that we were in your hand, and that

by closing it you could crush us to nothing. Are you determined to crush us? If you are, tell us so, that those of our nation who have become your children, and have determined to die so, may know what to do. In this case, one chief has said he would ask you to put him out of his pain. Another, who will not think of dying by the hand of his father or his brother, has said he will retire to the Chataughque, eat of the fatal root, and sleep with his fathers in peace.

"All the land we have been speaking of belonged to the Six Nations. No part of it ever belonged to the king of England, and he could not give it to you.

"Hear us once more. At Fort Stanwix we agreed to deliver up those of our people who should do you any wrong, and that you might try them and punish them according to your law. We delivered up two men accordingly. But instead of trying them according to your law, the lowest of your people took them from your magistrate, and put them immediately to death. It is just to punish the murderer with death, but the Senecas will not deliver up their people to men who disregard the treaties of their own nation."

Black Thunder, whose Indian name was Mackkatananamakee, was one of the most celebrated warriors of the Fox Tribe among the western Indians. An excellent speech was made by him to the American Commissioners who had assembled many chiefs in council at a place called The Portage, July, 1815, upon the state of their affairs. It was supposed that the Indians meditated hostilities against the whites. One of the American Commissioners, in opening the talk, unwisely accused the Indians of breach of former treaties. The first chief that answered, spoke with a tremulous voice which evidently portrayed guilt, or perhaps fear. Black Thunder's reply showed him equally indignant at the charge of the white man and at the cowardice of the chief who had preceded him. The speech was as follows: —

"My father, restrain your feelings, and hear calmly what I shall say. I shall say it plainly. I shall not speak with fear and trembling. I have never injured you, and innocence can feel no fear. I turn to you all — red-skins and white-skins, — where is the man who will appear as my accuser? Father, I understand not clearly how things are working. I have just been set at liberty. Am I again to be plunged into bondage? Frowns are all around me, but I am incapable of change. You, perhaps, may be ignorant of what I tell you, but it is a truth, which I call heaven and earth to witness. It is a fact which can easily be proved, that I have been assailed in almost every possible way that pride, fear, feeling, or interest could touch me — that I have been pushed to the last to raise the tomahawk against you, but all in vain. I never could be made to feel that you were my enemy. If this be the conduct of an enemy, I shall never be your friend. You are acquainted with my removal above Prairie du Chien. I went and formed a settlement and called my warriors around me. We took counsel, and from that counsel we have never departed. We smoked, and resolved to make common cause with the United States. I sent you the pipe, — it resembled this, — and I sent it by the Missouri, that the Indians of the Mississippi might not know what we were doing. You received it. I then told you that your friends should be my friends, — that your enemies should be my enemies, — and that I only awaited your signal to make war. If this be the conduct of an enemy, I shall never be your friend. Why do I tell you this? Because it is the truth, and a melancholy truth, that the good things which men do are often buried in the ground, while their evil deeds are stripped naked and exposed to the world. When I came here, I came to you in friendship. I little thought I should have to defend myself. I have no defence to make. If I were guilty, I should have come prepared; but I have ever held you by the hand, and I am come without excuses. If I had fought against you, I would have told you so; but I have nothing now to say here in your councils, except to repeat what I said before to my great father, the president of your nation. You heard it, and no doubt remember it. It was simply this: My lands can never be surrendered; I was cheated, and basely cheated, in the contract; I will not surrender my country but with my life. Again I call heaven and earth to witness, and I smoke this pipe in evidence of my sincerity. If you are sincere, you will receive it from me. My only desire is, that we should smoke it together, that I should grasp your sacred hand, and

I claim for myself and my tribe the protection of your country. When this pipe touches your lips, may it operate as a blessing upon all my tribe. May the smoke rise like a cloud and carry away with it all the animosities which have arisen between us."

It is worthy of statement that the issue of the council was peaceful, and in September following Black Thunder met the Commissioners at St. Louis, and executed a treaty of peace.

Another famous western Indian was Black Hawk. Shortly after a long period of fighting with the United States forces, he was finally captured and delivered to the whites. The following is said to be the speech which Black Hawk made when he surrendered himself to the agent at Prairie du Chien:—

"You have taken me prisoner with all my warriors. I am much grieved, for I expected, if I did not defeat you, to hold out much longer and give you more trouble before I surrendered. I tried hard to bring you into ambush, but your last general understands Indian fighting. The first one was not so wise. When I saw that I could not beat you by Indian fighting, I determined to rush on you, and fight you face to face. I fought hard. But your guns were well aimed. The bullets flew like birds in the air, and whizzed by our ears like the wind through the trees in the winter. My warriors fell around me; it began to look dismal. I saw my evil day at hand. The sun rose dim on us in the morning, and at night it sunk in a dark cloud and looked like a ball of fire. This was the last sun that shone on Black Hawk. His heart is dead and no longer beats quick in his bosom. He is now a prisoner to the white men; they will do with him as they wish. But he can stand torture and is not afraid of death. He is no coward. Black Hawk is an Indian.

"He has done nothing for which an Indian ought to be ashamed. He has fought for his countrymen, the squaws and papooses, against white men, who came, year after year, to cheat them and take away their lands. You know the cause of our making war. It is known to all white men. They ought to be ashamed of it. The white men despise the Indians and drive them from their homes. But the Indians are not deceitful. The white men speak bad of the Indian and look at him spitefully. But the Indian does not tell lies. Indians do not steal.

"An Indian who is as bad as the white men could not live in our nation; he would be put to death, and eat up by the wolves. The white men are bad schoolmasters; they carry false looks, and deal in false actions; they smile in the face of the poor Indian to cheat him; they shake them by the hand to get their confidence, — to make them drunk, to deceive them, and ruin their wives. We told them to let us alone and keep away from us, but they followed on and beset our paths, and they coiled themselves among us, like the snake. They poisoned us by their touch. We were not safe. We lived in danger. We were becoming, like them, hypocrites and liars, adulterers, lazy drones, all talkers and no workers.

"We looked up to the Great Spirit. We went to our great father. We were encouraged. His great council gave us fair words and big promises, but we got no satisfaction. Things were growing worse. There were no deer in the forest. The opossum and beaver were fled; the springs were drying up, and our squaws and papooses without victuals to keep them from starving. We called a great council and built a large fire. The spirit of our fathers arose and spoke to us to avenge our wrongs or die. We all spoke before the council-fire. It was warm and pleasant. We set up the war-whoop and dug up the tomahawk; our knives were ready, and the heart of Black Hawk swelled high in his bosom when he led his warriors to battle. He is satisfied. He will go to the world of spirits contented. He has done his duty. His father will meet him there and commend him.

"Black Hawk is a true Indian and disdains to cry like a woman. He feels for his wife, his children, and friends. But he does not care for himself. He cares for his nation and the Indians. They will suffer. He laments their fate. The white men do not scalp the head, but they do worse — they poison the heart; it is not pure with them. His countrymen will not be scalped, but they will, in a few years, become like the white men, so that you can't trust them, and there must be, as in the white settlements, nearly as many officers as men, to take care of them and keep them in order.

"Farewell, my nation! Black Hawk tried to save you and avenge your wrongs. He drank the blood of some of the whites. He has been taken prisoner, and his plans are stopped. He can do no more. He is near his end. His sun is setting, and he will rise no more. Farewell to Black Hawk."

A conspicuous war-captain among the Delawares, and particularly during the period of the Revolution, was a chief of the Wolf Tribe, whose Indian name was Hopocan, known among the whites as Captain Pipe. He seems to have wielded great influence both before and after the Revolution. At one time, in an expedition against the Americans, Captain Pipe went to Detroit, where he was received with respect by the British commander, who, with his attendants, was invited to the council house to give an account of past transactions. Captain Pipe was seated in front of his Indians, facing the chief officer, and held in his left hand a short stick to which was fastened a scalp. After the usual pause, he arose and spoke as follows:—

"Father" (then he stopped a little, and, turning towards the audience, with a countenance full of great expression, and a sarcastic look, said, in a lower tone of voice), "I have said father, although indeed I do not know why I am to call him so, having never known any other father than the French, and considering the English only as brothers. But as this name is also imposed upon us, I shall make use of it, and say" (at the same time fixing his eyes upon the commandment), "father, some time ago you put a war-hatchet into my hands, saying, 'Take this weapon and try it on the heads of my enemies, the Long-Knives, and let me afterwards know if it was sharp and good.' Father, at the time when you gave me this weapon, I had neither cause nor inclination to go to war against a people who had done me no injury, yet in obedience to you, who say you are my father, and called me your child, I received the hatchet, well knowing that if I did not obey, you would withhold from me the necessaries of life, without which I could not subsist, and which are not elsewhere to be procured but at the house of my father. You may perhaps think me a fool for risking my life at your bidding, in a cause, too, by which I have no prospect of gaining anything; for it is your cause and not mine. It is your concern to fight the Long-Knives. You have raised a quarrel amongst yourselves, and you ought yourselves to fight it out. You should not compel your children the Indians to expose themselves to danger for your sakes. Father, how many lives have been lost on your account? Nations have suffered and been weakened! Children have lost parents, brothers, and relatives! Wives have lost husbands! It is not known how many more may perish before your war will be at an end! Father, I have said that you may, perhaps, think me a fool for thus thoughtlessly rushing on your enemy. Do not believe this, father. Think not that I want sense to convince me that although now you pretend to keep up a perpetual enmity to the Long-Knives, you may before long conclude a peace with them. Father, you say you love your children, the Indians. This you have often told them, and indeed it is your interest to say so to them, that you may have them at your service. But, father, who of us can believe that you can love a people of a different color from your own better than those who have a white skin like yourselves? Father, pay attention to what I am going to say. While you, father, are setting me" (meaning the Indians in general) "on your enemy much in the same manner as a hunter sets his dog on the game, while I am in the act of rushing on that enemy of yours, with the bloody destructive weapon you gave me, I may perchance happen to look back to the place from whence you started me, and what shall I see? Perhaps I may see my father shaking hands with the Long-Knives; yes, with these very people he now calls his enemies. I may then see him laugh at my folly for having obeyed his orders, and yet I am now risking my life at his command. Father, keep what I have said in remembrance. Now, father, here is what has been done with the hatchet you gave me." (With these words he handed the stick to the commandant, with the scalp upon it, above mentioned.) "I have done with the hatchet what you ordered me to do, and found it sharp. Nevertheless, I did not do all that I might have done. No, I did not. My heart failed within me. I felt compassion for your enemy. Innocence (helpless women and children) had no part in your quarrels; therefore I distinguished — I spared. I took some live flesh, which, while I was bringing to you, I spied one of your large canoes, on which I put it for you. In a few days you will recover this flesh, and find that the skin is of the same color with your own. Father, I hope you will not destroy what I have saved. You, father, have the means of preserving that which with me would perish for want. The warrior is poor, and his cabin is always empty, but your house, father, is always full."

Heckewelder highly praised this speech, concluding his encomium as follows: "It is but justice here to say that Pipe was well acquainted with the noble and generous character of the British officer to whom this speech was addressed. He is still living in his own country, an honor to the British name. He obeyed the orders of his superiors, in employing the Indians to fight against us, but he did it with reluctance and softened as much as was in his power the horrors of that abominable warfare. He esteemed Captain Pipe, and, I have no doubt, was well pleased with the humane conduct of this Indian chief, whose sagacity in this instance is no less deserving of praise than his eloquence."

But probably the most noted specimen of Indian eloquence is that of Logan, the famous Mingo chief. Jefferson, in his notes on Virginia, published the facts alluded to in the speech of Logan. Logan was one of the most noted chiefs in Indian story. His name is still perpetuated among the Indians. He was a member of the Cayuga nation of the League of the Iroquois. For magnanimity in war and greatness of soul in peace, few, if any, in any nation ever surpassed Logan. He took no part in the French wars which ended in 1760 save that of peacemaker; was always acknowledged the friend of the white people until the year 1774, when his entire family was brutally and treacherously murdered by a party of whites under command of Captain Michael Cresap. The massacre was all the more dastardly and indefensible because it had no provocation. A bitter war followed in which Logan wreaked his vengeance to the fullest extent. A treaty of peace was finally concluded in a conference which resulted in said treaty, when the famous speech of Logan was made. It was not delivered in the camp of Governor Dunmore. Although desiring peace, Logan would not meet the whites in council, but remained in his own cabin until a messenger was sent to him to know if he would indorse the proposed treaty. He sent, in reply, the following:—

"I appeal to any white to say, if ever he entered Logan's cabin hungry, and he gave him not meat; if ever he came cold and naked, and he clothed him not.

"During the course of the last long bloody war, Logan remained idle in his cabin, an advocate for peace. Such was my love for the whites, that my countrymen pointed as they passed, and said, 'Logan is the friend of white men.'

"I had even thought to have lived with you, but for the injuries of one man. Colonel Cresap, the last spring, in cold blood, and unprovoked, murdered all the relations of Logan; not even sparing my women and children.

"There runs not a drop of my blood in the veins of any living creature. This called on me for revenge. I have sought it. I have killed many. I have fully glutted my vengeance. For my country I rejoice at the beams of peace. But do not harbor a thought that mine is the joy of fear. Logan never felt fear. He will not turn on his heel to save his life. Who is there to mourn for Logan? Not one!"

The writings of a hundred years ago abound with anecdotes illustrative of Indian character. Various phases are shown in the following, which have been selected from a large number of similar import.

Wit.—An Ottaway chief, known to the French by the name of Whitejohn, was a great drunkard. Count Frontenac asked what he thought brandy to be made of; he replied, that it must be made of hearts and tongues—"For," said he, "when I have drunken plentifully of it, my heart is a thousand strong, and I can talk, too, with astonishing freedom and rapidity."

Honor.—A chief of the Five Nations, who fought on the side of the English in the French wars, chanced to meet in battle his own father, who was fighting on the side of the French. Just as he was about to deal a deadly blow upon his head, he discovered who he was, and said to him, "You have once given me life, and now I give it to you. Let me meet you no more, for I have paid the debt owed you."

Recklessness.—In Connecticut River, about "200 miles from Long Island Sound, is a narrow of five yards only, formed by two shelving mountains of solid rock. Through this chasm are compelled to pass all the waters which in the time of the floods bury the northern country." It is a frightful passage of about 400 yards in length. No boat, or, as an author expresses it, "no living creature was ever known to pass through this narrow, except an Indian woman." This woman had undertaken to cross the river just above, and although she had the god Bacchus by her side, yet Neptune prevailed in spite of their united efforts, and the canoe was hurried down the frightful gulf. While this woman was thus hurrying to certain destruction, as she had every reason to expect, she seized upon her bottle of rum, and did not take it from her mouth until the last drop was quaffed. She was marvellously preserved, and was actually picked up several miles below, floating in the canoe, still quite drunk. When it was known what she had done, and being asked how she dared to drink so much rum with the prospect of certain death before her, she answered that she knew it was too much for one time but she was unwilling that any of it should be lost.

Justice. — A missionary, residing among a certain tribe of Indians, was one day, after he had been preaching to them, invited by their chief to visit his wigwam. After having been kindly entertained, and being about to depart, the chief took him by the hand, and said, "I have very bad squaw. She had two little children. One she loved well, the other she hated. In a cold night, when I was gone hunting in the woods, she shut it out of the wigwam and it froze to death. What must be done with her?" The missionary replied, "She must be hanged." "Ah!" said the chief, "go, then, and hang your God, whom you make just like her."

Magnanimity. — A hunter, in his wanderings for game, fell among the back settlements of Virginia, and by reason of the inclemency of the weather, was induced to seek refuge at the house of a planter, whom he met at his door. Admission was refused him. Being both hungry and thirsty, he asked for a morsel of bread and a cup of water, but was answered in every case, "No! you shall have nothing here. Get you gone, you Indian dog!" It happened, in process of time, that this same planter lost himself in the woods, and after a fatiguing day's travel, he came to an Indian's cabin, into which he was welcomed. On inquiring the way, and the distance to the white settlements, being told by the Indian that he could not go in the night, and being kindly offered lodging and victuals, he gladly refreshed and reposed himself in the Indian's cabin. In the morning the Indian conducted him through the wilderness, agreeably to his promise the night before, until they came in sight of the habitations of the whites. As he was about to take his leave of the planter, he looked him full in the face, and asked him if he did not know him. Horror-struck at finding himself thus in the power of a man he had so inhumanly treated, and dumb with shame on thinking of the manner it was requited, he began at length to make excuses, and beg a thousand pardons, when the Indian interrupted him, and said, "When you see poor Indians fainting for a cup of cold water, don't say again, 'Get you gone, you Indian dog!'" He then dismissed him to return to his friends. The author adds, "It is not difficult to say, which of these two had the best claim to the name of Christian."

Deception. — The captain of a vessel, having a desire to make a present to a lady of some fine oranges which he had just brought from "the sugar islands," gave them to an Indian in his employ to carry to her. Lest he should not perform the office punctually, he wrote a letter to her, to be taken along with the present, that she might detect the bearer if he should fail to deliver the whole of what he was entrusted with. The Indian, during the journey, reflected how he should refresh himself with the oranges and not be found out. Not having any apprehension of the manner of communication by writing, he concluded that it was only necessary to keep his design secret from the letter itself, supposing that would tell of him if he did not. He therefore laid it upon the ground and rolled a large stone upon it, and retired to some distance, where he regaled himself with several of the oranges, and then proceeded on his journey. On delivering the remainder and the letter to the lady, she asked him where the rest of the oranges were; he said he had delivered all. She told him that the letter said there were several more sent, to which he answered that the letter lied, and she must not believe it. But he was soon confronted in his falsehood, and begging forgiveness of the offence, was pardoned.

Shrewdness. — As Governor Joseph Dudley of Massachusetts was superintending some of his workmen, he took notice of an able-bodied Indian, who, half-naked, would come and look on, as a pastime, to see his men work. The governor took occasion one day to ask him why he did not work and get some clothes wherewith to cover himself. The Indian answered by asking him why he did not work. The governor, pointing with his finger to his head, said, "I work head work, and so have no need to work with my hands as you should." The Indian then said he would work if any one would employ him. The governor said he wanted a calf killed, and that, if he would go and do it, he would give him a shilling. He accepted the offer, and went immediately and killed the calf, and then went sauntering about as before. The governor, on observing what he had done, asked him why he did not dress the calf before he left it. The Indian answered, "No, no, Coponoh; that was not in the bargain; I was to have a shilling for killing him. Am he no dead, Coponoh?" (governor). The governor, seeing himself thus outwitted, told him to dress it and he would give him another shilling.

This done, and in possession of two shillings, the Indian goes directly to a grog-shop for rum. After a short stay, he returned to the governor and told him he had given him a bad shilling piece, and presented a brass one to be exchanged. The governor, thinking possibly it might have been the case, gave him another. It was not long before he returned a second time with another brass shilling to be exchanged. The governor was now convinced of his knavery, but not caring to make words at the time, gave him another, and thus the fellow got four shillings for one.

The governor determined to have the rogue corrected for his abuse, and, meeting with him soon after, told him he must take a letter to Boston for him and gave him half a crown for the service. The letter was directed to the keeper of bridewell, ordering him to give the bearer so many lashes, but mistrusting that all was not exactly agreeable, and meeting a servant of the governor on the road, the Indian ordered him, in the name of his master, to carry the letter immediately, as he was in haste to return. The consequence was, this servant got egregiously whipped. When the governor learned what had taken place, he felt no little chagrin at being thus twice outwitted by the Indian.

He did not see the fellow for some time after this, but at length, falling in with him, asked him by what means he had cheated and deceived him so many times. Taking the governor again in his own play, he answered, pointing with his finger to his head, "Head work, Coponoh, head work!" The governor was so well pleased that he forgave the whole offence.

Equality. — An Indian chief, on being asked whether his people were free, answered, "Why not, since I myself am free, although their king?"

Matrimony. — An aged Indian, who for many years had spent much time among the white people, both in Pennsylvania and New Jersey, one day, about the year 1770, observed that the Indians had not only a much easier way of getting a wife than the whites, but also a more certain way of getting a good one. "For," said he, in broken English, "white man court — court — may be one whole year — may be two years before he marry! Well — maybe then he get very good wife — but maybe not — maybe very cross! Well, now suppose cross! scold so soon as get awake in the morning! Scold all day! — scold until sleep! — all one — he must keep him! — White people have law forbidding throw away wife he be ever so cross — must keep him always! Well, how does Indian do? Indian, when he see industrious squaw, he go to him, place his two fore-fingers close aside each other, make two like one — then look squaw in the face — see him smile — this is all one he say yes! — so he take him home — no danger he be cross! No, no — squaw know too well what Indian do if he cross! throw him away and take another! — Squaw love to eat meat — no husband — no meat. Squaw do everything to please husband, he do everything to please squaw — live happy."

Toleration. — In the year 1791, two Creek chiefs accompanied an American to England, where, as usual, they attracted great attention, and many flocked around them as well to learn their ideas of certain things as to behold "the savages." Being asked their opinion of religion, or of what religion they were, one made answer that they had no priests in their country, or established religion, for they thought that upon a subject where there was no possibility of people's agreeing, and as it was altogether a matter of mere opinion, "it was best that every one should paddle his canoe his own way." Here is a volume of instruction in a short answer of a savage!

Justice. — A white trader sold a quantity of powder to an Indian, and imposed upon him by making him believe it was a grain which grew like wheat, by sowing it upon the ground. He was greatly elated by the prospect, not only of raising his own powder, but of being able to supply others, and therefore becoming immensely rich. Having prepared his ground with great care, he sowed his powder with the utmost exactness in the spring. Month after month passed away, but his powder did not even sprout, and winter came before he was satisfied that he had been deceived. He said nothing, but some time after, when the trader had forgotten the trick, the same Indian succeeded in getting credit of him to a large amount. The time set for payment having expired, he sought out the Indian at his residence and demanded payment for his goods. The Indian heard his demand with great complaisance, then looking him shrewdly in the eye, said, "Me pay you when my powder grow." This was enough. The guilty white man quickly retraced his steps, satisfied, we apprehend, to balance his account with the chagrin he had received.

Preaching against Practice. — John Simon was a Sogkonate, who, about the year 1700, was a settled minister to that tribe. He was a man of strong mind, generally temperate, but sometimes remiss in the latter particular. The following anecdote is told as characteristic of his notions of justice. Simon, on account of his deportment, was created justice of the peace, and when difficulties occurred involving any of his people, he sat with the English justice to aid in making up judgment. It happened that Simon's squaw, with some others, had committed some offence. Justices Almy and Simon, in making up their minds, estimated the amount of the offence differently. Almy thought each should receive eight or ten stripes, but Simon said, "No; four or five are enough — Poor Indians are ignorant, and it is not Christian-like to punish so hardly those who are ignorant, as those who have knowledge." Simon's judgment prevailed. When Mr. Almy asked John how many his wife should receive, he said, "Double, because she had knowledge to have done better;" but Colonel Almy, out of regard to John's feelings, wholly remitted his wife's punishment. John looked very serious, and made no reply while in presence of the court, but on the first fit opportunity remonstrated very severely against his judgment and said to him, "To what purpose do we preach a religion of justice, if we do unrighteousness in judgment?"

Characters contrasted. — An Indian of the Kennebeck tribe, remarkable for his good conduct, received a grant of land from the State, and fixed himself in a new township where a number of families were settled. Though not ill-treated, yet the common prejudice against Indians prevented any sympathy with him. This was shown at the death of his only child, when none of the people came near him. Shortly afterwards he went to some of the inhabitants and said to them, "When white man's child die, Indian man be sorry — he help bury him. When my child die, no one speak to me — I make his grave alone. I can no live here." He gave up his farm, dug up the body of his child, and carried it with him 200 miles through the forests, to join the Canada Indians!

A Singular Stratagem to escape Torture. — Some years ago the Shawano Indians, being obliged to move from their habitations, in their way took a Muskohge warrior, known by the name of old Scrany, prisoner. They bastinadoed him severely, and condemned him to the fiery torture. He underwent a great deal without showing any concern. His countenance and behavior were as if he suffered not the least pain. He told his persecutors, with a bold voice, that he was a warrior; that he had gained most of his martial reputation at the expense of the nation, and was desirous of showing them, in the act of dying, that he was still as much their superior as when he headed his gallant countrymen; that, although he had fallen into their hands and forfeited the protection of the divine power by some impurity or other, when carrying the holy ark of war against his devoted enemies, yet he had so much remaining virtue as would enable him to punish himself more exquisitely than all their despicable, ignorant crowd possibly could, and that he would do so, if they gave him liberty by untying him, and handing him one of the red-hot gun-barrels out of the fire. The proposal and his method of address appeared so exceedingly bold and uncommon that his request was granted. Then suddenly seizing one end of the red-hot barrel, and brandishing it from side to side, he leaped down a prodigious steep and high bank into a branch of the river, dived through it, ran over a small island, and passed the other branch, amidst a shower of bullets, and though numbers of his enemies were in close pursuit of him, he got into a bramble swamp, through which, though naked, and in a mangled condition, he reached his own country.

An Unparalleled Case of Suffering. — The Shawano Indians captured a warrior of the Anantoocah nation and put him to the stake, according to their usual cruel solemnities. Having unconcernedly suffered much torture, he told them with scorn that they did not know how to punish a noted enemy, therefore he was willing to teach them and would confirm the truth of his assertion if they allowed him the opportunity. Accordingly, he requested of them a pipe and some tobacco, which was given him. As soon as he had lighted it, he sat down, naked as he was, on the women's burning torches, that were within his circle, and continued smoking his pipe, without the least discomposure. On this, a head warrior leaped up and said they saw plain enough that he was a warrior and not afraid of dying, nor should he have died, only that he was both spoiled by the fire and devoted to it by their laws; however, though he was a very dangerous enemy, and his nation a treacherous people, it should be seen that they paid a reward to bravery, even in one who was marked with war streaks, at the cost of many of the lives of their beloved kindred. And then by way of favor he, with his friendly tomahawk, instantly put an end to all his pains.

Their Notions of Learning of the Whites. — At the Congress at Lancaster, in 1744, between the government of Virginia and the Five Nations, the Indians were told that, if they would send some of their young men to Virginia, the English would give them an education at their college. An orator replied to this offer as follows: " We know that you highly esteem the kind of learning taught in those colleges, and that the maintenance of our young men, while with you, would be very expensive to you. We are convinced, therefore, that you mean to do us good by your proposal and we thank you heartily. But you who are wise must know that different nations have different conceptions of things, and you will therefore not take it amiss if our ideas of this kind of education happen not to be same with yours. We have had some experience of it. Several of our young people were formerly brought up at the colleges of the northern provinces; they were instructed in all your sciences, but when they came back to us, they were bad runners; ignorant of every means of living in the woods; unable to bear either cold or hunger; knew nothing how to build a cabin, take a deer, or kill an enemy; spoke our language imperfectly; were, therefore, neither fit for hunters, warriors, nor counsellors; they were totally good for nothing. We are, however, not the less obliged by your kind offer, though we decline accepting it, and to show our grateful sense of it, if the gentlemen of Virginia will send us a dozen of their sons, we will take great care of their education, instruct them in all we know, and make men of them."

Success of a Missionary.—Those who have attempted to Christianize the Indians complain that they are too silent, and that their taciturnity was the greatest difficulty with which they have to contend. Their notions of propriety upon matters of conversation are so nice that they deem it improper in the highest degree even to deny or contradict anything that is said, at the time, and hence the difficulty of knowing what effect anything has upon their minds at the time of delivery. In this they have a proper advantage, for how often does it happen that people would answer very differently upon a matter were they to consider upon it but a short time! The Indians seldom answer a matter of importance the same day, lest, in so doing, they should be thought to have treated it as though it was of small consequence. We oftener repent of a hasty decision than that we have lost time in maturing our judgment. Now for the anecdote, which is as follows:—

A Swedish minister, having assembled the chiefs of the Susquehannah Indians, made a sermon to them, acquainting them with the principal historical facts on which our religion is founded; such as the fall of our first parents by eating an apple; the coming of Christ to repair the mischief; his miracles and sufferings, etc. When he had finished, an Indian orator stood up to thank him. "What you have told us," said he, "is all very good. It is indeed bad to eat apples. It is better to make them all into cider. We are very much obliged by your kindness in coming so far to tell us those things which you have heard from your mothers."

When the Indian had told the missionary one of the legends of his nation, — how they had been supplied with maize or corn, beans, and tobacco, — he treated it with contempt, and said, "What I delivered to you were sacred truths; but what you tell me is mere fable, fiction, and falsehood." The Indian felt indignant, and replied, "My brother, it seems your friends have not done you justice in your education; they have not instructed you in the rules of common civility. You see that we, who understand and practise those rules, believe all your stories. Why do you refuse to believe ours?"

Curiosity. — When any of the Indians come into our towns, our people are apt to crowd round them, gaze upon them, and incommode them where they desire to be private. This they esteem great rudeness and the effect of want of instructions in the rules of civility and good manners. "We have," say they, "as much curiosity as you, and when you come into our towns, we wish for opportunities of looking at you; but for this purpose we hide ourselves behind bushes where you are to pass, and never intrude ourselves into your company."

Rules of Conversation. — The business of the women is to take exact notice of what passes, imprint it in their memories (for they have no writing), and communicate it to their children. They are the records of the council, and they preserve tradition of the stipulations in treaties a hundred years back, which, when we compare with our writings, we always find exact. He that would speak rises. The rest observe a profound silence. When he has finished, and sits down, they leave him five or six minutes to recollect, that, if he has omitted anything he intended to say, or has anything to add, he may rise again and deliver it. To interrupt another, even in common conversation, is reckoned highly indecent.

Lost Confidence. — An Indian runner, arriving in a village of his countrymen, requested the immediate attendance of its inhabitants in council, as he wanted their answer to important information. The people accordingly assembled, but when the messenger had, with great anxiety, delivered his message and waited for an answer, none was given, and he soon observed that he was likely to be left alone in his place. A stranger present asked a principal chief the meaning of this strange proceeding, who gave this answer, "He once told us a lie."

A Serious Question. — About 1794, an officer presented a western chief with a medal, on one side of which President Washington was represented as armed with a sword, and on the other an Indian seen in the act of burying the hatchet. The chief at once saw the wrong done his countrymen, and very wisely asked, "Why does not the President bury his sword, too?"

Self-esteem. — A white man, meeting an Indian, accosted him as brother. The Red Man, with a great expression of meaning in his countenance, inquired how they came to be brothers. The white man replied, "O, by the way of Adam, I suppose." The Indian added, "Me thank him Great Spirit we no nearer brothers."

A Preacher taken at his Word. — A certain clergyman had for his text on a time, "Vow and pay unto the Lord thy vows." An Indian happened to be present, who stepped up to the priest as soon as he had finished, and said to him, "Now me vow me go home with you, Mr. Minister." The priest, having no language of evasion at command, said, "You must go then." When he had arrived at the home of the minister, the Indian vowed again, saying, "Now me vow me have supper." When this was finished, he said, "Me vow me stay all night." The priest, by this time thinking himself sufficiently taxed, replied, "It may be so, but I vow you shall go in the morning." The Indian, judging from the tone of his host that more vows would be useless, departed in the morning.

A Case of Signal Barbarity. — It is related by Black Hawk, in his life, that some time before the war of 1812, one of the Indians had killed a Frenchman at Prairie du Chien. "The British soon after took him prisoner, and said they would shoot him next day. His family were encamped a short distance below the mouth of the Ouisconsin. He begged permission to go and see them that night, as he was to die the next day. They permitted him to go, after promising to return the next morning by sunrise. He visited his family, which consisted of a wife and six children. I cannot describe their meeting and parting to be understood by the whites, as it appears that their feelings are acted upon by certain rules laid down by their preachers, whilst ours are governed only by the monitor within us. He parted from his wife and children, hurried through the prairie to the fort, and arrived in time. The soldiers were ready, and immediately marched out and shot him down."

Mourning Much in a Short Time. — A young widow, whose husband had been dead about eight days, was hastening to finish her grief, in order that she might be married to a young warrior. She was determined, therefore, to grieve much in a short time. To this end she tore her hair, drank spirits, and beat her breast, to make the tears flow abundantly, by which means, on the evening of the eighth day, she was ready again to marry, having grieved sufficiently.

How to evade a Hard Question. — When Mr. Gist went over the Alleghanies, in February, 1751, on a tour of discovery for the Ohio Company, an Indian, who spoke good English, came to him and said that their great man, the Beaver, and Captain Oppamyluah (two chiefs of the Delawares), desired to know where the Indian's land lay; for the French claimed all the land on one side of the Ohio River, and the English on the other. This question Mr. Gist found it hard to answer, and he evaded it by saying that the Indians and white men were all subjects to the same king, and all had an equal privilege of taking up and possessing the land in conformity with the conditions prescribed by the king.

Harmless Deception. — In a time of Indian troubles, an Indian visited the house of Governor Jenks of Rhode Island, when the governor took occasion to request him, that, if any strange Indian should come to his wigwam to let him know it, which the Indian promised to do; but to secure his fidelity, the governor told him that when he should give him such information he would give him a mug of flip. Some time after the Indian came again. "Well, Mr. Gobenor, strange Indian come my house last night!" "Ah," says the governor, "and what did he say?" "He no speak," replied the Indian. "What, no speak at all?" added the governor. "No, he no speak at all." "That certainly looks suspicious," said his excellency, and inquired if he were still there, and being told that he was, ordered the promised mug of flip. When this was disposed of and the Indian was about to depart, he mildly said, "Mr. Gobenor, my squaw have child last night." And thus the governor's alarm was suddenly changed into disappointment, and the strange Indian into a new-born papoose.

Mammoth Bones. — The following very interesting tradition concerning these bones among the Indians, will always be read with interest. The animal to which they belonged they called the big buffalo; and on the early maps of the country of the Ohio, we see marked, "Elephants' bones said to be found here." They were for some time by many supposed to have been the bones of that animal, but they are pretty generally now believed to have belonged to a species of animal long since extinct. They have been found in various parts of the country, but in the greatest abundance about the salt licks or springs in Kentucky and Ohio. There has never been an entire skeleton found, although the one in Peale's Museum in Philadelphia, was so near perfect, that, by a little ingenuity in supplying its defects with woodwork, it passed extremely well for such.

The tradition of the Indians concerning this animal is, that he was carnivorous, and existed as late as 1780 in the northern parts of America. Some Delawares in the time of the Revolutionary War visited the governor of Virginia on business, which having been finished, some questions were put to them concerning their country, and especially what they knew or had heard respecting the animals whose bones had been found about the salt licks on the Ohio River. "The chief speaker," continues our author, Mr. Jefferson, "immediately put himself into an attitude of oratory, and, with a pomp suited to what he conceived the elevation of his subject," began and repeated as follows : "In ancient times, a herd of these tremendous animals came to the Big-bone Licks, and began an universal destruction of the bear, deer, elks, buffaloes and other animals which had been created for the use of the Indians. The great man above looking down and seeing this was so enraged that he seized his lightning, descended to the earth, and seated himself on a neighboring mountain, on a rock of which his seat and the print of his feet are still to be seen, and hurled his bolts among them till the whole were slaughtered, except the big bull, who, presenting his forehead to the shafts, shook them off as they fell; but missing one at length, it wounded him in the side; whereon, springing around, he bounded over the Ohio, over the Wabash, the Illinois, and finally over the great lakes, where he is living at this day."

Such, say the Indians, is the account handed down to them from their ancestors, and they could furnish no other information.

Narrative of the Captivity and Bold Exploit of Hannah Duston.—The relation of this affair forms the XXVth article in the *Decennium Luctuosum* of the *Magnalia Christi Americana*, by Dr. Cotton Mather, and is one of the best written articles from his pen. At its head is this significant sentence, *Dux Fæmina Facti.*

On the 15th of March, 1697, a band of about twenty Indians came unexpectedly upon Haverhill, in Massachusetts, and as their numbers were small, they made their attack with the swiftness of the whirlwind, and as suddenly disappeared. The war, of which this irruption was a part, had continued nearly ten years, and soon afterwards it came to a close. The house which this party of Indians had singled out as their object of attack, belonged to one Mr. Thomas Duston, or Dunstan, in the outskirts of the town. Mr. Duston was at work at some distance from his house, at the time, and whether he was alarmed for the safety of his family by the shouts of the Indians, or other cause, we are not informed; but he seems to have arrived there time enough before the arrival of the Indians to make some arrangements for the preservation of his children; but his wife, who, about a week before, had been confined by a child, was unable to rise from her bed, to the distraction of her agonized husband. No time was to be lost; Mr. Duston had only time to direct his children's flight (seven in number), the extremes of whose ages were two and seventeen, and the Indians were upon them. With his gun, the distressed father mounted his horse and rode away in the direction of the children, whom he overtook but about forty rods from the house. His first intention was to take up one, if possible, and escape with it. He had no sooner overtaken them, than this resolution was destroyed, for to rescue either to the exclusion of the rest, was worse than death itself to him. He therefore faced about and met the enemy, who had closely pursued him. Each fired upon the other and it is almost a miracle that none of the little retreating party were hurt. The Indians did not pursue long, from fear of raising the neighboring English before they could complete their object, and hence the part of the family escaped to a place of safety.

We are now to enter fully into the relation of this very tragedy. There was living in the house of Mr. Duston, as nurse, Mrs. Mary Neff, a widow, whose heroic conduct in sharing the fate of her mistress, when escape was in her power, will always be viewed with admiration. The Indians were now in the undisturbed possession of the house, and having driven the sick woman from her bed, compelled her to sit quietly in the corner of the fire-place while they completed the pillage of the house. This business being finished, it was set on fire, and Mrs. Duston, who before considered herself unable to walk, was at the approach of night obliged to march into the wilderness and take her bed upon the cold ground. Mrs. Neff, too late, attempted to escape with the infant child, but was intercepted, the child taken from her, and its brains beaten out against a neighboring apple tree, while its nurse was compelled to accompany her new and frightful masters also. The captives amounted in all to thirteen, some of whom, as they became unable to travel, were murdered and left exposed upon the way. Although it was near night when they quitted Haverhill, they travelled, as they judged, twelve miles before encamping; "and then," says Dr. Mather, "kept up with their new masters in a long travel of an hundred and fifty miles, more or less, within a few days ensuing."

After journeying awhile, according to their custom, the Indians divided their prisoners. Mrs. Duston, Mrs. Neff, and a boy named Samuel Leonardson, who had been captivated at Worcester, about eighteen months before, fell to the lot of an Indian family consisting of twelve persons, — two men, three women, and seven children. These, so far as our accounts go, were very kind to their prisoners, but told them there was one ceremony which they could not avoid, and to which they would be subjected when they should arrive at their place of destination, which was, to run the gauntlet. The place where this was to be performed was at an Indian village 250 miles from Haverhill, according to the reckoning of the Indian. In their meandering course they at length arrived at an island in the mouth of Contookook River, about six miles above Concord, in New Hampshire. Here one of the Indian men resided. It had been determined by the captives, before their arrival here, that an effort should be made to free themselves from their wretched captivity, and not only to gain their liberty, but, as we shall presently see, something by way of remuneration from those who held them in bondage. The heroine, Duston, had resolved upon the first opportunity that offered any chance of success, to kill her captors and scalp them, and to return home with such trophies as would clearly establish her reputation for heroism, as well as insure her a bounty from the public. She therefore communicated her design to Mrs. Neff and the English boy, who, it would seem, readily enough agreed to it. To the art of killing and scalping she was a stranger, and that there should be no failure in the business, Mrs. Duston instructed the boy, who, from his long residence with them, had become as one of the Indians, to inquire of one of the men how it was done. He did so, and the Indian showed him, without mistrusting the origin of the inquiry. It was now March 31, and in the dead of night following, this bloody tragedy was acted. When the Indians were in the most sound sleep these three captives arose, and softly arming themselves with the tomahawks of their masters, allotted the number each should kill, and so truly did they direct their blows, that but one escaped that they designed to kill. This was a woman whom they badly wounded, and one boy for some reason they did not wish to harm, and accordingly he was allowed to escape unhurt. Mrs. Duston killed her master, and Leonardson killed the man who had so freely told him but one day before where to deal a deadly blow and how to take off a scalp.

All was over before the dawn of day, and all things were got ready for leaving this place of blood. All the boats but one were scuttled, to prevent being pursued, and, with what provisions and arms the Indian camp afforded, they embarked on board the other, and slowly and silently took the course of the Merrimack River for their homes, where they all soon after arrived without accident.

The whole country was astonished at the relation of the affair, the truth of which was never for a moment doubted. The ten scalps and the arms of the Indians were evidences not to be questioned, and the general court gave them fifty pounds as a reward, and numerous other gratuities were showered upon them. Colonel Nicholson, governor of Maryland, hearing of the transaction, sent them a generous present also.

Another phase of Indian peculiarity needs to be considered. We have alluded to the fact that the Indian had no written records. His history was preserved in tradition which was handed down from generation to generation, having been originally talked into their wampum belts, and placed in charge of the sachems or chiefs selected for that purpose, whose duty it was to be familiar with the traditions of the past and to be able at proper occasions and at frequent intervals to make them known to the nation in council. Among all the Indian tribes the custom seems to have prevailed to make certain records which were rudely carved on rocks or drawn upon the skins of animals which had been prepared for that purpose. These give to us the "picture writings" of the Indians. Brother Frank A. Bates of Lynn, Mass., who has given much time to the study and translation of these "picture writings," furnishes valuable information in relation to them, and to him we are indebted for what follows:—

Man in his primal stage had no thought beyond the present means of sustaining existence, and his advance toward civilization was recorded by the improvements in his implements of daily use. The first evidence of this advance is shown in an effort towards the artistic, in an endeavor to decorate these implements with a more or less crude portrayal of material objects. When he has reached that stage in which he attempts to convey his thoughts and wishes to others, he does so either by pantomimic gesture or an attempt at speaking, and a spoken language is at first but an attempt to imitate sounds which he hears and which are expressive of the thought which he desires to disclose. Soon he finds the necessity of leaving this expression in such form that it may be understood when he is not present; or, in his attempt to personally convey the thought, he makes an image of the object which he would describe and sees the value of this method, and his first attempts are likewise portraitures of material objects. This may be called the first stage of Pictography, as, for instance, the name *ca-hawk* (Delaware for goose) would be an imitation of the sound emitted by the bird and is expressed by a figure of the bird (Fig 1), and we see that a slight change in a figure makes another expression of a kindred thought, as Fig. 2, a man, is by an extension of the body lines made to represent a woman (Fig. 3), a fact apparent to all.

The sky (Fig. 4) is a curve drawn above, which is the way it appears to his untutored mind, and rain would be drops falling

from the sky (Fig. 5). For whatever purpose this may be extended does not now concern us.

The second stage would be reached when the man advanced in intelligence and became more versed in the use of these figures. Then he would commence to use these signs as symbols of some quality or characteristic, as, the deer would be emblematical of speed, and might be taken as the name-totem of a swift runner.*

Or a winged man would be an expression of a deity, as the ability to fly nearer the sun, the source of light and heat, hence divine, would be esteemed as a divine attribute.

There would be a still further advance when the imagination would be brought in play, as in the Ojibway figure of the Great Spirit (Fig. 6) which signifies everywhere.

---

* (NOTE. — An Indian child is first named from whatever incident first attracts the attention of the parent, after its birth. This name may stick throughout, or it may be changed when he has earned a name, as a reward for some deed of valor.)

The flaunting streamers used by the more intelligent, who became the medicine men, to hold the admiration and hence the respect of the masses, would soon become a signification of "Medicine," something uncanny, hence to be worshipped (Fig. 7), and a serpent, debased by his contact with the soil and deified by reason of his venomous properties, would be a fitting emblem, when joined to the above, of "Bad Medicine" (Fig. 8).

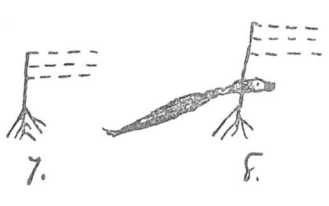

The "Medicine Lodge" would have its interior screened from the vulgar gaze by curtains, and soon would be signified as in Fig. 9.

Probably many of the old carvings were idle scrawls, and others commemorative of important events, as a time of famine or of plenty, matters which touched deeply to the heart of the simple son of the forest.

Plenty, or Sight, would be a dispensation of the good spirits, and Famine, Sickness, or Darkness the result of the machina-

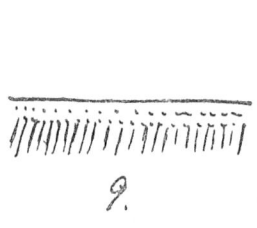
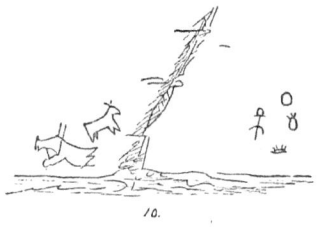

tions of the Evil Spirit or great serpent, whose fabulous poisonous breath parched the face of the earth, or by the great alligator, a symbol for a cold, dark desolation.

Indians were very ideal and superstitious, and attributed many commonplace events to the powers of the good or evil spirits.

Other pictures would be signboards of the road to trails, camps, or springs, or warnings for the benefit of travellers, as in Fig. 10, which was drawn at the entrance of a rocky trail in Cañon de Chilly, New Mexico. It signifies "Dangerous Passing" (a goat can go up, but a horse and rider would fall). If these figures at the right are a portion of the inscription, we might read, "A chief, of the totem of the Beaver was killed here," death being shown by the reversal of the name-totem. Others, again, would be records of deeds of great chiefs, or redoubtable warriors, engraved at their graves or near the scene of the combat. As the famous Dighton Rock is an Algonquin pictograph symbolic of some great event.

Most of these pictures, although crude, are correct in posture, and a knowledge of the sign language would explain many drawings.

Fig. 11 is emblematic of war, for his scalp-lock is in position and he holds the bow and arrow to dare any one to come and take it.

A line drawn from an object indicates an action, as Fig. 12 is indicative of sight. Fig. 13 shows the scalp, and the number of

lines indicates the number that the owner bears. Sometimes, when robes or other articles were used as a ground for the record, the color was indicative of the spirit of the drawing, and some of the paint on the faces would be expressive to him who understood.

Black is War, or Mourning. White is Peace, or Medicine. Red is also indicative of war, or passion, and is much affected by the young bucks. But these matters change in different tribes.

Some tribes keep a calendar of notable events, as is shown by Fig. 14 from the Dakota Calendar, which translated reads, "In this year the Uncpapas (a Sioux tribe) killed two Rees." The murderer is black, and the bow above shows the means of death. This, of course, is only an aid to the memory of the Medicine

Men and Chiefs. And so this might be carried out to an infinite end, as a vocabulary would be made.

Even at this late date, these pictures are used by the Indians, and indeed there are but few who can either read or write their own language in the sense in which civilized nations use the term.

As a further example of Indian picture writing, and in addition to the above account by Brother Bates, we give copies of totems recorded by the Indians on rocks and trees, as reproduced by Catlin in his description of the northwestern Indians written in 1832. It will be remembered that each of these totems represented the symbolic design of the tribe to which the Indian belonged who carved it. These totems were very plentiful around the red pipe-stone quarry, from which was obtained the material for the manufacture of their pipes. These totems were also found in the picture writings upon the robes worn by their leading chiefs. The robe was elegantly made, and the wearer literally carried upon his back, so that all could see, the history of his life and the brave deeds which he had accomplished.

Among the fascinating stories by J. Fenimore Cooper, not the least is that entitled "Last of the Mohicans," and in this is given an incident which illustrated the preserving power of the "totem" of the Indian among the people of his own tribe, the universal hospitality of the Indian race, and a vivid reference to Tamina, the great Indian chief selected as the patron saint of America by the Sons of Liberty, as elsewhere related fully in this history. The story runs as follows: The Huron chief, Cunning Fox, made a visit to a tribe of the Delawares to demand the return of captives who had escaped from the Hurons, and had been conveyed to the Delaware tribe. The Huron made his appearance, and when in full view of the Delawares he stopped, and made a gesture of amity by throwing his arm upward towards heaven, and then letting it fall impressively on his breast. He was encouraged to approach by similar indications of friendship. The Huron was welcomed by a chief of the Delawares, and after exchanging friendly salutations, the Delaware invited his guest to enter his lodge and share his morning meal. The invitation was accepted, and preparations were made for a council, all understanding that some important business must have brought the Huron to the Delawares. Demand was

Totems of the North American Indians.

made for the return of the captives, one of whom was a white woman loved by the Huron. The preliminary council was short, and the demand of the Huron was so extraordinary, that a solemn and formal assemblage was immediately called to make the final decision. Then the story thus proceeds:—

"It might have been half an hour before each individual, including even the women and children, was in his place. The delay had been created by the grave preparations that were deemed necessary to so solemn and unusual a conference. But when the sun was seen climbing above the tops of that mountain, against whose bosom the Delawares had constructed their encampment, most were seated; and as his bright rays darted from behind the outline of trees that fringed the eminence, they fell upon as grave, as attentive, and as deeply interested a multitude, as was probably ever before lighted by his morning beams. Its number somewhat exceeded a thousand souls.

"In a collection of so serious savages, there is never to be found any impatient aspirant after premature distinction, standing ready to move his auditors to some hasty and perhaps injudicious discussion, in order that his own reputation may be the gainer. An act of so much precipitancy and presumption would seal the downfall of precocious intellect forever. It rested solely with the oldest and most experienced of the men to lay the subject of the conference before the people. Until such a one chose to make some movement, no deeds in arms, no natural gifts, nor any renown as an orator, would have justified the slightest interruption. On the present occasion, the aged warrior whose privilege it was to speak, was silent, seemingly oppressed with the magnitude of his subject. The delay had already continued beyond the usual deliberative pause that always precedes such a conference; but no sign of impatience or surprise escaped even the youngest boy. Occasionally, an eye was raised from the earth, where the looks of most were riveted, and strayed toward a particular lodge, that was, however, in no manner distinguished from those around it, except in the peculiar care that had been taken to protect it against the assaults of the weather.

"At length, one of those low murmurs, that are so apt to disturb a multitude, was heard, and the whole nation arose to their feet by a common impulse. At that the door of the lodge in question opened, and three men issuing from it, slowly approached the place of consultation. They were all aged, even beyond that period to which the oldest present had reached; but one in the centre, who leaned on his companion for support, had numbered an amount of years to which the human race is seldom permitted to attain. His frame, which had once been tall and erect, like the cedar, was now bending under the pressure of more than a century. The elastic, light step of an Indian was gone, and in its place he was compelled to toil his tardy way over the ground, inch by inch. His dark, wrinkled countenance was in singular and wild contrast with the long, white locks on his shoulders, in such thickness as to announce that generations had probably passed away since they had last been shorn.

"The dress of this patriarch — for such, considering his vast age, in conjunction with his affinity and influence with his people, he might very properly be termed — was rich and imposing, though strictly after the simple fashion of the tribe. His robe was of the finest skins, which had been deprived of their fur, in order to admit of a hieroglyphical representation of various deeds in arms done in former ages. His bosom was loaded with medals, some in massive silver, and one or two even in gold, the gifts of various Christian potentates, during the long period of his life. He also wore armlets and cinctures above the ankles, of the latter precious metal. His head, on the whole of which the hair had been permitted to grow, the pursuits of war having so long been abandoned, was encircled by a sort of plated diadem, which, in its turn, bore lesser and more glittering ornaments, that sparkled amid the glossy hues of three drooping ostrich-feathers, dyed a deep black, in touching contrast to the color of his snow-white locks. His tomahawk was nearly hid in silver, and the handle of his knife shone like a horn of solid gold.

"So soon as the first hum of emotion and pleasure, which the sudden appearance of this venerable individual created, had a little subsided, the name of 'Tamenund' was whispered from mouth to mouth. Magua had often heard the fame of this wise and just Delaware; a reputation that even proceeded so far as to bestow on him the rare gift of holding secret communion with the Great Spirit, and which had since transmitted his name, with some slight alteration, to the white usurpers of his ancient territory, as the imaginary tutelar saint of a vast empire. The Huron chief, therefore, stepped eagerly out a little from the throng, to a spot whence he might catch a nearer glimpse of the features of the man whose decision was likely to produce so deep an influence on his own fortunes.

"The eyes of the old man were closed, as though the organs were wearied with having so long witnessed the selfish workings of the human passions. The color of his skin differed from that of most around him, being richer and darker, the latter hue having been produced by certain delicate and mazy lines of complicated and yet beautiful figures which had been traced over most of his person by the operation of tattooing. Notwithstanding the position of the Huron, he passed the observant and silent Magua without notice, and leaning on his two venerable supporters proceeded to the high place of the multitude, where he seated himself in the centre of the nation, with the dignity of a monarch and the air of a father.

"Nothing could surpass the reverence and affection with which this unexpected visit, from one who belonged rather to another world than this, was received by his people. After a suitable and decent pause, the principal chiefs arose, and, approaching the patriarch, they placed his hands reverently on their heads, seeming to entreat a blessing. The younger men were content with touching his robe, or even drawing nigh his person, in order to breathe in the atmosphere of one so aged, so just, and so valiant. None but the most distinguished among the youthful warriors even presumed so far as to perform the latter ceremony; the great mass of the multitude deeming it a sufficient happiness to look upon a form so deeply venerated, and so well beloved. When these acts of affection and respect were performed, the chiefs drew back again to their several places, and silence reigned in the whole encampment.

"After a short delay, a few of the young men, to whom instructions had been whispered by one of the aged attendants of Tamenund, arose, left the crowd, and entered the lodge which has already been noted as the object of so much attention throughout the morning. In a few minutes they reappeared, escorting the individuals who had caused all these solemn preparations toward the seat of judgment. The crowd opened in a lane; and when the party had re-entered, it closed again, forming a large and dense belt of human bodies, arranged in an open circle."

The council having been formed and everything being ready, the Huron made his address concluding with the demand for the return of his prisoners. It was decided that the white woman was the captive of the Huron. The aged chief, with exact justice, gave the verdict, "Justice is the law of the Great Manitto. My children give the stranger food. — Then Huron take thine own and depart."

The captive girl made an appeal to the aged chief without success. She then called attention to the fact that another prisoner was in the hands of the Delawares and asks that he be heard. Uncas, the chief referred to, was then brought forth, and when before him, the aged chief demanded, "With what tongue does the prisoner speak to the Manitto." Uncas replied, "Like his fathers with the tongue of the Delaware." Then followed a dialogue between Uncas and the patriarch, which was ended by the decision of the chief that Uncas should be given over to the torture. The novelist describes the rest of the remarkable scene in the following vivid language: —

"Not a limb was moved, nor was a breath drawn louder and longer than common, until the closing syllable of this final decree had passed the lips of Tamenund. Then a cry of vengeance burst at once, as it might be, from the united lips of the nation; a frightful augury of their ruthless intentions. In the midst of these prolonged and savage yells, a chief proclaimed, in a high voice, that the captive was condemned to endure the dreadful trial of torture by fire. The circle broke its order, and screams of delight mingled with the bustle and tumult of preparation. Heyward struggled madly with his captors; the anxious eyes of Hawk-eye began to look around him, with an expression of peculiar earnestness; and Cora again threw herself at the feet of the patriarch, once more a suppliant for mercy.

"Throughout the whole of these trying moments, Uncas had alone preserved his serenity. He looked upon the preparations with a steady eye, and when the tormentors came to seize him, he met them with a firm and upright attitude. One among them, if possible, more fierce and savage than his fellows, seized the hunting-shirt of the young warrior, and at a single effort tore it from his body. Then, with a yell of frantic pleasure, he leaped toward his unresisting victim, and prepared to lead him to the stake. But, at that moment, when he appeared most a stranger to the feelings of humanity, the purpose of the savage was arrested as suddenly as if a supernatural agency had interposed in the behalf of Uncas. The eyeballs of the Delaware seemed to start from their sockets; his mouth opened, and his whole form became frozen in an attitude of amazement. Raising his hand with a slow and regulated motion, he pointed with a finger to the bosom of the captive. His companions crowded about him in wonder, and every eye was, like his own, fastened intently on the figure of a small tortoise, beautifully tattooed on the breast of the prisoner, in a bright blue tint.

"For a single instant Uncas enjoyed his triumph, smiling calmly on the scene. Then, motioning the crowd away with a high and haughty sweep of his arm, he advanced in front of the nation with the air of a king, and spoke in a voice louder than the murmur of admiration that ran through the multitude.

"'Men of the Lenni Lenape,' he said, 'my race upholds the earth! Your feeble tribe stands on my shell! What fire that a Delaware can light would burn the child of my fathers,' he added, pointing proudly to the simple blazonry on his skin; 'the blood that came from such a stock would smoulder your flames! My race is the grandfather of nations!'

"'Who art thou?' demanded Tamenund, rising at the startling tones he heard, more than at any meaning conveyed by the language of the prisoner.

"'Uncas, the son of Chingachgook,' answered the captive modestly, turning from the nation, and bending his head in reverence to the other's character and years; 'a son of the great Unamis (Turtle).'"

Then followed the triumph of Uncas. All the captives with the exception of the white girl, were released, and such was the justice of the Indian race, the claim of the Huron for her return was recognized, and he was allowed to depart with his captive. He departed with tauntings which were received in silence by the Delawares. As long as their enemy and his victim continued in sight, the multitude remained motionless; but the instant he departed, a fierce and powerful passion seized them. The Huron had been informed that after a limited time the Delawares would be upon his trail, and within the next hour the preparation for the engagement upon the war-path went busily on.

In connection with what has been given in another part of this history, of the manner of enlistment for the war-path, the description of the scene which followed is worthy of reproduction, told as it is in language at once fascinating and literally correct in its description of this ancient custom of the Aborigines. The description is as follows: —

"A young warrior at length issued from the lodge of Uncas, and moving deliberately, with a sort of grave march, toward a dwarf pine that grew in the crevices of the rocky terrace, he tore the bark from its body, and then returned whence he came without speaking. He was soon followed by another, who stripped the sapling of its branches, leaving it a naked and blazed trunk. A third colored the post with stripes of a dark red paint; all which indications of a hostile design in the leaders of the nation were received by the men without in a gloomy and ominous silence. Finally, the Mohican himself reappeared, divested of all his attire except his girdle and leggings, and with one-half of his fine features hid under a cloud of threatening black.

"Uncas moved with a slow and dignified tread toward the post, which he immediately commenced encircling with a measured step, not unlike an ancient dance, raising his voice at the same time, in the wild and irregular chant of his war-song. The notes were in the extremes of human sounds, being sometimes melancholy and exquisitely plaintive, even rivalling the melody of birds — and then by sudden and startling transitions, causing the auditors to tremble by their depth and energy. The words were few and often repeated, proceeding gradually from a sort of invocation, or hymn to the Deity, to an intimation of the warrior's object, and terminating as they commenced, with an acknowledgment of his own dependence on the Great Spirit. If it were possible to translate the comprehensive and melodious language in which he spoke, the ode might read something like the following:—

"'Manitto! Manitto! Manitto!
Thou art great, thou art good, thou art wise;
Manitto! Manitto!
Thou art just.

"'In the heavens, in the clouds, oh! I see
Many spots — many dark, many red;
In the heavens, oh! I see
Many clouds.

"'In the woods, in the air, oh! I hear
The whoop, the long yell, and the cry;
In the woods, oh! I hear
The loud whoop!

"'Manitto! Manitto! Manitto!
I am weak — thou art strong; I am slow —
Manitto! Manitto!
Give me aid.'

"At the end of what might be called each verse he made a pause, by raising a note louder and longer than common, that was peculiarly suited to the sentiment just expressed. The first close was solemn, and intended to convey the idea of veneration; the second, descriptive, bordering on the alarming; and the third was the well-known war-whoop, which burst from the lips of the young warrior, like a combination of all the frightful sounds of battle. The last was like the first, humble and imploring. Three times did he repeat this song, and as often did he encircle the post in his dance.

"At the close of the first turn, a grave and high-esteemed chief of the Lenape followed his example, singing words of his own, however, to music of a similar character. Warrior after warrior enlisted in the dance, until all of any renown and authority were numbered in its mazes. The spectacle now became wildly terrific, the fierce-looking and menacing visages of the chiefs receiving additional power from the appalling strains in which they mingled their gutteral tones. Just then Uncas struck his tomahawk deep into the post, and raised his voice in a shout, which might be termed his own battle-cry. The act announced that he had assumed the chief authority in the intended expedition.

"It was a signal that awakened all the slumbering passions of the nation. A hundred youths who had hitherto been restrained by the diffidence of their years, rushed in a frantic body on the fancied emblem of their enemy, and severed it asunder, splinter by splinter, until nothing remained of the trunk but its roots in the earth. During this moment of tumult, the most ruthless deeds of war were performed on the fragments of the tree, with as much apparent ferocity as if they were the living victims of their cruelty.

"Some were scalped; some received the keen and trembling axe; and others suffered by thrusts from the fatal knife. In short, the manifestations of zeal and fierce delight were so great and unequivocal, that the expedition was declared to be a war of the nation.

"The instant Uncas had struck the blow he moved out of the circle and cast his eyes up to the sun, which was just gaining the point, when the truce with Magua was to end. The fact was soon announced by a significant gesture, accompanied by a corresponding cry; and the whole of the excited multitude abandoned their mimic warfare with shrill yells of pleasure, to prepare for the more hazardous experiment of the reality.

"The whole face of the encampment was instantly changed. The warriors, who were already armed and painted, became as still as if they were incapable of any uncommon burst of emotion. On the other hand, the women broke out of the lodges with the songs of joy and those of lamentation so strangely mingled, that it might have been difficult to have said which passion predominated. None, however, were idle. Some bore their choicest articles, others their young, and some their aged and infirm, into the forest, which spread itself like a verdant carpet of bright green against the side of the mountain. Thither Tamenund also retired with calm composure, after a short and touching interview with Uncas; from whom the sage separated with the reluctance that a parent would quit a long-lost and just-recovered child."

Probably the most remarkable specimen of this picture writing and also of the elegant dress worn by these Indians, is given in Catlin's description of the costume of Mah-to-toh-pa, a Mandan chief. The description is as follows: —

"The skirt was made of two skins of the mountain sheep, beautifully dressed and sewed together by seams which rested upon the arms; one skin hanging in front upon the breast, and the other falling down upon the back, the head being passed between them and they falling over and resting upon the shoulders. Across each shoulder and somewhat in the form of an epaulette was a beautiful band, and down each arm from the neck to the hand was a similar one of two inches in width (and crossing each other at right angles on the shoulder), beautifully embroidered with porcupine quills worked on the dress and covering the seams. To the lower edge of these bands the whole way, at intervals of half an inch were attached long locks of black hair, which he had taken with his own hand from the heads of his enemies whom he had slain in battle, and which he thus wore as a trophy and also as an ornament to his dress. The front and back of the skirt were curiously garnished in several parts with porcupine quills and paintings of the battles he had fought, and also with representations of the victims that had fallen by his hand. The bottom of the dress was bound or hemmed with ermine skins, and tassels of ermines' tails were suspended from the arms and the shoulders.

"The leggings, which were made of deer-skins, beautifully dressed and fitting tight to the leg, extended from the feet to the hips, and were fastened to a belt which was passed around the waist. These, like the skirt, had a similar band, worked with porcupine quills of the richest dyes, passing down the seam on the outer part of the leg, and fringed also the whole length of the leg with the scalp-locks taken from his enemies' heads.

"The moccasons were of buckskin, and covered in almost every part with the beautiful embroidery of porcupines' quills.

"The head-dress, which was superb and truly magnificent, consisted of a crest of war-eagles' quills, gracefully falling back from the forehead over the back part of the head, and extending quite down to the feet, set the whole way in a profusion of ermine, and surmounted on the top of the head with the horns of the buffalo, shaved thin and highly polished.

"The necklace was made of 50 huge claws or nails of the grizzly bear, ingeniously arranged on the skin of an otter, and worn like the scalp-locks, as a trophy, and as an evidence unquestionable that he had contended with and overcome that desperate enemy in open combat.

" His shield was made of the hide of the buffalo's neck, and hardened with the glue that was taken from its hoofs; its boss was the skin of a pole-cat, and its edges were fringed with rows of eagles' quills and hoofs of the antelope.

" His bow was of bone, and as white and beautiful as ivory; over its back was laid, and firmly attached to it, a coating of deers' sinews, which gave it its elasticity, and, of course, death to all that stood inimically before it. Its string was three-stranded and twisted of sinews, which many a time had twanged and sent the whizzing death to animal and to human victims.

" The quiver was made of a panther's skin, and hung upon his back, charged with its deadly arrows; some were poisoned and some were not; they were feathered with hawks' and eagles' quills; some were clean and innocent and pure, and others were stained all over with animal and human blood that was dried upon them. Their blades or points were of flints, and some of steel; and altogether were a deadly magazine.

" The lance or spear was held in his left hand; its blade was two-edged and of polished steel, and the blood of several human victims was seen dried upon it, one over the other; its shaft was of the toughest ash, and ornamented at intervals with tufts of war-eagles' quills.

" His tobacco-sack was made of the skin of an otter, and tastefully garnished with quills of the porcupine; in it was carried his k'nick-k'neck (the bark of the red willow, which is smoked as a substance for tobacco); it contained also his flint and steel, and spunk for lighting.

" His pipe which was ingeniously carved out of the red steatite (or pipe-stone), the stem of which was three feet long and two inches wide, made from the stalk of the young ash; about half its length was wound with delicate braids of the porcupine's quills, so ingeniously wrought as to represent figures of men and animals upon it. It was also ornamented with the skins and beaks of woodpeckers' heads, and the hair of the white buffalo's tail. The lower half of the stem was painted red, and

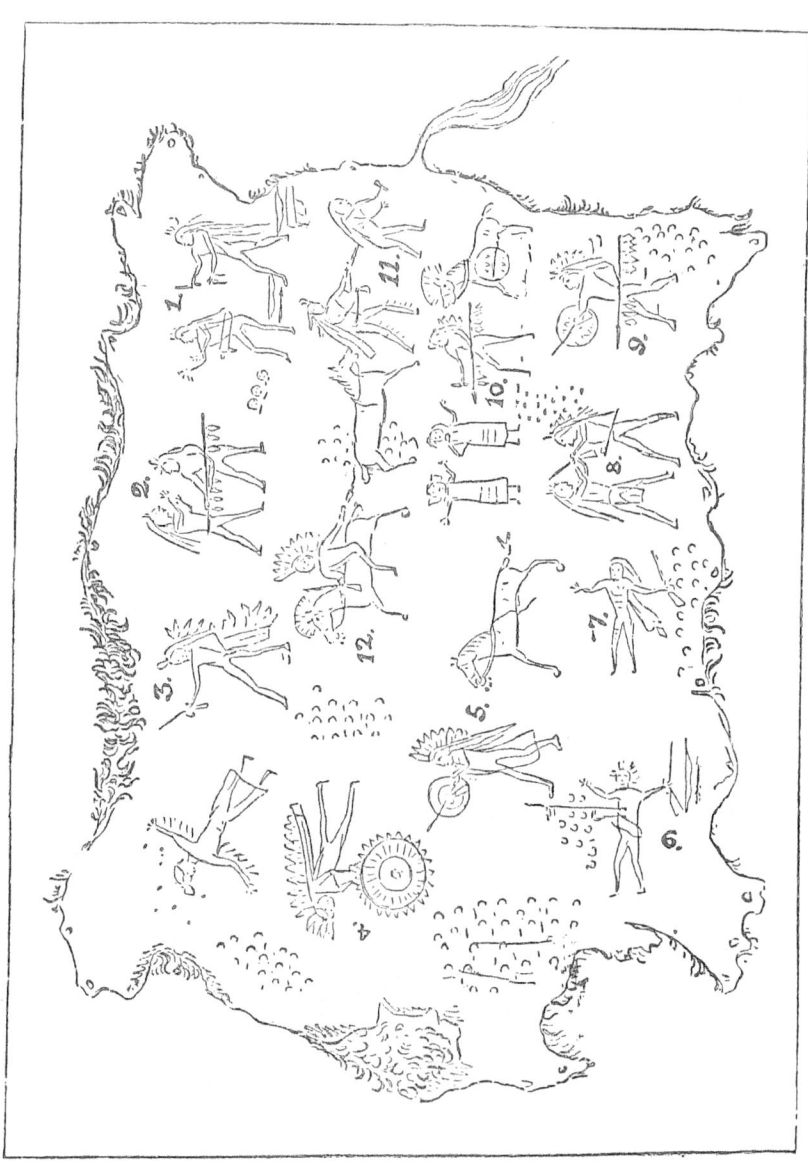

Robe of Mah-to-toh-pa, a Mandan Chief.

on its edges it bore the notches he had recorded for the snows (or years) of his life.

"His robe was made of the skin of a young buffalo bull, with the fur on one side, and the other finely and delicately dressed, with all the battles of his life emblazoned on it by his own hand.

"His belt, which was of a substantial piece of buckskin, was firmly girded around his waist, and in it were worn his tomahawk and scalping-knife.

"His medicine-bag was the skin of a beaver, curiously ornamented with hawks' bills and ermine. It was held in his right hand, and his Po-ko-mo-kon (or war-club), which was made of a round stone, tied up in a piece of rawhide, and attached to the end of a stick, somewhat in the form of a sling, was laid with others of his weapons at his feet."

The robe of Mah-to-toh-pa was really a record of the battles of his life, and besides being a remarkable specimen of Indian picture writing, is worthy of more extended mention as typical of the records preserved by Indian chiefs of the deeds in which they had been prominent personally. The interpretation of the various incidents recorded on the robe is given as follows: —

"1. Mah-to-toh-pa kills a Sioux chief. The three heads represent the three Riccarees, whom the Sioux chief had previously killed. The Sioux chief is seen with war-paint, black on his face. Mah-to-toh-pa is seen with the scalp of the Sioux on one hand, and his knife in the other, with his bow and quiver lying behind him.

"2. A Shienne chief, who sent word to Mah-to-toh-pa that he wished to fight him, was killed by Mah-to-toh-pa with a lance, in presence of a large party of Mandans and Shiennes. Mah-to-toh-pa is here known by his lance with eagles' quills on it.

"3. A Shienne killed by Mah-to-toh-pa after Mah-to-toh-pa had been left by his party badly wounded and bleeding; the twenty-five or thirty foot-tracks around, represent the number of Shiennes who were present when the battle took place; and the bullets from their guns represented as flying all around the head of Mah-to-toh-pa.

"4. Shienne chief with war-eagle head-dress, and a beautiful shield ornamented with eagles' quills killed by Mah-to-toh-pa. In this battle the wife of the Shienne rushed forward in a desperate manner to his assistance, but arriving too late, fell a victim. In this battle Mah-to-toh-pa obtained two scalps.

"5. Mah-to-toh-pa, with a party of Riccarees, fired at by a party of Sioux; the Riccarees fled — Mah-to-toh-pa dismounted and drove his horse back, facing the enemy alone, and killing one of them. Mah-to-toh-pa is here represented with a beautiful headdress of war-eagles' quills, and one on his horse's head of equal beauty; his shield is on his arm, and the party of Sioux is represented in front of him by the number of horse-tracks.

"6. The brother of Mah-to-toh-pa killed by a Riccaree, who shot him with an arrow, and then running a lance through his body, left it there. Mah-to-toh-pa was the first to find his brother's body with the lance in it; he drew the lance from the body, kept it four years with the blood dried on its blade, and then, according to his oath, killed the same Riccaree with the same lance; the dead body of his brother is here seen with the arrow and lance remaining in it, and the tracks of the Riccaree's horses in front.

"The following was, perhaps, one of the most extraordinary exploits of this remarkable man's life, and is well attested by Mr. Kipp and several white men, who were living in the Mandan village at the time of its occurrence. In a skirmish near the Mandan village, when they were set upon by their enemies, the Riccarees, the brother of Mah-to-toh-pa was missing for several days, when Mah-to-toh-pa found the body shockingly mangled, and a handsome spear left piercing the body through the heart. The spear was by him brought into the Mandan village, where it was recognized by many as a famous weapon belonging to a noted brave of the Riccarees, by the name of Won-ga-tap. This spear was brandished through the Mandan village by Mah-to-toh-pa (with the blood of his brother dried on its blade), crying most piteously, and swearing that he would some day revenge the death of his brother with the same weapon.

"It is almost an incredible fact, that he kept this spear with great care in his wigwam for the space of four years, in the fruitless expectation of an opportunity to use it upon the breast of its owner; when his indignant soul, impatient of further delay, burst forth in the most uncontrollable frenzy and fury, he again brandished it through the village, and said, that the blood of his brother's heart which was seen on its blade was yet fresh and called loudly for revenge. 'Let every Mandan' (said he) 'be silent, and let no one sound the name of Mah-to-toh-pa — let no one ask for him, nor where he has gone, until you hear him sound the war-cry in front of the village, when he will enter it and show you the blood of Won-ga-tap. The blade of this lance shall drink the heart's blood of Won-ga-tap, or Mah-to-toh-pa mingles his shadow with that of his brother.'

"With this he sallied forth from the village, and over the plains, with the lance in his hand; his direction was towards the Riccaree village, and all eyes were upon him, though none dared to speak till he disappeared over the distant grassy bluff. He travelled the distance of two hundred miles entirely alone, with a little parched corn in his pouch, making his marches by night, and laying secreted by days, until he reached the Riccaree village, where (being acquainted with its shapes and its habits, and knowing the position of the wigwam of his doomed enemy) he loitered about in disguise, mingling himself in the obscure throng; and at last, silently and alone, observed through the rents of the wigwam, the last motions and movements of his victim as he retired to bed with his wife; he saw him light his last pipe, and smoke it 'to its end'—he saw the last whiff and saw the last curl of blue smoke that faintly steeped from its bowl — he saw the village awhile in darkness and silence, and the embers that were covered in the middle of the wigwam gone nearly out, and the last flickering light which had been gently playing over them, when he walked softly but not slyly, into the wigwam and seated himself by the fire, over which was hanging a large pot with a quantity of cooked meat remaining in it, and by the side of the fire, the pipe and tobacco-pouch which had just been used; and knowing that the twilight of the wigwam was not sufficient to disclose the features of his face to his enemy, he very deliberately turned to the pot and completely satiated the desperate appetite, which he had got in a journey of six or seven days with little or nothing to eat; and then as deliberately charged and lighted the pipe, and sent (no doubt in every whiff that he drew through its stem) a prayer to the Great Spirit for a moment longer for the consummation of his design. Whilst eating and drinking, the wife of his victim, while lying in bed, several times inquired of her husband, what man it was who was eating in their lodge? to which, he as many times replied, 'it's no matter; let him eat, for he is probably hungry.'

"Mah-to-toh-pa knew full well that his appearance would cause no other reply than this, from the dignitary of the nation, for, from an invariable custom amongst these Northern Indians, any one who is hungry is allowed to walk into any man's lodge and eat. Whilst smoking his last gentle and tremulous whiffs on the pipe, Mah-to-toh-pa (leaning back, and turning gradually on his side, to get a better view of the position of his enemy, and to see a little more distinctly the shapes of things) stirred the embers with his toes (readers, every word of this was from his own lips, and every attitude and gesture acted out with his own limbs), until he saw his way was clear; at which moment, with his lance in his hands, he rose and drove it through the body of his enemy, and snatching the scalp from his head, he darted from the lodge, and quick as lightning, with the lance in one hand and the scalp in the other, made his way to the prairie. The village was in an uproar, but he was off, and no one knew the enemy who had struck the blow. Mah-to-toh-pa ran all night, and lay close during the days, thanking the Great Spirit for strengthening his heart and his arm for this noble revenge, and prayed fervently for a continuance of his aid and protection till he should get back to his own village. His prayers were heard, and on the sixth morning, at sunrise, Mah-to-toh-pa descended the bluffs, and entered the village amidst deafening shouts of applause, while he brandished and showed to his people the blade of his lance, with the blood of his victim dried upon it, over that of his brother, and the scalp of Won-ga-tap suspended from its handle.

"7. Riccaree killed by Mah-to-toh-pa in revenge of the death of a white man killed by a Riccaree in the fur-traders' fort, a short time previous.

"8. Mah-to-toh-pa, or four bears, kills a Shienne chief, who challenged him to single combat, in presence of the two war parties. They fought on horseback with guns, until Mah-to-toh-pa's powder-horn was shot away; they then fought with bows and arrows, until their quivers were emptied, when they dismounted and fought single-handed. The Shienne drew his knife, and Mah-to-toh-pa had left his; they struggled for the knife, which Mah-to-toh-pa wrested from the Shienne and killed him with it. In the struggle the blade of the knife was several times drawn through the hand of Mah-to-toh-pa, and the blood is seen running from the wound.

"This extraordinary occurrence also was one which admits of, and deserves, a more elaborate description, which will here be given as it was translated from his own lips, while he sat upon the robe, pointing to his painting of it, and at the same time brandishing the identical knife, which he drew from his belt, as he was showing how the fatal blow was given, and exhibiting the wounds inflicted in his hand, as the blade of the knife was several times drawn through it before he wrested it from his antagonist.

"A party of about 150 Shienne warriors had made an assault upon the Mandan village, at an early hour in the morning, and driven off a considerable number of horses, and taken one scalp. Mah-to-toh-pa, who was then a young man, but famed as one of the most valiant of the Mandans, took the lead of a party of fifty warriors, all he could at that time muster, and went in pursuit of the enemy. About noon of the second day they came in sight of the Shiennes, and the Mandans, seeing their enemy much more numerous than they had expected, were generally disposed to turn about and return without attacking them. They started to go back, when Mah-to-toh-pa galloped out in front upon the prairie, and plunged his lance into the ground; the blade was driven into the earth to its hilt. He made another circuit round, and in that circuit tore from his breast his reddened sash, which he hung upon its handle as a flag, calling out to the Mandans, 'What! have we come to this? We have dogged our enemy two days, and now when we have found them, are we to turn about and go back like cowards? Mah-to-toh-pa's lance, which is red with the blood of brave men, has led you to the sight of your enemy, and you have followed it; it now stands firm in the ground, where the earth will drink the blood of Mah-to-toh-pa. You may all go back, and Mah-to-toh-pa will fight them alone!'

"During this manœuvre, the Shiennes, who had discovered the Mandans behind them, had turned about and were gradually approaching, in order to give them battle. The chief of the Shienne war-party, seeing and understanding the difficulty, and admiring the gallant conduct of Mah-to-toh-pa, galloped his horse forward within hailing distance, in front of the Mandans, and called out to know, 'who he was who had stuck his lance and defied the whole enemy alone.'

"'I am Mah-to-toh-pa, second in command of the brave and valiant Mandans.'

"'I have heard often of Mah-to-toh-pa; he is a great warrior. Dares Mah-to-toh-pa to come forward and fight this battle with me alone, and our warriors will look on?'

"'Is he a chief who speaks to Mah-to-toh-pa?'

"'My scalps you see hanging to my horse's bits, and here is my lance with the ermine skins and war-eagle's tail.'

"'You have said enough.'

"The Shienne chief made a circuit or two at full gallop on a beautiful white horse, when he struck his lance into the ground, and left it standing by the side of the lance of Mah-to-toh-pa, both of which were waving together their little red flags, tokens of blood and defiance.

"The two parties then drew nearer on a beautiful prairie, and the full-plumed chiefs, at full speed, drove furiously upon each other, both firing their guns at the same moment. They passed each other a little distance and wheeled, when Mah-to-toh-pa drew off his powder-horn, and by holding it up, showed his adversary that the bullet had shattered it to pieces, and destroyed his ammunition. He then threw it from him, and his gun also, drew his bow from his quiver and an arrow, and his shield upon his left arm. The Shienne instantly did the same; his horn was thrown off, and his gun was thrown into the air; his shield was balanced on his arm, his bow drawn, and quick as lightning they were both on the wing for a deadly combat. Like two soaring eagles in the open air they made their circuits round, and the twangs of their sinewy bows were heard and the war-whoop as they dashed by each other parrying off the whizzing arrows with their shields. Some lodged in their legs and others in their arms, but both protected their bodies with their bucklers of bull's hide. Deadly and many were the shafts that fled from their murderous bows. At length the horse of Mah-to-toh-pa fell to the ground with an arrow in his heart. His rider sprang upon his feet, prepared to renew the combat; but the Shienne, seeing his adversary dismounted, sprang from his horse, and driving him back, presented the face of his shield toward his enemy inviting him to come on. A few shots more were exchanged thus, when the Shienne, having discharged all his arrows, held up his empty quiver, and dashing it furiously to the ground, with his bow and his shield, drew and brandished his naked knife.

"'Yes,' said Mah-to-toh-pa, as he threw his shield and quiver to the earth, and was rushing up. He grasped for his knife, but his belt had it not; he had left it at home. His bow was in his hand, with which he parried his antagonist's blow, and felled him to the ground. A desperate struggle now ensued for the knife; the blade of it was several times drawn through the right hand of Mah-to-toh-pa, inflicting the most frightful wounds, while he was severely wounded in several parts of the body. He at length succeeded, however, in wresting it from his adversary's hand, and plunged it in his heart.

"By this time the two parties had drawn up in close view of each other, and at the close of the battle Mah-to-toh-pa held up, and claimed in deadly silence, the knife and scalp of the noble Shienne chief.

"9. Several hundred Minatarrees and Mandans attacked by a party of Assinneboins all fled but Mah-to-toh-pa, who stood his ground, fired, and killed one of the enemy, putting the rest of them to flight, and driving off sixty horses. He is here seen with his lance and shield, foot-tracks of his enemy in front, and his own party's horse-tracks behind him and a shower of bullets flying around his head. Here he got the name of 'The Four Bears,' as the Assinneboins said he rushed on like four bears.

"10. Mah-to-toh-pa gets from his horse and kills two Ojibbeway women, and takes their scalps; done by the side of an Ojibbeway village, where they went to the river for water. He is here seen with his lance in one hand and his knife in the other, an eagle's-plume head-dress on his horse, and his shield left on his horse's back. His ill-will was incurred for awhile by asking him whether it was manly to boast of taking the scalps of women, and his pride prevented him from giving any explanation or apology. The interpreter, however, explained that he had secreted himself in the most daring manner, in full sight of the Ojibbeway village, seeking to revenge a murder, where he remained six days without sustenance, and then killed the two women in full view of the tribe and made his escape, which entitled him to the credit of a victory, though his victims were women.

"11. A large party of Assinneboins intrenched near the Mandan village, attacked by the Mandans and Minatarrees, who were driven back, Mah-to-toh-pa rushes into the intrenchment alone. An Indian fires at him and burns his face with the muzzle of his gun, which burst; the Indian retreats leaving his exploded gun, and Mah-to-toh-pa shoots him through the shoulder as he runs, and kills him with his tomahawk. The gun of the Assinneboin is seen falling to the ground, and in front of him the heads of the Assinneboins in the intrenchment; the horse of Mah-to-toh-pa is seen behind him.

"12. Mah-to-toh-pa between his enemy, the Sioux, and his own people, with an arrow shot through him, after standing the fire of the Sioux for a long time alone. In this battle he took no scalps, yet his valor was so extraordinary that the chiefs and braves awarded him the honor of a victory.

"This feat is seen in the centre of the robe. Head-dress of war-eagles' quills on his own and his horse's head; the tracks of his enemies' horses are seen in front of him, and bullets flying both ways all around him. With his whip in his hand he is seen urging his horse forward, and an arrow is seen flying and bloody, as it has passed through his body. For this wound, and the several others mentioned above, he bears the honorable scars on his body, which he generally keeps covered with red paint."

The material from which this chapter thus far has been taken, relates almost exclusively to the Indians composing the New England tribes and those tribes and nations living east of the Mississippi River comprised in the League of the Iroquois. The record given by Catlin of his travels among the Indians of the northwest in the years 1832-33, prove that in all essential matters the peculiarities and characteristics already mentioned are typical of the entire race of Red Men inhabiting the continent north of Mexico. At the time of his writings, substantially the whole territory west of Louisiana, Arkansas, Missouri, and Illinois was in the hands of the Indian tribes who then numbered, according to Catlin's estimate, about 2,000,000. His description of the people with whom he came in contact is worthy of reproduction.

"The Indians of North America," said he, "are coppercolored, with long black hair, black eyes, tall, straight, and elastic forms — are less than 2,000,000 in number — were originally the undisputed owners of the soil, and got their title to their lands from the Great Spirit who created them on it, — were once a happy and flourishing people, enjoying all the comforts and luxuries of life which they knew of, and consequently cared for, — were 16,000,000 in numbers, and sent that number of daily prayers to the Almighty, and thanks for his goodness and protection. Their country was entered by white men, but a few hundred years since; and 30,000,000 of these are now scuffling for the goods and luxuries of life over the bones and ashes of 12,000,000 of Red Men; 6,000,000 of whom have fallen victims to the small-pox, and the remainder to the sword, the bayonet, and whiskey; all of which means of their death and destruction have been introduced and visited upon them by acquisitive white men; and by white men also, whose forefathers were welcomed and embraced, in the land where the poor Indian met and fed them with 'ears of green corn and with pemican.' Of the 2,000,000 remaining alive at this time, about 1,400,000 are already the miserable living victims and dupes of the white man's cupidity, degraded, discouraged, and lost in the bewildering maze that is produced by the use of whiskey and its concomitant vices; and the remaining number are yet unroused and unnoticed from their wild haunts or their primative modes, by the dread or love of white man and his allurements."

All who have come in contact with the North American Indian in his native state, have borne testimony to the fact that he was honest, hospitable, faithful, brave, warlike even though cruel, revengeful, and relentless, and that he was an honorable, contemplative, and religious being. If the customs and ceremonies of the Indians present evidences of that which is dark and cruel, or of ignorant and disgusting excess of passion, it should be remembered in palliation that these customs and ceremonies came down to them by tradition from the dim past, and were as natural and proper to them as our customs and ceremonies of civilization to us. After intercourse for eight years, visiting and associating with some three or four hundred thousand of these people under an almost infinite variety of circumstances, Catlin bore witness to the very many and decidedly voluntary acts of hospitality and kindness bestowed upon him, and felt bound to pronounce them by nature a kind and hospitable people. He was welcomed in their country, and treated to the best they could give "without hope of fee or reward." He was escorted through the country of their enemies at hazard to their own lives, but under all circumstances of exposure "no Indian ever betrayed him, struck him a blow, or stole from him a shilling's worth of property."

A large number of legends have come down to us descriptive of the various dances and ceremonies of the northwestern Indians, all of which would be of great interest to the reader. A few of them will be appropriate as illustrating the peculiarities which made the Indian *sui generis*, and which justified the selection of the name by which he sometimes described himself, "Ongwee Hongwee."

Experiments by scientific men within the last few years to produce rain, during a season of long drought, have led to the participants in these experiments being called rainmakers. Among the Mandans, as late as 1832, the rainmakers were held in high repute. While the Mystery Men performed their rites inside of the lodge, young men were sent to the roof to stand there from sunrise to sundown commanding it to rain. If the attempt was fruitless he descended at night in disgrace. If he succeeded he acquired a lasting reputation as a Mystery or Medicine Man. The rainmakers never failed of success eventually as the ceremony continued from day to day until rain came.

The reason for this ceremony was apparent. The Mandans raised a great deal of corn, and in seasons of drought great disaster threatened the harvest. The Chiefs and Medicine Men were appealed to by the women to produce rain for the benefit of the corn. After delaying as long as possible, the demands of the women became so insistent that the Medicine Men assembled in the council house with all their mystery apparatus about them, with an abundance of wild sage and other aromatic herbs which they burned upon the fire prepared in order that the odors might ascend to the Great Spirit. No one was allowed within the council house where the ceremonies were performed except the Medicine Men, and the young men who had been selected as willing to make the attempt to produce rain. One by one each took his turn by lot to spend the day upon the top of the lodge, and to test the potency of his medicine. At the same time the doctors were burning incense in the wigwam below, and with their songs and prayers to the Great Spirit for success were sending forth grateful odors to Him "who lives in the sun and commands the thunders of Heaven." Finally the cloud appeared, and the fortunate brave, who, from the top of the lodge noticed its approach, drew upon himself the eyes of the whole village as he vaunted forth his superhuman powers, and, at the same time, commanded the cloud to come nearer, that he might draw down its contents upon the corn fields of his people. Finally the bow was bent, and the arrow, drawn to its head, sent to the cloud. In a few moments the rain fell in torrents. He then descended from his high place prepared to receive the honors and homage that were due to one so potent in his mysteries, and to receive the style and title of Medicine Man.

On the occasion above described after the rain had commenced falling, it continued to pour down in torrents until midnight, the thunder roared and the lightning flashed through a lodge and killed a beautiful girl. The new-made Medicine Man was in great trouble, for he knew that he was subject to the irrevocable degree of the chiefs and doctors whose vengeance was likely to fall without mercy upon the immediate cause of the disaster. Morning came and he soon learned from some of his friends the opinion of the wise men, and also the nature of the tribunal that was prepared for him. He sent for his three horses, and mounting the medicine lodge addressed the assembled villagers with these words: "My friends, I see you all around me, and I am before you; my medicine you see is great — it is too great

—I am young and I was too fast—I knew not when to stop. The wigwam of Mah-sish is laid low, and many are the eyes that weep for Ko-ka (the Antelope). Wak-a-dah-ha-hee gives three horses to gladden the hearts of those who weep for Ko-ka; his medicine was great—his arrow pierced the cloud and the lightning came! Who says the medicine of Wak-a-dah-ha-hee is not strong?" At the end of this sentence a unanimous shout of approbation ran through the crowd, and the brave descended amongst them greeted by shakes of the hand, and ever after he lived and thrived under the familiar and honorable title of Big Double Medicine.

The annual religious ceremony of the Mandans lasted four days. To the paleface this ceremony included scenes of great apparent cruelty and barbarity, but with the Indians themselves it was regarded as a great religious anniversary, and approved by the Great Spirit.

Catlin bore witness to the fact that all the Indian tribes visited by him were religious and worshipful, and did everything in their power to propitiate the Great Spirit. They all believed in the existence of a Great (or Good) Spirit, and an Evil (or Bad) Spirit, and also a future existence and future accountability for their virtues and vices in this world. In this respect the North American Indian seemed to have been one family; but there was a variance with regard to the manner and form, and time and place, of the accountability mentioned as to what constituted virtue and vice, and what were the proper modes of appeasing and propitiating the Good and Evil Spirits.

For instance, the Mandans believed in the existence of both a Great Spirit and an Evil Spirit; but they believed the Evil Spirit existed long before the Great Spirit, and was far superior in power. They believed in a future state and existence, and a future administration of rewards and punishments; but they believed these punishments were not eternal, but were commensurate with their sins. Living in a climate where they suffered from cold in the severity of their winters they very naturally reversed our ideas of heaven and hell. With them the torments of hell were from cold and not from heat, while heaven was supposed to be a warm and delightful place where nothing is felt but the keenest enjoyment, and where the country abounds in buffaloes and other luxuries of life. The Great Spirit they believed dwelt in the place of torment, for the purpose of meeting there those who had offended him, and increasing the agony of their sufferings. The Evil Spirit, on the contrary, they supposed to reside in Paradise still tempting the happy.

Three distinct objects were given for holding these religious ceremonies. First, as a celebration of the event of the subsiding of the flood. Second, for the purpose of dancing the Buffalo dance to the strict observance of which they attributed the coming of the buffaloes to supply them with food each returning season. Third, for the purpose of proving, by the ordeal of privation and torture, the courage of the young men of the tribe as they arrived at the age of manhood, and preparing them by extreme endurance for the duties of the war-path. Portions of the ceremonies were grotesque and amusing; but others tried, to the fullest extent, the courage and endurance of those upon which they were practised. The medicine or mystery lodge stood in the middle of the village, and was built exclusively for the purposes of the annual celebration. The time for the ceremony was on no particular day of the year, as they kept no record of days or weeks as do the palefaces, but was at a particular season designated by the full expansion of the willow leaves under the bank of the river. According to their tradition, "the twig that the bird brought home was a willow bough, and had full grown leaves on it," and the bird to which they alluded is the mourning or turtle dove, which they considered a medicine bird, and which they carefully guarded from harm even from their dogs who were instructed to do it no injury.

The ceremony of the first day commenced with great howling and screaming by the women and children. The whole community joined in the general expression of great alarm, as if in danger of instant destruction. In the midst of this din and confusion, way out on the prairie was seen approaching a man alone and nearly naked. A robe of willow skins hung back over his shoulders; on his head he had a splendid head-dress made of raven skins, and in his left hand he cautiously carried a large pipe which he regarded as something of great importance. He went to the mystery lodge, which he opened. He called to his assistance four men whom he appointed to clean out the lodge and put it in readiness for the ceremony about to take place, by sweeping it and strewing a profusion of green willow boughs over its floor, while sage and aromatic herbs were also scattered around, and over these were arranged buffalo and human skulls and other articles which were to be used during the ceremonies to follow. During the whole of the day, and while these preparations were being made, "the first or only man" went around through the village stopping in front of each lodge until the owner came out and asked who he was and what was the matter, to which he replied by relating the sad catastrophe which had happened on the earth's surface by the overflow of the waters. Saying that he was the only person saved from the universal calamity; that he launched his big canoe on a high mountain in the west where he now resides; that he had come to open the medicine lodge, for which he must receive a present of some edged tool from the owner of every wigwam, that it may be sacrificed to the water; if this was not done there would be another flood, and no one would be saved, as it was with such tools that the big canoe was made. He received a present from each, which was deposited in the medicine lodge, where they remained until the afternoon of the last day of the ceremony, when, as the final or closing scene, they were thrown into the river in the presence of the whole village as a sacrifice to the Spirit of the Water. On the third day the candidates for the torture, by which they were to prove their manhood and endurance, entered the mystery lodge. On the occasion which we are describing, about fifty entered the lists properly prepared for the test. Each carried in his right hand his medicine bag, while on the left arm hung his shield of bull's hide, and in his left hand were held his bow and arrows, and his quiver was hung on his back.

Having entered the mystery lodge, the first or only man delivered a short speech stimulating and encouraging them to trust to the Great Spirit for protection during the ceremonies and severe ordeal through which they were to pass. He then called in a medicine man whom he appointed master of ceremonies for the occasion, and who was designated by them O-kee-pah-ka-se-kah, keeper or conductor of ceremonies. To him was passed the medicine-pipe, and this appointment having thus been confirmed, the only man shook hands with him and bade him good-by, saying that he was going back to the mountains in the west, from whence he should assuredly return in just a year from that time to open the lodge again.

The Medicine Man took his position at the centre of the lodge. He cried to the Great Spirit all the time, and watched the young men who were to fast and thirst for four days and nights preparatory to the torture. Behind him on the floor were the scalping-knife, and a bunch of splints to be passed through the flesh of those who were to submit to the torture. Cords were let down from the roof to which the splints were to be attached, and by which they were to be hung up by the flesh.

The Buffalo dance was a part of the ceremony assigned principally to the third day, although it was danced four times on the first day, eight times on the second day, twelve times on the third day, and sixteen times on the fourth day. The principal actors in it were eight men with buffalo robes over their backs with the horns and hoofs attached, the body being in horizontal position, enabling them to imitate the actions of the buffalo while they were looking out of its eyes as through a mask. The bodies of the men were nearly naked, and all painted in the most extraordinary manner and similar to each other. The eight men were divided into four pairs, and took their positions at the four cardinal points. Between the groups were four other persons appropriately painted, two of whom represented night, and the other two represented day. These twelve persons were the only persons actually engaged in the dance, although a great number assisted in giving it proper effect.

On the first day this Bull or Buffalo dance was given one to each of the cardinal points, and the Medicine Man smoked his pipe in these directions. In like manner, twice on the second day, three times on the third day, and four times on the fourth day. Indeed a superstitious regard seems to have been paid to the number four. During the dances the Medicine Man, assisted by the old man, delivered a chant, sending forth their supplications to the Great Spirit for the continuation of his influence in sending them buffaloes to supply them with food during the year, and also keeping up the courage and fortitude of the young men in the lodge by telling them that the Great Spirit had opened their ears in their behalf.

On the fourth day was illustrated the driving away of the Evil Spirit. One of the tribe, painted in a hideous manner, represented the Evil Spirit. He came in among the people engaged in the ceremonies, all of whom fled from him with the greatest apparent fear and alarm. Finally the Evil Spirit was driven away by the women, and returned to the place from whence he came. The moral of the appearance of the Evil Spirit, was this : That in the midst of their religious ceremonies the Evil Spirit came for the purpose of doing mischief and of disturbing their worship ; that he was held in check and defeated by the superior influence and virtue of the medicine pipe, and at last driven in disgrace out of the village by the very part of the community whom he came to abuse. The close of the fourth day of the ceremonies was devoted to the tortures by which the bravery and endurance of the young man was tested. Splints were passed through the flesh of the arms, legs, and the breast. To those in the arms and legs were attached weights, buffalo heads, etc., which were allowed to remain until by suppuration they dropped out of their own weight. To the splints in the breast were attached the cords by which they were hoisted six or eight feet from the ground, remaining in that position until by their own weight they broke their flesh loose from the splints. After these tortures had been concluded the presents of edged tools which, as above stated, had been collected at the door of every man's wigwam, were taken by the Medicine Man to the bank of the river, when all the other medicine men attended him, and all the nation were spectators, and in their presence he threw them from a high bank into the water, from which they could not be recovered. This part of the affair took place exactly at sundown, and closed the scene, being the ending of the Mandans, religious ceremony.

This chapter has already exceeded the limit originally assigned ; but the subject has been so fascinating, and the mass of material at hand so great, that the difficulty has been to decide what to omit, rather than what to select. What has been presented is but a very small portion of that untouched. Our idea has been to present, as near as may be, a comprehensive sketch of Indian character in all its phases, trusting thereby, to arouse in the mind of the reader, sufficient interest to induce him to delve for himself in the mine of wealth at his command, illustrative of Indian character, Indian purity, Indian nobility alone and untarnished, and unspotted by contact with his so-called civilized conqueror.

Where extracts have been taken from publications long since out of print, some of them published more than one hundred years ago, or in which were quotations from writings and publications of the seventeenth and eighteenth centuries, we have thought proper to use the quaint language of the original writing rather than to change it to the modern idioms. As in the study of a history of a people much is learned from their habits and customs, so also an insight is gained into the forms and peculiarities of a certain time by the language then used. In this chapter as in other portions of the book, we have not hesitated to draw upon the material at command, making general acknowledgment of the source of our information, and claiming only the arrangement and adaptation to this history of the selections we have made.

Among the races of the earth, the North American Indian stands unique and remarkable. Whatever may have been the origin of the race, how many the ages of the evolution by which it descended from those prehistoric people that inhabited the country before it, it has left a record in the speaking books of the palefaces too vivid and remarkable ever to be effaced.

Brought into daily contact with the Indians, and being thereby made cognizant of their fearlessness, endurance and freedom from restraint, it is not too much to assume that the same inspiration of liberty was imbibed by those who composed the Patriotic Societies mentioned in the succeeding chapter, and suggested to them the idea of separation from the mother country and the establishment of a free government, which thought afterwards became crystallized into the United States.

Accustomed as we are to a reiteration of the brutal phrase "there is no good Indian except he be a dead Indian," simple justice would seem to compel us to learn something of this wonderful race, who in the imagery of their own expressive language, "are fast travelling to the shades of their fathers, towards the setting sun." If what has here been written will arouse that sense of justice which shall influence the reader to remember the virtues, and forget the faults, of this singular people, our object will have been accomplished. And if in the description given, we shall have brought to the members of our Order, even in a slight degree, some knowledge of the Original People, whose customs are perpetuated in the forms and ceremonies of our ritualistic work, we feel confident the result will be that they will have a stronger love and a more enduring fidelity for the Improved Order of Red Men, by which the memory of the Primitive Red Men will be preserved to the latest period of recorded time!

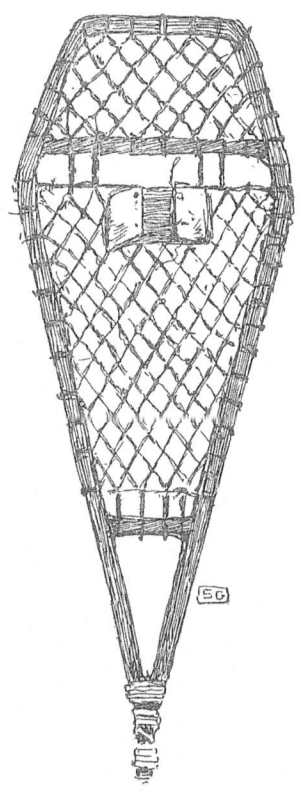

CHAPTER III.

PATRIOTIC SOCIETIES.

IN considering the traditional epoch of the history of our Order due notice must be taken of those patriotic organizations, frequently alluded to in these pages, formed, some at least, ten years previous to the Declaration of Independence, influential in all the colonies and all, or nearly all, using the forms and customs of the Indians for their mystic ceremonies. They certainly had a common origin and close communication for the same ultimate object, — the freedom and independence of the colonies. There is abundant evidence to justify this assumption. The population was too sparse to permit of such systematic work, in separate localities, harmoniously conducted, without some form of communication and union. This fact is made plain by investigation, and is surely sustained by the information herein given.

The first reliable information that we possess of the existence of a secret society which adopted and practised the forms and ceremonies, and wore the costumes of the "Children of the Forest," and which claimed a genuine Indian Chieftain as its tutelar saint and patron, is derived from the early history of the Colony of Maryland.

Some of the facts which we shall mention in the beginning of this chapter have been briefly commented upon; but we refer to them again at greater length, and substantiate them with additional proof. The people of the colonies, prior to the War of Independence, had suffered many indignities and wrongs at the hands of their rulers under the British Government.

History shows us that the presence of the English in any number or settlement in America, dates from the reign of James I. of England. At first, the settlers were privileged companies with royal letters-patent, but in reality independent, and as they were dissenters seeking a place of refuge from what they considered the grievance of the established church and the government, they took care not to convey the grievance with them as they would have done had they been really incorporated with the British empire. This course was at first allowed by Great Britain — until the advantage and value of the possessions in America were more thoroughly understood. Having once awakened to this knowledge, the policy of England was at once different, and all possessions acquired by the subjects of James I., either by conquest or occupation, were deemed to be held by them for the crown. This was exemplified in the early history of New Zealand. We refer now to the early settlement of the colonies. This course was a beneficent one for their growth upon foreign soil, as it must appear even upon cursory observation.

"There are many evils incident to any attempts at independent colonization. Colonists themselves when they rightly appreciate their own interests must see the advantage in the supremacy of the crown, or rather in that of the British Parliament, for the crown is only properly supreme over a territory which has been taken by conquest from another civilized power. The supremacy implies a right to protection much needed by small collections of men in distant regions."

Such was certainly true of the infant history of our country, and undoubtedly the fact that they were known as belonging to the English crown was an immense protection to the colonists against the claims of either France or Spain.

But while this was true of the infancy of America, the fact became patent that as the colonies grew and strengthened, financially, territorially, and in freedom of thought, they grew restive under this restraining influence, and disposed, if possible, to escape from it. Possibly the freedom of the Red Man was an incentive to this feeling, for the colonists saw that although they (the Indians) were governed by a Chief or Sachem, that this government was one in which all warriors had representation, and each was allowed a voice in the councils at which measures of government were decided. Added to this also was the change of attitude assumed by the English government, at first friendly, sympathetic, and helpful. The resources of the

New World no sooner came to be thoroughly understood than England became rapacious and grasping, and the colonists were regarded by the English as a mine from which, by unjust taxation, money could be continually raised.

This is shown by the subsequent history of the colonies. It could not be expected that men who had braved the perils of the ocean, and the unknown dangers of the New World, would tamely submit to such a course. Continued criticism among themselves of these causes, although smothered protests to such acts, engendered in them a spirit of opposition which grew stronger even from the secrecy which its existence made necessary. The colonists strongly resented having laws made for them and taxes levied upon them, in which they had no voice. Harsh and tyrannical measures provoked a spirit of opposition and enmity to the crown, and although its laws and edicts had been submitted to, yet this submission partook of the form and spirit of sullen compliance, totally devoid of allegiance or recognized duty to a sovereign, and it was looked upon as a stern and compulsory necessity from which there was no escape except through rebellion and revolution.

Among the most offensive acts of England, and the one most detrimental to the interests of the colonies, was the Navigation Act. This was passed in the year 1660. "By this act the American colonists were compelled to ship their staples to England alone, they were forced also to buy all their European goods there, and the carrying trade was confined to English vessels."

The injustice of this act will be seen at once. The colonists already had a thriving business in ship-building and in commerce. This was ruined by the act, and the loss naturally produced great indignation against the mother country.

England would not allow the colonies to produce anything that would interfere with her own manufactures. The colonists having plenty of beaver skins made a great many hats; this was forbidden by England. They said that America would soon supply the world with hats. The colonists manufactured iron. The English stopped that also; they said that the Americans had no right to manufacture even a nail for a horseshoe.

The Navigation Act, of which we have spoken, was more bitterly resented than any act of the English government, for, as we have said, it was the most hurtful. In order to see that the measures of this act were carried out, England created a large number of custom-house officers, and to assist them in finding smuggled goods, they obtained Writs of Assistance, which were neither more nor less than legal permits to enter and search any man's house. No free people could submit to this. All these acts were but the forerunner of that struggle which was to result in the freedom forever of the colonies.

England now attempted to tax the colonies in order to meet the expense arising from the French and Indian wars, by imposing a tax on articles imported into the colonies. This was, of course, resisted. Angered by the actions of the colonists, and determined to force submission and revenue from them, England, in 1765, passed an act known as the Stamp Act which levied a tax on all paper vellum and parchment used in the colonies. No document could be legal without a stamp. There was also passed, about the same time, the Quartering Act. A standing army was ordered for the colonies, and the people were required to provide the troops with quarters, bedding, fire-wood, drinks, soap, and candles.

This dastardly act roused to a burning fire the indignation and resentment which had smouldered so long in the hearts of the colonists.

It may be mentioned here, as an instance of how strangely history repeats itself, and also, the changes that years made, that in the United States a stamp tax was imposed for the first time after the war of the Southern rebellion, and that earlier than this, about the year 1779, in the State of Maryland, a tax was levied upon her people to meet the expenses resulting from the Revolutionary war. This tax was endured the more cheerfully because it was part of the price of liberty, and men knew that no price was too dear for that blessing.

Although opposition had not as yet taken the form of open hostility, still in secret men brooded over their wrongs, and, when it could be done with safety, counselled and consulted with each other as to the means of freeing themselves from the obnoxious rule of the mother country.

Gradually these secret councils took the form of regularly organized meetings, which in turn resolved themselves into a secret society styled by its members "the Sons of Liberty." So instinctive was this feeling in the hearts of all the members of this society, that the name "Sons of Liberty" was chosen as symbolical of the sentiment and as indicative of the liberty and freedom they longed for. The precise date of the formation of this society cannot now be traced; but that it had an existence at least ten years previous to the Declaration of Independence is proved by the action of its members relative to the odious Stamp Act, sought to be imposed upon the American colonies in the year 1765.

At the beginning of this chapter the statement was made that the first information of a society which claimed a genuine Indian chieftain as its tutelar saint and patron, was derived from the early history of the colony of Maryland. This, as the text subsequently indicated, referred to the Saint Tamina Society, organized at Annapolis in 1771. It would be more proper to say that the society of Sons of Liberty on that date changed its name to that of Saint Tamina Society. In addition to what is elsewhere stated concerning the Sons of Liberty, it is proper to add a further account of this society.

Colonel Isaac Barrè was a member of Parliament for several years following 1761. He was among the few who opposed the passage of the Stamp Act, which passed Parliament by a vote of five to one, for which service he afterwards received the thanks of the province. In a speech on February 6, 1765, Barrè had called the opposing parties in the colonies "the Sons of Liberty," which name was immediately afterwards adopted by the society. While the *precise date* of organization, therefore, may not be stated, it was evidently at or previous to the year 1765, and the time of assuming the name " Sons of Liberty," subsequent to February, 1765. The organization took a leading part in all patriotic movements between 1765 and the Declaration of Independence. On the 14th of August, 1765, Andrew Oliver, brother-in-law of Governor Hutchinson, was hung in effigy from the old elm known as the Liberty Tree which stood on Washington street, Boston, Mass., facing what is now the beginning of Boylston street. " This pageant," we are told, "had been prepared by a party of Boston mechanics called Sons of Liberty who, prompted by the intense feeling of the hour, devised this method to express it. The 14th of August became a memorable anniversary for the Sons of Liberty, who eight years later in 1773, celebrated it by 'a festivity' on Roxbury Common." The opposition which the Stamp Act received was sufficient finally to secure its repeal by an act of Parliament, February 21, 1766, that received the approval of the king March 17, 1766. Throughout the colonies the news of the repeal "was received with every conceivable demonstration of joy." "The principal demonstrations took place in Boston, on May 19, 1766. An obelisk was erected on the Common and decked with lanterns; Hancock illuminated his house and discharged fireworks in front of it from a stage; and this was responded to by similar demonstrations by the Sons of Liberty at the workhouse."

The society of the Sons of Liberty in Boston exercised commanding influence and when, on the 1st of October, 1768, several hundred British soldiers were landed at Long Wharf, and marched as far as the Common where a portion of the troops encamped, the remainder were "allowed by the Sons of Liberty, later in the day, to occupy Fanueil Hall."

There is record of a dinner given by the Sons of Liberty at Dorchester, August 14, 1769.

Many and important were the events that transpired, some of which are repeated in contemporaneous history, but concerning the minor details of which there is much obscurity, owing to the exceeding delicacy of the position occupied by the colonists, and the absolute secrecy necessary as regards the personal identity of the patriots engaged in many of the proceedings of those times. Finally came Thursday, December 16, 1773. The Old South Church was filled to suffocation, more than 2000 people being in the building. The meeting had been called because of the arrival of three vessels loaded with tea which it had been proposed to land in defiance of the expressed wishes of the people, who refused to pay the tax the representatives of the king had attempted to collect thereon. The ships were moored off Griffin's Wharf, now Liverpool Wharf, near the foot of Pearl Street. Addresses were made by Samuel Adams, Young,

Roe, Quincy, and others. It was unanimously resolved that the tea should not be landed. Besides the large crowd in the church, it is estimated that more than 7000 people had gathered on the outside. Messengers were sent to the governor to try to persuade him to arrange for the return of the vessels without an attempt to land the tea. About six o'clock the messengers returned and reported that they were unsuccessful. The record from which we quote continues : —

"No sooner had he concluded than Samuel Adams arose and said : 'This meeting can do nothing more to save the country.' Instantly a shout was heard at the porch ; the war-whoop resounded, and a band of forty or fifty men, disguised as Indians, rushed by the door, and hurried down toward the harbor, followed by a throng of people ; guards were carefully posted according to previous arrangements around Griffin's Wharf to prevent the intrusion of spies. The 'Mohawks,' and some others accompanying them, sprang aboard the three tea-ships and emptied the contents of three hundred and forty-two chests of tea into the bay, 'without the least injury to the vessels or any other property.' No one interfered with them ; no person was harmed ; no tea was allowed to be carried away. There was no confusion, no noisy riot, no infuriated mob. The multitude stood by and looked on in solemn silence, while the weird-looking figures, made distinctly visible in the moonlight, removed the hatches, tore open the chests, and threw the entire cargo overboard. This strange spectacle lasted about three hours, and then the people all went home, and the town was as quiet as if nothing had happened. The next day the fragments of the tea were seen strewn along the Dorchester shore, carried thither by the wind and tide. A formal declaration of the transaction was drawn up by the Boston committee ; and Paul Revere was sent with despatches to New York and Philadelphia, where the news was received with the greatest demonstrations of joy. In Boston the feeling was that of intense satisfaction proceeding from the consciousness of having exhausted every possible measure of legal redress before undertaking this bold and novel mode of asserting the rights of the people."

Two stanzas describing these events may be aptly inserted here from a poem by Oliver Wendell Holmes.

> "Fast spread the tempest's darkening pall;
> The mighty realms were troubled;
> The storm broke loose, but first of all
> The Boston teapot bubbled.
>
> "The lurid morning shall reveal
> A fire no king can smother,
> When British flint and Boston steel,
> Have clashed against each other."

There is record that in March, 1774, twenty-eight and one-half chests of tea were disposed of by similar "Indians." Under date of January 10, 1774, Samuel Adams wrote to James Warren concerning a lot of tea cast on shore from a vessel wrecked off of the back of Cape Cod, and which had been brought up from the cape and landed at Castle William. The letter goes on to say: "It is said that the Indians this way, if they had suspected the Marshpee tribe would have been so sick at the knee, would have marched on snow-shoes to have done the business for them."

We are particular in mentioning these facts to show, that the Sons of Liberty did make use of the forms and customs of the Indians as a disguise in the patriotic work in which they were engaged. Undoubtedly their leading spirits had determined upon separation from the mother government. But until public sentiment had been sufficiently educated to sustain an open declaration of independence, it was necessary that a mantle of secrecy should be thrown upon their acts, which if successes were patriotic, but if failures were treasonable.

We call attention to the fact that Paul Revere was sent by the Boston committee with despatches to New York and Philadelphia. This corroborates the claim we have made, that these societies were united by secret modes of communication, and were in full harmony and communion in the common work in which they were engaged. The connection between the Sons of Liberty and the Saint Tamina Society of Annapolis, Maryland, is clear and distinct. While the Saint Tamina Society of Maryland was the first, of which we have record, to use the name of an Indian as the patron saint of America and of the said organization, the Sons of Liberty was the first organization, of which we have record, to use the disguise of Indians and presumably their forms and customs for the patriotic purposes for which they were organized.

From the beginning the organization seems to have been inspired by the purest and most lofty patriotism, and by a desire to do everything that should be done for the benefit of the colonists, while at the same time, as we have remarked, laying the foundation for a government that should be independent of Great Britain and properly guard the mighty continent which had come into their possession as a great heritage, and whose possibilities for future grandeur and power they even then dimly foresaw and realized.

The Non-Importation Act of 1770 was warmly supported by the Sons of Liberty; and in the *Boston Gazette* of February 19, 1770, there is a quaint account of a sewing-circle composed of 45 daughters of liberty, who met at the house of Rev. Mr. Moorhead and spun 232 skeins of yarn. It is mentioned that their entertainment was wholly of American production, except a little wine, etc. "The whole was concluded with many agreeable tunes and liberty songs, with great judgment; fine voices performed and animated on this occasion in all the several parts by a number of the Sons of Liberty."

During the siege of Boston the famous Liberty-tree, under which the Sons of Liberty used to hold their meetings, was cut down "amidst the sneers and taunts of the soldiers and tories, who had not forgotten its almost personal symbolism." In 1833 the old Liberty-Tree Tavern stood upon the spot. In later days this in turn gave place to the present business block now occupying the site and on the face of which is a tablet bearing a representation of the famous Liberty-tree and an appropriate inscription.

Whether the persons who composed the Sons of Liberty actually took part in the hanging in effigy of Mr. Hood, who was appointed Stamp Master at Annapolis, Maryland, in the year 1765, is not clearly proved by history; but that a general meeting or convention of several societies of the Sons of Liberty did take place in the town of Annapolis, Md., in the year 1766, is fully authenticated by the following account taken from Ridgely's Annals of Annapolis:

"In March, 1766, the Sons of Liberty, from Baltimore, Kent,

and Anne Arundel counties, met at this place, and made a written application to the chief justice of the provincial court, the secretary and commissary general and judges of the land office, to open their respective offices, and to proceed as usual in the execution of their duties. This demand was complied with, and the Stamp Act virtually became null and void."

These associations, called "the Sons of Liberty," existed among the Northern and Middle Colonies. They were very active, and thoroughly frightened the officers appointed to distribute the stamps.

Another writer says: "They opposed the distribution of British stamps in Maryland; formed themselves into associations called "Sons of Liberty," drove the stamp distributers from the Province, and warned all the officials at Annapolis not to attempt the execution of the Stamp Act anywhere upon the soil covered by Lord Baltimore's charter."

At this time there existed several organizations among the foreign citizens of Annapolis and other sections, each of which had adopted the patronage of some saint of European extraction, and designated the society by his name, as Saint George's Society, Saint Andrew's Society, and Saint David's Society. These were all loyal to the crown of Great Britain, and it was at first in ridicule of them that the Sons of Liberty claimed the patronage of an undoubted American, an Indian Chief or King named Tamina or Tamanend, and traced a legend of his life and exploits, much of which was derived from his own descendants.

In the year 1771, the Society of Sons of Liberty adopted the title of "Sons of Saint Tamina, or Saint Tamina Society," and set apart the first day of May as their anniversary.

We quote from our former authority, Mr. Ridgely, in his Annals of Annapolis, who says:

"In this year (1771), and for many years later, there existed in the town of Annapolis, a society called 'The Saint Tamina Society,' who set apart the first day of May in memory of Saint Tamina, their patron saint, whose history is now lost in fable and uncertainty. It was usual, on the morning of this day, for the members of the Society to erect in some public location in the city, 'a May-pole,' and to decorate it in a most tasteful manner with wild flowers, gathered from the adjacent woods, and forming themselves in a ring around it, hand in hand, perform the 'war-dance,' with many other customs which they had seen exhibited by the 'Children of the Forest.' It was also usual, on this day, for such of the citizens as chose to enter into the amusements, to wear a piece of bucktail in their hats, or in some conspicuous part of their dress. General invitations were given out, and a large company usually assembled during the course of the evening, and whilst engaged in the midst of a dance, the company would be interrupted by the sudden intrusion of a number of the Saint Tamina Society, habited like Indians, who, rushing violently into the room, singing war songs and giving the 'whoop,' commenced dancing in the style of that people. After this ceremony, they made a 'collection of money, and retired evidently well pleased with their reception and entertainment.'"

After the close of the Revolutionary War, the Societies known as the Sons of Saint Tamina, or Sons of Liberty (the titles being synonymous) having achieved their object, namely, the freedom of their country from a monarchical yoke, became less prominent in public affairs as organized bodies; and it was not until the agitation among the people, arising from the difference of opinion in regard to adopting a permanent form of government, became the all-absorbing topic among all classes, and made it necessary, in their opinion, for consolidating their ranks, that they again assumed commanding influence.

The condition of the country after the close of the war was to some alarming and deplorable, and had it not been that over all the glorious banner of freedom and liberty waved, and that there were men prominent at that time whose thought and aim was the public good, much trouble would have resulted in the colonies. For eight long years the colonies had been the scene of continued strife and bloodshed, and while it resulted in the achievement of the political independence of the United States, it had undoubtedly done much to change the character of the people. It has been said "that an army is always corrupt, and always corrupts the society which holds it in its bosom." While we are not prepared to entirely indorse this sentiment, we can say that undoubtedly any body of troops quartered for any length of time in a vicinity leaves an indelible impress upon the locality, — not always for the best.

It seems inconsistent with common sense, and yet experience proves its truth, that a body of troops whose business it is to preserve and enforce the laws of a land, often spreads through a community a spirit of lawlessness hitherto unknown among its citizens. Such a spirit was rife at the end of the Revolutionary War, and was one of the elements with which those who strove for the common good had to contend. The condition of the country at large was deplorable. Education had been almost entirely neglected during the war, and irreligion and infidelity had been introduced.

"The Revolution opened the door to infidelity in two ways. First, by introducing foreign fashions, habits and modes of feeling, thinking and acting—a practical infidelity. And, secondly, by introducing from England and France, but especially the latter, an open opposition to Christianity. The atheistical philosophy of Goodwin, Rousseau, Voltaire, and others was spread in the United States during the revolution with a fearful rapidity."

But there were infidel writers in our own country. Ethan Allen's "Oracles of Reason" had already appeared. Thomas Paine's "Common Sense" written to aid the Revolution, with much truth had inculcated some error and paved the way for his other and more objectionable writings. The effect of all these evil influences was long felt in the country.

Of the condition of the colonies at this time Dr. Ramsay, of South Carolina, wrote in his History of the Revolution: —

"On the whole, the literary, political, and military talents of the United States have been improved by the Revolution; but their moral character is inferior to what it was. So great is the change for the worse that the friends of good order are loudly called upon to exert their utmost abilities in extirpating the vicious principles and habits which have taken deep root during the convulsion."

It could not but be expected that some time would elapse, and great care and good judgment be required, before the government of the colonies could be settled as far as possible, upon a uniform and common plan. This had been the hope, at least, of those most prominent in the late struggle. It must not be forgotten, however, that while the majority of Americans revolted against the English yoke, yet upon American soil there were others who felt differently. England had many friends and supporters on American soil — some who would gladly have continued under her sway and government. Others there were, who, objecting to the rule of England, still preferred a monarchical form of government, and would gladly have established a throne and monarchy within the confines of America.

It is known that the government of the country during the Revolutionary War consisted of what was called the Continental Congress, composed of members deputed by the several colonies. They held their sessions at Philadelphia during the greater part of the period.

A committee was appointed to draft a declaration of the sentiment of this Congress with regard to the independence of the colonies. This committee reported the Declaration of Independence, which on the 4th of July, 1776, was adopted. "By this instrument the thirteen American colonies declared themselves free and independent under the name of the Thirteen United States of America."

"This Declaration of Independence was received everywhere throughout the Union with tokens of appreciation. Such was the spirit of the majority, though it must be admitted there were those who viewed the whole matter in a very different light."

These were, of course, the element we referred to, and while not powerful enough to effect such a change as they desired, were still strong enough to occasion much trouble and anxiety among the colonists. The country was burdened with an immense debt of over forty millions of dollars. Efforts were made to reduce this. Opposition, however, for the time prevented any plan proposed being executed. Only time, prudent measures, and admonition could bring order out of such a chaos. That this was done, the history of our country shows.

Happy indeed, for our record as a nation, that there should have lived at that time General George Washington, for to all classes of people, "whether federal or not, (for by this name the friends of the federal government were known,)" he was acceptable as the first President of the United States. "Had he been as ambitious as Napoleon, or even as Bolivar or Francia, he might have been dictator for life as well as they. Such a course was proposed to him in 1782, when it was believed that the country was not yet ready for anything but a qualified monarchy; but he turned from it with disdain."

With such a state of affairs in this beloved land, it was apparent to the minds of those patriotic men who had so valiantly upheld their country's cause, that it behooved the Sons of Saint Tamina to be ever watchful in the interests of their beloved country, and so we find them again rallying under the banner of their patron saint.

They saw, with alarm, that in their midst were many who, although opposed to foreign rule, and although they had entered freely into the War of Independence, were, nevertheless, strongly imbued with principles of royalty. Added to this, ambition held sway among many of the popular leaders, and more than one aspirant to a crown and sceptre could have been found, and who would have gained many supporters. When, finally, a proposition to elect a President and Congress for life was made, this element of the people, deservedly called the "popular element of the people," took alarm, and when, in addition to this, the Society of the Cincinnati was formed, the constitution of which made membership hereditary, which was a strong anti-republican feature and obnoxious to the masses, the defenders of freedom recognizing the fact that, "Eternal vigilance is the price of liberty," instituted or rather reinstated, the old society of the Sons of Saint Tamina under the name of "Tammany Society or Columbian Order."

We will now refer briefly to the Society of the Cincinnati, as we have mentioned the effect its organization had upon the mind of the general public. It was composed chiefly, if not entirely, of the military, and, indeed, owed its existence to a desire on the part of the officers of the Revolutionary army at the close of the War, to perpetuate the bonds of friendly feeling which their continued and constant intercourse had created, and also that they might have some spot or trysting place where, in after years, they might meet to revive old associations, renew old friendships, and perpetuate, through posterity, the record of those deeds by which such wonderful results had been achieved. General Knox was the originator of the idea which led to the formation of the Society. He first obtained General Washington's approval of the plan. A meeting of officers was held, and a committee appointed to draft a plan for the formation of the Society. They did so, and at a meeting held at the house of General Steuben, near Newburg, N. Y., on the 13th of May, 1783, the plan which they had formulated was adopted. Their idea of naming the Society after the famous Roman, Cincinnatus, was well taken, for there was, in many respects, a similarity between his life and theirs. History tells us that this noted Roman lived about five hundred years previous to the birth of Christ. Among his countrymen, he was so noted for his integrity and honesty, that he was chosen by the Roman Senate as Consul. So great was the simplicity of the man that, when messengers were sent to appraise him of his election to this office, they found him tilling the soil of his farm. At the expiration of his term of office, he returned to his former simple mode of life, as Washington did, only to be again and again called to assume the leadership and control of a people to whom he was devotedly attached.

The points of resemblance of character between him and their beloved Washington; his mode of life which had its counterpart in many of theirs (for in laying down the sword, many took up the ploughshare); and his devoted patriotism, made him in their eyes, a worthy model and name-giver to the Society of which they expected such happy results. This idea was shown in their incorporation, for at this meeting before spoken of, they reported that, "the officers of the American army, having generally been taken from the citizens of America, possess a high veneration for the character of that illustrious Roman, Lucius Quintius Cincinnatus, and being resolved to follow his example by returning to their citizenship, they think they may, with propriety, denominate themselves the " Society of the Cincinnati."

Care was also taken to state distinctly and fully the object for which the society was designated.

"To perpetuate, therefore, as well the remembrance of this vast event as the mutual friendship which had been formed under the pressure of common dangers, and, in many instances, cemented by the blood of the parties, the officers of the American army do hereby, in the most solemn manner, associate, constitute, and combine themselves into one society of friends, to endure as long as they shall endure, or any of their eldest male posterity; and in failure thereof the collateral branches, who may be judged worthy of becoming its supporters and members."

There was to be one general society, which was sub-divided into State societies, these to be farther divided into districts.

"The State Society was expected to meet annually on the first Monday in May, so long as they should deem it necessary, and afterwards at least once in every three years."

Its object, besides cementing "the cordial affection subsisting between the officers," was "to extend the most substantial acts of beneficence, according to the ability of the society, towards those officers and their families, who, unfortunately, may be under the necessity of receiving it."

The fund from which this benefit was derived was made up by each officer paying to the Treasurer of his State's Society "one month's pay," and the interest of the fund thus created was used to alleviate the wants of the distressed.

They also embodied within their constitution the following glowing principles:

"An incessant attention to preserve inviolate those exalted rights and liberties of human nature, for which they fought and bled, and without which the high rank of a rational being is a curse instead of a blessing. An unalterable determination to promote and cherish, between the respective States, that unison and national honor so essentially necessary to their happiness and the future dignity of the American empire."

Its officers consisted of President, Vice-President, Secretary, Treasurer, and Assistant Treasurer. These were elected annually by a majority vote of the members.

General Washington was the first President and held that position for 16 years. After his death General Alexander Hamilton succeeded him. He held the position six years. Death also relieved him from the duties of the office, the duel with Aaron Burr terminating his life.

It would seem from the standpoint of to-day that the fact of such men as Washington, General Knox, and others of like character and position being connected with the Society of the Cincinnati would have been sufficient to give it a hold upon the public favor, and probably this would have been so but for the following causes. It will be seen that by the constitution or plan of the Society, its members were pledged to maintain in undisguised harmony the union of the States. This was not altogether pleasing to many who were sticklers for distinct State sovereignty, for as yet the Articles of Confederation were practically untried, and many preferred a form of independence and freedom in State government.

Secondly, it was exclusive, being intended for the perpetuation of kind feeling between "the officers of the American Army," which, of course, debarred many from membership.

Thirdly, it savored to many of a return to the customs at least of royalty, in the transmission of hereditary rights, and also as unjustly elevating the military above the mass of the people.

Consequently the "Society of the Cincinnati" was denounced by the mass of the people, who regarded it as harmful to the good and liberty of the nation. Not here was to be found material to furnish the bone and sinew which had been so helpful in the late war. Not here was to be found a society which would be in hearty sympathy with the demands and needs of a common people. Not here, but from among themselves, must this material be found, and, accordingly, in the minds of a faithful few of Tamina's band, this idea finally blossomed into fruit in the resuscitation of the old society.

The need having been recognized of a society for the protection of the rights of the people at large, or the masses of the people, the Sons of Saint Tamina being ready to undertake the formation of such a society, the result was, as we have said, the organization of the Saint Tamina Society or Columbian Order.

The question of government was the all-absorbing topic of the day, and we find that the discussion of adopting the Federal Constitution really divided the country into two distinct parties. Prominent men, among whom were Jay, Hamilton, and Chancellor Livingston, were strenuous in advocating it upon the ground that it was the most energetic government they could obtain. They were as strongly opposed by men equally prominent, among whom were George Clinton, Governor of New York, Robert Yates, and others. "The opponents of the Constitution did not profess to be adverse to a confederation, but they looked upon the project before them as an attempt at consolidation, and the erection of an irresponsible power to destroy the sovereignty of the States."

History shows us that the Constitution was adopted, that the Tammany Society was formed, and that it numbered for years among its ranks moderate men of both parties (Federal and anti-Federal). Being composed of the more conservative element of both parties, it was, of course, free from any charge of being "a party institution." As the years go on, we will see in tracing its history that this trait or characteristic changed, and that in the administration of Jefferson, it became distinctly known as the organ of one party, or as embracing within it the characteristics peculiar to one political party of the United States.

The formal organization of this association took place on the twelfth day of May, 1789, in the city of New York, and was accomplished principally through the efforts of William Mooney, an American by birth, but of Irish descent, who had been a leader among the "Liberty Boys" during the Revolution. He entered into the Revolutionary War with the enthusiastic spirit characterizing the race of which he was a descendant, and upon the close of the struggle was still as ready as at its beginning to serve his country in whatever way he could. After the war he entered into mercantile life on Nassau Street, New York City, as an upholsterer, but afterwards moved to Maiden Lane, and still later to Chatham Street. Through all his life he was an active partisan, and was rewarded substantially by the party whose cause he espoused.

The first constitution of this Society declared that it was formed "to connect in indissoluble bonds of Friendship, American brethren of known attachment to the political rights of human nature and the liberty of the country."

The following account of the formation of this Society is taken from its history written by R. G. Horton, Esq., and published by authority of the Tammany Society of New York in 1867.

On the twelfth day of May, 1789, about two weeks after General George Washington had taken the oath of office as first President of the United States in the balcony of the old City Hall, at the foot of Nassau Street, in the city of New York, the organization known as the Tammany Society or Columbian Order was instituted. Various parties had existed before and during the Revolution in different sections of the country under the name of Sons of Saint Tammany or Tamina. This body was organized by William Mooney, whose purpose in so doing was patriotic and purely republican, and the constitution provided by his care contained a solemn asservation, which every member was required to repeat and subscribe to, "that he would sustain the State institutions, and resist the consolidation of power in the general government."

Mooney, in the first instance, intended to do no reverence to Tamina, the distinguished and honored native American chieftain. His idea was to confer the honor upon Columbus, the discoverer of America, as evidenced by the name of the Society, which was to be styled the "Columbian Order," and to the public belongs the credit of naming it the Saint Tammany Society, the uninitiated supposing it to be one of the many Saint Tamina Societies that were scattered throughout the South and West.

Seeing that the Indian name was popular, Mooney and his associates concluded to give Columbus a second place in the title of the Order. They therefore accepted the Red Chieftain as their divinity, and named their organization the Tammany Society or Columbian Order. Although the Society afterwards became purely a political institution, it was not so at its organization. As we have before said, the feature of distinct party affiliation was introduced during the time of Jefferson. Until then, it was composed of men of different political opinions. It incorporated a benevolent feature in its organization, as its charter shows, and in the earlier days of its existence, the Tammany Society was made the means of rendering assistance to needy and worthy objects. Soon, however, its attractions became of a social nature, owing to its meetings being held at public houses, and conviviality often took the place of patriotism and benevolence.

The Society having been instituted on the twelfth day of May, that day was adopted as the anniversary of the Order, instead of the first of May previously celebrated by the old Saint Tamina Societies, and the anniversary of the formation of the Society was celebrated by a grand festival on the banks of the Hudson River.

On that occasion, tents or wigwams were erected about two miles from the city of New York, for the reception and accommodation of the brethren, the calumet of peace was smoked, and the tomahawk was buried. After engaging in various Indian dances, and other recreations so popular at the time, until the close of the day, the company returned to the city, where the amusements were continued.

The officers or chiefs for the first year of the Societies were as follows : Grand Sachem, William Mooney; Sachems, White Mattack, Oliver Glenn, Philip Hone, James Tylie, John Campbell, Gabriel Furman, John Burger, Jonathan Pierce, Thomas Greenleaf, Abel Hardenbrook, Courtlandt Van Beuren, and Joseph Godwin ; Treasurer, Thomas Ash ; Secretary, Anthony Ernest ; Wiskinkie, or Doorkeeper, Gardiner Baker.

The Society adopted Indian forms, ceremonies, and costumes, and divided the year into seasons and the seasons into moons. The season of Snow embraced the months of December, January, and February; the season of Blossoms, March, April, and May ; the season of Fruits, June, July, and August ; and the season of Hunting, September, October, and November.

All the transactions of the Society were dated from three eras : First, its own organization ; second, our national independence ; third, the discovery of America.

In the formation of the 13 Tribes into which the Society was divided, 13 Sachems were elected, from which number one was selected as the Grand Sachem. All of their customs were borrowed from Indian tribes, which were then so numerous in the country, and it was claimed that this was done to conciliate, as far as possible, those tribes of red men who were devastating the defenceless frontiers, and this did, in fact, prove of some avail during the year following the institution of the Society, averting, in all probability, a bloody war with the Creek Indians.

Mention is made in the records of the society of the " Council Fire," "Calumet" or pipe of peace, and the " Tomahawk " which was always buried when the pipe of peace was smoked.

PATRIOTIC SOCIETIES. 169

The manner of admission was by being proposed at one meeting, and elected at the next, and it required the vote of every member present to elect an applicant. The initiation fee was three dollars, and the annual dues one dollar. At the initiation of a candidate, the ceremony was enlivened by the singing of the following ode or chant: —

ODE.

"Sacred's the ground where Freedom's found,
 And Virtue stamps her name;
Our hearts entwine at Friendship's shrine,
 And Union fans the flame;
  Our hearts sincere
  Shall greet you here,
  With joyful voice
  Confirm your choice.
 Et-hoh! Et-hoh! Et-hoh!"

The division of the Society into thirteen branches denominated Tribes, was in imitation of the thirteen nations of Saint Tamina's kingdom, and when it was found by a coincidence that this number corresponded with the thirteen original States of the Union, a name or "totem" was given to each State, of which the following record has been preserved: —

New York was given the Eagle; New Hampshire, the Otter; Massachusetts, the Panther; Rhode Island, the Beaver; Connecticut, the Bear; New Jersey, the Tortoise; Maryland, the Fox; Pennsylvania, the Rattlesnake; Delaware, the Tiger; Virginia, the Deer; North Carolina, the Buffalo; South Carolina, the Raccoon; and Georgia, the Wolf.

When a member joined the Society, he either chose one of these Tribes as he preferred, or he was assigned to one by the Grand Sachem.

At the installation or raising up of the Grand Sachem, there was sung the "Et-hoh" or sacred song, commencing

"Brothers our council fire shines bright, Et-hoh!"

Every applicant for membership was required to be vouched for by a member "that he was a true republican, and firmly attached to the Constitution of the United States."

The Society adopted the word *Friendship* for its motto, after the example of the old Order of Saint Tamina, whose watchword was *Freedom*, and those mottoes have been preserved in the present Improved Order of Red Men, with the addition of the motto *Charity*, thus suggesting the chain of connecting links — Sons of Liberty, 1765; Sons of Saint Tamina, 1771; Saint Tamina Society, 1789; Society of Red Men, 1813-16; Improved Order of Red Men, 1833.

In the year 1789-90, a matter of dispute arose between the United States government and the Creek Indians, which for a time threatened serious consequences, and in order to bring about a settlement of the difficulty, Col. Marinus Willett, was sent by Congress to confer with Alexander McGilvey, a halfbreed of great influence with that nation, and induced him, together with about thirty chiefs of the Creeks, to accompany him to the city of New York on a visit to the Great Father, General Washington. The Tammany Society, on learning of the proposed visit, and desirous to conciliate the Indians, determined to receive them with a great display of ceremony and savage pomp. The members were accustomed to dress in Indian costumes, and on this occasion wore feathers, moccasins, and leggings, painted their faces in true Indian style, and sported huge war-clubs, knives, and tomahawks.

The following report of Colonel Willet to the United States military authorities, is found on page 112 of the *Military Actions of Colonel Willett* in the Congressional Library at Washington, D. C. : —

"On Tuesday, the 20th, I left Philadelphia at the dawn of day — arrived at Elizabeth Point at four o'clock in the afternoon, from which place just at dusk I set out for New York in a row-boat, landed at White Hall rock between nine and ten o'clock. Set out again for Elizabeth Town Point at two o'clock in the morning, at which place I arrived at six o'clock, where I found a sloop which had been sent from New York to transport us to that place. Embarked on board the sloop with the Indians for New York. We landed about noon, near the coffeehouse, and were received with great splendor by the Tammany Society in the dress of their Order; conducted up Wall Street past the Federal Hall where Congress was in session, and with great pomp and parade escorted to see the President. The

Indians, with additional parade, visited the Minister of War and Governor Clinton, where an elegant entertainment finished the day."

In addition to what is detailed in Colonel Willett's report, it may be stated that the Indians were also conducted to the Wigwam of the Tammany Society, on entering which, they were so surprised at the preparations made to receive them, and at the number (as they supposed) of their own race present, that they "uttered a whoop," which almost terrified the people, including the mock Indians. They seemed overjoyed by the manner in which they were treated, so much so that they performed a dance and sang the "Et-hoh" song, an Indian ode sung only on great occasions.

The Calumet of Peace was smoked, and so well were they pleased by the speech delivered to them by the Grand Sachem, William Pitt Smith, in which he told them that "although the hand of death was cold upon the two great chiefs Tamina and Columbus, yet their spirits were still walking to and fro in the wigwam," that they gave him the title of "Tuliva Mico" or Chief of the White Town.

In the evening they were taken to the theatre by the members of the Society, and before their departure to their own territory, they entered into a treaty of peace and friendship with Washington, the "Beloved Sachem of the Thirteen Fires," as they termed him.

Thus it may be said that the dreaded war with this nation, at that time one of the most powerful, was averted and peace secured, mainly through the efforts of the Tammany Society. In June, 1790, the Society established a museum for the purpose of collecting and preserving everything of historical value. This was called the Tammany Museum, and every member of the Society had free access to it for himself and family. After changing hands several times, this museum formed the foundation of what was afterwards called Scudder's Museum. In the year 1805, the Society was incorporated under the name of "the Tammany Society." It maintained its Indian organization and continued to use Indian costumes, ceremonies, and habits as late as the year 1811, and we read that on May 13, 1811, corner of Nassau and Frankfort Streets, they laid the corner-stone of their new hall, and marched from their old wigwam in "Martling's Long Room," in Indian file, wearing their aboriginal costumes. Martling's Long Room was situated at the corner of Spruce and Nassau Streets. The new hall was occupied by the Society until its removal in 1867 to the present Tammany Hall.

During the war of 1812-14, the members of the Tammany Society offered their services in the defence of the city of New York, and repaired in a body to the forts, volunteering and performing patriotic duty and the labor of erecting and manning the redoubts against the British. After peace was declared, the Society relapsed into a political organization, and has since remained so, exerting a powerful influence in political circles.

One fact in connection with the Society worthy of honorable record, and which should be ever remembered by the American people with gratitude, occurred in the year 1807-8.

During the War of the Revolution, the British prison ships at "Wallabout" were crowded with prisoners, and from inhuman treatment, scanty food, and, in many cases, no food at all, together with the ravages of disease, the Americans had died at a fearful rate, and their bones had been permitted to bleach upon the shores. Repeated calls had been made upon Congress to bury these bones at the public expense, which, however, were unheeded. The Tammany Society at length determined to perform the sacred duty of interment, and appointed a committee to carry this determination into effect. The magnitude of the undertaking can best be realized from the following stanza from the pen of Phillip Freneau, a most gifted poet of Revolutionary times, the college-mate and warm friend of President Madison:—

> "Each day at least six carcases we bore,
> And scratched their graves upon the shore;
> By feeble hands the graves were made—
> No stone memorial o'er their corpses laid.
> In barren sands and far from home they lie—
> No friend to shed a tear in passing by;
> O'er the mean tombs the insulting Britons tread,
> Spurn at the sand, and curse the Rebel dead."

By the most reliable accounts, not less than 11,500 souls perished on board the prison ships moored in the East River.

Paine predicted that before America would submit to England, the bones of 3,000,000 of her citizens would whiten her shores. So far was this prediction verified, that the bones of 11,500 victims to British cruelty had indeed whitened the shores of Wallabout, and were buried by the Tammany Society.

"Tammany Society took up the subject in 1803," and endeavored to obtain assistance from Congress, without success. Finally, in 1807, "when it became evident that Congress would do nothing" in the matter, a committee called "the Wallabout Committee" was appointed, to take measures for carrying the long-contemplated design of interment into effect. This committee reported in 1808, and immediate measures were taken to carry into effect their suggestions. The corner-stone of the tomb was laid on the 13th of April, 1808, when a grand and imposing procession was formed under the direction of Major Aycregg, Grand Marshal. The military companies and civic societies united with the Tammany Society and proceeded to the spot, where Joseph D. Fay, the orator of the day, delivered an eloquent and impassioned oration. Referring to those who had perished for the love they bore their country, he said: "On this day we lay the corner-stone of their tomb. Their ashes hitherto have been blown about like summer's dust in the whirlwind. But the marble column shall rise on this spot, and tell to future ages the story that they had to choose death or slavery, and that they nobly elected the former. The curious mariner shall point to it in silent admiration, as he passes at a distance, and posterity shall call it 'the tomb of the Patriots.'"

The result being completed, the Society fixed on the 25th of May of the same year, for consigning the bones to their final resting-place; but the weather proving too stormy, the ceremony was postponed until the 26th, when one of the largest and most magnificent funeral pageants which this city has ever witnessed took place. Garret Sickles was the Grand Marshal of the day. The first feature in the procession was a trumpeter mounted on a black horse, carrying in his hand a black flag, upon which was inscribed in letters of gold, "Mortals, avaunt! 11,500 Spirits of the Martyred Braves! Approach the tomb of Honor, of Glory, of Virtuous Patriotism!"

"Then followed the military under command of Brigadier-

General Morton, and immediately after, the Wallabout Committee, each member with a bucktail in his hat. Then came the Tammany Society, headed by Benjamin Romaine, Grand Sachem, with all the insignia of their Order, making a most impressive display. The municipal governments of New York and Brooklyn came next (De Witt Clinton was then mayor of the city) followed by the Governor of the State, D. D. Tompkins, and Lieutenant-Governor John Broome, members of Congress, military and naval officers of the United States, and finally all the various civic societies of the city. The procession proceeded through the principal streets, crossed to Brooklyn, and moved to the vault in Hudson Avenue, near York Street, which was to contain the remains of the patriot dead. Dr. Benjamin De Witt delivered the oration, which he had prepared at the request of the Tammany Society. After its conclusion, the coffins were deposited in the tomb, and the procession returned to the city."

By this act this Society, which as "the Sons of Liberty" had assisted in the defence of their country's rights, and as the Sons of Saint Tamina had protected the claims of the people at large, delivered their beloved country from "the disgrace which justly attached to our country for the neglect which it showed to the memory of these brave men," and added fresh laurels to their ever-increasing fame as the Tammany Society or Columbian Order.

The extended description given of the Tammany Society of New York is justified by the fact that it is the only branch of the patriotic organizations founded in the latter half of the eighteenth century which has maintained an unbroken existence from its institution down to the present time. That period of its history which has been here related covers the time when it was really a patriotic and benevolent institution, and before it had been changed from its original purposes into a political organization. It is hardly necessary to add that, of course, there is not the slightest connection between the Tammany Society of New York and the Improved Order of Red Men except the common origin in the patriotic societies existing over 100 years ago.

To properly understand the prominent place occupied by the Societies of Saint Tammany from 1771 to 1820, it is necessary to refer briefly also to mention made of them in the con-

PATRIOTIC SOCIETIES. 175

temporaneous history of the city of Philadelphia. It will be remembered that branches of the organization existed throughout the colonies, from the period of the revolution until, with the exception of the Saint Tammany Society of New York, they ceased to exist. They all seem to have been originally patriotic and benevolent societies. The element of decay was introduced when they turned from benevolent to political purposes. Apparently they could not exist both as fraternal organizations and as factors in politics. The Tammany Society of New York is the only survivor, and is the concentration of Democratic politics.

In Westcott's History of Philadelphia, frequent mention is made of the Tammany Societies that existed in that city, and with due credit to this source of our information, we make the following extracts.

In chronicling the events of 1772, Mr. Westcott states that the Tammany Society, afterwards of much importance, first as a patriotic body and afterwards as a political association, was established in this year. On Friday, May 1st, "a number of Americans, Sons of King Tammany, met at the house of James Byrnes to celebrate the memory of that truly noble chieftain, whose friendship was most affectionately manifested to the worthy founders and first settlers of this province. After dinner the circulating glass was crowned with wishes loyal and patriotic, and the day concluded with much cheerfulness and harmony." The account from which this was evidently copied goes on to say, "it is hoped that from this small beginning a society may be formed of great utility to the distressed, as this meeting was more for the purpose of promoting charity and benevolence than mirth and festivity."

It will be noticed that this organization took place in 1772, only one year later than the organization at Annapolis, Md. It is more than probable that like the society at Maryland this Tammany Society of Philadelphia was a transformation of a body previously organized as the Sons of Liberty. The Sons of Liberty certainly existed in Philadelphia, because, according to Westcott, a circular was addressed by them to William Coxe of Philadelphia, who had been appointed stamp-master for East Jersey. A delegation from the Sons of Liberty waited upon him and asked him to resign, saying, "If, sir, you refuse our very reasonable request, it will be disagreeable both to you and to us." This communication was dated December 27, 1765. This citation also proves the existence of the Sons of Liberty in Philadelphia in the year 1765 contemporary with the branch of the same society existing in Boston in that year.

The celebration of the Tammany Society in 1772 must have been successful, because in 1773 we are told that it resolved to extend the interest which was manifested in its objects, and for that purpose a circular was sent to 126 of the most prominent individuals in the city, among whom may be mentioned Chief Justice Chew, Rev. Jacob Duché, Rev. Thomas Coombe, Rev. William White, John Dickinson, James Allen, Andrew Allen, Gov. William Franklin (of New Jersey), Gov. James Hamilton, Thomas Mifflin (afterward Major-General and Governor of the State), Lieutenant-Governor Richard Penn, David Rittenhouse (the astronomer), Joseph Reed, and Thomas Wharton, Jr. (each afterward *President* of the State), and many others of like prominence. The circular inviting these gentlemen to be present was as follows : —

"APRIL 28, 1773.

"SIR : As all nations have for seven (several?) centuries past adopted some great personage remarkable for his virtues and loved for civil and religious liberty as their tutelar saint, and annually assembled at a fixed day to commemorate him, the natives of this flourishing province, determined to follow so laudable example, *for some years past* have adopted a great warrior, sachem and chief named Tammany, a fast friend to our forefathers, to be the tutelar saint of this province, and have hitherto on the 1st of May done the accustomed honors to the memory of so great and celebrated a personage. And for this purpose you are requested to meet the children and associate Sons of Saint Tammany at the house of Mr. James Byrnes, to dine together and form such useful charitable plans for the relief of all in distress as shall then be agreed upon."

This circular is susceptible of two interpretations. One is, that those from whom it issued desired to impress the gentlemen to whom it was sent with the fact that the Sons of Tammany had a strength much greater than was actually the fact. The language will also bear the interpretation that *"for some years past"* it had been in existence, and had done homage to the memory of Tammany. This latter view is at variance with the record made by Mr. Westcott that the Tammany Society was established May 1, 1772, but the original data, from which that statement was copied, may have been furnished by some one not familiar with the facts. If we admit the probability that there had been an organization which, "*for some years past,*" had adopted Tammany as its tutelar saint, then its organization would antedate the Society at Annapolis, which in 1771 was organized out of the previously existing Sons of Liberty.

Among various other public actions celebrated during the year 1779, mention is made of St. Tammany's Day, and the "observance of this noted anniversary on the 1st of May by the Sons of St. Tammany." They seem to have had as their guests, "their adopted brethren of St. Patrick, St. Andrew, and St. George," and they had a dinner at the old theatre, Southwark.

Among the popular celebrations of the year 1783, was the appropriate observance on Thursday, May 1, of the anniversary of St. Tammany, "the tutelar Saint of Pennsylvania," at the country seat of Mr. Pole on the Schuylkill by 250 "Constitutional Sons of St. Tammany," who were decorated with bucktails and feathers. At noon thirteen Sachems or Chiefs were appointed, who selected a head Chief and Scribe. The ceremony of burying the tomahawk, in token that the war with England had ended, was then performed, each man casting a stone upon its grave, after which the calumet, or pipe of peace, was smoked. The bowl of the pipe was a huge ram's horn, gilded with thirteen stars, and its stem a reed six feet in length decorated with peacock feathers. In a cabin set apart for that purpose a feast was prepared for the members. At one end of this cabin was a portrait of St. Tammany, and besides this there was a design of the siege of Yorktown, and portraits of Washington and Rochambeau. Thirteen toasts were drunk to the accompaniment of artillery salutes and three cheers, which, when the army and Washington were named, swelled spontaneously to thirteen. At the toast to "The friends of liberty in Ireland," and "The tuning of the Harp of Independence," thirteen cheers were again given, and the band struck up "St. Patrick's Day in the Morning." After the drinking of toasts had ended, the Chief sang the first verse of the original song for St. Tammany's day, — a composition in vogue in the special celebrations long before the revolution, — and the remaining stanzas were sung by Mr. Leacock. The song thus referred to was as follows: —

SONG FOR SAINT TAMMANY'S DAY.

Of Andrew, of Patrick, of David, and George,
    What mighty achievements we hear!
While no one relates great Tammany's feats,
Although more heroic by far, my brave boys,
    Although more heroic by far.

These heroes fought only as fancy inspired,
    As by their own stories we find;
Whilst Tammany, he fought only to free
From cruel oppression, mankind, my brave boys,
    From cruel oppression, mankind.

When our country was young, and our numbers were few,
    To our fathers his friendship was shown;
(For he e'er would oppose whom he took for his foes),
And he made our misfortunes his own, my brave boys,
    And he made our misfortunes his own.

At length, growing old, and quite worn out with years,
    As history doth truly proclaim,
His wigwam was fired, he nobly expired,
And flew to the skies in a flame, my brave boys,
    And flew to the skies in a flame.

Other songs in honor of the saint were sung, and the warriors, highly pleased with the gaiety of the Chief, bore him on their shoulders from the green into his cabin amid the shouts of all present. The colors of France and Holland, and the State flag of Pennsylvania, had been raised in the morning on separate staffs. These were struck after sunset at a signal from the cannon. The Chief and his Sachems then marched into the city in Indian file, the band playing "St. Tammany's Day." They saluted the French Minister in passing, and proceeded to the Coffee-House, where, after giving three cheers, they dispersed and returned to their homes.

On the 1st of May, 1784, another celebration was held at the country seat of Mr. Pole, when the State flag was hoisted with the colors of France and the Netherlands on either side, the ceremony being accompanied by a salute with a cannon. The usual toasts were drunk, and on their way home from the banquet the Sons of St. Tammany saluted General Washington who was dining with Robert Morris, at Lemon Hill, with music, cheers, and firing of cannon. The Ministers of France and the Netherlands were complimented in a similar manner.

At the celebration in the following year, 1785, which was held at the country seat of Mr. Beveridge on the Schuylkill, "The compliments of General Washington for the respects paid him in the previous year being communicated by the Secretary, produced thirteen cheers which came from the heart." One of the features of this celebration was the raising of a new flag with a painting of St. Tammany upon it.

On the 11th of April, 1786, the Sons of St. Tammany received at their wigwam on the Schuylkill the famous Seneca Chief "Corn Planter," who with five other Chiefs had arrived in Philadelphia on the way to New York in order to secure action by Congress upon certain matters of interest to their nation. What followed is thus described: "About three o'clock in the afternoon the Tammany Sachems waited on 'Corn Planter' and his companions at the Indian Queen Tavern, and attended the Chiefs separately to a rendezvous near the wigwam. Three others of the Indians were escorted by a company of militia. On the arrival of the Sachems cannons were fired and flags hoisted. Corn Planter then made a speech in which he expressed himself in strong terms of amity and friendship for the whites, and after a salute of thirteen guns and three cheers from the company, which numbered about 2000 persons, a circle was formed about the 'council fire' and the pipe of peace was smoked. A libation of wine was poured out in honor of St. Tammany, after which Corn Planter and the other Indians performed the war dance followed by a peace dance in which the Tammany Sachems and militia officers participated. One of the Sachems then replied to Corn Planter's speech in fitting terms, a salute was fired, the colors struck, and the Indians escorted back to town."

St. Tammany day was celebrated by the Society on the 1st of May at the wigwam in the usual manner. Charles Biddle, Vice-

President of the State, was elected Sachem, and hailed as Tammany. The names of the other Sachems, together with the Indian titles conferred upon them, are recorded as follows:— Jonathan Bayard Smith, "Iontonque"; Alexander Boyd, "Tataboucksey"; Thomas Nevill, "Hoowamente"; Frederick Phile, "Pechemelind"; Daniel Heister, "Towarraho"; William Coates, "Deunquatt"; Joseph Dean, "Shuetongo"; William Thorpe, "Simougher"; Emanuel Eyre, "Tediescung"; Zachariah Endress, "Shamboukin"; Thomas Proctor, "Kayashuta"; and Elias Boys, "Hyngapushes." At this celebration a portrait of Corn Planter was presented by Mrs. Eliza Phile to the Sachem "Iontonque," Jonathan Bayard Smith, and an ode was recited by Brother Prichard, which we reproduce as follows:—

ODE.

When superstition's dark and haughty plan
Fettered the genius and debased the man,
Each trifling legend was as truth received;
The priest invented and the crowd believed;
Nations adored the whim in stone or paint,
And gloried in the fabricated saint.
Some holy guardian, hence, each nation claims—
Gay France her Denis, and grave Spain her James.
Britons at once two mighty saints obey;
Andrew and George maintain united sway.
O'er humbler lands the same odd whim prevails—
Ireland her Patrick boasts, her David, Wales.
We, Pennsylvanians, these old tales reject,
And our own saint think proper to elect.
Immortal Tammany, of Indian race,
Great in the field, and foremost in the chase,
No puny saint was he, with fasting pale,
He climb'd the mountain and he swept the vale;
Rushed through the forest with unequalled flight—
Your ancient saints would tremble at the sight—
Caught the swift boar, and swifter deer with ease,
And worked a thousand miracles like these.
To public views he added private ends,
And loved his country most, and next his friends.
With courage long he strove to ward the blow,
(Courage we all respect e'en in a foe),
And when each effort he in vain had tried,
Kindled the flame in which he bravely died!

CAPTURED BY THE BRAVES.

> To Tammany let well filled horns go round;
> His fame let every honest tongue resound:
> With him let every generous patriot vie
> To live in freedom or with honor die!
> Nor shall I think my labors too severe,
> Since ye, wise Sachems, kindly deign to hear.

On the way back to the city the members of the Society stopped at the residence of Benjamin Franklin and paid its respects to that honorable statesman.

At the celebration by the Jeffersonians in honor of the acquisition of Louisiana, held May 12, 1804, mention is made that "the Tammany Society paraded with 'the Tribe of Pennsylvania' and sixteen others." Mention is also made of "the incorporated St. Tammany" as being among the societies which paraded.

In 1806 the Tammany Society at its meeting in May, "proceeded in great state to the wigwam at Rowland Smith's, Spring Garden, bearing the general flag of the General Council of Sachems, the property flag of each tribe, and the peculiar insignia of the Society,—the Great Key, the Bugle Horn, the Calumet, and the Sheathed Tomahawk." The affair was rendered more imposing by the appearance of a new band of music composed of performers upon six clarionets, four flutes, two horns, two bassoons, one bass drum, a psaltery, and some violins. Dr. Michael Leib was Grand Sachem.

When, in 1814, the Committee of Defense thought that "field fortifications" should be thrown up on the western side of the city of Philadelphia, a public call was made for volunteers to perform the labor necessary. Hearty enthusiasm was shown, and all classes of society joined the organizations in a body, and among those who thus responded were four hundred members of the Tammany Society on one occasion, and one hundred and thirty on another.

There were other celebrations of Saint Tammany's Day, but enough has been given to indicate the nature of the festivities which marked these occasions. It will be noticed that the leading members and officers of these organizations were men prominent in social and political affairs, but at first this tendency to political action was controlled by patriotic impulses and inspired with the desire to complete the organization of the

Republic which had been founded as a result of the Revolutionary War. The Tammany Societies wherever they existed seem to have been opponents of everything tending towards monarchy, or which in the slightest degree would cripple the complete civil and religious liberty gained in the establishment of the new government.

As an indication of the gradual change taking place in the objects controlling the Tammany organizations as early as 1796, we quote the following from Mr. Westcott:—

"To the national societies may be added 'the Society of Saint Tammany, or the Columbian Order.' Before the Revolution an association bearing this name was social and patriotic. It continued firmly patriotic in its ceremonies and proceedings during the contest of the Revolution, and for some years afterwards. In 1796 there appeared publicly the first notices that the Tammany Society had become a political society in Philadelphia. It met February 20 of that year at the wigwam No. 63 North Fourth Street. In 1800 the wigwam was in Harmony Court,—probably at Northwest corner of Whalebone (or Hudson's) Alley."

The drift of the Society towards political action may also be inferred from an attack made on Governor McKean who was assailed on account of his participation as "Grand Sachem" at the anniversary celebration of the Saint Tammany Society held May 12, 1800, at the Buck Tavern in Moyamensing. The "longtalk" was made by Dr. John Porter, and among the other Sachems present besides McKean were Israel Israel and Colonel John Barker. The Colonel Barker here named afterwards became General, and it was his son, Captain James N. Barker, an officer of the regular army, who commanded the garrison at Fort Mifflin, assisted by Lieutenant Williams, at the time when it is claimed the Society of Red Men was organized there. Captain Barker resigned from the army after the close of the War of 1812, was made an alderman of the city of Philadelphia, and afterwards elected Mayor. While we have no evidence of the fact, it may be that Captain Barker was a member of the Saint Tammany Society in which his father was so prominent. Assuming this, the connection between the Societies of Sons of Saint Tammany and the Society of Red Men is unbroken and complete.

In addition to the Tammany Societies existing in New York

PATRIOTIC SOCIETIES. 183

and Philadelphia, it is proper to mention the branch of the organization in the city of Baltimore, Md. In 1805 there existed in that city a branch of the Saint Tammany Society, or Columbian Order, fashioned after that of New York in 1789, and purely a political organization. This branch was established in the "Month of the Corn" and "year of discovery of America, 314," and its existence can be traced through several subsequent years.

The constitution of this Society, organized at Baltimore in 1805, was published in the pamphlets of the Maryland Historical Society, Vol. XXVI., indexed 385. From this constitution we give extracts sufficient to indicate how the Society was governed.

It declared that its purpose was to "connect in indissoluble bands of patriotic friendship citizens of known attachment to the political rights of human nature, and the liberties of this country." Every member before initiation was required to come under a solemn obligation to maintain the constitution of the Society, and to preserve its secrets. The presiding officer was designated as Grand Sachem, and there were as many Sachems as States in the Union, who with the Grand Sachem, formed a council for the government of the body. There was a treasurer and secretary, and the quorum consisted of a number equal to the number of States. The number of Tribes into which the Society was divided also corresponded with the number of States, and each Tribe took the name of a State. The place of meeting was called a wigwam, and in the year 1808 this wigwam was located at North Calvert Street near the City Spring, in what was known as the Octagon Building. The constitution provided that the election of officers should take place at the first stated meeting in May, annually. In the absence of the Grand Sachem his duties for the time being were devolved upon the "Father of the Council." The admission fee was fixed at not more than 1000 cents, nor less than two dollars, to be paid on the signing of the Constitution. Applications for membership were referred to a committee for examination, and upon the report of said committee a ballot was taken, and if not more than two black to every sixteen white balls appeared, the candidate was elected. He was required to attend for admission within six months or his election was declared void. Provision was made for a new ballot in case of rejection on account of falsehood or mistake. Otherwise he could not be proposed a second time in the Society. Crimes against the Society were declared to be betraying the secrets, slander, embezzlement, or flagrant breach of civil laws; but no person could be expelled except after due trial. The regular meetings of the Society were held the first Thursday evening of each month, "and the 12th day of May shall be observed as the anniversary of the Society, on which a longtalk shall be delivered by a brother appointed for that purpose." The doorkeeper was styled "The Winskinki." He was directed to admit no person not personally known to him to be a member, nor unless he presented "the characteristic word" of the Society, nor to allow any member to leave the wigwam without leave of absence having been first obtained from the Grand Sachem. One significant clause of the By-Laws, which was certainly an improvement on the New York Society, and had a beneficent effect by preventing debauchery among the members, declared that "no drink stronger than water shall be admitted into the wigwam."

An account of a meeting of the Tammany Society in Baltimore, in 1807, appeared in the *Baltimore American*, a leading daily of that city, from which we extract as follows:—

"MAY 23, 1807.

"At an adjourned meeting of the Tammany Society, held at their Wigwam on the 21st of the month of Flowers, nineteen brethren were elected Sachems for the ensuing year, and a meeting of Sachems being held and an allotment being made, the following was the result:—

"Grand Sachem, John Barkson; New Hampshire, Sachem Small; Connecticut, Sachem Aitken; Delaware, Sachem Niles; Kentucky, Sachem George; Georgia, Sachem McClure; Vermont, Sachem Sinclair; Pennsylvania, Sachem Craig; Virginia, Sachem Bland; Tennessee, Sachem Snyder; Rhode Island, Sachem Fulton; New Jersey, Sachem Stewart; Ohio, Sachem Hewitt; South Carolina, Sachem Chase; Massachusetts, Sachem Williams; New York, Sachem Moore; Maryland, Sachem Peelin; North Carolina, Sachem Maris."

The Society maintained a fitful existence for a short time and then, like the other branches of the organization, seems to have gone out of existence.

The St. Tamina Society organized out of the Sons of Liberty

at Annapolis in 1771, maintained its existence as late as 1810, because in the *Maryland Republican*, a newspaper published at Annapolis, Maryland, in the years 1809-10, appear the notices of the weekly meetings of the Tamina Society of that city. On the 12th of May, 1810, a longtalk was delivered before the Society by Mr. John S. Skinner, which longtalk was subsequently published in the *Maryland Republican*. The longtalk was so acceptable to the members of the Society that on the "12th day of the Month of Blossoms, the Year of Discovery 318," a resolution was unanimously adopted, "that the thanks of this society be presented to Brother John S. Skinner for the appropriate longtalk delivered by him, and that he be requested to furnish a copy for publication."

The address was accordingly published in the *Republican* for May 19, 1810, and a copy is before us as we write. In the longtalk the speaker referred in eloquent terms to the days of the Revolution, claiming that the society which he addressed was directly descended from the St. Tamina Society of the olden time. We make a few quotations as follows:—

"Brothers, our Society takes its name from a celebrated Indian chief of the Delaware Tribe who was, like Logan, renowned for his illustrious qualities and like him also 'the friend of the white man.' Its symbols are properly borrowed from the aboriginal Americans whose state when discovered presented a model of perfect freedom if not primeval innocence and affection. It was instituted by a sturdy band of inflexible patriots, who secretly assembled together amidst surrounding horrors of British desolation through the Revolutionary War, to commune over the affairs of their country, and to watch the motion of its enemies. From this fountain sprung forth many waters, out of this beginning has grown that chain of institutions of which we are a component link, and which we have this day met to brighten and to celebrate." . . . "Secrecy was properly imposed on each member at his admission, thus far resembling the social dinners at Sparta, where, when the Spartan youth entered, the oldest man present pointed to the door and said, 'No one word spoken in this company goes out there.'"

A large portion of the address is devoted to the political character of the Society, and much sound advice is given the members as to their duties as citizens. He said:—

"Brothers, beware of abusing the elective franchise, that is the great bulwark of your freedom, the main pillar of your patriotic edifice, a fortress from which you can rake your political enemies and defend forever the eternal principles of truth, justice and equal rights. When we approach the polls, let us guard against the seductive arts of the office-hunter and the more baneful pretensions of the masked usurper, hatching his schemes of aggrandizement and tyranny, aided by all the servile or deluded followers which art or gold can secure. Such men have 'the words of Jacob and the hands of Esau.'"

The celebration at which this longtalk was delivered occurred only two years before the outbreak of the War of 1812-14. Already the shadow of the coming conflict hovered over the country. The insolence of England aroused a storm of indignation among the people, and it was evident that war could not be long postponed. In reference to this and to seeming vacillation in the councils of the Nation, he spoke as follows : —

"Brothers, if there exist such solid reasons for union and vigilance at home is there not ample cause to send our scouts, perhaps our warriors, to watch and punish foreign aggressions beyond the great waters? I thought, did we not all expect, that unless ample reparation was made us, the tomahawk which lies concealed beneath the council fire of our great wigwam would have been unburied when our (national) Sachems assembled in the month of Beavers. We thought that they who had treacherously rejected the friendly wampum, and insolently refused to smoke the Calumet of Peace, ought not to have passed unpunished. We thought the bloody scalps of our brethren slain in the Chesapeake would have roused apathy itself. But some evil birds have been flying among us — some old squaws seem to have been admitted in disguise into the Council of our Sachem, and to have turned our wrongs into jest for fear of the battle. I have no hope of brightening your honor until these old squaws are kept at home to hill their corn and dress their potatoes. I have notched a list of our wrongs, but unredressed as they are likely to be, I fear their rehearsal would drive us into despair and rage and convert this jocund society into a mourning scene. With England we have whiffed the pipe of peace, but as soon as our back was turned she struck us with the tomahawk and drew the scalping knife. She pretends to great honor and lofty views, but all is hollow, false and faithless and inconsistent. In England is a government 'uniting the mock modesty of a bloody sceptre with the little traffic of a merchant's counting-house, wielding a truncheon in one hand and picking a pocket with the other.' Against France, too, we have much ground for complaint. Her injuries may be likened to the Severn, but the crimes of England are huge as the Chesapeake, or vast as the great waters of whose undived empire she boasts. Our Tribes will not always submit to injury. *They will yet rise in their fury, sing the war song and 'terrible as the mountain storm' they will rush upon their enemies.*"

In view of the war that so shortly ensued, the concluding words of the above paragraph seem almost prophetic, and during the two years of blood and conflict which marked that page of our nation's history, the blood of the Sons of St. Tammany was freely shed as the price of freedom, and, as events have since proved, of lasting peace with our old enemies. Whether from fear or policy, the hand of England no longer grasps the tomahawk, and for many great suns between the two nations the smoke from the calumet of peace has ascended to the Great Spirit.

John S. Skinner, who delivered this oration, was born in 1772 in Anne Arundel County, Md. It has been claimed that he was a member of the Society in the latter years of his life, but as we are unable to find any record giving the date of his admission we cannot vouch for the truth of this claim. His life was full of interesting episodes, not the least memorable being that connected with the War of 1812. He was one of the friends who accompanied Francis Scott Key when with others he sought the release of his friend, the aged Dr. Beams, detained a prisoner by the British. He was a particular friend of Mr. Key and his family. It was while on this mission to the British fleet, under a flag of truce, that Key wrote the immortal national hymn, the "Star Spangled Banner." Brother Skinner was a man of considerable literary ability, and in the year 1818 published a periodical called *The Censor*. In the year 1819, in company with Samuel Sands, he edited the *American Farmer*, and in 1829 published and owned the *Turf Register*. He was closely identified with the best interests of the State of Maryland, and in the year 1825 was secretary of a convention called to discuss means best calculated to promote the prosperity of the State. He was postmaster of the city of Baltimore for many years, which position he filled most acceptably. Of him it may with truth be said that he needs no eulogy as a good man and a useful citizen.

It is now proper to mention still another society which used the forms and ceremonies of the Indians, and which is brought to our notice under the name of the "Kickapoo Amicable Association," which existed in the city of Washington, D. C., in the year 1804, and which not only adopted the usages, forms, ceremonies, and costumes of the Indian race, but also gave to its members Indian names and, following the custom of the

Indian race, bestowed the name of an animal or other natural object upon them. Among the manuscripts of the "Oldest Inhabitants' Association" of Washington, Vol. I., is a document which is a copy of the original certificate of membership issued to a member of this association named Washington Boyd, under date of October 20, 1804. The document is in a cipher, made by spelling backwards the words composing the certificate. The certificate reads as follows:—

"For Verbea, or the Beaver, Washington Boyd, Esq., United States of America.

"*To the Members of the Kickapoo Amicable Association, Greeting:*

"Know ye that we, the Kickapoos of Washington City, reposing due confidence in the benevolent and humanizing disposition of our beloved friend the Beaver, have adopted him and given him this in the name of our ancient and honorable fraternity according to the rules of our association.

"J. Lamb, *Secretary Washington Tribe.*
"LONG LIVE THE KICKAPOOS!"

This chapter would be incomplete without giving an account of the celebrated Indian chief who was canonized as the patron saint of America, and after whom the Tamina (or Tammany) Societies herein described were named. In the work of Mr. Horton already referred to, the legend of Tamina is attributed to the researches of the late Dr. Samuel L. Mitchell, and it is from this account that the following legend is taken.

Long before the discoveries of Ferdinand de Soto or La Salle, or even before the fancied voyage of Bœhem, Tammany and his people inhabited that extensive and fertile tract of land west of the Alleghany Mountains, and extending northward of the Ohio river. The remains of monuments and other vestiges of art, which are now found in that section were owing, it is said, to the skill of Tammany. In his youth he was famed for his exploits as a hunter and warrior, and, from beyond the Father of Waters to the Great Salt Lake, his deeds were recounted at every council fire. He waged for many years a war with his mortal enemy, the Evil Spirit, and during this time his prowess and courage exceeded, if possible, all that is related in ancient story and song of the Grecian Hercules. This Evil Spirit took every occasion to annoy the great Chief, and first caused poison sumach and stinging nettles to grow in the land, which diffused virulent exhalations through the air, poisoning his people, and puncturing them when they went to hunt. Tammany, after various efforts to destroy them, finally took advantage of an excessive drouth, set fire to the prairies, and consumed the venomous plants, which burned with so much rapidity that the Evil Spirit himself, who was skulking about, was sorely singed by the flames. In revenge for this, his enemy sent innumerable rattlesnakes to infest the land, which Tammany destroyed by sowing the seeds of the ash-tree upon the grounds, and cured their bites by seneka-root and plantain. After this, he brought large droves of mammoths and other huge animals from behind the great lakes, and turned them loose upon the Tammanial territories. These beasts caused great devastation among the people of Tammany. They were swift and ferocious, and arrows fell blunted from their sides, so tough and impervious were their skins. But Tammany was not to be frustrated. He caused salt to be sprinkled at different places throughout his dominions, and in the paths of the animals, as they went to these licks (as they are called to this day), he caused large pits to be dug which were concealed by means of trees and leaves. Into these they fell and were killed, being impaled upon the points of sharpened trees, and their bones are yet found there, to confirm the truth of the story.

His enemy was mortified and enraged at his disappointment in his endeavors to injure Tammany, and now tried another expedient to effect his purpose. He had a large dam thrown across the lake, near where the city of Detroit now stands, causing a great rising of the waters of lakes Huron and Michigan, which was intended to deluge the country south of it, where lay the territory of Tammany. He also threw another across at Niagara, raising the waters of Lake Erie. The disastrous effects which might have resulted from this, Tammany averted by opening the drains in which the waters of the Miami, the Wabash, and the Alleghany now run, and by cutting a ditch which at present forms the channel of the Ohio. For this he was pronounced by his adoring people "the savior of his country." The lakes gradually subsided, but the rapids of

Detroit and the falls of Niagara still remain as monuments of the astonishing event!

After this, the Evil Spirit stirred up the red men of the East and the North against Tammany, and a long and bloody war ensued; but they were at length defeated, and a great number taken prisoners. When they found themselves in the power of Tammany, they expected, of course, to be put to the most cruel tortures and lacerations; but each one had prepared himself for the horrible execution, and like Alkmoonac, had determined to sing his death-song, while gashes were separating limb from limb, and blazing splinters stuck into his flesh. But what was their surprise when they learned that the victorious Chief had determined to spare their lives! He ordered them to be brought to his wigwam, where he delivered to them a discourse so full of good reason and sound sense that they were heartily ashamed of their own villainy.

But the Evil Spirit was determined not to give up yet, and so implacable was his enmity against Tammany, that he resolved to waylay and attack him himself. Tammany, however, knew by the moving of the bushes where his enemy was secreted, and pretending not to notice the discovery, he advanced, and with his hickory staff he dealt a blow upon his adversary which made him bellow out with pain; and, to follow the exact words of the legend, "they clinched, and dreadful was the crashing of timber which they trod down in the scuffle. Never since the times when the giants piled mountain upon mountain were there such exertions of animal strength. For the space of more than a league square not a tree was left standing—all were crushed and trampled flat by the combatants. At length, after unceasing exertions for fifty days, Tammany, skilfully taking advantage of the hiplock, threw him head and shoulders on the ground, and endeavored to roll him into the Ohio and drown him; but an immense rock standing in the way, he could not effect it. He then seized him by the throat, and would certainly have strangled him, had not his wrist and thumb been so sprained and weakened that they could not gripe him hard enough to stop his breathing. Tammany by this time grew faint and exhausted, which the Evil Spirit perceiving, slipped out of his hands; but, as he departed he was told to confine himself to the cold and remote regions of Labrador and Hudson's Bay, and was threatened with instant death if he should ever be caught showing his face on this side of the great lakes."

After this, Tammany devoted himself to the arts of peace. He brought maize, beans, and tobacco from their uncultivated states, and domesticated plum trees and onions, and introduced many other improvements in agriculture. By these things he endeared himself to his people. His government was of the patriarchal kind, mild, but firm. His people looked up to him as their father, and referred all their differences and disputes to him. His decisions were always law. Plenty pervaded his land, and his people were contented and happy. Their watchword was "Tammany and Liberty."

About this time, Manco Capac, the great Inca of Peru and the descendant of the Sun, who had heard of the wisdom and powers of Tammany, dispatched messengers inviting him to an interview, the place of which he would mention might be Mexico, a spot about equidistant from the dominions of each, where he wished to consult him on a form of government which he was about to establish for the Peruvian nation. Tammany, before departing to have this talk with the illustrious Sachem of the Andes, called together his tribes, which amounted to thirteen, and delivered the following sententious precepts to each : —

"CHILDREN OF THE FIRST TRIBE: The EAGLE should be your model. He soars above the clouds, loves the mountain-tops, takes a broad survey of the country round, and his watchfulness in the daytime lets nothing escape him. From him learn to direct your thoughts to elevated objects, to rise superior to the fogs of prejudice and passion, to behold in the clear atmosphere of reason all things in their true light and posture, and never expose yourself to be surprised while the sun shines, in a fit of drowsiness or slumber.

"CHILDREN OF THE SECOND TRIBE: The TIGER affords a useful lesson for you. The exceeding agility of this creature, the extraordinary quickness of his sight, and, above all, his discriminating power in the dark, teach you to be stirring and active in your respective callings, to look sharp to every engagement you enter into, and to let neither misty days nor stormy nights make you lose sight of the worthy object of your pursuit.

"CHILDREN OF THE THIRD TRIBE: You are to pay good attention to the qualities of the DEER. He possesses uncommon readiness of hearing — can judge of sounds at a great distance. In like manner open ye your ears to whatever is passing; collect the substance of distant rumors, and learn before dangers surround your corn-fields and wigwams what is going on at a distance.

"CHILDREN OF THE FOURTH TRIBE: There is one quality of the WOLF to which I would call your attention. His wide extent of nostrils catches the atoms floating in the air, and gives him notice of the approach of his prey or his foe. Thus when power grows rank, and like a contagion sends abroad its pestilent streams, I see the WOLF, like the myrmidons of Tammany, the first to rouse, turn his head and snuff oppression in every breeze.

"CHILDREN OF THE FIFTH TRIBE: You, my children, are to take useful hints of the BUFFALO. He is one of the strongest animals in the wilderness; but strong as he is he loves the company of his kind, and is not fond of venturing upon distant excursions. This is wise in the buffalo, and wise it will be in you to imitate him. Operate in concert, stand together, support one another, and you will be a mountain that nobody can move; fritter down your strength in divisions, become the spirit of parties, let wigwam be divided against wigwam, and you will be an ant-hill which a baby can kick over.

"CHILDREN OF THE SIXTH TRIBE: That social and valuable creature, the DOG, offers something for you to profit by. The warmth of his attachment, the disinterestedness of his friendship, and the unchangefulness of his fidelity, mark him as the object of your kindness and imitation. Do but love with half the warmth, sincerity and steadiness with which these, your constant hunting companions, love you all, and happiness, comfort, and joy will make your land their dwelling-place, and ye shall experience all the pleasure that human nature can bear.

"CHILDREN OF THE SEVENTH TRIBE: You are to take pattern after the BEAVER. His industry merits your regard. Forests must be cleared, hills levelled, rivers turned to accomplish your plans. Labor and perseverance overcome all things; for I have heard old people say their ancestors assisted in making the sun, immense as he appears, by collecting into a heap all the fire-flies and glow-worms they could find; and the moon, whose light is fainter and size smaller, was in like manner formed by gathering into a pile all the fox-fire or phosphoric rotten wood they could procure.

"CHILDREN OF THE EIGHTH TRIBE: The SQUIRREL, my children, offers something profitable to you. It is his practice, as he has a foresight of winter, to collect acorns, chestnuts, and walnuts and carry them in large quantities to his hole. In like manner it becomes you to look forward to the winter of life, and have some provision necessary for yourselves at that needy time. This you may enjoy at your firesides, while all around you frost rends the trees asunder, and the white powder lies so thick upon the ground that you cannot venture out without your snow-shoes.

"CHILDREN OF THE NINTH TRIBE: You are to learn a lesson from the FOX. He looks well before him as he travels, examines carefully the ground he treads upon, and takes good care that his enemies do not come upon him by surprise. Such keen examination will guard you from difficulties; and, if in the course of nature, you shall be, in spite of all this, beset by them, nothing will more effectually enable you to extricate yourselves.

"CHILDREN OF THE TENTH TRIBE: The TORTOISE, who supports on his back the world we inhabit, offers a world of instruction to you. Were it not for his benevolence in keeping afloat on the immense ocean in which he swims, this land we inhabit would soon go to the bottom; and the displeasure he feels when men lead lives of idleness and vice, when they quarrel and injure their neighbors and families, has induced him more than once to dip a part of his shell under the water, and drown a set of wretches no longer fit to live. If, then, you wish to attain a long life, be honest, upright and industrious.

"CHILDREN OF THE ELEVENTH TRIBE: I recommend to your attention the wholesome counsel derived to man from the EEL. He was never known to make a noise or disturbance in the world, nor to speak an ungentle sentence to a living creature. Slander never proceeded from his mouth, nor doth guile rest under his tongue. Are you desirous, my children, of modest stillness and quiet? Would you like to live peaceably among men? If such be your desires, learn a lesson of wisdom from the EEL, who, although he knows neither his birth nor his parentage, but is cast an orphan upon creation, yet shows by his strength and numbers the excellence of the mode of life he has chosen.

"CHILDREN OF THE TWELFTH TRIBE: I shall point out for your improvement some excellent traits in the character of the BEAR. He is distinguished for his patient endurance of those inconveniences which he finds it impossible to ward off. Thus when scarcity threatens your country with famine — when disease among the beasts strew your hunting-grounds with carcases — when insects destroy your beans, and worms corrode the roots of your corn — when the streams refuse their accustomed supplies, or when the clouds withhold their rain, bear with patience and resignation whatever necessity imposes upon you. Show yourselves men; for it is adversity which gives scope to your talents.

"CHILDREN OF THE THIRTEENTH TRIBE: I call your attention to the economy of the BEE. You can observe among those creatures a discipline not surpassed by anything the woods afford. Idlers, vagrants, and embezzlers of public property have no toleration there. Regularity and method pervade every department of their government. Borrow from them an idea of arrangement in business; and above all derive from their instructive example that alchemy of mind, which, by an operation somewhat analogous to the production of nectar from venom, converts private feelings into public advantages, and makes even crimes and vices ultimately conducive to public good."

After delivering these precepts to his tribes, Tammany departed for his interview with the Inca, which proved to be most interesting and beneficial to all parties. On returning to his native country, he found his old enemy had taken advantage of his absence, and had instilled notions of idleness and dissipation into the minds of his people. On account of this, diseases had broken out among them, which required all his skill and sagacity to subdue. This, however, he eventually succeeded in doing, and lived, after he had accomplished it, many years in great happiness and wonderfully beloved by his people. At last, after arriving at an unusual age, that universal palsy, which, in the natural course of things, immediately precedes death, terminated his life without either sickness or pain, and he expired without a sigh or a groan. Great honors were paid to his memory. After more ceremony than was ever shown to any corpse before, they committed the body of Tammany to the ground, after their manner, and raised over it a large mound of earth. Curious antiquarians have detected the spot, though they know not its design or use, for he lies within the great Indian fort, near Muskingum, beneath the hillock which they have so often admired — a monument for size and labor second to nothing of the kind save the Pyramids of Egypt.

Such is the legendary history of Tammany. Of his real life we know but little, but that little upsets much of the poetry of the foregoing account, as we doubt not an explicit, unvarnished narrative of the deeds of Hercules and Ajax would many of the remarkable exploits which have been attributed to them by the pens of the classic poets. One statement informs us that Tammany, or, as captious orthographists contend, Tamanend, was settled within the bounds of Pennsylvania when William Penn came to America; that he lived then near the Schuylkill, but at the time of his death resided in Bucks County, near Doylestown, and is buried near a spring about four miles from the latter place. It is believed, though not positively known, that Tamanend was present at the great council under the elm tree at Shakamaxon, upon Penn's first arrival in this country. All the chiefs of the tribes of the Lenni Lenape were there, and it is not at all probable that so distinguished a king as Tammany would have been absent. As, however, there was no treaty signed at the first interview, which was only intended for the purpose of exchanging assurances of friendship, the names of those present have never been preserved. The first treaty for the purchase of lands, made by Penn with the Indians, is dated April 23, 1683, and in that Tamanend and Metamequam relinquished their right and title to a tract lying between Pennypack and Neshaminy creeks. In the great treaty, by which a large portion of Pennsylvania was acquired, dated the 30th of May, 1685, the name of Tamanend does not appear. From this we infer that he must have deceased between these years. This opinion is strengthened by the fact that all accounts of him agree in the statement that he died but a short time after Penn settled in this country — indeed, Penn himself related, in his account of the first settlement of Pennsylvania, that "he found him an old man, yet vigorous in mind and body, with high notions of liberty, but easily won by the suavity and peaceable address of the governor." Another account, differing only slightly from the above, represents him as a noted chief of the Delaware nation, the head of the powerful confederacy of the Lenni Lenape, and his wigwam stood where Princeton College is now located.

At all events, Tammany was disposed to cultivate the friendship of the palefaces, and had the sagacity to perceive that their knowledge of the mechanical and agricultural arts rendered them much superior to his own people in power and intelligence. That he lived to a great age, is universally attested by all accounts, both historical and legendary. Cooper, in his novel, the "Last of the Mohicans," represents him as referring to his age in the following beautiful manner. At the death of Uncas, he exclaims — " My day has been too long. In the morning, I saw the sons of Unamis happy and strong, and yet, before the night has come, have I lived to see the last warrior of the wise race of the Mohicans." He is sometimes represented as an Iroquois chieftain, and one of the first converted to Christianity by the French missionaries; and it has been stated that he was actually enrolled among the saints of the calendar. But this is a mistake. Tammany was not an Iroquois, but belonged to the confederacy of the Lenni Lenape, and was doubtless a Delaware.

Various spellings of his name are given, Tamina, Tammany, Tammanen, Temeny, Tamanend, Tamané, Tamaned, by the different authors and historians who have written concerning his history; but modern usage has accepted "Tammany" as the correct orthography.

Tammany was, however, without any question, one of the most distinguished Red Men who ever lived. He was kind, merciful, and brave. He taught his children to cultivate the arts of peace, as well as to subdue their enemies. Under his reign, the confederacy of the Lenni Lenape became powerful and mighty. Then living to a remarkable age — so great as to be called "Tamanend of many days " — he was looked upon as a patriarch, and reverenced with all that strength of affection which the sons of the forest always bestowed upon their chieftains. Such was the man whom the patriots of the Revolution adopted as their tutelar saint ; and if they could not claim that he had performed miracles, they could at least point to him as one who had rendered good service both to his own people and to the whites, and who, while he endeavored to live in peace with all men, would suffer neither wrong nor abuse, nor submit to a loss of his liberty or his rights.

This chapter should not be closed without calling attention to the fact that the Tammany Societies which we have described were organized no further north than New York. We have discovered no trace of them in the New England States. In that section of the country all the patriotic work previous to the Revolution, and while the struggle was going on, was done, as we have shown, by the Sons of Liberty. It will be remembered that Tammany was a chief of the Lenni Lenape. Their hunting grounds covered the tract of land including Pennsylvania, Delaware, and part of Maryland. While, therefore, it was natural for the Sons of Liberty in those States to transform themselves into St. Tammany Societies, the influence was not equally strong with the Sons of Liberty in New England.

It will be noticed that the title of Red Men had not entered into the nomenclature of the famous Tamina (or Tammany) Societies described in this chapter. These words as a part of the title of our organization do not appear until the formation of the Society of Red Men at Fort Mifflin in 1813, concerning which full information is given in the succeeding chapter. We have shown with sufficient clearness to satisfy reasonable criticism the history of the Order through its traditional period, from the Sons of Liberty of 1765 and the St. Tamina Society of Annapolis in 1771, down to the War of 1812. It may be asked why it was necessary to change the name of the Society if the connection was as we claim between its membership and that of the Tammany Societies existing previously. It is a sufficient answer to this query to call attention to the fact that originally the Tammany Societies were formed for social and benevolent purposes. They became perverted from the original idea, and largely political in their general nature. When a reorganization was desired along the lines of the original affiliation, to carry out the principles of patriotism and benevolence, it was natural that a new name should be selected to avoid whatever of odium had become connected with the old Society mainly through taking active part in politics. The desire to retain the features taken from the manners and customs of the Indians doubtless suggested the use of the name "Red Men." We feel justified in making the claim that the suggestion which led to this selection of the name of "Red Men" for the organization formed at Fort Mifflin, came from knowlege of, indeed *actual membership* in, the previous organizations known as St. Tammany Societies that existed as recorded in this chapter, and this is further sustained by the evidence submitted to the G. C. U. S., and upon which was based its action declaring 1771 as the date of the origin of the Order. It must be remembered, also, that the information herein stated has been gathered from the fragmentary accounts of these various societies given in the papers of the time. We know even in our own days how little information of the interior history of an organization appears in the public press. It is not surprising, therefore, that we are unable to command the absolute historic data to establish beyond question the connection between the Tammany Societies which we have described and the Society of Red Men that succeeded them.

Having due regard, therefore, to the meagre and fragmentary nature of the accounts published in the contemporaneous papers, the wonder is that so much of interest and historical value has been preserved rather than that it is impossible to identify the individuality which would make the connection between the Tammany Societies and their successor absolute and complete. One thing is certain, from the very political nature of the Tammany Societies in their second stage, they included the energetic, ambitious party leaders of that time.

When the War of 1812 broke out we find the names of members of these Societies prominent among those who rallied a second time for the defence of our country. It is not improbable that the garrison at Fort Mifflin contained many who were members of the Tammany Societies, although we cannot positively establish that fact.

With these explanatory remarks we close this chapter, and proceed to the consideration of that Society formed in 1813 which became the successor of the St. Tamina Society of 1771, and the connection link between the Patriotic Societies of the Revolution and the Improved Order of Red Men of 1834. We pass from the region of tradition to supposition and present for the consideration of the reader information at once interesting and instructive concerning the second period in the History of our Order from 1813 to 1834.

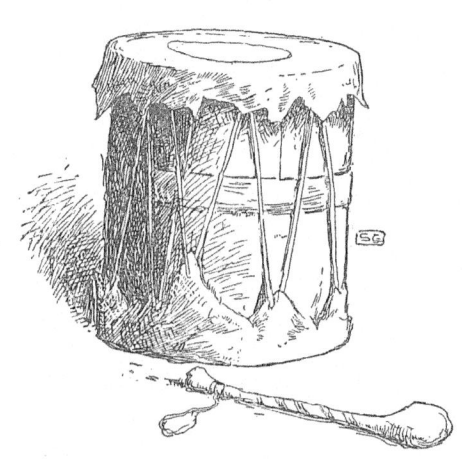

CHAPTER IV.

SOCIETY OF RED MEN (1813-1833).

WE come now to the second epoch in the history of the Improved Order of Red Men, and to the consideration of those societies, whose origin was claimed to be in 1813, and which existed from 1816 down to 1833 ; which used the name of Red Men, and included in their membership many who were afterwards members of the Improved Order of Red Men, established at Baltimore in 1833. This portion of our history is based upon documents in the possession of the Great Council of the United States, to which access has been had by those under whose direction this history has been prepared, and which have already been used to establish the claim that the origin of the Improved Order of Red Men dated from 1813 at Fort Mifflin, on the Delaware River near Philadelphia.

The researches of Past Great Incohonee Morris H. Gorham were directed to the establishment of this claim. An address by Past Great Incohonee Hugh Latham, at Lancaster, Pa., October 21, 1857, referred to certain vague traditions which pointed to Fort Mifflin as its birth-place, and to the interval between the years 1812 and 1815 as the time of its birth.

In that part of the history devoted to extracts from the printed records of the Great Council of the United States, a detailed statement is made of the action taken by said body towards establishing the date of the Order, and obtaining possession of certain documents said to be in the hands of parties formerly members of the Society of Red Men, and to the subsequent acquisition of these documents, and their use by Brother Gorham and the authors of the present history.

The documents referred to had remained in the possession of Mr. James J. Loudenslager, a gilder and carver by trade, from the year 1831 until April 7, 1866, when they were acquired by

Brother Gorham in behalf of the Great Council of the United States.

The documents thus opportunely recovered are fragmentary in their nature, and not as full and complete as is necessary to positively establish historical facts. They contained sufficient, however, to fully illustrate what has been termed herein the second epoch in the history of the Improved Order of Red Men. Among the documents may be mentioned the Minute Book of the Society of Red Men, an account book between the Society and its members, printed notices of meetings, and other papers of a nature similar to what societies of this kind issue and use in the transaction of their business. Scattered through these books and papers are the names by which the members were known. The Society followed the Indian custom by giving to each paleface adopted a new name. This new name was used invariably when referring to the brother, and unless in possession of the key, the personal identity of each brother was safely hidden. If a brother was appointed to serve on a committee, the record would be made something after this fashion: "Voted, that a committee consisting of 'Black Wampum,' 'Split Log,' and 'Split Log's Brother,' be appointed to arrange an entertainment for the society at its next council fire."

Meagre though these documents are, they furnish sufficient evidence to establish the existence of the Society of Red Men, and, further, that many of its members "sent on mission to distant States," furnished in one instance the nucleus around which was gathered the reorganization in the present form of the Improved Order of Red Men.

Fort Mifflin is situated on the Delaware River, about four miles below Philadelphia, and was the only defensive work between that city and the Capes. It was an old British fort of the Revolution, and was located on the southeast extremity of Mud Island, a little below the mouth of the Schuylkill River. It was a strong redoubt, of irregular form, constructed of stones, bricks and earth, and was mounted with heavy guns. This fort still stands, but has been greatly strengthened and improved.

Fort Mifflin was garrisoned during the War of 1812, for a time, by a military company composed of the sons of the lead-

SOCIETY OF RED MEN.

ing citizens of Philadelphia. The organization was known by the name of "Junior Artillerists." At Fort Mifflin and among these volunteers originated the "Society of Red Men." This claim is based partly upon the Preamble of the Constitution of the "Red Men's Society of Pennsylvania," adopted at its reorganization in 1816 and which we reproduce as follows: —

PREAMBLE.

"We hold it as a sacred truth, that all men are born equally free, and are endowed by their great and beneficent Creator with the right of enjoying and defending their lives and liberties, and of pursuing their own happiness, so far as they conform to the known salutary principles laid down in the Constitution and laws of our beloved country.

"Impressed with a strong sense of the paramount duties we owed to our country for the blessings of liberty, civil and religious, which we enjoyed by the successful termination, by our forefathers, of the War of Independence, many of us entered into her services early in the year 1813 (as well as subsequently), and marched as volunteers from this city, Philadelphia, to garrison Fort Mifflin, then commanded by Captain James N. Barker and the lamented Lieutenant (Alexander John) Williams, (2) at a time of general alarm, and when our city was menaced by a British force.

"At that fort originated the Society of Red Men; instituted not only for social purposes, but to relieve each other in sickness or distress; and in the event of battle, solemnly pledged at all personal hazards firmly to adhere to each other in defence of our country's cause.

"Several years having elapsed, and many members expressing a wish that we should extend the views of the early members by forming ourselves into a Benevolent Society to relieve the distresses of each other, our wives, and children, we, therefore, whose names are hereunto subscribed, do declare that we have associated ourselves into a Benevolent Society, by the name, style, and title of the Red Men of Pennsylvania, pledging ourselves to observe the following rules and regulations with honor and good faith."

Fortunately we are able to sustain the claim made that the Society of Red Men originated at Fort Mifflin as above stated, in another and strongly corroborative manner. As will appear in this chapter, the Society of Red Men celebrated several important occasions as feast days of the Order. Among these were Washington's Birthday, February 22, and Saint Tamina Day, May 12. On February 22, 1825, Puyumannawaton, or "Great Light of the Council Fire," delivered "a talk" before the Red Men of Pennsylvania, a copy of which is among the documents in our possession. After eulogizing William Penn for his honesty and honor in his intercourse with the primitive Red Men, and Washington for his great wisdom and soldierly conduct, he uses language as follows: "I wish now to take a brief glance at the origin of our institution. In 1813, when a second attempt was made by Great Britain to subjugate the United States, a number of volunteer warriors from this city repaired to Fort Mifflin to repel, as far as they had power, the encroachments of the enemy. It was at this post, then commanded by Captain James N. Barker, that our present institution was formed. The original founders wished, by identifying themselves by name with the Aborigines of the country, to show their attachment to the soil they inhabited, which they held either by birth or adoption."

This declaration, taken in connection with the Preamble already quoted, is evidence sufficient of the organization at Fort Mifflin of a society of Red Men. When we learn the prominent position occupied by the person from whose talk we have quoted, it will be seen that he could not have been mistaken in the statement made by him. The member of the Society who made this talk was Joseph Kite, and as late as November, 1822, he was the Grand Recording Scribe of the Society. The name of Joseph Kite appears on the Muster Roll of the "Independent Blues," commanded by Captain William Mitchell, which company served on garrison duty with the "Junior Artillerists" at Fort Mifflin in March, 1813. From this it would be fair to assume that he was one of the original founders of the Society at the Fort. Mr. Kite was a printer by profession and a Quaker by descent. He seems to have been a man of warm heart and high character. He was an enthusiastic Red Man and his writings, as preserved in the minutes and communications by him to the officers of the Society, show a deep veneration for the Great Master of Life, and from his qualities of mind and heart, he seems to have justified the peculiar appropriateness of the title by which he had been invested,—"Great Light of the Council Fire." In 1823 he removed to Wilmington, Delaware, where he organized a Tribe which, as early as the 18th of the second moon, had adopted 86 palefaces.

From the information hereafter given, it will be learned that the Society of Red Men, like the St. Tammany Societies preceding it, used the forms and ceremonies and the language of the primitive Red Men. Indeed, for some time, the Society of Red Men and a branch of the St. Tammany Society existed together in the city of Philadelphia, and the names of several individuals appear upon the roll of membership in each of the two organizations at the same time. We feel justified, therefore, in asserting the claim that the inspiration which led to the selection of the name of " Red Men " for the organization formed at Fort Mifflin came from knowledge of, and probable membership in, the previous organizations known as St. Tammany Societies that existed from 1771. This fact is further sustained by the evidence submitted to the G. C. U. S., and upon which was based its action declaring 1771 as the date of the origin of the Order. With this preliminary statement we pass to the consideration of the work of the Society of Red Men as detailed in the Minute Book and other documents in the possession of the Great Council of the United States.

Early in the History of the Society we find the loss of its early records deplored. They seem to have fallen into the hands of persons not members of the organization, and it is presumed they were never recovered, because the first written record in the Minute Book is under date of 1821. Among the documents is a muster roll and account book, the latter containing the names of members of the organization and the dates of certain charges against them for dues, and credits of cash paid.

On some of the accounts credits are given for the year 1816. It was in this year also that a notice was inserted in a Philadelphia newspaper calling for a meeting of the members of the Society for the purpose of reorganization. This would indicate that the reorganization took place in the latter part of 1816. The scattering of the garrison of Fort Mifflin, and the discharge of the soldiers among whom the Society had been organized, at the close of the war, would account for the period between 1813 and 1816 while the Society was lying dormant. It is sufficiently explicit, however, to say that the reorganization took place in 1816. The account book referred to contains the names of 76 members, while in the latter part of the book are given the names of the members and the Indian name with its translation, assigned to each on his adoption into the Society. The custom seems to have prevailed also, on the death or discharge of a member, to confer his name and title upon some other member, or upon a paleface at adoption.

There were ten officers of the Society, as follows: Generalissimo, First and Second Captain-Generals, Grand Recording Scribe, Treasurer, Grand Door-Keeper, and four Tryors, who were sometimes called Warriors. The Generalissimo was the presiding officer of the Society with almost absolute power in the matter of decisions on the ceremonies and legislation of the Society. The First and Second Captain-Generals were the special aids of the Generalissimo to assist him while present and act for him in his absence, performing duties similar to those now exercised by the Junior and Senior Sagamores. There was a limitation to their power, however, unless acting under special authority from the Generalissimo in certain cases. Thirteen members constituted a quorum. Membership was limited to citizens of the United States, and admission was denied to any person owning or holding a slave.

Applicants for membership were proposed by a brother and referred to a committee which inquired into the character and fitness of each applicant and ascertained if he was a citizen of the United States. The report having been made, a ballot was taken which the laws required to be unanimous or the applicant was rejected. It was not customary to initiate candidates on the night of election, although the constitution was sometimes suspended to permit this to be done.

At the admission of a candidate he was placed in charge of the Grand Door-Keeper who made the necessary preparations and presented him to the Generalissimo. He was required to answer certain questions regarding his own citizenship and principles, and his motive in desiring to become a Red Man. His answers being satisfactory he was by unanimous consent allowed to proceed.

When he was put to trial, to test his sincerity and to prepare his mind for the instruction about to be given, he was warned that "Red Men were men without fear, and that none but such could be engrafted on the Tribe." Having "passed the ordeal, and come out as a man should who knows no fear," he was

THE RAIN MAKER.

again presented to the Generalissimo for further instructions. Among the instructions quoted as coming from the old manuscripts may be mentioned these: "Red Men administer no oaths binding you to any political or religious creed; they bind neither your hands nor your feet; as you enter their wigwam so you depart, a free man." . . . "Here we sit in the full confidence of each other's friendship, bound together by the strong ties of brotherly love. The motto of the Society is Freedom, and while claiming its privileges and blessings for ourselves, we aim no less than to exert Toleration to others."

"Being thus united as Red Men, prudence admonishes us to exact from those who would become affiliated with us a simple pledge of honor, as an assurance of fidelity and trustworthiness." . . . "Are you willing to give such assurance?" The answer being favorable the instructions continued. "Then, sir, looking upon you as a man of honor, one who regards his word as binding on his conscience as an oath possibly can be, we bid you proceed, and caution you that all you may hear or see in the wigwam are the secrets of Red Men, and must be kept inviolate."

During the ceremony he underwent the Rite of Investiture, in which a new name was conferred upon him by which he was always referred to in the councils of the Tribe. He was required to remember this name, and record is made of the expulsion of one unfortunate brother who had forgotten his name of adoption on the night of admission.

The names conferred seem to have had reference to the calling or profession of the palefaces adopted. For instance, William Muirhead was the proprietor of a house of public entertainment, and he received as his name Withea of Missouri or "Hospitality." Sometimes the relationship of a father and son or of two brothers was indicated by the name assigned, as for instance, William Marley, who was given the name signifying "Moose Deer" while his son was called "Young Moose Deer."

It will be noticed that the titles used by the officers of the Society were military in their character. This may have been due to the military origin of the organization, and the fact that soldiers exclusively organized it. In the secret ceremonies of the organization Indian titles alone were used.

The means of communication between the central organization and its branches in the various States were limited, and this required a large number of subordinate officers, each of whom had his own staff of assistants. These officers ranged from the Generalissimo, who was the Commander-in-Chief of all of the Red Men, and the presiding chief of the Society while in council, down through the various grades of Captain-General, Lieutenant-General, etc., to the brothers of the Order. The grades of rank were indicated by emblems worn upon badges consisting of a bright red ribbon about twelve inches long and two and one-fourth inches wide. The emblems upon the badges were formed by variations of six-pointed and five-pointed stars, scalping knife and tomahawk, with silver and gold bullion fringe.

The records speak of Generalissimo, First and Second Captain-Generals, six Lieutenant-Generals, twenty Major-Generals, forty Brigadier-Generals, and an unknown number of Brevet Brigadier-Generals, Lieutenant-Colonels, Colonels, etc. The Lieutenant-Colonels, of whom there were one hundred or more, were aids to the superior officers. Besides these there were ten Kings, several Half-Kings, ten Majors, nine Brevet-Majors, nineteen Captains, twelve Brevet-Captains, seven Lieutenants, six Sachems, seventeen Chiefs, twenty-five Old Men in Council, and three Squaw Sachems.

It must be remembered that each of these in addition to his military title had the Indian name and its signification, as conferred upon him at the time of his adoption.

By the assistance of these subordinate officers the Society was extended into various parts of the country. The documents and records of the Society contain the reports made by these brothers "absent on mission" and indicate with a clearness sufficient for all practical purposes, the places where branches of the organization were established. The means of communication between distant parts of the country being at that time very crude, this multiplicity of officers and complicated system of official machinery was adopted by the founders of the Society to "lengthen the chain of friendship," and "extend its principles." The rule seems to have been that whenever a qualified brother intended to visit a distant locality either for temporary or permanent residence, he was given the necessary authority to instruct palefaces or establish a Tribe if opportunity should offer, just as at the present time a Deputy Great Incohonee may be appointed for the purpose of establishing a Tribe of the Improved Order of Red Men in territory where none exists. If his residence was to be temporary, he was recorded as being "on mission." If he succeeded in organizing a Tribe or branch of the Society at his new residence, then he was recorded as being "on command" or "commanding."

As an illustration of what is here stated, there is a record of Joseph Higginbottom whose Indian name was Nescoureaosca, or "Black Cat's Father." He was thirty-second Brigadier-General and fifteenth Aid to the Generalissimo. He is on the record as being "on mission to Virginia." A number of other brothers are recorded as being "on mission," but the locality is not stated.

Early in the year 1818, it is recorded that Minowakanton, or "Ironstone," fifth Major-General, John M. Burns, received a commission and was appointed "General-in-Chief of all the Southern Tribes," and on the "twelfth moon of Snows" of that year, he kindled a council fire in the city of Charleston, S.C. The tribe thus organized in Charleston, it is stated, prospered beyond all expectation until the month of Heat, 1820, when, owing to a local disease, the members became scattered and the Tribe broken up. John M. Burns, in a letter to the Generalissimo, at that time "Black Wampum," under date of the month of Leaves, the 5th, 1826, says: —

"I was appointed in 1818, General-in-Chief of all the Southern Tribes, by our lamented Generalissimo, 'Split Log.' Since the death of that great counsellor I have not held any communication with the Northern Tribes. Our Tribe held their council fire in the month of Snows, the 12th, 1818, and prospered beyond all expectations, and continued so until the month of Heat, 1820, but owing to a local disease coming among the Tribe which proved fatal and carried off my chief aids, 'Peruvian Bark' and 'Mainspring,' which caused a great chasm in the Council. They were buried with the usual honors of Red Men, beneath the wigwam, with their tomahawks. The plague continued, which caused the Tribe to scatter all over the wilderness, taking

with them their squaws and papooses, and since that have never been re-united, although I have often been solicited to call them together : but I find it difficult in consequence of the Tribe being squandered all over the great Forest. 'Eagle Eye' holds an appointment under government in Maryland, and 'Walk-in-the-Water' has another in Florida, and 'Little Oak' has an appointment in Mexico ; so you will see that it is hard to form the Tribe after losing so many warriors and learned counsellors. However, I shall always obey the orders of the Generalissimo and subscribe myself,
"Your Red Brother,
"MANOWHUCKINGTON or 'GENERAL IRONSTONE.'"

The institution of this Tribe at Charleston is peculiar for another fact, for it will be remembered that the third article of the By-Laws declared that no person owning or holding a slave could be admitted.

Without attempting to give in proper chronological order, the assignments of the various officers on mission, mention may be made of various commissions issued to show the introduction of the Society into various places. William Smart, known as Wampalooshewaytie, or "Wheat Straw," was promoted to the rank of Colonel on the 14th of March, 1821, and sent on mission to Alabama, although no record is made of the result. In like manner certain officers are recorded as being commissioned to command in New Jersey, although the date is not stated. Elisha L. Antrim, Major-General, Voibisonthe, or "Strong Water," is entered on the roll as commanding in New Jersey. The probabilities are that the Order was established in that State about the time that it was taken to South Carolina, between 1818 and 1821.

There is likewise an uncertainty as to the exact date of the introduction of the Society into the State of New York. The name of Kanytariys of Oneida, or "Light Wood," eleventh Brigadier-General, Richard Lough, appears on the roll as "commanding in New York." Under date of the 10th, fourth moon, 1823, on page 69 of the Minute Book, there is record of the admission into the Philadelphia Society of a certain number of persons who were entered as lumber merchants. There is also among the original papers, dated September 26, 1824, a list of 64 members as compiled by John B. Sarzien, whose Indian name was Annenenwago, or "Balsam Apple," who is entered as Colonel commanding of the New York Tribe.

We find recorded the application for recognition of "the benevolent Tribe of Nassau, established in the village of Brooklyn on the Island of Nassau, in the State of New York; and to form a mutual and friendly correspondence with the Tribe." This authority was unanimously granted, as shown by subsequent references in the minutes and correspondence with the Tribe.

It is assumed that a Tribe was established at Lancaster, Pa., some time between 1819 and 1821, and among the documents preserved, is a letter signed by "Smooth Stone," General at Lancaster, written to the Generalissimo. The letter concludes as follows: "We have formed our little wigwam into a beneficial society, and wish very much that you would do the same. We have a dollar admission, and three five penny bits a month, which goes into our funds for the relief of a distressed or sick brother, and we are intending shortly to raise it."

On page 16 of the Minute Book the fact is recorded that "Wetahoopeto, or 'Yellow Cat,' George Taylor, was brevetted from the rank of Brigadier to that of Major-General, and received a special certificate with power to make Red Men in New Orleans and to initiate them into the signs of the Tribe, with a request that he should, from time to time, report to the Red Men of Pennsylvania, the situation of the nation over which he is appointed Sachem."

The Order was introduced into Delaware by Joseph Kite, whose Indian name, as previously stated, was Puyumannawaton, or "Great Light of the Council Fire." While the precise date of the institution in that State cannot be given, we find his name recorded as having attained the rank of twenty-ninth Brigadier-General and as "commanding in Delaware," and on page 55 of the Minute Book, under date of the 18th of the second moon, 1823, it is stated that "the Chief of the Delaware Tribe reported that since he had received power to initiate brethren, that 86 persons had been adopted in the Tribe and received the appropriate signs."

Reading, Pa., may claim to have had a branch of the organization which continued its existence long after the reorganization of the Society into the Improved Order of Red Men at Baltimore in 1833. On page 147 of the Minute Book it is recorded that "the Generalissimo having confidence in our Brother Bowstring (whose other name was Nementon, George Priest, Tailor), resident in the Borough of Reading, in the State of Pennsylvania, promoted him to the rank of Brigadier-General, and gave to him full powers to open a wigwam in the Borough of Reading, and to initiate, with strict precaution and in due form, into the Reading Tribe of Red Men, all such white men as wish to become Red Men, if on examination they shall meet the approbation of the Council sitting at his council fire."

This Tribe maintained a prosperous and long-continued existence, although not alluded to in the records of the Mother Society. On the 9th of October, 1849, the Great Council of Pennsylvania of the Improved Order of Red Men instructed its Great Chief of Records to correspond with the Tribe of Red Men at Reading for the purpose of inducing them to come under the jurisdiction of said Great Council. Nothing definite seems to have been accomplished, and on the 10th of April, 1850, the matter was transferred by the Great Council from the Great Chief of Records to the Committee of Correspondence. However, action was taken January 16, 1851, when a resolution was adopted as follows:—

"*Resolved*, That they be admitted on the payment of the charter fee, and that their past chiefs be not entitled to seats in this Great Council until they shall have passed the stumps in the Improved Order of Red Men."

On the 15th of September, 1854, the matter was brought to the attention of the Great Council of the United States by a series of resolutions in which the organization was referred to as the "Ancient" Order of Red Men, located in the city of Reading, Pa. This term was used not because it was the title of the Tribe, but to distinguish it from the *Improved* Order of Red Men. The Society at Reading was the "Reading Tribe of Red Men." Again, on the 19th of October, 1854, immediately following the council of the Great Council of the United States, the Great Council of Pennsylvania adopted resolutions for carrying into effect the legislation of the Great

Council of the United States. It may be assumed that the ancient organization was absorbed by the Improved Order soon after, as there is no further reference to the matter on record.

A Tribe was organized at Germantown, Pa., now the city of Philadelphia, for, on page 303 of the Minute Book is recorded the fact that "Brother Big Buttonwood Tree (Muskekittee Wahtawaw) was appointed Chief of the Germantown Tribe."

A Tribe must have existed also at Albany, N.Y., for on page 341 of the Minute Book it is recorded that "Brigadier-General 'Northern Warrior' was appointed Chief of the Albany Tribe, and in due form, and in open council (by a warrant handed to him), permitted and empowered to open a wigwam, etc., in the city of Albany, in the State of New York, under the title, and name of the Albany Tribe of Red Men, etc., dated 13th day of the 6th moon, 1826."

Concerning the introduction of the Society of Red Men into the city of Baltimore, and the institution there of branches which afterwards, through the individuals composing them, became the foundation for the reorganization into the Improved Order of Red Men, we defer extended mention until we reach the chapter devoted to the establishment of the Order in Maryland. It is sufficient at this time to state that the Society of Red Men was organized in Baltimore, and that at least two of its most prominent members moved to that city from Philadelphia, one of whom, Richard Marley, afterwards became Great Incohonee of the Improved Order of Red Men.

The other, William Muirhead, held high rank in the Order in Philadelphia. His Indian name was Withea of Missouri or "Hospitality."

The first Generalissimo of the Order was Francis Shallus, whose Indian name was Yeougheowanewago or "Split Log." He was born about the year 1773. He was possessed of considerable literary talent, and in 1817 published a work in two volumes entitled "Chronological Tables for every day in the year." It is also stated that he was an engraver, and that he personally engraved the plates on which were printed the early notes of the old United States bank.

Mr. Thomas J. Loudenslager, from whom were obtained the

old documents relating to the Society of Red Men, is quoted as authority for the statement that Mr. Shallus, through his maternal grandmother, was a direct descendant of the Indian race, and that to this fact was due the great interest he felt in establishing the Society upon the manners and customs of that race. The early literature of the Order shows the mark of his ability, and the legislation was undoubtedly shaped by his desires and influence.

When the Society was reorganized in 1816 the Preamble indicates that the intention was to make it a benevolent Society exactly as it is at the present time, in which should be paid a regular, stipulated amount each week in cases of sickness or disability, which payment should be made as a right and not as a gratuity. For this purpose the admission fee was fixed at $2.00 and the dues at 25 cents per month. For some reason which is not recorded the original idea was changed and the payment of a stipulated amount weekly was discontinued, and the Society became purely charitable, dispensing relief to needy members when requested. References are frequent in the Minute Book where the needy condition of some Brother is brought to the attention of the Society, and either direct appropriation from the funds made to relieve him, or a committee chosen to raise funds for that purpose.

Francis Shallus had been a member of Philadelphia Lodge, No. 72, F. & A. M., from August 13, 1803, to April 9, 1808, at which latter date he resigned his membership. It would seem from this that he was not a member of the Masonic Fraternity at the time of the establishment of the Society of Red Men. Whether his connection with that organization influenced the change from a beneficial to a charitable organization the records do not indicate, but that the change was made is abundantly shown by the documents in our possession. Mr. Shallus "was intensely American in sentiment and feeling, and a close student of American history, particularly that portion of it treating of the manners and customs of its primitive inhabitants." His familiarity with the Masonic Fraternity probably gave him the experience necessary for outlining the structure of the organization which he instituted; but there is nothing in the ritualistic work, the forms and ceremonies, the legislation, or the interior workings, to suggest in the slightest degree the Masonic Fraternity. The Society of Red Men, like its successor, the Improved Order of Red Men, stands original and distinct from any other existing organization.

Francis Shallus died on the 12th day of November, 1821, after a painful illness, in the 48th year of his age. Every effort seems to have been made by the Society to render proper tribute of respect to the memory of the dead Generalissimo; but the records indicate that some wrangling occurred by reason of which the eulogy on the character and services of the Generalissimo, which had been provided for, was not delivered.

During the illness of the Generalissimo it is evident that much anxiety was felt among the members about the safety of the papers and documents belonging to the Society which were then in his possession, and at the council held November 7, 1821, a resolution was passed providing for the appointment of a committee to request from the Generalissimo all papers, books, and documents in his possession relating to the business of the Red Men's Society. Had it been possible to obtain these papers, as contemplated in that resolution, there is not the slightest doubt but that the complete connection between the Society of Red Men of 1816 and the organization at Fort Mifflin would have been established, as well as information beyond price concerning the correspondence between the Generalissimo and the members of the Society "on mission," to whom he had intrusted the work of establishing branches of the organization in distant States.

On page 3 of the Minute Book, under date of July 7, 1822, is recorded a resolution which was adopted providing for the appointment of a committee to inquire concerning the paper and books formerly in the possession of the late Generalissimo, and report at the next meeting, the committee consisting of "Great Light of the Council Fire," "Racer," and "Deep River." July 9, 1822, this committee made a report which was as follows:—

To the Red Men in Council assembled.

The Brothers, by you delegated, to inquire for, and collect, the papers and documents of the Red Men of Pennsylvania, lay upon your Council board the following Report:—

By a train of unfortunate events, following each other in rapid succession, the papers and documents of Red Men, came into the possession of White Men. — The Committee are not disposed to dwell upon the causes; — the individual most implicated having passed the dark river which lies at the foot of the Hill of Life! A Red Man has with trouble and Expense redeemed them, or a portion of them, for it is impossible yet to ascertain in what direction the winds of Misfortune may have wafted them. The Brother who holds what has been collected of them has asked no remuneration but your committee deem he should have remuneration — for they know that the Great Spirit, the good Manetho, delights in justice! it is the mantle that envelopes him when he sits upon his throne! They have therefore come to this conclusion, —

That $2.62½ be paid to Brother Otter and that the documents of the Tribe of Columbia be delivered to the Generalissimo — and request that a new Committee be appointed to search if other records may be found, and to report to any succeeding Council Fire.

PUYUHTOMMAKON, or, GREAT LIGHT OF COUNCIL FIRE.
DEEP RIVER
WANKAPONCHET, or THE RACER
The Committee.

Dated, the 8th day of the Seventh Moon, 1822.

The above extract is printed just as it appears on the Minute Book, the punctuation and capitalization being followed. Several errors appear, one of the most notable being in the name of "Great Light of the Council Fire," which should be Puyummannawaton instead of as above recorded.

The report was adopted, and "Black Wampum" and "Otter" were added to the committee. A subscription was taken up among the Brothers present by which $2.92½ were collected and given to the committee for the purpose of reimbursing Brother "Otter" for the amount of money which he had paid out as reported by the committee. The Brother "Black Wampum" here referred to was George Knorr, who succeeded Francis Shallus as Generalissimo, and whose Indian title was Lappopetung or "Black Wampum." The committee seems to have met with partial success in recovering the documents because under date of December 23, 1823, a resolution was adopted providing for "a book into which should be entered in regular form all the Minutes in the hands of the Generalissimo, or elsewhere existing and attainable, and the Minutes of all future Council Fires of the Red Men within the city of Philadelphia and its suburbs."

SOCIETY OF RED MEN. 215

On the 22d of January, 1824, the Grand Recording Scribe Wiverwaski, or "Red Oak," reported that all the Minutes up to that date had been copied into a book which he presented for the inspection of the members, the Minutes commencing with the 25th of the sixth Moon, 1822, and continuing down to January 24, 1824. For some reason, possibly because they were not then "attainable," this book does not include early Minutes of the 7th, 9th, 14th, and 20th, of November, 1821, which still exist in manuscript form. A committee was appointed to examine the book, and on February 3d the committee reported that the examination had been made and that "the thanks of the Tribe were due to Brother 'Red Oak' for his zeal, diligence, and general correctness in transcribing the previous Minutes." The Minute Book here referred to lies before us as we write, the Minutes therein recorded slightly faded during the years that have passed, but as plain and legible as when written 69 years ago. They form a connecting link with the past of inestimable value, and give information concerning the Society of Red Men not to be obtained elsewhere, and without which the preparation of this period of the History of the Improved Order of Red Men would have been impossible.

Francis Shallus, as already stated, was succeeded in the position of Generalissimo, by George Knorr, who had been First Captain-General under him, and whose name appears on the Minute Book, and the documents of the Society, as Lappopetung or "Black Wampum." Mr. Knorr was a baker by trade, whose residence and place of business at the time he attained the rank of Generalissimo was on Sixth street between Market and Arch. His election took place, probably, some time between November 30 and December 12, 1821. The record of his election must have been in the Minutes which were not recovered, among the documents in the possession of the white men as above referred to.

The Minute Book at this period indicates the prosperity then attending the Society. Not only was a council held regularly each month, but special and adjourned councils were frequently necessary in order to receive applications from white men and arrange for their initiation. As an indication of the growth of the Society, and the manner of proposition and of conferring a new name upon the newly admitted Brother, we submit the following record for the 25th of the fifth Moon, 1822, at which time we find this entry: "The following white men were proposed, and after going through the usual forms were accepted and initiated," viz.:—

Name.	Name Received.	Proposed by
John Douglass, Magistrate	Flinty Warrior	Otter.
Joseph Keene	Malt	Hard Bread.
Samuel Douglass	War Pole	Otter.
Michael Kneas	Big Axe	Great Chief.
William Taylor	Silver Heels	White Wolf.
William Warwick	War Club	Otter.
Joseph Crumback	Black Rock	Otter.
James Vandergrift	Black Fox	Bird Tail King.

We could quote innumerable similar instances scattered through the Minute Book, which would virtually require a reproduction of the records; but the above is sufficient to indicate the fact that only the new name given a Brother was used to describe him after his admission, and that when a white man was proposed his name and occupation were inserted in the record together with the name of the Brother proposing him and the name assigned to him by the Society. We find a slip of paper among the documents stating that at a certain period, the number of members shown upon the Minute Book was found by actual count to be 584, and it was thought that these did not include all. This, of course, had reference only to the home Society at Philadelphia.

It is proper to consider the charitable work of the organization, and abundant evidence of this is given in the Minute Book. During the five years of the history of the Society therein recorded in detail, frequent applications for assistance from needy brothers are considered. Sometimes the application is made by the individual himself, and at others by some brother in his behalf. It may be well to refer to a few of these instances, as an evidence of the work done by the Society, and the manner in which action was taken at each succeeding council.

Under date of July 1, 1823, a petition was received from Brother Abbitiby, or "Frog," notifying the Tribe that he was sick, and that his family was in distress. The application for relief bore the indorsement of "Little Painter," vouching for Brother "Frog" as an industrious, honest, sober, and well behaved gentleman. This was further subscribed to by "A. H. R.," who felt himself in duty bound to give Brother "Frog" the character of an honest man. By this it will be inferred that good character was a passport to favor when relief was needed or requested from the Society. The report at the next meeting showed that Brother "Frog" was ill and had a wife and two children to maintain, and that his situation required immediate aid. An amount was collected from the members present to be paid to him.

The case above cited is typical of many similar recorded in the Minute Book. The plan of relief seems to have required that application should be made to the Society either by the brother himself or by some other brother in his behalf. This application was indorsed by one or more brothers, a committee was appointed to make proper investigation, and on the report of the committee a collection for the relief of the petitioner was taken up among the members present. In nearly every case recorded, the condition of the applicant seems to have justified the relief given.

Among the cases thus relieved may be mentioned, also, that of "Blue Hills," who applied for aid, stating he had a wife and three small children to support, and that he had lost the use of his arms. The committee appointed to investigate the case found that it was deplorable indeed. He had not been able to do anything towards the support of his family for the preceding five months, and had been under the necessity of selling his household furniture to procure bread for his wife and children. When the committee entered his room it found him lying on an old rug with a pillow under his head. His arms were of little or no service to him, and he could not feed himself. A collection was at once taken up, and the afflicted brother relieved.

Not only was the charity conferred upon sick and disabled brothers, but the watchful care of the organization was also extended to the widows and orphans of those who had crossed the dark river.

As early as November 19, 1822, record is made of a special council fire kindled at the wigwam of Brother "Turtle Shell" to make arrangements for attending the funeral of Brother Hassunimesut or "Mulberry." At this council it was resolved to attend the funeral of the late brother. This seems to indicate that "burying the dead" was also an object of affiliation.

On Sunday afternoon, April 18, 1824, about seventy of the brethren attended the funeral of Brother Andastakas, or "Badger," John M. Boddy, in accordance with the request of the brother made prior to his death. On the return of the members to the Wigwam a collection was taken up for the assistance of the late brother's widow and orphans. On the following day the amount was presented to the widow, who returned her grateful acknowledgments for it to the Red Men's Society. Various other allusions are made to similar action on the part of the Society, but the attendance at funerals was evidently purely voluntary, for, on December 13, 1825, a committee was appointed to consider the propriety of establishing a rule requiring attendance of members at the funeral of deceased Red Men.

Under date of January 6, 1826, the following was adopted:—

"*Resolved*, That hereafter all monies drawn from the funds of the Red Men's Society, or that shall be voluntarily contributed by the brethren individually, for the relief of distressed brothers, shall be paid over to the applicant, by the person presenting the petition, in the presence of the Grand Recording Scribe, or in his absence the Assisting Scribe, or some other brother, whom the presiding-officer may appoint for that purpose; and that a written acknowledgment (from the applicant) for the money paid to him, or them, shall be produced at the first meeting after payment has been made."

January 10, 1826, a voluntary subscription was taken up in aid of the family of "Calumet Man," and in addition thereto the sum of ten dollars was appropriated from the funds of the Society for the same charitable purpose. In accordance with the resolution above recorded, a receipt was subsequently presented from the widow, for the donations received by her from the Society amounting to $15.38.

We have referred to this phase of the organization to illustrate the manner adopted by the Society for providing relief. It must be remembered by those familiar with the systematic work of modern beneficial societies that at the time of which we are writing these societies were in embryo. The Independent Order of Odd Fellows was organized in 1819, three years later than the reorganization of the Society of Red Men. In many characteristics the two organizations were similar. The meeting places were the large rooms, or halls, connected with the taverns or places of public entertainment, for the very good reason that no other meeting places existed. The beneficial work of these organizations was an evolution from the circumstances that called them into existence.

The experience of the early days, as recorded in the Minute Book of the Society of Red Men, showed the necessity of a regular system for mutual relief, as otherwise the burden came upon the generous and the faithful. The faithful were constant in their attendance at the councils of the Society. Being constant in their attendance, their generosity was appealed to in every case requiring relief. This suggested the adoption of regulations, whereby a regular contribution should be made by each member, to provide a fund from which assistance could be donated as required. Voluntary contributions continued, but there was always provision made for larger donations in cases of extreme need. Thus out of this experience has come the magnificent financial system of the present day, under which, it may with truth be said, that "we visit the sick, relieve the distressed, bury the dead, and educate the orphan."

The frailty of human nature does not lack for illustration even in a beneficial Society. Doubtless this may be accounted for by the fact that an organization banded together for the highest and best duties that can engage the thought of men, must still depend on human nature for the material by which it is managed. No patent process has yet been devised by which the individual man, narrow of brain, sordid of nature, selfish of impulse, can suddenly be transformed into a model of generosity simply by being admitted into a fraternal or benevolent institution. The most that can be hoped for is to attract as large a proportion as possible of individuals, in whose hearts beat the impulse of humanity and the desire to benefit mankind, and to give to each other mutual relief and assistance; keeping out, as far as possible, the selfish and designing. Thus we may unite, for a common purpose, men of kindred thought and sympathy, and thereby accomplish by united effort the good which with individual action is impossible.

We have made the above statement to explain the fact, that through the Minute Book appears frequent record of the discipline inflicted upon delinquent brothers. The extreme penalty was inflicted when for any dereliction a Brother was "tomahawked." This was the figurative term used by the Society for the word "expelled," and this fact should be borne in mind by those members of the Improved Order of Red Men who are prone to use the nomenclature of the Order in a slipshod and meaningless manner. The records show that the discipline of the Society was inflicted on men of high rank as well as on the more humble members. Yet, notwithstanding the necessity for this discipline, the Society continued to increase in strength and in general prosperity, as is proved by the constant accession of new members.

It is necessary at this time to consider that phase of the organization clearly made manifest in the records on the Minute Book, and indicative of the elements of conviviality which seem to have been inseparable from all fraternal organizations of that period. This convivial element, it is claimed, finally produced such a degeneration in the Society as to disgust the better element, and cause the reorganization in its present form, and the incorporation of the word "Improved" in its title. While this may all be true, criticism is in a measure disarmed by the fact already stated that conviviality was not confined to the Society of Red Men alone, and by the further notable fact that the legitimate benevolent work of the Society was never interfered with or sacrificed to gratify convivial inclinations. The Minute Book and manuscript records show that during the period of more than 10 years almost every Council was "adjourned for social purposes." At no time, however, is there any record that refreshments were taken into the wigwam or permitted there while the council fire was burning, or that any funds of the organization were appropriated for that purpose. It is undoubtedly true, that after the council fire was quenched, and "social purposes" were indulged in, some of the members had, what may be truthfully designated, "a halcyon and vociferous time." There were bounds beyond which the members could not pass in their hilarious celebrations, because the Minute Book records the punishment of members who allowed their unfortunate appetites to get the better of their reason, and were guilty of conduct meriting condemnation and punishment.

As has already been remarked the most convenient places for holding the Councils of the Society were public taverns, and many members were keepers of these places. Naturally the bar attached to these taverns was a constant source of temptation to the brethren assembled. While such a condition of affairs could not exist in 1893, it must be remembered that it was considered entirely proper in 1823, and must be judged by the customs and opinions of that time rather than by those of the present day.

Among the documents preserved is a copy of a notice, issued early in 1821, calling for a meeting of the brethren at the corner of 10th and Arch Streets, when a "Free and Easy will commence." This call is signed Yeogheowanewago, or "Split Log," Generalissimo, that being the name and title of Francis Shallus.

Among the documents are copies of songs written for use at the Red Men's "Free and Easy." We give these songs as follows: —

RED MEN'S SONG.

TUNE — *Tars of Columbia.*

Ye Sons of Columbia to Freedom Aspire.
While cheerful we sit round our Grand Council Fire,
Our heroes departed shall have the first toast,
And next our loved country — our pride and our boast.

CHORUS. — For her cause we'll defend until our lives end,
For Red Men their country will never desert
While Fame nerves their arm or blood warms their heart.

When the General has kindled the Fire so bright,
His commands we'll obey with joy and delight;
If he orders our Tribe the hatchet to wield,
Our war-song we'll sing, and repair to the field.

CHORUS. — To combat with those who are Liberty's foes,
For Red Men are always fearless and bold,
Be't in Midsummer's heat or in stern Winter's cold.

No party dissensions our Councils distract;
Each Red Man is free to think, speak and act;
For Freedom's our motto, Toleration our aim;
Friendship our watchword, and Red Men our name.

CHORUS. — Then smoke the pipe of peace, and bid all discord cease;
May the chain of the Red Men never lose a link,
But extend and increase till Creation shall sink.

Now, let every Red Man, a bumper in hand,
Around our Council Fire in due order stand —
Fill your glasses, my boys, drink the toast I will give,
Here's to all faithful Red Men and long may they live.

CHORUS. — For our Council Fire never will expire,
While we have power the hatchet to raise,
Or breath left to kindle its vestal-like blaze.

The following was sung to the tune of

SANDY AND JENNY.

Hail Red Men and Brethren! hail this happy night,
Here assembled in Council our Wigwam looks bright:
Your Grand Chief, altho' far advanced in years,
Before you again on his duty appears.

His Generals on each side, in new array stand,
Always ready and willing to obey or command;
The Warriors at their station in martial array,
Are ready at a call to come forth and obey.

The fears of a White Man, to test and to try,
To their station the Warriors like light'ning do fly;
Their Tomahawk, War-Club, and Long Knife display,
Take charge of the stranger and lead him away.

Now as Freedom's our motto, toleration our aim,
Friendship our watchword, Red Men our name,
Let sobriety, good order, always be found here,
In Freedom's cause fight, as Red Men without fear.

And again Brethren Red Men, permit me to say,
When you enter a Wigwam leave discord away;
For no party dissensions can here a place find,
No broils nor no quarrels, you'll leave those behind.

> Now as Red Men united in sweet Friendship's band,
> If a poor worthy brother who in need of it stand,
> Asks relief, give your mite, be it large be it small,
> For good actions like those Manitou rewards all.
>
> When our business is finish'd, be it short be it long,
> Let's be merry together and sing a good song,
> Drink a little strong water our strength to increase,
> Spend the evening together in friendship and peace.

Among the members there seem to have been some who appreciated a practical joke, for we find a manuscript song, endorsed "Obadiah Porritt, Plumber, Reading," evidently sung to the tune of "Derry Down," of which the following is a copy and which may be properly entitled

WHEAT SHEAF'S NARROW ESCAPE.

> "Wheat Sheaf" is a baker, oft it has been said,
> Around this fair city he serves out his bread;
> Of loaves that are large, and loaves that are small,
> And cakes nicely sweetened, he can please you all.
>   Derry Down.
>
> For which the good people, with little delay,
> Call on Brother "Wheat Sheaf" and give him his pay;
> One day being merry, as I have been told,
> He had all his pockets well filled up with gold.
>   Derry Down.
>
> To a meeting of Red Men he went in full spunk,
> Where, with singing and drinking, he got pretty drunk;
> Two wily young Red Men, so sly, and so proud,
> While he lay asleep, slipped him into a shroud.
>   Derry Down.
>
> On the top of a board they laid him full tight,
> Then went to the surgeon in dead of the night;
> "We have brought you a baker, just fit for dissection —
> A plump little fellow, he'll suit to perfection."
>   Derry Down.
>
> The doctor, well pleased, said, "What is your price?"
> "A guinea apiece," both cried in a trice;
> Then quick by the doctor the guineas were paid,
> And in a dark room the poor baker was laid.
>   Derry Down.

After locking the door, he went to bed with his wife ;
"To-morrow," said he, "I shall use my long knife."
Thus the baker and doctor both peaceably lay,
Till birds by their melody hailed a new day.
    Derry Down.

The baker got dry, became anxious for drink ;
He tried for to move, but he hardly could think ;
So tight was he bound, from his feet to his head,
He thought for awhile that he surely was dead.
    Derry Down.

At last he got angry, he used all his strength,
And bursting the cords, he was loosened at length ;
Looks round for a pitcher, got hold of a skull
He tried for to drink, but it was as dry as a hull.
    Derry Down.

He fumbled around, but naught could descry,
Save bones of all sizes lay piled up so high ;
Amid these sad trials, he frightened was, sure,
When he heard the doctor approaching the door.
    Derry Down.

It unlocked ; was opened, and who should be there,
The doctor, with his long knife ; he sunk in despair ;
But recovering, he gave him a pretty hard thump,
To the foot of the stairs it sent the doctor quite plump.
    Derry Down.

"Wheat Sheaf," rushed to the street with lion-like sway,
He knocked over all that obstructed his way ;
He never again got so drunk, it is said ;
Nor the doctor bought a baker till he knew he was dead.
    Derry Down.

The following is added as an example of the

RED MEN'S PARTING SONG.

As Red Men, oft together again may we meet,
In Friendship united, with discord at our feet,
No party dissensions, nor broils of any kind
Shall enter our wigwam, we will leave them behind.

CHORUS. — For Freedom's our motto, Toleration our aim,
    Friendship's our watchword, Red Men our name ;
    If danger should threaten, together we'll fly,
    As Red Men, we'll conquer without fear, or die.

Our wigwam's in good order; our Council fire bright,
To brighten Friendship's sweet chain, we've assembled to-night;
Then may this bright chain of Friendship ne'er lose a link,
But extend and increase 'till creation shall sink.

CHORUS. — For Freedom's our motto, etc.

When the General commands, with pride Red Men obey;
But a tyrant over Red Men shall never hold sway;
As Red Men independent we together will fight,
With our Tomahawk, our War Club, and our Scalping-knife bright.

CHORUS. — For Freedom's our motto, etc.

In Brother ——'s wigwam how pleasantly we sit,
We drink and we sing, and talk while the moments by flit:
Our landlord's kind and good, his wish is all to please —
He keeps good gin and brandy, he keeps good bread and cheese.

CHORUS. — Then, Red Men united, enjoy life while you can,
Old age is coming on, and life's but a span;
Then fill your cans and glasses, a toast now I'll give,
"Success to Red Men's squaws, and happy may they live."

And when our part here we have acted in love,
And we shall be called to the wigwam above,
May the Great Spirit guide us to that happy land,
Where, as brothers united, we'll join in one band.

CHORUS. — For Freedom's our motto, etc.

And if in life's journey a Red Man you shall find
In sore distress, then to him be good and kind;
And if 'tis in your power to assuage his grief,
Stretch forth the hand of Friendship and give him relief.

CHORUS. — For Freedom's our motto, etc.

For in Friendship united, Red Men will stand,
In Friendship as brothers, joined hand in hand;
And if in life's journey a Red Man you shall find
In distress, we again say, be to him good and kind.

CHORUS. — For Freedom's our motto, etc.

Of course these songs abound in allusions to the prominent idea of all social gatherings at that time, wherein the wine cup held full sway. It is no reproach upon the organization to record historical facts. While we are not called upon to defend anything that is wrong, we feel it may with truth be said, that the convivial element of the Society of Red Men at the period at which we write was no more pronounced and had no more control upon the patriotic, fraternal, and benevolent work of the organization than have similar practices existing at the present time at social gatherings of institutions, the proudest in our land, and in whose membership the best and highest of our citizens are proud to claim affiliation. Let it always be remembered that, however enticing the "Free and Easy" was to the brothers after the council fire had been quenched, the work of the organization was faithfully performed, and all duties of fraternity and benevolence properly attended to before the "Free and Easy" opened, and the conviviality and the worship of Bacchus began.

There is one other fact, not only proper to mention in connection with the Society of Red Men, but absolutely necessary, in order that proper credit may be given. The Tammany Societies, as we have said, degenerated into political organizations. So far as the records of the Society of Red Men give evidence, but one attempt was made to use that organization as a political machine. As this was the first and only attempt, and as it evidently came to a disastrous conclusion, it is proper to give the facts concerning it. They are these: At a council held on the 26th of the sixth moon, 1822, John Douglass, Magistrate, was proposed for membership and initiated, receiving the name of Okamkan, or "Flinty Warrior." This name had been held previously by Lieutenant John McKinney, deceased, and was now transferred to Mr. Douglass, proving what we have elsewhere claimed that a name given to one brother was sometimes conferred afterward upon another when the brother to whom it was first given had died or had been expelled from the Society. At the time of his admission Mr. Douglass was a candidate for sheriff for Philadelphia County, and undoubtedly thought that admission to the Society of Red Men would assist his chances of election by bringing to his support the influence of that organization. At a slimly attended meeting of the Society a committee was chosen to advance the interests of Brother "Flinty Warrior." When the movement became thoroughly understood, a feeling of determined opposition was manifested. The previous action was reconsidered and then indefinitely postponed. Thus ended the first and only attempt, as far as the documents show, to use the Society of Red Men to advance the political fortunes of any of its members. It may also be remarked that the name of "Flinty Warrior" does not again appear on the minutes or papers of the Society of Red Men. In connection with this incident it is proper to quote here from the original manuscript a longtalk given by "Great Light of the Council Fire," which has direct allusion to this attempt to subvert the Society to partisan ends, and which contains sound advice that may well be heeded in our present organization. It is as follows, with italics and capitalization as in the original: —

"*To The Red Men of Pennsylvania:*

"*Brothers.* When a *white man* is adopted in our tribe, whatever be his years, he is a *young man*, and we cannot immediately recognize him as a *Sachem.* He must primarily declare himself '*void of fear.*' This fear alludes only to the body, for every Red Man must stand in fear of offending the *Great Manitou* by ill deeds, — and it is given as a warning to the warrior, to be brave in battle, but to do nothing which will offend the *Great Spirit.*

"*Red Men.* We have assembled in *General Council* around a *Fire of Peace*. Let us smoke the *Calumet*, bury the *Tomahawk*, and have our *talks*. Let all who have aught to say be quickly heard. Red Men in council are always attentive to those who speak. They deliberately weigh and maturely reply. It is said that a *white man* of fair character, and who is said to have been a good warrior in *white men's wars*, asks for your support, and wishes to be adopted by our tribe. Let him be adopted. But *Red Men* will let the tree bud and blossom before they decide on the fruit. They will let the spring be planted before they become its supporters. Before the ground is tilled they will expect no increase.

"*Brothers.* When a White Man visits your *Wigwam* smoke with him the *Calumet of Peace.* But let him not lead *your tribe, or nations*, until you know him well.

"This Talk, Brothers, is not meant to throw a tree in the way of any Traveller. Let them all journey on. But let us not afford assistance to one stranger and deny it to another."

Various anniversaries were celebrated by the Society of Red Men, the first of which mention is made being the birthday of Lieutenant Alexander John Williams, of the 21st Regiment of the United States Artillery when at Fort Mifflin, and who was subsequently promoted to the rank of captain and assigned to duty at Fort Erie, where he was killed on the 14th of August, 1814, in the glorious and successful defence of that fortification.

He was not quite 24 years of age at the time of his death, but had lived long enough to prove himself a hero, and to merit and receive the plaudits of his fellow-citizens. The claim is not made that he was a member of the Society organized at Fort Mifflin, but that his birthday was celebrated by the Society which would indicate that such was the fact.

We have already referred to Captain James N. Barker, who was in command at Fort Mifflin in 1813, and to the fact that he was the son of General John Barker, who had been a prominent member of the Sons of St. Tammany. Captain Barker became mayor of the city of Philadelphia in 1819. The testimony of Richard Marley, Past Great Incohonee, while living, is quoted as proof of the claim that Mayor Barker was a member of the Society of Red Men.

The birthday of Washington was frequently celebrated by the Society, and as early as the 17th of the 12th moon, 1822, there is record of the appointment of a committee to take in charge the proper observance of February 22, 1823. The records of subsequent councils show the action taken in the time intervening between that date and 1824, when again the anniversary was appropriately observed.

On the 23d of the second moon, 1824, a "Grand Monthly Council Fire" was lit at the wigwam of Brother "Free and Easy," for the purpose of doing honor to the memory of Washington. Generalissimo Lappopetung, or "Black Wampum," George Knorr, presided. Brother Shekoghell of Specra, or "Big Turtle," Daniel E. Scott, delivered a longtalk suitable to the occasion. After this the brethren adjourned for supper. The members were evidently pleased with the success of the celebration, as upon pages 149, 150, and 151 of the Minute Book is an extended account thereof, with expressions of thanks to the committee having the matter in charge, and recommendations for the publication of the longtalk of Brother "Big Turtle."

A similar observance of Washington's Birthday was held in 1825, when was delivered the longtalk of Puyumannawaton, or "Great Light of the Council Fire," from which we have quoted the allusion to Fort Mifflin as the place where the Society of Red Men was organized.

SOCIETY OF RED MEN. 229

In connection with these observances of Washington's Birthday, may be given the following song, the authorship of which is attributed to the James N. Barker, already alluded to in this chapter: —

> " When Freedom on the battle storm
>   Her weary head reclined,
> When round her fair, majestic form
>   The serpent slavery twined;
> Amid the din, beneath the cloud,
>   Great Washington appeared;
> His daring hand rolled back the shroud,
>   And thus the suff'rer cheered:
>
> " ' Burst, burst thy chains! be great! be free!
>   In giant strength arise!
> Stretch, stretch thy pinions, Liberty,
>   Thy flag nail to the skies.
> Clothe, clothe thyself in glory's robe!
>   Let stars thy banner gem;
> Rule, rule the sea! — possess the globe! —
>   Wear victory's diadem.
>
> " ' Tell, tell the world a world is born,
>   Another orb gives light,
> Another sun illumines the morn,
>   Another star the night;
> Be just, be brave, and let thy name,
>   Henceforth, Columbia be;
> Wear, wear the fadeless wreath of fame,
>   The wreath of liberty!'
>
> " He said, and lo! the stars of night
>   Forth to the banner flew;
> And morn, with pencil dipped in light,
>   Its blushes on it drew.
> Columbia's chieftain grasped the flag,
>   The standard sheet unfurl'd,
> Flew with it to his native skies,
>   And waved it o'er the world."

There does not appear in the records in our possession any legislation by which the celebration of St. Tammany Day, the 12th of May, as a holiday or anniversary of the Society was required in the Constitution or Laws. But all through the records in the Minute Book, in every year from 1823 down to 1827 inclusive, votes are recorded providing for a proper observance of this day. When the various societies of St. Tammany, which existed from 177- down to 1822 in Philadelphia, became broken and disorganized, it is quite certain that the membership became absorbed in the Society of Red Men. There is positive evidence to show that men were members of both Societies at the same time in 1818, and inasmuch as the St. Tammany Societies observed the birthday of their patron saint with great pomp and ceremony, nothing was more natural than that the custom should have been engrafted upon the regulations of the Society of Red Men. We will present extracts from the Minute Book showing the action taken for a proper observance of St. Tammany's Day.

On page 72 of the Minute Book, under date of April 29, 1823, record is made of the appointment of a committee "to receive subscribers' names, of our different brethren, that will be inclined to take dinner, etc., on the 12th of May next," and the committee appointed in accordance with this vote, consisted of "Snow Clad Mountain," "Big Turtle," "Bull's Horns," "Hickory Sapling," and "White Cat Fish," with full powers to fill all vacancies. This committee reported progress on the 6th of May and further at the council of May 8. The grounds of Judge Peters at Mantua Village were secured, and the dinner was furnished by Brother "Hospitality," William Muirhead, at a cost of fifty cents each. Brother "Big Turtle," delivered a longtalk previous to the dinner.

Again, at the Monthly Grand Council held on April 6, 1824, a committee of five was appointed "to take order on the proposed dinner for Red Men on St. Tammany's Day. Brothers 'Big Turtle,' 'Red Oak,' 'Live Oak,' 'Cedar Bush,' and 'Peppermint' were appointed with full power to fill all vacancies if any should occur." This committee subsequently reported on April 20, that "they could not find a more suitable and convenient place than the one they used the last anniversary of St. Tammany; they therefore recommend the same place for the present contemplated festival, and that the dinner be provided, by some brother, similar to the former." The committee was discharged and another appointed consisting of Brothers "Red Oak," "Peppermint," "Live Oak," "Son of Vulcan," and "Red

Belt" "for the purpose of inquiring what brothers will propose and make order the dinner on said day and on what terms they will furnish the same." It was unanimously agreed that the dinner take place at Mantua Village, as was done at the last festival of St. Tammany in 1823. At the council held April 23, the committee was directed to examine a place at Kane's (Kaighn's) Point, and report at the next council whether the same was preferable to Mantua Village, and also to report on what terms the dinner could be obtained per man. The committee accordingly reported on April 27, "that Brother Hospitality offers to furnish a dinner at Mantua Village at the rate of 75 cents per man and each to pay for his drink separately." Brother Hickory Sapling declined to bid for the dinner, as he was unable to furnish it on that day. The committee also reported that strict search had been made on the Jersey shore agreeably to the request made by the Council April 23. As the result of its investigation it made report as follows:—

"At Kane's point, a tavern keeper (a white man) offer'd to furnish a dinner in the woods, at the back of his house, at 50 cents per man, and if it should rain, he then would entertain them in his house, and every man pay for whatever liquor he may think proper to call for.

"They then viewed a place at Newtown Creek, which place the Red Men can obtain permission to use, on said day, with the use of a kitchen and a spring house, free of expense.

"At this place we shall have to provide ourselves, in every respect, with all necessaries, provisions, liquors, etc. An estimate of which, and the supposed amount thereof, is also laid before the present Council, for their determination.

"Your Committee after much fatigue, etc., are happy that they are able to make the foregoing report, and now beg, that they may be discharged."

The committee was discharged as requested, and it was voted to reconsider the action about taking dinner in the woods at Mantua Village, and a committee of five was appointed to make inquiry if any other brother would undertake to furnish a dinner "and to make report at the next council." This committee consisted of Brothers "Big Turtle," "Weaver of Shoes," "Peppermint," "Cassia Sprig," and "Wooden Foot." At the next council of April 30 the committee again reported as follows:—

"They had enquired of many Red Men (Tavern keepers), but that Brother 'Hospitality' was the only person who would furnish a dinner on

St. Tammanie's day, and be likely to give general satisfaction; his proposal was 75 cents per man, and each to pay for his own drink.

"Committee further reported, that they had maturely considered existing circumstances and that, after having conference with many of the brethren, did find the current opposition running against dining at Mantua Ville, for various reasons that had been suggested to the Society, therefore, they do recommend the reconsideration of the report which was made by the Committee, who examined the place, at Newtown Creek. Your Committee further recommend the reorganization of that Committee, and that your present Committee will render them every assistance in their power, if necessary."

The recommendation was carried out and the two committees were consolidated and it was voted to take dinner at Newton (Newtown) Creek.

"The two Committees being now joined as one, they are hereby requested, and enjoined, to do all that may be in their power, to obtain subscribers, to appoint caterers, regulate, obtain, do and direct all that they can devise; for the general good, the comfort, harmony, ease and enjoyment of all the brethren that may think proper to join in the celebration of the day of the birth of our Titular Saint."

On May 4 the committee reported "that they had engaged a 'Team Boat,' to convey our brethren to Newtown Creek on the 12th of the fifth moon, and to return back again to Philadelphia, for the sum of five dollars. That they recommend to the council that our brethren do meet on the said 12th day at eight o'clock, A.M., and to start positively at the hour of nine o'clock. They also recommend that notices be published at various taverns which are kept by our brethren for the purpose of making known to Red Men what time and at what place they are to meet on the said 12th instant." The recommendations of the committee were adopted and the committee given power to carry out the wishes of the Society. On page 186 of the Minute Book appears the following record: —

"Agreeably to General Orders, the brethren met at the Wigwam of Brother 'Hospitality,' between the hours of 8 and 9 o'clock, A.M., on the 12th of the 5th moon, 1824; from thence they proceeded on board of a Team boat, which was employed for the purpose of conveying such of our brethren to Gloucester point as thought proper to celebrate (at Newtown Creek), the festival of Tammany (our Tutilar Saint). After landing at Gloucester point, the brethren marched in single file, under command of the Generalissimo, through the Forest, until they arrived at the appointed spot; and after the brethren had received refreshment, a council fire was lit; the following white man was proposed, and after going through the usual and necessary forms, he was initiated: Joseph Wigmore, occupation, Silver Smith, proposed by Br. 'Weaver of Shoes,' name received 'Green Walnut Tree.' After which, the Council adjourned to social purposes, and a little before 6 o'clock, P.M., the brethren proceeded and went on board the Team boat, and landed at about 9 o'clock in Philadelphia."

We have given the legislation leading up to the celebration on this occasion considerably in detail so that our readers may understand the importance which was attached not only to the anniversary itself, but to the proper arrangements to be made for a celebration of the event that should be pleasing to the members of the society.

On page 259 of the Minute Book, under date of April 4, 1825, record is made of the appointment of the usual committee "to select a convenient place for the Red Men to celebrate the anniversary of St. Tammany," as follows: "Brothers 'Red Oak,' 'Brown Stout,' 'White Cat Fish,' 'Wild Turkey,' and 'Peppermint.'" At the next council held April 15, the committee reported, and it was voted "that the Red Men celebrate St. Tammany's Day at the wigwam of Brother Pine Grove, and agreeably to his offer take a repast at twenty-five cents per man for their eating." At the next council held April 19, a committee was appointed "to receive subscribers for the celebration of St. Tammany's Day." The committee consisted of Brothers "Red Oak," "Wheat Sheaf," "Peppermint," "Chief of the Northern Tribe," and "Strawberry Bush." ("Chief of the Northern Tribe" was General Thomas Snyder.) At the next council, April 26, it was formally voted "that the Red Men take dinner at Brother 'Pine Grove's' on the 12th day of May, that being the anniversary of St. Tammany; at the charge of fifty cents each for his dinner." Subsequently arrangements were made for the brethren to assemble at the house of Brother "Hickory Sapling" at one o'clock, and proceed thence to Brother "Pine Grove's," "and every brother to wear his badge." Arrangements were made also for a publication of General Orders to call the brethren to assemble on St. Tammany's Day. The General Orders were usually printed on sheets of convenient size for posting in houses of entertainment and other public places. Among the old documents are several of these.

HEAD-QUARTERS.

GENERAL ORDERS!

Attention Red Men.

YOU will assemble in Grand Council Fire, at the Wigwam of Brother HICKORY SAPLING, (Sign of General Jackson) Race near Eighth street, on THURSDAY next, the 12th instant, at 12 o'clock, noon, in due order, with the full Insignia of your Tribe, and Badge of your Rank, fully prepared to take up the line of march to Celebrate the

Anniversary of Tammany,

The Tutelar Saint of Red Men.

☞ A Repast and other Entertainments will be provided by Brother *PINE GROVE*, at his Wigwam, Harmony Hall Hotel, Bush-Hill, suitable for the occasion. Tickets can be had of the Committee of Arrangement, and at Pine Grove's Wigwam.

N. B. The Generals are requested to report themselves on that day, as in case of neglect they will be superceded by new appointments.

BY ORDER,

Lappopetung, or BLACK WAMPUM;
GENERALISSIMO.

Wiuerwaski; or *Red Oak,*
2d Lieut. Gen. Grand Recording Scribe, R. M. P.

Fifth Moon, 9th, 1825.   *Bull-Frog,* Pr.

SOCIETY OF RED MEN. 235

A copy of the sheet, on which were printed the General Orders above referred to, is before us as we write, and on the opposite page is a reproduction of this identical notice for the celebration of May 12, 1825. For some reason there appears to be no record of the observance of St. Tammany's Day in the year 1826. But at the council held April 3, 1827, "King of the Western Tribe," "Meridian Sun," "Black Wampum," "Tombstone's Brother," and "Son of Vulcan" were appointed a committee "to consider and report a plan for the celebration of St. Tammany's Day." This committee reported at the next council, April 6, "no progress, and beg to be discharged," which was agreed to. On page 407 of the Minute Book it is recorded that a subscription list was opened to receive such names of members as wished to dine on St. Tammany's Day. On May 11 a resolution was adopted "that such brethren as will make it convenient to celebrate St. Tammany's Day will dine at Brother 'Hospitality's.'" On page 412 of the Minute Book it is recorded that "the Generalissimo presided on the 12th of the 5th moon, 1827, (being St. Tammany's Day) at the wigwam of Brother 'Hospitality,' where a handsome dinner was provided which gave general satisfaction to the brethren that were present, and for his attention, etc., in providing the same, Brother 'Hospitality' received the unanimous thanks of the meeting."

Inasmuch as the Minute Book contains no records of a later date than May 15, 1827, it is impossible to give any further account of subsequent celebrations of St. Tammany's Day, and the scattered fragments of the minutes preserved outside the Minute Book do not cover the months of April and May, and therefore give no information on the subject.

Our readers are familiar with the fact of the visit to the United States, in 1824, of General Lafayette, and it is interesting to here record the action taken by the Society of Red Men to assist in rendering proper honor to the distinguished guest of the nation. For this purpose General Orders were issued and posted in public places inviting the members to attend a council to be held on August 24, 1824, to make arrangements for joining in the procession in honor of General Lafayette.

About this same time the records mention the organization

of a rifle company to be composed entirely of Red Men, and on the Minute Book, page 190, under date of May 25, 1824, it is recorded that "a committee was appointed to take into consideration, etc., the forming of a Rifle Company of Red Men, to report thereon at our next council fire," and the committee appointed for this purpose consisted of the Generalissimo and Brothers "Lookout," "Peppermint," "Hickory Sapling," "Strawberry Bush," "Hospitality," "Hot Iron," and "Red Buck." This committee reported at the subsequent council held May 29, and the report was received and laid over until the Grand Monthly Council which was held June 1, 1824. On this date, page 192 of the Minute Book, it is stated that "the committee that was appointed to receive subscribers for the raising a Rifle Corps of Red Men made a communication to the council which was read and approved. Committee desired permission to add five or six to the present committee (if they should find the same necessary). Their desire was unanimously granted, with a request that the committee should exert themselves in collecting subscribers, so that the Corps may be formed as speedy as possible." At subsequent councils shown on page 197 of the Minute Book, the committee reported that they had advertised "that they would meet, etc., at certain wigwams three times each week to receive subscribers," and "that they had 36 members on their list."

The Minute Book does not give much further information in relation to the Red Men's Rifle Corps. Fragmentary documents indicate that the Corps was known to the outside world as the "Morgan Rifle Rangers." The names of the officers were George Knorr, "Black Wampum," Captain; Richard Loudenslager, "Old Warrior," Lieutenant; William Leitmann, "Peppermint," First Sergeant; Jacob Wolf, "Sheep Stealer," Second Sergeant; George Ziegler, "Wolf Catcher," Third Sergeant. Upon a poster inviting the members of the Society to attend a special council August 29, to consider the propriety of making arrangements to receive Lafayette, it was noted that "a meeting of the Red Men's Rifle Corps will be held at Brother 'Hospitality's' on Monday next, August 23, 1824."

The uniform worn by the "Rangers" is described as "a green frock or overshirt, and leggings trimmed with yellow fringe;

a fur cap, with deer's tail in lieu of feathers or pompons and moccasons."

The next mention of the reception in honor of Lafayette appears on page 202 of the Minute Book, at the council held under date of August 24, 1824, wherein "It was agreed That a Procession of Red Men should take place in honor of General De La Fayette's visiting Philadelphia, provided, that a sufficient number of brethren will attend, whereby the procession shall appear truly respectable." At the same council it was unanimously agreed that a committee of 15 be appointed, with full powers to fill vacancies, "to examine whether a sufficient number of brethren can be obtained to form a respectable procession, and that they report their opinion thereon at the wigwam of Brother 'Black Bottle,' on the evening of the 28th instant." The committee appointed in accordance with this action represented the city proper, Northern Liberties, and Southwark, and was as follows:—

For the City—Lieutenant-General "Old Warrior," Brigadier-General "Hospitality," Lieutenant-General "Red Oak," Brigadier-General "Peppermint," Brigadier-General "Black Bottle," Brigadier-General "Wheat Sheaf's Brother."

For Northern Liberties — Brigadier-General "Strawberry Bush," Brigadier-General "Blue Crane," Brother "Wolf Dog," Brother "Bold Warrior."

For Southwark — Brigadier-General "Black Rat," Brigadier-General "Deer Skin," Brother "War Club," Brother "Black Rock."

At the council held August 28, a preamble and resolutions were unanimously adopted as follows:—

"WHEREAS, The Red Men of the State of Pennsylvania are anxious, in common with their fellow citizens, to pay that respect, and give that reception to the national guest, the brave and patriotic General La Fayette, who was the associate in arms of our late Grand Sachem, General George Washington; he in his youth left his friends and country, at his own expense, volunteered his services and shed his blood, to obtain for us the liberty and Independence which we now so happily enjoy; therefore,

"*Resolved*, By the Red Men of Pennsylvania, That we will embrace the present opportunity (being, perhaps, the last time that will ever offer) to pay that respect due to one whom we look upon as the champion of Liberty, the friend of Freedom, and the benefactor of America.

"*Resolved*, That we will devote the day of his arrival exclusively to his reception.

"*Resolved*, That we will on the day of the procession, appear at such place as may be hereafter designated, with the full insignia of our Tribe and badge of our rank, the Revolutionary cockade, and the La Fayette badge.

"*Resolved*, That the Grand Recording Scribe, under the direction of the Generalissimo, invite the Reading, Lancaster and Delaware Tribes, to attend on the occasion; and all brothers belonging to other Tribes, who may be in the city or vicinity, are particularly requested to join in the procession.

"*Resolved*, That the above proceedings be published in the city papers.

"By order of   'BLACK WAMPUM,' *Generalissimo*.
"Signed by   WIVERWASKI, or 'Red Oak,' *Lieutenant General*,
"*Grand Recording Scribe*."

No record is made of any action taken by the Tribes at Reading or Delaware, but a reply was received from Lancaster of which the following is a copy:—

"MR. KNORR, *Baker, Sixth or Fifth Street, between Market and Arch Streets, Philadelphia.*

"DEAR SIR AND BROTHER: We have received your 'Talk' of the 1st of the Ninth Moon, and note its contents. It has pleased the Generalissimo, 'Smooth Stone,' to appoint us a committee for the purpose of addressing you, and to return to you individually our sincere thanks for the attention you have so politely honored us with. It will, however, be impossible for the brethren of Lancaster to participate with you in paying their respects to the illustrious La Fayette, and the patron of universal Liberty. Some, however, of our Tribe are desirous of visiting Philadelphia, for the purpose of paying their respects, in common with the rest of the citizens, to General La Fayette, and will join in procession with you.

"We are, sir, with sentiments, yours, etc.,
"SPRUCE, *Major-General* 1st *Aid to the Generalissimo*.
"BACKENSIGA, *Lieutenant Colonel and* 6th *Aid*.
"SAGASAUNAY, *Major-General*.
"LANCASTER, 7th of the Ninth Moon, 1824."

At the council held August 31, 1824, a committee of arrangements was appointed and authorized to have badges prepared to be purchased at the option of the brethren, the committee consisting of "Big Canoe Builder," Grand Marshal, with "Spike Driver," "White Oak Club," "Black Bottle," "Screw Auger," "Shooting Stick," and "Heart of Erin" as assistants. At the next council, September 3, this committee reported that they had prepared "certain articles suitable for and to be used in the contemplated procession in honor of our nation's guest, General La Fayette," and further "that the same will be in readiness by Wednesday the 8th instant." Among these articles may be mentioned "a staff on which to fix the banner of the Order, with a liberty cap upon the top which shall be gilt and the staff stained red."

Under date of September 3, 1824, a communication was received by the Generalissimo inviting the Rifle Corps to unite with the regiment of citizen volunteers, and inviting the Generalissimo to attend a meeting of the board of officers on that evening at Mr. Holt's tavern, for the purpose of making final arrangements for the parade.

On September 7, 1824, it was "resolved that a committee of five be appointed consisting of 'King Tom,' 'Hospitality,' 'Fox,' 'White Oak Club,' and 'Strawberry Bush,' whose duty it shall be to confer with the Councils, and in concert with them ascertain and fix the station the Red Men shall occupy in the contemplated grand procession in honor of our justly distinguished nation's guest, the beloved, venerated La Fayette." This committee evidently corresponded with the Committee of Councils, for a letter was received by the committee of which the following is a copy:—

"SEPTEMBER 11th, 1824.

"GENTLEMEN: Your note of the 8th inst. was laid before the Committee of Councils, who desire me to say that a place in the procession for the reception of General La Fayette will be assigned by lot to the Red Men, who are invited to appoint a deputy to draw for them, at the Common Council Chamber, corner of Fifth and Chestnut Streets, on Wednesday next, the 15th inst., at three P.M.

"Yours respectfully,
"JOSEPH S. LEWIS, *Chairman.*

"Messrs. Thomas Waterman, William Muirhead, William Simpson, M. M. Donohew."

Brother "White Oak Club" was appointed to represent the Red Men at the drawing referred to, and as the result of his performance of that duty he made the following report:—

"*To the Generalissimo and Members of the Society of Red Men.*

"Agreeably to lot I have, on the part of the Society, drawn No. 4 for the procession in honor of La Fayette, being the number preceding the lowest number drawn on the day appointed.

"M. M. DONOHEW, or 'White Oak Club.'"

We have before us as we write the original of this report, and upon it is affixed the square piece of paper with the figure 4 on it in ink, being the identical number drawn by "White Oak Club" as stated in his report.

At the council held September 10, "the marshals agreeably to their duty produced the banners, liberty cap, marshals' rods, etc., which were duly approved of." The proceedings of the committee were read, and a copy of the letter addressed to the Committee of the City Councils, which received general satisfaction. September 14 it was on motion

"*Resolved*, That the thanks of the Society be presented to the marshals for their attention and diligence in providing the sufficient articles which they were particularly requested to attend to and obtain."

"Whereupon the Generalissimo in the name of the Society tendered them thanks accordingly." At this same council it was also resolved "that Brother 'Fawn Deer' be authorized and requested to engage the contemplated music for the approaching grand procession in honor of the nation's guest."

At the council held September 17, a resolution was adopted as follows:—

"*Resolved*, That in addition to the Society's badge, Revolutionary cockade, and La Fayette badge, each Red Man in procession will carry in his hand a sprig of Laurel; and that the marshals take order for procuring a sufficiency of Laurel for the occasion."

Further action was taken at the council held September 24, when it was voted that two brothers be appointed to carry the standard on the day of the procession, and Brothers "Hard Walnut Knot" and "Bold Warrior" were appointed by the Society as standard bearers. At the same meeting Brothers "Strawberry Bush," "Wheat Sheaf," and "Cherokee Warrior" were appointed to carry the implements and to guard the banner. Evidently none but good Red Men were permitted to appear upon occasions of this kind, for we find that it was voted "on motion by Brother 'Byron' that Brother 'Long Pen' should be notified not to walk in the procession of Red Men to welcome General La Fayette until some (supposed) charges were cleared up." At the succeeding council of September 27, it was reported that the First Marshal, Brother "Big Canoe

Builder," was hurt and unable to attend the procession, and Brother "Hard Walnut Knot" was appointed in his place. At this council notice was given by the Generalissimo "to meet at the house of Brother 'Hickory Sapling's' to-morrow morning at seven o'clock, to make collections towards paying the music, and then proceed in procession." Accordingly on the following morning a council fire was lit at the wigwam of Brother "Hickory Sapling," and collection taken up towards defraying the expenses of music engaged, the amount realized being $6.83. The Society then adjourned, and proceeded to join the procession on the Frankford Road.

It is not necessary to enter into an extended description of the magnificent ovation given to Lafayette on the occasion mentioned. Our purpose has been to give in detail the part taken by the Society of Red Men, and to show that it was an organization of considerable importance in the city of Philadelphia at that time. There is also evidence to indicate that in this procession the Society was represented not only by the Rifle Corps but also by the members themselves in a body. While refraining from giving a full description of the scenes and events attending the reception, we will quote an ode composed for the occasion by Mr. Benjamin Mayo, and sung by a group of twenty-four boys and twenty-four girls stationed at an arch at the corner of Fourth and Vine Streets as the general approached. The ode was as follows:—

ODE.

Strike the cymbal! roll the tymbal!
Sound the trumpets! beat the drums!
Loudly singing, cheerily singing,
Lo! the patriot hero comes!
Great Commoner, slighting honor,
Here the youthful hero came,
Aiding strangers, braving dangers,
Human freedom was his aim.
Troops come prancing, see, advancing—
All Columbia's sons and daughters
Greet the hero! land and waters—
Streamers streaming, shouts proclaiming
Far and near, the hero's name.
God of thunder, rend asunder
All the power that tyrants boast!

> What are nations — what their stations —
> When compared with Freedom's host?
> What are mighty monarchs now,
> While at Freedom's shrines we bow?
> Pride of princes, strength of kings,
> To the dust fair Freedom brings!
> Hail him! hail him! let each exulting band
> Welcome Fayette to Freedom's happy land!
> All hail him! all hail him! all hail him!

We have already stated that the Minute Book has no record in it beyond page 413, at which time is recorded a council held at the wigwam of Brother "Struggler" on the 15th of the fifth moon, 1827. For an account of the Society during the time intervening from 1827 to 1832, we are compelled to rely upon the fragmentary manuscript minutes still preserved, and upon personal conversations with Mr. Thomas J. Loudenslager held by Brother Gorham. It will be remembered that it was from Mr. Loudenslager that the documents were obtained from which have been given the extracts contained in this chapter relating to the Society of Red Men.

From the sources mentioned we learn that on September 2, 1827, a committee consisting of "Red Oak," "Chief of the Northern Tribe," and "Fair Play" was appointed to have the dresses of the Society properly repaired. At this same council the report was read, and a committee previously appointed for the purpose of drafting a new Constitution and code of By-Laws for the future government of the Society, but further action thereon was deferred "until our next council." As the minutes of "our next council" have not been preserved there is nothing to indicate the nature of this report nor of the Constitution and Laws adopted.

November 13, 1827, a council was held, at which the Second Captain-General presided. Four candidates were initiated, — George Grier, book printer, "Fair Play's Brother;" George Allison, "White Metal;" James M. Benckart, musician, "Great Joy;" and Samuel P. Mitchell, Captain-Major, "Bold Soldier." Then come minutes of a council held at the wigwam of Brother "Chief of the Northern Tribe," General Thomas Snyder, on November 16, at which Generalissimo "Black Warrior" presided. A charge having been produced against "Dry Berry,"

SOCIETY OF RED MEN. 243

for revealing the secrets of the Red Men under very aggravating circumstances, it was resolved that he be declared unworthy of any longer remaining a Red Man. The Generalissimo stated that there would be no council fire lighted until the first Tuesday in next month in consequence of the dresses being out of repair. The council on December 4, 1827, was held at the wigwam of Brother "Hickory Sapling." The only action taken at this council was to reconsider the resolution of the previous council relating to Brother "Dry Berry," and a committee of three, consisting of "Turkey Foot Warrior," "Full Moon," and "Long Pen," was appointed to investigate the charges against the brother, and to report at the next council the facts of the case with their opinion thereon.

The next council of which we have record was held at the wigwam of Brother "Hospitality" on December 18, 1827. A candidate was initiated, but nothing else of importance seems to have been done. December 21 a council was held at the wigwam of Brother "Morning Star," at which five white men were elected and initiated, and Brother "Dove's Foot" was appointed "Chief of the Southern Tribe."

A break now occurs in the minutes, and we have nothing until November 29, 1830, when a council fire was kindled at the house of General Thomas Snyder, Third Street, near Coates, Lieutenant-General "Old Warrior" presiding. The loss of the minutes covering the time intervening between December 21, 1827, and November 29, 1830, is peculiarly unfortunate, as their existence would serve to make plain many points now obscure, and give information not only concerning the existence of the parent society at Philadelphia, but action taken to extend it into other cities, and the communications received therefrom sent by brothers "on mission" or "on command." We can only infer that during this time Generalissimo Lappopetung, or "Black Wampum," George Knorr had resigned, or at least that a vacancy had occurred, because in the minutes it is stated that a resolution was adopted to make a nomination for Generalissimo. The "Old Warrior" mentioned as presiding over the council held November 29, 1830, was Richard Loudenslager, father of "Young Red Eagle," Thomas J. Loudenslager, from whom Brother Gorham obtained the books and papers of the society in behalf of the Great Council of the United States, after a period of thirty-five years. It is assumed that Richard Loudenslager joined the Society in the interval between 1818 and 1822. The only instance where his name appears on the Minute Book is that which names him as Lieutenant of the Red Men's Rifle Corps or Morgan Rifle Rangers.

At this same council of November 29, 1830, a committee was appointed to obtain the books, implements, dresses and large painting belonging to the Society. This committee consisted of "Chief of the Northern Tribe," "Hospitality," and "Wheat Sheaf."

December 13, 1830, a council was held at the wigwam of Brother "Blue Crane," in the Northern Liberties, "Wheat Sheaf" presiding. The committee previously appointed reported that the dresses and large painting had been procured, and were in the hands of Brother "Chief of the Northern Tribe," and the books, papers, etc., were in the hands of "Robin Hood," or Bashaba of Piscataqua, Henry Knorr. Two brothers were added to the committee, "Blue Crane" and "White Brandt." At this council nominations were made of candidates for Generalissimo. The brothers placed in nomination being "Pine Grove," Charles Clements; "Hickory Sapling," Chalkley Baker; "Strawberrry Bush;" "Hospitality," William Muirhead; "Blue Crane," "Wheat Sheaf," and "Bull Frog." The council adjourned until Monday evening, December 20, 1830, but of that meeting we have no record.

Then comes the council of January 7, 1831, held at the house of Brother "Wheat Sheaf," "Old Warrior" presiding. At this council four candidates were adopted, and the meeting adjourned to meet on the following Monday evening, January 12, 1831. This meeting was held at the wigwam of Brother "Hospitality," who had removed from his old quarters in Bank Street to the Cosmopolite Hotel on Cherry Street above 6th. At this council a report was made by the committee chosen for that purpose, that possession had been obtained of the books and papers belonging to the Society from Brother "Bull Frog," and that they were now in the possession of the Grand Recording Scribe. They had not recovered the dresses, large painting, and other articles. Brother "Chief of the Northern Tribe"

RETURN OF THE HUNTERS.

had promised to be present at the meeting, but had failed to appear.

January 31, a meeting was held at the wigwam of Brother "Hospitality," at which it was resolved that Brother "Chief of the Northern Tribe," as treasurer of the Society, prosecute Jacob Wolf, "Wheat Sheaf's Brother," for the articles which he holds, they being the property of the Red Men.

No later minutes than those above given exist. It will be seen that the successor of George Knorr, "Black Wampum," must have been selected, as nominations had been regularly made in December to fill the vacancy. The last minutes in our possession, being those of January 21, 1831, were signed "Young Red Eagle," who appears to have been the last Grand Recording Scribe. It will be remembered that this was the name of Thomas J. Loudenslager, and that it was in his possession that the property of the Society passed when it finally ceased to exist. It is to his care we are indebted for the knowledge we now possess, and for the priceless treasures presented by him to our Order. He is cited as authority for the statement that his father, Richard Loudenslager, "Old Warrior," was elected Generalissimo of all the Red Men December 20, 1830. Some doubt is expressed as to the correctness of this date, although the fact of his election may be accepted as beyond dispute. In 1866, Mr. Loudenslager assigned as the cause of the ultimate decline of the Society in Philadelphia the acquisition of too many members of a certain class, "who were so clannish and offensively aggressive that they disgusted the better class of members, who withdrew from the Society, and it finally ceased to exist." He spoke with much earnestness on this subject, and gave evidence that his early love for the Society had revived, or rather had never waned. As to the time of the dissolution of the Society, he could not state the precise date with absolute certainty, but as nearly as he could recall the closing events of the Society, it was in the latter part of 1832 or early in 1833.

It will be remembered that in 1832 the nation was visited by the Asiatic cholera, and the presence of that terrible scourge in our country made it extremely difficult to maintain the existence of any organization, much less secure additions to its membership. But, as will be shown later, while the parent Society died out in Philadelphia, offshoots therefrom maintained an organization in other localities, and served to preserve the principles and objects for which it was founded. Upon this point Brother Gorham remarks: "It will be found by the light of subsequent history, that although it was thought that the Improved Order of Red Men had a different individual existence apart from that of the old Society of Red Men in Philadelphia, yet it was a legitimate offshoot or scion of the parent stem, branches of which were still in active existence, which, had either of them seen fit, might have successfully disputed the rights of the younger branches to precedence, and have asserted their right to exercise eminent jurisdiction over 'all Red Men wherever their Tribes existed.'" The authority upon which this claim is based will be given in the succeeding chapter, wherein will be recorded the establishment of the Order in Maryland, and its reorganization into its present form as the Improved Order of Red Men.

In closing this chapter, we feel that the material herein presented cannot fail to be of deep interest to every member of our Order. We think we have established all we have claimed for the Society of Red Men as a legitimate successor of the old Tammany Societies of the Revolution. What will follow brings us within the domain of positive fact as obtained from existing records.

CHAPTER V.

ORGANIZATION AT BALTIMORE.

THE third epoch in the history of the Order, which we will now consider, covers that part of the chronology for the verification of which we have written records that are beyond question. We have tried thus far to show these facts: that there was a link of common sympathy and common inspiration connecting the earliest patriotic societies, existing previous to and at the time of the Revolution, with the Society of Red Men formed in 1813; that the Society of Red Men existed from its organization down to a period subsequent to 1830; and that from these various societies resulted the institution of the fraternal and benevolent organization now known by the name of The Improved Order of Red Men. What has been presented thus far is certainly sufficient to justify the claim we make and to satisfy every member of the organization of the patriotic, noble, and inspiring origin of our Order.

A confusion of dates makes it difficult to state positively when the first tribe was organized in Baltimore. One authority claims that on the 12th of March, 1834, the Society of Red Men, Tribe of Maryland, No. 1, was organized at the house of D. McDonald, on Bond Street, Fell's Point. This is stated, it is claimed, on the authority of manuscript in the handwriting of John L. Booker, who was Great Chief of Records of the Great Council of the United States from its organization down through many years until 1866.

The conflicting claims as to which Tribe was first organized have been ably stated; and in order that a fair judgment may be given, we shall present here the evidence sustaining each claim, and leave our readers to judge as to which may justly bear the credit of priority.

The passage of years often leaves a very perplexing uncertainty in the minds of those interested in an object or an event as to many circumstances connected therewith, and sometimes this uncertainty occurs about those things most important. Particularly is this so where the subject in question is one of vital interest to a comparatively few. A matter of national importance leaves its impress upon the heart of that nation so indelibly that it can never be effaced, and about the details of which there can be little doubt or uncertainty; but in matters of interest to a comparatively few, or where records are for a great measure dependent upon oral testimony, or where inclination, procrastination, or indifference interferes with the transmission of authoritative evidence, mistakes often occur. Differences of opinion are apt to spring up, productive, often, of endless, and sometimes needless, discussion. We find this to have been the case in the history of our beloved Order.

In tracing the Improved Order of Red Men back to the institution of the first Tribe, we find a slight difference of opinion as to the date of that event, arising out of the information given by the two members of that Tribe who were considered the best authorities on the subject, and the most reliable in their data relative to the early days of the Order; namely, Past Great Sachem George A. Peter, and Past Great Senior Sagamore John F. Weishampel.

Brother George A. Peter was one of *the original charter members*, and Brother John F. Weishampel was adopted into the Tribe during the *first three moons of its existence*. The former gives the date as occurring during the year 1833, while the latter asserts that the Tribe was formed in 1834.

It is probable that Brother Peter dated the organization of the Tribe from its first preliminary meeting, held in December, 1833, while Brother Weishampel fixes the date from the time when the Tribe was actually placed in operation, which must have been early in 1834, as both agree it took place in the winter season.

It is recorded in another chapter that several associations under the title of Red Men had existed in various parts of the country prior to the organization of the Improved Order of Red Men, whose objects were either of a political or convivial character.

The first reason — the defence of the liberty of the people —

which in years past had caused to spring into existence "the Sons of Liberty," and later on "the Sons of Saint Tammany," had passed away. America was free; was independent. Hence in the minds of the people at large, political societies had not the strong hold they once had held. The evil effects of societies, purely and simply for convivial purposes, was so patent that the most reputable classes of the community turned from them with disgust and abhorrence, and it was realized by those interested in the continuance of the Order that, if the society of Red Men was to be successful, it must be planned upon a different basis, and governed by different principles, from either of the preceding types quoted. Benevolence — Charity — must be its redeeming feature, which, in the golden light that beamed forth from the kindly acts of its members, would reflect a halo even upon the principles of Freedom and Friendship, which were to constitute with it *the triune* under which the new society, arising, phœnix-like, from the ruins of the old, would secure success.

A society of a convivial character had been formed in Baltimore, Md., about the year 1833, the members of which met weekly in a room over a tavern, on Bond Street, Fells Point. In reference to this society the following is quoted from a pamphlet prepared by Brother John F. Weishampel, Sr., containing a long talk delivered by him on Saint Tammany's Day, May 12, 1837, in Trinity Church, in the city of Baltimore. In his pamphlet, Brother Weishampel also gives a description of the society referred to in the following clear and comprehensive language. He says: "For some length of time prior to organizing the present Improved Order of Red Men, there existed in Baltimore, Md., a lodge, or society, called Red Men. They had their wigwam, or place of meeting, in the garret of a tavern. They met once a week, paid their dues, and initiated new members if any were on hand. After the business was over, the rest of the evening was spent in singing, telling yarns, making speeches, and convivial enjoyment, in which *the decanter* figured largely. The object of the society appeared to be *only* convivial entertainment." The object of the society was thus objectionable to many. "Several gentlemen who had been induced to join the lodge, but who did not favor such a course, withdrew as soon as they discovered the nature and object of the society," and it soon afterwards broke up.

Among those who had become members, in ignorance of the prevailing bad element composing the Tribe, were George A. Peter and William T. Jones, who, observing the evil effects exerted by the society upon its membership, yet admiring the beauty of the traditional Indian features of its ceremonies, determined to revive the interest of the members, and instil into their minds the usefulness and strength that could be infused into an association founded upon the basis of sobriety, virtue, and mutual assistance in time of need, benevolence, care for the sick, relief of the widow and orphan, and a total absence of those pernicious practices which had proven so fatal to the former societies.

They associated themselves with several other members of the old society, among whom the names of the following have been preserved: John E. Stansbury, G. H. Mittnacht, Peter B. Lucas, J. Friedenwald, and A. Lowe. These brethren, using their influence among their paleface friends, and those of their old associates in the defunct society upon whom they could depend for support in their laudable enterprise, urged the immediate formation of a new Order.

Several preliminary meetings were held, at which plans, rules, and regulations for the organization and government of the Society were presented and discussed. "These meetings were held at Elisha Snike's Temperance House, located on Thames Street, Baltimore, Md., at which the final organization took place."

The Tribe being now duly organized, the selection of a name became the all-important consideration; and Brother George A. Peter proposed the name of *Logan Tribe, No. 1, Order of Red Men.* This title was afterwards changed to *Logan Tribe, No 1, Improved Order of Red Men.* But of this we will speak a little later on.

Thus after the adoption of the title was Logan Tribe, No. 1, announced to the community as an association formed for mutual fraternity and benevolence, taking for its motto

"FREEDOM, FRIENDSHIP, AND CHARITY."

The early experience of the Order was not, however, devoid of difficulty and annoyances from those who, having been among the bad element of the old society, but by fair promises had gained admission into the new one. Such trouble was frequent, and at last culminated in an attempt to eject the Sachem (Brother George A. Peter, the first Sachem of the Tribe) from the stump. This attempt was opposed by the other members of the Tribe, and the malcontents were forcibly expelled from the wigwam; and thus ended their membership.

In conformity with the Indian character of the organization, the officers received the titles of chiefs of veritable Indian tribes. The presiding chief was styled the Sachem; and the others graded as Sagamores, Prophet, Chief of Records, Keeper of Wampum, Guards of the Forest and Wigwam, Sannaps, Warriors, and Braves.

The council fire was always kindled *in the centre* of the wigwam, and during its burning strict order and decorum was enjoined upon the members. It was always quenched at the close of the session of the Tribe.

Dates were computed according to the Jewish method, using the year of the world, or, as it was called, *the great sun of the world;* and this continued for many years, until changed by the Great Council of the United States in the year 1865 for that of *the great sun of discovery* 374, dating from the discovery of America by Columbus. This change of method of computation recognized the connecting link between the Improved Order of Red Men and the earlier societies elsewhere mentioned.

The term for a year was "a grand sun," afterwards changed to "great sun."

The months followed the regular calendar order, but with an added title significant of the season, as follows: January, *Cold moon;* February, *Snow moon;* March, *Worm moon;* April, *Plant moon;* May, *Flower moon;* June, *Hot moon;* July, *Buck moon;* August, *Sturgeon moon;* September, *Corn moon;* October, *Travelling moon;* November, *Beaver moon;* December, *Hunting moon.*

The term "*moon*" was used instead of "*month.*" Weeks and days were termed "*seven suns*" and "*suns.*" *Money* was called "*Wampum*," and divided into denominations of *fathoms, yards, feet,* and *inches*.[1]

A *fathom* was one dollar and a half; *a yard,* seventy-five cents; *a foot,* twenty-five cents; and *an inch* was *two and one-twelfth cents.*

These denominations were afterwards changed by the Great Council of the United States, as follows:—

A *fathom* was fixed at *one dollar,* a *foot* at *ten cents,* and *an inch* at *one cent.* *Fathoms* and *inches* were generally the only denominations used. The chiefs of the Tribe were elected every three moons, and meetings were held once in every seven suns.

The council fire of Logan Tribe was kindled on the sleep of the second sun (Monday), in the wigwam of Elisha Snike's house on Thames Street, and the meetings were well attended for several *great suns.* The first act of Logan Tribe after its organization was to pass a law that no council fire should be kindled in any wigwam where " Fire Water " (liquor) was sold. The knowledge of this fact but adds to the lustre which already brightens our Order's fair fame. Recognizing the benefits to be derived from temperance, they inculcated its principles in the teachings and laws of their Order. In these days when such warfare is waged against the liquor traffic, it is pleasing to know the position the organizers of our Order took upon this question. For upon whatever side of this important issue we stand, whether for or against the temperance question, *all* must deplore the result of excessive use of liquor.

This prohibitory measure on the part of the organizers of Logan Tribe No. 1 struck at once at the root of the evil so fatal to the former Red Men Societies; many of the old members were reformed through the efforts of the members of the new Tribe, and it speedily rose in the estimation of the public. After Logan Tribe had been in existence about one great sun, and there had also been instituted Metamora Tribe, No. 2, it was deemed advisable to apply to the Maryland Legislature for a charter, so that the Tribe could be recognized as an important body. Brother John F. Weishampel, Sr., was appointed to draw up the petition, and in so doing prepared the papers in

[1] Proceedings Great Council of United States.

ORGANIZATION AT BALTIMORE. 253

the name of the "Improved Order of Red Men," thus transposing the original title, "Order of Improved Red Men." In this connection an extract of Brother Weishampel's pamphlet is here quoted: —

"The Tribe increased in membership, and about a year after its organization it was resolved to apply to the Maryland Legislature for a charter, and John F. Weishampel was appointed to draw up and print the petition for that purpose. He did so, and on all copies he printed the name of the Order as it stood upon the record, except one for his own use, and in that he transposed the terms Order and Improved, and rendered the name *Improved Order of Red Men*. He then collected all the copies of the petition to which other members had obtained signatures, and, cutting off the names, attached them to his own copy, in which the change above named stood. The memorial went to the Legislature, and a charter was granted to Logan Tribe of Maryland, No. 1, of the Improved Order of Red Men. None of the members seemed to notice the alteration in the name and it therefore remained so."

Thus we see that a successful stratagem to meet the views of a single member defeated the intention of the founders of the Order in adopting the title first proposed.

(There seems to have been a mistake regarding the charter of Logan Tribe. The Acts of the Assembly of Maryland do not show a charter granted to Logan Tribe *alone*, and no charter was granted by the Legislature of Maryland until the session of 1837 or 1838, in the month of March, which charter was granted after a meeting of Logan and Metamora Tribes, jointly, on May 20, 1835, the result of which was the forming of the Great Council of Maryland, after which, of course, the officers of that body were elected. In the charter granted the names of members of both Tribes appear.)

In the peculiar wording of the charter, Logan Tribe is mentioned as "Logan Tribe of Maryland, No. 1, Improved Order of Red Men," and this peculiarity has given rise to a statement in some quarters that the first Tribe was called "Maryland Tribe, No. 1," and by some writers has been so referred to. This, however, is a mistake, as no such Tribe as "Maryland Tribe, No. 1," ever had an existence in the Improved Order of Red Men.

After an existence of varied successes and failures, Logan Tribe finally became very popular, its peculiar features of charity and benevolence enlisted the attention of the palefaces, and it attained a large membership.

An application was made to the Tribe for authority to establish another Tribe in a section of the city more centrally located. This was granted, and on the 22d day of June, 1834, Metamora Tribe, No. 2, was instituted, and held its meetings in a wigwam located at the corner of West Baltimore Street and Tripolet's Alley (now Post-Office Avenue), and selected the sleep of the 4th sun (Wednesday) for the kindling of the council fires. The charter members of Metamora Tribe, No. 2, have already been given. This Tribe promised well at first, and succeeded in increasing its membership with considerable rapidity. It was, however, short lived, as the records show that in 1840 the Great Council of Maryland declared the Tribe defunct.

Soon after the organization of Metamora Tribe, No. 2, it was deemed best to form a higher body, to be known as the *Grand Council of Maryland*, in order that the laws and practices, as well as the ceremonies of the Order, should be under a common controlling authority so as to insure uniformity, as the authority of Logan Tribe over Metamora Tribe was not always strictly acknowledged or observed by the younger Tribe. Accordingly delegates were selected from each of the two Tribes (see long-talk of J. F. Weishampel), and on May 20, 1835 (or 20th sun, Flower moon, 5595), they assembled in the old wigwam on Thames Street, Baltimore, Md. The Grand Council of Maryland was then and there organized and selected (as already given).

It will be seen that Edward Lucas held two positions, which it appears was allowed in the early days of the Order, as the same thing occurred in 5598 (A.D. 1838), when Past Sachem John Miller held the position of Grand Keeper of Wampum, and also that of Grand Prophet. The former title having been changed from "Chief" to "Keeper of Wampum," and the word "Worthy" prefixed to the titles of the grand chiefs. (*See charter of Pocahontas Tribe, No. 3, of Maryland.*)

On the 12th sun, Flower moon, 5598, or May 12, 1838, a dispensation for a new Tribe was granted to the following appli-

ORGANIZATION AT BALTIMORE. 255

cants: J. Lysher, William Burke (then Grand Sachem), T. Hynes, Peter Green, W. G. Cook, J. C. Chamberlain, and George W. Stauffer, to form Pocahontas Tribe, No. 3, and it was instituted on the same date. This was the first Tribe organized under the authority of the Grand Council of Maryland.

The Order was now firmly established, and seemed to be on the high road to prosperity. Its members were zealous and untiring in their efforts to increase its numbers, and its peculiar ceremonies being so attractive, there was always a good attendance at the council fires.

The regalia consisted of a collar and apron, and in the grand sun 5604 (or A.D. 1844), the following was adopted as the only Regalia of the Order: Collars. — For initiatory degree, pink (afterwards changed to orange); second degree, blue; third degree, scarlet. Aprons. — Color, scarlet, trimmed with the color of the degree of the wearer. Regalia for officers. — Sachem, scarlet collar trimmed with gold; Sagamore, scarlet collar trimmed with silver; Prophet, a white sash worn over the right shoulder to the left side.

In grand sun 5617 (A.D. 1857) the present regalia was adopted. (*See Proceedings of Great Council United States.*)

The number of Tribes did not increase for several years, which is strange for an Order of such intrinsic worth. But the members seemed to concentrate their efforts upon building up the Tribes already formed, adding to their numerical strength, and making them capable of self-support, without too great a tax upon their individual wampum belts, an example worthy of imitation in later years when so many skeleton Tribes have been formed. Another advantage resulting from this small but continuous growth in membership was that all members of the Tribes became perfectly acquainted with the work of the Order, and therefore better able to instruct new brethren admitted.

While the Order had been to some extent successful, it was, of course, in its infancy and comparatively unknown even in Baltimore. A desire began to grow in the minds of its members to have it more generally known to the community at large, and at the same time to celebrate its anniversary with due honor. After much serious consideration, for it was felt to be a momentous question in the history of the Order, it was decided about the close of grand sun 5596 that a public anniversary celebration should be held, and arrangements were made that the 12th sun of the Flower moon, 5597 (May 12, 1837), Saint Tammany's Day, should be celebrated by a public display of the Tribes, and it was determined that an oration suitable to the occasion should be delivered with attendant ceremonies, consisting of a parade, etc.

We quote from the pamphlet of Brother Weishampel an account of this anniversary: —

"P. S. John E. Stansbury was chosen Chief Marshal, and Past Sachem J. F. Weishampel orator of the day. Dr. J. Bonfield acted as Prophet *pro tem*. These rode in a barouche at the head of a long and imposing procession that marched through a number of streets of the city to the Trinity Church in Old-Town, where the longtalk was delivered to a large audience of members of the Order and paleface citizens of both sexes. After the oration, the procession re-formed and proceeded to a pleasant grove, where they partook of the refreshments provided for the occasion and had an orderly enjoyment till toward the going down of the sun, when they formed again, proceeded to their wigwams and disbanded and sent their players on horns, pipes, and drums home. This was the first public anniversary celebrated by the Order."

About one grand sun subsequent to the anniversary above mentioned, the Order was called upon to mourn the loss of one of its oldest members, Past Great Sachem William T. Jones, who left the hunting grounds of earth after a lingering illness, in 1838. His death was a sad loss to the Society, by whom he was respected and loved. He was active always in the interest of the Order, and when the "Great Council of Maryland came into existence he was chosen the first Sachem of that body. So unbounded was the confidence in him that for most of the time he was entrusted with the wampum belt, without ever being required to give further security than simply to be willing to take charge of the funds as treasurer." He died on the 8th sun, Flower moon, 5598 (May 8, 1838), aged thirty-nine grand suns, leaving a widow and orphans, also a large circle of friends to mourn his departure.

In the demise of Brother Jones the Order suffered a severe loss, for although he had for a long time been debarred by illness from mingling with his brethren around the council fire, yet they remembered his early active services, so faithfully rendered and by them so highly appreciated. His funeral took place on the 9th sun, Flower moon, 5598 (May 9, 1838), and was attended by a large concourse of friends, the Grand Council of Maryland, the members of the Tribes, and also by the Grand Lodge, and Union Lodge, No. 16, of the Independent Order of Odd Fellows, of which he was an honored member.

The records of the Grand Council of Maryland show that during the grand sun 5600 (A.D. 1840), the charter of Metamora Tribe, No. 2, was revoked and the Tribe declared defunct, although the reasons for this act are not definitely given or explained, and the Order was thus reduced *to two Tribes*, Logan, No. 1, and Pocahontas, No. 3.

In the month of September, 5601 (A.D. 1841), a new Tribe, named Metamora, No. 4, was instituted, the charter members being: Louis Weaver, Christian Benner, Jacob Weisner, A. Leutz, and C. Hilsbury. The Tribe was instituted on or about the 17th of the month, and continued to work under the authority of the Grand Council of Maryland until Plant moon, grand sun 5610 (1850), when, on account of a difficulty arising between the Grand Council and the Tribe, the membership decided to withdraw from the Order and form the nucleus of the organization known as the Independent Order of Red Men, composed entirely of Germans.

At a session of the Grand Council held April 28, 5603 (A.D. 1843) the question of celebrating Saint Tammany's Day was taken into consideration, and a committee was appointed to make necessary preparations for a procession. On May 5, of the same year, the committee reported favorably, and a resolution was adopted to have a parade and engage two bands of music, but no further authentic record can be found of the affair.

In September, 5603 (A.D. 1843), a new Tribe, to be known as Powhattan Tribe, No. 5, was petitioned for by the following applicants: Samuel Halfpenny, Henry Slater, James Seward, T. Bangs, and George Sables. This was duly instituted, and has become one of the most successful and flourishing Tribes in the Order. At this writing it is considered one of the wealthiest Tribes in existence, owning its own wigwam, known as Pocahontas Hall, located on the corner of Pratt and Bond

Streets, Baltimore, Md. The wigwam is a large, commodious building, admirably adapted to the purposes for which it was built, and is often used by the Great Council of Maryland for the kindling of its great sun council fires.

For another great sun after the institution of Powhattan Tribe, the Grand Council seems by the records to have kindled its council fires each moon, and sometimes even more frequently.

At a special council fire, held on April 19, 5604 (A.D. 1844), the question of celebrating Saint Tammany's Day was again discussed, and at a special session held on April 26, of that year, the Representatives from the several Tribes reported adversely, and the matter was indefinitely postponed. (*See Proceedings of the Great Council of Maryland, Vol. I.*) The members of the Order, however, seemed to be of the opinion that a demonstration of some kind would be of benefit to the Order, and the subject of holding a "peace dance" or ball, was frequently discussed. On the minutes of the Grand Council fire kindled December 13, 1844, the following resolution appears as having been adopted :—

"*Resolved*, That this Great Council will not permit the Tribes under its jurisdiction to have or to hold any procession, ball, or other public exhibition, in the wigwam or elsewhere, without first obtaining permission from this Great Council."

It is evident that permission was granted for the proposed ball, as in Cold moon, 5605 (January, 1845), the exact date is not on record, "a peace dance" or public ball was held at Washington Hall, located on Baltimore Street, adjoining the bridge over Jones Falls (now Monumental Theatre). It was given under the auspices of Pocahontas Tribe, and proved a most successful event in the history of the Order, having the effect, not only of exhibiting to the public the fraternity of Red Men in its brightest aspect, but also of adding to the wampum belt of the Tribe. "The Master of Ceremonies" was Professor Charles Spies, now a member of Ottawa Tribe, No. 16.

From this public demonstration of the Order good results soon followed, and a large increase of membership was added to the Tribes. The impetus thus given awakened an interest outside the hunting grounds of Baltimore, and communication was opened with several gentlemen of Washington, D.C., which

ORGANIZATION AT BALTIMORE.

resulted in a petition for the institution of a Tribe in the District of Columbia, known as Powhattan Tribe, No. 1, and located in the city of Washington. The laws of the Great Council made it necessary that at least five members of a new Tribe should be members of the Order, and in obedience to this law, five members of Pocahontas Tribe, No. 3, of Baltimore, took temporary cards of withdrawal from their own Tribe and went to Washington to form the new Tribe. The names of these brethren were William H. Ford, T. G. Miller, John L. Booker, William G. Gorsuch, and Louis Bonsal. After forming the Tribe they initiated the requisite number of palefaces to put it in working order, and then rejoined their own Tribe. This event marks the first extension of the Order outside of Maryland. Of those devoted brethren who aided in this extension, Past Great Sachem William H. Ford is still a faithful member of the Order in Pocahontas Tribe, No. 3, while another, Past Great Incohonee William G. Gorsuch, was the first Great Sachem Incohonee of the Great Council of the United States, and the father of Susquehanna Tribe, No. 27, of Baltimore, Md.

The next step of importance was the institution of Uncas Tribe, No. 6, in the hunting grounds of Baltimore, which located its wigwam at the corner of Front and Gay Streets, the charter being issued to the following Chiefs : G. T. Laws, J. Adams, W. Smuller, P. Metz, W. A. Allen, J. Coburn, George F. Sables, J. C. Boyd, and J. Kettrich. This event occurred early in the great sun 5605 (A.D. 1845).

On the 18th sun, Snow moon, 5605 (February 18, 1845), Osceola Tribe, No. 2, of the District of Columbia, was instituted in the town of Alexandria, on a petition signed by five members of the Great Council of Maryland, who, as in a former case, took withdrawal cards for the purpose. Their names were William G. Gorsuch, John Meisner, John L. Booker, George F. Sables, and James Pruden. These brethren went to Alexandria and established Osceola Tribe, No. 2, of the District of Columbia, and afterwards rejoined their own Tribe.

During the same grand sun a third Tribe was instituted in the District of Columbia, known as Anacostia Tribe, No. 3, by members of Powhattan Tribe, No. 1, among whom were William Tucker, A. G. Herold, Peyton Page, and Joseph Mundree. This

Tribe was instituted in Buck moon or Corn moon, the precise date being uncertain, in grand sun, 5605 (A.D. 1845), as appears from the report of the Great Council of D.C., which was shortly afterwards organized.

Three Tribes having been instituted in the District of Columbia, measures were taken to form a Great Council of that jurisdiction, placing these Tribes under its direct control, with the agreement that the supreme authority of the Order should be vested in the Great Council of Maryland until such time as the Great Council of the United States should be formed. Accordingly a petition was sent to the Great Council of Maryland requesting that body to institute the Great Council of the District of Columbia. The Great Sachem called a special council fire of the Great Council of Maryland to consider the matter, on the 30th sun, Sturgeon moon, 5605 (August 30, 1845), when the petition was read and the application granted. The names of the petitioners were as follows: From Powhattan Tribe, No. 1, John A. Stephenson, Z. K. Offutt, and T. H. Wannart; from Osceola Tribe, No. 2, Hugh Latham, Lewis H. Hopkins, and John Howell; from Anacostia Tribe, No. 3, William Tucker, Peyton Page, and A. G. Herold.

Immediate steps were taken to form the Great Council, and, on the 4th sun, Beaver moon, 5605 (November 4, 1845), it was instituted by the great chiefs of the Great Council of Maryland, Great Sachem James Purden being the instituting officer. The following Great Chiefs were elected and installed (the term "raised up" not then being in vogue): Worthy Great Sachem, Joseph Wannels; Worthy Great Senior Sagamore, William Tucker; Worthy Great Junior Sagamore, John A. Stephenson; Worthy Great Prophet, James Mundell; Worthy Great Chief of Records, John Howell: the other great chiefs were elected at a subsequent meeting.

This being the first Great Council instituted outside of Maryland, the charter, or warrant of authority, under which it worked is worthy of reproduction. It was as follows:—

Charter Granted to the Great Council of the District of Columbia by the

GREAT COUNCIL OF MARYLAND, IMPROVED ORDER OF RED MEN.

Know Ye, That

Whereas, The General Assembly of the State of Maryland at the session of the said body held in the years of 1837 and 1838, did pass an act incorporating the Great Council of the Improved Order of Red Men of the State of Maryland, which Act is to be found in Chapter 181 of the said enactments;

And, *whereas*, The said Great Council of Maryland has, by virtue of the power vested in it, established three subordinate Tribes of the said Improved Order of Red Men in the District of Columbia;

And, *whereas*, The said subordinate Tribes: — Powhattan No. 1, Osceola No. 2, and Anacostia No. 3, all of the District of Columbia, have in due form respectively petitioned the Great Council of Maryland for the privilege to constitute a Great Council of the District of Columbia of the Improved Order of Red Men, and for a charter to protect it in the lawful discharge of its duties and the maintaining of its rights and privileges,

Therefore, the said Great Council of Maryland does hereby grant to the said applicants represented by John A. Stephenson, Z. K. Offutt and T. H. Wannart of Powhattan Tribe, No. 1; Hugh Latham, Lewis H. Hopkins and John Howell of Osceola, No. 2; William Tucker, Peyton Page and A. G. Herold of Anacostia, No. 3, the privilege to organize a Great Council of the District of Columbia of the said Order, and grants to it the exercise of all the rights, privileges and powers to preside over and govern the said Tribes, and all other Tribes the said Great Council of the District of Columbia may hereafter establish in the said District, according to the usage of the Order. And the said Great Council shall further have the right to become a body politic. And the said Great Council shall be considered to possess the power to participate with the Great Council of Maryland in the establishment of a Great Council of the United States of the said Improved Order of Red Men. But the said Great Council of the District of Columbia shall not have power to alter any of the usages and customs or principles of the said Order without the approbation and concurrence of the other Great Councils, or the Great Council of the United States, that are or may be hereafter established.

In ratification of all the above dispensations and agreement, the said Great Council of Maryland does on this third sun of the first seven suns in Beaver moon of the grand sun 5605 (November 4, 1845), duly install the following chiefs into the respective offices of the said Great Council of the District of Columbia, viz. : — Joseph Wannels, Great Sachem ; William Tucker, Great Senior Sagamore ; John A. Stephenson, Great Junior Sagamore ; James Mundell, Great Prophet ; John Howell, Great Keeper of Records ; and , Great Keeper of Wampum.

This charter to remain in full force so long as the said Great Council of the District of Columbia complies with the conditions and requirements herein specified, and so long as at least five Past Sachems of good standing of the Tribes working under its jurisdiction are members of the same. Otherwise, this charter is declared forfeited and of none effect, and is to be returned to the source from which it emanated.

Given by virtue of a unanimous resolution passed by the Great Council of Maryland, assembled in Logan Wigwam in the city of Baltimore, on the 6th sleep of the third seven suns of Travelling moon in the grand sun 5605, and signed and delivered in the city of Washington by the undersigned chiefs of the Great Council of Maryland, on this third sun of the second seven suns of Beaver moon in the grand sun 5605, with the seal of the Great Council of Maryland affixed thereto.

Attest : — JAMES PURDEN, M. W. G. Sachem.
GUSTAV OTTO, M. W. G. Sen. Sag.
WILLIAM H. HOOPER, M. W. G. Jun. Sag.
WILLIAM G. GORSUCH, Prophet *pro tem*.
JOHN MEISER, Keeper of Records.
——— WERNER, Keeper of Wampum.

For some time previous to this organization of the Great Council of the District of Columbia, and doubtless in anticipation of that event, the minds of the members of the Great Council of Maryland had been occupied with the subject of forming a supreme body to be known as the Great Council of the United States. The necessity of having a higher or supreme organization with control and authority over the Great Councils which might be organized to spread the Order in other hunting grounds, and whose organization, judging from the spirit manifested, seemed probable in the near future, was at length brought more forcibly to the notice of the membership by a communication from the Great Council of the District of Columbia to the Great Council of Maryland, relative to the right and authority of the former to grant charters to new Tribes. The Great Council of Maryland had reserved the right of granting charters and instituting new Tribes in all localities except the District of Columbia, and, consequently, any attempt to execute this power on the part of the Great Council of the District of Columbia, would have resulted in a conflict of authority, and to avoid such conflict it was determined to organize the Great Council of the United States with supreme authority over all Great Councils, and to organize Tribes outside of Maryland and the District of Columbia. But this important step was not taken without great deliberation, the membership of the Order seemingly desiring to avoid any unfavorable result that may follow undue haste or inconsiderate action.

In the early part of Cold moon, 5606 (January, 1846), a resolution was adopted by the Great Council of Maryland to appoint a committee to inquire into the expediency of forming the Great Council of the United States, and should that committee determine that it was necessary and expedient, it was empowered to take such steps necessary toward that object and report the action taken to the Great Council. The committee consisted of Great Sachem Gustav Otto, Past Great Sachem James Purden, Past Great Sachem George Ketler, and Past Great Sachem George Fastie. The committee made a favorable report on the 7th sun of Corn moon, 5606 (September, 1846), having had the matter under consideration for the space of seven months. The report was accepted and the committee continued. The Great Council passed a resolution that none should be eligible to membership in the Great Council of the United States, except Past Great Sachems, and acting on this resolution the committee seems to have formed its members into a permanent body as a nucleus for the formation of the Great Council, and sent a communication to the Great Council of Maryland on the 13th sun of Beaver moon, 5606 (November 13, 1846), requesting that body to send a Past Great Sachem to represent it at a meeting of the self-constituted Great Council of the United States. The Great Council of Maryland, however, ignored the request and annulled the resolution making Past Great Sachems alone eligible as members of the proposed Great Council of the United States, and elected three members, not Past Great Sachems, as Representatives to said Great Council, and instructed each Tribe to send one Past Sachem as a delegate to form the supreme body. A communication was also sent to the Great Council of the District of Columbia, requesting that body to send delegates; but the Great Council of the District declined to take part, and so informed the Great Council of Maryland. This resulted in the passage of a resolution by the Great Council of Maryland, "that the Great Council of the United States shall be forthwith opened," and the Great Chief of Records was instructed to so notify the Great Council of the District of Columbia.

In the meantime applications had been received to institute

two new Tribes in Baltimore, — Wacusta, No. 7, and Philip, No. 8. The former, however, from some cause not explained was never instituted. The latter was duly organized and a charter granted to the following applicants: Past Great Sachem Gustav Otto, and Past Sachems D. Lustre, L. Weber, A. Ballauf, and J. L. Muhlhoffer, together with a number of brethren from Logan Tribe. The Tribe was instituted in the latter part of 5606 (1846). An application was also received from a number of members to form Mohegan Tribe, No. 9, at Cumberland, Md., which was granted.

At this time the Order consisted of the Great Council of Maryland, Logan Tribe, No. 1, Pocahontas Tribe, No. 3, Metamora Tribe, No. 4, Powhattan Tribe, No. 5, Uncas Tribe, No. 6, and Philip Tribe, No. 8, of Maryland; the Great Council of the District of Columbia, Powhattan Tribe, No. 1, Osceola Tribe, No. 2, Anacostia Tribe, No. 3, and Shawnee Tribe, No. 4, of the District of Columbia.

Shortly after, a change was made in the numbering of the Tribes under the District of Columbia, and they became known as follows: Powhattan Tribe, No. 1, and Anacostia Tribe, No. 2, of Washington, D.C.; Osceola, No. 1, and Shawnee, No. 2, of Virginia.

We have nearly completed the early history of our beloved Order from its earliest origin up to the time of the organization of the Great Council of the United States.

With pleasurable pride we have noted its advance, its increase of Tribes, its added membership, its wise administration of power in small jurisdictions, until, grown stronger and larger, it was deemed advisable to combine in one supreme body, with representation from all smaller executive bodies, the authority and control of the Order at large. So was formed, as we will now read, the Great Council of the United States.

Until this period, the Great Council of Maryland had held supreme sway, from, or through the right of priority, and justly so, for a body, which resulted from the forming of the Improved Order of Red Men should have supreme control of it, in its infancy at least, until its noble principles were so familiar to its members, that they were fitted to go among strangers and establish branches, and teach the golden principles of Freedom, Friendship, and Charity.

As the Order grew older, the members of the different Tribes began to feel a desire for a Great Council in which all should meet on an equal footing, without the prestige of priority which the Great Council of Maryland had always held, and which, from its birth as we have shown, had been its right.

The civil charter of the Great Council of the United States was granted to the Order by the Legislature of the State of Pennsylvania, for this reason: that the Legislature of Maryland would not grant a charter to any corporate body unless the applicants were all residents of the State, and the applicants for the charter of the United States were not all from Maryland. The Great Council of the State of Maryland was incorporated by the Legislature on the 14th sun, Worm moon 5598 (session 1837–1838). The Great Council of Maryland having been given a legal existence, forthwith issued charters to Logan Tribe, No. 1, and Metamora Tribe, No. 2. These charters bore the date, 21st sun, Worm moon, G. S. 5598 (March 21, 1838).

It may not be out of place to give a copy, in our retrospective, of the first charter issued by this august body. It is as follows:—

CHARTER

Granted by the Great Council of Maryland

of the

Improved Order of Red Men.

Organized		*Incorporated*
on the		*on the*
12*th day of May,*	(Illustration.)	14*th day of March,*
A.D. 1836.		A.D. 1838.

To all Whom it May Concern:

Know ye that the Great Council of Baltimore and State of Maryland doth hereby grant this Charter or Dispensation to the following Brothers of the said Improved Order of Red Men, viz.: William T. Jones, P. R. Hilditch, George A. Peter, John Miller, George Fastie, Jones Fridewald, Giles Harkiness and John Hugget, the said Brothers all residing in the city of Baltimore, and in the State of Maryland, to establish a Tribe of the said Order in the said city, to be hailed and known by the title of Logan Tribe, No. 1, who, being duly formed, are hereby authorized and empowered to initiate into the mysteries of the said Order any person or persons duly and regularly proposed, and elected agreeably to the General Laws adopted or amended by this Great Council, as they, the said Great Council, shall from time to time hereafter alter, amend, or adopt; and to administer to all Brothers who are known to be of good character and standing in society, the privileges and benefits arising therefrom: and they, the said Logan Tribe, No. 1, are hereby empowered by the said Great Council to enact By-Laws in accordance with the General Laws, and subject to all amendments of the said Great Council of the Improved Order of Red Men, for the government of their said Tribe; and, provided that the said Logan Tribe, No. 1, do in all matters and points act according to the usages and customs adopted by the Great Council, and they, the said Logan Tribe, No. 1, are hereby bound to adhere to and support the articles or amendments as aforesaid of this Great Council, and adhering to and supporting the articles delivered with this Charter or Dispensation; and in default of which, the said Great Council, at their decision, may declare, or take away, or suspend as null and void, and of none effect, this Charter, as the said Council are fully empowered so to do by an Act passed by the Legislature of the State of Maryland on the 14th day of March, A.D. one thousand eight hundred and thirty-eight.

In witness whereof, we, the officers of the said Great Council, have hereunto subscribed our names and affixed the seal of the Great Council of Maryland, in the United States of America, the 21st day of March, one thousand eight hundred and thirty-eight.

WILLIAM B. BURKE, W. G. S.
GEORGE FASTIE, W. G. S. S.
AUGUST KETLER, W. G. J. S.
JOHN MILLER, W. G. P.
THOMAS HENNA, W. G. C. of R.

From some unexplained cause, the charter of Pocahontas Tribe, No. 3, was not issued until the 27th sun, Hunting moon, of the same year (December 27, 1838), although the then presiding Great Sachem was a member of that Tribe. (*See charter of Pocahontas Tribe, No. 3.*)

In the case of Logan Tribe, No. 1, and Metamora Tribe, No. 2, this act of the Great Council was a secondary act of authority. Logan Tribe, No. 1, and Metamora Tribe, No. 2, derived its rights and powers from its institution as a branch of the Order from Logan Tribe, No. 1, which, when the Great Council was formed, of course, surrendered all its former authority as the head of the Order, and became itself subordinate to the higher power of the Great Council of Maryland, formed by Representatives from both Tribes, in grand sun 5595 (A.D. 1835). In issuing the charters of the Tribes here referred to, the Great Council inserted the names of the chiefs of the Tribe who occupied the stumps at the date of issuing these charters, and *not to the original members* who applied to have the Tribes instituted, and this has given rise to a seeming confusion of dates, and led some brethren astray when attempting to arrive at the date of original formation and seniority of the first Tribe. No one disputes that George A. Peter, and William T. Jones were original members of Logan Tribe, No. 1, at its institution, but the charter of Logan Tribe, No. 1, contains the following:—

FREEDOM, FRIENDSHIP, CHARITY.

THE GREAT COUNCIL OF MARYLAND IMPROVED ORDER OF RED MEN.

TO WHOM IT MAY CONCERN:

Know that the Great Council of Maryland, Improved Order of Red Men, doth grant this Charter to the following Chiefs: Charles Treusch, Christie Druff, Louis Toenis, Peter Nagle, William Segnell, J. W. Kratz.

Issued this 21st sun Worm moon, grand sun 5598.

To be known and hailed as Logan Tribe, No. 1, Improved Order of Red Men, etc., etc.

Thus, it will be seen that neither of the names, George A. Peter nor William T. Jones, appear on the charter, and the only date is grand sun 5508, 21st Worm moon. No date of the common era appears anywhere in the charter, and upon the seal which is twice affixed, once in plain impress, and again in the colors of the Order, the date 20th sun, Flower moon, G. S. 5598, the date of the organization of the Grand Council of Maryland, can be distinctly seen.

At the present writing, A.D. 1893, this charter is still in existence, a venerable document, discolored by age, but in good state of preservation, being glued to a strong linen or canvas back to prevent injury, and is signed by William B. Burke, Great Sachem, George Fastie, Great Senior Sagamore, and other great chiefs of the Great Council of Maryland.

The charter of Pocahontas Tribe, No. 3, still hangs in the wigwam, even more venerable in appearance than that of the defunct Logan Tribe, yet still perfectly legible, and bears the words "Organized on the 12th day of May, 1838," on the left-hand side of the vignette, and the date, March 14, 1838, on the right, the latter being the date of the incorporation of the Great Council of Maryland, by the Maryland Legislature.

The charter is signed by the following Great Chiefs: W. B. Burke, Worthy Great Sachem; George Fastie, Worthy Great

Senior Sagamore; August Ketler, Worthy Great Junior Sagamore; John Miller, Prophet; Thomas Hanna, Worthy Great C. of R.; John Miller, Worthy Great K. of W.; and it is issued to the following chiefs of the Tribe: William B. Burke, Zefhemiah Lyster, Peter Green, Thomas Hines, George W. Stauffer, W. E. Cook, J. M. E. Chamberlain.

On the accuracy of the dates pertaining to the institution of these three first Tribes depends the correctness of the history of the Order. Many of the early records of the Order have been lost, or more probably, wantonly destroyed, as they *have never been seen by any member of the Order since their removal from the office of the Great Council of the United States in the Great Sun of Discovery* 375, at which time a new Great Chief of Records was elected, and a portion of the manuscript records were concealed or destroyed. Several attempts have been made to recover them, or gain some information as to their whereabouts, but no positive information has been obtained by any one. It is the absence of these records which has caused dispute and confusion of dates and localities heretofore, existing prior to the research contained in this work, obtained after the expenditure of time, labor, and money, from old books, documents, charters of the old Tribes, records, and manuscripts, and evidence and information derived from the oldest living members of the Order, as well as contemporaneous historical data, as shown by the following letter from G. A. Peter, *the founder of the Order:* —

CINCINNATI, Sept. 17, 1872.

PAST GREAT SACHEM, GEORGE W. LINDSAY:

Esteemed Brother: — Having examined your report of the origin of the Improved Order of Red Men, from the information I received from Brother Muirhead formerly of Philadelphia and other old members of the Order, *I think that you are very accurate in its history, and from and after the organization of the Improved Order of Red Men* I can certify to its correctness in organization of the Improved Order of Red Men. We severed our connection with the old Society of Red Men that was instituted in Baltimore by Brother William Muirhead, he having subscribed to an agreement to become a member and support the Improved Order of Red Men.

Yours fraternally in the bonds of F. F. and C.

GEORGE A. PETER.

Brother George A. Peter was the first Sachem of Logan Tribe, and Brother William T. Jones, the first Great Sachem of the Improved Order of Red Men.

ORGANIZATION AT BALTIMORE.

A letter written by Brother George A. Peter to one of the compilers of this work, contributes much to the settlement of this point, it having been at one time disputed by Brother John F. Weishampel, who was misled by his recollections, dating back some forty years, and he mistook the chieftaincies, awarding to Brother Jones the credit of founding the Improved Order of Red Men, which credit indisputably, in the light of other evidence, belongs to Brother George A. Peter.

The writer has on many occasions consulted with Brother Richard Marley, prior to his death, who was one of the earliest members of the Order, and whose active membership made him a most reliable authority. He always most emphatically stated that Brother George A. Peter was the first Sachem of Logan Tribe, No. 1, and other aged members of that Tribe corroborate Brother Marley's statement.

This distinguished honor was conferred on Brother Peter for his earnest, honest, and devoted work in reclaiming the name of Red Man from the disgrace and obloquy into which it had fallen among other societies, and for his success in organizing the first Tribe of the Improved Order of Red Men. He was foremost in the work, and his name will be revered as the founder of the Order so long as Redmanship has a place in the hearts of its members.

It may not be out of place to say here, that from time to time, during the thirteen great suns preceding the organization of the Great Council of the United States, applications were received and petitions granted to form Tribes in distant hunting grounds, special authority being given to brothers deputized for the purpose. But when the Great Council of the United States was organized, there existed no Tribes of the Improved Order of Red Men anywhere except in Maryland, District of Columbia, and Virginia.

We are thus brought down to the period when a supreme body seemed necessary with authority, shared equally, in a representative capacity, by all the Great Councils and other bodies subordinate to it. In chapters VII and VIII is given the history of that supreme body, named the Great Council of the United States, from its institution in 1847 down to the present time.

CHAPTER VI.

ORGANIZATION AT BALTIMORE. ANOTHER VERSION.

In justice to all concerned, it seems necessary to state claims made somewhat at variance with those in the preceding chapter. The facts and claims thus stated are those made by the late Past Great Incohonee, Morris H. Gorham.

It must be remembered that the time of which we are writing was sixty years ago, and that many of the dates given are based upon human memory, always faulty, of the matters stated, and lacks the verification of the official documents and records, which, but for their unfortunate disappearance, might establish the exact facts beyond dispute. All we can do is to present the conflicting claims, the argument given to sustain each, and then leave the reader to judge which rests upon the soundest presumption of plausibility. With this end in view the following is given as the evidence fairly stated of the counter-claim concerning the Tribe at Baltimore.

In a preceding chapter an account was given of the approximate date, at which branches of the Society of Red Men were established in different parts of the country. The facts there stated indicate that Minowakinton, or "Iron Stone," John M. Byrns (Burns), 5th Major-General, was General-in-Chief of all the southern Tribes in 1818, at which time he organized a Tribe at Charleston, South Carolina, which became broken up by reason of the plague in 1820, and which was apparently never reorganized. In his letter to the Generalissimo in 1826 he recites this fact, and states that "Walk-in-the-Water" held an appointment under the government in Florida, "Little Oak" in Mexico, and "Eagle Eye" in Maryland. The "Eagle Eye" referred to, as shown by the Muster Roll, was Marinus W. Pike. On another Roll "Iron Stone" is entered as "commanding in Maryland." From this it is inferred that when he left Charleston, on account of the epidemic prevailing in that city, he pro-

ENLISTING FOR THE WAR-PATH.

ceeded to Baltimore, and by virtue of his seniority of rank, assumed command of the Red Men in Maryland. An explanation has already been given of the different significations of "on mission" and "commanding" or "on command." The fact that his name was entered upon the roll as "commanding" in Maryland, also indicates the existence of the society of Red Men there as early as 1820, even if not established in 1818 by Byrns on his way south. As a further proof of the existence of the Order in Maryland at the time named, references may be had to a letter dated May 13, 1820, by Yeougheowanewago, or "Split Log," Francis Shallus, Generalissimo, and addressed to "Split Log's Brother," Metawa of Chippewa, late Poscopsahee or "Black Cat," Grand Chief of the Mandans, Brigadier-General by Brevet, now 5th Major-General, "commanding in Maryland." The ink in which the words to Split Log's Brother, Metawa of Chippewa, are written, is very much brighter than the balance of the superscription which has perceptibly faded. This letter was found among the papers of Richard Marley after his death. From these the inference has been drawn that it was addressed to Brother Marley. If this was so, then Richard Marley must have been in command of a Tribe in Maryland at that time, but on page 209 of the Minute Book, is entered among others, admitted under date of September 14, 1824, the name of "Richard Marley, Cordwainer," proposed by "Hospitality," name received Metawa, or "Moose Deer's Brother."

Again, on October 28, 1857, the late Past Great Incohonee Hugh Latham, in an address delivered at Lancaster, Pa., reported in the *Conestoga Chief*, of October, 1857, stated that "our worthy brother Past Great Incohonee, Richard Marley, was a Major-General, and called Eagle Eye." Having removed to Baltimore, he was appointed Chief of the Maryland Tribe, with the title of "Split Log," and, agreeably to instructions, caused a council fire to be kindled in that city in June, 1820. It is presumed Brother Latham obtained this information from Brother Marley, and it is asserted that in lapse of time between 1820 and 1857 some confusion of dates must have occurred in the account of Brother Marley, as the statement quoted is in conflict with the documents in existence. On Muster Rolls Nos. 2, 3, and 4, the name of Richard Marley is entered as

Major-General "commanding in Maryland"; but on these Muster Rolls appears no date to indicate the time of appointment, or when such command was exercised or held. The title given Brother Marley on these rolls is neither "Eagle Eye" nor "Split Log," but "Split Log's Brother." "Eagle Eye" was the name of Marinus W. Pike, and "Split Log" was the name of Francis Shallus, the first Generalissimo of the Society. It is possible, however, that Brother Marley was mistaken as to the date of kindling the council fire in Maryland.

There were no less than five members of the Society in Philadelphia by the name of Marley; and, recalling the custom already alluded to in the former chapter, of expressing consanguinity by the title given to a member at adoption, we may infer that William Marley, whose name appears on Roll No. 1, under date of February 4, 1817, with the title of Toxus of Norridgewock, or "Moose Deer," was undoubtedly the father of William Cooper Marley, whose name appears on Roll No. 2, with the title of Norridgewrigwock, or "Young Moose Deer," and that he was the brother of Richard Marley, whose name appears on Roll No. 2, with the title of Metawa of Chippewa, or "Moose Deer's Brother," and subsequently, having attained the rank of 3d Major-General, as "commanding in Maryland," with the new sub-title of "Split Log's Brother."

The superscription upon the letter cited indicates that it was addressed to the "5th Major-General." The 5th Major-General was John M. Byrns, Minowakinton, or "Iron Stone." It is claimed that there would be less likelihood of confusion of rank than a confusion of names, as the name held by one brother, as we have already seen, was frequently transferred to another upon the death of the original holder, or upon the occasion of his severing his connection with the Society. From all these data, it is claimed that Richard Marley could not have organized a Tribe in Maryland in 1820, four years before his admission to the Society, as recorded on page 209 of the Minute Book.

Among other names given in connection with the Order in Baltimore, at different dates, are Dr. Matthias Lopez, Captain Jacob Warner, Jacob Winn, John Flaherty, "Light Stick," "Little Wasp," "Wolf Rapid," John Braceland, "Bald Eagle's Eye," Benjamin Vantassel, David Sweetman, Captain Moore,

"Iron Face," and Jacob Johnston. These are the only names appearing on the Muster Roll and records in connection with Maryland. Where the records give the real name of the brother, we have quoted it; and where the real name is not given, we have quoted the title by which he was designated on the Roll. On information said to have been furnished by Richard Marley, it is stated that the Tribe already established at Baltimore in 1820 continued in operation until about the year 1824, when it became dormant. In 1829, an effort was made to revive it, under the direction of Richard Marley, 3d Major-General, and was successful to the extent that the Tribe attained a membership of about 150. It continued to exist for a period of three or four years, with alternating success and depression, until it finally expired.

In 1833, William Muirhead, whose name in the Society of Red Men was Withea of Missouri, or "Hospitality," resided in Baltimore. This fact is stated upon the authority of Past Great Incohonee Richard Marley, who also is quoted as the authority for the statement that William Muirhead established the Society in Baltimore in the year 1833. It is alleged that this statement was confirmed by Thomas J. Loudenslager, of Philadelphia, in 1866. It will be remembered that the latter gentleman was admitted in 1824, and was the last Grand Recording Scribe when the Society in Philadelphia ceased operations. The statement attributed to him is that William Muirhead "held the commission of Brigadier-General under George Knorr, the second Generalissimo of the Society, and that he had gone to Baltimore, and established the Society there in 1833 or 1834." A further verification of this fact is given by manuscripts furnished by the late John L. Booker, who was Great Chief of Records of the Great Council of Maryland, and Great Chief of Records of the Great Council of the United States.

William Muirhead must have joined between the years of 1818 and 1821. His name is not on the old Account Book of 1816, and the first mention of his name is upon manuscript minutes dated November 7, 1821. He had attained the rank of Brigadier-General and aid to the Generalissimo. He was an active and earnest member of the Order, and was for many years proprietor of a well-known house of public entertainment in Bank Street (opposite Elbow Lane), between Chestnut and Market streets. It is known by the sign of Robert Burns. Whatever weakness may have been assigned to William Muirhead in the latter days of his life, common justice requires that proper tribute should be rendered to his faithful services to the Society of Red Men from the time of his being admitted until the establishment of the Tribe at Baltimore, out of which grew the first Tribe of the Improved Order of Red Men.

It is stated that Muirhead, having established himself permanently in Baltimore, with the assistance of his son Robert, began to get together a sufficient number of former brothers of the Tribes to revive the Society in that city, and that on March 12, 1834, "his purpose was fully accomplished by the organization of the Society of Red Men, Tribe of Maryland, No. 1, at the house of D. McDonald on Bond Street, Fell's Point."

About this time the name of William T. Jones appears in connection with the Order, and he was an able and willing assistant to Muirhead in his work of organizing the above-named Tribe. He is described as a respectable citizen of Fell's Point, where for many years he carried on the business of a shipping master, in which occupation he won the respect particularly of the seamen, and when he became a Red Man he was given the title of "Seaman's Friend." John F. Weishampel, Sr., of Lancaster, Pa., is quoted as additional authority for the fact of the organization of the Tribe above mentioned, and we have already quoted from his address in 1837 concerning the events leading up to the withdrawal of himself and others to whom, as he alleged, the associations were distasteful. In the same address he makes a further statement as follows : —

"Some time after, in the grand sun of 1834, Mr. William T. Jones proposed to a number of his friends, some of whom had belonged to the lodge of Red Men just mentioned, to organize a new Tribe of Red Men, upon the principle of a Beneficial Order; and soon a number joined him in the enterprise, and 'Logan Tribe, No. 1, of Red Men' was formed. At what time in the grand sun I do not distinctly remember. But it did not go long until they found that the convivial character of the old lodge had unjustly attached itself to the new Order, and that on that account many persons refused to join it. It was then agreed upon that we would change the name. And to kill the prevailing prejudice, it was proposed by one member to lay aside the name 'Red

Men' and adopt the cognomen of 'Aborigines' (the original inhabitants). But one old man, Peter B. Lucas, who had a little impediment in his speech, objected to that, 'for,' said he, 'I can't say Abborigdegenerees.' The name 'Order of Improved Red Men' was then proposed and adopted. At the next council fire J. F. Weishampel, Sr., proposed to reconsider the former action upon the name, and to place the qualifying term 'Improved' upon the Order, instead of upon the members, and so suggested the transposition to 'Improved Order of Red Men.'"

Mr. Weishampel, in the document from which this quotation is made, states that Mr. William T. Jones was the founder of the Order, and that the organization was effected in his house, and that he was also the first Sachem of Logan Tribe, and that during his term of service as Sachem he himself (Weishampel) was initiated. Mr. Weishampel also recalls among the members at that time the names given on page 146, as among the members of Logan Tribe.

(We have already referred to the convivial element prominent in the organization, and shown it was no more applicable to the Society of Red Men than the kindred Societies of that time. While the members as individuals may have passed the "decanter" too frequently, yet this was not done during the burning of the council fire, but when all the regular business had been concluded.)

In the pamphlet of Mr. Weishampel, from which these quotations have been made, is contained an address delivered on St. Tammany's Day, May 12, 1837, to which fuller reference is necessary later. In the concluding portion of this address, after referring to the fact that the Order was a beneficial society, he uses these significant words:—

"I am not prepared to say how much wampum has been paid out for charitable purposes since the organization of our young Order, of but three years' existence. The number of members is about 250. Many of us have dear paleface squaws and papooses, and these, when we are dead, will share, as a matter of right, all the advantages, rights, and benefits which are secured to them by its organic laws. And let me add, that before a half-hundred grand suns have rolled round, the Improved Order of Red Men will most likely have extended to all the States and Territories of our great country, and then come back to Maryland and hold a semi-centennial celebration in Baltimore, where the Order was organized in the grand sun 1834, in a wigwam on Thames Street, Fell's Point."

As additional evidence of the existence of the Tribe established by William Muirhead, reference is made to a code of laws adopted by the "Red Men's Society, Tribe of Maryland, No. 1." The motto upon these By-Laws was, "True religion and brotherly love is this: to visit and assist the widows and fatherless in affliction, and to keep one's self unspotted from the world." Surely no organization could have foundation on a purer or more lofty sentiment than is contained in this motto.

The Preamble stated that the members united themselves "for mutual benefit." Article 1 declares that "the name, style or title of this Order shall be 'The Red Men of the Tribe of Maryland, No. 1.'" Then follow twenty-two articles, defining the machinery by which the Society should be managed. Without giving these articles in detail, we will refer to the points covered by them. Meetings were to take place every Monday at 7 o'clock in winter and 8 o'clock in summer. Five brothers constituted a quorum. There were five officers, Generalissimo, First Captain-General, Second Captain-General, Treasurer, and Recording Scribe, and the Generalissimo was given power to appoint two Major-Generals, four aids, three warriors, and a Grand Recording Scribe. The first Captain-General had power to appoint two aids, and the Second Captain-General one aid. The term of office was three months. The Generalissimo presided, assisted by the two Captain-Generals. The duties of the Recording Scribe and Treasurer were those usually performed by such officers. The initiation fee was one dollar, and no person was eligible under 21 or over 45 years of age. The dues were twenty-five cents a month. Applications for membership were required to be in writing, countersigned by a brother, and accompanied by one-half of the initiation fee. The application was referred to a committee to make necessary inquiries, and at its report a ballot was had, and one-third of the ballots being opposed the applicant was rejected. The members became beneficial in twelve months, and were then entitled to receive three dollars per week during disability, provided application was made to the proper officer and his dues were paid. "If, however, his indisposition seemed to have originated from immoral conduct, his benefit shall be withheld until his case be investigated and laid before the Council." Provision was made for paying benefits to distant members on the testimony of a physician or two respectable witnesses. In case of death, the elective officers had power to allow twenty dollars to defray the funeral expenses, the money to be paid to the widow or nearest relative. The fund for this purpose was provided by assessing each brother twenty-five cents. Provision was made for suspension for non-payment of fines, and any member in arrears for thirteen weeks forfeited his benefits. Article 22 provided that "any member being guilty of immoral conduct whereby the Society may be disgraced, attempting to impose on it, or divulge the secrets of the Order, may be suspended or expelled as the Council may think proper."

The "By-Laws" were more properly rules of order governing debate, although among them were several important general regulations. Among other provisions was one fixing a penalty of fifty cents upon any member who introduced a political or religious dispute. Section 18 was significant inasmuch as it provided that "every *Ancient Red Man*, applying to become a member of this council fire, shall send a written application by a brother, etc." On the death of a brother it was provided that each member should attend his funeral and furnish himself with a badge of red ribbon, with appropriate inscription, to wear on the left breast.

The constitution, from which the above extracts are taken, was printed by R. J. Matchet, Baltimore, in the year 1835, about one year subsequent to the alleged organization of the Tribe.

Section 18 of the By-Laws, in its reference to "*Ancient Red Men*," is cited as a verbal acknowledgment of the existence of the former organization bearing the name of Red Men, and having similar features, and avowing the same general principles of which the Tribe of Maryland was the successor. Attached to this constitution were printed forty-five names, and among these may be mentioned John Buckingham, Stephen Burgess, George Fastaff (Fastie?), William T. Jones, Peter B. Lucas, William Muirhead, and George A. Peter. Two of the members, named John Buckingham, "Gannynipper," and William Muirhead, "Hospitality," had been members of the Society of Red Men in Philadelphia.

Following the organization of this Tribe, it is claimed on the authority of the manuscript records of the Great Council of Maryland, that early in the year 1835, the members of Maryland Tribe, No. 1., took the necessary preliminary steps towards "lengthening the chain of friendship," and establishing a supreme authority for the Order. Six delegates were chosen by the Tribe and given ample power for the purpose. Three of these were Past Chiefs, and three others were Representatives The Past Chiefs were William T. Jones, William Muirhead, and Charles Skillman, and the Representatives were George A. Peter, Captain Joseph Branson, and Edward Lucas. The account from which this is taken goes on to state that "on the 20th day of the 5th moon in the season of Blossoms, 1835," the Past Chiefs and Representatives just named assembled in the "old wigwam" on Thames Street, Fell's Point, in pursuance of their appointment, when Past Chief "Seaman's Friend," William T. Jones, was called to the chair; "Links of Union," George A. Peter, was appointed Scribe, and "Cock of the Walk," Joseph Branson, took the Sagamore's seat. At a subsequent meeting an election was held, which resulted in the choice of "Seaman's Friend," William T. Jones, for Grand Sachem; "Hospitality," William Muirhead, Grand Senior Sagamore; "True Verdict," Edward Lucas, Grand Junior Sagamore; "Cock of the Walk," Joseph Branson, Grand Prophet; "Links of Union," George A. Peter, Grand Scribe; "True Verdict," Edward Lucas, was also elected Grand Chief of Wampum, and "Camel's Hair," Charles Skillman, was appointed Grand Guard of Wigwam.

At a meeting of the Grand Council, held May 25, 1835, a resolution was adopted declaring the supremacy of the Grand Council, and providing for the punishment of brothers who might attempt to set up an opposition Council.

(It must be remembered that at this time the Tribe at Reading was in existence, and continued so as late as the year 1850, although it is fair to presume that Brother Muirhead was unable to secure communication with the Reading Tribe, and hence presumed that it became defunct like the mother Tribe at Philadelphia. Otherwise there would have been good ground to dispute the legitimacy of the assumption

ORGANIZATION AT BALTIMORE.

of supreme authority by the Grand Council formed in Maryland.)

At a meeting of the Grand Council, held May 28, 1835, "Cock of the Walk," Captain Joseph Branson, presented a constitution which was slightly amended and adopted. At a special council convened June 6, a new form of initiation was presented by Brother "Camel's Hair," Charles Skillman, which was referred to a committee which reported June 12, when the form was adopted, and on the 18th of the same month all the members present at said meeting received the "Grand Council Degree" after which they were instructed in the "First Degree of the Society."

June 10, 1835, a council was held at the usual place, and an application was received from Brothers Samuel Reed, Samuel Armer, William Rods, Robert Farrell, John A. Lockwood, John A. Smith, D. H. Harmon, F. W. R. Broaders, James G. McGibbon, Thomas Towson, and Robert McClelland for dispensation to open a second Tribe to be styled Metamora Tribe, No. 2, and on June 22, 1835, the Grand Chiefs instituted Metamora Tribe, No. 2, at the house of Brother F. W. R. Broaders in Pratt Street.

Mention is now made of the unfortunate circumstances which resulted finally in the extinction of Tribe of Maryland, No. 1. Accounts differ as to what these circumstances were, but the inference is given that with some members the social features of the Society too frequently degenerated into excesses. By reason of this, William T. Jones, Peter R. Hilditch, George A. Peter, John Miller, George Fastie, Jones Friedewald, Giles Harkiness, John Hugget, and others withdrew and petitioned the Grand Council of Maryland for a dispensation to open a new Tribe. It is asserted that they were tenacious to retain their numerical position and post of honor in the Order, and that the Grand Council, yielding to their wish, granted the dispensation, naming them "Logan Tribe, No. 1." Under this title they were instituted by the Grand Chiefs, May 12, 1836, as is shown by a reprint of said charter. (Assuming the correctness of this claim, the Tribe should have been No. 3, instead of No. 1.)

The authority from which we are quoting claims "that the

Tribe of Maryland was not in existence in the year 1833, but was organized March 12, 1834; second, that George A. Peter was not admitted to membership in said Tribe until May 19, 1834, as shown by the Booker manuscript (a copy of which is in the possession of the editor); third, that Logan Tribe, which was formed by the withdrawing members of the Tribe of Maryland, was not organized until May 12, 1836, as shown by its charter; fourth, that the Grand Council of Maryland was organized at the 'old wigwam' in Thames Street, Fell's Point, May 20, 1835; that, inasmuch as the Grand Council of Maryland has never ceased to exist down to the present time, but has created by its dispensation, or charter, every Tribe in Maryland since its own organization, and derives its own existence from and through the delegates of the old Tribe of Maryland, No. 1, which Tribe existed by authority of the mother Tribe at Philadelphia, by which the commission to institute it was issued, the Grand Council of Maryland, by reason of the failure of the Reading Tribe to assert its right to priority, is the only true and legitimate successor to the authority and rights of the 'old' Society of Red Men, which title, by virtue of its sovereign power, it changed to 'The Order of Improved Red Men' and exercised supreme authority over the Order, until the organization of the Great Council of the United States."

The same authority, and for the same reasons given, disputes the claim that George A. Peter, afterwards Great Incohonee of the G. C. U. S. "was the brother who *first gave the name* Improved Order of Red Men to our Order." How that name was adopted appears in the preceding chapter.

It is claimed on the authority of John F. Weishampel, Sr., that William T. Jones was the founder and first Sachem of the Order.

CHAPTER VII.

GREAT COUNCIL OF UNITED STATES (1847–1880).

WITH this chapter begins the record of the Great Council of the United States, from the preliminary organization down to the last council held up to the time this history is written.

An interest necessarily attaches to all the early incidents attending the organization, and to the individuals who associated themselves together for that purpose.

On the " 1st sleep of the 5th seven suns of Cold moon, 5607," which in the common era corresponds to Monday, January 30, 1847, a meeting was held at Uncas Wigwam, Baltimore, in accordance with a resolution previously adopted by the Great Council of Maryland. At this meeting were present Past Grand Sachems George Fastie, Louis Bonsal, John Meiser, James Purden, Gustav Otto, and William G. Gorsuch. Other representatives admitted were as follows: Grand Sachem John L. Booker; Grand Junior Sagamore J. Thomas Laws; Past Sachem Charles Tydings; Past Sachems Stephen Burgess, of Logan Tribe, No. 1; William H. Ford, of Pocahontas, No. 3; — Halfpenny, of Powhattan Tribe, No. 5; William Somerville, of Uncas, No. 6; J. Muhlhoffer, of Philip, No. 8.

Past Grand Sachem Fastie was chosen Chairman, and Grand Sachem Booker, Secretary.

The chairman stated that the object of the meeting was the institution of a Great Council of the United States of the Improved Order of Red Men.

Past Grand Sachems Gorsuch, Bonsal, Meiser, and Otto and Representative Halfpenny were appointed a committee to draft a Constitution, By-Laws, and Rules of the Order for the government of the Great Council, and also a form of prayer. A committee was appointed to procure a room for the meetings of the body, and the council fire was quenched to meet on the 1st sleep, 2d seven suns, Snow moon.

Pursuant to this the Great Council again assembled at Uncas Wigwam.

The Representative of Metamora Tribe, No. 4, was admitted. The committee on the meeting place for the Great Council reported that Uncas Wigwam could be obtained, and it was voted that the meetings be held at that place until further orders. The Committee on Constitution made its report, which was considered and part of it was adopted. An adjournment was then made for one seven suns. At this adjournment the Constitution was further considered, and the council fire was quenched until the 1st sleep of the 1st seven suns of Worm moon. At this meeting the remainder of the Constitution was adopted. By-Laws, Rules of the Order, and a Prayer were adopted, and it was then voted to nominate chiefs for the ensuing grand sun. The election was deferred until the 1st sleep of the 3d seven suns of Worm moon. The acting Keeper of Records was directed to notify the Great Council of the District of Columbia, and also the Tribe at Cumberland, of the proceedings of the Great Council.

At the council held on the 1st sleep, 3d seven suns, Worm moon, Grand Junior Sagamore Z. K. Offutt and Past Sachems Joseph Mundell and Y. P. Page of the Great Council of the District of Columbia, and James Nokes of Anacostia Tribe, No. 3, of the District of Columbia, were admitted as Representatives.

The election of chiefs was then held, which resulted in the following choice, being the first chiefs recorded of the Great Council of the United States: —

Grand Sachem Incohonee . . . . WILLIAM G. GORSUCH.
Grand Sagamore . . . . GUSTAV OTTO.
Grand Prophet . . . . Z. K. OFFUTT.
Grand Keeper of Records . . . . JOHN L. BOOKER.
Grand Keeper of Wampum . . . . STEPHEN BURGESS.
Grand Tocakon . . . . WILLIAM H. FORD.
Grand Minewa . . . . J. MUHLHOFFER.

They were duly raised up to their respective positions by Past Grand Sachem Meiser.

It will be noticed that the titles adopted differed slightly from those now in use. The word "grand," as will subsequently appear, was afterwards changed to "great." We have

WILLIAM G. GORSUCH, FIRST GREAT INCOHONEE.

thought it best to follow the usage of the Great Council until the date of the change, in order to preserve the chronology and nomenclature.

At this council measures were taken to supply the necessary funds for carrying on the work of the Great Council, and it was voted to adopt certain unwritten language and to procure a seal for the Great Council.

The Great Council met again on the 1st sleep of the 1st seven suns, Plant moon. G. S. Incohonee Gorsuch presided. At this council a communication was received from Shawnee Tribe, No. 5 (now No. 2), of Winchester, Virginia. This is the first mention of that State in the G. C. U. S. records.

A committee of three was appointed to revise the work of the Order.

Arrangements were made for supplying State Great Councils and each Tribe and Representative with copies of the printed matter issued by the Great Council, and also to provide for a revenue through the sale of visiting cards and the like.

The next council was held on the 1st sleep of the 4th seven suns, Flower moon, G. S. Incohonee Gorsuch presiding.

At this council Representatives were admitted from Powhattan Tribe, No. 1, of Washington, D.C., and Osceola Tribe, No. 2, of Alexandria, D.C. (When Alexandria was set off from the District of Columbia, and became a part of the State of Virginia, Osceola Tribe, No. 2, then became No. 1 of that reservation.)

The Great Council of the United States asserted its supremacy to the extent of ordering that the name of the Great Council, State of Maryland, be stricken out of all obligations used by this body, and Great Council of the United States inserted in lieu thereof until the committee on revision was prepared to report.

A petition was received from Osceola, Shawnee, and Mohawk Tribes asking that permission be given and a charter granted to organize a Great Council in the State of Virginia, to be located at Winchester, Frederick County, and the prayer of the petitioners was granted.

The next council was not held until the 1st sleep of the 3d seven suns, of Buck moon, 5607, when the Great Council was called to order by G. S. Incohonee Gorsuch. Past Sachem

John Fry of Tecumseh Tribe, No. 1, of Pennsylvania, was admitted as a Representative. Brother Fry was the father of the present (1892) Great Sachem of the reservation of Pennsylvania. This is the first representation in the G. C. U. S. from the reservation of Pennsylvania, and marks the beginning of what is now the most numerous branch of our Order.

The committee on revision appointed in Flower moon, reported an initiatory ceremony, which was adopted. They also reported a form of charter for State Great Councils and Tribes, which was adopted.

At this council permission was given to Tecumseh Tribe, No. 1, of Pennsylvania, to initiate palefaces at the rate of three fathoms, two yards of wampum, for the space of one moon. This being translated means $5 each.

The next council was held at Metamora Wigwam on the 4th Monday of Sturgeon moon, 5607. At this council two Representatives of Virginia were admitted who afterwards left the imprint of their genius upon the records of their Great Council, as well as on those of the Great Council of the United States. One of these was Past Sachem C. A. B. Coffroth, and the other, Past Grand Sachem Hugh Latham, afterwards Great Incohonee of the Great Council of the United States.

The question of a higher branch of the Order seems to have even then been considered by many of the members, because at this council a petition was presented, which, after considerable debate, was laid on the table, asking the Great Council to establish a higher degree into which should be admitted only brothers who had received all of the degrees of the Tribe.

This desire has manifested itself from time to time at various succeeding councils of the G. C. U. S. The establishment of Beneficial Degree Councils and the Chieftains' League are indications of it, as well as the agitation to have all the work of the Order in Tribes done in the Chief's degree.

The records indicate that the business of the Great Council was not concluded at one council, and that not only evening but day sessions were held during that same seven suns.

At the subsequent councils among the business transacted was the adoption of the report of the committee on revision, in relation to the ceremonies of the degrees, and a form of kindling and quenching fires; also the appointment of a committee for the selection of a suitable ode, to be used at the kindling of the council fire.

At this council Philip Tribe, of Washington, withdrew its Representative, the reason being that he was "found asleep in the council." Evidently the Tribe believed that a Red Man when on duty should never sleep.

A form of raising up chiefs was adopted, as were also amendments to the Constitution, By-Laws, and Rules of Order. At this council also the sum of $25 was appropriated as compensation for the Grand Keeper of Records. Arrangements were made for translating and printing the ritual in the German language, and a committee was chosen to carry the vote into effect.

Up to this time the councils of the Great Council had been held in the hunting grounds of Baltimore, but it was decided that the next council fire should be kindled in the hunting grounds of Washington, D.C.

The record thus far considered is made up from fragmentary portions that were collected many great suns ago, and put into permanent form, as covering the period of the preliminary organization of the G. C. U. S.

Commencing with the council held at Washington in grand sun 5608 (1848), we enter upon the more formal period of the history of the Great Council. Either more attention was paid to the keeping of records, or more care exercised in preserving them, because there are no omissions from that time to the present.

1848.

The council fire was kindled on the 26th of Plant moon, 5608, in the wigwam of Powhattan Tribe, No. 1, of Washington, D.C., the Worthy Grand Sachem Incohonee Gorsuch presiding.

The longtalk of W. G. S. Incohonee Gorsuch reported that the spread of the Order had been steady and progressive. During the grand sun five Tribes had been instituted, all in a flourishing condition. These Tribes were Tecumseh, No. 1, of Norristown, Metamora, No. 2, of Lancaster, Leni Lenape,

No. 3, of Philadelphia, and Kuequenaku, No. 4, of Philadelphia, Pa., and Delaware, No. 1, of Washington, Del.

He reported the Order in Maryland in a prosperous condition. Virginia was also commended for the progress made.

Charters were granted to the Tribes which had been instituted during the grand sun.

A committee was appointed to procure regalia for the chiefs.

On a ruling of the W. G. S. Incohonee, the Great Council refused to receive a communication from a Tribe, on the ground that the same should come through the Great Council of the State, thus establishing the power of the State Great Council.

The Great Council declined to approve a provision in a code of laws submitted from Metamora Tribe, No. 2, of Pennsylvania, which sought to provide that "no soldier of a standing army, seaman, or mariner, shall be admitted to membership, and should any member voluntarily enlist as a soldier, or enter on board any vessel as a seaman or mariner, he shall thenceforth lose his membership."

A committee was appointed to prepare a form for the Raising up of chiefs for the G. C. U. S.

The Great Council then went into an election of great chiefs for the ensuing grand sun, the result being as follows:—

W. G. S. Incohonee,	Hugh Latham, P. G. S.,	Alexandria, Va.
W. G. Sagamore,	E. L. Thomas, P. S.,	Cumberland, Md.
W. G. Prophet,	James Purden, P. G. S.,	Baltimore, Md.
W. G. Keeper of Records,	John L. Booker, P. G. S.,	" "
W. G. Keeper of Wampum,	Stephen Burgess, P. S.,	" "
W. G. Tocakon,	Robert Hamilton, P. S.,	" "
W. G. Minewa,	Wm. B. Entwisle, P. S.,	" "

It was unanimously resolved that the future councils be held in the city of Baltimore.

The Committee on Regalia made a report which was adopted, that the regalia for members of the G. C. U. S. be a scarlet collar trimmed with gold lace, and fixed thereto with gold cord, the letters "U. S. G. C." meaning the United States Great Council.

The grand chiefs whose election was recorded above were raised up to their respective positions.

Appended to the records is the first report of the Grand

Keeper of Records, giving statistical information concerning the Order. By this report there were under the jurisdiction of the G. C. U. S. the Great Councils of Maryland, District of Columbia, and Virginia, and four Tribes in Pennsylvania, and one in Delaware. The number of members in good standing was 1168. During the grand sun 344 had been admitted, 66 rejected, 77 suspended, 13 admitted by card, 10 withdrawn by card, and 16 had died.

The amount expended for the relief of brothers was 1705 fathoms 7 feet and 5 inches, and for the relief of widows and orphans, 1539 fathoms 2 feet and 5 inches. For the education of orphans, 17 fathoms. The total amount reported received by Tribes during the grand sun was 5396 fathoms 5 feet and 4 inches. The present fathom, equal to one dollar, is here meant.

1849.

The council fire of the Great Council of the United States was kindled at the wigwam of the Great Council in Plant moon, G. S. 5609, W. G. S. Incohonee Hugh Latham presiding.

The W. G. S. Incohonee submitted an elaborate and interesting longtalk, covering the administration of affairs under his charge during the grand sun. He reported the Order in a prosperous condition, and gradually increasing in numbers and respectability.

He reported that dispensations had been granted to organize four Tribes in the State of New York and two in Pennsylvania.

The Tribes in New York were Oneida, No. 1, Osceola, No. 2, and Oneactah, No. 4, all of New York City, and Metamora, No. 3, of Brooklyn. These Tribes were instituted by the W. G. S. Incohonee in person.

He reported that on his arrival in New York he found that some of the petitioners had been associated under the name of the "Order of Red Men" without being aware of the existence of the Improved Order of Red Men until a very short period before making application to the G. C. U. S. for dispensations.

In view of their manly course in at once acknowledging the supremacy of the Improved Order, he recommended the granting of a Great Council charter without the usual fee; a recommendation which was subsequently endorsed by the G. C. U. S.

He also reported the institution of Pocahontas Tribe, No. 5, at Philadelphia, and Mohegan Tribe, No. 6, at Waynesboro, Pa. He mentioned the receipt of an application for a Great Council for Pennsylvania, to be located in Philadelphia. He also stated that he had received inquiries from New Orleans, Louisiana, and Columbia, Pa., relative to the Order, and concluded with a grateful acknowledgment of the assistance rendered by Grand Keeper of Records Booker during the grand sun.

A proposition was presented and referred to the Committee on Petitions proposing the establishment of a branch of the Order to be known as Chiefs of the Mountain. Membership was to be restricted to members of the Order, and it was to be subordinate to the rules and regulations of the Great Council of the United States. The proposition was rejected. Permission was given to Kuequenaku Tribe, No. 4, of Pennsylvania, to change its name.

Upon a favorable report of the Committee on Petitions, it was voted to grant a charter for the institution of the Great Council of Pennsylvania. It is worthy of mention that among the petitioners for a charter for the Great Council of Pennsylvania was the name of William Beesley Davis, afterwards Great Incohonee of the Order, and John Fry, father of the present Great Sachem of that reservation.

A very flattering vote was adopted extending the thanks of the Great Council to W. G. S. Incohonee Latham for the "very distinguished and impartial manner in which he has discharged his duty, his gentlemanly deportment and competency, which will ever be appreciated by the brothers composing this body."

The chiefs for the ensuing grand sun were elected and raised up to their respective positions as follows: —

W. G. S. Incohonee,	JOHN F. SMITH, P. G. S.,	Virginia.
W. G. Sagamore,	WM. BEESLEY DAVIS, P. S.,	Pennsylvania.
W. G. Prophet,	B. W. FERGUSON, P. S.,	Maryland.
W. G. Keeper of Records,	JOHN L. BOOKER, P. G. S.,	"
W. G. Keeper of Wampum,	STEPHEN BURGESS, P. G. S.,	"
W. G. Tocakon,	JOHN MCCAULEY, P. S.,	District of Columbia.
W. G. Minewa,	R. A. MCALLISTER, P. S.,	Maryland.

It was decided that the travelling expenses of the W. G. S. Incohonee in attending the councils of the G. C. U. S. be paid by that body.

Past Grand Sachem Burgess having tendered his resignation as Grand Keeper of Wampum, to which he had just been raised, Past Sachem Jesse H. Magruder, of Maryland, was elected to fill the vacancy and duly raised up.

From the reports submitted by the Great Councils of Maryland, District of Columbia and Virginia, and from the Tribes under the immediate jurisdiction of the G. C. U. S., statistics are collated of the work of the grand sun as follows: Number of members, 2146; adopted, 663; rejected, 62; admitted by card, 48; withdrawn, by card, 149; died, 23; suspended, 121; expelled, 45; paid for relief of brothers, 3123 fathoms 2 feet 5 inches; paid for relief of widows and orphans, 2404 fathoms 5 feet; paid for the education of orphans, 46 fathoms; total receipts of Tribes, 11,752 fathoms 1 foot.

The business of the Great Council having been concluded the council fire was quenched, to be rekindled at Baltimore, in Plant moon, G. S. 5610.

1850.

The Great Council assembled at the Great Council wigwam, Baltimore, in Plant moon, G. S. 5610, W. G. S. Incohonee John F. Smith presiding.

Among those admitted at this council was Past Grand Sachem Robert Sullivan, who afterwards became Great Incohonee.

At this time the G. C. U. S. seems to have permitted proxy representation, a custom not now in vogue.

At this council New Jersey for the first time was represented, by Bernhard McCormack, who appeared for Arreseoh Tribe, No. 1, of Newark, N. J.

In his longtalk the Worthy Grand Sachem Incohonee tendered his heartfelt congratulations upon the strength and position the Order had assumed since the last council, being in a more prosperous and healthy condition than ever before. For this he stated that thanks should be returned to that Great Spirit "whose eye never slumbers nor sleeps." He reported the institution of the Great Council of Pennsylvania, on the 23d of Flower moon, G. S. 5609, in the city of Philadelphia. He also reported the institution of the Great Council of New York. He reported the organization of Arreseoh Tribe, No. 1, at Newark, N.J.; the work having been done by Past Sachem Albert Fisher, Jr., W. G. J. S. of the G. C. of New York. He also made a report, that, on a recent visit to Baltimore, he was informed that it had pleased Metamora Tribe, No. 4, late under the jurisdiction of the Great Council of Maryland, to sever the connection which existed between said Tribe and the Great Council, by surrendering their charter, books, etc., and declaring themselves an "Independent Order of Red Men," and not knowing the cause which prompted said action, he recommended that the case of Metamora Tribe be taken under special advisement.

The affair thus mentioned by the Great Incohonee was referred to a special committee which subsequently reported that the matter was considered with some diffidence, inasmuch as the Tribe was under the jurisdiction of the Great Council of Maryland, and there had been no action on the part of said Great Council. From information received it appeared that said Tribe pursued a legal and proper course in surrendering its charter, and it was to be regretted that circumstances should have caused the withdrawal of any portion of our Order at a time when the prospects were so flattering. The committee, while refraining from condemning the withdrawal (for every Tribe or brother had a perfect right to withdraw or remain), expressed its most emphatic condemnation of the action of the former brothers in assuming a part of the name of the Order in the establishment of another organization. The committee recommended to the entire brotherhood to abstain from any intercourse whatever with the brothers as an institution, and recommended the adoption of resolutions expressing the will of the Great Council, which were adopted, as follows:—

"*Resolved*, That no brother of this Order (under this immediate jurisdiction, or under the jurisdiction of a Great Council holding a charter from this body), shall be permitted to hold membership with the Order known as the Independent Order of Red Men.

"*Resolved*, That any brothers persisting in associating themselves with the Independent Order of Red Men be expelled forthwith."

A committee was appointed to draft a Form of Dedication.

At this council for the first time Representatives were admitted from the Great Councils of Pennsylvania and New York.

A complete revision of the Constitution was adopted.

New charters in place of those formerly held were granted to the Great Councils of Maryland and the District of Columbia.

The time of kindling and quenching the council fire of the G. C. U. S. was changed from Plant moon to Corn moon, and it was decided that the chiefs elected at this council should serve until the regular council in Corn moon, G. S. 5611.

The Constitution adopted seems to have provided for several new chiefs, among them being a Grand Junior Sagamore, a Grand Tocakon and a Grand Minewa.

The chiefs elected and raised up for the ensuing term were as follows : —

W. G. S. Incohonee,	WILLIAM BEESLEY DAVIS,	Pennsylvania.
W. G. Senior Sagamore,	ROBERT SULLIVAN,	Maryland.
W. G. Junior Sagamore,	JOHN WITHERELL,	New York.
W. G. Prophet,	JOHN CARTER,	District of Columbia.
W. G. Keeper of Records,	JOHN L. BOOKER,	Maryland.
W. G. Keeper of Wampum,	B. W. FERGUSON,	Maryland.

The W. G. S. Incohonee appointed William Tucker, of D. of C., W. G. Tocakon, and A. Gibbs, of Pennsylvania, W. G. Minewa.

The Committee on Design of Cards was directed to furnish the Great Council at its next council a suitable form of card with the probable cost of the plate thereof.

The Committee on Revision reported favorably upon an application for a Tribe to be located in the city of Camden, N.J.

The matter of a revised ritual and a proposed new regalia was laid over until the special council in Corn moon.

One matter considered at this council was important enough to be mentioned here at length. We submit the action of the Great Council in full as it stands alone in the history of the Order. The report is as follows : —

" *To the Great Council of the United States, Impd. O. R. M.* :

" The Committee on Credentials report, that the certificate from Metamora Tribe, No. 2, of Lancaster, Pa., in favor of Bro. Wm. B. Fahnestock, is in form, but from information received, are compelled to inform this Great Council that Bro. Fahnestock has never served in the seat of Sachem, but that he is in possession of the Past Sachem's degree, conferred by the Great Council of Pennsylvania, in accordance with permission from the Great Sachem Incohonee of this Great Council. For certain reasons, it was desirable on the part of Metamora Tribe, that Bro. Fahnestock should be present at the Great Council this session. This is a novel case, and one which we hope may never occur again. In view of all the circumstances, the committee are reluctantly constrained to recommend that Bro. Wm. B. Fahnestock be permitted to visit this Great Council during the present session, and would offer the following resolution:

"*Resolved*, That Bro. Wm. B. Fahnestock be allowed a seat in this Great Council, but that he is not permitted to vote on any question, nor allowed to address this Great Council unless by a unanimous vote.

"Wm. G. Gorsuch,
"Hugh Latham,
"Henry Cryss."

The following resolution was also adopted:—

"*Resolved*, That in the passage of the report of the committee recommending the admission of Bro. Wm. B. Fahnestock, this Great Council does not make this a precedent for any future action for this body."

The statistics of the Order as given by the report of the W. G. Keeper of Records showed that the Order existed in Maryland, District of Columbia, Virginia, Pennsylvania, and New York.

The number of Tribes was 45, in which there had been 1255 initiations, 139 suspensions, and 27 expulsions, leaving the number of members at the time of the report, 3175. There were expended for the relief of brothers, 4015 fathoms and for the relief of widows, 2358 fathoms. In addition to this 103 fathoms were expended for the education of orphans.

Further explanation seems appropriate concerning the reasons which caused the separation from the Order of Metamora Tribe, No. 4, of Maryland, and the subsequent organization of the "*Independent* Order of Red Men" as a rival to the "*Improved* Order of Red Men."

So many great suns have passed since this action was taken, that full particulars need not be suppressed through fear of misconstruction. The facts will show that the G. C. U. S. acted with calmness and good judgment, and in the difference of opinion between the Tribe and the G. C. U. S. simply upheld its own dignity, while the Tribe exhibited a stubborn determination to ignore all obligations taken and to disobey the laws of the Order.

Metamora Tribe, No. 4, had refused to pay benefits, in accordance with the laws of the Tribe, on the plea that the party was not entitled. The party thereupon appealed from the action of the Tribe to the Great Council of Maryland. That body carefully investigated the case, and, after a calm, equitable consideration, sustained the appeal, and directed the Tribe to satisfy the claim. This the Tribe refused to do, and appealed to the G. C. U. S., where, after a searching investigation, that body resolved to sustain the action of the Great Council of Maryland, and directed the Tribe to obey the mandate thereof.

Metamora Tribe, No. 4, rather than comply with the decision of the higher two bodies, and do that which seemed to both to be only an act of justice, defiantly refused to obey, and at once took steps to forsake the parent organization and institute a new one to be termed the "Independent Order of Red Men."

As the new departure worked only in the German language, they appealed to, and received, support from those of that nationality only. A number of German Tribes in Philadelphia and elsewhere were importuned to cast their lot with the so-called "Independents," but in vain, for in nearly every instance they remained true to the principles of Freedom, Friendship, and Charity, and faithful chiefs of the Improved Order of Red Men.

The new venture was introduced into New York, New Jersey, Pennsylvania, Maryland, Ohio, West Virginia, Illinois, Missouri, Louisiana, California, Massachusetts, Rhode Island, and a few other States, and at one time had 12,000 members. During the last ten great suns a number of their Tribes (or "Stamms," as they are called) becoming dissatisfied with their management, surrendered their charters, squared their accounts, and became bodily, and separately by adoption, Tribes and members of the Improved Order of Red Men, and, with pleasure we record it, have proved excellent workers in our Order.

Over forty great suns have passed since the departure of No. 4, and at this time it seems but a ripple upon the wave of prosperity that has come to our Order, when we look back upon the separation that then took place.

A special council of the G. C. U. S. was kindled at Uncas wigwam, Baltimore, Md., on the 10th of Corn moon, G. S. 5610. In the absence of W. G. S. Incohonee Davis, the council fire was kindled by W. G. Senior Sagamore, Robert Sullivan.

The peculiar position of Brother William B. Fahnestock, upon whom had been conferred the degree of Past Sachem as previously recorded, again came before the G. C. U. S. upon a request from Metamora Tribe, No. 2, of Pennsylvania, that Brother Fahnestock be accorded the rights and privileges of a Representative in the G. C. U. S.

A preamble and resolutions were submitted which recited the fact that Brother Fahnestock had written, and presented to the Committee on Revision of the Work of the Order, an entire new set of degrees for the Tribe, and declared that he be permitted to take a seat as a Representative from Metamora Tribe, with all the privileges of a Past Sachem, in the G. C. U. S. The matter was disposed of by allowing to Brother Fahnestock the same privileges as were accorded at the last council of the G. C. U. S.

The report of the Committee on Revision of the Work of the Order was considered, and the Great Council adopted a ritual as presented by Past Sachem Fahnestock, and forms for instituting a Tribe, for introducing members into the G. C. U. S., for raising up chiefs of the G. C. U. S., for introducing Past Sachems and Representatives in State Great Councils, for a funeral ceremony, and for dedication of wigwams.

The subject of regalia occupied considerable of the time of the Great Council. The following style was finally adopted : —

The regalia for the P. G. Incohonee shall be a sash with a pouch attached, composed of scarlet and purple silk velvet, running from end to end with a small band of gold cord over the seam, a gold jewel suspending an eagle with a tomahawk in its talons depending from the centre of lower edge.

Belt. — Four inches wide, color of the sash, with the letters P. G. I. embroidered thereon.

Regalia of P. G. Sachem. — Sash as above, with the exception of the emblems.

Aprons. — A half skirt of purple silk velvet trimmed with gold bullion fringe, an eagle bearing in his beak a scroll with the name of the State embroidered in front.

Regalia of a P. Sachem. — Sash as above of scarlet velvet, trimmed with gold bullion fringe, with the emblems of the degrees embroidered thereon.

Aprons. — Of scarlet velvet, with the name of the State encompassed by a wreath embroidered thereon, trimmed with gold bullion fringe.

Regalia for Initiatory Degree . . . . Green sash.
" " Brave's " . . . . Orange "
" " Warrior's " . . . . Blue "
" " Chief's " . . . . Scarlet "

Trimmed with silver lace.

Aprons. — Color of the degree, with the emblems of the degree embroidered thereon. Trimmed with silver bullion fringe.

The funeral regalia to be left discretionary with the State Great Councils.

Permission was denied Delaware Tribe, No. 1, of Wilmington, Delaware, to have a procession in costume, although permission was granted to have a procession.

A regalia was presented to retiring W. G. S. Incohonee Latham.

1851.

The Great Council assembled at Osceola wigwam, Baltimore, Md., in Corn moon, G. S. 5611, W. G. S. Incohonee W. Beesley Davis presiding.

Among the Representatives admitted at this council was Richard Marley of Maryland, who afterwards became Great Incohonee of the Order. For the first time a Representative was received from the reservation of New Jersey, in the person of Selden Dickinson, from Arreseoh Tribe, No. 1, of Newark, N.J.

The ritual prepared by Brother Fahnestock, adopted at the special council previously held, seems to have been too elaborate for proper delineation; and a resolution was adopted to the effect that a committee be appointed to inquire into the expediency of remodelling the entire work of the Order.

This committee later in the council reported that the necessity for remodelling the entire work of the Order was imperative, and recommended that a committee of five be appointed to make such alterations in the work as shall meet the wants and capacities of the brotherhood.

At this council a petition was received from Arreseoh, No. 1, Leni Lenape, No. 2, and Red Bird, No. 3, of New Jersey, asking for a Great Council for the State of New Jersey, and the petition was subsequently granted.

The W. G. S. Incohonee in his longtalk had referred to difficulties in the reservation of New York. The matter was referred to the Committee on the State of the Order, which subsequently reported that the Great Council of New York was defunct, and but one Tribe remained in existence. They recommended that a chief of this body be sent to New York to reclaim the property of the Order, and to attach Manhattan Tribe to this Great Council. The report was adopted.

Dispensations had been granted during the grand sun for the institution of Miami Tribe, No. 1, Cincinnati, and Tecumseh Tribe, No. 2, Springfield, Ohio. An application for a Tribe at Ironton, Ohio, was received at the council and it was voted that the matter be referred to the incoming W. G. S. Incohonee.

The chiefs elected and appointed and raised up for the ensuing grand sun were as follows:—

W. G. Incohonee,	ROBERT SULLIVAN,	Maryland.
W. G. Senior Sagamore,	WILLIAM TUCKER,	District of Columbia.
W. G. Junior Sagamore,	JNO. A. WILLARD,	Delaware.
W. G. Prophet,	DANIEL CHAMBERS,	Virginia.
W. G. Chief of Records,	JNO. L. BOOKER,	Maryland.
W. G. Keeper of Wampum,	B. W. FERGUSON,	Maryland.
W. G. Tocakon,	SELDEN DICKINSON,	New Jersey.
W. G. Minewa,	J. T. BRADLEY,	District of Columbia.

At this council an elaborate plan for a so-called higher degree was submitted by the Representatives from the Great Council of Maryland, which was indefinitely postponed.

It was voted that a committee of three be appointed to procure and present to the next council of the G. C. U. S. a design for a charter plate, with an estimate of the probable cost.

It will be seen that the principal work engaging the attention of the G. C. U. S. at this council was a ritual of the Order and the style of regalia to be adopted. While the ritual prepared by Brother Fahnestock was of a high order of merit as a literary production, experience proved that it was not adapted for general use among the members of the Order, most of whom could not be expected to have that special training necessary for the proper rendering of the work.

The subject of regalia was finally settled to the satisfaction of all, and the regalia adopted at this council continued in use many great suns, and was considered very neat and appropriate.

From the statistical records from Great Councils we submit the following summary of the work done for the 18 moons ending 1st Buck moon, G. S. 5611. The record contains reports from Great Councils only, and therefore gives the statistics from Maryland, District of Columbia, Virginia, and Pennsylvania. As an indication of the growth of the Order in Pennsylvania, it may be observed that the number of Tribes at this time in that reservation had increased to 21. The totals of the statistics were as follows: Number of Tribes, 59; initiations, 2131; suspensions, 259; expulsions, 74; rejections, 169; admitted by card, 57; withdrawn by card, 110; deaths, 43; number of members, 4709; expended for the relief of brothers, 6590 fathoms 5 feet; expended for relief of widows, 2734 fathoms 2 feet 5 inches; expended for education of orphans, 138 fathoms.

1852.

The council fire of the G. C. U. S. was kindled at Osceola wigwam, Baltimore, Md., in Corn moon, G. S. 5612, W. G. Incohonee Robert Sullivan presiding.

Among the Representatives admitted at this council were Thomas A. Bosley, of Ohio, and Joseph Pyle, of Delaware, each of whom subsequently became Great Incohonee of the G. C. U. S. Brother Pyle is the present honorable and honored Great Keeper of Wampum of the United States.

The States from which Representatives were admitted at this council were Maryland, Virginia, Pennsylvania, Ohio, Delaware, and the District of Columbia.

W. G. Incohonee presented his longtalk which congratulated the Great Council upon the flattering success and progress that had been experienced during the grand sun.

At the council held on the 15th sun an invitation was accepted from Pocahontas, No. 3, Baltimore, Md., tendered through P. G. I. William G. Gorsuch, to partake of the hospitality of the Tribe at a reception and banquet to be given on that sleep. The occasion is worthy of mention as being the first time upon which such formal hospitality was tendered to, and accepted by, the G. C. U. S.

The chiefs elected and appointed and raised up to their

respective positions for the ensuing grand sun were as follows: —

W. G. Incohonee,	WM. TUCKER, P. G. S.,	District of Columbia.
W. G. Senior Sagamore,	LOUIS BONSAL, P. G. S.,	Maryland.
W. G. Junior Sagamore,	T. B. DISNEY,	Ohio.
W. G. Prophet,	JOSEPH MYERS,	New Jersey.
W. G. Chief of Records,	JOHN L. BOOKER,	Maryland.
W. G. Keeper of Wampum,	B. W. FERGUSON,	Maryland.
W. G. Tocakon,	GEORGE PERCY,	Virginia.
W. G. Minewa,	J. W. PATTERSON,	Delaware.

At this council a petition was presented from several Tribes located in and near the city of Philadelphia, Pa., asking that the Great Council of that body be located in the city of Philadelphia inasmuch as the kindling of its council fire in Lancaster, Columbia, and Harrisburg, compelled a long journey on the part of a majority of the members of Tribes, in order to attend the councils of the Great Councils. The Great Council declined to grant the prayer of the petitioners.

The Committee on the Revision of the Ritual, appointed at the last council, reported that it had been unable to attend to the work entrusted to it, and at this council many propositions were submitted having in view the adoption of some method by which a satisfactory ritual could be adopted. Many of the propositions appeared in the work as revised, and others never again saw the light of day. Among these matters, one is deserving of mention, being a proposition submitted by Representative George Percy, of Virginia, that a committee be appointed to which shall be referred the expediency and propriety of establishing a Pocahontas degree, to be conferred upon the wives of such brothers as may apply for the same; and such committee is required to report at the next council.

Upon the report and recommendation of the Committee on the State of the Order, the action of the W. G. Incohonee was approved in relation to organizing and reorganizing the Great Council of the State of New Jersey, and charters were granted to the Great Councils of New Jersey and Ohio. The action of the W. G. Incohonee was also approved in relation to the petition for a Tribe at Ironton, Ohio.

Favorable action was taken upon the proposition to share the expense of maintaining an office for the W. G. Chief of Records.

The statistical report of Great Councils to the Great Chief of Records of the G. C. U. S. furnished the following very interesting information. The whole number of Tribes attached to the Great Councils of Maryland, Virginia, Ohio, District of Columbia, New Jersey, and Pennsylvania was 68, and in addition there were two Tribes in Delaware and two in Kentucky. Initiations, 1004; suspensions, 324; expulsions, 88; rejected, 92; admitted by card, 68; withdrawn by card, 74; deaths, 34; number of members, 4276; expended for relief of brothers, 6163 fathoms; expended for relief of widows, 2957 fathoms; expended for the education of orphans, 136 fathoms 5 feet. Maryland still retained her position as number one among the Great Councils, both in Tribes and membership, Pennsylvania being second.

1853.

The council fire of the G. C. U. S. was kindled in Osceola wigwam, Baltimore, Md., at the 10th run of the 13th sun, Corn moon, G. S. 5613, W. G. Incohonee William Tucker presiding.

Representatives were admitted from Maryland, Virginia, Pennsylvania, New Jersey, Delaware, Ohio, Kentucky, and the District of Columbia. Among the number were Past Great Sachems George A. Peter, representing the Great Council of Ohio, and William R. Burns, representing the Great Council of New Jersey, each of whom afterwards became Great Incohonee of the G. C. U. S.

By the revisions of the laws that up to this time had taken place the title "Grand" had been changed to "Great." The prefix "Sachem" to the title of "Incohonee" had been dropped, but the prefix "Worthy" was retained for all the great chiefs of the G. C. U. S.

The Great Incohonee presented his longtalk, of which we make the following summary: —

He reported the organization of Osceola Tribe, No. 1, at Fayetteville, N.C., on the 9th sleep of Travelling moon, G. S. 5613 (October 9, 1853). This was the first of several attempts to establish the Order in that reservation. Each successive attempt met with failure and it was not until many great suns after that an organization was perfected, resulting in the Tribes now existing in that reservation.

The rivalry between the Tribes in Philadelphia and those outside had culminated in the holding of a council by one faction at Philadelphia and another at Columbia, and the suspension of three of the Tribes, and the W. G. Incohonee referred to the conflict as a matter needing the attention of the G. C. U. S.

The institution of Keokuk Tribe, No. 3, of Delaware, by "Past Sachem" Joseph Pyle, was reported, as was also information of an attempt to reorganize the Order in New York "whether sanctioned by the G. C. U. S. or not."

In relation to the condition of the Order in New York, which at the last council had been referred to him, he reported that he had secured the work, which had been retained in the hands of a brother in New York City, upon payment of a claim for expenses amounting to $6.66. He also obtained the books of the defunct Great Council of New York, and of several defunct Tribes, and placed Manhattan Tribe, the only one left, under the immediate jurisdiction of the G. C. U. S. This Tribe, shortly after, also became defunct, and its work was reclaimed.

He reported the organization of the Great Council of New Jersey on the 1st of Travelling moon. Leni Lenape Tribe, of Camden, not having been notified, the organization was effected with the understanding that if not entirely satisfactory, a subsequent reorganization would be made. All difficulties were amicably adjusted, and on the 26th of Hunting moon (December 26, 1851), the reorganization was made with Brother McCormick as Great Sachem.

He referred to the organization of Osceola Tribe, No. 2, Delaware City, Delaware, Algonquin, No. 3, of Columbus, Ohio, Chickasaw Tribe, No. 1, of Newport, Kentucky, and Black Hawk Tribe, No. 2, of Covington, Kentucky. The date of the introduction of the Order into Kentucky was 29th Hot moon, G. S. 5612 (June 29, 1852). The first Prophet of Black Hawk Tribe, No. 2, was A. J. Francis, afterwards sixteenth Great Incohonee of the G. C. U. S.

He also recorded the institution of the Great Council of Ohio at Cincinnati on the 7th sleep of Plant moon, G. S. 5612

(April 7, 1852), by Past Great Sachem George A. Peter. The Great Senior Sagamore was Samuel S. McGibbons, and 21 great suns later his trail led him into the reservation of Massachusetts, where he renewed his membership and became attached to the Order in that State, in Sagamore Tribe, No. 2, of Lynn. Brother Peter, as elsewhere noted, was the seventh Great Incohonee of the G. C. U. S.

For the first time the Great Chief of Records submitted a written report, covering the transactions of his chieftaincy during the grand sun. From this we extract as follows: —

In obedience to instructions, he had arranged jointly with the Great Council of Maryland for the expense of hiring and fitting up an office suitable for his work. He had procured a seal and press of a design that he trusted would meet with approval. He had attended to the other instructions concerning printing and distributing the Constitution and General Laws of the Order.

Accompanying his written report was a summary of reports from State Great Councils. That of New Jersey was reported to be incomplete, and the statistics from Tribes in Kentucky, North Carolina, and Delaware were not included. From this summary we learn that the number of tribes was 74; initiations, 1231; suspensions, 345; expulsions, 109; deaths, 31; admitted by card, 78; withdrawn by card, 86; number of members, 5242; expended for relief of brothers, 7199 fathoms 1 foot; expended for relief of widows, 2658 fathoms 1 foot.

The Great Chief of Records of the Great Council of Pennsylvania presented a communication stating that all the difficulties in that reservation had been amicably adjusted, and that matters were now being conducted in a harmonious manner.

In accordance with its own request the Committee on Revision was discharged.

The Committee on procuring a charter plate reported that they had been unable to procure a design, as no appropriation had been made by the G. C. U. S. to carry out the vote under which the Committee was appointed, and the report was accepted and the Committee discharged.

A proposition by George Percy that the Great Council of the United States take into consideration the propriety or impropriety of having the facts of the rise and progress and present condition of the Order published for the use of the members of the Order throughout the United States was rejected.

Had the action proposed by Brother Percy, having in view the collection of facts in relation to the origin and history of the Order, been adopted, the task of the compilers of this history would have been much easier and possibly unnecessary. All disputed points could have been decided by the testimony of those who organized the Improved Order of Red Men, and who if not members of, were fully conversant with, the societies of Red Men that existed, down to a short time at least, previous to 1834. Many important documents then in existence were afterwards lost, and have never since been found, their mysterious disappearance indicating design rather than accident on the part of those responsible therefor.

The Great Council proceeded to the election of great chiefs, who were duly elected and raised up to their respective positions. The elected and appointed chiefs for the ensuing grand sun were as follows: —

W. G. Incohonee,	GEORGE A. PETER, P. G. S.,	Ohio.
W. G. Senior Sagamore,	WILLIAM R. BURNS, P. G. S.,	New Jersey.
W. G. Junior Sagamore,	JOHN H. BARLOW,	Kentucky.
W. G. Prophet,	J. EDWARDS,	Pennsylvania.
W. G. Chief of Records,	JOHN L. BOOKER,	Maryland.
W. G. Keeper of Wampum,	WILLIAM G. GORSUCH, P. G. I.,	Maryland.
W. G. Tocakon,	JOSEPH PYLE,	Delaware.
W. G. Minewa,	DAVID SIEGLE,	Virginia.

All amendments to the Constitution were postponed for one grand sun, and a committee of five was appointed to revise the Constitution, By-laws, and Rules of Order.

The vexing question of a proper ceremonial for the Order was temporarily disposed of by the offer of a premium for a satisfactory ritual, to be competed for only by members of the Order.

The following preamble and resolutions were presented and adopted. They are self-explanatory and indicate a desire, even forty great suns ago, to unite under one head all bodies of Red Men in the United States.

"*Whereas*, From information received, it appears that there are certain Tribes of the Ancient Order of Red Men, located in the city of Reading, Pa., who are desirous of becoming connected with the Improved Order of Red Men, but who under existing laws are disabled from so doing, inasmuch as they at present are compelled to pay percentage on all money at present in their wampum belt, therefore,

"*Resolved*, That the G. C. of Pa. be and is hereby authorized to make overtures to them looking to their connection with our Order.

"*Resolved*, That the G. C. of Pa. be authorized to grant them a Charter, and confer the degrees upon all who are at present in the possession of the degrees in their own body, on application for the same and the payment of the Charter fee."

Representative George Percy seems to have been undismayed by his former unsuccessful attempt to induce the G. C. U. S. to adopt a degree for the female relatives of brothers of the Order. He again submitted the proposition; but the Great Council refused to listen to the brother, and laid his motion upon the table.

The above motion is the second mention or intimation of a desire to establish a branch of the Order into which could be admitted the female relatives and friends of members. It was not until 33 great suns later that the law was adopted that established the Degree of Pocahontas, now recognized as a very valuable adjunct to our Order.

A committee was appointed to procure a design for a charter and report at the next council, it being afterwards decided to take the design on the travelling card and enlarge it to a suitable size, and print a sufficient number of copies to supply the Order.

A committee was appointed to make application to the Legislature of Maryland for an act of incorporation for the G. C. U. S.

1854.

The council fire of the G. C. U. S. was kindled at Osceola wigwam, Baltimore, Md., at the 10th run of the 12th sun, Corn moon, G. S. 5614, W. G. Incohonee George A. Peter presiding.

Among the Representatives admitted at this council for the first time were Andrew J. Baker, of Pennsylvania, and Daniel W. Carter, of Delaware, each of whom afterwards became Great Incohonee.

The Committee on Credentials reported Representatives present from the Great Councils of Maryland, District of Columbia,

Ohio, Virginia, Kentucky, Pennsylvania, and New Jersey, and from Tribes in Delaware.

From the longtalk of the Great Incohonee, we present the following summary : —

He congratulated the Great Council on the continued increase and prosperity of the Order. It had reached the banks of the Mississippi, and was speeding on towards the Pacific coast. Eight Tribes, one Degree Council, and one Great Council had been organized during the grand sun. Three additional States were included among the Tribes referred to, namely, Indiana by Seneca, No. 1, at Metamora, 3d sun Snow moon, G. S. 5614 (February 3, 1854); Illinois by Pocahontas, No. 1, at Paris, 1st sun, Worm moon, G. S. 5614 (March 1, 1854); Iowa by Camanche, No. 1, Dubuque, 5th sun Hot moon, G. S. 5614 (June 5, 1854).

The Great Council of Kentucky was instituted at Newport on the 9th sleep of Sturgeon moon, G. S. 5614 (August 9, 1854). Great Sachem George W. Ford, elected at this time, afterwards became ninth Great Incohonee of the G. C. U. S.

He had appointed Past Sachem A. Curry Vice Great Incohonee of California, with power to establish two Tribes; but the project had fallen through because of inability to forward the necessary supplies.

He mentioned the receipt of an application from Lafayette, Oregon, for a Tribe at that place; but the organization had not been perfected, for want of a competent brother in that locality to do the work.

He referred to another attempt to establish the Order in New York by the institution of Metamora Tribe at New York City.

The longtalk also expressed regret that the council fire of Osceola Tribe, No. 1, of North Carolina, had become extinct.

The question of a charter plate for Great Councils, and subordinate branches of the Order, was finally settled at this council by the adoption of the design now in use for travelling cards, suitably enlarged and filled.

The action of the W. G. Incohonee in establishing Tribes as reported in his longtalk was approved, and charters granted to the respective Tribes and to the Great Council of Kentucky.

A form of raising up of chiefs was adopted.

A committee of three was appointed for the purpose of forming a general recognition sign for this Order and report, if possible, at the present council.

A form for raising up of chiefs for State Great Councils was presented and adopted. The chiefs for the ensuing grand sun elected and appointed and raised up were as follows: —

W. G. Incohonee,	WM. R. BURNS, P. G. S.,	New Jersey.
W. G. Senior Sagamore,	JOHN T. BRADLEY, P. G. S.,	District of Columbia.
W. G. Junior Sagamore,	J. EDWARDS,	Pennsylvania.
W. G. Prophet,	JOSEPH PYLE,	Delaware.
W. G. Chief of Records,	JOHN L. BOOKER,	Maryland.
W. G. Keeper of Wampum,	WM. G. GORSUCH, P. G. I.,	Maryland.
W. G. Tocakon,	C. C. MILLS,	District of Columbia.
W. G. Minewa,	C. S. SMINCK,	New York.

Arrangements were made for providing suitable regalia and emblems for the chiefs and members of the G. C. U. S., and for printing and issuing proper forms for reports from State Great Councils and Tribes working under the immediate jurisdiction of the G. C. U. S., and of the form for raising up of chiefs of State Great Councils.

From the statistical reports from Tribes and Great Councils, as presented by the Great Chief of Records, we gather the following information, the reports from the Great Councils of the District of Columbia, Ohio, and from Tribes in Illinois not being included through informality. From the returns made we find, that the number of Tribes was 94; initiations, 1767; admitted by card, 102; suspensions, 480; expulsions, 65; withdrawn by card, 110; deaths, 51; members, 6251; expended for relief of brothers, 9798 fathoms; expended for relief of widows, 4661 fathoms 5 feet; expended for the education of orphans, 434 fathoms 5 feet.

1855.

The council fire of the G. C. U. S. was kindled at Osceola wigwam, Baltimore, Md., at the 10th run of the 11th sun, Corn moon, G. S. 5615, W. G. Incohonee, William R. Burns presiding.

The Committee on Credentials reported a representation present from the Great Councils of Virginia, Pennsylvania,

New York, Maryland, Ohio, District of Columbia, and Kentucky, and from Tribes in Delaware and New York.

Among the Representatives admitted for the first time at this council may be mentioned Morris H. Gorham of Pennsylvania, Paxon Coats of Ohio, and George W. Ford of Kentucky, each of whom afterwards became Great Incohonee of the G. C. U. S.

In the longtalk of the W. G. Incohonee presented at this council, we find the following: —

He recorded the institution of Cherokee Tribe, No. 4, at Edinburg, and Miami Tribe, No. 5, at Franklin, Indiana, and the institution of the Great Council of Indiana, on the 11th of Flower moon, G. S. 5615 (May 11, 1855).

Permission had been granted to Seneca Tribe, No. 1, to change the hunting grounds of the Tribe from Metamora to Brookville, Indiana.

Camanche Tribe, No. 1, of Dubuque, Iowa, had ceased to work, and its books and property had been surrendered to the G. C. U. S.

He expressed hope that with a revival of business, friends in the Eastern States with whom he had corresponded, would be able to establish the Order in their section.

The question of a proper ritual for the Order seems still to have bothered the G. C. U. S., for we find that the committee on that subject selected at a previous council made a report which was received and laid upon the table.

By a supplementary report of the Committee on Credentials, Past Great Sachem George W. Lindsay, of Maryland, was admitted for the first time. He afterwards became Great Incohonee.

Provision was made for printing and distributing the proceedings of the G. C. U. S. from its organization.

The great chiefs for the ensuing grand sun were elected and appointed and raised up as follows: —

W. G. Incohonee,	GEORGE W. FORD, P. G. S.,	Kentucky.
W. G. Senior Sagamore,	JOSEPH BARTON, P. G. S.,	Pennsylvania.
W. G. Junior Sagamore,	C. S. SMINCK,	New York.
W. G. Prophet,	J. W. MCNELL,	Virginia.
W. G. Chief of Records,	JOHN L. BOOKER,	Maryland.

W. G. Keeper of Wampum,	William G. Gorsuch, P. G. I.,	Maryland.
W. G. Tocakon,	Paxon Coats,	Ohio.
W. G. Minewa,	J. P. A. Entler,	Virginia.

A charter was granted for the Great Council of Indiana, whose institution was referred to in the longtalk of the W. G. Incohonee. A revised Constitution submitted by the committee appointed at the previous council was finally laid upon the table.

From the statistical reports from Great Councils, as presented by Great Chiefs of Records, we learn there were 102 Tribes; initiations, 1539; admitted by card, 461; suspensions, 457; expulsions, 159; withdrawn by card, 84; deaths, 87; number of members, 7220. Maryland still held the lead, with 20 Tribes and 2635 members, with Pennsylvania a close second, with 24 Tribes and 1676 members. The amount expended for relief of brothers was 11,318 fathoms 5 feet; expended for relief of widows, 3360 fathoms 3 feet 6 inches; expended for the education of orphans, 302 fathoms 8 feet 2 inches.

1856.

The council fire was kindled at Red Men's Hall, Baltimore, Md., at the 10th run, 9th sun, Corn moon, G. S. 5616, P. G. I. Hugh Latham presiding in the temporary absence of the W. G. Incohonee, George W. Ford, who entered immediately after the kindling of the council fire.

At this council Missouri was represented for the first time, by James O. Alter, of Hiawatha Tribe, No. 1, St. Louis.

The W. G. Incohonee submitted his longtalk, which among other things mentioned the following: —

The past grand sun had been one of peace and quiet, of plenty and prosperity. Our hunting grounds had been largely extended, they now reaching far into the Sunny South, and the mighty West drawing nearer every sun. Missouri in the West and Louisiana in the South were now numbered with the chosen Red Men of the forest. V. G. I. Joseph Pyle reported the institution of Cherokee Tribe, No. 4, of Wilmington, Del., and of the Great Council of Delaware on the 19th of Hunting moon, G. S. 5616 (December 19, 1856).

In person he had instituted Osyka Tribe, No. 1, at New Orleans, La., on the 12th sleep of Beaver moon, G. S. 5615 (November 12, 1855), and Hiawatha Tribe, No. 1, at St. Louis, Mo., on the 11th sleep of Worm moon, G. S. 5616 (March 11, 1856).

He referred to the cost of instituting Tribes as being a bar to growth, and recommended action that would remove the obstacle.

He had received correspondence from Kansas and Texas about the Order, but no Tribe had yet resulted therefrom.

A resolution was presented and referred to the Committee on the State of the Order, suggesting a card for the wives of Red Men. The Committee reported that the important and grave changes necessary in the work of the Order, if the proposition should be adopted, made it inexpedient.

Charters were granted to the various Tribes organized during the past grand sun and to the Great Council of Delaware.

A committee was appointed to revise the laws regulating the regalia of the Order, and define more clearly the emblems of the various chiefs.

The committee subsequently made a report recommending sash, belt, and apron, with distinguishing jewels, and in the five colors, — purple, scarlet, blue, orange, and green, according to rank. The report was adopted.

The Great Council accepted an invitation to participate in the ceremonies attending the laying of the corner-stone of the new Custom House, Wheeling, Va. (now W. Va.).

Chiefs of the G. C. U. S. for the ensuing grand sun were elected and appointed and raised up as follows: —

W. G. Incohonee,	Louis Bonsal, P. G. S.,	Maryland.
W. G. Senior Sagamore,	Daniel W. Carter, P. G. S.,	Delaware.
W. G. Junior Sagamore,	Chris. Weistenberg, P. G. S.,	Pennsylvania.
W. G. Prophet,	John W. McNell,	Virginia.
W. G. Chief of Records,	John L. Booker, P. G. S.,	Maryland.
W. G. Keeper of Wampum,	Wm. G. Gorsuch, P. G. I.,	Maryland.
W. G. Tocakon,	A. Britton,	Pennsylvania.
W. G. Minewa,	James O. Alter,	Missouri.

A new constitution for the Great Council was considered in Committee of the Whole and adopted.

The special Committee on Revision of Ritual having reported against any change, the report was accepted and the committee was discharged; but the question of a proper ritual seems to have been still undecided, for the Great Council adopted resolutions offering a premium for a ritual of three degrees.

Arrangements were made for printing and promulgating the Constitution adopted at this council.

From the reports of State Great Councils to the G. C. U. S., we find that the number of Tribes was 99; initiations, 1596; suspensions, 734; expulsions, 159; deaths, 59; admitted by card, 53; withdrawn by card, 50; number of members, 7953; total amount expended for relief of brothers, 10,417 fathoms and 75 inches; expended for relief of widows, 3803 fathoms and 25 inches; expended for education of orphans, 321 fathoms 75 inches.

1857.

The council fire of the G. C. U. S. was kindled at Red Men's Hall, Baltimore, Md., at the 9th run of the 8th sun, Corn moon, G. S. 5617, W. G. Incohonee Louis Bonsal presiding.

Representatives from the Great Councils of Maryland, Ohio, Virginia, Kentucky, and Delaware were admitted and instructed. Among those thus admitted for the first time was Past Great Sachem A. J. Francis, who afterwards became Great Incohonee of the G. C. U. S.

The W. G. Incohonee presented his longtalk, which among other things mentioned the following: —

After congratulating the Great Council upon the commanding position which the Order was assuming, he referred to the legislation that would engage the attention of the G. C. U. S. Among those prominent in importance was the old, but ever new, question of a proper ritual for the Order. An attempt had been made to adjust difficulties existing in the Great Council of the District of Columbia, and while this seemed at one time to approach success, subsequent events proved that desirable result more than dubious. He reported the organization of another Tribe at St. Louis. The Great Council of Indiana had ceased to exist, and what Tribes remained were placed under the immediate jurisdiction of the G. C. U. S.

The Order had become extinct in Iowa in the preceding grand sun.

The committee upon the subject of ritual, appointed at the previous council, reported, but presented nothing definite, and was discharged.

The chiefs elected and appointed and raised up for the following grand sun were as follows:—

W. G. Incohonee,	DANIEL W. CARTER, P. G. S.,	Delaware.
W. G. Senior Sagamore,	J. H. TATSAPAUGH,	Virginia.
W. G. Junior Sagamore,	J. EDWARDS,	Pennsylvania.
W. G. Prophet,	A. J. FRANCIS, P. G. S.,	Kentucky.
W. G. Chief of Records,	JOHN L. BOOKER, P. G. S.,	Maryland.
W. G. Keeper of Wampum,	W. G. GORSUCH, P. G. I.,	Maryland.
W. G. Tocakon,	A. S. WALTON,	Maryland.
W. G. Minewa,	JNO. F. METZ,	Pennsylvania.

The Great Council voted to participate in a body in the procession to be held at Lancaster, Pa., on the 21st Travelling moon, G. S. 5617 (October 21, 1857).

Another committee on ritual was appointed to report at the next council.

The record for this grand sun contains no statistical reports from the respective Great Councils.

1858.

The council fire of the G. C. U. S. was kindled at Red Men's Hall, Baltimore, Md., at the 10th run of the 14th sun, Corn moon, G. S. 5618, P. G. I. Hugh Latham presiding in the temporary absence of the W. G. Incohonee. W. G. Incohonee Carter subsequently entered and assumed his position.

Among the Representatives admitted at this council for the first time, were George B. Colflesh of Maryland, William B. Eckert, of Pennsylvania, and Joshua Maris, of Delaware, each of whom afterwards became Great Incohonee of the G. C. U. S.

The great chiefs elected and appointed and raised up for the ensuing grand sun were as follows:—

W. G. Incohonee,	PAXON COATS, P. G. S.,	Ohio.
W. G. Senior Sagamore,	JOSEPH PYLE,	Delaware.
W. G. Junior Sagamore,	A. S. WHITE,	New Jersey.
W. G. Prophet,	GEO. R. COFFROTH, P. G. S.,	Virginia.

GREAT COUNCIL OF UNITED STATES. 311

W. G. Chief of Records, JOHN L. BOOKER, P. G. S., Maryland.
W. G. Keeper of Wampum, WILLIAM G. GORSUCH, P. G. I., Maryland.
W. G. Tocakon, GEORGE P. OLIVER, Pennsylvania.
W. G. Minewa, J. D. RADCLIFFE, North Carolina.

The W. G. Incohonee submitted his longtalk.

He referred to the financial panic of 1857 as affecting the growth and prosperity of the Order. He mentioned efforts made to revive the Order in Indiana, and the continued difficulties in the District of Columbia. The efforts to keep the Order alive in the State of New York had again been unsuccessful, and the extinction of the Tribes there had followed. A new Tribe had been instituted in North Carolina, and the Order was reported as in good condition in Louisiana and Missouri, an application for a charter for a Great Council in the latter State being among the probabilities of the near future.

He reported the organization of the first Tribe ever organized in the New England States, Narragansett Tribe, No. 1, at Hartford, Conn., which was instituted by great Chief of Records John L. Booker, on the 19th sleep of Buck moon, G. S. 5617 (July 19, 1857).

He called attention to the new work which the Committee on Ritual had prepared, and which was ready for the action of the G. C. U. S.

Narragansett Tribe, No. 1, of Hartford, Conn., above referred to in the longtalk of the W. G. Incohonee, had a fitful existence for a short time, and then its council fire became extinct.

The ever-present question of the ritual again engaged the attention of the G. C. U. S. Upon the report of the special committee appointed at the previous council, that but one work had been received by the committee for consideration, and they felt constrained to report against its adoption, it was voted again to offer a premium for a satisfactory ritual.

Southerland's Manual was adopted as a standard of parliamentary law for the use of the G. C. U. S.

From the statistical reports from State Great Councils and Tribes, we glean the following information: Number of Tribes, 105; initiations, 1437; rejections, 136; suspensions, 520; expulsions, 138; reinstated, 18; admitted by card, 42; withdrawn by card, 68; died, 71; number of members, 7742; amount expended for relief of brothers, 13,503 fathoms 25 inches; expended for widows and orphans, 5640 fathoms 75 inches; expended for education, 863 fathoms 50 inches.

During the grand sun, 13 Tribes had been instituted, and 19 had become defunct. Of the latter number, 11 were in the reservation of Pennsylvania, in which some unfortunate dissensions had arisen that left this baneful imprint upon the prosperity of the Order in that State. Appended to the proceedings for this grand sun, is a complete list of the 105 Tribes in existence at this time in the States of Maryland, Pennsylvania, Kentucky, Virginia, Ohio, New Jersey, Delaware, Louisiana, Missouri, Mississippi, Connecticut, and North Carolina, and in the District of Columbia.

1859.

The council fire of the G. C. U. S. was kindled at Red Men's Hall, Baltimore, Md., at the 9th run of the 14th sun, Corn moon, G. S. 5619, W. G. Incohonee Paxon Coats presiding.

Representatives were present from Maryland, Pennsylvania, Virginia, Ohio, New Jersey, Delaware, and Kentucky.

A Committee on Ceremonial was appointed to consider a new ritual that had been received by the Great Chief of Records.

The W. G. Incohonee presented his longtalk, which, among other things, referred to the following:—

He stated the condition of the Order in the various reservations, Pennsylvania standing at the head, with an increase of five Tribes and 1008 members. He reported the institution of the Great Council of Missouri in a somewhat informal manner by the V. G. Incohonee of that State, on the 18th Hunting moon, G. S. 5618 (December 18, 1858). In the State of Indiana, Cherokee Tribe, No. 4, of Edinburg, had been resuscitated with bright prospects for future success. A new Tribe in the same State, Camanche Tribe, No. 7, had been instituted at Dearborn. He had received the charter and other effects of Camanche Tribe, No. 1, Dubuque, Iowa. He also made official report of the institution of Natchez Tribe, No. 1, of Natchez, Miss., and of Minnehaha Tribe, No. 2, of St. Louis, which had not been reported at the previous council of the G. C. U. S.

A special committee of three was appointed to carry out the provisions of a series of resolutions to the effect that a special committee of three be appointed to report during the present session: 1st. The date of the Institution and Constitution of the Order in the hunting grounds of the palefaces. 2d. The date of the Institution of the Great Council of the United States. 3d. Such other statistics of the Order as the committee may deem pertinent.

In this same connection, later in the council, the Special Committee was authorized to purchase the "Muster Roll," containing the names of the founders of the Order of Red Men at Fort Mifflin; and such other documents relative to the origin and history thereof as they may deem worthy of preservation, to be placed in the archives of the Great Council of the United States.

The chiefs elected and appointed and raised up for the ensuing grand sun were as follows:—

W. G. Incohonee,	ANDREW J. BAKER, P. G. S.,	Pennsylvania.
W. G. Senior Sagamore,	JAMES N. TYRACK,	Kentucky.
W. G. Junior Sagamore,	E. L. LUNSFORD, P. G. S.,	Virginia.
W. G. Prophet,	JOHN M. REUTER,	Missouri.
W. G. Chief of Records,	JOHN L. BOOKER, P. G. S.,	Maryland.
W. G. Keeper of Wampum,	WM. G. GORSUCH, P. G. I.,	Maryland.
W. G. Tocakon,	W. F. WEHL,	Delaware.
W. G. Minewa,	WILLIAM KINER,	New Jersey.

The Special Committee on Ceremonial reported in favor of a ritual which had been presented by Brother John Esten Cook, of Richmond, Va.

The report was adopted, and it was ordered that the new ritual go into operation on the 1st sun of Cold moon, G. S. 5620 (January 1, 1860). Arrangements were made for printing and distributing the new ritual.

From the statistical reports from State Great Councils and Tribes to the G. C. U. S., we obtain the following information: Number of Tribes, 115; initiations, 1822; rejections, 124; suspensions, 831; reinstated, 55; admitted by card, 110; withdrawn by card, 78; expulsions, 381; died, 71; number of members, 9266; Tribes instituted, 7; Tribes defunct, 6; amount expended for relief of brothers, 13,311 fathoms; expended for widows and orphans, 3373 fathoms 25 inches; expended for education, 419 fathoms 5 feet.

1860.

The council fire of the G. C. U. S. was kindled at Red Men's Hall, Baltimore, Md., at the 9th run of the 11th sun, Corn moon, G. S. 5620, W. G. Incohonee Andrew J. Baker presiding.

The Committee on Credentials reported Representatives present from Maryland, Pennsylvania, Virginia, Ohio, New Jersey, Missouri, Kentucky, Delaware, and the District of Columbia.

The longtalk submitted by the W. G. Incohonee was a much more comprehensive document than had hitherto been given by the presiding chief of the Great Council. It gave a complete and detailed account of his efforts to bring the work and literature of the Order into harmonious symmetry, and the results secured. Among the matters touched upon may be mentioned the following: —

He reported a preliminary organization for a Great Council in Louisiana on the 5th sun of Snow moon, G. S. 5620 (February 5, 1860).

Arrangements had been made for collecting the charters and private work of the Tribes in North Carolina, which had ceased to work. Illinois had been brought into line once more by the organization of a Tribe at Nashville, Washington County. He detailed several visitations made by him in the reservations of Ohio, Kentucky, Virginia, Maryland, and Delaware. He reported that the new ritual had not met with the general approbation hoped for, but still by a large majority of the members was preferred to the old one. He recommended the appointment of a competent committee to revise the whole ritual of the Order.

The Great Chief of Records submitted a written report detailing the routine of work of his chieftaincy during the grand sun. Accompanying this was the statistical report of State Great Councils and Tribes, the reports of three Tribes being missing. From these reports, we glean the following: Num-

ANDREW J. BAKER.

JOSEPH PYLE.

GEORGE W. LINDSAY.

ADAM SMITH.

PAST GREAT INCOHONEES.

ber of Tribes, 94; initiations, 1559; suspensions, 683; expulsions, 82; rejections, 72; admitted by card, 123; withdrawn by card, 120; died, 57; number of members, 9096; expended for relief of brothers, 15,065 fathoms; expended for relief of widows, 7890 fathoms; expended for education, 440 fathoms.

An invitation was accepted to attend a celebration given under the auspices of the Great Council of Pennsylvania at Philadelphia on the 23d sun of Flower moon, G. S. 5621 (May 23, 1861).

The chiefs elected and appointed and raised up for the ensuing great sun were as follows: —

W. G. Incohonee,	RICHARD MARLEY, P. G. S.,	Maryland.
W. G. Senior Sagamore,	R. M. HAYES,	Ohio.
W. G. Junior Sagamore,	JOSHUA MARIS,	Delaware.
W. G. Prophet,	ABRAM F. HAAS,	Pennsylvania.
W. G. Chief of Records,	JOHN L. BOOKER, P. G. S.,	Maryland.
W. G. Keeper of Wampum,	WM. G. GORSUCH, P. G. I.,	Maryland.
W. G. Tocakon,	JOHN D. MOORE,	New Jersey.
W. G. Minewa,	S. RIANHARD,	Delaware.

It was voted that a committee of five be appointed to procure an act of incorporation from the State of Maryland for the G. C. U. S.

A form for kindling and quenching the council fire of State Great Councils was adopted.

The committee appointed to make inquiry into the date of the introduction of the Order, etc., not being prepared to report, it was voted that the committee be continued until the next Corn moon council.

A special committee of three was ordered, as advised by W. G. Incohonee Baker in his longtalk, to revise the entire ritual of the Order and report at the next council of the G. C. U. S.

The Great Chief of Records was authorized to procure photographs of all P. G. Incohonees, and to have them suitably framed and placed in the office of the Great Chief of Records.

A duplicate charter for the Great Council of Ohio was granted to replace the original, which had been lost.

1861.

The council fire of the G. C. U. S. was kindled at Red Men's Hall, Baltimore, Md., at the 9th run of the 10th sun, Corn moon, G. S. 5621, W. G. Incohonee Richard Marley presiding.

Among the Representatives admitted for the first time at this council were Angus Cameron and William B. Eckert of Pennsylvania, each of whom afterwards became Great Incohonee of the G. C. U. S. Representatives were admitted from the Great Councils of Maryland, Pennsylvania, Ohio, New Jersey, Missouri, Kentucky, and Delaware.

The longtalk submitted by the W. G. Incohonee referred to the disturbed political condition of the country at this time, but in a tone which proved that the spirit of fraternity rose above sectional strife, and that, though divided politically by the events of that unfortunate period in the history of our country, the hearts of all true Red Men were united without regard to locality.

The longtalk of the W. G. Incohonee gave a report of his acts in establishing the Order at Richmond, Ind., and the gathering in of the books and other property of Tribes that had become extinct in various reservations. It also gave the decisions rendered. He complained of the meagre returns received from the V. G. Incohonees owing to the troubled condition of the country. Concerning the only Tribe in New England, he said that understanding that the Great Chief of Records was to visit one of the Eastern States, he requested him to extend his journey to Hartford, Conn., for the purpose of obtaining the Work, etc., of Narragansett Tribe, No. 1. He succeeded in obtaining the Work of the Order, but in consequence of the late Chief of Records of the Tribe removing to Massachusetts he could not obtain the Ledger and Journal of the Tribe.

The Great Chief of Records gave an account of his stewardship during the grand sun, and of his compliance as far as possible with the instructions given him at the last council. Among other things he had procured the photographs of P. G. Incohonees Hugh Latham, of Virginia; George A. Peter, of Ohio; William P. Burns, of New Jersey; George W. Ford, of Kentucky; Paxon Coats, of Ohio; Louis Bonsal, of Maryland, and Andrew J. Baker, of Pennsylvania. "The remainder would have been procured had it not been that through political difficulties, the artist thought it prudent to remove from the State."

The Great Chief of Records further said, that owing to the unsettled condition of affairs, the usual statistical reports from the Great Councils had not been prepared and therefore could not be submitted.

For several great suns under the Constitution it had been necessary that the council fire of the G. C. U. S. should be kindled at Baltimore, Md. At this council an amendment was adopted permitting the kindling at such place as may be fixed by the Great Council.

The chiefs elected and appointed and raised up for the ensuing grand sun were as follows: —

W. G. Incohonee,	JOSEPH PYLE, P. G. S.,	Delaware.
W. G. Senior Sagamore,	L. SCHLOSS,	Ohio.
W. G. Junior Sagamore,	LEWIS C. PIERCE, P. G. S.,	Pennsylvania.
W. G. Prophet,	MORRIS H. GORHAM, P. G. S.,	Pennsylvania.
W. G. Chief of Records,	JOHN L. BOOKER, P. G. S.,	Maryland.
W. G. Keeper of Wampum,	WM. G. GORSUCH, P. G. I.,	Maryland.
W. G. Tocakon,	CHAS. F. WILLITS,	New Jersey.
W. G. Minewa,	EDWARD R. MCCAIN,	Maryland.

The Special Committee on Ritual reported progress.

The special committee appointed at the previous council to procure an act of incorporation for the G. C. U. S. was continued with the addition of two members.

A form was adopted for kindling and quenching the council fire of a Beneficial Degree Council.

A report having been called for from the Committee on the Origin of the Order, etc., Representative Gorham of Pennsylvania, of the Committee, stated cause for delay in making the report, and it was voted that the Committee be continued one grand sun, and that Representative Gorham be substituted as Chairman of the Committee.

1862.

No council of the G. C. U. S. was held in G. S. 5622 (1862). The war between the North and the South was occupying the minds of all the people of the country. The disturbed condition of affairs in the city of Baltimore made it imprudent to kindle the council fire in that city, and no other place having been fixed upon at the preceding council, under the Constitution it could be kindled only at Baltimore. It was therefore deemed best to omit the council for this grand sun.

1863.

The council fire of the G. C. U. S. was kindled at Red Men's Hall, Baltimore, Md., at the 9th run of the 8th sun, Corn moon, G. S. 5623, Great Incohonee Joseph Pyle presiding.

The Committee on Credentials reported Representatives present from the Great Councils of Pennsylvania, Maryland, New Jersey, Ohio, Kentucky, and Delaware, and the District of Columbia.

The Great Incohonee submitted his longtalk, covering the administration of his chieftaincy during the last two grand suns. He congratulated the Order that, notwithstanding the disturbed condition of affairs in the country at large, the Order had not lost ground, but was steadily and surely advancing. He viewed in detail the various matters which had engaged his attention, and the efforts made by him to gather in the work from defunct Tribes, to establish new Tribes, and to encourage those that seemed to be faltering in the good work, and explained the cause for not kindling the preceding grand sun council fire.

The western part of Virginia having been set off as a separate State, known as West Virginia, he had placed Logan Tribe, No. 21, of Wheeling, under the immediate jurisdiction of G. C. U. S., for the reason that no Great Council could legally exercise jurisdiction in two States.

The Committee on the New Ritual made a report and presented a thorough revision.

The report of the committee was accepted and considered in Committee of the Whole and finally adopted, thus giving to the Order a complete, symmetrical, and attractive ceremonial which stood the test of experience for a number of great suns.

The chiefs elected and appointed and raised up for the ensuing grand sun were as follows : —

W. G. Incohonee, A. J. FRANCIS, P. G. S., Kentucky.
W. G. Senior Sagamore, CHRIS. WEISTENBERG, P. G. S., Pennsylvania.

W. G. Junior Sagamore,	W. Limeburner,	New Jersey.
W. G. Prophet,	Joshua Maris, P. G. S.,	Delaware.
W. G. Chief of Records,	John L. Booker, P. G. S.,	Maryland.
W. G. Keeper of Wampum,	Wm. G. Gorsuch, P. G. I.,	Maryland.
W. G. Tocakon,	Wm. Chidsey,	Ohio.
W. G. Minewa,	James A. Cooper,	District of Columbia.

A report having been called for from the Committee on the Origin of the Order, the Chairman of that committee stated that it was not prepared to report at this council, and it was voted that the committee be continued for one grand sun.

The balance of the council was consumed in the ordinary routine work, action on the reports of committees, and in perfecting the unwritten work necessary to accompany the revised ritual.

From the statistical report presented by the Great Chief of Records, we find that the number of Tribes was 81 ; initiated, 763; rejected, 52 ; suspended, 1060; expelled, 283 ; reinstated, 9 ; admitted by card, 42 ; withdrawn by card, 58 ; died, 146 ; number of members, 6156. There seems to have been no returns of the amount expended for the relief of brothers and widows and orphans and for education.

A resolution was adopted providing for holding the next grand sun council in the hunting grounds of Philadelphia, Pa.

1864.

The council fire of the G. C. U. S. was kindled at Pocahontas wigwam, Philadelphia, Pa., in Corn moon, G. S. 5624, W. G. Incohonee A. J. Francis presiding.

The Committee on Credentials reported Representatives present from Maryland, Ohio, New Jersey, Delaware, Kentucky, West Virginia, Missouri, and the District of Columbia.

The Great Incohonee submitted his longtalk, and gave in detail the matters which had engaged his attention during the preceding grand sun. Among these was the institution of California Tribe, No. 1, at San Francisco.

The Great Chief of Records submitted a report of his actions during the grand sun and the measures taken by him for printing and distributing the new ritual adopted, and other supplies furnished through his office. He also referred to a Degree Work received from P. G. I. George A. Peter, of Cincinnati, Ohio, entitled "Degree of the Daughters of Powhatan," with a request that same be printed and laid before the G. C. U. S. at this council. He had not complied with the request because he had no power so to do.

The following preamble and resolutions were presented by Representative Morris H. Gorham, and are here given as marking the initiative of a movement of historical interest in the Order.

"*Whereas*, The Improved Order of Red Men is purely American in its origin, ritual, and traditions, being based upon the customs and antiquities of the Aborigines of this continent; and, *whereas*, the discovery of America forms an epoch alike grand in the history of the Paleface and the Red Man, it therefore suggests itself as the appropriate period from which to compute dates in this Order; therefore,

"*Resolved*, That the computation of time now in use be, and is hereby abolished in this Order.

"*Resolved*, That all documents of this Order be dated from the year of the discovery of America by Columbus, the style to be G. S. D. (or Grand Sun of the Discovery).

"*Resolved*, That the Grand Sun shall commence on the first sun of the Corn moon."

The resolutions were referred to the Committee on the State of the Order, which afterwards reported recommending that they be laid over until the next grand sun council, which recommendation was adopted.

The chiefs elected and appointed and raised up for the ensuing grand sun were as follows:—

W. G. Incohonee,	ANGUS CAMERON, P. G. S.,	Pennsylvania.
W. G. Senior Sagamore,	MOSES L. MERRILL, G. S.,	District of Columbia.
W. G. Junior Sagamore,	AUGUST ROETTGER,	West Virginia.
W. G. Prophet,	A. C. DIBOLL,	Ohio.
W. G. Chief of Records,	JOHN L. BOOKER, P.G.S.,	Maryland.
W. G. Keeper of Wampum,	WM. G. GORSUCH, P.G.I.,	Maryland.
W. G. Tocakon,	CHAS. HEBEL,	Kentucky.
W. G. Minewa,	JAMES G. KING, P. G. S.,	New Jersey.

Past Great Incohonee Andrew J. Baker, Past Great Sachem, afterwards Past Great Incohonee, Morris H. Gorham, and Past Sachem A. F. Haas, the committee under whose direction the new ritual had been prepared, were appointed a special committee to prepare a Sachem's and a Prophet's degree, and report them to the next Great Council.

At this council further action was taken towards procuring from the proper authority an act of incorporation for the G. C. U. S.

No statistical summary was published with the proceedings for this grand sun.

1865.

The council fire of the G. C. U. S. was kindled at Red Men's Hall, Baltimore, Md., at the 9th run of the 12th sun, Corn moon, G. S. 5625, Great Incohonee Angus Cameron presiding.

The Committee on Credentials reported Representatives present from Maryland, Pennsylvania, Delaware, New Jersey, Ohio, Kentucky, West Virginia, Louisiana, and the District of Columbia.

Among those present at this council for the first time was Past Sachem James A. Parsons of New Jersey, who afterwards became Great Incohonee.

The committee referred to the fact that Past Great Incohonee Hugh Latham and two other Representatives appeared accredited to the G. C. U. S. from the Great Council of Virginia, their credentials being without the seal of said Great Council, said seal having been destroyed by fire, and the Representatives were admitted by a vote of the Great Council.

Thus after the four years of weary waiting, of hardship and struggle, of civil war and fraternal strife, the country at large was once more united and all sections of the country in which the Order existed were again represented around the council fire of the G. C. U. S.

The Great Incohonee submitted his longtalk, reporting in detail his acts during the grand sun, among which may be mentioned a new Tribe, Cornstalk, No. 2, at Wheeling, W. Va.; the reorganization of a new Tribe, Tecumseh, No. 4, of Baton Rouge, La.; the issuing of charters for the Great Council of the District of Columbia, and several Tribes voted at the preceding council, and the reorganization of the Great Council of Virginia on the 15th of Sturgeon moon, G. S. 5625 (August 15, 1865).

The inclination to adopt a degree for female relatives of members of the Order again made its appearance by the submission of resolutions therefor from the District of Columbia, upon which it was decided to be inexpedient to legislate.

The chiefs elected and appointed and raised up for the ensuing grand sun were as follows:—

W. G. Incohonee,	THOS. A. BOSLEY, P. G. S.,	Ohio.
W. G. Senior Sagamore,	ALFRED SHAW,	Louisiana.
W. G. Junior Sagamore,	JOHN D. MOORE,	New Jersey.
W. G. Prophet,	WILLIAM R. MCFARLANE,	Delaware.
W. G. Chief of Records,	JOHN L. BOOKER, P. G. S.,	Maryland.
W. G. Keeper of Wampum,	WM. G. GORSUCH, P. G. I.,	Maryland.
W. G. Tocakon,	R. C. MCCRACKEN,	Kentucky.
W. G. Minewa,	JOHN B. SHANER,	Virginia.

The Special Committee on Ritual submitted a report of progress, which was adopted, the committee continued and the vacancy caused by the withdrawal from the Order of Brother A. F. Haas, filled by the appointment of Past Great Sachem E. F. Stewart of Pennsylvania.

The same committee was ordered to prepare a new form for raising up chiefs of the G. C. U. S.

The revised Constitution was considered in Committee of the Whole and adopted.

The resolutions submitted at the last council in relation to changing from the Jewish calculation of time were taken up and amended by adding after the word "discovery," the words "the year 1492 be considered the year 1, and the year 1865 as the year 374, so that the year may be always ascertained by subtracting 1491. Also the word 'Corn' erased and 'Cold' inserted."

The legislation of the Great Council seems to have provided for a Committee on Returns and Reports, and this committee submitted a summary of the reports presented by State Great Councils and Tribes under the immediate jurisdiction of the G. C. U. S., from which we gather the following information: Number of Tribes, 85; initiations, 1246; suspensions, 330; expulsions, 21; admitted by card, 49; withdrawn by card, 36; died, 91; number of members, 7835; amount expended for relief of brothers, 12,811 fathoms 97 inches; expended for relief of widows, 4740 fathoms 40 inches; expended for education, 486 fathoms 75 inches.

By the legislation adopted at this council the term of the chiefs of the G. C. U. S. was extended from one grand sun to two grand suns, but it was voted that this change should affect the chiefs elected at the succeeding council.

The subject of incorporation of the G. C. U. S. again engaged attention, and a committee was instructed to procure an incorporation of this Great Council by the State of Pennsylvania.

The Great Council seems to have had some difficulty in gathering wampum sufficient to meet the necessary expenses, and to relieve itself from similar embarrassment in the future a resolution was adopted to the effect "that this Great Council will not pay any mileage until relieved from debt, and that the several States and Tribes in this jurisdiction be requested to pay the mileage of their own Representatives for future sessions."

1866.

The council fire of the G. C. U. S. was kindled at Red Men's Hall, Baltimore, Md., at the 9th run of the 11th sun, Corn moon, G. S. D. 375, M. W. Incohonee Thomas A. Bosley presiding. For the first time the new style of dating was used, the G. S. D. 375 being equivalent to A.D. 1866.

The Committee on Credentials reported Representatives present from Delaware, Virginia, West Virginia, Kentucky, New Jersey, Ohio, Missouri, Pennsylvania, and the District of Columbia. Among the Representatives admitted for the first time at this council was Past Sachem Thomas K. Donnalley, the present (1892) Great Incohonee, and Thomas J. Francis, of New Jersey, the present Great Prophet of the United States.

The Committee appointed to procure an Act of Incorporation for the G. C. U. S. reported that the charter had been secured as directed by the Great Council.

By a vote of the Great Council, the report and the Act of Incorporation were accepted.

The M. W. Great Incohonee presented his longtalk, which among other things mentioned the following: Dispensations had been granted for the organization of Ontario Tribe, No. 6, at St. Louis, Mo.; Leni Lenape Tribe, No. 2, at Camden, New Jersey; Swamp Eagle Tribe, No. 1, Marshall, Texas; Manhattan Tribe, No. 2, San Francisco, Cal.; Tippecanoe Tribe, No. 8, Patriot, Ind.

The Great Council of Missouri had been reorganized on the 24th sleep of Snow moon, G. S. D. 375 (February 24, 1866).

The Great Chief of Records submitted a report of the routine work of his chieftaincy, together with a tabulated statement of membership and receipts.

Great Chief of Records John L. Booker, who had served the Great Council from its organization down to the present time, withdrew his name as a candidate for re-election. Morris H. Gorham, of Pennsylvania, the brother who was elected to succeed him, afterwards became Great Incohonee, and the imprint of his zeal and love for the Order has been left in indelible marks upon its ritual and laws.

Charters were granted to the Great Council of Missouri, and to the various Tribes enumerated in the longtalk of the Great Incohonee.

A resolution was adopted to the effect "that there being property belonging to this Great Council, and the Great Council of Maryland, held jointly, and now in the possession of P. M. W. Great Chief of Records Jno. L. Booker, a committee be appointed to examine, and divide the same."

This action has a significance from the fact that many important documents that would have shed light upon the origin and early history of the Order were in possession of the retiring Great Chief of Records, Brother Booker. These documents disappeared and have never been found. Their loss is irreparable.

The Committee on Revision of Ritual submitted a report which was a revision of the work, and promised at next council to present the Sachem's and Prophet's degrees, with a new funeral ceremony.

The ceremonial presented by the committee was considered in Committee of the Whole and unanimously adopted.

It was voted that the next council of the G. C. U. S. be held at Philadelphia, Pa.

Great Chief of Records Gorham, from the Committee on date of the Institution of the Order in the Hunting Grounds of the

Palefaces, stated that he had prepared a report, but was unable to get the names of the other members of the committee affixed to it; whereupon Representative Cameron moved that four additional members be added to the committee, in order to obtain a majority report, which was agreed to. The M. W. Great Incohonee appointed on the committee, Representatives Cameron, of Pennsylvania; Ford, of Maryland; Ditman, of Virginia; and McFarlane, of Delaware. The report was then read, unanimously adopted, and the M. W. Great Chief of Records instructed to have the same printed with the forthcoming proceedings of the G. C. U. S.

The report above referred to is the first attempt to give to the world a history of the origin of the Improved Order of Red Men.

After detailing the legislation preceding the selection of the Committee, all of which has been covered by the matter given in this chapter, the report proceeds as follows: —

We shall consider the first inquiry, under what we shall term THE TRADITIONAL OR UNCERTAIN PERIOD of the history of our affiliation; and waving for the time the generic term Order, will, for the sake of greater accuracy, use the term *Society*, as applied to it in the earlier documents now extant.

Passing to the consideration of the first inquiry propounded in the resolutions, we have to deplore the loss of the original record of their transactions and other early papers, which would have settled beyond dispute the date of the institution of the Society in the hunting grounds of the palefaces.

As early as 1821, we find the loss of these documents regretted and complained of. In November of that year a Committee was appointed to "inquire into whose possession the papers appertaining to the Red Men" had fallen. The said committee reported on the 9th of August, 1822, that "by a train of unfortunate events, following each other in rapid succession, the papers belonging to the Red Men had come in possession of white men." They "were not disposed to dwell upon the cause" leading thereto, "the individual[1] most implicated having passed the dark river, which lies at the foot of the hill of life." "A Red Man" had "with trouble and expense recovered a portion of them," and it was impossible to tell in what direction the winds of misfortune had wafted the remainder.

There exists in the recollection of some of the older members of the present day an early tradition — once popular — which points to Fort Mifflin, on the Delaware River, as the birthplace of the Society, and that sometime during the period intervening between the years 1812 and 1814 was the time of the kindling of its first Council fire.[2]

---

[1] Francis Shallus, first Generalissimo.
[2] The Preamble to the Constitution and By-Laws names the year 1813.

The circumstance which this tradition assigns as the stimulating cause of its first organization, grew out of the bitter animosity which has been engendered between the *war* and *anti-war* parties during those eventful years in American history.

The spirit of hatred, strife and distrust which embittered the feeling of the conflicting factions, was not long confined to the civil community outside, but passing as it were unseen by the sentinels, it made its appearance and disseminated its demoralizing influence among the soldiers of the garrison. Some of the more influential and patriotic of the volunteers [1] within the Fort, viewing with apprehension and fear the threatening consequence of the powers at work among them to their country and its free institutions, and rising above the machinations of party to the true level of patriotism, proposed and effected among the soldiers the organization of a *Secret Society*, fortified by signs, grips and passwords, the object of which was to dispel discord and disseminate friendship. Their efforts, as we are told, were attended with the happiest results; for in a very short time after their organization was completed a marked change was visible in the tone and temper of the garrison. Where before had been distrust, hatred and the manifestations of angry passion, was now kindness, good fellowship, and brotherly regard—amity of sentiment and unity of purpose prevailing in every heart, as the soldiers of Fort Mifflin emerged from the council of Red Men, where they had pledged themselves to patriotism and fraternity.

At the close of the war their Council fire was necessarily quenched, the garrison disbanded, and the volunteers returned to their homes. But recollections of the past, the charms of an association so patriotic in its origin and purpose, and which had been productive of so much good in the past, when the dark mantle of adversity hung like a pall upon the country, with the natural desire to perpetuate and extend it, were the incentives to revive the Society.[2] Accordingly, a call was inserted in one or more of the newspapers of Philadelphia for a council of the Red Men, which resulted in the organization of what was subsequently known as the "Tribe of Columbia of the Society of Red Men of Pennsylvania."[3]

Such, in brief, is substantially the traditional history of the origin of our affiliation, as preserved (among others) in the recollection of our venerable brother and colleague, P. G. I. Marley. Brother Richard Marley was admitted and adopted by the *Society* on the evening of the 9th of September, 1824, and received the name *Moose Deer's Brother*, and therefore was acquainted with many of the principal members, and familiar with the origin and history they would ascribe to it. Besides, there is *internal* evidence found in the military character of the organization, as will appear

---

[1] Captain James N. Barker, and Lieut. Williams. The former was Commandant of the Fort, and subsequently (in the year 1819) was Mayor of the city of Philadelphia. The latter, having attained the rank of Captain, was slain in the defence of Fort Erie August 14, 1814.—(Preamble to Constitution and By-Laws.)

[2] Preamble to Constitution and By-Laws.

[3] Manuscript Record.

in another part of this report, which proves it to have been the work of military men.[1]

But whilst the Society is fortunate in the possession of the tradition, preserved in part at least by brother Marley, and verified to some extent by authentic documentary evidence, your Committee are not prepared to limit its origin to as late a date as the war of 1812–15. Indeed, there is in the records of the Society presumptive as well as contemporaneous external evidence that it originated at a much earlier day; and it is as probable that it took its rise during the Revolutionary War as during that of 1812–15, and the origin attributed to the Society at Fort Mifflin may have been but the *reorganization of pre-existing fraternal elements* by the volunteers for kindred purposes.

DRAKE, in his "History and Biography of the North American Indians," speaking of Tammany, says: "The fame of this great man extended even among the whites, who fabricated numerous legends concerning him. . . . In the Revolutionary War his enthusiastic admirers dubbed him a Saint, and he was established under the name of Saint Tammany, the patron Saint of America. His name was inserted in some of the calendars, and his festival celebrated on the *first* day of May in every year. On that day a numerous Society of his votaries walked together in procession through the streets of Philadelphia, their hats decorated with buck-tails, and proceeded to a handsome rural place out of town, which they called the *Wigwam*, where, after a *longtalk* or Indian speech had been delivered, and the calumet of peace and friendship had been duly smoked, they spent the day in festivity and mirth. After dinner, Indian dances were performed on the green in front of the Wigwam, the calumet was again smoked, and the company separated."

There were two days in the calendar of our early Red Men which were held sacred — the 22d of February and the 12*th day of May*. Of the first it is unnecessary, for the purpose of this report, to say anything further. Of the latter, we may remark that it was invariably observed as a *feast*. [It is worthy of note in this place that the By-Laws of 1817 fixes the birthday of Captain Williams, who fell in defence of Fort Erie on the 14th of August, 1814, as the day for holding the "anniversary meetings of the Society."] The particular day, however, is left blank in those laws, and subsequent documentary evidence shows their feasts to have been observed on the 12*th day of May*, Saint Tammany's day. On the morning of the 12th of May, the Red Men's Society assembled at a designated place, — usually at the house of a member, — and, decorated with the badges and insignia of their rank, with banners flying, and to the sound of stirring music took up their line of march through the streets of the city, and proceeded to some previous secured rural spot, within convenient distance, where the day was spent in the manner described in the quotation just cited. The fact of their having invariably celebrated the feast of Saint Tammany in the ostentatious and public manner just described, will easily account for their having been known

---

[1] Since writing the Report, the Chairman of the Committee has come in possession of a copy of the Preamble, and some of the old Laws, which verify the truth of the tradition referred to.

to the community outside as the SAINT TAMMANY SOCIETY. Public notice of their assembling on that occasion was given in the newspapers of the day, and by quaint Red Handbills, worded in the peculiar phraseology of the Society, which were posted on the street corners, in public houses, and other public places. The quotation we have made, from Drake's "History and Biography," fixes upon the *first of May* as the feast of Saint Tammany; but the original documents in the possession of the Chairman of your Committee, and which will be considered more at length in their proper place in this report, incontestably prove the day observed to have been the 12th of May.

The Wigwam, which our author refers to as the place of holding the feast, was located on Bush Hill, then out of the city, and was kept by a gentleman of the name of Clements,[1] who was known also among the members of the Society as brother *Pine Grove*. The house was known to the community at large as Harmony Hall, which name was given to it by the proprietor in honor of the Bush Hill Band of Musicians, of which he was the leader. Subsequently it was called the "Wigwam," from the fact that the Red Men had secured a large room in the old Stone Building, which they made their permanent place of meeting, having fitted it up beautifully with appropriate scenic decorations and effects necessary for the celebration of their quaint and romantic rites.[2] Prior to their occupation of this Wigwam, they had no permanent place of assembling, but kindled their council fires — as the old manuscript records show — first at the house of one brother, and then at that of another. Nor was it their uniform practice to celebrate the feast of their tutelar Saint at the Wigwam, as intimated by our author, but wherever convenient or fancy might dictate. Long before the Wigwam became their abode, they celebrated the natal day of their Aboriginal Saint in the groves of New Jersey, or other rustic localities on the Pennsylvania side of the Delaware River.

From these considerations, your Committee cannot resist the conclusion that the "Saint Tammany Society," referred to in the quotations we have made from Drake's "History and Biography of the North American Indians," were identical with the Red Men, — one and the same Society — and this conclusion is strengthened by still another fact. There is associated with the name of the Saint Tammany Society a *political* characteristic, which is also attached to the recollection of the early Red Men. It is true, indeed, that there is still preserved a sentiment which was enjoined on the candidate at his admission — that "Red Men administered no oaths, binding . . . to any political or religious creed: they bind neither your hands nor your feet; as you enter their Wigwam, so you depart — a free man."

But in understanding and construing this preliminary injunction, we must bear in mind that the Society rested upon a *national* basis; that whether we adopt the theory that it originated among the volunteers of Fort Mifflin in 1812–15, or regard it as the successor of a still earlier Society existing among the *Soldiers of the Revolution*, national politics formed a conspicuous feature

---

[1] Familiarly known as Father Clements.

[2] The Tribe at this time was largely composed of musicians, literati, and actors.

of the organization. Down as late as 1817, and even in 1827, this feature is clearly visible in it. An old report of a Committee, appointed to inquire into the character and *principles* of an applicant for membership, settles this question in the following emphatic words: "That he is a *citizen*; of good moral character, and of uniform and correct *political* principles, and is well entitled to a seat in the Wigwam."

In the manuscript records of the 6th of July, 1822, we find a motion adopted, "That a Standing Committee of twelve be appointed as an advance post, to superintend the election of brother *Flinty Warrior*,[1] and to report if anything unfavorable should be circulated against him."

On page 94, manuscript records, 1823, we find it resolved, That the names of the *Committee of Vigilance* be not published until after their next meeting. On page 95, same date, we find that houses had been secured for the distribution of tickets by the Red Men *on the day of election*. Again, on page 96, we find that the Committee appointed to procure suitable houses for the issuing of tickets in support of our brother *Flinty Warrior*, be indefinitely postponed.[2]

In an old copy of By-Laws,[3] preserved in the archives of the Great Council of the United States, the complexion of the political bias — indicated thus early in the Order — is clearly shown by a provision disqualifying persons who were not citizens, or who either *owned or held slaves*, from becoming members.

Thus far the Society was no doubt political — taking its rise among military men, who were thoroughly imbued with American sentiments; and prior to the development of the intensely bitter animosity and local prejudices, which at a latter day grew out of the agitation of the slavery question, it was considered national without being political in any partisan sense: and hence the injunction already quoted from the early Ritual.

We have thus presented all the positive and presumptive evidence in our possession, or accessible to us at this time, which can shed any light upon the inquiry as to the date of the institution of the Society into the hunting grounds of the palefaces; and as the second and third inquiries of the first resolution will be answered incidentally in this report, we deem it unnecessary to give them special consideration, and proceed to examine the proposition contained in the second resolution, namely: "The purchase of the 'Muster Roll,' and such other documents as may be deemed worthy of preservation."

There appears to have existed among some of the older members of the Society, from an early day, a tradition that an original instrument, called the "Muster Roll," containing the names of the founders of the Society at Fort Mifflin, or a copy of the same, was in existence in the city of Baltimore, and

---

[1] John Douglass, magistrate.

[2] The Generalissimo, *Black Wampum*, had delivered a *longtalk* against using the name of the Red Men's Society to further the election of young and inexperienced brothers.

[3] Article II. None but citizens of the United States can become members. Art. III. No person owning or holding slaves can become members. — (Old Laws.)

was in possession of the late Logan Tribe, No. 1. Shortly after the appointment of your Committee, the present Chairman, in company with G. C. of R. Booker, visited Fell's Point, for the purpose of making inquiry concerning it, and if possible to purchase it. Their visit, however, was fruitless; and from new light which they have since received, they cannot believe any such document ever existed in Baltimore. The Committee have shown that the origin of the Society may have been anterior to the war of 1812–15, and they have also shown, by documentary evidence, that most of the earlier papers, which would have thrown light upon the history of the Society, were lost as early as 1821. The oldest manuscript document in existence, so far as we are aware, is an Account Book, quarto post, containing 96 pages, and the accounts of seventy-six members, with their Indian or characteristic titles. Most of these accounts open on the 24th of January, 1817, and continue until March 3, 1818. The next document we have to notice we shall, for the sake of convenience, denominate the "Muster Roll." This "Muster Roll" is composed of a number of pass-books, 12mo, containing a list of the given or Indian names of the members. It is incomplete, without date, running perhaps over a series of years, and containing, at a rough estimate, five thousand names. Many of the names are wholly obliterated, others partly so, whilst still others can only be deciphered by the aid of a magnifying-glass.

It was the custom of these early Red Men, when adopting a new member, after the manner of the Indians, to take away his old name and invest him with a new one, by which he was ever afterwards known upon the books, and in all councils, assemblages or gatherings of the fraternity; and hence it is difficult at times to identify the individuals who were enrolled as members. Occasionally, however, the initials, and even the full name of a brother, may be found entered upon these old and musty pages. Among the few others we find the name of Richard Marley, with the rank of Third Major General, and who is our present venerable Past Great Incohonee. This document, or "Muster Roll," when it came into the hands of our Chairman, was closely tied between the leather covers of an old 12mo book, bearing an inscription on the outside, in heavy ink marks, too much obliterated to be deciphered, excepting the date (1812), which is yet bold and distinct. On the inside is the name of Matthew Zahm, Lancaster, Pennsylvania.

The next paper claiming our attention is the "General Orders," issued by the Generalissimo[1] from Stratton's Hotel, Philadelphia, and bears date September 15, 1820. This document promulgates and defines the badges [2] and insignia to be worn by, as well as fully enumerates the several ranking officers. From it we learn there were twenty grades of ranking officers, commencing with the Lieutenant, and ascending upward to the Generalissimo. These officers were for the government of the external or general operations of the Society; whilst for local and ceremonial purposes they were arranged

---

[1] Francis Shallus.

[2] A bright red ribbon, with emblem of rank embroidered in gold, silver, or blue, according to the rank of wearer.

somewhat differently, and of course were not so numerous. Assuming the council fire to be kindled, and the Tribe in working order, we find the officers arranged in the following order: the Generalissimo, or, as he is otherwise termed, *Yeoughwannawago*, and his two Captain-Generals; the Chief and his four Tryors; the Grand Treasurer, Grand Recording Scribe, and the Grand Doorkeeper.

Next we have manuscript memoranda [1] of the original ceremony of initiation, which, with the verbal explanations given to the Chairman of your Committee, places us in full knowledge of, as we now term it, the old *Unwritten Work*. The ceremony appears to have been committed to memory, and was then transmitted traditionally from one to another. It was only in rare instances, as when organizing Tribes at a distance, that memoranda in writing were allowed to be made; and, indeed, the *true* and *false* countersigns were only permitted to be communicated by the Generalissimo or his Special Deputy.

In a circular, or small poster, bearing date April 14, 1821, we have preserved an original impression of the Red Men's Seal. In this document, too, which contains the names of sixty-five brothers, the evidence of the introduction into the Society of a corroding element, which finally brought about the decline not only of the Tribe of Columbia, but also of the branch Societies generally throughout the several States — we mean their organization for *social purposes*.

Passing from the initiatory ceremony, we come to the records of the 7th, 9th, 14th and 20th of November, 1821, containing the announcement of the death of the Generalissimo, Francis Shallus, and the proceedings had in relation thereto.

We now proceed to notice the Book of Records of the "Red Men's Society." This is a bound volume of 710 pages quarto post, containing 413 written pages of minutes of the Society, commencing on the 25th of June, 1822, and ending on the 15th of May, 1827, and an unfinished alphabetical list of the given and proper names of members. In addition to these, we have the original manuscript minutes, from which those recorded in the book were copied in a neat and legible hand. We have, also, loose manuscript records of the 12th of December, and the 24th and 31st of January, 1831. These are the latest records of the old organization, so far as your Committee are aware, that have been preserved; and the above-mentioned records comprise all of that kind of documentary evidence of their proceedings now in existence. There are, however, a few other papers which may be regarded as supplemental to, or explanatory of them, and which are important as shedding light upon portions of the early history of the Society. They will be noticed as we proceed.

Thus far our observations, since the reorganization in 1817, have been directed to the consideration of the Society and its documentary evidence, as it existed in Philadelphia. From this locality it radiated and spread into

---

[1] A copy of this memoranda may have led to the misapprehension about the Muster Roll being in Baltimore.

different sections of the country, North and South. Of the exact time of its introduction into some localities we are able to speak only with probability, whilst its existence in other places rests upon positive documentary evidence.

From a letter written by Ironstone, Fifth Major-General, or *Minowakaton*, whose correct name was John M. Burns, we learn that as early as 1818 he was appointed, by Francis Shallus, General Chief of *the Southern Tribes*. And from the fact that Shallus died in 1821, and the further fact that Ironstone declares, in the letter referred to, that since the death of that great and good counsellor he has held no communication with the Northern Tribes, we conclude that Tribes were established in the South soon after his appointment, indeed, some of them may have existed prior to it. From the same letter we learn that a Tribe was established in Charleston, South Carolina, and continued in existence until 1820, when, owing to some local disease, which decimated their ranks, they ceased operations.

It is highly probable, from the concurrent evidence we have, that simultaneously with the organization of the Tribe in Charleston, it was introduced into Baltimore, Maryland. In an address delivered by P. G. I. Hugh Latham, at Lancaster, Pennsylvania, on the 21st of October, 1857, it is stated, speaking of brother Richard Marley, that, "having removed to Baltimore, he was appointed Chief of the State of Maryland, with the title of *Split Log*, and agreeable to instructions, caused a council fire to be kindled in June, 1820." Upon these statements your Committee have to remark, first, that by reference to the "Muster Roll" already referred to, we find the name of Richard Marley entered as Third Major-General, with the title of *Split Log's Brother*. Second, on page 209 of the Red Men's Minute Book, we find this record: "14th of the 9th Moon, 1824, the following white men were proposed; and after going through the usual and necessary forms, were received and initiated: Richard Marley, cordwainer, proposed by *Hospitality* — name given *Moose Deer's Brother*." Brother Marley must, therefore, have been a member some considerable time to have reached the rank of Third Major-General, and could by no possibility have kindled a council fire in Baltimore in June, 1820, seeing he was not admitted to membership until September 14, 1824. Your Committee, therefore, from what has already been stated in Ironstone's letter, — from the fact that the names, titles, and marks of rank of brothers in Baltimore are of frequent occurrence on the "Muster Roll," and from the absence of any minutes of the organization of the Society in that place in the Record Book, between the years 1821 and 1831 — are of the opinion that the Society was established in that city as early at least as 1818 to 1820.[1]

On the 24th of August, 1822, *Wetehoopeta*, or *Yellow Cat*, was brevetted from the rank of Brigadier to that of Major-General, and commissioned to "kindle a council fire in New Orleans, to make Red Men, and give them all necessary instructions," and he was required to "report from time to time to

---

[1] That Brother Marley did kindle a council fire in Baltimore is not questioned; but the Society several times ceased to exist in that city, and was as often revived.

the Red Men of Pennsylvania the condition of the *nations* over which he was appointed Sachem."

About the year 1820 or 1821, the Society was established in the State of Delaware, for we find on page 55 of the manuscript record this minute: "The Chief of the Delaware Tribe reports, that since he had received power to initiate brethren, that eighty-six persons had been adopted in the Tribe, and received the appropriate signs." But we cannot find anywhere in the records, from that date back to the opening of the book on the 25th of June, 1825, any mention of the commission authorizing its organization; and hence our conclusion, that it must have taken place about the time named, and during *that period* of which the records are lost.

From the original manuscript petition of *Tall Birch Tree, — Never Fear's Son* — [who was made a Red Man under *Split Log,*] for recognition by the "Mother Tribe" in Philadelphia, and bearing date the 12th Moon, 1825, we learn that the "Benevolent Tribe of Nassau," in the village of Brooklyn, Island of Nassau, and State of New York, had been previously organized. It, however, asked to be recognized, and received a grant of power from the Tribe of Columbia, at Philadelphia.

For the sake of proper connection in the subject-matter of this portion of our report, it is necessary we should diverge from regular chronological order, and refer to the printed *Proceedings* of the present Great Council of the U. S. On p. 3, vol. i, session 5609, G. Incohonee Latham, speaking of Tribes in New York, from which petitions had been received, says: "On my arrival in New York, I found that some of the petitioners had been associated together under the name of the 'Order of Red Men,' without being aware of the existence of the *Improved* Order of Red Men, until a short period previous to making their application to this Great Council for dispensations." From this portion of the report to the Great Council of the United States, we infer that these Red Men of New York were regarded as mere waifs upon the tide of Society — children whose paternity was unknown, either to themselves or others; and, indeed, a similar condition of facts will be found to have existed relative to the origin of the Red Men in Maryland. We trust, however, that this report of your committee may be found sufficiently demonstrative of the true source from which they sprung, and conclusively prove that they have all flowed from the same original fountain head, viz.: "The Tribe of Columbia," at Philadelphia.

We find upon the record of the 13th of June, 1826, page 341, that Brigadier-General Northern Warrior was appointed "Chief of the Albany Tribe, and in due form, in open council, by a warrant handed to him, permitted and empowered to open a Wigwam in the city of Albany, in the State of New York, under the title and name of 'The Albany Tribe of Red Men.'"

We are unable to indicate the precise date of the institution of the Society in New Jersey; and from the fact that there is no mention of it upon the record, we infer it to have been prior to the 25th of June, 1822. On the "Muster Roll" we find that *Strong Water*, the Seventh Major-General, was the Commander in that jurisdiction.

There are numerous strong indications that the Society of Red Men had been diffused over a much wider extent of country than we have mentioned; but as these indications are not in themselves *conclusive* upon that point, we forbear presenting them.

Returning to Pennsylvania, where at this day it is remembered traditionally by the outside community as Saint Tammany's Society, we find it radiating from Philadelphia to Germantown, Lancaster, and Reading. Indeed, it existed in the latter place until a comparatively late date. We find on p. 8, vol. i, session of 5609, printed *Proceedings* of the Great Council of Pennsylvania, a preamble and sundry resolutions looking to a *union* with the "Ancient Order of Red Men," located in the borough of Reading, Pennsylvania, with the present *Improved* Order.

Your Committee have already shown the Society to have been taken to Baltimore as early, at least, as 1820; but it existed there only with alternating success, and for a time, when it ceased to exist. Certain it is, that it was not successfully and permanently established in that city until the year 1834. On the 12th of March of that year William Muirhead, an old and active member of the Tribe at Philadelphia, acting under the authority of a commission granted by *Black Wampum*, or Generalissimo George Knorr, reorganized it under the name of the Red Men's Tribe of Maryland. From causes which appear to have been the bane of the Society in all sections where it had been introduced, but which it is unnecessary for present purposes to enlarge upon, this Tribe also languished, until at length a determination upon the part of a few of the members to reform existing abuses was not only developed, but carried out. Accordingly, a meeting of the Past Chiefs and Representatives, selected for that purpose, convened at the old Wigwam, on Thames Street, Fell's Point, Baltimore, on the 20th day of May, 1835. The names of the brethren present at this convention were: William T. Jones, or *Seamen's Friend*; Wm. Muirhead, or *Hospitality*; Charles Skillman, or *Camel's Hair*. These were Past Chiefs. The Representatives present were: George A. Peter, or *Link of Union*, who is still a member of the Order, and resides in the State of Ohio; Captain Joseph Branson, or *Cock of the Walk*, who still resides in Baltimore, and Edward Lucas, or *True Verdict*.

At the meeting just referred to, the Grand [1] Council of Maryland and of the United States, was completely organized, and the hitherto "Society of Red Men" announced to the world as the IMPROVED ORDER OF RED MEN.[2]

---

[1] By subsequent legislation the word *Grand*, wherever it occurs, was abandoned, and adherence had to the less pretentious but equally significant word Great, as expressing more correctly the idea intended to be conveyed by the aboriginal Red Men.

[2] As another organization claiming to be RED MEN is in existence, it is proper to note that in Grand Sun 5609 a difficulty occurred between Metamora Tribe, No. 4, and the Great Council of Maryland, which determinated in the severance of that Tribe from the Improved Order. The Tribe thereupon assumed the title of "Independent Order of Red Men." Subsequently, 5612, a similar difficulty occurred in Pennsylvania, with a like result. These latter connected themselves with the Independents. These disaffected Tribes — indeed, the entire so-called Independent Order — *are exclusively* German.

The first chiefs chosen by the Grand Council were: Grand Sachem, *Seamen's Friend*; Grand Senior Sagamore, *Hospitality*; Grand Junior Sagamore, *True Verdict*; Grand Chief of Records, *Link of Union*; Grand Chief of Wampum, *True Verdict*; Grand Prophet, *Cock of the Walk*.

It may be noticed here that a material and marked change was effected in the interior arrangement of the organization. The military succession and titles were abandoned, and new ones adopted in their stead. The reorganization and change were effected without regard to, or apparent knowledge of, the existence of the fraternity elsewhere.

We have shown already in this report, by the record of the Great Council of the United States, that the "Red Men's Society" existed in New York down to 5609; and we have shown by the *Proceedings* of the Great Council of Pennsylvania that it continued in that jurisdiction as late as the same date, so that had there been a disposition so to do, the act of the Tribe in Maryland, assuming *supreme* power and changing the organization, might well have been questioned. These acts, however, passed unchallenged; the Improved Order absorbed the Society in New York, whilst its authority has been established in Pennsylvania, and the succession cannot now be disputed.

The Order in Maryland and vicinity having increased, it became necessary to organize a National Body, independent of and superior to local or State jurisdiction. This was accomplished on the first sleep, third seven suns, — Moon, 5607.

We have thus endeavored to sketch, as rapidly as the nature of our subject would allow, a summary of the history of our affiliation from the earliest period of its existence down to the date of its authentic records, which are open and accessible to all who may be curious enough to examine them. If we have exhibited delay and tardiness in making this report, it has been on account of the almost insurmountable difficulties we had to encounter. When we entered upon our task, the history of the Order was unknown. Its early documents were buried in oblivion, and the knowledge of their existence had passed, as it were, to the tomb with the generation that preceded us. The best sources of information known to us were but vague, uncertain and contradictory traditions, which had become interpolated and rendered more uncertain by the lapse of time. These we have had to analyze, weigh and compare in order to ascertain their exact value. Many of the more important documents, which were unknown to us, we have exhumed, as it were, from the grave of the past, where they have been buried for the last thirty-five years, and they must present the history of our Order in a new and more important light. Had we presented our report at an earlier session, and relieved our minds from its consideration, those documents, with the invaluable historical information they contain, would in all human probability have remained buried in oblivion.

In view of the importance of these recovered documents, it is but just that the meed of praise should be awarded to each person who may have contributed towards their recovery.

In the month of April last, Charles Sweed, a member of Chattahoochee Tribe, No. 17, of Philadelphia, happening to meet a friend who was in conversation with an old gentleman sixty-five years of age, the conversation turned upon Societies, and finally upon Redmanship. Mr. Thomas J. Loudenslager (name of the old gentleman) stated that he thought he was the oldest Red Man in Philadelphia; that he was the Grand Recording Scribe of the Society when it ceased operation, late in 1831, or the beginning of 1832; that he was authorized to, and did collect what remaining books, papers and documents he could, which he had preserved since that time in the original case belonging to the Society. This information brother Sweed at once communicated to the Chairman of your Committee (who is also a member of Chattahooche Tribe). After several visits he succeeded in purchasing from Mr. Loudenslager the case and documents for the Great Council of the United States, at a net cost of fifty dollars.

Another document of some importance, referred to in this report, is the report of the Committee on the charter and principles of Calvin Berden, in 1818. This was obtained from Mr. Abram Britain, formerly a Representative to this Body, and a former member of Shawnee Tribe, No. 8, of Pennsylvania.

We also acknowledge our indebtedness to Mr. William B. Smith, of Philadelphia, for much valuable information communicated to our Chairman concerning the "Tribe of Columbia" in that city. He was familiar with many of the former members of that Tribe, and his statements help to fill up a blank in its documentary history.

In drawing this lengthy report to a close, it is proper we should say that we have left much, very much, untold. With a view of placing all the facts before the members of our fraternity in a more comprehensive and popular form, our Chairman is now engaged in preparing a full and complete history of the Order, which will be presented for your approval in due time.

Having, as we believe, complied with the terms of the resolutions under which we were appointed, we now place the result of our labors in your hands, and ask to be discharged.

Respectfully submitted, in the bonds of Freedom, Friendship and Charity.

MORRIS H. GORHAM,
WM. G. GORSUCH,
ANGUS CAMERON,
CHARLES DITMAN,
WM. R. MCFARLANE,
WM. H. FORD.

BALTIMORE, *Corn Moon*, G. S. D. 375.

By its action upon the report of a committee the Great Council declared against "non-beneficial" membership.

The chiefs elected and appointed and raised up for the ensuing term were as follows; —

M. W. G. Incohonee,   Joshua Maris, P. G. S.,   Delaware.
M. W. G. Senior Sagamore,   John D. Moore, P. G. S.,   New Jersey.
M. W. G. Junior Sagamore,   John B. Shaner,   Virginia.
M. W. G. Prophet,   William R. McFarlane,   Delaware.
M. W. G. Chief of Records,   Morris H. Gorham, P. G. S., Pennsylvania.
M. W. G. Keeper of Wampum,   William Benson, P. G. S.,   Maryland.
M. W. G. Tocakon,   Thomas Rich,   District Columbia.
M. W. G. Minewa,   Geo. W. Lindsay, P. G. S.,   Maryland.

The resolution of a former council, by which Southerland's Manual was adopted as the parliamentary law of the G. C. U. S., was rescinded, and Cushing's Manual was substituted.

The office furniture owned but not used by the G. C. U. S. was donated to the Great Council of Maryland.

As a mark of respect to the retiring Great Chief of Records and Great Keeper of Wampum, the Great Council adopted a series of very flattering Resolutions.

It was voted, That this Great Council direct a strict adherence to the technical phraseology of our Order, in the transaction of all business.

From the statistical reports from Great Councils and Tribes under the immediate jurisdiction of the G. C. U. S., we extract the following information: Number of Tribes, 111; adopted, 2394; rejected, 174; suspended, 313; admitted by card, 123; withdrawn by card, 99; died, 88; number of members, 10,238; expended for relief of brothers, 14,322 fathoms 25 inches; expended for relief of widows, 2118 fathoms 75 inches; expended for education, 301 fathoms 25 inches.

1867.

The council fire of the G. C. U. S. was kindled at Red Men's Hall, Philadelphia, Pa., on the 10th sun of Corn moon, G. S. D. 376, M. W. Great Incohonee Joshua Maris presiding.

The Committee on Credentials reported Representatives present from Maryland, Pennsylvania, New Jersey, Kentucky, Louisiana, Indiana, Missouri, Delaware, Ohio, Virginia, and the District of Columbia.

The longtalk of the Great Incohonee was an elaborate document, touching upon many important matters, and making many important recommendations,

He reported the organization of Tecumseh Tribe, No. 1, of Nashville, Tenn.; Cherokee Tribe, No. 1, Atlanta, Ga.; Pocahontas Tribe, No. 1, Detroit, Mich.; Alknooma Tribe, No. 2, Nashville, Tenn.; Narragansett Tribe, No. 5, New Orleans, La.; and Iroquois Tribe, No. 9, Brookville, Ind.

The Great Chief of Records submitted a written report of his actions during the interim, and of the measures taken to remove the property of the Great Council from Baltimore to Philadelphia.

The term "Most Worthy" was stricken from the titles of Chiefs of the Great Council.

It was resolved that Tammany's Day, the 12th sun of Flower moon be observed by the Order as a holiday.

It was voted "that the Great Chiefs be authorized to proceed and recover the original book of records and other papers of this Great Council."

This has reference to the difficulty attending the transfer of property from the former Great Chief of Records as already alluded to.

It was decided to kindle the next council fire in the hunting grounds of Cincinnati, Ohio.

At this council the old manner of computing wampum, whereby a fathom represented $1.50, was changed to the present form, under which a fathom represents $1.00, a foot, 10 cents, and an inch, 1 cent.

From the statistical reports of State Great Councils, and Tribes under the immediate jurisdiction of the G. C. U. S., we gather the following: Number of Tribes, 128; adopted, 3080; rejected, 193; suspended, 624; expelled, 208; reinstated, 50; admitted by card, 114; withdrawn by card, 161; died, 138; Past Great Sachems, 81; Past Sachems, 1333; Tribes instituted, 17; Tribes extinct, 4; number of members, 12,160; amount expended for relief of brothers, 16,496 fathoms 35 inches; expended for relief of widows, 8291 fathoms 55 inches; expended for education, 258 fathoms 30 inches; total receipts of Tribes, 74,320 fathoms 56 inches.

1868.

The council fire of the G. C. U. S. was kindled at Red Men's

Hall, Cincinnati, Ohio, on the 8th sun of Corn moon, G. S. D. 377, Great Incohonee Joshua Maris presiding.

The Committee on Credentials reported Representatives present from Maryland, Pennsylvania, Ohio, Delaware, New Jersey, Kentucky, Louisiana, Indiana, Michigan, West Virginia, Tennessee, California, and the District of Columbia.

Among those who were admitted for the first time at this council was Past Sachem Adam Smith of California, who afterwards became Great Incohonee of the G. C. U. S.

The Great Incohonee submitted an exceedingly interesting longtalk, which contained many valuable recommendations, decisions, and suggestions for the benefit of the Order.

He began by expressing thankfulness for the prosperous results attending the Order during the past grand sun. He made official announcement of the death of John D. Moore, of New Jersey, Great Senior Sagamore of the G. C. U. S., and also of Past Great Incohonee Robert Sullivan, of Baltimore, Md.

During the grand sun he had issued dispensation for 19 Tribes, one Degree Council and one Great Council, for all of which he recommended that charters be granted. The Tribes were located one in Louisiana, four in Texas, six in California, seven in Tennessee, and one in Michigan. Besides these the council fire of Wyandotte Tribe, No. 8, Richmond, Ind., had been re-kindled.

The Degree Council and the Great Council referred to were located in California.

He urged legislation which should require the selection of nothing but aboriginal names for Tribes, that in his opinion being fitting and proper, and in accordance with the traditions upon which the Order was founded. He suggested that the word "Improved" be dropped from the title of the Order, and that the word "Society" be used in place of "Order;" and that the word "great" be substituted for "grand" as being more appropriate and more in conformity with the origin and history of the Order.

The first paper ever published in the name of the Order and asking its support is referred to as follows: —

"It affords me great pleasure to announce that a newspaper, entitled *The Calumet*, is published fortnightly in San Francisco, under the auspices of the Improved Order of Red Men of California, and is devoted to the interests of the Order. It professes to be the organ of the Improved Order of Red Men, and is justly entitled to such credit. It is well managed and ably conducted, and so far to the membership has proved intensely interesting. In short, it may safely be regarded as both an honor and a benefit to the Order. It deserves encouragement, and should receive the patronage of the entire Brotherhood."

The Great Chief of Records presented a written report detailing the measures taken for distributing supplies to the Order, and other measures for carrying out the votes of the Great Council in relation to printing and securing proper quarters for the office of the G. C. of R.

Petitions were received from, and charters granted for, Tribes and Great Councils in the States of Indiana, Texas, California, and Tennessee.

For several councils the G. C. U. S. had been unable to liquidate the arrearages of mileage due to former Representatives. At this council the matter was satisfactorily adjusted, and warrants drawn for the full amount, thus placing the G. C. U. S. free from debt in this particular.

The run for the election of great chiefs having arrived, the Great Incohonee decided that Past Sachems were eligible to the position of presiding chief of the G. C. U. S. An appeal having been taken from this decision, it was reversed by the Great Council, thereby establishing the law that none but a Past Great Sachem is eligible to the position of Great Incohonee.

The chiefs elected and appointed and raised up for the ensuing grand sun were as follows: —

Great Incohonee,	JAMES A. PARSONS, P. G. S.,	New Jersey.
Great Senior Sagamore,	GEORGE W. LINDSAY, P. G. S.,	Maryland.
Great Junior Sagamore,	ADAM SMITH,	California.
Great Prophet,	JOSEPH PYLE, P. G. S.,	Delaware.
Great Chief of Records,	MORRIS H. GORHAM, P. G. S.,	Pennsylvania.
Great Keeper of Wampum,	WILLIAM BENSON, P. G. S.,	Maryland.
Great Tocakon,	JOHN W. HERBERT,	Pennsylvania.
Great Minewa,	JOHN G. SNYDER, P. G. S.,	Ohio.

The Great Council refused to adopt an amendment to the laws giving the rank and honors of a Past Sachem to a brother serving in the capacity of Chief of Records of his Tribe for five successive grand suns. This is mentioned as being the first attempt in that direction towards legislation which was finally embodied in the laws of the Order.

The Great Council refused to strike out the word "Improved" from the title of the Order.

It was voted "that P. G. S. Morris H. Gorham be permitted to dispose of Diplomas published by him until this Great Council may see proper to supersede the same, and that Great Councils or Tribes working under this jurisdiction may authorize the fixing of their respective seals to such Diplomas."

Appropriate resolutions were adopted in memory of the late Great Senior Sagamore John D. Moore.

The Great Chief of Records of the G. C. U. S. was ordered to issue a new charter for the Great Council of Maryland to replace that "lost or made way with by the late G. C. of R. John L. Booker."

The Committee on Ritual submitted a report which was considered in secret session and presumably adopted.

It was voted that the distinctive regalia of the appointed Warriors in a Tribe should be a blue sash of uniform size and shape with the regalia of the other chiefs, with a club as the emblem. That of the Braves should be of orange color, the deer's antlers as the emblem, and aprons of the color of the degree to which the wearer has attained.

It was ordered that the next council fire be kindled in the hunting grounds of St. Louis, Mo.

Upon the recommendations of the Great Incohonee it was voted that all Tribes hereafter chartered by this or any Great Council shall have for their titles Indian names, and that the words "great sun" be substituted for "grand sun" in the calendar.

The committee recommended that the title of the presiding chief of the G. C. U. S. be changed from "Great Incohonee" to "Great Tododaho," but the Great Council refused to adopt the suggested change.

The titles of the Great Chiefs were further simplified by striking out the prefix "M. W."

From the statistical reports we extract the following information: Number of Tribes, 168; adopted, 4366; rejected, 279; suspended, 787; expelled, 240; admitted by card, 274; withdrawn by card, 272; died, 117; Tribes instituted, 38; Tribes extinct, 19; number of members, 19,491; Past Great Sachems, 104; Past Sachems, 1826; total receipts of Tribes, 112,901 fathoms 3 inches; expended for relief of brothers, 20,661 fathoms 13 inches; expended for relief of widows and orphans, 6386 fathoms 99 inches; expended for education of orphans, 493 fathoms and 3 inches.

The great sun just closed had brought marked prosperity to the Order. Its membership had now reached nearly 20,000, covering 15 States. The financial affairs of the Great Council were in a gratifying condition, and everything pointed to a satisfactory and prosperous growth in the immediate future.

1869.

The council fire of the G. C. U. S. was kindled at Red Men's Hall, St. Louis, Mo., on the 14th sun of Corn moon, G. S. D. 378, Great Incohonee James A. Parsons presiding.

The Committee on Credentials reported Representatives present from Maryland, Pennsylvania, Ohio, Delaware, New Jersey, Virginia, Kentucky, California, Michigan, Missouri, and Texas.

The Great Incohonee submitted his longtalk, from which we glean the following: —

He reported the Order as being in a generally prosperous condition. During his term Great Councils had been instituted in Indiana, Tennessee, and Texas.

The Great Council of Indiana was instituted at Patriot on the 19th sun of Hot moon, G. S. D. 378 (June 19, 1869).

The Great Council of Texas was instituted at Marshall on the 5th sleep of Cold moon, G. S. D. 378 (Jan. 5, 1869).

The chiefs of the Great Council of Tennessee are not given in the longtalk of the Great Incohonee, as the report of the Vice Great Incohonee by whom the Great Council was instituted had been mislaid.

The Great Incohonee reported the organization of new Tribes in West Virginia, Michigan, Louisiana, Illinois, and Winnebago Tribe, No. 1, at Athens, Ala.

The death of Past Great Incohonee Richard Marley was referred to in appropriate language.

Charters were granted to the various Tribes and Great Councils instituted during the great sun.

Petitions were presented for a Tribe to be located at Selma, Ala., and for a Great Council in West Virginia, and the prayers of the petitioners were granted.

It was ordered that the next council fire be kindled in the hunting grounds of Baltimore, Md.

Among the States into which the Independent Order of Red Men had been carried was California, and some confusion of the Improved Order and the Independent Order had arisen, which was manifested by resolutions presented from the Great Council of California urging some modification of the name of the Order so as to prevent such confusion in the future. The matter was referred to the Committee on the State of the Order. This Committee reported on the two propositions submitted by the Great Council of California in relation to the union of the two Orders, that such a union would be desirable and doubtless in time would be effected, but that overtures from the Independent Order, and indications favorable to such reunion with the Improved Order, would be first desired, and the time for action evidently had not yet come.

The Great Council of California also urged the adoption of a degree into which could be admitted the wives, mothers, sisters, and daughters of brothers of the Chief's Degree. The Committee on the State of the Order reported favorably upon this recommendation; but the Great Council of the United States was not prepared to favor it, and the report of the Committee was laid upon the table.

The Great Chief of Records submitted his longtalk, which gave in detail the action taken by him in printing and issuing rituals and constitutions during the great sun. He also mentioned the removal of the office of the Great Chief of Records to No. 56 North Seventh Street, Philadelphia.

A resolution was adopted abolishing the apron as a part of the regalia of the Order.

The following resolution was referred to the Committee on the State of the Order, which subsequently made a favorable report, and the resolution was laid over under the rules : —

"*Resolved*, That State Great Councils are hereby authorized to confer the Past Sachem's Degree upon the Chief of Records of any Tribe, who shall have served five consecutive great suns in that position."

From the statistical reports of State Great Councils and Tribes under the immediate jurisdiction of the G. C. U. S., we glean the following information: Number of Tribes, 213; adopted, 5160; rejected, 309; suspended, 1219; expelled, 108; reinstated, 78; admitted by card, 352; withdrawn by card, 421; died, 159; number of members, 19,571; Past Great Sachems, 74; Past Sachems, 1945; Tribes instituted, 41; Tribes extinct, 10; amount expended for relief of brothers, 30,785 fathoms and 4 feet; expended for relief of widows, 8941 fathoms; expended for education, 265 fathoms 55 inches; total receipts of Tribes, 152,201 fathoms 82 inches.

Tribes were reported from 17 States and the District of Columbia. Pennsylvania had reached Tribe No. 110; Maryland, Tribe No. 44; Ohio, Tribe No. 47; Virginia, Tribe No. 33; New Jersey, Tribe No. 15; Kentucky, Tribe No. 12; California, Tribe No. 28; Tennessee, Tribe No. 9, and Indiana, Tribe No. 13.

1870.

The council fire of the G. C. U. S. was kindled at Red Men's Hall, Baltimore, Md., on the 6th sun of Corn moon, G. S. D. 379, Great Incohonee James A. Parsons presiding.

The Committee on Credentials reported Representatives present from Maryland, Pennsylvania, Ohio, Delaware, New Jersey, California, Michigan, Missouri, West Virginia, Indiana, Tennessee, and the District of Columbia.

The Great Incohonee submitted the longtalk of his doings for the past great sun, from which we extract the following information:—

"The progress of our Order during the past great sun has been unparalleled during its whole existence. In some of the older jurisdictions the increase can be numbered by the thousands, whilst in many new hunting grounds our council fires have been lighted and bid fair to burn brightly as beacons to 'many of the paleface nations' that they may clearly see the trail that leads them to the 'Light of our councils,' and the brother whose path may lead him to the setting sun will be cheered by their light and welcomed by the 'sound of the tomahawk' on his way 'across the continent,' whilst towards the Sunny South new council fires have been kindled that will vie in brightness with those in other parts of our country, and also in the North the brother whose way may lead him across the once trackless snow, may find the trail of the Improved Red Man and be greeted by the bright light of the burning 'Council Brand.'

"The Order has been introduced into four new jurisdictions, and the council fires of our Tribes are brightly burning in twenty-one States."

Under his direction the Great Council of West Virginia had been instituted on the 27th of Cold moon, G. S. D. 379 (January 27, 1870).

Under his direction, also, new Tribes had been organized in Alabama, Louisiana, and Mississippi.

The Order had also been planted in Oregon by the institution of Oregonian-Pocahontas Tribe, No. 1, which was organized at Jacksonville, Ore., on the 16th of Plant moon, G. S. D. 379 (April 16, 1870). This Tribe was quickly followed by La Lake Tribe, No. 2, at Ashland, and Multnomah Tribe, No. 3, at Portland. When it is considered that the brother who instituted these Tribes was compelled to travel over 1500 miles, mostly by stage, and over a rough country, with heavy expense and very great labor, the indomitable spirit that resulted in their institution may well be commended.

He also reported the institution of Piute Tribe, No. 1, at Carson City, Nevada, on the 18th of Buck moon, G. S. D. 379 (July 18, 1870).

The great chiefs elected and appointed and raised up for the ensuing term were as follows: —

Great Incohonee,	WILLIAM B. ECKERT, P. G. S.,	Pennsylvania.
Great Senior Sagamore,	ADAM SMITH, P. G. S.,	California.
Great Junior Sagamore,	CHARLES S. BETTS, P. G. S.,	Ohio.
Great Prophet,	JOSEPH PYLE, P. G. I.,	Delaware.
Great Chief of Records,	JOSHUA MARIS, P. G. I.,	Delaware.
Great Keeper of Wampum,	WILLIAM BENSON, P. G. S.,	Maryland.
Great Tocakon,	BERNARD SHANLEY,	West Virginia.
Great Minewa,	GREGORY B. KITELY,	Kentucky.

By a supplementary report of the Committee on Credentials, Past Great Sachem James P. Riely was admitted for the first time, as a Representative from Virginia. He afterwards became Great Incohonee of the G. C. U. S.

The desire was again manifested to unite the two Orders of Red Men by a communication from the reservation of California, which urged the Great Council to adopt legislation looking to the union of the Independent Order of Red Men with the Improved Order of Red Men. The time was not ripe for this movement and nothing resulted.

The new Tribe at Jacksonville, Ore., made known its desire for a side degree into which could be admitted the wives and daughters of members of the Order. The communication was referred to the Committee on the State of the Order, which subsequently reported favorably, with a resolution directing that such a degree be prepared for wives and daughters. The report of the Committee was amended by striking out "and daughters." Pending further amendments, the subject was laid upon the table until the next great sun council of the G. C. U. S.

The name of Past Great Sachem Charles C. Conley appears for the first time upon the record of this Great Council. At a subsequent session, Brother Conley was admitted as a Representative, and at the council held at Boston, Mass., in G. S. D. 399 (1890), he was given the rank and honors of a Past Great Incohonee for meritorious service.

It was voted that a committee of three be appointed to present a design or designs for a suitable and appropriate Badge, Mark or Totem, for the members of the Order.

Charters were granted to the various Tribes that had been instituted since the last great sun.

The proposition to merge the Independent Order of Red Men with the Improved Order of Red Men was decided adversely.

Upon a proposition submitted that all of the business of the Tribe should be transacted in the Chief's Degree, the Committee on the State of the Order reported a resolution, which was adopted, which in substance stated that the Great Council deemed it unwise and detrimental to the good of the Order to make the proposed change in the work. The matter was given its quietus for the time, but has been considered at various subsequent councils of the G. C. U. S.

The Great Council, by a very decisive vote, refused to restore the apron formerly used as a part of the regalia of the Order.

The special committee appointed to collate the laws of the Great Council of the G. C. U. S. submitted a report which was adopted, and it was ordered that the same committee collate the proceedings of the present council, so that the Digest may be brought down to the latest possible date.

The general laws for the government of the new degree of the Order, to be known as the "Council of Sachems," was reported, and the consideration thereof postponed until the next great sun council.

It was decided that the council fire of the next Great Council be kindled in the hunting grounds of Philadelphia.

From the statistical reports of State Great Councils and Tribes under the immediate jurisdiction of the G. C. U. S., we glean the following information: Number of Tribes, 296; adopted, 6519; rejected, 394; suspended, 1949; expelled, 138; reinstated, 96; admitted by card, 329; withdrawn by card, 439; died, 169; number of members, 23,784; Past Great Sachems, 102; Past Sachems, 2370; Tribes instituted, 70; Tribes extinct, 27; amount expended for the relief of brothers, 48,643 fathoms 19 inches; expended for relief of widows, 12,192 fathoms 52 inches; expended for education, 373 fathoms 88 inches; total receipts of Tribes, 181,925 fathoms 85 inches.

1871.

The council fire of the G. C. U. S. was kindled in Philadelphia, Pa., on the 12th sun, Corn moon, G. S. D. 380, Great Incohonee William B. Eckert presiding.

The Committee on Credentials reported Representatives present from Maryland, Pennsylvania, Ohio, Delaware, New Jersey, California, Michigan, Missouri, West Virginia, Indiana, Virginia, Kentucky, Wisconsin, Louisiana, Mississippi, Nevada, Tennessee, and the District of Columbia, being the largest number of reservations up to this time represented in the G. C. U. S.

The Great Incohonee submitted his longtalk covering the transactions of the preceding great sun.

He reported the organization of new Tribes in Mississippi, Nevada, Wisconsin, New York, Alabama, and Louisiana.

By the organization of Mohawk Tribe, No. 1, at New York

City, the Order was again planted in that reservation and this time upon a permanent basis, as the Order there has existed and flourished from that time to the present.

The Great Chief of Records submitted a complete report of the transactions of his chieftaincy during the great sun, touching upon the routine work which he had performed and the measures he had adopted to carry out the instructions of the Great Council.

From the statistical portion of his report we extract the following information: Number of Tribes, 348; adopted, 6630; rejected, 367; suspended, 2607; expelled, 320; reinstated, 187; admitted by card, 366; withdrawn by card, 466; died, 238; number of members, 26,945; Past Great Sachems, 108; Past Sachems, 2534; Tribes instituted, 51; Tribes extinct, 13; amount expended for relief of brothers, 51,321 fathoms 31 inches; expended for relief of widows and orphans, 12,500 fathoms 80 inches; expended for education, 478 fathoms 5 feet; total receipts of Tribes, 213,723 fathoms 62 inches.

The place used for the temporary wigwam of the G. C. U. S. seems to have been inconvenient, as another place was obtained and the further councils of the body were continued at Pocahontas wigwam, northwest corner of Fourth and Walnut Streets.

The committee chosen at a previous council to prepare a badge, or totem, for the use of members of the Order, made a report recommending the design submitted by Brother Isaac Bedichimer of Miantonomo Tribe, No. 45, of Philadelphia, Pa., which was adopted. A *fac simile* of the badge is here presented.

Resolutions were adopted providing for the appointment of a committee to procure a new set of regalia for the chiefs of the Great Council on the ground that it was "for the good of the Order that the chiefs of the Great Council should present a becoming appearance to palefaces on all public occasions."

The longtalk of the Great Keeper of Wampum showed that the total receipts of the Great Council for the great sun had been 5378 fathoms and 26 inches, and the amount expended was 3313 fathoms and 30 inches, leaving a balance on hand of 2064 fathoms and 96 inches. He also reported that the arrearages of mileage, for the payment of which the Great Council had provided, had been adjusted.

An amendment of importance was one affecting the representation in the Great Council. The effect of the amendment adopted was to reduce the representation very materially by a change in the ratio for each Great Council.

The Great Council refused to strike out the word "Improved" from the title of the Order.

The Committee on the State of the Order submitted a report on the ritualistic work which was subsequently considered in Committee of the Whole, but no material change in the ritual was made.

The Committee on Diploma submitted a report, recommending that the Diploma published by Morris H. Gorham be "adopted as the authorized Diploma of the Order," which recommendation was adopted.

The financial affairs of the G. C. U. S. had reached the very pleasing condition that permitted an investment of 500 fathoms after paying all indebtedness of the Great Council.

The recommendation of the Great Incohonee relating to conferring the degree of Past Sachem upon the first Prophet of a Tribe at its institution or organization was endorsed by the Great Council.

The proposition in relation to a uniform password was defeated, but again presented in the form of an amendment to the laws to be acted upon at the succeeding great sun council.

A proposition to permit Past Sachems, not Representatives, to visit the G. C. U. S. during its council was rejected as detrimental to the interests and materially interfering with the transaction of business of the Great Council.

Notwithstanding that the Order was founded upon the manners, traditions, and customs of the Aborigines of the American Continent, the Great Council adopted a report of the Committee on the State of the Order to the effect that under the laws as they then existed, North American Indians were not eligible to membership.

Among the charters granted was one for Saux Tribe, No. 2, to be located at Des Moines, Ia.

The city of Nashville was selected as the place for kindling the next great sun council fire.

The Committee on Regalia was directed to report at the next great sun council a suitable standard or flag for the Order.

1872.

The council fire of the G. C. U. S. was kindled in Suwanee wigwam, Nashville, Tenn., in Corn moon, G. S. D. 381, Great Incohonee William B. Eckert presiding.

The Committee on Credentials reported Representatives present from 16 States and the District of Columbia. Nevada, Wisconsin, and Massachusetts were represented for the first time in the G. C. U. S. Among the Representatives admitted for the first time was Past Sachem Thomas J. Francis of New Jersey, subsequently Great Incohonee of the G. C. U. S.

The committee appointed for that purpose reported having purchased regalias for the chiefs of the Great Council at an expense of 208 fathoms.

The Great Incohonee submitted his longtalk for the previous great sun.

He reported the institution of the Great Council of Michigan in the hunting grounds of Detroit on the 10th of Flower moon, G. S. D. 381 (May 10, 1872).

Also the Great Council of New York, in the city of New York, on the 19th of Sturgeon moon, G. S. D. 381 (August 19, 1872).

Also the Great Council of Rhode Island, in the city of Providence, on the 20th of Sturgeon moon, G. S. D. 381 (August 20, 1872).

During the interim, he had also issued dispensations for seven new Tribes in New York, five in Rhode Island, one in Mississippi, two in Nevada, and one in Michigan. He had also issued dispensations by which the Order was introduced for the first time into the respective reservations named : for Washakie Tribe, No. 1, Salt Lake City, Utah ; Osage Tribe, No. 1, Fort Scott, Kansas ; Chemakum Tribe, No. 1, Port Townsend,

Washington Territory, and Manataug Tribe, No. 1, Marblehead, Mass.

The Great Incohonee renewed the recommendation for a universal password, and also recommended that only Past Great Incohonees be eligible to fill the position of Great Prophet, and that the form for instituting Tribes be revised and approved.

The Great Chief of Records submitted a report in detail of the transactions of his chieftaincy during the great sun, and told of the manner in which he had carried out the instructions of the Great Council in relation to advertising the badge adopted, distribution of printed matter, and the like. He recommended the altering of the Seal of the Great Council, so that the date thereon should conform with the new system of dating adopted by the Order. The recommendation was subsequently approved and the necessary authority given.

The statistical abstract accompanying his report furnishes the following information: Number of Tribes, 422; adopted, 8654; rejected, 499; suspended, 2603; expelled, 103; reinstated, 227; admitted by card, 284; withdrawn by card, 525; died, 246; number of members, 31,540; Past Great Sachems, 119; Past Sachems, 3160; Tribes instituted, 72; Tribes defunct, 11; amount expended for relief of brothers, 58,502 fathoms 13 inches; expended for relief of widows and orphans, 13,853 fathoms 30 inches; expended for education, 401 fathoms 38 inches; total receipts of Tribes, 236,900 fathoms 68 inches.

The Great Council accepted an invitation, from the committee representing the Great Council of Tennessee, to visit the State Capitol Building, and also the tomb of Ex-President James K. Polk.

The chiefs elected and appointed and raised up for the ensuing term were as follows: —

Great Incohonee,	JAMES P. RIELY, P. G. S.,	Virginia.
Great Senior Sagamore,	CHARLES S. BETTS, P. G. S.,	Ohio.
Great Junior Sagamore,	WILLIAM F. MEACHAM,	Tennessee.
Great Prophet,	PAXON COATS, P. G. I.,	Ohio.
Great Chief of Records,	JOSHUA MARIS, P. G. I.,	Delaware.
Great Keeper of Wampum,	WILLIAM BENSON, P. G. S.,	Maryland.
Great Tocakon,	JOSHUA D. BAKER,	Pennsylvania.
Great Minewa,	FRANK W. ANDERTON,	Ohio.

The Special Committee on Regalia, appointed at the preceding council, was continued and instructed to report at the next council.

The report of the Special Committee on Ritual, creating a "Council of Sachems," was presented, which was considered in secret council. The substance of the action taken was the adoption of a resolution to the effect that the Great Council deemed it inexpedient at present to adopt any other degrees than those now incorporated in the ritual.

The Great Council again refused to adopt a universal password.

The report of the Committee on Finance showed a very gratifying condition of the wampum belt of the G. C. U. S. Including the balance from the last great sun of 2064 fathoms and 96 inches, the total receipts had been 11,598 fathoms and 62 inches, of which there had been paid out 4085 fathoms and 26 inches, including the 500 fathoms invested according to the instruction of the last council of the G. C. U. S., leaving a balance of 7513 fathoms and 36 inches. From this amount, appropriations were recommended, including 500 fathoms to add to the amount already invested, of 6655 fathoms and 74 inches, leaving 847 fathoms and 62 inches for ordinary contingent expenses.

Charters were ordered to be issued for the Great Councils and Tribes instituted during the great sun.

It was voted that in the event of the inability of a Representative elected to attend this Great Council, the Great Sachem of the reservation shall be empowered to appoint a qualified member of his Great Council to serve during the succeeding council of this Great Council.

Important action was taken by the Great Council upon a case, the points of which are these : A Great Council held an election at which one brother received 15 votes and another brother received 14 votes. At an adjourned council, a protest was offered against the validity of the election, and the protest was sustained and a new election ordered. In the election which followed, the brother elected at the first council failed to receive a majority of the votes, and his unsuccessful competitor at the first ballot was elected. From this action the first brother appealed. The Committee on Grievances reported that the appeal should be dismissed, but the Great Council adopted a resolution which declared that the action of the Great Council in setting aside the election was incorrect and illegal, and that the first-named brother was legally elected. The Great Council further recommended that the said brother be raised up to the chieftaincy to which he had been elected.

Wilmington, Del., was selected as the place for kindling the next great sun council fire.

Great Senior Sagamore Adam Smith was honored by a vote of thanks for his good work in establishing the Order on the Pacific Coast.

1873.

The council fire of the G. C. U. S. was kindled at the Masonic Temple, Wilmington, Del., on the 9th sun of Corn moon, G. S. D. 382, Great Incohonee James P. Riely presiding.

The Committee on Credentials reported credentials for Representatives received from 21 States and the District of Columbia.

The Great Incohonee submitted his longtalk.

He reported the institution of the Great Council of Nevada on the 6th of Cold moon, G. S. D. 382 (January 6, 1873).

Also the Great Council of Oregon, which was instituted on the 23d of Buck moon, G. S. D. 382 (July 23, 1873).

Dispensations for additional new Tribes had been issued during the great sun, two in Illinois, one in Alabama, two in Massachusetts, two in Georgia, one in North Carolina, and four in Mississippi.

Official report was also made of the institution of Sho-sho-nee Tribe, No. 1, at Lincoln, Neb., on the 31st of Travelling moon, G. S. D. 381 (October 31, 1872).

The Great Chief of Records submitted an interesting report stating the action taken by him during the interim to carry out the instructions of the G. C. U. S. He referred to the condition of the Order and the rapid increase of the Tribes, membership, Tribal property, and the amount expended for relief, the figures received by him showing that there had been an increase of 57 in the number of Tribes and 4708 in the number of members. There had also been an increase of 62,960 fathoms and 83 inches in the receipts of Tribes, and 25,295 fathoms and 52 inches in the amount expended for relief.

The statistical abstract accompanying his report furnished the following information: Number of Tribes, 479; adopted, 9395; rejected, 588; suspended, 3300; expelled, 223; reinstated, 271; admitted by card, 359; withdrawn by card, 589; died, 324; number of members, 36,248; Past Great Sachems, 125; Past Sachems, 3810; Tribes instituted, 77; Tribes defunct, 8; amount expended for relief of brothers, 77,059 fathoms and 87 inches; expended for relief of widows and orphans, 19,815 fathoms and 8 inches; expended for education, 419 fathoms and 48 inches; total receipts of Tribes, 299,861 fathoms and 51 inches.

A committee of three was appointed to revise the form of raising up of chiefs, and also to prepare a form for public raising up of same, and for the institution of new Tribes, and also for the institution of Great Councils.

The question of uniting the several Orders of Red Men again engaged the attention of the Great Council by the presentation of a communication from the Arkansas Tribe Independent Order of Red Men; but the Great Council decided not to act in the matter of consolidation until the subject should be presented by some State or National organization.

The Great Council again refused to strike out the word "Improved" from the title of the Order.

The Special Committee on Regalia and Jewels submitted a report which under the laws was laid over for action at the succeeding great sun council, when it was adopted. By this report the regalia and jewels of the Order were brought into symmetrical proportions and relations one to the other, and have been changed but slightly since.

It was voted inexpedient to establish a head-dress to be worn by members of the Order on public occasions.

The city of Indianapolis, Ind., was selected as the place for kindling the next great sun council fire of the G. C. U. S.

The arrangements made for entertaining the Great Council by the Great Council of Delaware were more elaborate than had been experienced up to this time. Resolutions of thanks were adopted. The address of welcome on behalf of the Great Council of Delaware was made by Past Great Incohonee Joseph Pyle, to which a fitting response was made by Great Incohonee Riely.

1874.

The council fire of the G. C. U. S. was kindled at Indianapolis, Ind., on the 8th sun, Corn moon, G. S. D. 383, Great Incohonee James P. Riely presiding.

Previous to the formal kindling of the council fire, an address of welcome was delivered by Will C. David, Great Sachem of Indiana, to which a fitting response was made by Great Incohonee Riely.

A communication was received from the Great Keeper of Wampum William Benson of Maryland, stating his inability to be present at this council, and resigning from the chieftaincy of Great Keeper of Wampum.

The Committee on Credentials reported that credentials had been received from 22 States, one Territory, and the District of Columbia.

Among the Representatives admitted at this council was Great Sachem Charles H. Litchman, representing the Great Council of Massachusetts, who afterwards became Great Incohonee of the G. C. U. S.

The Great Incohonee presented his longtalk.

During the great sun a dispensation had been issued for the Great Council of Massachusetts, which was instituted in the hunting grounds of Marblehead on the 23d sun of Hunting moon, G. S. D. 382 (December 23, 1873).

Dispensations had also been issued for additional Tribes in Utah and Washington Territories, and in Mississippi and North Carolina.

The Order had been established in South Carolina by the institution of Catawba Tribe, No. 1, at Columbia, on the 5th sun of Snow moon, G. S. D. 383 (February 5, 1874). Two additional Tribes had also been instituted in South Carolina.

The Great Chief of Records presented his longtalk, which contained a brief account of the Order in each reservation.

From the statistical abstract accompanying his report, we

glean the following information: Number of Tribes, 560; adopted, 779; rejected, 553; suspended, 3642; expelled, 214; reinstated, 312; admitted by card, 492; withdrawn by card, 706; died, 318; number of members, 39,953; Past Great Sachems, 129; Past Sachems, 4363; Tribes instituted, 94; Tribes extinct, 11; amount expended for relief of brothers, 75,817 fathoms and 99 inches; expended for relief of widows and orphans, 20,593 fathoms and 67 inches; expended for education, 663 fathoms and 52 inches; total receipts of Tribes, 308,838 fathoms and 96 inches.

A communication was received from the Secretary of the Washington National Monument Society, asking the aid of the G. C. U. S. in soliciting subscriptions from the Tribes in the Order towards the completion of the unfinished monument to Washington at the National Capitol. The communication was referred to a committee which subsequently reported, recommending the matter to the favorable consideration of the Tribes for such voluntary contributions as they felt able to make.

A communication was received from the Great Council of California, urging the necessity and expediency of a union of the Orders of Red Men in the United States. The matter was referred to a committee, and on its report the Great Council voted to adhere to its previous action, which was in effect that whenever a proposition presenting a definite plan of action came to the G. C. U. S. from any organization having due authority, the G. C. U. S. would act thereon.

The proposition to transact all the business of Tribes in the Chief's Degree was renewed, and met the usual fate of defeat.

A proposition to institute a side degree for ladies was received from the Great Council of Michigan, and referred to a special committee. The committee subsequently reported inexpedient to legislate, and the report was adopted.

The Great Council again refused to adopt the universal password.

Announcement was made of the death of Vice Great Incohonee A. Curry, of Carson City, Nev., a brother, by whose untiring energy and zeal the Order was introduced into that State, and appropriate resolutions were adopted in commemoration of his services.

The chiefs elected and appointed and raised up for the ensuing term were as follows : —

Great Incohonee,	GEORGE W. LINDSAY, P. G. S.,	Maryland.
Great Senior Sagamore,	MORRIS H. GORHAM, P. G. S.,	Pennsylvania.
Great Junior Sagamore,	J. P. H. WENTWORTH, P. G. S.,	California.
Great Prophet,	PAXON COATS, P. G. I.,	Ohio.
Great Chief of Records,	JOSHUA MARIS, P. G. I.,	Delaware.
Great Keeper of Wampum,	JOSEPH PYLE, P. G. I.,	Delaware.
Great Tocakon,	JOHN DUMBELL,	Pennsylvania.
Great Minewa,	CHRISTIAN SEIBKE,	West Virginia.

A proposition from the Great Council of Tennessee to establish a uniform, for the use of members, was considered and rejected.

Since the paper published in the interest of the Order at San Francisco under the name of the *Calumet* had become defunct, there had been no publication issued in the interest of the Order. At this council, however, notice was given that the publication had been commenced at Easton, Pa., of a paper called the *Council Brand*, under the management of brother, now Past Great Sachem, T. D. Tanner. The matter was referred to the Committee on the State of the Order, which subsequently made a report which was adopted, commending it to the favorable consideration of the brotherhood.

A committee was chosen to compile and revise the laws of the G. C. U. S.

The report of the Committee on Regalia and Jewels, submitted at the last great sun council, was taken up and adopted.

The Committee on Finance submitted its report, by which it was shown that, including the balance on hand from the last Great Council of 1888 fathoms and 52 inches, there was available an amount of 5858 fathoms and 55 inches. Appropriations were recommended amounting to 5723 fathoms and 97 inches, leaving a balance of 134 fathoms and 58 inches in addition to 1000 fathoms invested in the Utah Savings Bank of Baltimore, Md. Among the recommendations of the Committee was one for an appropriation of 3500 fathoms for mileage and per diem of the Representatives in attendance at this council. This was amended to make the amount 4500 fathoms.

It was voted that the next great sun council fire be kindled in the hunting grounds of Richmond, Va.

We have already mentioned the action of the G. C. U. S. at a previous council by which membership was denied to members of the Indian race, notwithstanding the fact the ritual of the Order is founded on the manners, traditions, and customs of the Aborigines of the American Continent. Among the cases considered by the Committee on Appeals and Grievances at this council was one involving the question of permitting membership to two applicants who were descendants of the Indian race. Opekasset Tribe, No. 122, of Pennsylvania, had adopted the two persons referred to, and by direction of the Great Council of Pennsylvania the persons were afterwards expelled. The Tribe appealed to the G. C. U. S., and the Committee on Appeals and Grievances sustained the appeal, and directed the Great Council of Pennsylvania to re-admit the two persons.

In secret council forms for instituting Great Councils and for raising up of chiefs of Tribes were adopted. In regular council it was voted that with the approval of the Great Incohonee or Great Sachem, permission be granted Tribes to use in public the new form for raising up of chiefs.

Action was taken at this Great Council which was very far reaching in its effect, and had influence upon the Order during the succeeding six great suns not contemplated by those by whose votes said action prevailed. The Committee on Finance had recommended an appropriation of 3500 fathoms for mileage and per diem. In addition to this there were left on deposit in the Savings Bank 1000 fathoms which could have been used judiciously for the extension of the Order, and the payment of necessary expenses; but the Great Council voted to apply this also to the payment of mileage and per diem, and thus deprived the incoming great chiefs of all means for propagating and strengthening the Order. As a result, the efforts of the great chiefs were nearly paralyzed, and the growth of the Order completely checked. It will be noticed by the statistical abstracts that a steady growth for many great suns had been recorded, until at the council in 1874 the number had reached 39,953. The full effect of the unwise legislation here referred to did not begin to be felt until after the report was made for the council held in 1875. At this latter council the highest point in membership in the history of the Order up to this time was reached, the membership then being 40,504. From this point it receded with each succeeding great sun, until G. S. D. 388 (December, 1879), when it had fallen off to 27,214. By this time, with stringent economy, the funds at the disposal of the chiefs of the G. C. U. S. had begun again to accumulate. There was more wampum for legitimate expenses, and for use in propagating the principles of the Order. The increase begun in 1879, has continued until the membership has finally been brought to the magnificent proportions of the present time, when, according to the latest reports received by the Great Chief of Records, it is about 140,000.

1875.

The council fire of the G. C. U. S. was kindled in the wigwam of Pocahontas Tribe, No. 14, at Richmond, Va., on the 14th of Corn moon, G. S. D. 384, Great Incohonee George W. Lindsay presiding.

Previous to the formal kindling of the council fire, on behalf of the Great Council of Virginia, P. G. I. James P. Riely delivered an address of welcome, to which a fitting response was made by Great Incohonee Lindsay.

The Committee on Credentials reported that credentials had been received from 23 States and the District of Columbia.

The Great Incohonee submitted his longtalk for the past great sun.

He reported the organization of additional Tribes in Alabama, Illinois, Wisconsin, North Carolina, and Mississippi, and the rekindling of the council fire of Cherokee Tribe, No. 1, of Georgia.

The Order had been introduced into the State of New Hampshire by the institution of Paugus Tribe, No. 1, at Rollingsford, and into the State of Minnesota by the institution of Minnehaha Tribe, No. 1, at St. Paul.

The Order had become defunct in Nebraska by the extinction of the council fire of Sho-Sho-nee Tribe, No. 1, of Lincoln. The reason for this extinction was given as improper instruction at the time of organization.

The Tribes in Louisiana and in the State of Texas had become extinct through the ravages of the yellow fever, one Tribe at Shreveport reporting that five of the seven chiefs had died with the disease. This is also reported to have caused considerable difficulty in reclaiming the work and books of the extinct Tribes.

The longtalk of the Great Chief of Records was submitted, which contained a brief summary of the condition of the Order in each reservation.

By unanimous vote, Philadelphia was selected as the place for kindling the next great sun council fire.

A ritual for "a Council of Squaws" was presented and referred to a committee, but the Great Council was not ready to adopt the innovation and the proposition was defeated.

The question of a suitable uniform for public parade was introduced by the Representatives from Massachusetts, but the Great Council was not yet ready to approve, and therefore subsequently adopted the report of the committee to which the matter was referred, that it would be injudicious at this time to recommend the adoption of any uniform other than the present regalia of the Order. The same action was taken in relation to a similar proposition to adopt a uniform head-dress to be worn by members of the Order on public occasions.

The Committee on Revision and Compilation of the Laws presented its report, which was considered, and a complete code of laws adopted. After which the same Committee was directed to revise and compile the Digest, and report thereon at the next great sun council.

An important matter acted upon at this council was the adoption of the flag or standard of the Order as follows : —

1st. The Flag or Standard, of the Improved Order of Red Men, shall be in the form of an oblong square or parallelogram, in the proportion of seven long to five wide.

2d. It shall consist of a white field, five wide and seven high, attached to which shall be four horizontal bars, of equal width, the aggregate width of the four being equal to the height of the field.

3d. The color of the bars respectively shall be green, orange, blue and scarlet, the green bar being at the bottom, and the others placed above it in the order above enumerated.

4th. A purple stripe, of one-half the width of one of the bars, shall enclose the entire circumference of the flag, the outer edge of the purple stripe (except where attached to the staff) shall be trimmed with fringe composed of the emblematic colors in the flag.

5th. Upon the base or lower edge of the white field shall be delineated the upper section of the globe, showing portions of the eastern and western continents, the date G. S. D. 1 appearing immediately above the globe on the edge of the field next the staff, and the date of the common era appearing in like manner and position on the opposite edge of the field.

6th. Above the globe and in the centre of the field shall appear the American eagle, bearing the emblems of our Order in his talons, and in his beak a scroll or ribbon containing the legend or motto of our Order, "Freedom, Friendship and Charity," and upon his breast the shield or escutcheon, with the four emblematic bars, and a field upon which shall appear the four mystic characters, T. O. T. E.

7th. Above the eagle shall appear thirteen stars; upon the horizontal bars may appear the name of the Great Council of the United States, the Great Council of a State or of the Tribe to be designated by it.

8th. The staff shall be surmounted by the eagle of the Order, and shall be decorated with cord and tassels displaying the emblematic colors of the Order.

Resolved, That the foregoing described flag be, and it is hereby declared, the flag or standard of the Improved Order of Red Men.

The following is an engraving of the flag above described:—

The report of the Committee on Finance showed that the expenses for the preceding great sun had exceeded the receipts in the sum of 14 fathoms and 70 inches. Among the appropriations was one of 1835 fathoms and 45 inches for the unpaid bills of the past fiscal great sun. This left available for mileage and per diem of Great Chiefs and Representatives in attendance at the present council only 2700 fathoms.

Charters were granted to the various Tribes for which dispensations had been issued during the great sun.

From the statistical abstract presented by the Great Chief of Records we present the following information: Number of Great Councils, 19; Number of jurisdictions having Tribes but no Great Council, 16; total number of Tribes, 582; adopted, 6643; rejected, 393; suspended, 5460; reinstated, 385; admitted by card, 375; withdrawn by card, 550; died, 344; number of members, 40,504; Past Great Sachems, 145; Past Sachems, 4935; Tribes instituted, 58; Tribes extinct, 22; amount expended for relief of brothers, 91,520 fathoms and 77 inches; expended for relief of widows and orphans, 20,167 fathoms and 24 inches; expended for education, 463 fathoms and 95 inches; total receipts of Tribes, 315,245 fathoms and 30 inches.

1876.

The council fire of the G. C. U. S. was kindled in the wigwam of the Chattahoochee Tribe, Girard Avenue, Philadelphia, Pa., on the 12th of Corn moon, G. S. D. 385, Great Incohonee George W. Lindsay presiding.

Previous to the kindling of the council fire the Great Council was welcomed to the hunting grounds of Pennsylvania by Past Great Incohonee A. J. Baker, in an interesting longtalk, to which appropriate response was made by Great Incohonee Lindsay.

The Great Chief of Records on behalf of Great Junior Sagamore Wentworth presented to the G. C. U. S. a beautiful tomahawk, which was accepted in fitting terms by the Great Incohonee.

The Committee on Credentials reported that credentials had been received from 32 reservations.

The Great Incohonee submitted his longtalk.

He had given dispensations for additional Tribes in Mississippi, New Hampshire, Illinois, and Kansas. The Order had been introduced into the reservation of Maine by the institution of Squando Tribe, No. 1, at Biddeford.

The Order had also been reorganized in Nebraska by the institution of Omaha Tribe, No. 2, at Omaha.

The Great Chief of Records submitted his longtalk, which, as usual with this chief, was an exhaustive summary of the transactions of his chieftaincy during the great sun, and a condensed statement of the condition of the Order in the United States.

Accompanying his report was the statistical abstract, from which we learn there were 18 Great Councils and 17 reservations having no Great Council; total number of Tribes, 558; adopted, 3195; reinstated, 220; admitted by card, 122; rejected, 245; suspended, 3543; expelled, 112; withdrawn by card, 343; died, 255; number of members, 39,516; Past Great Sachems, 146; Past Sachems, 4897; amount expended for relief of brothers, 55,546 fathoms and 64 inches; amount expended for relief of widows and orphans, 22,936 fathoms and 38 inches; expended for education, 382 fathoms and 31 inches; total receipts of Tribes, 197,496 fathoms and 19 inches; Tribes instituted, 20; Tribes extinct, 20.

From the State of Indiana came a proposition, which, for the first time, brought to the attention of the Great Council a plan for engrafting upon the laws of the Order a system of life insurance for its members. The proposition, together with other suggestions from other Representatives, was referred to the Special Committee on Insurance which subsequently reported a law governing the Widows and Orphans' Benefit Fund. The report of the Committee was accepted, and consideration thereon postponed until the next great sun council.

The city of Columbus, Ohio, was selected as the hunting grounds in which the next great sun council fire should be kindled.

The chiefs elected and appointed and raised up for the ensuing great sun were as follows : —

Great Incohonee,	ADAM SMITH, P. G. S.,	California.
Great Senior Sagamore,	WILL C. DAVID, P. G. S.,	Indiana.
Great Junior Sagamore,	CHARLES H. LITCHMAN, P. G. S.,	Massachusetts.
Great Prophet,	ANDREW J. BAKER, P. G. I.,	Pennsylvania.

Great Chief of Records,   JOSHUA MARIS, P. G. I.,   Delaware.
Great Keeper of Wampum, JOSEPH PYLE, P. G. I.,   Delaware.
Great Tocakon,   JAMES A. MOSS, P. G. S.,   Pennsylvania.
Great Minewa,   CHARLES S. BETTS, P. G. S.,   Ohio.

A committee of three was appointed to prepare a new form of funeral ceremony, and report the same at the next great sun council in printed form.

At this council provision was made for translating the ritual into the French language.

At this council, also, a proposition was offered having in view the establishment of a Permanent Fund for the G. C. U. S., and laid over under the rules until the next great sun council.

A ceremony for laying corner-stones of wigwams was adopted.

1877.

The council fire of the G. C. U. S. was kindled at Columbus, Ohio, on the 11th sun of Corn moon, G. S. D. 386, Great Incohonee Adam Smith presiding.

Previous to the formal kindling of the council fire, Representative Joseph Dowdall, of Ohio, welcomed the Great Council to the hunting grounds of Columbus, in an appropriate longtalk, to which Great Incohonee Smith responded.

The Committee on Credentials submitted its report, by which it was learned that credentials had been received from 23 States and the District of Columbia. Among those admitted as Representatives for the first time at this council were Charles C. Conley, of Pennsylvania, who afterwards was declared Past Great Incohonee for meritorious service, and William H. Hyronemus, of Tennessee, who afterwards became Great Incohonee of the G. C. U. S.

The longtalk of the Great Incohonee was presented, which gave an account of the matters that had come under his jurisdiction during the great sun. Among other things mentioned was the introduction of the Order at the Hawaiian Islands, by the institution of Hawaiian Tribe, No. 1, at Honolulu. It may be here mentioned in passing, that this Tribe flourished for a few great suns but finally became extinct. It included among its members King Kalakaua and some of the leading people of the Island.

GREAT COUNCIL OF UNITED STATES. 365

He reported the institution of three additional Tribes in Illinois, one in Kansas, and one in Georgia.

He made formal mention of the death of Past Great Incohonee Angus Cameron, of Pennsylvania. He earnestly recommended a revision of the ritualistic work of the Order. He also recommended consideration of the subject of taxation and representation, and that the Vice Great Incohonee in charge of a State reservation at the time a new council is instituted, be made the Great Prophet of said Great Council, with the title and rank of Past Great Sachem.

The Great Chief of Records submitted his usual elaborate and comprehensive report of matters coming under his jurisdiction.

The statistical abstract accompanying the report of the Great Chief of Records showed that there were Great Councils in 18 States and the District of Columbia; Tribes under the immediate jurisdiction of the G. C. U. S. in 14 States and 2 Territories; total number of Tribes, 557; adopted, 4288; reinstated, 313; admitted by card, 326; rejected, 233; suspended, 6431; expelled, 184; withdrawn by card, 410; died, 381; number of members, 36,422; Past Great Sachems, 166; Past Sachems, 5124; amount expended for relief of brothers, 85,751 fathoms and 44 inches; expended for relief of widows and orphans, 33,640 fathoms and 88 inches; expended for education, 317 fathoms and 96 inches; total receipts of Tribes, 300,680 fathoms and 57 inches; Tribes instituted, 18; Tribes extinct, 12.

The provisions of the local committee of Columbus for the entertainment of the G. C. U. S. were very elaborate, and the hospitality will long be remembered by those present.

The trial through which the Order was passing is also indicated by the report of the Great Keeper of Wampum, who deplored the fact that the receipts for the great sun had fallen much below the estimated income, owing, no doubt, to the great depression of business all over the land, and that the Tribes and State Great Councils have not ordered supplies as anticipated by the Finance Committee. The progress of the Order was not only seriously retarded, but absolutely prevented, through lack of necessary wampum in the hands of the chiefs of the G. C. U. S., to properly extend it through the land.

At this council a proposition came from Indiana to adopt a uniformed side degree for the Order which should use the Continental (1776) Soldiers' uniform as the distinguishing badge or emblem of said degree. The Great Council refused to endorse the proposition.

At this council a new departure was made in the adoption of a beneficiary law, under whose provisions it was expected that a sum not exceeding 2000 fathoms would be paid to the beneficiaries of a deceased member. As the law then adopted differs materially from that afterward in operation, we deem it unnecessary to make more than this passing allusion to the legislation adopted.

The Representative from Nebraska, in an eloquent longtalk, presented various articles used by the aboriginal people of this country, which were accepted with the grateful thanks of the Great Council, and the articles deposited with the Great Chief of Records, to await the future action of the G. C. U. S. This is the first attempt by the Great Council of the United States to make a collection of Indian relics.

The article laid over from the last great sun council, establishing a Permanent Fund for the Order, was taken up and adopted.

Resolutions of respect to the memory of P. G. I. Angus Cameron were adopted.

The special committee on that subject submitted a form for a funeral ceremony. The matter was considered briefly, and finally referred to the next great sun council.

1878.

The council fire of the G. C. U. S. was kindled at Red Men's Hall, Baltimore, Md., on the 10th of Corn moon, G. S. D. 387, Great Incohonee Adam Smith presiding.

Previous to the formal kindling of the council fire, an address of welcome to the visiting Chiefs and Representatives was delivered by Great Sachem John H. Bennett, to which Great Incohonee Smith appropriately responded.

The Committee on Credentials reported that credentials had been received from 22 States.

The longtalk of the Great Incohonee was submitted, in which he congratulated the Great Council that, although the great sun just passed had not been one of marked prosperity, neither had it been altogether one of clouds and darkness.

He reported the institution of the Great Council of Illinois at Pekin on the 13th of Hot moon, G. S. D. 387 (June 13, 1878).

During the great sun dispensations had been granted by him for additional Tribes in Illinois and Georgia.

Among the matters which he earnestly recommended to the consideration of the Great Council was the importance of making provisions to send a qualified chief into the several portions of the Great Reservation of the United States to instruct weak Tribes; for a revision of the ritual; changes in the Beneficiary Law; for a union between the branches of the Order of Red Men, and for the reduction of the charter fee of State Great Councils. He reported that the applications for membership in the Beneficiary Association, adopted at the previous council, had not been as numerous as had been desired and anticipated.

The Great Chief of Records submitted a longtalk of the transactions of his chieftaincy, which was full and complete.

From the statistical abstract presented by the Great Chief of Records, we glean the following information: Great Councils, 19; reservations without Great Councils, 17; total number of Tribes, 525; Tribes instituted, 9; Tribes reorganized, 5; Tribes extinct, 46; adopted, 2575; reinstated, 414; admitted by card, 367; rejected, 108; suspended, 6266; expelled, 97; withdrawn by card, 496; died, 303; Past Great Sachems, 172; Past Sachems, 4622; amount expended for relief of brothers, 73,073 fathoms and 35 inches; expended for relief of widows and orphans, 3358 fathoms and 6 inches; expended for burial of dead, 22,205 fathoms and 4 inches; expended for education, 224 fathoms and 48 inches; total receipts of Tribes, 257,427 fathoms and 21 inches; amount invested by Tribes, 195,820 fathoms and 97 inches; amount in Tribal wampum belts, 49,737 fathoms and 83 inches.

A lengthy communication was submitted from the Great Council of California, urging a union between the Independent Order and the Improved Order of Red Men. The matter was referred to a committee which subsequently reported in favor of referring the matter to a special committee with authority to sit during the recess, and consult with such similar committee as may be appointed by the Independent Order, and to submit a full report at the next great sun council, together with such detailed law for the union of the two Orders as may be agreed upon by such joint committee should an agreement be reached.

At this council the proposition was again submitted for the preparation of a degree for the wives, daughters, and sisters of brothers who had attained the Chief's Degree. The time for such action had not yet arrived, however, and the Great Council again voted that it was inexpedient to legislate.

The attention of the Great Council was called to the epidemic of yellow fever then prevailing in some of the Southern States, and a contribution was made by each Representative present, and it was also voted that an appeal be issued to the Order requesting a liberal contribution for the benefit of sufferers from the epidemic, said sums to be forwarded as directed by the Great Incohonee.

The Great Council again adopted a resolution that it was inexpedient to adopt a dress uniform for funerals, parades, balls, etc.

The recommendation of the Great Incohonee, in relation to arranging for visits to isolated Tribes, bore fruit in the adoption of a resolution appropriating 200 fathoms to be used for the contingent expenses of the Great Incohonee, and for the expense of qualified chiefs that may be appointed by him to visit, instruct, and encourage such Tribes. By this action was begun a custom which has continued with marked benefit down to the present time, and which doubtless resulted eventually in turning the tide of adversity into the prosperity that afterwards came to the G. C. U. S.

Various changes were made in the Beneficiary Law tending to perfect it, and make it more attractive to members of the Order.

A Committee on Revision of the Ritual was appointed, thus attempting to again open a question which had received its quietus for several great suns.

It was voted that the next great sun council be held in the hunting grounds of New York, N.Y.

MORRIS H. GORHAM.

CHARLES H. LITCHMAN.

GEORGE B. COLFLESH.

WILLIAM H. HYRONEMUS.

PAST GREAT INCOHONEES.

The chiefs elected and appointed and raised up for the ensuing great sun were as follows:—

Great Incohonee,	Morris H. Gorham,	Pennsylvania.
Great Senior Sagamore,	Charles H. Litchman,	Massachusetts.
Great Junior Sagamore,	George B. Colflesh,	Maryland.
Great Prophet,	Hugh Latham,	Virginia.
Great Chief of Records,	Joshua Maris,	Delaware.
Great Keeper of Wampum,	Joseph Pyle,	Delaware.
Great Tocakon,	William H. Hyronemus,	Tennessee.
Great Minewa,	John W. Linck,	Indiana.

1879.

The council fire of the G. C. U. S. was kindled in the hunting grounds of New York, N.Y., on the 9th of Corn moon, G. S. D. 388, Great Incohonee Morris H. Gorham presiding.

The Committee on Credentials reported that credentials had been received from 24 States and the District of Columbia. Among the Representatives admitted for the first time at this council were Ralph S. Gregory, of Indiana, afterwards Great Incohonee of the G. C. U. S., and Andrew H. Paton, the present Great Senior Sagamore of the G. C. U. S.

The longtalk submitted by the Great Incohonee was an admirable document, replete with interesting matter, much of which was of great value as indicating the scheme followed in establishing the ritual and laws of the Order.

He brought to the attention of the Great Council the death of Past Great Incohonee Paxon Coats of Ohio.

He reported his action concerning the institution of Tribes in Georgia and Florida and the reorganization of Osceola Tribe, No. 7, at Shreveport, La.

He also reported the introduction of the Order into the reservation of Colorado by the institution of Rising Bow Tribe, No. 1, at Central City.

Among the recommendations made by him was one in relation to the establishment of a fund for aged and indigent members, and another in favor of a universal password.

He deprecated the propositions for amending the ritual, and the abuse of candidates in the degree work. He endorsed the propositions to work in the Chief's Degree, and to drop the prefix "Improved" from the title of the Order,

The longtalk of Great Incohonee Gorham is of peculiar interest even at the present date. In a comparatively short time after his services as Great Incohonee, the brother was suddenly called to the hunting grounds above; but the imprint that his zeal and love for the Order left upon its legislation and ritualistic work cannot easily be effaced, and will remain as long as the members of the Order preserve the ancient landmarks.

The Great Chief of Records submitted his longtalk for the preceding great sun. Among other things he stated that he had carried out the will of the Great Council in communicating with the Gross Stamm of the Independent Order of Red Men at its annual session at Trenton, N.J., and received a reply that the body had adjourned before the proposition had been received, and consequently no action had been taken thereon.

He submitted a list of the members of the Order that had attached themselves to the Beneficiary Association, and gave a detailed statement of the operations of that adjunct to the Order during the preceding great sun.

From the statistical abstract of the Great Chief of Records we glean the following information: Great Councils, 20; reservations having no Great Council, 12; adopted, 3017; reinstated, 482; admitted by card, 157; expelled, 69; withdrawn by card, 210; died, 84; suspended, 5263; number of members, 28,075; Past Great Sachems, 176; Past Sachems, 5035; Tribes instituted, 8; Tribes reorganized, 7; Tribes extinct, 37; total number of Tribes, 505; amount expended for relief of brothers, 79,811 fathoms and 76 inches; expended for relief of widows and orphans, 2761 fathoms and 39 inches; burial of the dead, 15,811 fathoms and 74 inches; expended for education, 152 fathoms and 10 inches; other Tribal disbursements, 105,840 fathoms and 55 inches; total receipts of Tribes, 234,049 fathoms and 66 inches; invested by Tribes, 75,228 fathoms and 97 inches; in Tribal wampum belts, 59,631 fathoms and 46 inches.

In the longtalk of the Great Keeper of Wampum a report was made of the amount contributed for the Yellow Fever Fund, giving in detail the names of each individual subscriber, and of each Tribe in the United States that made a contribution. The total amount raised was 841 fathoms and 28 inches. Fortunately very few among those afflicted were members of the Order, and

GREAT COUNCIL OF UNITED STATES. 371

consequently the demand upon the Fund was limited to 61 fathoms and 54 inches, leaving a balance of 779 fathoms and 74 inches. This balance was placed in the wampum belt of the G. C. U. S., as a relief fund to be drawn upon by the chiefs of the Great Council whenever in their judgment a meritorious case for relief is presented.

An elaborate plan was submitted by a Representative from Maryland, providing for two classes of membership in the Improved Order of Red Men to be styled "Active" and "Nonactive." The matter was referred to a committee, but the Great Council declined to enter upon the radical changes necessary to carry out the objects proposed.

The Great Council again refused to adopt the proposed change by which the business of the Tribes should be done in the Chief's Degree.

In like manner, the wise suggestion of the Great Incohonee, in relation to the establishment of a fund for aged and infirm members, received an adverse report from the Committee on the State of the Order, which report was adopted by the Great Council.

Charters were granted to the Tribes for which dispensations had been ordered during the interim.

It was voted that the next great sun council be held in the hunting grounds of Boston, Mass.

One of the most pleasing features of this council was a fraternal visit made to it by David B. Woodruff, Supreme Chancellor of the Knights of Pythias. He was welcomed to the fraternal greetings of the Great Council by Great Prophet Hugh Latham of Virginia, and to the fraternal words of greeting thus extended to him the visitor responded in a very felicitous manner.

The agitation of several great suns, for the adoption of a universal password, finally was rewarded with success at this council by the adoption of the proposed amendment.

The Great Council endorsed a proposition permitting in States or Territories where no Great Council existed, by and with the consent of the Great Incohonee, Tribes to attach themselves to the nearest Great Council until such time as said States and Territories contain sufficient Tribes to form a Great

Council. While said Tribes are thus attached, they shall be subject to the laws and regulations of such Great Council.

Appropriate resolutions in memory of Past Great Incohonee Paxon Coats were adopted. Similar resolutions were also adopted in relation to other Great Chiefs and Representatives whose departure had been reported to the Great Council.

1880.

The council fire of the G. C. U. S. was kindled at Boston, Mass., on the 14th of Corn moon, G. S. D. 389, Great Incohonee Morris H. Gorham presiding.

The Great Council was welcomed to the State and City in an eloquent talk by Great Sachem Nicholas Pitman, and a fitting response was made by Great Incohonee Gorham.

The Committee on Credentials reported that credentials had been received from 19 Great Councils and seven reservations in which no Great Council existed.

The longtalk of the Great Incohonee, like that of the preceding great sun, was full of valuable information and important suggestions. He gave in detail his official acts during the great sun, such as the appointment of Vice Great Incohonees, official promulgation of the universal password, the decisions made during the great sun, and other routine work. He recommended that the Great Council reserve to itself the exclusive right to print and supply the several reservations with certified receipts to be used in connection with the universal password. He also renewed his recommendation that the business of the Tribes be transacted in the Chief's Degree, and also that a fund be provided for aged and infirm members.

He reported the institution of the Great Council of Georgia at Atlanta on the 6th of Hunting moon, G. S. D. 388 (December 6, 1879).

He also reported that dispensations had been issued for two additional Tribes in Colorado, and one each in Texas and Florida. Also the introduction of the Order into Arizona Territory by the institution of Maricopa Tribe, No. 1, to be located at Phœnix, Maricopa County, Arizona.

In announcing the death of Past Great Incohonee George A.

GREAT COUNCIL OF UNITED STATES. 373

Peter, of Ohio, he gave some intensely interesting information of the manner in which the Order was introduced into Maryland, and showed the connecting link between the society of Red Men that existed in Pennsylvania, and the organizations in Maryland, out of which came the present Improved Order of Red Men.

The Great Chief of Records submitted his longtalk which as usual covered a detailed statement of his work during the great sun, and the measures taken by him to carry out the various resolutions of instruction of the G. C. U. S. A new system of accounts recommended by the Committee on Finance at the previous great sun council had been adopted, and the report as rendered by the Great Chief of Records was clear and explicit, covering every item of receipt and expenditure.

From the statistical abstract presented by the Great Chief of Records, we obtain the following information: Great Councils, 21; reservations without a Great Council, 12; Tribes instituted, 18; Tribes reorganized, 2; Tribes extinct, 30; total number of Tribes in existence, 491; adopted, 3679; reinstated, 477; admitted by card, 273; suspended, 4139; expelled, 72; withdrawn by card, 347; died, 282; number of members, 27,214; Past Great Sachems, 168; Past Sachems, 5250; amount expended for relief of brothers, 71,237 fathoms and 84 inches; expended for relief of widows and orphans, 8694 fathoms and 67 inches; expended for burial of the dead, 18,072 fathoms and 64 inches; expended for education of orphans, 255 fathoms and 22 inches; expended for other Tribal purposes, 102,481 fathoms and 85 inches; total receipts of Tribes, 244,276 fathoms and 22 inches; invested by Tribes, 117,511 fathoms and 16 inches; in Tribal wampum belts, 69,142 fathoms and 2 inches.

The number of members reported by the Great Chief of Records was the smallest since the decrease began in G. S. D. 383. This period may be termed the "low tide" in the affairs of the Order. From this time the tide turned, and wise, prudent, and economical legislation began to have its effect both in the financial affairs of the G. C. U. S., and in the discipline and energy among the members at large.

Radical changes were made in the laws of the Great Council, by which the number of Representatives was largely decreased, and by which representation was restricted entirely to Great Councils.

The proposition to create a fund for aged and infirm members of the Order was approved by the Committee on the State of the Order, but in the opinion of the committee it was a matter for local legislation. The subject was finally referred to a special committee to report at the next great sun council.

A special committee on the subject submitted resolutions of respect to the memory of Past Great Incohonee George A. Peter, of Ohio.

The chiefs elected and appointed and raised up for the ensuing great sun were as follows: —

Great Incohonee,	CHARLES H. LITCHMAN,	Massachusetts.
Great Senior Sagamore,	GEORGE B. COLFLESH,	Maryland.
Great Junior Sagamore,	WILLIAM H. HYRONEMUS,	Tennessee.
Great Prophet,	HUGH LATHAM,	Virginia.
Great Chief of Records,	JOSHUA MARIS,	Delaware.
Great Keeper of Wampum,	JOSEPH PYLE,	Delaware.
Great Tocakon,	JOSEPH W. CLYMER,	Pennsylvania.
Great Minewa,	RALPH S. GREGORY,	Indiana.

It is worthy of remark at this time that the brother elected at this council to the important position of Great Incohonee was the first in the history of the G. C. U. S. to pass successively through the chieftaincies of Great Junior Sagamore, Great Senior Sagamore, and Great Incohonee. Other chiefs were elected as Great Incohonee who had at times filled both of the other chieftaincies, but Great Incohonee Litchman was the first to pass successively from one to the other. The custom thus adopted has been continued down to the present time. Whatever contest is good-naturedly made, occurs in a kind and fraternal spirit over the election to the chieftaincy of Great Junior Sagamore. It is assumed, and perhaps rightly, that the brother elected for that chieftaincy is qualified to advance step by step, until crowned with the highest honors in the power of the G. C. U. S. to bestow.

It is also worthy of remark that the Great Council unanimously re-elected as Great Prophet Past Great Incohonee Hugh Latham, of Virginia. For three great suns preceding this council, Brother Latham had been able to attend the G. C.

U. S. only by the exercise of an indomitable will that arose superior to bodily infirmities. It is within the truth to say that his determination to be present at the council at Boston lessened even the few suns that he might have been expected to live. No influence was sufficient to prevail upon him to remain at home, and how great the sacrifice made was hardly realized until, in but a little more than one moon, the sad tidings was communicated to the Order that the Great Spirit had called him home.

[The editor of this history may be pardoned this digression, for the relations between him and Past Great Incohonee Latham were those of intimate personal friendship, and nearer that of father and son than even brothers in our grand fraternity. He was placed in nomination for each successive chieftaincy by Past Great Incohonee Latham, and when the brother arose at the council in Boston "to complete," as he said, "the work commenced at Philadelphia in 1876 when he first placed in nomination 'the little chick from Massachusetts,'" his feebleness of body, which was manifest, and the shadow which all felt was even then upon him, added a solemnity to the occasion which will never be forgotten by those present.]

The Great Senior Sagamore, on behalf of the Committee on Entertainment of Massachusetts, stated that the arrangements for the entertainment of the Great Council of the United States had been frustrated, and that he was authorized to present to the G. C. U. S. the fund of 100 fathoms contributed for that purpose by the Great Councils of Massachusetts and Rhode Island, and the donation was accepted with the thanks of the Great Council.

While the Great Council was assembled, a sad event occurred, being the sudden death of the wife of Great Incohonee Gorham, and resolutions were adopted expressing the sympathy of the Great Council with the bereaved great chief.

Amendments were made in the Beneficiary Law to strengthen it, and make it further applicable to the needs and wishes of those whose membership was solicited.

It was voted that the next great sun council be held in the hunting grounds of Annapolis, Md.

With this record of the year 1880, ends the first section of the History of the Order under the jurisdiction of the Great Council of the United States. While the membership had run down from 40,504 to 27,214, prudent legislation and wise economy in the management of the finances of the Order had laid the foundation for the gratifying success hereafter to be recorded. The members who participated in the deliberations of the Great Council of the United States, during the period to which we refer, will remember the anxiety felt at that time, and the great pleasure with which was hailed the change for the better, that began immediately at the quenching of the council fire of 1880.

CHAPTER VIII.

THE GREAT COUNCIL OF THE UNITED STATES (1881–1892).

THE fluctuating fortunes of the Order have been shown by the facts thus far given, and it is very gratifying to here record the turning-point in the downward trail of the Order, and the beginning of that era of prosperity which has continued until, at the time these lines are written, the membership numbers nearly five times that of the Order at the quenching of the council fire in 1880.

We have alluded to the causes which led to the decline. Crippled by a depleted treasury, the great chiefs of the Great Council of the United States were powerless to increase the Order, or even to maintain it. Now, by rigid economy, wampum began, slowly but surely, to accumulate, and wisely expended started the impetus which continues as yet unchecked.

From 1875 to 1880, the membership of the Order steadily decreased. For the first time in seven great suns, the reports for 1881 showed a gain, and from that time to 1893 the percentage of increase in Tribes, Great Councils, and members has been wonderful. New State Great Councils have been formed, the older Great Councils have worked with renewed vigor, and, where feeble and struggling on the border of complete dissolution, have become among the strongest reservations of the Order. In all New England, at the council of 1880, there were but 495 members. At the present writing there are not far from 24,000 members in the New England Tribes.

Among other reservations which showed a phenomenal growth, during the period now to be considered, may be mentioned Indiana, Illinois, New Jersey, New York, Ohio, Georgia, and Pennsylvania.

With this increase in members came also a marked improvement in the standing and influence of the Order in the respective localities where its branches were established. From being comparatively obscure and unknown, the Order advanced to the front rank among similar fraternal organizations, and not infrequently passed them in some reservations, in the rivalry for public favor and support.

With the increase in Tribes and membership came an increase in the income of the Great Council of the United States, and means were supplied for the propagation of the Order, thus extending it into new hunting grounds and insuring its stability everywhere.

The continued extracts from the records of the Great Council of the United States, which follow, indicate how this pleasant result was achieved.

1881.

The council fire of the G. C. U. S. was kindled in the Hall of the House of Delegates at the State House, Annapolis, Md., on the 13th of Corn moon, G. S. D. 390, Great Incohonee Charles H. Litchman presiding. After the formal kindling of the council fire a recess was taken, until the setting of the sun, in order to take part in the exercises which had been arranged by the Committee on Reception representing the Great Council of Maryland and Chesapeake Tribe, No. 32, of Annapolis. These exercises consisted of prayer by the Rev. William S. Southgate; addresses of welcome by the Hon. James T. Briscoe, Secretary of State, Hon. Thomas E. Martin, Mayor, and Brother William T. Iglehart; a "Welcome Ode"; music by the Naval Academy Band; a poem by Past Great Sachem William Louis Schley, and a benediction. The ceremonies were in the State House grounds, and were attended by a large number of the citizens of Annapolis. The Great Incohonee responded for the Great Council.

On again assembling in council, the Committee on Credentials submitted its report, from which it was learned that credentials had been received from ten Great Councils. Representatives from other Great Councils held over from the preceding great sun council.

The longtalk of the Great Incohonee was presented. He referred to the turn in the tide in the history of the Order;

gave a record of his decisions during the great sun; and recommended the liberal use of documents for propagating the Order, and the appointment of a special committee to gather and compile material for a full and complete history of the Order.

He suggested that the minimum age for the admission of a paleface might be reduced without detriment to the Order.

He reported the institution of the Great Council of New Hampshire at Manchester on the 13th of Plant moon, G. S. D. 390 (April 13, 1881).

He spoke of the limited number of visits he had been able to make, even in response to urgent invitations from distant Tribes, and urged that if provision to meet the expense of such visitations could be made, the result would be for the benefit of the Order.

He spoke a kind word for the Beneficiary Plan, and urged the Representatives present to lend it their support and encouragement.

He renewed a recommendation of his predecessor, that the name of the Order be amended by dropping the word "Improved."

He made official announcement of the death of Past Great Incohonee and Great Prophet Hugh Latham, of Virginia.

The Great Chief of Records submitted his longtalk, giving a detailed account of the routine work of his chieftaincy, and a statement of the receipts and expenditures. He also spoke of the limited success which as yet had attended the Beneficiary Plan.

As a matter of historical interest he contributed the fact, that at least two of the first great chiefs of this body were yet living and in good standing in the Order, — Brothers Gorsuch and Ford. The former was an attendant at this Council.

From the statistical abstract, accompanying the report of the Great Chief of Records, we glean the following information: Great Councils, 22; reservations without Great Councils, 14; Tribes instituted, 12; Tribes reorganized, 6; Tribes extinct, 37; total number of Tribes in existence, 470; adopted, 4390; reinstated, 461; admitted by card, 254; suspended, 3651; expelled, 53; withdrawn by card, 203; died, 295; total number of members, 28,366; Past Great Sachems, 187; Past Sachems, 3535; amount expended for relief of members, 67,802 fathoms and 10 inches; expended for relief of widows and orphans, 6057 fathoms and 79 inches; expended for burial of dead, 20,310 fathoms and 42 inches; expended for education of orphans, 181 fathoms and 30 inches; disbursed for other purposes, 94,835 fathoms and 36 inches; total receipts of Tribes, 248,796 fathoms and 57 inches; invested by Tribes, 126,936 fathoms and 93 inches; in Tribal wampum belts, 38,432 fathoms and 38 inches.

Past Great Incohonee, Adam Smith, of California, presented to the council sundry Indian relics which were accepted and placed in the archives of the G. C. U. S.

The improved financial condition of the G. C. U. S., at this time, as indicated by a resolution submitted by the Committee on Finance, and adopted by the Great Council, led to the appropriating of 600 fathoms, instead of the usual appropriation of 100 fathoms to be added to the Permanent Fund of the Order. The Committee also adopted the suggestion of the Great Incohonee by appropriating 200 fathoms for the contingent expenses of that great chief.

A favorable report was made by the Judiciary Committee in relation to striking out the word "Improved" from the title of the Order, but the amendment of the laws to that effect was laid over for one great sun.

The proposition for transacting the work of Tribes in the Chief's degree also received a favorable report from the Committee on the State of the Order, and a resolution was adopted asking the various State Great Councils to express an opinion as to the advisability of the proposed change.

The Great Council again refused to adopt any other uniform than the regalia then used.

The Special Committee on the subject reported favorably upon the idea of establishing a fund for aged and infirm members, and requested to be continued for one great sun for final report. The report of the Committee was adopted.

Elaborate resolutions of thanks were adopted as an expression of the gratitude of the Great Council for the hospitality with which the members thereof had been entertained by the Red Men of Annapolis.

Arrangements were made for issuing a charter to the Great Council of Louisiana.

Appropriate resolutions were adopted concerning the death of Past Great Incohonee and Great Prophet Hugh Latham, of Virginia.

The Special Committee on the subject was authorized to continue during the great sun recess and prepare a circular descriptive of the Order for use among palefaces; and to collect material for a history of the Order.

Easton, Pa., was selected as the place for kindling the next great sun council fire.

Past Great Incohonee Morris H. Gorham, of Pennsylvania, was unanimously elected Great Prophet to fill the vacancy caused by the death of Past Great Incohonee Hugh Latham, of Virginia.

The Committee appointed at the preceding great sun council to consider the question of a new ritual for Degree Councils, was at its request continued for another great sun.

1882.

The council fire of the G. C. U. S. was kindled at Easton, Pa., on the 12th of Corn moon, G. S. D. 391, Great Incohonee Charles H. Litchman presiding.

Previous to the formal kindling of the council fire, an address of welcome was delivered by Past Sachem Thomas D. Tanner on behalf of the two Tribes of that city, to which an appropriate response was made by Great Incohonee Litchman.

After the kindling of the council fire, the Committee on Credentials reported that credentials had been received from 17 reservations.

The Great Incohonee submitted his longtalk, which stated that during the year he had made an extensive journey across the Continent, visiting the Order, and being royally received in thirteen great reservations.

He recommended that the first Great Prophet of State Great Councils be made a Past Great Sachem by dispensation at the end of the term; that the word "Improved" be stricken from the title of the Order; that the charter fee of Tribes be increased; and that the Prophets of Tribes be elected from Past Sachems.

He reported the institution again, of the Great Council of Louisiana, and the probability that a Great Council would soon be instituted in each of the States of Colorado and Florida. On the other hand, the Great Council of Rhode Island was reported to be in a feeble condition.

One dispensation granted by him, by which Squantum Tribe, No. 1, of Biddeford, Me., was attached to the jurisdiction of the Great Council of New Hampshire, was the first consolidation of this kind in the history of the Order, and was in accordance with a vote adopted by the Great Council but a few great suns before. The precedent thus established has been subsequently followed in other reservations with marked benefit to the isolated Tribes thus attached.

He spoke of the probabilities of revival of the Order in Nebraska, Connecticut, and Utah.

The Great Chief of Records submitted his longtalk, reporting that there had been a larger increase than reported at the last great sun council, and that the tide of prosperity seemed to have set in.

From the statistical abstract, accompanying the report of the Great Chief of Records, we glean the following information: Great Councils, 22; Reservations without a Great Council, 12; total number of Tribes, 465; adopted, 4148; reinstated, 444; admitted by card, 99; suspended, 2604; expelled, 47; withdrawn by card, 173; died, 276; total number of members, 29,965; Past Great Sachems, 178; Past Sachems, 5620; amount expended for relief of members, 81,200 fathoms and 22 inches; expended for relief of widows and orphans, 16,654 fathoms and 43 inches; expended for education, 132 fathoms and 76 inches; expended for other purposes, 99,248 fathoms and 68 inches; total Tribal receipts, 270,551 fathoms and 43 inches; invested by Tribes, 148,760 fathoms and 73 inches; in Tribal wampum belts, 45,920 fathoms and 55 inches.

He reported quite a handsome increase in the membership of the Beneficiary Association, there having been an addition of 241 to its list, the membership at the time of the report being 473.

The Special Committee on the subject of establishing a fund for aged and infirm members submitted a report, which, at the request of the Committee, was laid over until the succeeding great sun council. It was then taken up, and the substance of it incorporated in the laws. The report was as follows : —

The committee to whom was referred the matter of arranging and devising a plan for a continued membership by brothers over the age of fifty great suns, whose Tribes shall become extinct, and for the creation of a charitable fund for the sole use and benefit of such aged brothers, have had the same under consideration and beg leave to report the following:

That any Tribe which shall hereafter become extinct for any cause whatever, containing within its membership at the time of its extinction a member or members in good standing and severally entitled to a withdrawal card therefrom, according to the laws of the Order, and who shall, within the three moons next after the extinction of such Tribe, make application for and receive such withdrawal card, shall, within the three moons next after the procurement of such withdrawal card, make application for membership, according to the law of the Order, to the proper Tribe, and in case such application to such Tribe shall be refused on account of age or infirmity of such applicant, then, and in that case, said Tribe shall receive such brother, if otherwise worthy, under the regulations hereafter provided.

If such brother, upon his application to such Tribe, shall be rejected on account of his age and infirmity as aforesaid, and shall otherwise be found worthy and accepted by such Tribe, he shall then and thereafter be and become a member of said Tribe, subject to all the rights and privileges thereof, except said Tribe shall not be liable to such brother for benefits when unable to follow the hunt, and funeral expenses and donations and provisions made for the members of such Tribe other than such brother. Such brother upon being so received into such Tribe shall pay to the Keeper of Wampum of such Tribe, and shall regularly thereafter, pay his dues as other members are required to do. Such Keeper of Wampum shall keep all such dues and fees so paid by such brother as a separate fund to be expended as hereinafter made and provided.

There shall be assessed and collected from each member of every Tribe at the beginning of each great sun two inches, which sum, together with the admission fee and dues of such brother when so collected, shall be remitted by the Keeper of Wampum of each Tribe to the Great Keeper of Wampum of the jurisdiction wherein such Tribe is located, accompanying which shall be a report stating from what source and for what purpose said wampum was collected. The wampum so collected shall be held by the Great Keeper of Wampum as a special fund for the relief of such brother. Such brother shall receive benefits and assistance from said funds when unable to follow the hunt, according to the law in force on that subject in the jurisdiction wherein his Tribe is located. But such brother shall not receive such assistance except upon the application in his behalf, of the Keeper of Wampum and the recommendation of his Tribe, under the seal of such Tribe, to the Great Keeper of Wampum. The Great Keeper of Wampum, upon such application, shall send the wampum so to be paid said brother to the Keeper of

Wampum of his Tribe, who will pay the same to such brother and take his receipt therefor.

Such Keeper of Wampum shall, as to said fund, keep an account with each Tribe wherein shall appear the names of all such brothers and report the same to the State Great Council and to the Great Council of the United States at each council thereof.

The wampum herein provided for such brothers shall at all times be governed by the amount in the wampum belt, but shall in no case exceed three fathoms per seven suns, and each of the several Great Councils shall determine from time to time in what manner said fund shall be paid or disposed of, not exceeding three fathoms per seven suns to each brother as herein provided.

The special committee to prepare a circular to use in spreading the Order among palefaces made a report which was adopted. The circular briefly set forth the aims and objects of the Order, and gave information necessary to guide palefaces who desired admission to Tribes, or who wished to form new Tribes.

A new applicant for favor, in the shape of a publication in the interest of the Order, having made its appearance, the Great Council adopted the following:—

Resolved, That this Great Council recommends to the favorable consideration of the Order everywhere, *The Wampum Belt*, issued in the interests of the Improved Order of Red Men, by Brother Charles H. Litchman, of Marblehead, Mass.

The chiefs elected for the ensuing great sun were as follows:—

Great Incohonee,	GEORGE B. COLFLESH, P. G. S.,	Maryland.
Great Senior Sagamore,	WM. H. HYRONEMOUS, P. G. S.,	Tennessee.
Great Junior Sagamore,	RALPH S. GREGORY, P. G. S.,	Indiana.
Great Prophet,	ADAM SMITH, P. G. I.,	California.
Great Chief of Records,	JOSHUA MARIS, P. G. I.,	Delaware.
Great Keeper of Wampum,	JOSEPH PYLE, P. G. I.,	Delaware.

The chiefs-elect were raised up to their respective stumps, with the exception of the Great Incohonee, who was detained at home by the illness of one of his family.

P. G. I. Andrew J. Baker, acting temporarily as Great Incohonee, ruled that the Great Incohonee-elect, not having been raised to his stump, could not exercise the powers conferred by the laws upon a Great Incohonee, and that therefore the appointees by him for Great Tocakon and Great Minewa, could not be raised up; and that it rested with the Great Senior Sagamore to fill the vacant stump, and to appoint to said chieftaincies.

The Great Senior Sagamore declined, under the circumstances, to make the appointments.

It was then voted that the Great Prophet, the Past Great Incohonees resident in Baltimore, and such other chiefs as may attend, be instructed to raise up the Great Incohonee-elect, and the chiefs he may appoint, at a special council to be convened at some suitable time and place in Baltimore, Md.

This duty was performed on the 23d sun of Corn moon, at which time the Great Incohonee-elect was raised up. The great chiefs appointed and raised up at the same time were William Louis Schley, P. G. S., of Maryland, Great Tocakon, and Charles C. Conley, P. G. S., of Pennsylvania, Great Minewa.

The Great Council selected Atlantic City, N. J., as the place for kindling the next great sun council fire.

The law relative to the fiscal great sun of the G. C. U. S. was amended so as to make the great sun end on the first sun of Buck moon instead of the first sun of Cold moon.

1883.

The council fire of the G. C. U. S. was kindled in the Masonic Hall, Atlantic City, N. J., on the 11th of Corn moon, G. S. D. 392, Great Incohonee George B. Colflesh presiding.

An address of welcome on behalf of the Red Men of New Jersey was delivered by Past Great Sachem D. C. Vannote, of New Jersey, to which a fitting response was made by the Great Incohonee.

The Committee on Credentials reported that credentials had been received from 18 Great Councils.

The Great Incohonee submitted his longtalk, in which he made official announcement of the sudden death of Past Great Incohonee Morris H. Gorham, of Philadelphia, Pa.

He reported 6 new Tribes organized under the immediate jurisdiction of the G. C. U. S. in the States of Texas, Kansas, North Carolina, and Iowa. The remainder of the report covered the routine work of his chieftaincy.

The longtalk of the Great Chief of Records was the most satisfactory which had been received for many great suns.

He reported a substantial increase in the Beneficiary Association, the number of members at the end of the fiscal sun being 874, and the amount paid to beneficiaries of deceased members, 3186 fathoms and 53 inches.

From the statistical abstract we glean the following information: Number of Great Councils, 23; reservations without a Great Council, 14; total number of Tribes, 462; adopted, 9106; reinstated, 814; admitted by card, 352; suspended, 3404; expelled, 66; withdrawn by card, 250; died, 398; total number of members, 35,217; Past Sachems, 5439; Past Great Sachems, 181; amount expended for relief of members, 112,380 fathoms and 82 inches; expended for relief of widows and orphans, 9151 fathoms and 63 inches; expended for burial of the dead, 32,164 fathoms and 22 inches; expended for education of orphans, 250 fathoms and 25 inches; expended for other Tribal purposes, 159,068 fathoms and 26 inches; total receipts of Tribes, 402,312 fathoms and 40 inches; amount invested by Tribes, 374,443 fathoms and 46 inches; in Tribal wampum belts, 62,598 fathoms and 67 inches.

An interesting feature of this council was the presentation and placing upon the records of numerous testimonials of affection and esteem from State Great Councils in memory of Past Great Incohonee Morris H. Gorham, whose sudden death had been announced by the Great Incohonee.

It will be remembered that for many great suns the question of consolidating the outside organizations of Red Men with the Improved Order had been brought up. The report of the Committee on the State of the Order upon this subject explained the situation, as it then existed, fully, and favored consolidation under certain regulations. The report was adopted, the Great Council thereby placing itself on record as willing to welcome them all to membership, allowing them individually to hold the same relative honors in this Order they had earned in the others.

The members of the Great Council were the recipients of unremitting attention on the part of the brothers of New Jersey, and their gratitude found expression in appropriate resolutions.

A special committee of three was appointed to search for a proper Indian word signifying "brother," which might be used by the Order.

The report of a Committee on the Revision of the Constitution and Laws of the Order made its report, which was considered in Committee of the Whole, and after being considerably amended the further consideration was postponed until the next great sun council.

The special committee on that subject presented a report upon the death of Past Great Incohonee Morris H. Gorham, and a page of the Record of this Great Council was dedicated to his memory.

Springfield, Ill., was selected as the place for kindling the next great sun council fire.

1884.

The council fire of the G. C. U. S. was kindled in the Hall of the House of Representatives, in the Capitol Building at Springfield, Ill., on the 9th of Corn moon, G. S. D. 393, Great Incohonee George B. Colflesh presiding.

Previous to the kindling of the council fire, an eloquent longtalk was delivered by Past Great Sachem Owen Scott, of Illinois, in which he welcomed the G. C. U. S. to the hunting grounds and hearts of the Red Men of Illinois. A fitting and appropriate response was made by Past Great Incohonee Chas. H. Litchman, who spoke for the Great Council in the absence of the Great Incohonee by reason of temporary illness.

The Committee on Credentials reported that credentials had been received from 18 Great Councils, besides 4 holding over from the previous great sun council. Among those admitted for the first time at this council, was Past Great Sachem Thomas E. Peckinpaugh, of Ohio, the present Great Incohonee of the United States.

The Great Incohonee presented his longtalk for the previous great sun. He gave official announcement of the institution of the Great Council of Florida, on the 13th of Snow moon, G. S. D. 393 (February 13, 1884).

He also reported that a dispensation had been issued for institution of the Great Council of Colorado.

He also reported that the Great Spirit in His wisdom had again seen fit to remove from the hunting grounds of earth a chief of the Great Council of the United States, Great Chief of Records, and Past Great Incohonee Joshua Maris, and also made official mention of the death of Past Great Incohonee Daniel W. Carter, who, at the time of his death, was Chief of Records of the Great Council of Delaware.

He reported the organization of new Tribes under the jurisdiction of the G. C. U. S. in Florida, South Carolina, Iowa, Colorado, and Kansas, and the introduction again of the Order into Arkansas, by the institution of Mineola Tribe, No. 1, at Hot Springs.

The Great Chief of Records, *pro tem.*, Joseph A. Bond, of Delaware, presented his longtalk.

From the statistical abstract, accompanying the report of the Great Chief of Records, we glean the following interesting information: Great Councils, 24; reservations where no Great Council existed, 13; total number of Tribes, 528; adopted, 9067; reinstated, 534; admitted by card, 332; suspended, 3091; expelled, 47; withdrawn by card, 275; died, 340; total number of members, 41,497; amount expended for relief of members, 102,051 fathoms and 30 inches; expended for relief of widows and orphans, 4892 fathoms and 14 inches; expended for the burial of the dead, 27,920 fathoms and 29 inches; expended for education of orphans, 194 fathoms and 28 inches; other Tribal disbursements, 138,808 fathoms and 31 inches; total receipts of Tribes, 363,951 fathoms and 70 inches; invested by Tribes, 458,574 fathoms and 4 inches; in Tribal wampum belts, 146,743 fathoms and 22 inches.

He reported that there had been an addition of 754 names to the Beneficiary Association, and there had been paid out during the great sun 4726 fathoms and 50 inches, to beneficiaries of deceased members.

A special committee of five was appointed, to take into consideration the conflict of opinion alleged to exist as to the origin and early history of the Order, and report at the next great sun council. In this connection a copy of the history upon which Past Great Incohonee Morris H. Gorham of Pennsylvania had been at work at the time of his sudden death, was presented to the Great Council, received by that body, and referred to the Special Committee on the History of the Order here alluded to.

The further consideration of the Revised Constitution and Laws was resumed at this council, and the Constitution and General Laws as then amended were adopted and promulgated.

Charters were ordered to be issued for the Great Councils of Iowa, Colorado, Florida, and Kansas, and for the various Tribes in Arkansas, Florida, South Carolina, Iowa, and Kansas.

The Special Committee on selecting some appropriate Indian word signifying "brother," reported the result of their researches. They found many terms of a general fraternal sense, but none of the desired specific meaning, and therefore made no recommendation.

The Special Committee on Resolutions in memory of the late Great Chief of Records, Joshua Maris, P. G. I., submitted a report, which was adopted. The same committee presented resolutions upon the death of Past Great Incohonee Daniel W. Carter, which were also adopted. A memorial page was set aside for each of the chiefs named.

The chiefs elected and appointed and raised up for the ensuing term were as follows:—

Great Incohonee,	Wm. H. Hyronemus, P. G. S.,	Tennessee.
Great Senior Sagamore,	Ralph S. Gregory, P. G. S.,	Indiana.
Great Junior Sagamore,	Louis Beckhardt, P. S.,	New York.
Great Prophet,	Charles H. Litchman, P. G. I.,	Massachusetts.
Great Chief of Records,	Charles C. Conley, P. G. S.,	Pennsylvania.
Great Keeper of Wampum,	Joseph Pyle, P. G. I.,	Delaware.
Great Tocakon,	Luke S. Rosencrance, P. G. S.,	New York.
Great Minewa,	Addison Knickerbocker, P. G. S.,	Illinois.

Permission was given to translate the Ritual of the Order into the Danish language, provided that no expense was thereby incurred, and provided further, that the translation should be the property of the G. C. U. S.

Numerous changes were made in the laws governing the Beneficiary Association.

From this council dates the custom now in vogue of a standing Committee on Finance, which meets previous to the kindling of the council fire of the G. C. U. S., for the examination of the books and accounts, and for the purpose of making such recommendations to the G. C. U. S. as the exigencies of the Order seem to require.

The hunting grounds of Elmira, N.Y., were selected as the place for kindling the next great sun council fire.

1885.

The council fire of the G. C. U. S. was kindled in the wigwam of Massasoit Tribe, No. 14, at Elmira, N.Y., on the 8th of Corn moon, G. S. D. 394, Great Incohonee William H. Hyronemus presiding.

The Committee on Credentials reported that credentials had been received from 21 Great Councils.

The Great Incohonee submitted his longtalk.

He reported the institution of the Great Council of Colorado on the 23d sun of Sturgeon moon, G. S. D. 393 (August 23, 1884).

He also reported the institution of the Great Council of Kansas, in the city of Parsons, on the 17th of Hunting moon, G. S. D. 393 (December 17, 1884).

He also reported the institution of the Great Council of Iowa in the city of Oskaloosa, on the 18th of Hunting moon, G. S. D. 393 (December 18, 1884).

Another Tribe had been instituted in the reservation of Texas, and the Order had been introduced into Montana by the institution of Silver Bow Tribe, No. 1, Butte City, and into Wisconsin by the institution of Oshkosh Tribe, No. 1, at Oshkosh.

He also referred to a pleasant tour made by him through the Southern States, on which occasion he was the guest of the members of the Order in that section of the country. Among the recommendations made were the establishment of a home for the aged and indigent Red Men and their widows, and that the Great Council hold its councils every two great suns.

The longtalk of the Great Chief of Records was a full and explicit statement of the work done by him since the last great sun council. From the statistical abstract, accompanying the report of the Great Chief of Records, we learn that the number of Great Councils was 25 ; reservations where no Great Councils existed, 9; total number of Tribes, 543 ; adopted, 6633 ; reinstated, 344 ; admitted by card, 298 ; suspended, 4465 ; expelled,

76; withdrawn by card, 355; died, 403; total number of members, 43,619; Past Great Sachems, 215; Past Sachems, 6668; amount expended for relief of members, 109,476 fathoms and 20 inches; expended for relief of widows and orphans, 3473 fathoms and 95 inches; expended for burial of the dead, 29,788 fathoms and 61 inches; expended for education of orphans, 679 fathoms and 86 inches; other Tribal disbursements, 160,814 fathoms and 63 inches; total receipts of Tribes, 360,163 fathoms and 13 inches; invested by Tribes, 495,966 fathoms and 58 inches; in Tribal wampum belts, 100,546 fathoms and 15 inches.

He reported a great falling off in the membership of the Beneficiary Association.

The improved condition of the financial affairs of the G. C. U. S. may be learned from the statement in the longtalk of the Great Keeper of Wampum, that the total receipts for the great sun, including balance on hand at last settlement, were 10,814 fathoms and 36 inches.

We have already referred to the fact that at various times attempts had been made to induce the G. C. U. S. to adopt a side degree into which could be admitted the wives and female relatives of the members of the Order. At this council a communication was received from the Great Council of Massachusetts, asking that permission be granted for a degree to which female relatives of the members of the Order could be admitted, and that a code of laws be adopted governing the same. The proposition was referred to a special committee which subsequently reported in favor of the proposed action. This report was adopted, and the committee submitted a further report later in the council, with the rules and regulations for the government of the Degree of Pocahontas thus established, the same to go into effect after the first of the Cold moon, G. S. D. 395 (January 1, 1886). Under the appropriate chapter, further allusion will be made to this important action of the G. C. U. S.

Up to the present time the regalia and jewel for a Past Great Incohonee had not been defined with sufficient clearness, and at this council a resolution was adopted describing what they should be.

The question of a uniform degree again claimed the attention of the G. C. U. S., and the matter was referred to the Committee on the State of the Order, which subsequently reported general laws governing a uniform rank to be known as the "Knights of Tammany," with a uniform appropriate. The matter was adopted, with the proviso that no part of it should be used until a ritual therefor had been approved by the G. C. U. S.

A badge to be worn at funerals in lieu of regalia was adopted.

It was voted to kindle the next great sun council fire in the hunting grounds of Detroit, Mich.

The Great Council again refused to adopt the proposition that the business of the Tribes should be transacted in the Chief's Degree.

A pleasing feature of this council was an address of welcome on behalf of the city of Elmira by His Excellency David B. Hill, then Governor of the State.

1886.

The council fire of the G. C. U. S. was kindled in Harmonic Hall, Detroit, Mich., on the 14th of Corn moon, G. S. D. 395, Great Incohonee William H. Hyronemus presiding.

Previous to the formal kindling of the council fire, addresses of welcome were made by Past Sachem John M. Herz and Great Sachem William W. Tanner, to which an appropriate response was made by Great Incohonee Hyronemus.

The Committee on Credentials reported that credentials had been received from 22 reservations.

The Great Incohonee presented his longtalk, which opened with congratulations that the Order had made a gain during the great sun of nearly 8000 members. He especially complimented Massachusetts, New York, Pennsylvania, and New Jersey for the work done in those reservations. He reported the Great Council of Kentucky in a crippled condition, with only one Tribe in good working order. Among his recommendations was one that the Tribes in the reservations of Connecticut, Rhode Island, and Vermont be placed under the jurisdiction of the Great Council of Massachusetts. He made official announcement of the death of Past Great Incohonee William Beesley Davis. He also made report of his visitations through the Southern States, and the hospitality with which he was there received.

RALPH S. GREGORY.

CHARLES C. CONLEY.

THOMAS J. FRANCIS.

THOMAS K. DONNALLEY.

PAST GREAT INCOHONEES.

The Great Chief of Records presented an extended longtalk of the transaction of his chieftaincy during the great sun.

From the statistical abstract, accompanying the longtalk of the Great Chief of Records, we glean the following information: Number of Great Councils, 24; reservations having no Great Council, 12; total number of Tribes, 591; adopted, 12,506; reinstated, 612; admitted by card, 328; suspended, 5587; expelled, 55; withdrawn by card, 300; died, 489; total number of members, 50,263; Past Great Sachems, 223; Past Sachems, 7115; amount expended for relief of members, 136,144 fathoms and 50 inches; expended for relief of widows and orphans, 5412 fathoms and 80 inches; expended for burial of the dead, 37,150 fathoms and 48 inches; other Tribal disbursements, 164,444 fathoms and 79 inches; total Tribal receipts, 450,469 fathoms and 60 inches; Tribal investments, 596,271 fathoms and 79 inches; in Tribal wampum belts, 106,915 fathoms and 86 inches.

His report of the Beneficiary Association showed that the membership was gradually falling off, and that it had not met with the success its friends fondly hoped.

He reported the Order in Arkansas, Kentucky, and Rhode Island as in feeble condition, if not defunct.

The report in the longtalk of the Great Keeper of Wampum showed the financial affairs of the G. C. U. S. to be in a healthy condition, with ample wampum to meet current expenses.

A new charter was granted to the Great Council of Virginia, to replace the original, lost or destroyed during the war.

The Committee on History of the Order, previously appointed, reported progress, and requested further time, which was granted.

The chiefs elected and appointed and raised up for the ensuing great sun were as follows:—

Great Incohonee,	RALPH S. GREGORY, P. G. S.,	Indiana.
Great Senior Sagamore,	THOMAS J. FRANCIS, P. G. S.,	New Jersey.
Great Junior Sagamore,	THOMAS K. DONNALLEY, P. G. S.,	Pennsylvania.
Great Prophet,	GEORGE B. COLFLESH, P. G. I.,	Maryland.
Great Chief of Records,	CHARLES C. CONLEY, P. G. S.,	Pennsylvania.
Great Keeper of Wampum,	JOSEPH PYLE, P. G. I.,	Delaware.
Great Tocakon,	THOS. E. PECKINPAUGH, P. G. S.,	Ohio.
Great Minewa,	A. ANDREWS, P. S.,	California.

The recommendation of the Great Incohonee was approved, placing the reservations of Connecticut, Rhode Island, and Vermont under the jurisdiction of the Great Council of Massachusetts, and the request of the Great Council of Georgia was granted, placing the reservations of South Carolina and Alabama under the jurisdiction of said Great Council until such time as the States named should be in condition to erect and maintain a State Great Council.

Various amendments to the Beneficiary Association Law were presented, considered, and adopted.

It was voted that the council fire of the next great sun council be kindled in the hunting grounds of Wilmington, Del.

One of the important actions of this council was the adoption of rules governing a uniformed degree for the Order, to be known by the title of the "Chieftains' League," and the ceremony to be used therein to be that already adopted for Beneficial Degree Councils, with slight alteration. This action was practically the completion of that begun at the preceding great sun council, the new title being in place of "Knights of Tammany," accepted at that time.

A memorial upon the death of Past Great Incohonee William Beesley Davis was adopted.

A committee of five was appointed to prepare a plan for the erection of a home for Red Men.

At this council a Ritual for the Degree of Pocahontas was presented and adopted.

As an indication that the Great Council did not confine its charitable operations solely to the members of the Order, it may be mentioned that at this council an appropriation of 100 fathoms was made in aid of the sufferers by the earthquake in Charleston, S.C.

1887.

The council fire of the G. C. U. S. was kindled in Odd Fellow's Hall, Wilmington, Del., on the 13th of Corn moon, G. S. D. 396, Great Incohonee Ralph S. Gregory presiding.

Previous to the formal kindling of the council fire, the Great Council was welcomed to the reservation of Delaware by Past Great Incohonee Joseph Pyle, who was followed by John M.

Whitford, Deputy Grand Master of the Independent Order of Odd Fellows, who for the Order he represented welcomed the Great Council to the State. A fitting and appropriate response was made by Great Incohonee Gregory.

The Committee on Credentials reported that credentials had been received from 24 Great Councils.

The Great Incohonee submitted his longtalk.

During the great sun he had issued a proclamation in which he had declared that the work of the Chieftains' League would be issued on and after the first sun of Cold moon, G. S. D. 396 (January 1, 1887), and the work of the Degree of Pocahontas on and after the 15th sun of Cold moon, G. S. D. 396 (January 15, 1887), and that in accordance with the action of the G. C. U. S., he had placed the reservations of Connecticut, Rhode Island, and Vermont under the jurisdiction of the Great Council of Massachusetts, and the reservations of South Carolina and Alabama under the jurisdiction of the Great Council of Georgia.

A dispensation had been granted for the institution of a Tribe in Toronto, Can., being the first Tribe instituted on this Continent outside of the limits of the United States.

He reported the organization of the Great Council of Connecticut on the 1st of Sturgeon moon, G. S. D. 396 (August 1, 1887).

He also announced the organization of a Chieftains' League in Pennsylvania and another in New Jersey.

The correspondence between him and the Chiefs, in the various parts of the great reservation of the United States, was given in full.

The longtalk of the Great Chief of Records was a very interesting document. He reported that almost every reservation showed an increase in membership, the net gain for the great sun being about 13,000.

From the statistical abstract, accompanying the longtalk of the Great Chief of Records, we glean the following information: Number of Great Councils, 24; reservations without a Great Council, 12; adopted, 18,411; reinstated, 575; admitted by card, 564; suspended, 5749; expelled, 79; withdrawn by card, 512; died, 476; total number of members, 63,200; Past

Great Sachems, 242; Past Sachems, 8120; amount expended for relief of members, 143,445 fathoms and 3 inches; expended for relief of widows and orphans, 5191 fathoms and 88 inches; expended for burial of the dead, 35,541 fathoms and 48 inches; other Tribal disbursements, 210,075 fathoms and 10 inches; total receipts of Tribes, 560,582 fathoms and 57 inches; Tribal investments, 573,312 fathoms and 65 inches; in Tribal wampum belts, 167,351 fathoms and 97 inches.

His report of the Beneficiary Fund was not very encouraging as to its condition or hope for the future.

Charters were granted for the new Tribes at Toronto, Can., and Minneapolis, Minn., and for the Great Council of Connecticut.

The reservation of Wisconsin was placed under the jurisdiction of the Great Council of Illinois.

The rules governing the Degree of Pocahontas were amended so as to permit membership to members of the Improved Order of Red Men of the Chief's Degree in good standing in their Tribes, and to any women over 18 years of age of good moral character. Also that past officers of organizations that were in existence prior to the promulgation of the Degree of Pocahontas, said bodies having accepted the provisions of the law, were declared to be entitled to the rank and honors of Past Chiefs, and Great Councils were required to make out and present to the Great Chief of Records of the G. C. U. S. a report every great sun of the Councils of the Degree of Pocahontas under their jurisdictions. Previously the membership had been restricted to members of the Order of the Chief's Degree and their immediate relatives.

The Special Committee on History of the Order submitted majority and minority reports as follows:—

Majority Report.

Great Chiefs and Brothers: Your Committee to whom was referred the origin and early history of our organization, known to-day as the Improved Order of Red Men, respectfully submit the following report as the result of our investigation: During Worm moon, G. S. D. 395, they met according to appointment in the city of Baltimore with all members of the Committee present, when it was duly organized by the selection of A. S. Williams, of Tennessee, as Chairman, and G. C. of R. Charles C. Conley, of Pennsylvania, as Secretary.

Brothers P. G. I. George W. Lindsay and P. S. William G. Hollis, representing respectively the "Gorham" and "Lindsay" Histories of the Order were present with all their manuscripts and authorities for the establishment of their different theories, all of which were cheerfully placed in the hands of your Committee for their scrutiny and investigation; Bros. Lindsay and Hollis remaining with the Committee for the purpose of explaining any matter pertaining to the manuscript and documents that might not be of themselves sufficiently clear to the minds of the Committee, for which assistance your Committee gratefully acknowledge their obligation.

Your Committee find from the various documents and proofs submitted, that there existed during the early history of our American country many societies of men formed for the purpose of attaining a higher degree of religious, social, and political freedom, than was accessible through the ordinary avenues of civil life as tolerated by the authority emanating from the throne of royal rulers; the guiding principles and leading features of which were derived in a great measure from the manners, customs, and traditions of the Aborigines of the American Continent. It seems conclusive from the evidence extant that the American paleface was early imbued with many of the commendable characteristics that marked the nature of the North American Indian or Red Man of the forest; so much so that they soon commenced to manifest an admiration for many of his traits of character, and to inscribe them upon their banners as worthy of the emulation of all true lovers of liberty, home, and friends. Among the most prominent characteristics exhibited by the nature of the North American Indian, and which seemed to meet a heartier response from the bosom of the primitive American paleface, was his love of freedom, devotion to friends, and implicit faith and confidence in the "*Kishe Manitou*," the *Great Spirit*, in whose hands he claimed all power to exist. Hence we need not marvel that our early ancestors, who were at the time, and had been for many great suns previous, writhing under the galling yoke of British tyranny, should so readily learn to admire and partake of a principle that sought to alleviate their suffering, and establish an intercourse among them that might ultimately destroy oppression and bring relief in its happiest and most acceptable form; hence the Boston Boys as the "Sons of Liberty," with bucktails and other marks of the aboriginal Red Man of the forest, are found asserting in a practical way the principle inculcated by such precepts, in making Boston harbor the receptacle for *high taxed British tea*. Again are found the Tammany Societies or Columbian Order, organized as early as 1771, and existing in several States, with rituals and guide book composed almost entirely of ideas drawn from the original inhabitants of the American Continent. These several and different societies, so far as your Committee has been able to ascertain, existed as individuals so far as their allegiance to a source of higher authority of the Order was concerned; in other words, each adopted such rules and regulations for their own government as they deemed wise and expedient, and consistent with the objects and purposes of their several societies. These societies continued to exist in one form or another as to name and title from great sun to great sun down through the several periods and trying changes of our American government, gathering as time rolled on more and more of the true American idea as demonstrated by the untutored Red Man of the forest, making very little progress, if any, towards consolidation, or the establishment of a head by and through which they could have a concert of action, until after the war of 1812, when a society was organized in the city of Philadelphia, known as Red Men, some time between 1815 and 1817 A.D., which created a line of chiefs or officers clothed with power and invested with a commission from what was known as the Mother Tribe, to make or create Red Men wherever in the forest of life opportunity was offered. For a more perfect description of the Order and its *modus operandi*, see Gorham's "History of the Improved Order of Red Men." While this society was of later birth than the many others mentioned, it seemed to be controlled by the same spirit that actuated those before it.

Social and political features. — But while the facts were that way, many virtues and benevolent ideas seemed to make way into the meetings and take hold of the hearts and minds of the members, until they were persuaded to feel that their mission was not circumscribed by the mere lines of political and social distinction, but was capable of taking position in the front ranks of benevolent and charitable institutions with an abundant amount of crude material from the manners, customs, and traditions of the American Indian, out of which to mould and shape a ritual that would not only compare favorably with that of like institutions, but possess a peculiarity that makes it especially interesting, and at the same time endears it to every American heart — since it would be the first secret benevolent organization of American birth, owing no allegiance to other lands or country for any part of its construction — but conceived in hope, born of liberty, and reared under the blessed influences of America's free institutions; facts which attest the sagacity, good judgment, and patriotism of its progenitors, and justly entitle them to a high place upon the scroll of public benefactors and the sincere gratitude of thousands who have been the recipients of its munificent bounty and multiplied thousands yet to follow who may become the happy beneficiaries of its benign influences.

These societies continued to multiply in number and interest, until they were found in many States of our Union, and became so important a factor in the affairs of our country that it became necessary, in order to make their work more effective, to establish direct communication with each other, and adopt a plan of action by which their proceedings would be uniform and in keeping with the objects and purposes of the Order. On that line of march these societies continued to move forward in that semi-connected manner until G. S. D. 342, in the city of Baltimore, Md., the Improved Order of Red Men was announced to the world as a fraternal and benevolent organization, fully equipped and amply prepared to assume its share of the responsibilities resting upon secret institutions, and to discharge every obligation with zeal and fidelity. To ascertain the success attained in that direction, go ask the thousands of worthy and noble Improved Red Men, who each seven suns assemble around the burning council fire of Freedom, Friendship, and Charity, and there enjoy the sweet benefits of our beloved Order.

Your Committee have also carefully examined the works prepared and written upon the origin and history of the Improved Order of Red Men by our worthy and faithful brothers, P. G. I.'s Morris H. Gorham and George W. Lindsay, with a view of determining if possible which of the two contained the most correct and authentic account of the source and early history of our Order. While your Committee feel justified in cheerfully commending P. G. I. Gorham's History to the Improved Order of Red Men, and all others who may desire knowledge and information upon the subject of our organization, as a work complete in many respects and justly entitled to the name it bears, as well as a credit to its lamented author, they are of the opinion from the facts and circumstances adduced, that the work is in error, and not sustained by the authorities presented to your Committee, when it fixes Fort Mifflin as the place, and 1813 as the time where and when the Improved Order of Red Men originated.

The manuscript of the proposed History of the Order by P. G. I. George W. Lindsay establishes the fact conclusively that there were societies of Red Men formed for social and political purposes by palefaces as far back as 1771, which societies continued to grow and multiply in one form and another until October 14, 1833, when the Improved Order of Red Men was organized and given to the world as an endowed benevolent institution which stands to-day as a witness thereof.

Respectfully submitted, in F. F. & C.,

> ALBERT S. WILLIAMS,
> JOSEPH PYLE,
> CHAS. C. CONLEY,
> J. H. BENNETT.

MINORITY REPORT.

While there is much in the report of the majority of the Committee to which I do not object, I feel it my duty to give briefly the reasons why I cannot concur in the conclusions of my colleagues.

In my opinion the information at hand may be considered under three heads ; —

1. Tradition.
2. Supposition.
3. Fact.

When we deal with the traditions of that period which gave birth to the American Republic, we find in existence societies of various kinds, and holding various names. These were the masks behind which the men of those days concealed their actions. These actions if successful made them heroes; if failures made them traitors. Hence, until the arbitrament of war decided whether they should be crowned or hung, they from motives of prudence concealed their identity by the fictitious names used in the societies alluded to. The nomenclature of the Indian Tribes was admirably adapted and naturally applied for that purpose. This will explain why the ceremonies of nearly all these societies partook so largely of the characteristics of the ceremonies of the Indian Race.

I fail to find any evidence that these societies were known or called Orders of *Red Men* in any sense that could justify the claim that our present Improved Order of Red Men is in any way connected with them, or is the lineal descendant thereof.

With the organization formed at Fort Mifflin, commences what I call the era of supposition in the history of our Order.

It is possible, and perhaps probable, that among those who formed this society of Red Men were those who had been members of the earlier Tammany Societies of the Revolutionary period. No evidence of this fact has to my knowledge been produced.

For several years the record is sufficiently clear and unbroken to substantiate the claim that from them came the inspiration, the suggestion, the names and titles, and indeed the very personality by which the Tribes were organized, which in the city of Baltimore formed the Improved Order of Red Men.

This brings us to the era of fact and to the date from which the historical record is complete.

I could sustain what is here stated by copious extracts from the documents submitted to your Committee, but I do not care to weary you.

I submit the following as my conclusions:—

1. The very able, instructive, and interesting compilation of

Past Great Incohonee Lindsay, while a very valuable contribution to the legendary lore concerning the societies which existed prior to 1812, does not prove them the origin of our Order.

2. The History of Past Great Incohonee Gorham does conclusively prove the existence of a Society of Red Men at Fort Mifflin during the war of 1812. It also furnishes strong circumstantial evidence of continuity of existence down to very near the time of the formation of the Improved Order of Red Men at Baltimore in the year 1833. It also proves, and the proof is strengthened by documents in existence, that members of the organization which grew out of that at Fort Mifflin, subsequently participated in the organization of Tribes that formed the Improved Order of Red Men, the officers by which some of these Tribes (if not all) were organized acting under authority conferred by those who were active in the Tribes existing from 1813 to 1830.

If you wish to launch upon the unknown sea of fanciful tradition to find an origin for our Order, you will go to the closing years of the 18th century and find it there. If you wish to have an origin with at least a plausible foundation, I think you will be justified in claiming a beginning at Fort Mifflin in 1813.

If you wish to be exactly and historically correct, truth will compel you to halt at the formation of the Improved Order of Red Men at Baltimore in 1834, and declare that the true origin of our Order.

While I may not be able to be present personally and submit this report, I ask for it your kind consideration.

I offer the following for your action :—

Resolved, That in the facts presented to your Committee nothing has been added to the knowledge already gained which would require any additional action by the Great Council of the United States.

Yours fraternally,

CHAS. H. LITCHMAN, *Committee.*

The Great Council, after considerable deliberation, adopted the report of the majority, thus declaring that there was reasonable foundation for the claim, that our Order has its origin in the societies existing from the time just prior to the American

GREAT COUNCIL OF UNITED STATES. 403

Revolution. Guided by this action of the Great Council of the United States, this History has been prepared, and its conclusions and deductions, as far as sustained by evidence and documents obtainable, have been recorded, by the compilers.

An appropriation of 500 fathoms was made for the contingent expenses of the Great Incohonee, Great Senior Sagamore, and Great Junior Sagamore during the ensuing great sun.

It was voted that the next great sun council fire be kindled in the hunting grounds of Chicago, Ill.

Among the resolutions of thanks adopted upon report of the Committee on State of the Order was one extended to his Excellency Governor B. T. Biggs, of the State of Delaware, for his eloquent and hearty address of welcome, his Honor C. B. Rhoads, mayor of the city of Wilmington, and to Past Great Incohonee Joseph Pyle, at whose beautiful home the members of the Great Council had been entertained during the council.

An appropriation of 200 fathoms was made, to be used by the trustees of the Beneficiary Fund for the extension and building up of the membership thereof.

At this council a special committee was appointed to have prepared a certificate of membership to be issued under the direction and authority of the G. C. U. S.

1888.

The council fire of the G. C. U. S. was kindled at the Palmer House, Chicago, Ill., on the 11th of Corn moon, G. S. D. 397, Great Incohonee Ralph S. Gregory presiding.

Previous to the formal kindling of the council fire, Past Great Sachem Owen Scott, on behalf of the Great Council of Illinois, welcomed the Great Council of the United States to the reservation of Illinois, and a proper response was made by Great Incohonee Gregory.

The Committee on Credentials reported that credentials had been received from 23 Great Councils.

The Great Incohonee submitted his longtalk, which commenced by congratulating the Great Council that the numerical strength of the Order had increased 18,000 during the preceding great sun, and that all differences, dissensions, factions, and discords had gracefully submitted to the principles of Freedom, Friendship, and Charity.

He reported the Chieftains' League and the Degree of Pocahontas as prospering and increasing rapidly.

He also reported the institution of the Great Council of Rhode Island, and presented in detail the history of the Order during the great sun.

The Great Chief of Records submitted his longtalk, which also congratulated the Great Council on the progress made during the great sun.

He brought to the attention of the G. C. U. S. the deaths of Past Incohonee William G. Gorsuch, of Maryland, and Past Great Incohonee James P. Riely, of Virginia. Brother Gorsuch was the first Great Incohonee of the Order.

He also reported the organization of two additional Tribes in Washington Territory and the reorganization of Osceola Tribe, No. 1, in North Carolina.

The correspondence received by him indicated that Great Councils would soon be organized in the reservations of Alabama and Maine.

He also reported that the Degree of Pocahontas had already become very popular. Councils had been instituted in California, Connecticut, Illinois, Indiana, Massachusetts, Nevada, New Hampshire, New York, Ohio, Oregon, Pennsylvania, Virginia, and West Virginia.

From the statistical abstract submitted with the longtalk of the Great Chief of Records we glean the following information: Number of Great Councils, 25; reservations without Great Councils, 4; adopted, 22,813; reinstated, 611; admitted by card, 2310; suspended, 6546; rejected, 616; expelled, 103; withdrawn by card, 2477; died, 674; total number of members, 78,781; Past Great Sachems, 262; Past Sachems, 9062; total number of Tribes, 896; amount expended for relief of members, 159,449 fathoms and 16 inches; amount expended for relief of widows and orphans, 6988 fathoms and 65 inches; expended for burial of the dead, 46,443 fathoms and 31 inches; other Tribal disbursements, 300,278 fathoms and 96 inches; total Tribal receipts, 682,414 fathoms and 11 inches; Tribal investments, 667,643 fathoms and 53 inches; in Tribal wampum belts, 243,712 fathoms and 91 inches.

No further progress could be reported concerning the Beneficiary Fund, although the balance in the reserve fund had increased to 790 fathoms and 48 inches.

The growth of the Order was made manifest in the increased receipts of the G. C. U. S., the amount received during the great sun being 12,428 fathoms and 27 inches.

A proposition was submitted in behalf of Brother Lee C. Hascall for a publication of a history of the Order, and the matter was referred to the Committee on the State of the Order. Upon the report of that committee the proposition as submitted was in substance adopted, and a committee of three appointed to prepare the necessary material. It may be stated in passing that it is under the authority herein mentioned that the present History was prepared and published.

The chiefs elected and appointed and raised up for the ensuing term were as follows: —

Great Incohonee,	THOMAS J. FRANCIS, P. G. S.,	New Jersey.
Great Senior Sagamore,	THOS. K. DONNALLEY, P. G. S.,	Pennsylvania.
Great Junior Sagamore,	THOS. E. PECKINPAUGH, P. G. S.,	Ohio.
Great Prophet,	RALPH S. GREGORY, P. G. I.,	Indiana.
Great Chief of Records,	CHARLES C. CONLEY, P. G. S.,	Pennsylvania.
Great Keeper of Wampum,	JOSEPH PYLE, P. G. I.,	Delaware.
Great Tocakon,	ANDREW H. PATON, P. G. S.,	Massachusetts.
Great Minewa,	R. T. DANIEL, P. S.,	Georgia.

The committee appointed at the previous great sun council to prepare a Diploma of membership reported that the owner of the Diploma originated by the late Past Great Incohonee Morris H. Gorham, was willing to make an agreement with the G. C. U. S. to pay into the wampum belt 15 inches as a royalty for each certificate issued. The committee recommended that the proposition be accepted. This the Great Council refused to do, and referred the matter to a special committee of three. This committee subsequently reported a review of the legislation of the G. C. U. S. under which the original publication of the Diploma by Brother Gorham was permitted, and recommended that the committee be continued until the next great sun council, in order that the exact rights of all parties concerned might be ascertained and reported to the Great Council.

Charters were granted for the Great Councils of Rhode

Island, Maine, and Alabama and for Tribes in North Carolina, Washington, and Oregon.

The Tribes in the reservation of Kentucky were placed under the jurisdiction of the Great Council of Ohio.

The Great Chiefs were authorized to prepare a design for a signal or flag that may be used by members of the Order who are mariners, it being suggested that the signal combine the four colors of the Order, green, blue, orange, and red.

It was voted that the next great sun council fire be kindled in the hunting grounds of Baltimore, Md.

The Special Committee on Memorials to Past Great Incohonee William G. Gorsuch and Past Great Incohonee James P. Riely made a report, which was adopted.

Two hundred fathoms of wampum were appropriated for the yellow fever sufferers of Florida, and an appeal to the Order for funds was authorized.

A charter was granted to the Great Council of Illinois to replace the original lost or destroyed.

Legislation was adopted at this council perfecting the rules governing the Degree of Pocahontas.

1889.

The council fire of the G. C. U. S. was kindled at Red Men's Hall, Baltimore, Md., on the 10th of Corn moon, G. S. D. 398, Great Incohonee Thomas J. Francis presiding.

Previous to the formal kindling of the council fire Past Great Sachem John H. Bennett on behalf of the Great Council of Maryland welcomed the G. C. U. S. to Baltimore. The remarks of welcome were fittingly responded to by Great Incohonee Francis.

The Committee on Credentials reported that credentials had been received from 26 Great Councils.

The Great Incohonee submitted his longtalk, which was a full and complete record of the business coming under his supervision during the great sun.

He had authorized the institution of the Great Council of Maine in the hunting grounds of Bath on the 25th sleep of Travelling moon, G. S. D. 397 (October 25, 1888).

In person he had instituted the Great Council of Alabama in the hunting grounds of Birmingham on the 19th of Beaver moon, G. S. D. 397 (November 19, 1888).

He spoke of the many visitations he had made in various reservations, and of action taken by him to relieve distress caused by an epidemic of yellow fever in Florida, and by the terrible floods at Johnstown, Pa., and elsewhere. He detailed the correspondence that had been received by him in relation to the Diploma of the late Brother Gorham formerly issued under the authority of the G. C. U. S.

An unfortunate difficulty in the reservation of Illinois had arisen which called for prompt action on his part, and which at one time threatened to rupture the pleasant relations that should exist between Tribes and a Great Council and between a State Great Council and the G. C. U. S. It may be said in passing that reason and common sense finally prevailed, and brothers who had been antagonistic to each other came together in the spirit of harmony and fraternity, differences were adjusted and forgotten, and the reservation of Illinois placed again on the road to enduring prosperity.

The longtalk of the Great Chief of Records showed that the membership of the Beneficiary Association had gradually decreased, although the reserve fund showed that the system under which the Association was conducted was sound from a business standpoint.

He referred to action which had been taken for the relief of sufferers by yellow fever, and stated that the amount which had been received in response to an appeal for their aid was 817 fathoms and 5 inches. The action of the Great Council in this matter, he said, had received the warmest praise in the reservation of Florida, the people and the press of the State having united in giving highest credit to the Improved Order of Red Men for its generous and well-directed assistance.

He recommended that the unexpended balance of the fund raised be placed in bank as a special fund to be used by the great chiefs whenever a case of emergency may arise requiring instant relief.

He also referred to the action of the Order in connection with the flood at Johnstown, Pa., the amount raised by voluntary subscription from various Tribes being 1693 fathoms and 85 inches, including a donation of 250 fathoms from the G. C. U. S., the total amount having been paid to the Great Chief of Records of Pennsylvania to be disbursed among the sufferers by the flood.

He called attention to the success which had attended the introduction of the Chieftains' League and the Degree of Pocahontas.

From the statistical abstract, accompanying his longtalk, we glean the following information: Number of Great Councils, 28; reservations without a Great Council, 3; adopted, 18,779; reinstated, 236; admitted by card, 2025; suspended, 9808; rejected, 857; expelled, 116; withdrawn by card, 2196; died, 697; total number of members, 88,442; Past Great Sachems, 261; Past Sachems, 10,360; total number of Tribes, 976; amount expended for relief of members, 149,648 fathoms and 70 inches; expended for relief of widows and orphans, 4590 fathoms and 67 inches; expended for burial of the dead, 40,700 fathoms and 68 inches; other Tribal disbursements, 257,424 fathoms and 10 inches; total receipts of Tribes, 654,074 fathoms and 60 inches; Tribal investments, 727,008 fathoms and 14 inches; in Tribal wampum belts, 326,242 fathoms and 85 inches.

The Trustees of the Beneficiary Fund made a report in which they expressed regret that the efforts to increase the interest in the Fund had not met with the success desired. There had been a slight decrease in membership, and the total of the reserve and general fund was 935 fathoms and 46 inches.

The reservation of the State of Nebraska was placed under the jurisdiction of the Great Council of Iowa, with the hope that the Order in that reservation might be resuscitated.

The Special Committee on Digest made a report, and submitted the Digest which had been prepared, which was accepted by the Great Council.

The Committee on Finance submitted a report which stated the total amount received during the great sun was 15,360 fathoms and 78 inches.

The Special Committee on Diploma submitted an exhaustive report which detailed the exact situation and the relation borne by the G. C. U. S. to the matter. The report concluded with a recommendation that the Order should adopt and issue an Official Diploma, or give fair field and no favor to all members who wished to manufacture and sell Diplomas to members.

The Great Council decided to issue an Official Diploma, and to offer a premium for a design.

It was voted that the next great sun council fire be kindled in the hunting grounds of Boston, Mass.

The Great Council voted unanimously to grant charters to Manataug Tribe, No. 1, of Marblehead, Mass., and Seattle Tribe, No. 2, of Seattle, Wash., to replace originals destroyed by fire. The charter of Manataug Tribe was granted by the G. C. U. S., because the original charter of said Tribe had been granted by said body.

At this council a large number of amendments were presented containing propositions to amend the laws governing Chieftains' Leagues, and suggesting uniforms and other matters of interest to the League. After consuming a great deal of time upon the consideration of these various propositions, the Great Council adopted a resolution giving the Chieftains' League an independent organization, with the qualification that none but Red Men in good standing should be admitted thereto or continue as members thereof.

The Great Council adopted the recommendation of the Great Chief of Records that the balance of the Yellow Fever Fund be set apart as a Benevolence Fund to be at the disposal of the great chiefs, and to be used in cases of great emergency for the benefit of the Order.

The Great Council refused to adopt an amendment permitting the admission of palefaces under 21 great suns of age.

1890.

The council fire of the G. C. U. S. was kindled at Encampment Hall, No. 724 Washington Street, Boston, Mass., on the 9th of Corn moon, G. S. D. 399, Great Incohonee Thomas J. Francis presiding.

Previous to the formal kindling of the council fire, Great Sachem Charles H. Symonds, on behalf of the Great Council of Massachusetts, and the Order in that State, heartily welcomed the members of the G. C. U. S. to the hospitality of the Order in the reservation. The address of welcome was responded to in a fitting manner by Great Prophet Ralph S. Gregory.

The Committee on Credentials reported that credentials had been received from 27 Great Councils.

The Great Incohonee submitted his longtalk, covering the transactions of the preceding great sun. It embraced a full and detailed statement of the decisions made by him, and the correspondence had with various chiefs and great chiefs throughout the Order.

He reported that North Carolina had again renewed its interest in the Order by the institution of three Tribes in that reservation.

Dispensations had also been issued for another Tribe in Oregon, at Portland.

During the great sun he had made official visitations in New Jersey, West Virginia, Michigan, Pennsylvania, Connecticut, New York, Maine, and Virginia.

He called the attention of the G. C. U. S. to an evil which had crept into the Order in the form of what purported to be "a mock adoption for the Improved Order of Red Men." He believed such a matter detrimental to the best interests of the Order, and called for such action as the Great Council saw fit to take. He also condemned gift concerts and lotteries as an infraction of the laws of the Great Council.

Among the interesting matters touched upon in the longtalk was a report received from one of his Vice Great Incohonees who had endeavored to introduce the Order into Denmark, but had failed because of its isolation from the parent body, and the consequent difficulty of keeping the necessary close and constant connection, and because of the fact that the Order being wholly American, the patriotic sentiment which is so much an element of its strength at home would be entirely lacking in Denmark.

The longtalk of the Great Chief of Records was very interesting, showing the transactions of his chieftaincy during the great sun. The success of the Degree of Pocahontas was indicated by the fact that there were 11,302 members in the degree, according to the latest reports received.

He gave a detailed statement of the Beneficiary Fund, and showed that there had been paid to the beneficiaries during the six great suns it had existed the sum of 44,944 fathoms and 20 inches. The membership had been reduced so low that notices had been sent to the members thereof requesting an expression of opinion as to the advisability of winding up the concern. There had been received 62 answers, of which 16 were for continuance, and 46 against continuance.

From the statistical abstract, accompanying the longtalk, we glean the following information: Number of Great Councils, 28; number of Tribes, 1078; reservations without a Great Council, 3; adopted, 19,978; reinstated, 1003; admitted by card, 891; suspended, 9983; rejected, 816; expelled, 128; withdrawn by card, 1236; died, 784; total number of members, 97,164; amount expended for relief of members, 233,069 fathoms and 4 inches; expended for relief of widows and orphans, 9655 fathoms and 71 inches; expended for burial of the dead, 51,866 fathoms and 56 inches; other Tribal disbursements, 337,458 fathoms and 50 inches; total receipts of Tribes, 925,731 fathoms and 92 inches; Tribal investments, 803,813 fathoms and 1 inch; in Tribal wampum belts, 359,272 fathoms and 91 inches.

For the first time there was included in the longtalk of the Great Chief of Records a summary of the condition of Councils of the Degree of Pocahontas. The statistical abstract showed that the degree had been established in 18 States; total number of Councils, 145; adopted, 5015; reinstated, 25; admitted by card, 109; suspended, 896; rejected, 136; expelled, 4; withdrawn by card, 344; died, 61; total number of members, 11,302; Past Chiefs, 328; amount expended for relief of members, 2169 fathoms and 18 inches; expended for relief of widows and orphans, 225 fathoms and 99 inches; expended for burial of the dead, 666 fathoms and 16 inches; expended for other Council purposes, 20,285 fathoms and 22 inches; total Council receipts, 36,509 fathoms and 69 inches; Council investments, 9174 fathoms 53 inches; in Council wampum belts, 11,843 fathoms and 4 inches.

The Trustees of the Beneficiary Fund showed that the membership had dwindled to 97, and that the total balance on hand in the reserve fund and general fund was 1046 fathoms and 55 inches.

The chiefs elected and appointed and raised up for the ensuing term were as follows:—

Great Incohonee, Thos. K. Donnalley, P. G. S., Pennsylvania.
Great Senior Sagamore, Thos. E. Peckinpaugh, P. G. S., Ohio.
Great Junior Sagamore, Andrew H. Paton, P. G. S., Massachusetts.
Great Prophet, Thomas J. Francis, P. G. I., New Jersey.
Great Chief of Records, Charles C. Conley, P. G. I., Pennsylvania.
Great Keeper of Wampum, Joseph Pyle, P. G. I., Delaware.
Great Tocakon, George E. Green, P. G. S., New York.
Great Minewa, James Johnson, P. S., Colorado.

For the first time in the history of the Great Council there was but one nominee for each chieftaincy, and each brother nominated was unanimously elected.

Action was taken by the G. C. U. S. at this council without precedent in the history of that body. It was the grant by unanimous vote, of the title and honors of Past Great Incohonee to Past Great Sachem and Great Chief of Records Charles C. Conley, of Pennsylvania, for meritorious service.

The Committee on History of the Order reported that a conference had been held with Brother Hascall, who had signified his acquiescence in the terms suggested by the Great Council, and who further desired that the History should include the Digest of the Order. The Committee thought this could not be done without permission from the G. C. U. S., which said committee recommended should be granted. The report of the committee was adopted and the requisite permission given.

A charter was granted for the Great Council of South Carolina.

The Great Council adopted the report of the Committee on State of the Order in relation to "a mock adoption ceremony" and other burlesque ceremonies to the effect that "such burlesque ceremonies detract from the dignity of, and tend to lower the Order, in the estimation of those not connected with the Improved Order of Red Men, and should be condemned."

Similar action was taken in connection with gift concerts and similar enterprises given under the name and auspices of the Order.

Cleveland, Ohio, was selected as the place of kindling the next great sun council fire.

The Committee on Diploma made a report and presented a design for an Official Diploma, which was adopted.

A committee of three was appointed to revise and codify the Constitution and Laws of the G. C. U. S., including the laws governing the Beneficiary Fund.

A feature of the entertainment of the chiefs and members at this council was a grand exemplification of the work of the various degrees at Mechanics' Hall under the direction of the Great Council of Massachusetts, with the Great Council of the United States as special guests and in the presence of 5000 members of the Order. The work was very finely rendered, the various degrees being exemplified by the following Tribes: —

WINNEPURKET TRIBE, No. 55, of Lynn, Adoption Degree.
KENNEPAUKENIT TRIBE, No. 58, of Natick, Hunter's Degree.
WAPITI TRIBE, No. 65, of Boston, Warrior's Degree.
AGAWAM TRIBE, No. 5, of Tapleyville, Chief's Degree.

The Great Council adopted very complimentary resolutions of thanks for the courtesies extended by the members of the Order in Massachusetts.

The laws governing the Beneficiary Fund were changed so that the Great Chief of Records and Great Keeper of Wampum and one member of the Fund, who shall also be a member of the G. C. U. S., should constitute the Board of Trustees.

1891.

The council fire of the G. C. U. S. was kindled at Cleveland, Ohio, on the 8th of Corn moon, G. S. D. 400, Great Incohonee Thomas K. Donnalley presiding. His Honor William S. Rose, mayor of the city, in warm and cordial words welcomed the members and their ladies to the city of Cleveland, and the remarks of welcome to the G. C. U. S. were responded to by Past Great Incohonee Charles H. Litchman, of Massachusetts.

O. S. Cheney, Great Sachem of Ohio, delivered an address of welcome on behalf of the Order in the State, which was appropriately responded to by Great Incohonee Donnalley.

The council fire was then formally kindled,

The Committee on Credentials reported that credentials had been received from 28 Great Councils.

The Great Incohonee submitted his longtalk, in which he reported the institution of the Great Council of South Carolina at Columbus on the 17th of Beaver moon, G. S. D. 399 (November 17, 1890).

He also reported the institution of the Great Council of Nebraska at Lincoln on the 9th of Buck moon, G. S. D. 400 (July 9, 1891).

He had granted dispensations for two additional Tribes in Washington, and another Tribe in Oregon, and had personally introduced the Order into the Indian Territory by the institution of Choctaw Tribe, No. 1, at Hartshorne, Gaines County, on the 9th of Hot moon, G. S. D. 400 (June 9, 1891).

He reported action taken by him concerning a spurious organization which had appropriated a part of the name of the Order, and which had been started by an expelled member of the Improved Order of Red Men.

He spoke of the rapid growth of the Degree of Pocahontas.

During the great sun he had met with members of the Order in 21 reservations.

He expressed regret that the resolution of the Great Council in G. S. D. 386 (1877), for the collection and preservation of trophies and antiquities of the Aborigines of America had not been more fully carried out, and he urged the various State Great Councils to carry out the spirit of this resolution while yet such trophies and antiquities could be procured.

The Great Chief of Records submitted an exhaustive report of the condition of the Order and the transactions of his chieftaincy during the great sun.

Concerning the Beneficiary Fund he said it was gradually dying out, but had honestly filled its obligations to the widows and orphans.

From the statistical abstract, accompanying his report, we glean the following information: Total number of Great Councils, 29; total number of Tribes, 1244; adopted, 22,954; reinstated, 963; admitted by card, 901; suspended, 11,921; rejected, 1064; expelled, 157; withdrawn by card, 1403; died, 857; total number of members, 107,644; Past Great Sachems,

325; Past Sachems, 13,258; amount expended for relief of members, 248,547 fathoms and 21 inches; expended for relief of widows and orphans, 6457 fathoms and 70 inches; expended for burial of the dead, 59,984 fathoms and 92 inches; expended for other purposes, 419,299 fathoms and 61 inches; total Tribal receipts, 958,520 fathoms and 46 inches; Tribal investments, 866,564 fathoms and 32 inches; in Tribal wampum belts, 392,470 fathoms and 22 inches.

From the statistical abstract, accompanying the reports from the Councils of Pocahontas, we glean the following information: Total number of Councils, 194; adopted, 4636; admitted by card, 84; reinstated, 162; suspended, 1367; expelled, 18; withdrawn by card, 386; deceased, 83; rejected, 111; Past Chiefs, 630; total number of members, 14,168; expended for relief of members, 4323 fathoms and 92 inches; expended for burial of the dead, 994 fathoms and 80 inches; Council receipts, 41,769 fathoms and 49 inches; invested by Councils, 29,166 fathoms and 56 inches.

The Great Chief of Records also reported that, in accordance with the authority given at the last great sun council, the Diploma of the Order had been perfected and issued.

From the longtalk of the Great Keeper of Wampum, we learn that the wampum received during the great sun was 16,812 fathoms and 84 inches. The Permanent Fund had increased to 2474 fathoms and 88 inches. The total funds of the G. C. U. S. amounted to 19,267 fathoms and 24 inches.

The Special Committee on History of the Order reported that a careful collation of all the material at hand had been made, abstracts of the entire records of the Great Council prepared, and the foundation laid for a most thorough and exhaustive history of the Order. This matter had been placed in the hands of the publisher, by the committee, and it was hoped that during the ensuing great sun the history would be published.

The Committee on Revision of the Laws reported a thorough and complete revision of the Constitution and Laws governing the Order, together with a code of procedure to govern trials. This report was considered by the Great Council, amended in various parts, and finally adopted as amended.

Various propositions having been received for translating the ritual, the Great Council voted that it was inexpedient to have the ritual translated in other than as at present, the German and French languages.

A very pleasing feature of the gathering at this council was the presentation to Past Great Sachem M. A. Marks, and to his wife and child, on behalf of the members of the G. C. U. S., of beautiful testimonials, as tokens of appreciation of their efforts to make pleasant the visit of the Great Council to Cleveland.

Resolutions were adopted as expressive of the sentiment of the Great Council towards the Chieftains' League in its present form.

It was voted that the next great sun council fire be kindled in the hunting grounds of Atlanta, Ga.

The Great Council, having been invited to participate in a jubilee celebration to be given in the hunting grounds of Philadelphia, Pa., on the 12th, 13th, and 14th of Travelling moon, G. S. D. 400 (October 12, 13, and 14, 1891), the Great Council adopted the following:—

The undersigned, members of the committee to which was referred the matter of the contemplated "Jubilee Celebration," in the hunting grounds of Philadelphia, Pa., on the 12th, 13th, and 14th of Travelling moon, beg leave to report as follows:—

The Great Sun of Discovery, that within which Christopher Columbus discovered America, is entitled to appropriate commemoration by all who dwell upon the land which he made known to the world. The national government and the various States will join in a World's Fair, as a proper recognition of the vast importance of that great epoch in the history of the world, and of its far-reaching influences on the destinies of mankind.

When Columbus knelt on the soil of the newly discovered land, and returned thanks to the God of his faith for safe deliverance and the successful issue of his voyage, he was met and welcomed by a strange and hitherto unknown race, peaceful, and in their way industrious, contented, and happy. They owned and controlled this great American continent, the "Original People" of our land. Upon the manners, tradition, and customs of that race, which will soon be known only in tradition and history, our Order has been founded. What more fitting, then, than an appropriate observance by the Improved Order of Red Men, of that great historical event which gave to the nations of the earth its greatest and grandest member? We feel and believe that the Great Council of Pennsylvania is entitled to all credit and honor for its prompt recognition of the importance of this event, and as the largest of our great reservations, for its generosity in undertaking the responsible duty of observing the Great Sun of Discovery 400, in a manner at once suitable to the occasion and honorable to the Order. We congratulate the Tribes of that jurisdiction upon the opportunity presented to them to make in the sight of the palefaces of that reservation a demonstration that cannot fail, under the prudent and intelligent management selected, to win the favor of the paleface nation, and to gain unbounded honor and credit to themselves and to the Order at large. We also think that the least this Great Council should do is to be represented at the proposed gathering, to the end that the whole Order may officially recognize an event of such great importance. We therefore present and recommend the adoption of the following : —

Resolved, That the Great Council of the United States sends fraternal greeting to the Order in Pennsylvania, and commends its energy and prudent forethought in arranging for an appropriate observance of Great Sun of Discovery 400, a movement which, successfully conducted, will return great honor to our whole Order.

Resolved, That the great chiefs of the Great Council of the United States, be and are hereby authorized to attend said commemorative jubilee as the official representatives of this Great Council, and of the Order at large.

Resolved, That the members of the Order, within convenient distance, are fraternally urged to cordially and earnestly co-operate with the management for the purpose of making this celebration one of the memorable events in our Order, and one that shall redound to the honor and prosperity of the Improved Order of Red Men.

In this connection it may be said that the jubilee was held as indicated, and passed off to the great credit of the Order in that reservation, and to the great satisfaction of all who were fortunate enough to participate.

Charters were ordered issued to the Great Councils and Tribes that had been instituted during the interim.

While the report of the Committee on Revision of the Laws was under consideration, a motion was made to repeal the article establishing a Permanent Fund. The matter was referred to a special committee to report a law devoting the fund to the building of a home for widows and orphans of the Order. In accordance with this the law was reported and unanimously adopted, which appears elsewhere in the full Constitution as printed. In this connection and for the purpose of bringing the matter to the attention of the Order in a proper and official manner, the Great Council unanimously adopted the following : —

Unto all men it is appointed once to die. It is proper that the living should in a fitting manner commemorate the virtues of the dead and give proper tribute to their memory. It seems right, therefore, that our Order perform this duty by setting apart one sun each great sun upon which may be observed the memory of the dead. For this purpose be it

Resolved, That each State Great Council be, and is hereby urged to set apart one sun in each great sun, at such time as local climate and other considerations may suggest, which sun shall be known as "Donation Day," upon which the members of the Order, through their respective Tribes, either by strewing flowers upon the graves of departed brothers, holding councils of sorrow, or in such other appropriate manner as each Tribe may determine, shall honor the memory of their dead.

Resolved, That upon Donation Day each Tribe be requested to make a donation, either by appropriation or voluntary contribution, the sum so collected to be forwarded through the Great Chief of Records of the State to the Great Chief of Records of the United States for investment by the Trustees of the Permanent Fund for the Widows' and Orphans' Home.

Resolved, That, for the purpose herein mentioned, Tribes are hereby authorized to make appropriations from their wampum belts.

Resolved, That each Great Council, and in the interval between the adoption of these resolutions and a council thereof, the Great Chiefs of said Great Council shall have authority to adopt and promulgate regulations needed for the successful conduct of the objects herein contemplated.

The Committee on Beneficiary having reported in favor of distributing to the members of the Fund the amount on hand in the general and reserve funds, the Great Incohonee ruled that the Great Council had no power to take away the vested rights of a member of the Fund, and that the dissolution of the Association could only be affected by the members themselves.

The Representatives from Georgia extended a cordial invitation to the members of the G. C. U. S. to bring with them at the next great sun council their wives and daughters, assuring them that the citizens of Atlanta and the Red Men of Georgia would spare no pains nor leave anything undone to make their stay a pleasant and delightful one in the beautiful Southland.

The Special Committee on Revision of the Laws was given permission to revise the Digest.

Probably no council of the Great Council in recent years had been of such great importance to the Order as that held at Cleveland. In the revision of the laws submitted and amended by the Great Council and then adopted, many radical changes were made, yet all inspired by a desire to gain for the Order the best possible good. The rapid growth during the preceding great sun had supplied the wampum belt of the Great Council with funds adequate for all legitimate purposes of the Order. The spirit of economy was manifested in a desire to reduce the amount of *per capita* tax; but after a full consideration of the matter it was deemed advisable to continue the income of the G. C. U. S. at the old rate, in order that the growth and prosperity so pleasing to all may not be retarded, but that ample provision may be made for still greater prosperity in the immediate future.

1892.

The Great Council assembled in the Senate Chamber of the State Capitol building, Atlanta, Ga., on the 13th of Corn moon, G. S. D. 401.

Addresses of welcome were delivered by Past Great Sachem R. T. Daniel; Hon. F. D. Bradwell, State Commissioner of Education; Hon. M. A. Hemphill, Mayor of the city; and Y. A. Wright, Great Sachem.

Responses were made by Great Incohonee Donnalley, and other Great Chiefs and members of the G. C. U. S.

The Great Chiefs, 93 Representatives, 4 Past Great Incohonees, and 15 Past Great Sachems, representing 30 State Great Councils, responded to roll-call.

The longtalk of the Great Incohonee reported the institution of 2 Tribes in North Carolina; 2 in Wyoming; 1 in Utah; 3 in Washington; and 6 in Oregon.

He recommended the adoption of a badge for veteran Red Men, to be worn by those who had held membership for 21 successive great suns; and the selection of a date on which the members of the Order might meet at the World's Fair, to make a demonstration in honor of Discovery Day — the date to be designated *Red Men's Sun.*

He reported visits to many reservations and suggested increased appropriation for his successors.

He also reported that the Beneficiary Fund membership had become reduced to 72, and recommended legislation which would close its affairs.

He commented on the weakness of the funeral and seven suns benefit system of the Order, and suggested that radical changes were necessary to bring the dues charged and benefits promised into scientific relation to each other.

He also recommended the appointment of one or more great chiefs to exemplify the work when called upon.

The longtalk of the Great Chief of Records showed that 349 fathoms 15 inches of wampum had been contributed by the Order for the Permanent Fund for the Widows' and Orphans' Home. The Beneficiary Fund receipts had been 150 fathoms; expenditures, 126 fathoms. The summary of statistics was as follows: Number of Great Councils, 30; Tribes, 1424; adopted, 28,619; reinstated, 1125; admitted by card, 1202; suspended, 13,407; expelled, 172; withdrawn, 1809; died, 1136; present membership, 122,314; Tribal receipts, 1,002,972 fathoms 96 inches; expended for relief of brothers, 298,091 fathoms 23 inches; relief of widows and orphans, 14,280 fathoms 19 inches; burial of dead, 73,073 fathoms 41 inches; other expenditures, 492,602 fathoms 59 inches; total funds of Tribes, invested and in wampum belts, 1,220,576 fathoms 86 inches.

Number of Councils, Degree of Pocahontas, 241; membership, 16,813; adopted, 5040; admitted by card, 88; reinstated, 221; suspended, 1952; expelled, 16; withdrawn, 721; died, 119; Council receipts, 45,644 fathoms 68 inches; expended for relief of members, 8011 fathoms 89 inches; burial of dead, 1400 fathoms 20 inches; other expenditures, 24,021 fathoms 98 inches; invested and in wampum belts, 42,783 fathoms 54 inches.

The longtalk of the Great Keeper of Wampum presented a statement of assets of the G. C. U. S. as follows: Balance for contingent expenses, 18,479 fathoms 33 inches; Permanent Fund, 3237 fathoms 2 inches; Beneficiary Fund, 1260 fathoms 34 inches; Yellow Fever Fund, 659 fathoms 59 inches.

The committee to collate the material for the Official History of the Order was continued to such time as its work should be completed.

The proposition that all Tribal work should be transacted in the Chief's Degree was ruled out of order as not properly before the Great Council.

A motion to permit adoption of candidates under 21 great suns of age was defeated.

A motion to permit the wearing of a badge in lieu of regalia in Tribal councils was defeated.

An amendment to the Constitution was adopted whereby the

Committee on Constitution and Laws became a standing committee to act during the recesses of the Great Council.

A Badge for Veteran Red Men, as suggested by the Great Incohonee, was adopted, and patented for the exclusive use of the G. C. U. S. An engraving of the badge is herewith presented.

It was voted that the next great sun council fire be kindled in Des Moines, Iowa.

It was voted to be unwise and impolitic to translate or print the rituals in any language other than those in which they are now printed.

Charters were granted to the Tribes instituted the past great sun, and for a Great Council to be instituted in Oregon.

A duplicate charter was granted to the Great Council of Illinois to replace the original, lost or destroyed.

The Great Incohonee ruled that the reservations of Minnesota, Wisconsin, and Ontario had reverted to the control of the Great Council of the United States.

The Committee on Revision was authorized to prepare and have printed a new form for raising up chiefs; and also to issue a new Digest revised to date.

The same committee was ordered to present a form for indoor use at funerals of members of the Order.

A complete revision of the laws, for government of the Degree of Pocahontas, and of Tribes under the immediate jurisdiction of the G. C. U. S. was adopted.

A special committee was appointed to report at the next great sun council upon the subject of Dues and Benefits, and to present a plan of operations.

It was voted that if the members of the Beneficiary Fund will unanimously consent, the same shall be dissolved, and its reserve funds shall be equitably distributed to its members.

The Great Incohonee was authorized to appoint "Exemplifiers," to instruct the Order in the ritualistic work.

The Committee on Revision was directed to revise the ceremony for dedication of wigwams.

The chiefs for the ensuing term were elected and appointed, and raised up as follows: —

Great Incohonee,	THOMAS E. PECKINPAUGH, P. G. S.,	Ohio.
Great Senior Sagamore,	ANDREW H. PATON, P. G. S.,	Massachusetts.
Great Junior Sagamore,	ROBERT T. DANIEL, P. G. S.,	Georgia.
Great Prophet,	THOMAS K. DONNALLEY, P. G. I.,	Pennsylvania.
Great Chief of Records,	CHARLES C. CONLEY, P. G. I.,	Pennsylvania.
Great Keeper of Wampum,	JOSEPH PYLE, P. G. I.,	Delaware.
Great Tocakon,	JOSEPH C. SUIT, P. G. S.,	Indiana.
Great Minewa,	E. D. WILEY, P. G. S.,	Iowa.
Great Guard of Forest,	GEORGE T. FOWLER, P. G. S.,	Maryland.

With the record thus presented of the council held at Atlanta, ends the written record of the G. C. U. S. down to the latest date previous to the publication of this History. It leaves the Order in the full tide of prosperity, with the probability that the reports to be received for the fiscal year ending June 30, 1893, will reach fully 140,000 members. The condition of the Great Council of the United States was never as good, there is ample wampum for all the legitimate uses, the Order is stronger than ever in its history, and the future looks bright and prosperous for still larger additions in membership, and far wider influence and prosperity.

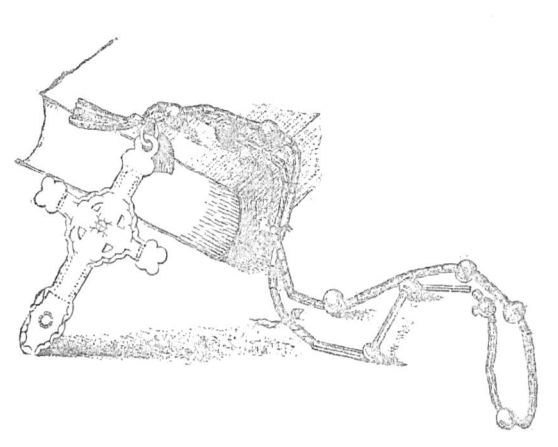

THOMAS E. PECKINPAUGH, GREAT INCOHONEE.

CHAPTER IX.

STATE GREAT COUNCILS AND TRIBES.

The complete history of each State reservation, under the jurisdiction of the Great Council of the United States, would be largely a volume of repetitions of experiences; covering, of course, periods which vary in length, and results which differ in measure; but nearly all having the same general characteristics. The original Great Councils have made almost uninterrupted progress numerically, financially, in social influence, and in all that give stability and popularity to the Improved Order of Red Men. The great majority of those admitted later have likewise prospered and continued. A few have struggled for a time in vain or misdirected effort. Some have begun anew and built success over the ashes of preceding failure. Out of the 33 States in which Great Council fires have been kindled since the beginning, 30 have at this time Great Council fires burning brightly; dispensation has been granted for another; and in several States and Territories, Tribes are flourishing with prospects of early applications from some of them for Great Council charters.

The record of the Great Council of the United States covers the legislative action which governed all, and suggests the trail over which all have journeyed. This chapter, therefore, deals only with the brief statistical outlines of State beginnings and present conditions.

Maryland. — This was the first Great Council instituted; the date being 20th of Flower moon, G. S. 5595 (May 20, 1835). On the 14th of Worm moon, G. S. 5598, it became an incorporated body under the laws of the State of Maryland, and claimed, and, as the Great Council of Maryland, exercised, supreme authority over the Order until the organization of the Grand Council of the United States in G. S. 5607 (1847).

The standing of the Tribes in the reservation on the 30th of Hot moon, G. S. D. 401, was as follows: —

Number of Tribes	54
Membership	4,110
Past Sachems	792
Past Great Sachems	25
Past Great Incohonees	3
Wampum invested	75,689 fathoms 57 inches.
Wampum in belts	7,923 fathoms 78 inches.
Total funds	67,765 fathoms 79 inches.

Pennsylvania. — This is the second reservation into which the Improved Order of Red Men was introduced; it being a fact of record that John F. Weishampel, of Logan Tribe, No. 1, of Baltimore, having been authorized so to do in G. S. 5599 (1839), instituted Tammany Tribe, No. 1, of Shippensburg, Pa., probably in the same grand sun. There is no further record of the existence of this Tribe, except a reference to it in the Maryland records in 5602 (1842), and the inference is that its life was of very brief duration. The Order in the reservation was revived on the 14th of Hot moon, G. S. 5607 (1847), by the institution of Tecumseh Tribe, No. 1, at Norristown. The next grand sun, Metamora Tribe, No. 2, of Lancaster; Leni Lenape Tribe, No. 3, Kuquenaku Tribe, No. 4, and Pocahontas Tribe, No. 5, of Philadelphia, were instituted. In G. S. 5609 (1849), Mohegan Tribe, of Waynesboro, was instituted. On the petition of Tecumseh, Leni Lenape, Kuquenaku, and Pocahontas Tribes, a charter was granted by the Great Council of the United States, in Plant moon, G. S. 5609, and on the 23d of Flower moon, the Great Council of Pennsylvania was instituted, being the fourth in numerical order. The reservation soon took first rank in number of members, and has continued to maintain the lead.

The standing of the Tribes in the reservation on the 30th of Hot moon, G. S. D. 401, was as follows: —

Number of Tribes	317
Membership	30,495
Past Sachems	4,982
Past Great Sachems	25
Past Great Incohonees	3
Wampum invested	401,454 fathoms 61 inches.
Wampum in belts	37,860 fathoms 75 inches.
Total funds	439,315 fathoms 36 inches.

Virginia. — This is the third reservation into which the Order was introduced, Brother Weishampel having instituted Pocahontas Tribe, No. 1, at Wheeling, in grand sun 5599. There is no further record of this Tribe, except the fact that a member of it was authorized the next grand sun to institute Natchez Tribe, No. 1, Mississippi. In grand sun 5605 (1845), Osceola Tribe, No. 2, was instituted at Alexandria, and later placed under the jurisdiction of the Great Council of District of Columbia, which became No. 1, of Virginia, when the Great Council fire of that State was kindled. Shawnee Tribe, No. 5, of Winchester, was instituted in Corn moon, G. S. 5606 (1846), and soon after Mohawk Tribe, No. 6, was instituted, both, by and under the jurisdiction of the Great Council of the District of Columbia. These Tribes became respectively Nos. 2 and 3 of the Great Council of Virginia. The Great Council of Virginia was the first instituted by the Great Council of the United States, and was the third Great Council in numerical order. Its first council fire was kindled in Buck moon, 5607 (1847). The three Tribes to whom the charter was issued were Osceola, No. 1; Shawnee, No. 2; and Mohawk, No. 3. The Great Council was not represented in the G. C. U. S. during the period 5621 to 5624 inclusive, but was reorganized and again admitted in G. S. 5625 (1865).

The standing of the Tribes in the reservation on the 30th of Hot moon, G. S. D. 401, was as follows: —

Number of Tribes	47
Membership	2,678
Past Sachems	440
Past Great Sachems	10
Wampum invested	1,066 fathoms 96 inches.
Wampum in belts	17,111 fathoms 86 inches.
Total funds	18,178 fathoms 82 inches.

Mississippi. — The records of the Great Council of Maryland show that Brother Pailey Sharp, of Wheeling, Va., was commissioned in Corn moon, G. S. 5600 (1840), to institute Natchez Tribe, No. 1, at Vicksburg, Miss. This would make that reservation the fourth in which the Order was planted. There is no further record of this Tribe, nor is the reservation mentioned again until G. S. 5619, at which time we learn that a

Tribe, of the same name and number, had been instituted during the preceding grand sun at Natchez, but the fact had not been mentioned at the previous grand sun council. Tahlequah Tribe, No. 2, and Choctaw, No. 3, were instituted in G. S. D. 379. Tishomingo Tribe, No. 4, was instituted at Corinth, on the 7th of Hot moon, G. S. D. 381. In G. S. D. 382, four Tribes were instituted — Iuka, No. 5, of Iuka, Minnehaha, No. 6, of Kossuth, Chickasaw, No. 7, of Rienzi, and Osceola, No. 8, of Burnsville. Red Cloud Tribe, No. 9, was instituted at Chapel Hill Meeting-House, on the 10th of Snow moon, G. S. D. 383. The council fire of Mohawk Tribe, No. 10, was kindled at Pittsboro, in Flower moon, G. S. D. 384; and in the same great sun, Hiawatha Tribe, No. 11, was instituted at Coffeeville. Choctaw, Tishomingo, and Chickasaw Tribes became extinct this great sun. At the Great Sun Council of the G. C. U. S. in G. S. D. 387, all the Tribes were reported as extinct, because of a combination of circumstances, the sickness of the Vice Great Incohonee in charge, and the disorganized political conditions. No attempt has since been made to establish the Order in Mississippi.

Louisiana. — This appears to be the fifth reservation into which the Order was introduced. Brother Pailey Sharp, who had been, nearly three grand suns before, commissioned to kindle the council fire of Natchez Tribe, No. 1, of Mississippi, with five others, petitioned in Worm moon, G. S. 5603 (1843), for a charter to institute Mohican Tribe, No. 1, of Bayou Sara, La. The charter was granted by the Great Council of Maryland. This Tribe, if instituted, appears to have failed of continuance, there being no further record of it. In 13 grand suns from the time Brother Sharp and others petitioned for Mohican Tribe, No. 1, of Bayou Sara, Osyka Tribe, No. 1, was instituted at New Orleans. During the following grand suns, the Order prospered, and a preliminary organization of a great council was effected in Snow moon, G. S. 5620 (1860). The civil war which soon followed seems to have prevented the formal institution of the Great Council, and to have caused the disbandment of all its Tribes except Osyka, No. 1, and for a time the Order was dormant in this State. Tecumseh Tribe, No. 4, of Baton Rouge, was instituted in G. S. 5625 (1865), and

STATE GREAT COUNCILS AND TRIBES. 427

the Order in Louisiana began again to increase. Narragansett Tribe, No. 5, was instituted at New Orleans in G. S. D. 376. Another Tribe was instituted in G. S. D. 377, but its council fire was allowed to go out. Tribes Nos. 6 and 7 were instituted in G. S. D. 378. All these except Osyka Tribe, No. 1, and Osceola Tribe, No. 7, soon became extinct; but in G. S. D. 380, Tunica Tribe, No. 8, of Shreveport, was instituted. On account of the yellow-fever epidemic in G. S. D. 384, all but Osyka Tribe, No. 1, became extinct. In G. S. D. 388, the council fire of Osceola Tribe was rekindled. Tuscarora Tribe, No. 9, was instituted in G. S. D. 390. On the 3d of Cold moon, G. S. D. 391, Pocahontas Tribe, No. 10, was instituted at New Orleans.

The Great Council fire of Louisiana was rekindled on the 30th of Cold moon, G. S. D. 391. The hunting grounds of Texas and Arkansas are under the jurisdiction of the Great Council of Louisiana.

The standing of the Tribes of this reservation on the 30th of Hot moon, G. S. D. 401, was as follows:—

Number of Tribes	8
Membership	417
Past Sachems	88
Past Great Sachems	8
Wampum invested	1,020 fathoms.
Wampum in belt	2,303 fathoms 2 inches.
Total funds	3,323 fathoms 2 inches.

District of Columbia. — The first Tribe to be instituted in this reservation was Powhatan Tribe, No. 1, of Washington. Its council fire was kindled in Cold moon, G. S. 5605 (1845), by Past Great Sachem Louis Bonsal and Past Sachem John L. Booker, of Maryland. Anacostia Tribe, No. 3, of Washington, was instituted soon after. On the petition of these two Tribes and Osceola Tribe of Alexandria, Va., the Great Council of the District of Columbia was instituted on the 4th of Beaver moon, G. S. 5605. This Great Council was subordinate to the Great Council of Maryland, and was required to obtain its permission to institute Tribes in Virginia. The Order grew very rapidly in this reservation at this time, and the Great Council of Virginia was an early result of its efforts. In G. S. 5619 (1859), the Great Council fire of the District of Columbia, by reason of internal dissensions became extinct, but it was rekindled in G. S. 5624 (1864), and has burned continuously from that date.

The standing of the Tribes in the reservation on the 30th of Hot moon, G. S. D. 401, was as follows:—

Number of Tribes	6
Membership	300
Past Sachems	70
Past Great Sachems	10
Wampum invested	366 fathoms 55 inches.
Wampum in belts	1,108 fathoms 54 inches.
Total funds	1,475 fathoms 9 inches.

Delaware.— Delaware Tribe, No. 1, of Wilmington, was instituted on the 31st of Hunting moon, G. S. 5607 (1847). Osceola Tribe, No. 2, of Delaware City, was instituted on the 24th of Hunting moon, G. S. 5612 (1852); Keokuk Tribe, No. 3, of Wilmington, on the 15th of Beaver moon, G. S. 5613 (1853); and Cherokee, No. 4, of Wilmington, on the 10th of Beaver moon, G. S. 5616 (1856). The Great Council fire was kindled on the 19th of Beaver moon, G. S. 5616, by Joseph Pyle, Vice Great Incohonee. It has had continuous and successful existence.

The standing of the Tribes in the reservation on the 30th of Hot moon, G. S. D. 401, was as follows:—

Number of Tribes	28
Membership	2,536
Past Sachems	442
Past Great Sachems	20
Past Great Incohonees	1
Wampum invested	20,721 fathoms 73 inches.
Wampum in belts	4,755 fathoms 46 inches.
Total funds	25,477 fathoms 19 inches.

New York.— The first four Tribes in this reservation were all instituted in Sturgeon moon, G. S. 5608 (1848), the four council fires being kindled on the same sun by W. G. S. Incohonee Latham in person. Many of the petitioners were up to date associated as Tribes of the "Order of Red Men," without being aware of the existence of the Improved Order of Red Men. These Tribes were Oneida, No. 1, Osceola, No. 2, and Oneactah, No. 4, of New York City, and Metamora, No. 3, of Brooklyn.

In Travelling moon, G. S. 5610 (1850), the Great Council was instituted. The Great Council was declared defunct in G. S. 5611 (1851), when but one Tribe remained. Two grand suns later this Tribe also went out of existence. The Order was revived in New York by the institution of Metamora Tribe, on the 1st of Beaver moon, G. S. 5614 (1854); but was again reported extinct in G. S. 5617 (1857).

A third and successful attempt to plant the Order in this State was made in G. S. D. 380, when Mohawk Tribe, No. 1, and Cherokee Tribe, No. 2, of New York City were instituted. Montauk Tribe, No. 3, of Williamsburg; Wyoming, No. 4, Mendota, No. 5, Metamora, No. 6, Manhattan, No. 7, and Tecumseh, No. 8, all of New York City, and Mineola, No. 9, of Brooklyn, followed in rapid succession, and were all reported to the great sun council of the G. C. U. S. in G. S. D. 381. On the 19th sun, Sturgeon moon, G. S. D. 381, the Great Council fire was kindled, and from that time the Improved Order of Red Men has increased and prospered in New York. The reservation of Ontario was at one time under the jurisdiction of this Great Council.

The standing of the Tribes in the reservation on the 30th of Hot moon, G. S. D. 401, was as follows:—

Number of Tribes	160
Membership	11,110
Past Sachems	1,030
Past Great Sachems	18
Wampum invested	187,920 fathoms 1 inch.
Wampum in belt	25,734 fathoms 70 inches.
Total funds	213,654 fathoms 71 inches.

New Jersey. — The first Tribe instituted in New Jersey was Arreseoah, No. 1, at Newark, in Worm moon, G. S. 5610 (1850). Leni Lenape Tribe, No. 2, of Camden, was instituted soon after. Then followed Red Bird Tribe, No. 3, of Newark, and Chemanitou, No. 4, and Moax, No. 5, of Trenton. The records of the G. C. U. S. relate that the Great Council fire was kindled first in Travelling moon, G. S. 5611 (1851), and that, because of a misunderstanding which prevented the co-operation of Leni Lenape Tribe at this date, a reorganization and reinstitution were effected on the 26th of Hunting moon, G. S. 5611. On the other hand, it is indicated by the records of the Great Council of New Jersey, that the date of institution of the Great Council was on the 26th of Hunting moon, G. S. 5610 (1850). The Order grew slowly in this reservation, and at the end of 30 great suns had only reached 2100 members. From that number, however, the advance has been very rapid, and to-day New Jersey is second among Great Councils in number of members.

The standing of the Tribes in the reservation on the 30th of Hot moon, G. S. D. 401, was as follows:—

Number of Tribes	143
Membership	15,644
Past Sachems	1,598
Past Great Sachems	20
Past Great Incohonees	2
Wampum invested	187,920 fathoms 1 inch.
Wampum in belts	25,734 fathoms 70 inches.
Total funds	213,654 fathoms 71 inches.

Ohio.— The first two Tribes in this reservation were Miami, No. 1, of Cincinnati, and Tecumseh, No. 2, of Springfield, both instituted in G. S. 5611 (1851). Algonquin Tribe, No. 3, of Columbus, was instituted the following grand sun. Great Council charter was granted for Ohio, in G. S. 5612 (1852). Ohio thus became the pioneer Great Council of the West, and has grown and flourished, until now it is among the strong jurisdictions of the Order. The hunting grounds of Kentucky are included in the Great Council reservation.

The standing of the Tribes in the reservation on the 30th of Hot moon, G. S. D. 401, was as follows:—

Number of Tribes	75
Membership	5,117
Past Sachems	793
Past Great Sachems	20
Wampum invested	30,290 fathoms 51 inches.
Wampum in belts	17,405 fathoms 82 inches.
Total funds	47,696 fathoms 33 inches.

North Carolina.— John L. Booker, Great Chief of Records of the United States, kindled the council fire of the first Tribe in this reservation on the 9th of Travelling moon, G. S. 5613 (1853). This Tribe was Osceola, No. 1, of Fayetteville, which lived only one grand sun. Between G. S. 5613 and G. S. 5618 (1858), a second Tribe was probably instituted and went out of existence; because the Order is reported as "revived" in that State in G. S. 5618 by the institution of Weccamaw Tribe, No. 3, at Wilmington. Again, however, the council fires failed to burn, and in G. S. 5620 (1860) the Order was declared extinct in North Carolina. Wyoming Tribe, No. 4, was instituted at Wilmington on the 28th of Buck moon, G. S. D. 382. The next Tribe was Black Hawk Tribe, No. 5, of Wilmington, instituted on the 1st of Flower moon, G. S. D. 383. In G. S. D. 384, three tribes were instituted — Pee Dee, No. 6, at Laurinburg, Pocahontas, No. 7, at Brooklyn, and Matchepungo, No. 8, at Fayetteville. The council fires of all except Wyoming Tribe, No. 4, were reported quenched in G. S. D. 387. Wyoming Tribe surrendered in G. S. D. 391, but in that great sun two other Tribes were instituted — Matchepungo, No. 8, revived at Fayetteville, and Cherokee, No. 9, of Wilmington. On the 21st of Sturgeon moon, G. S. D. 397, the council fire of Osceola Tribe, No. 1, was relighted at Raleigh. Matchepungo Tribe, No. 8, had, in the meantime, again disbanded. In the following great sun, Chippewa Tribe, No. 2, was instituted at South Mills. Junaluska Tribe, No. 3, of Asheville, and Sapona Tribe, No. 4, of Greensboro, were instituted in Plant moon, G. S. D. 399. Eyota Tribe, No. 5, of Wilmington, was instituted in Cold moon, G. S. D. 401, and soon after, the council fire of Narragansett Tribe, No. 6, was lighted at Old Trap. The Tribes reported in good standing on the 30th of Hot moon, G. S. D. 401, were Chippewa, No. 2, Eyota, No. 5, Narragansett, No. 6, and Cherokee, No. 9.

Kentucky. — Chickasaw Tribe, No. 1, of Newport, and Black Hawk, No. 2, of Covington, were both instituted in G. S. 5612 (1852). Pocahontas Tribe, No. 3, of Newport, and Kentucky, No. 4, of Louisville, were instituted in the following grand sun. The Great Council fire was lighted on the 9th of Sturgeon moon, G. S. 5614 (1854). The Order in Kentucky flourished many great suns, but finally began to lose interest and membership, and was not represented in the G. C. U. S. after G. S. D. 389. In G. S. D. 395, but one Tribe was reported in the State — Miami, No. 17, of Newport. The Great Council fire had long before ceased to burn. In G. S. D. 397, Kentucky was placed under the jurisdiction of the Great Council of Ohio, and the standing of its Tribes on the 30th of Hot moon, G. S. D. 401, is included in the statement given for that reservation. During its existence as a Great Council, Kentucky furnished two Great Incohonees to the G. C. U. S.

Indiana.— The Order had a brief existence in this reservation from Snow moon, G. S. 5614 (1854), to G. S. 5617 (1857). In Snow moon, G. S. 5614, the council fire of Seneca Tribe, No. 1, was kindled at Metamora. Between that time and Flower moon, G. S. 5615 (1855), four Tribes were instituted at Laurel, Terre Haute, Edinburg, and Franklin. A Great Council was instituted on the 11th of Flower moon; but in two grand suns the Tribes all ceased to work, and the Great Council surrendered its charter. In G. S. 5619 (1859), the Order was resuscitated in the jurisdiction by the rekindling of the council fire of Cherokee Tribe, No. 4, of Edinburg, and the institution of Comanche Tribe, No. 7, of Aurora, and Wyandotte Tribe, No. 8, of Richmond. In less than three grand suns, the Order had again lapsed in Indiana. A third attempt to establish the Order in this State was made in G. S. D. 375, when Tippecanoe Tribe, No. 8, of Patriot, was instituted. In the next great sun, Iroquois Tribe, No. 9, was instituted at Brookville. In G. S. D. 377, Wabash Tribe, No. 10, of Lafayette, and Kanahwaga, No. 11, of Attica, were instituted, and Wyandotte, No. 8, of Richmond, was resuscitated. This gave the Order its third and successful start, and on the 19th of Hot moon, G. S. D. 378, its Great Council fire was rekindled.

The standing of the Tribes in the reservation on the 30th of Hot moon, G. S. D. 401, was as follows:—

Number of Tribes	103
Membership	8,632
Past Sachems	635
Past Great Sachems	19
Past Great Incohonees	1
Wampum invested	48,508 fathoms 21 inches.
Wampum in belts	20,087 fathoms 19 inches.
Total funds	68,595 fathoms 40 inches.

Illinois.— The Improved Order of Red Men was introduced into Illinois by the institution of Pocahontas Tribe, No. 1, at Paris, on the 1st of Worm moon, G. S. 5614 (1854). This Tribe soon ceased to exist, and the Order here was not revived until G. S. 5620 (1860), when a Tribe was instituted at Nashville. The Nashville Tribe soon disbanded, however, and no effort to introduce the Order into the State again succeeded until G. S. D. 378, when Seminole Tribe, No. 3, of Mason, was instituted. Somonauk Tribe, No. 4, was instituted at Chicago, in Hunting moon, G. S. D. 381, and Modoc Tribe, No. 5, was instituted at Effingham on the 3d of Plant moon, G. S. D. 382. The council fire of Seminole Tribe had been quenched in the meantime. Shawnee Tribe, No. 6, was instituted at Quincy on the 24th of Beaver moon, G. S. D. 383; and on the 9th of Plant moon, G. S. D. 384, Pawnee Tribe, No. 7, was instituted at Mattoon. In Snow moon, G. S. D. 385, Chickasaw Tribe, No. 8, was instituted at Neoga; and in Flower moon, Potawatamie Tribe, No. 9, was instituted at Oakland City. Four tribes were added in the next two great suns, and on the 13th of Hot moon, G. S. D. 387, the Great Council fire was kindled. The hunting grounds of Wisconsin and Minnesota are both within the jurisdiction of the Great Council of Illinois.

The standing of the Tribes in this reservation on the 30th of Hot moon was as follows:—

Number of Tribes	44
Membership	2,170
Past Sachems	283
Past Great Sachems	7
Wampum invested	5,716 fathoms 97 inches.
Wampum in belts	5,373 fathoms 73 inches.
Total funds	11,090 fathoms 70 inches.

Iowa. — The stay of the Order in Iowa at its first appearance was of very short duration. Camanche Tribe, No. 1, of Dubuque, was instituted on the 5th of Hot moon, G. S. 5614 (1854), and was reported at the next grand sun council of the United States as having surrendered its charter. Saux Tribe, No. 2, of Des Moines, was instituted on the 20th of Corn moon, G. S. D. 381. Black Hawk Tribe, No. 3, was instituted on the 16th of Travelling moon, G. S. D. 382, but surrendered its charter within a few great suns. Iowa Tribe, No. 4, was instituted at Oskaloosa on the 22d of Snow moon, G. S. D. 392. During the next great sun Osceola Tribe, No. 5, was instituted at Davenport in Plant moon, and Wapello Tribe, No. 6, at Cleveland, on the 28th of Hot moon.

The Great Council fire of Iowa was kindled on the 18th of Hunting moon, G. S. D. 393. The reservation of Nebraska was placed under the jurisdiction of Iowa, and by its well-directed and energetic efforts several Tribal council fires were soon kindled, and a Great Council instituted in that State.

The standing of the Tribes in this reservation on the 30th of Hot moon, G. S. D. 401, was as follows:—

Number of Tribes	33
Membership	1,481
Past Sachems	137
Past Great Sachems	7
Wampum invested	560 fathoms 45 inches.
Wampum in belt	3,689 fathoms 71 inches.
Total funds	4,250 fathoms 16 inches.

Missouri.— The first appearance by the order in Missouri was in G. S. 5616 (1856), when Hiawatha Tribe, No. 1, of St. Louis was instituted. Minnehaha Tribe, No. 2, of St. Louis, was instituted during the same grand sun. Tribe No. 2 soon quenched its council fire, which was relighted in G. S. 5618 (1858). No record of the institution of Tribe No. 3 appears, but Cherokee Tribe, No. 4, was instituted in G. S. 5618, and a Great Council was informally instituted on the 18th of Hunting moon, G. S. 5618. At the grand sun council of the G. C. U. S. succeeding, a charter was granted for the Great Council of Missouri, notwithstanding the informality of its organization and institution. The Great Council lapsed soon afterward; but in G. S. D. 373 was reorganized. Again the Great Council of Missouri disbanded, but its council fire was kindled for the third time on the 24th of Snow moon, G. S. D. 375, and it has continued to date without further disaster.

The standing of the Tribes in the reservation on the 30th of Hot moon, G. S. D. 401, is as follows:—

Number of Tribes	8
Membership	298
Past Sachems	74
Past Great Sachems	12
Wampum invested	9,157 fathoms 8 inches.
Wampum in belts	1,931 fathoms 76 inches.
Total funds	11,088 fathoms 84 inches.

STATE GREAT COUNCILS AND TRIBES.

Connecticut. — The Order failed of continuance in this reservation from its first appearance, which was by the institution of Narragansett Tribe, No. 1, at Hartford, on the 19th of Buck moon, G. S. 5618 (1858). In G. S. 5621 (1861) this Tribe was reported to the G. C. U. S. as extinct.

The second introduction of the Order here was in G. S. D. 395. The reservation of Connecticut had been placed within the jurisdiction of the Great Council of Massachusetts; and by the efforts of its great chiefs Hammonassett Tribe, No. 1, was instituted at New Haven on the 1st of Beaver moon, G. S. D. 395. In a few seven suns the Tribe had more than 500 members; and enthusiasm for the Order spread so rapidly, that in less than ten moons, nine large Tribes were flourishing in the State, had withdrawn from the Great Council of Massachusetts, and had been instituted as the Great Council of Connecticut.

The standing of the Tribes in the reservation on the 30th of Hot moon, G. S. D. 401, was as follows: —

Number of Tribes	20
Membership	2,347
Past Sachems	123
Past Great Sachems	6
Wampum invested	4,207 fathoms 13 inches.
Wampum in belt	5,066 fathoms 78 inches.
Total funds	9,273 fathoms 91 inches.

West Virginia. — Before the war of 1861 this had been a part of the great reservation of Virginia; but having been set apart by the civil government as an independent State, the only Tribe existing there in G. S. 5623 (1863), Logan, No. 21, of Wheeling, came under the jurisdiction of the G. C. U. S., and took the number 1 of West Virginia. Cornstalk Tribe, No. 2, of Wheeling, was instituted during the G. S. 5625 (1865), and Black Hawk Tribe, No. 3, was instituted in G. S. D. 378. At the following Council of the G. C. U. S. a charter for Great Council was issued, and on the 27th sun of Cold moon, G. S. D. 379, the Great Council was instituted.

The standing of the Tribes in the reservation on the 30th of Hot moon, G. S. D. 401, was as follows: —

Number of Tribes	20
Membership	1,115

Past Sachems	158
Past Great Sachems	15
Wampum invested	none
Wampum in belts	5,233 fathoms 66 inches.
Total funds	5,233 fathoms 66 inches.

California. — The first mention of the Order in connection with California was a report by W. G. Incohonee Peters in G. S. 5614 (1854), that he had appointed Past Sachem A. Curry, Vice Great Incohonee, with authority to institute two Tribes in that reservation. There appears to be no official record of his doings in this connection, but there is a tradition in California that he established a Tribe at Red Dog. If he did, its life was of short duration. Among the many Red Men in California in G. S. 5623 (1863) were Brothers Adam Smith, Lando, and Weis, who, with a number of palefaces, organized California Tribe, No. 1, of San Francisco, which was instituted on the 9th of Beaver moon, in G. S. 5623. Manhattan Tribe, No. 2, quickly followed, but lived only a short time. Hiawatha Tribe, No. 3, was next instituted in Corn moon, G. S. D. 376. Then followed Manzanita, No. 4, with 400 charter members. California, No. 1, soon died, and another No. 1, working in the German language, was instituted. In G. S. D. 377, six flourishing Tribes were in existence, and the Great Council was instituted. This has always been the largest Great Council west of the Mississippi River, and by the efforts of its members much of the preliminary work has been done for the planting of the Order in the further western jurisdictions.

The standing of the Tribes in the reservation on the 30th of Hot moon, G. S. D. 401, was as follows:—

Number of Tribes	36
Membership	2,636
Past Sachems	373
Past Great Sachems	18
Past Great Incohonee	1
Wampum invested	71,766 fathoms 50 inches.
Wampum in belts	5,782 fathoms 2 inches.
Total funds	77,548 fathoms 52 inches.

Texas. — The Order was introduced into Texas by the institution of Swamp Eagle Tribe, No. 1, at Marshall, in G. S. D. 375. Four Tribes were instituted in G. S. D. 377, and on the

5th of Cold moon, G. S. D. 378, its Great Council fire was kindled. Choctaw Tribe, No. 5, was instituted in G. S. D. 380. The Great Council made no report; and the Great Incohonee demanded its effects in the following Great Sun. Choctaw Tribe, No. 5, of Starrville, was the only Tribe in the State then reported to be in existence. In G. S. D. 387, Choctaw Tribe also ceased to exist. The order in Texas was revived in G. S. D. 392, by the institution of Caddo Tribe, No. 8, at Dallas. In Corn moon of the same great sun, Osceola Tribe, No. 9, was instituted at Waco. The name Osceola was soon after changed to Waco. Seminole Tribe, No. 10, was instituted at Dallas, in Cold moon, G. S. D. 395. The hunting grounds of Texas were now under the jurisdiction of the Great Council of Louisiana. Caddo, No. 8, and Waco, No. 9, were the only Tribes in Texas on the 30th of Hot moon, G. S. D. 400. The statement of standing of Tribes in Louisiana on the 30th of Hot moon, G. S. D. 401, covers Texas, which yet remains within the jurisdiction of the Great Council of Louisiana.

Tennessee. — The history of the Order in this reservation began in G. S. D. 376, with the institution of Tecumseh Tribe, No. 1, at Nashville. The Order had a very rapid growth here, as is evidenced by the fact that at the great sun council of the G. C. U. S. in G. S. D. 377, the Great Incohonee reported the addition of seven Tribes in that jurisdiction. Their application for a Great Council charter was then granted; the Great Council was instituted soon after; and a very large number of Tribes was instituted. The rapid growth of the Order in these hunting grounds did not continue; and for a long time the membership gradually reduced in number. In the recent great suns, however, new life and energy has appeared, and a steady increase is shown.

The standing of the Tribes in the reservation on the 30th of Hot moon, G. S. D. 401, was as follows: —

Number of Tribes	5
Membership	275
Past Sachems	25
Past Great Sachems	9
Past Great Incohonee	1
Wampum invested	1800 fathoms 90 inches.
Wampum in belts	297 fathoms 95 inches.
Total funds	2097 fathoms 95 inches.

Georgia.— Cherokee Tribe, No. 1, of Atlanta, instituted in G. S. D. 376, was the beginning of the Order here. The institution of Nickajack, No. 2, followed in G. S. D. 378. Then came Modoc Tribe, No. 3, in G. S. D. 379, all of Atlanta. All surrendered their charters after a time, but were resuscitated. In G. S. D. 387, the reports showed Cherokee, No. 1, Modoc, No. 3, Chattahoochie, No. 5, and Choctaw, No. 6, in existence. The G. C. U. S., in 388, issued a charter for the Great Council of Georgia, and it was instituted on the 6th of Hunting moon of that great sun. Alabama and South Carolina were placed under its jurisdiction in G. S. D. 395; and the great chiefs of Georgia instituted eight Tribes in the former and five in the latter State.

The standing of the Tribes in the reservation on the 30th of Hot moon, G. S. D. 401, was as follows:—

Number of Tribes	41
Membership	3,401
Past Sachems	75
Past Great Sachems	9
Wampum invested	5,765 fathoms.
Wampum in belts	11,541 fathoms 99 inches.
Total funds	17,306 fathoms 99 inches.

Michigan.— Pocahontas Tribe, No. 1, was instituted at Detroit, in G. S. D. 376.

In five great suns the number of Tribes had increased to four, the additions being, Tecumseh, No. 3, Chippewa, No. 4, and Red Cloud, No. 5, all of Detroit. Tribe No. 2 had existed at Grand Haven, but had dissolved. In Worm moon, G. S. D. 381, dispensation was issued for a Great Council charter, and on the 10th of the following Flower moon, the Great Council was instituted. The Order has progressed slowly but steadily in Michigan from that date.

The standing of the Tribes in the reservation on the 30th of Hot moon, G. S. D. 401, was as follows:—

Number of Tribes	20
Membership	1,113
Past Sachems	115
Past Great Sachems	12
Wampum invested	1,131 fathoms 91 inches.
Wampum in belts	2,106 fathoms 74 inches.
Total funds	3,238 fathoms 65 inches.

STATE GREAT COUNCILS AND TRIBES.

Alabama. — The first Tribe in Alabama was Winnebago, No. 1, at Athens, instituted in G. S. D. 378. A Tribe at Selma, Powhatan, No. 2, followed in the same great sun. On the 18th of Sturgeon moon, G. S. D. 380, Cherokee Tribe, No. 3, was instituted at Fort Hampton. Seminole Tribe, No. 4, was instituted at Clutsville, in Cold moon, G. S. D. 382. In G. S. D. 383, the council fires of two Tribes were kindled — Creek, No. 5, of Courtland, and Etawa, No. 6, of Hillsboro. Only Powhatan Tribe, of Selma, survived in G. S. D. 388, but in G. S. D. 391, it was also reported dissolved. Cherokee Tribe, No. 3, was resuscitated at Elkmont, in G. S. D. 392, but dissolved soon after. This reservation having been placed in charge of the Great Council of Georgia, in G. S. D. 396, eight Tribes were instituted within a few moons at Brownville, Anniston, Montgomery, Pratt Mines, Birmingham, Dolomite, Warrior, and Tuscombia. On the 19th sun of Beaver moon, G. S. D. 397, the Great Council of Alabama was instituted.

The standing of the Tribes in this reservation on the 30th of Hot moon, G. S. D. 401, was as follows: —

Number of Tribes	23
Membership	1,003
Past Sachems	122
Past Great Sachems	4
Wampum invested	590 fathoms.
Wampum in belts	2,273 fathoms 40 inches.
Total funds	2,863 fathoms 40 inches.

Oregon. — The Order began its work in Oregon by the institution of Oregonian-Pocahontas Tribe, No. 1, in G. S. D. 379, at Jacksonville; which was immediately followed by the institution of La Lake Tribe, No. 2, at Ashland, and Multnomah Tribe, No. 3, at Portland. Oneonta Tribe, No. 4, of Portland, was instituted on the 15th of Beaver moon, G. S. D. 381, and in Buck moon, G. S. D. 382, the Great Council of Oregon was instituted. The last report made by this Great Council was in G. S. D. 391, when six Tribes were reported in good standing. In G. S. D. 400, however, Oregonian-Pocahontas Tribe, No. 1, of Jacksonville, and Williamette, No. 6, of Portland, again appear in the records of the G. C. U. S. Minnehaha Tribe, No. 2, was instituted, at Portland, on the 6th of Worm moon, G. S. D. 399; and in the following great sun, Himaly Tribe, No. 3, was instituted at Albina. Winona, No. 4, and Chinook, No. 5, of Portland, Concomley, No. 7, of Astoria, Kamiakin, No. 8, of Salem, Modoc, No. 9, of Portland, and Mohawk, No. 11, of Albany, followed in rapid succession, and a charter was granted by the G. C. U. S., at Atlanta, in Corn moon, G. S. D. 401, for the institution of the Great Council of Oregon.

Nevada. — Piûte Tribe, No. 1, was instituted at Carson City, Nevada, on the 18th of Buck moon, G. S. D. 379. On the 19th of the succeeding Corn moon, Pocahontas Tribe, No. 2, of Virginia City was instituted, and in Hot moon, G. S. D. 380, Minnehaha Tribe, No. 3, of Reno, was instituted. Washoe Tribe, No. 4, of Washoe City, was instituted on the 15th of Flower moon, G. S. D. 381; and on the 7th of Buck moon, G. S. D. 381, Shoshone Tribe, No. 5, of Elko, was instituted. The Great Council fire was kindled on the 6th of Cold moon, G. S. D. 382. The Order has worked under the disadvantages of a sparsely settled country, and has made little gain in numbers.

The standing of the Tribes in this reservation on the 30th of Hot moon, G. S. D. 401, was as follows: —

Number of Tribes	4
Membership	156
Past Sachems	44
Past Great Sachems	7
Wampum invested	1,600 fathoms.
Wampum in belts	845 fathoms 74 inches.
Total funds	2,445 fathoms 74 inches.

Wisconsin. — The Order was introduced first into this reservation in G. S. D. 380, by the institution in Cold moon of Milwaukee Tribe, No. 1, and of Mendota Tribe, No. 2, of Madison, in Flower moon. The council fire of the latter was soon quenched. Black Hawk Tribe, No. 3, was instituted at Milwaukee, in G. S. D. 384. In G. S. D. 387, the Great Chief of Records reported that the Tribes of Wisconsin had disbanded. Again in G. S. D. 393, the State having been placed under the jurisdiction of the Great Council of Illinois, the great chiefs of that reservation instituted Oshkosh Tribe, No. 1, at Oshkosh, in

Worm moon. The reports for Hot moon, G. S. D. 397, showed that Black Hawk Tribe, No. 2, of Beloit, Mohawk, No. 3, of Janesville, Hiawatha, No. 4, of Waukesha, Passyunk, No. 5, of Milwaukee, Winnebago, No. 6, of Fond du Lac, Kishwaukee, No. 7, of Milwaukee, Minissine, No. 8, of Madison, Sioux, No. 9, of Whitewater, and Rickapoo, No. 10, of Richland Centre, had all been instituted within the great sun. Only Hiawatha and Minissine Tribes were in existence, however, in one great sun thereafter. The standing of the Tribes in Wisconsin, on the 30th of Hot moon, G. S. D. 401, is contained in the statement given for the Great Council of Illinois, on that date.

Rhode Island. — Beginning on the 8th of Beaver moon, G. S. D. 380, with the institution of King Philip Tribe, No. 1, at Providence, the Order made rapid strides in this reservation. On the 22d of Cold moon, G. S. D. 381, Canonicus Tribe, No. 2, was instituted at Warwick. On the 19th of the same moon, Miantonomah Tribe, No. 3, was instituted at Providence. In Plant moon following, Wampanoag Tribe, No. 4, was instituted at Pawtucket, and Narragansett, No. 5, at Natick. On the 20th of Sturgeon moon, G. S. D. 381, the Great Council was instituted, being the first in New England. It flourished for a few great suns, when interest began to flag, and members to fall away, until in G. S. D. 391 the Order was reported extinct in Rhode Island. In G. S. D. 396, Rhode Island having been placed in charge of the Great Council of Massachusetts, the great chiefs of that State resuscitated several of the old Tribes, and kindled council fires of new ones, so that in G. S. D. 397, there were more than 800 Red Men in the State, and the Great Council fire was kindled a second time, in Sturgeon moon.

The standing of the Tribes in this reservation on the 30th of Hot moon, G. S. D. 401, was as follows: —

Number of Tribes	10
Membership	1,272
Past Sachems	97
Past Great Sachems	5
Wampum invested	6,886 fathoms 85 inches.
Wampum in belts	3,921 fathoms 61 inches.
Total funds	10,812 fathoms 46 inches.

Utah. — The first introduction of the Improved Order of Red Men to the reservation of Utah, was by the institution of

Washakie Tribe, No. 1, at Salt Lake City, on the 4th of Worm moon, G. S. D. 381. The next Tribe instituted was Pocatallo, No. 2, of Salt Lake City, in G. S. D. 383. In G. S. D. 385, Pocatallo Tribe was declared extinct. Two great suns later, Washakie Tribe, also, ceased to kindle its council fires. A second attempt to plant the Order in Utah was made on the 22d of Worm moon, G. S. D. 391, by the institution of Wasatch Tribe, at Salt Lake City; but the Tribe lived only a few moons.

(The council fire of Washakie Tribe, No. 1, of Salt Lake City, was relighted on the 8th of Buck moon, G. S. D. 401.)

Kansas. — Osage Tribe, No. 1, of Fort Scott, was the first Tribe instituted in the State, the date being 10th of Buck moon, G. S. D. 381. Panionkee Tribe, No. 2, was instituted at Girard, on the 1st of Worm moon, G. S. D. 385. In the following great sun, the Great Incohonee reported the institution of Delaware Tribe, No. 3, at Leavenworth. In G. S. D. 392, the institution of three Tribes was reported, Neosho, No. 4, at Emporia, Tawacanie, No. 5, at Cherokee, and Mohawk, No. 6, at Parsons. Hiawatha Tribe, No. 7, was instituted at Arkansas City, in G. S. D. 393. The Great Council fire was lighted on the 17th of Hunting moon, G. S. D. 393.

The standing of the Tribes in the reservation on the 30th of Hot moon, G. S. D. 401, was as follows: —

Number of Tribes	18
Membership	1092
Past Sachems	107
Past Great Sachems	9
Wampum invested	3,908 fathoms 88 inches.
Wampum in belts	1,255 fathoms 71 inches.
Total funds	5,164 fathoms 59 inches.

Washington. — Chemakum Tribe, No. 1, of Port Townsend, was instituted in G. S. D. 381; Clalm Tribe, No. 2, was instituted at New Dungeness, in G. S. D. 383. In the following great sun, Wa Shella Tribe, No. 3, was instituted at Port Ludlow. Snake Tribe, No. 4, of Vancouver, was instituted on the 15th of Plant moon, G. S. D. 391, but was extinct in G. S. D. 393. Clalm and Wa Shella Tribes survived but a short time. In G. S. D. 397, Seattle Tribe, No. 2, was instituted at Seattle, and Kumtux, No. 3, was instituted at Vancouver. Clallam Tribe,

No. 4, was instituted at Port Angelus, on the 18th of Hot moon, G. S. D. 400. Snoqualmie Tribe, No. 5, was instituted in the same great sun, and was quickly followed by Lummi, No. 6, at New Whatcom, Snohomish, No. 7, at Snohomish, and Piute, No. 8, of Vancouver. These Tribes were all in good standing on the 30th of Hot moon, G. S. D. 401.

Massachusetts. — The Order was introduced into this State on the 1st of Sturgeon moon, G. S. D. 381, by the institution of Manataug Tribe, No. 1, of Marblehead. Sagamore Tribe, No. 2, of Lynn, was instituted on the 28th of Worm moon, G. S. D. 382; and on the 27th of Hot moon, G. S. D. 382, Naumkeag Tribe, No. 3, of Salem, was instituted. On the petition of these three Tribes the Great Council was instituted on the 23d of Hunting moon, G. S. D. 382. The Order in the State grew slowly, its gains of new Tribes and members being offset by losses of old Tribes and members for several great suns. At the first report after institution the Great Council showed 221 members, and in G. S. D. 389, seven great suns after, there were but 151 members reported. From this point the Order had steady and sometimes rapid gain. In G. S. D. 400, it stood second among Great Councils in number of members, and at last report third. Connecticut, Rhode Island, and Vermont were placed under its jurisdiction with the result that a Great Council with 9 Tribes and nearly 1600 members, was organized in Connecticut within one great sun; and another with 7 Tribes and over 800 members, in Rhode Island within two great suns. Several Tribal council fires have also been kindled in Vermont, and a Great Council is in prospect for the near future.

The standing of the Tribes in this reservation on the 30th of Hot moon, G. S. D. 401, was as follows: —

    Number of Tribes   110
    Membership   14,601
    Past Sachems   1,026
    Past Great Sachems   16
    Past Great Incohonee   1
    Wampum invested . . . . . . 50,202 fathoms 41 inches.
    Wampum in belts . . . . . . 12,204 fathoms 30 inches.
    Total funds . . . . 62,406 fathoms 71 inches.

Nebraska. — Shoshonee Tribe, No. 1, of Lincoln, was instituted on the 31st of Travelling moon, G. S. D. 381; but for lack of instruction the interest of its members flagged, and it soon surrendered its charter. The second attempt to plant the Order here was in G. S. D. 385, Omaha Tribe, No. 2, being instituted at Omaha on the 3d of Plant moon, G. S. D. 385, which six great suns later discontinued its reports to the G. C. U. S. The reservation of Nebraska having been placed under the charge of the Great Council of Iowa, the chiefs of that Great Council instituted Shawnee Tribe, No. 1, of Tecumseh, Yah Nun Dah Sis, No. 2, of Omaha, and Sioux, No. 3, of Lincoln during the great sun ending 30th Hot moon, G. S. D. 399. Five other Tribes were instituted within a few moons, and on the 9th of Buck moon, G. S. D. 400, the Great Council of Nebraska was instituted.

The standing of the Tribes in this reservation on the 30th of Hot moon, G. S. D. 401, was as follows:—

Number of Tribes	14
Membership	838
Past Sachems	32
Past Great Sachems	2
Wampum invested	192 fathoms 50 inches.
Wampum in belts	937 fathoms 65 inches.
Total funds	1,130 fathoms 15 inches.

South Carolina. — Three Tribes were instituted in this reservation in G. S. D. 383: Catawba, No. 1, of Columbia, on the 5th of Snow moon, Chicora, No. 2, on the 26th of Cold moon, and Tuscarora, No. 3, of Newberry, on the 29th of Flower moon. In G. S. D. 385, only Chicora Tribe remained. On the 5th of Cold moon, G. S. D. 393, Zuni Tribe, No. 4, was instituted at Florence, but was reported extinct the next great sun. In G. S. D. 396, the hunting grounds of South Carolina were placed under the jurisdiction of the Great Council of Georgia, which, in Hot moon, G. S. D. 399, reported five Tribes in South Carolina: Chicora, No. 2, at Columbia, Black Hawk, No. 5, at Graniteville, Kiowa, No. 6, at Charleston, Cherokee, No. 7, at Clifton, and Choctaw, No. 8, at Langley. On the 17th of the following Beaver moon, the Great Council of South Carolina was instituted.

The standing of the Tribes in the reservation on the 30th of Hot moon, G. S. D. 401, was as follows:—

STATE GREAT COUNCILS AND TRIBES. 445

Number of Tribes 6
Membership 605
Past Sachems 42
Past Great Sachems 2
Wampum invested . . . . 114 fathoms 50 inches.
Wampum in belts . . . . 791 fathoms 98 inches.
Total funds . . . . 906 fathoms 48 inches.

Minnesota. — The council fire of Minnehaha Tribe, No. 1, of St. Paul, was kindled on the 2d of Plant moon, G. S. D. 384. It had an existence of a few great suns, but in G. S. D. 390, was declared extinct. The reservation of Minnesota having been placed under the jurisdiction of the Great Council of Illinois, the chiefs of that Great Council instituted Hiawatha Tribe, No. 2, at Minneapolis, in Travelling moon, G. S. D. 395. Cherokee Tribe, No. 3, was reported, in G. S. D. 399, as instituted at Minneapolis. The standing of the Tribes in Minnesota on the 30th of Hot moon, G. S. D. 401, is included in the statement given for the Great Council of Illinois.

New Hampshire. —The first Tribal council fire kindled in New Hampshire was of Paugus Tribe, No. 1, of Salmon Falls. The institution of the Tribe was in Flower moon, G. S. D. 384. Two other Tribes were instituted in the reservation during the great sun, — Kankamagus, No. 2, at Dover, on the 5th of Travelling moon, and Samoset, No. 3, at Rochester, on the 29th of Beaver moon. Newichewannock Tribe, No. 4, was instituted at Portsmouth, on the 9th of Worm moon, G. S. D. 385. The council fire of Samoset Tribe was reported quenched in G. S. D. 387. Passaconaway Tribe, No. 5, of Manchester, was instituted on the 12th of Plant moon, G. S. D. 390. The Great Council of New Hampshire was instituted on the 13th of Plant moon, G. S. D. 390. The reservation of Maine was placed within the jurisdiction of the Great Council of New Hampshire, and there remained until the 25th of Travelling moon, G. S. D. 397, when the members of that State withdrew to form the Great Council of Maine.

The standing of the Tribes in this reservation on the 30th of Hot moon, G. S. D. 401, was as follows : —

Number of Tribes 21
Membership 2,221
Past Sachems 221

Past Great Sachems	9
Wampum invested	6,844 fathoms 94 inches.
Wampum in belts	2,253 fathoms 40 inches.
Total funds	9,098 fathoms 34 inches.

Maine. — The Order was first introduced into this jurisdiction by the institution of Squando Tribe, No. 1, at Biddeford, on the 6th of Beaver moon, G. S. D. 384. This Tribe became attached to the Great Council of New Hampshire by the consolidation of the two States into one jurisdiction. Soon afterward, however, it surrendered its charter. Nine Tribes were instituted in the hunting grounds of Maine under the new dispensation, when in G. S. D. 397, permission was given for the withdrawal of Maine to form a Great Council. On the 25th of Travelling moon the Great Council fire was lighted.

The standing of the Tribes in the jurisdiction on the 30th of Hot moon, G. S. D. 401, was as follows: —

Number of Tribes	21
Membership	1,754
Past Sachems	117
Past Great Sachems	4
Wampum invested	5,091 fathoms 68 inches.
Wampum in belts	2,301 fathoms 72 inches.
Total funds	7,393 fathoms 40 inches.

Hawaiian Islands. — The Order was introduced into the Hawaiian Islands by Great Incohonee Adam Smith, who, in person, kindled the council fire of Hawaiian Tribe, No. 1, at Honolulu, in G. S. D. 386. The Tribe existed about ten great suns, at the end of which time its council fire ceased to burn. It was reorganized in G. S. D. 396, but continued for only a few moons, when its council fire was again quenched.

Florida. — Osceola Tribe, No. 1, was instituted in the hunting grounds of Starke, Fla., in Buck moon, G. S. D. 388. Wacassassa Tribe, No. 2, of Bronson, was instituted in Flower moon, G. S. D. 389, but surrendered its charter in the next great sun. Three tribes were instituted in G. S. D. 390: Seminole, No. 3, at Palatka, on the 4th of Sturgeon moon, Yemassee, No. 4, at Waldo, on the 23d of Sturgeon moon, and Lulloosa Tribe, No. 5, at Hawthorne, on the 14th of Travelling moon. Yemassee and Lulloosa Tribes surrendered their charters in

G. S. D. 392. Miccosookee Tribe, No. 6, of Enterprise, was instituted in Beaver moon, G. S. D. 392, and Lulloosa Tribe was revived. On the 2d of Snow moon, G. S. D. 393, the Great Council of Florida was instituted.

The standing of the Tribes in the reservation on the 30th of Hot moon, was as follows: —

Number of Tribes	6
Membership	210
Past Sachems	35
Past Great Sachems	2
Wampum invested	400 fathoms.
Wampum in belts	415 fathoms 7 inches.
Total funds	815 fathoms 7 inches.

Colorado. — Rising Bow Tribe, No. 1, of Central City, was instituted in G. S. D. 388. In G. S. D. 389, Rising Sun Tribe, No. 2, was instituted at Nevadaville, and Blazing Arrow Tribe, No. 3, was instituted at Idaho Springs. Arapahoe Tribe, No. 4, of Caribou, was instituted in Cold moon, G. S. D. 391. Ouray Tribe, No. 5, of Denver, was instituted on the 26th of Hot moon, G. S. D. 393. The Great Council fire was kindled on the 23d of Buck moon, G. S. D. 393.

The standing of the Tribes in the reservation on the 30th of Hot moon, G. S. D. 401, was as follows: —

Number of Tribes	23
Membership	1,291
Past Sachems	142
Past Great Sachems	6
Wampum invested	16,693 fathoms 45 inches.
Wampum in belts	6,997 fathoms 74 inches.
Total funds	23,691 fathoms 19 inches.

Arizona. — Dispensation was issued in Corn moon, G. S. D. 388, for the institution of Maricopa Tribe, No. 1, at Phœnix; but the Tribe never reported to the Great Council, and its name soon disappeared from the roll of Tribes.

Arkansas. — Mineola Tribe, No. 1, of Hot Springs, was instituted in G. S. D. 393. It made no report after G. S. D. 394, and in G. S. D. 395 was reported extinct. In G. S. D. 396, the State was placed within the jurisdiction of the Great Council of Louisiana.

Montana. — Silver Bow Tribe, No. 1, was instituted at Butte City, in Beaver moon, G. S. D. 392. Its name was by dispensation changed to Navahoe. The council fire was in G. S. D. 396 reported quenched.

New Mexico. — Montezuma Tribe, No. 1, of Las Vegas, was instituted in G. S. D. 395, but failed to keep its council fire burning.

Vermont. — The Order was introduced into this reservation in G. S. D. 395, by the great chiefs of Massachusetts, the State having been placed under the jurisdiction of the Great Council of Massachusetts. The first Tribe instituted was Ascutney Tribe, No. 1, of Bellows Falls. The Tribes existing on the 30th of Hot moon, G. S. D. 401, were Ascutney, No. 1, of Bellows Falls, Quonekticut, No. 2, of Brattleboro, Cascadnac, No. 4, of White River Junction, Hocco Mocco, No. 5, of Bradford, Mohegan, No. 6, of Bennington, Pequiot, No. 8, of West Randolph, and Algonquin, No. 9, of St. Johnsbury. The standing of its Tribes on the 30th of Hot moon, G. S. D. 401, is included in the statement given for the Great Council of Massachusetts.

Province of Ontario. — The province of Ontario having been placed under the jurisdiction of the Great Council of New York, its great chiefs organized Missiosigee Tribe, No. 1, at Toronto, in G. S. D. 396, and its council fire was kindled by Great Chief of Records Charles C. Conley, on the 1st of Sturgeon moon. In G. S. D. 399 its council fire was reported quenched. There is now, therefore, no council fire burning outside the limits of the United States.

Indian Territory. — The Order has been established here but one great sun — Choctaw Tribe, No. 1, having been instituted at Hartshorne, on the 9th of Hot moon, G. S. D. 400.

Wyoming. — Cheyenne Tribe, No. 1, of Cheyenne, was instituted on the 9th of Beaver moon, G. S. D. 400. The council fire of Wahsatch Tribe, No. 2, was kindled at Laramie City, on the 29th of Worm moon, G. S. D. 401. Both council fires are burning brightly.

CHAPTER X.

BIOGRAPHIES.

As the written history of any country is incomplete without a knowledge of the individuals through whose agency the affairs of government have been conducted, so in an organization for fraternal, benevolent, or social purposes the personality of the individuals composing it, and under whose control it has advanced either to prosperity or adversity, are so closely interwoven with every detail of its history as to make it impossible to correctly give that history without giving also information of its prominent members.

It seems to have been the rule that all organizations founded upon the inspiration of a desire to benefit mankind, and for the diffusion of the principles of benevolence and charity, have been organized by men in humble ranks in life. From the bitterness of their own personal experience, they have seemed to realize how powerless is man as an individual to cope with those forces which tend to degrade him in the social scale, and comprehend in its full force the trite saying, "In union there is strength." The founders of these organizations have sought to bring together kindred spirits, men actuated by the same unselfish motives, and by their united efforts do for the individual what he alone and unaided would be unable to accomplish.

The history of the Improved Order of Red Men is no exception to the general rule. It will be found that the brothers who, with unselfish devotion to Freedom, Friendship, and Charity, planted the seeds of our fraternity, were men in humble walks in life, whose names are not blazoned upon the pages of our country's history, but who, modest and unassuming, with hearts full of the desire to benefit humanity, joined themselves together in an organization which should accomplish for them and their successors the good it was their ambition to secure.

These short biographies are given so that the members of the Order in the present generation may learn something concerning the founders of the Order, and, by reading of their devotion and self-sacrifice, be inspired with equal fidelity to the principles of our fraternity.

With these preliminary and introductory remarks, we present the biographies of the following Past Great Incohonees: —

Past Great Incohonee William G. Gorsuch. — William G. Gorsuch was born in Baltimore County, Md., in June, 1804, and was adopted in Pocahontas Tribe, No. 3, of that city. He was one of the six Past Great Sachems of Maryland who met January 30, 1847, and organized the Great Council of the United States, of which he was elected the first Great Incohonee.

September 13, 1869, he was elected Great Keeper of Wampum, and was continued in that chieftaincy 12 great suns. For a number of terms he was Representative to the Great Council of the United States, the last time of his service as such being 1875. He also served as Great Keeper of Wampum of Maryland for 17 years.

He died in the city of Baltimore, October 7, 1887. A short time before his death, two of his associate Past Great Incohonees visited him at his home. He spoke feelingly of the past and future prospects of the Great Council of the United States, and made grateful reference to the many acts of kindness the members had manifested towards him, and the love he always had for the Order and its principles. At parting he warmly pressed the hands of his visitors, and as tears coursed down his furrowed cheeks at the thought that the friendly tie would soon be severed, he said: "My work is done, but the Order still moves on. I am waiting for the boatman to take me home. I have been in this room three years. I have not murmured. It is all right. It is all right. Good-by, and may God bless you!"

He was in the Great Council at its birth, and was permitted to live long enough to see it have under its jurisdiction 65,000 members. He was kind and genial in his nature, and was revered and respected by all who knew him, as a brother and friend, and as an honored and honorable member of the community in which he lived.

BIOGRAPHIES.

Past Great Incohonee Hugh Latham. — Hugh Latham was born in Washington, D.C., April, 1812, but his parents moved to Alexandria, Va., while he was very young. In early life he learned, and worked at the trade of shoemaking; but late in 1845, or early in 1846, he became the first agent for the *Baltimore Sun* south of the Potomac, and was also the first agent for the Adams Express Company in that city. He became a member of the Order as charter member of Powhatan Tribe, No. 1, District of Columbia; and in the year 1845, when the Order was introduced into Alexandria, Va., he was one of the members who assisted in the organization of Osceola Tribe, then No. 2, of the District of Columbia, now No. 1, of Virginia, and he was chosen the first Sachem of that Tribe. Upon the organization of the Great Council of the District of Columbia he was elected Grand Sachem, as it was then called. When the Great Council of Virginia was formed, he withdrew, and joined that body. He was admitted to the Great Council of the United States in 1847, and at once took the rank in that body to which his great ability and commanding talents entitled him. At the time of his entry into that body, some opposition had begun to manifest itself to the claim of supreme authority made and exercised by the Grand Council of Maryland. His wisdom, skill, prudence, and ability prevailed with the Representatives, and shaped the legislation which finally gave to the Great Council of the United States the supreme power it now possesses, while, at the same time, retaining for each State Great Council exclusive jurisdiction over its own reservation. At the election of chiefs, in 1848, he was elected the second Great Incohonee of the Order. His administration was marked with zeal and ability, and, indeed, from his admission until his death, he was a leading and influential member of the Great Council of the United States. He served on its most important committees, and helped to frame its legislation and unwritten work. To enumerate his labor would be to reproduce the history of the important legislation of the Great Council of the United States. He was twice elected Great Prophet; first, in 1888, and again in 1890. It is the exact truth to say that in the deliberations of the supreme body of the Order he had few equals and no superiors as a sound, eloquent, and logical debater.

He was a master of invective and sarcasm when these qualities were necessary to rebuke an unwise antagonist or to defeat a noxious measure. Of him with truth it has been said, "as a man he was genial and courteous, a true type of the Virginia gentleman; a firm and generous foe; keen and ready in repartee, and unsparing in his unscathing denunciation of sham and pretence." In civil life he was repeatedly honored by election to the City Council of Alexandria, and he was the first Mayor of that city after the late Civil War. He died October 25, 1880, and was buried with the honors of the Order, the Great Incohonee and many other of the Great Chiefs and Past Great Chiefs of the Great Council of the United States being present at his funeral.

Past Great Incohonee John F. Smith. — John F. Smith was born in Middlebury, Va., and was a member of Algonquin Tribe, No. 1, of that State. He was admitted to the Great Council of the United States, April 4, 1849, and was elected Great Incohonee at that council. The information possessed by us concerning Brother Smith is very meagre, and we are unable to give the date either of his birth or death, and as far as we know he may be now living. From those who were his associates during his connection with the Great Council of the United States, we learn that he was an efficient chief, and discharged the duties of Great Incohonee in a manner that met the approbation of the members of the G. C. U. S. His manner was pleasant and genial, and his decisions, while Great Incohonee, were rendered with great fairness and clearness of judgment. He must have possessed qualities of mind that commended him to his associates to receive the exalted rank of Great Incohonee on the occasion of his first admission into the G. C. U. S.

Past Great Incohonee William Beesley Davis. — William Beesley Davis was born in Salem, N.J., December 2, 1820. He first became a member of the Order by adoption in Kuequenaku Tribe, No. 4, at its institution in Plant moon, G. S. 5608, and while a member of that Tribe was elected Great Sachem of Pennsylvania, and Great Incohonee of the United States. He afterwards took an active part in organizing and instituting Black Hawk Tribe, No. 26, of Philadelphia, to which he was attached at the time of his death. He was an ardent and industrious student, and graduated with high honors from Pennsylvania University, and for many years successfully practised his profession in the city of Philadelphia, where he was highly respected not only as a physician, but as a sterling and able citizen. He took an active part in society matters, and was for many years a member of Kensington Lodge, No. 211, F. and A. M., of which he was an honored Past Master. He proved himself eminently a scholar and a gentleman, though modest and retiring in his general deportment. He was firm in his convictions, and proved a faithful member of our Order in its early days. After a wasting illness, which he bore with calm and Christian resignation, he passed from the hunting-grounds of earth, the 7th of Worm moon, G. S. D. 395 (March 7, 1886), and was buried in South Cedar Hill Cemetery, Philadelphia. His funeral was attended by a large number of members of the Masonic Fraternity and the Improved Order of Red Men, as well as a large circle of his friends, among whom he was universally admired and respected. The Great Council of the United States and the Great Council of Pennsylvania were represented by many of their members.

Past Great Incohonee Robert Sullivan. — Robert Sullivan was born in the city of Baltimore, Md., in the year 1814. He became a member of Pocahontas Tribe, No. 3, of Baltimore, but the precise date of his adoption, we are unable to give. As early as 1850, he had attained the rank of Past Grand Sachem of the Grand Council of Maryland, and was admitted to the G. C. U. S. in Plant moon, 1850, and at the same council was elected W. G. Senior Sagamore. At the succeeding council in 1851 he was elected W. G. Incohonee. He died September 24, 1867. He was a painter by trade, and won material success at his calling. For many years he served the city of Baltimore as a member of the City Council, and was also for a long time Superintendent of Druid Hill Park, a position requiring judgment, care, and executive ability. He is described as a man of fine personal appearance, good physique, and pleasant, affable manners, and his good heart and gentlemanly conduct drew to him the loyal friendship of all who knew him. While his connection with the Order was comparatively brief, yet it was of sufficient length to impress all the members whom he met, with his sterling worth and executive ability.

Past Great Incohonee William Tucker. — William Tucker was born in the city of Washington, D.C., in the year 1813. He was admitted to the Order in 1845 as a charter member of Anacostia Tribe, No. 3, District of Columbia, and was admitted as a Representative of that Tribe in the Great Council of Maryland, on October 10, 1845. His name also appears as one of the three from his Tribe, on a petition for a charter to the Great Council of the District of Columbia which was chartered in that same year. The meagre records of the G. C. U. S. do not give the precise date of his admission into that body, but he was elected W. G. Senior Sagamore in 1851, and W. G. Incohonee in 1852. He followed the trade of a pump and block maker, and built up a large business in the city of Washington and vicinity. He was an active worker in the Order while he remained a member. We are unable to give the date when his membership ceased, or the date of his death.

Past Great Incohonee George A. Peter. — George A. Peter was born in Baltimore, Md., February 14, 1809. He was one of the historical characters of the Improved Order of Red Men. Another authority gives the date of his birth as February 1, 1808. He was a member of one of the branches of the Society of Red Men. At the institution of the "Grand Council of Maryland, Society of Red Men," he was chosen Grand Chief of Records. In G. S. D. 349 (1840), he removed to St. Louis, Mo., but remained there only a few moons, and then went to Cincinnati, Ohio, where he located permanently. He secured the organization of Miami Tribe, No. 1, at Cincinnati, on the 9th of Corn moon, G. S. 5611 (September 9, 1851), of which Tribe he remained a member until he died. When the Great Council of Ohio was organized, he became Great Sachem, which entitled him to admission into the Great Council of the United States, and his name is recorded among the Representatives admitted at the council held in 1853. At the Council of 1854, he was elected Great Incohonee. He died September 30, 1879. Brother Peter was a practical paper-hanger and decorator, and in his trade showed skill, ability, and fidelity, which endeared him to all with whom he came in contact. He was prominent in other fraternal

BIOGRAPHIES.

organizations, being a member of Ohio Lodge, No. 1, and Wiley Encampment of the I. O. O. F. In civil life, in his adopted city of Cincinnati, he was known and respected by his fellow-citizens, by whom he was repeatedly selected as a member of the school board and of the City Council. He was also Mayor of the village of Riverside, a suburb of Cincinnati. This brief sketch gives but faintly a memorial of Past Great Incohonee George A. Peter. The name given him on his admission to the Society of Red Men was "Link of Union." This is a peculiarly apt name for the brother, as in his personality he was indeed a "link of union" between the old organization and the new.

Past Great Incohonee William R. Burns. — William R. Burns was the eighth Great Incohonee of the Order. The information concerning this brother at our command is very meagre. He was a charter member of Moax Tribe, No. 5, which was instituted October 1, 1851. In 1853 he was admitted to the Great Council of the United States, representing the Great Council of New Jersey, and at the same council was elected W. G. Senior Sagamore. In 1854, by which time he had attained the rank of Past Great Sachem of New Jersey, he was elected W. G. Incohonee. Almost immediately after the termination of his chieftaincy, his connection with the Order was severed. We are not in possession of any data concerning him after that time.

Past Great Incohonee George W. Ford. — We have no information as to the date of the birth or death of Brother George W. Ford. The first information concerning him given, is residing at Newport, Ky., and it is probable that he was a member of Chickasaw Tribe, No. 1, of Newport, which was instituted June 29, 1852. He was admitted to the Great Council of the United States in 1855, by which time he had attained the rank of Past Great Sachem of Kentucky, and at that council was elected W. G. Incohonee. Brother Ford was an active and zealous Red Man during his connection with the Order. He gave his personal attention to the institution of Tribes while holding the position of W. G. Incohonee, and among the Tribes instituted by him was Osyka, No. 1, of New Orleans, La. Brother Ford is recorded as having been a generous, frank, good-hearted man, a kind friend, and a capable chief in the Great Council of the United States.

Past Great Incohonee Louis Bonsal. — Louis Bonsal was born in Baltimore, Md., June 17, 1818. He was elected a member of Pocahontas Tribe, No. 3, of Maryland, December 23, 1840, and remained a member of that Tribe for a period of more than 50 years until its dissolution. In Travelling moon, G. S. D. 401 (October, 1892), shortly after the dissolution of the Tribe, he passed from the hunting grounds of earth, and through no fault of his own was not a member of the Order at that time. His advanced age, being over 74 years, precluded his admission into any other Tribe, and the local legislation of the reservation of Maryland did not provide for continuing the membership of aged members of the Order. Brother Bonsal held almost every position in his Tribe, and was also Great Chief of Records, and Great Sachem in the Great Council of Maryland. He assisted at the organization of the Great Council of the United States in January, 1847, and was elected Great Incohonee, September 10, 1856. While Great Incohonee he aroused considerable opposition by issuing a charter to Powhatan Tribe, No. 1, of Washington, D.C., but having the courage of his convictions he was not deterred by threats nor moved from his purpose by angry words. In early youth Brother Bonsal served his apprenticeship as a book-binder, but on reaching his majority established himself in business in a book and stationery store which he continued for several years. He moved from Baltimore to the country for a short period, and on his return engaged in the grocery business, which he continued for many years. Brother Bonsal merited and received the loyal affection of his brothers in the Order, with whom he was connected through many great suns. As stated, he died at a ripe old age, in the full fruition of a good life well spent, and beloved by all who knew him.

Past Great Incohonee Daniel W. Carter. — Daniel W. Carter was born in Salem, N.J., October 24, 1820. His admission to the Order occurred in the early history of that reservation, and he was admitted to the Great Council of the United States in 1854. In 1856 he was elected W. G. Senior Sagamore, and in 1857, W. G. Incohonee, of the G. C. U. S. He died April 23, 1885, and at the time of his death held the position of Great Chief of Records of the Great Council of Delaware. At the age of 12 years, by reason of the death of his father, he was compelled to go among strangers and earn his livelihood. He was apprenticed to learn the trade of a tanner and currier, and at the age of 21 entered into a partnership which continued until 1854, when he removed to Wilmington, Del., where he again engaged in the business of tanner and currier. Subsequent to 1861 he was superintendent of several influential firms. He held many positions of trust and honor in the city of Wilmington, and in all the offices filled by him, either as a member of the Order or as a citizen, he won the confidence and respect of all his associates.

Past Great Incohonee Paxon Coats. — Paxon Coats was born June 24, 1815, near New Hope, Bucks Co., Pa. In 1841 he moved to St. Louis, Mo., and, in 1842, established himself permanently in the city of Cincinnati, where he engaged in the business of a distiller. In 1843 he established the business of burning and grinding charcoal for use in rectifying, still continuing the business of a distiller. A short time previous to his death he returned to Pennsylvania, and died in the city of Philadelphia, June 6, 1879, in the 64th year of his age, at the home of his nephew William Coats. He was adopted in Miami Tribe, No. 1, of Cincinnati, Ohio, and advanced rapidly through the various chieftaincies, until he was admitted into the Great Council of the United States at the council held in 1856. In September, 1858, he was elected Great Incohonee. Brother Coats was a good citizen, and though unfortunate in his business relations near the end of his life, he always retained the respect and confidence of his intimate personal friends.

Past Great Incohonee Andrew J. Baker. — Andrew J. Baker was born January 20, 1828, at Passayunk, now a part of the city of Philadelphia, Pa. His early education was obtained in the old Passayunk Seminary. When but ten years old, his father died, and at the age of 12 he was compelled to assist in the support of the family. He afterwards learned the trade of metal turner and subsequently that of gas-fitter. He resided in Richmond, Va., for a short time, and while working at his trade of gas-fitter put up the first gas-pipe used in that city. While residing there he assisted at the institution of Pocahontas Tribe, No. 14, and regularly attended its Councils. He was one of the petitioners for the charter of Wyoming Tribe, No. 7, and was adopted at its institution, September 22, 1849, being the youngest member adopted. The original name of the Tribe was Weccacoe, but it was changed, in 1854, to Wyoming. He was admitted to the Great Council of Pennsylvania, October 9, 1849. He served as Sachem of his Tribe from August 5, 1850, and subsequently served as Chief of Records for several terms, and on January 2, 1862, he was raised up as Keeper of Wampum, which chieftaincy he has held since that time. He passed through various chieftaincies in the Great Council of Pennsylvania, and has been repeatedly elected Representative from that body to the G. C. U. S. in which he was admitted for the first time in 1854. He served as Great Chief of Records of Pennsylvania for a period of 14 great suns, during which time 180 Tribes were instituted, besides a number whose council fires had ceased to burn, and were rekindled during that time. Brother Baker has instituted or taken part in the institution of more than 200 Tribes in Pennsylvania, besides several in New Jersey and New York. Acting under the authority of Great Incohonee Parsons, he instituted the Great Council of West Virginia, January 27, 1870. In the Great Council of the United States, Brother Baker served on most of the important committees, and has had a prominent part in shaping its laws and perfecting its ritual and other ceremonies. In company with the late P. G. I. Gorham, he prepared the ritual which, with the modifications recently adopted, remains in use at the present time. Brother Baker has been present at every council of the G. C. U. S., since his admission to that body, and has also attended every regular council of the Great Council of Pennsylvania for more than forty great suns. While Brother Baker has more closely identified himself with the Improved Order of Red Men than with any other organization, he is also a Past Grand of Southern Lodge, No. 41, of the I. O. O. F., and is also Past Master of Lafayette Lodge, No. 71, and of St. John Chapter, No. 32, of the Masonic Fraternity. Brother Baker has not taken active part in politics, although he has occasionally served as a member of the Common Council of the city of Philadelphia. For a number of years he was a member of the Philadelphia Grays. During the late Civil War, he held a commission as first lieutenant in one of the emergency regiments of Pennsylvania, although his regiment was not called into active service. In the Volunteer Fire department, in Philadelphia, he was a member of the Old Diligent Fire Engine Company for about 20 years, and still holds a position of trust in the relief association of the veteran firemen of that city. Brother Baker is the senior surviving Past Great Incohonee now connected with the Order. He is a man of strong will and resolute purpose, active, energetic, and earnest in the support of what he believes for the best interest and welfare of the Order. At the same time, he is strong in his personal friendships, and those who obtain his confidence find him a warm and loyal friend.

Past Great Incohonee Richard Marley. — Richard Marley was born in the city of Philadelphia, Pa., November 12, 1791. Early in life, he was apprenticed to the trade of a shoemaker, at which he became an expert, and upon his removal to Baltimore, he opened a ladies' shoe store, in which venture he was successful, and in which he continued during his life. The Minute Book of the Society of Red Men shows the admission, September 14, 1824, of "Richard Marley, Cordwainer," proposed by "Hospitality," name received, Mattawa, or "Moose Deer's Brother." Among his papers, at the time of his death, was found a letter dated Philadelphia, May 13, 1820, and signed by the Generalissimo, directed to "Split Log's Brother," 5th Major-General commanding in Maryland. Brother Marley was among those who assisted at the organization of a Tribe in Baltimore, of the Society of Red Men, out of which grew the Improved Order of Red Men. He afterwards became a charter member of Ottawa Tribe, No. 16, in November, 1849. He was admitted to the Great Council of the United States in 1851, and was elected W. G. Incohonee in 1860, having previously obtained the rank of Past Great Sachem in the Great Council of Maryland. Not only was Brother Marley prominent in the Improved Order of Red Men, but he was among the earliest members of the Independent Order of Odd Fellows, and attained the rank of Past Grand Sire in that organization corresponding to the rank of Past Great Incohonee in our Order. He died May 7, 1867, at the age of 78, and from both of the organizations named, many joined at his funeral in doing all possible honor to his memory. With Brother George A. Peter, Brother Marley shared the honor of being the positive living element connecting the new organization with the old, and throughout his membership did all in his power to advance the prosperity of the Improved Order of Red Men.

Past Great Incohonee Joseph Pyle. — Joseph Pyle, the present Great Keeper of Wampum of the Great Council of the United States, was born in the township of Sunbury, Pa., in 1826. When but three weeks old his parents moved to Delaware, where, at the age of 17, he was apprenticed to learn the leather trade. He afterwards worked as a journeyman at his trade, and evidently used his brain as well as his hands in his daily toil, because several valuable patents were invented by him for the more facile manipulation of leather. In 1847 Brother Pyle was adopted in Delaware Tribe, No. 1, from which he withdrew to become a charter member of Keokuk Tribe, No. 3. As Vice Great Incohonee he organized the Great Council of Delaware. He was admitted to the Great Council of the United States in 1852, and in 1861 was elected Great Incohonee. In 1874 he was elected to the position of Great Keeper of Wampum of the G. C. U. S., to which position he has been unanimously elected at every succeeding election. Brother Pyle is Past Grand Master and Past Grand Patriarch of the I. O. O. F., Past Grand Archon of the Order of Heptasophs, and Past Grand Patriarch of the Sons of Temperance. In early life he served as a member of the City Council, until the pressing demands of business claimed all his attention, when he declined further honors in that direction. For the same reason he has repeatedly declined to accept the nomination for Mayor of the city. He has also been mentioned as a candidate for the Governor of the State of Delaware. He is a member of the board of education of Wilmington. Brother Pyle is a Methodist, and has been superintendent of the Sunday-school for 30 years, and President of the board of trustees for 26 years of St. Paul's M. E. Church. Brother Pyle is President of the C. & J. Pyle Co., manufacturers of patent leather, of Wilmington, and, as a member of this firm, has built up a handsome fortune. From the day of his admission to the Order Brother Pyle has been an active worker for the Red Men. He has the confidence and esteem of every member of the Order who has the honor and pleasure of his acquaintance. He is held in high esteem by the members of the Great Council of the United States, and will undoubtedly remain in his position as long as he cares to accept an election, or until the Great Spirit in his wisdom shall call him from the hunting grounds of earth.

Past Great Incohonee A. J. Francis. — We have absolutely no information concerning Brother A. J. Francis other than that he was admitted into the Great Council of the United States at the council held at Baltimore, Md., in Corn moon, 1857, at which time he was reported as a Past Great Sachem of Kentucky. At the council held at Baltimore, in 1863, he was elected W. G. Incohonee. He resided in Covington, Ky. Personally he was modest and unassuming; but his recommendations as Great Incohonee indicate that he possessed firmness of character, and a kind and generous disposition.

Past Great Incohonee Angus Cameron. — Angus Cameron was adopted into Chattahoochee Tribe, No. 17, in the city of Philadelphia, on the 4th of Sturgeon moon, G. S. D. 368 (August 4, 1859), for the purpose of qualifying him to become one of the charter members of Miquon Tribe, No. 50, in the same city, which was instituted on the 11th of the same moon, at which time he was elected its first Senior Sagamore. He became a member of the Great Council of Pennsylvania, January 18, 1860, where his zeal, devotion, and talents at once marked him as destined for distinguished honors in our beloved Order. In 1862 he was elected Great Senior Sagamore of the Great Council of Pennsylvania, and by reason of the absence of the Great Sachem of that Body in the army, Brother Cameron was required to perform the duties of that position for nearly two great suns. Brother Cameron withdrew from Miquon Tribe, No. 50, and became a charter member of Kawanio-Chee-Keteru Tribe, No. 190, at its institution October 16, 1872. He continued one of its most active and useful members until his death. Brother Cameron was admitted into the Great Council of the United States in 1861, and in September, 1864, he was elected Great Incohonee, being the third from Pennsylvania to receive that distinguished honor. He died January 18, 1879, at Philadelphia, Pa. Brother Cameron was a man of unusual force of character; possessed of enlarged and liberal views, of great natural ability, of wide business experience, and of educational qualifications of a high order. He was a man whose judgment and opinion were frequently appealed to on questions of doubt and uncertainty. He was ever ready and willing to assist and encourage the timid and retiring, to aid in bringing out the talent of those whom he believed to be of good intentions, but he most heartily despised the sham and pretender. The indelible impress of his mind is stamped upon many of our laws and our legislation, and will remain as long as our council fire continues to burn. His highest ambition, as a Red Man, was to elevate our Order to a higher plane, and a purer moral atmosphere.

Past Great Incohonee Thomas A. Bosley.—Thomas A. Bosley was born in Baltimore, Md., February 8, 1817; but he subsequently removed to Cincinnati, Ohio, where he died May 2, 1888. At what time he connected himself with our Order we are unable to state; but the records show that he was for many years an active member in its interests. He became a member of Miami Tribe, No. 1, of Cincinnati, and held membership therein when he was admitted into the Great Council of the United States at the council held in 1852, and was elected Great Incohonee in 1865. He was also prominent in the Independent Order of Odd Fellows and the Knights of Pythias, and other similar organizations, in all of which he showed the energy and enterprise characteristic of him as a man. He was a paper-hanger and house decorator by trade, and as such established a successful business. During his chieftaincy as Great Incohonee an act of incorporation, of the Great Council of the United States, was obtained from the Legislature of Pennsylvania, the same being approved by Governor Curtin of that State, March 30, 1866. Under this charter authority was gained not before possessed to hold the councils of the G. C. U. S. in any State it saw fit, and to locate its principal office as it might elect within said limits. Brother Bosley died of inflammatory rheumatism May 2, 1888, beloved by all who knew him.

Past Great Incohonee Joshua Maris.—Joshua Maris was born in Willistown Township, Chester Co., Pa., April 7, 1832, and died in Wilmington, Del., August 13, 1884. He was educated at the Academy at Newark, Del., in the schools of Wilmington, and at Dickinson College, Carlisle, Pa. Upon completing his studies, he pursued the profession of a teacher until 1856, when he studied law in the office of Chancellor Daniel M. Bates of Delaware, and was admitted to the Delaware Bar in 1859, continuing the practice of law until his death. In 1859 he was elected Clerk of the City Council, and was twice re-elected to the same position. In 1863 he was elected Mayor of Wilmington and the following year for a second term. In 1871 he was elected President of the City Council for two years, and re-elected to the same position for a second term. In 1872 he was a member of the Legislature from New Castle County, and served on several important committees. He was admitted in Keokuk Tribe, No. 3, of Wilmington, April 28, 1853, and remained a member of that Tribe until March 26, 1868, when he withdrew to become a charter member of Lenape Tribe, No. 6. He was admitted to the Great Council of Delaware January 14, 1856, and passed through the various chieftaincies of that Great Council. He was admitted into the Great Council of the United States September 10, 1862, and was elected Great Incohonee September 11, 1866, being the first Great Incohonee to serve two successive great suns, the change in the law to that effect commencing with his chieftaincy. In September, 1870, he was elected Great Chief of Records of the G. C. U. S., which position he held until his death, which occurred August 13, 1884. He was prominent in other fraternal organizations, but the Improved Order of Red Men received the largest portion of his care and attention. His administration of public and fraternal duties won the esteem and lasting friendship of all fortunate enough to associate with him.

Past Great Incohonee James A. Parsons. — James A. Parsons was born in Atlantic County, N.J., April 16, 1837. His parents subsequently removed to Medford, N.J., and in 1854 to Camden, where Brother Parsons resided and grew to manhood. In 1860 he went to Richmond, Va., where he continued in the stove and tinware business until the breaking out of the Civil War, when, from his open and expressed Union sentiments, he was compelled, in April, 1861, to leave at such short notice that he left behind him his business and other effects. He returned to Camden, where he resided until 1878, when he removed to Philadelphia, his present abiding place. Brother Parsons was adopted into Leni Lenape Tribe, No. 2, of New Jersey, June 27, 1860, being elected Chief of Records December 30, 1863. Largely through his earnest, persistent, personal efforts the apathy then existing in the Tribe was removed, and it now has a membership of over 800. He continued Chief of Records until his election as Great Sachem, in January, 1868. He continued a member of Leni Lenape Tribe until January, 1881, when he withdrew and became a member of Ottawa Tribe, No. 15. On becoming a resident of Philadelphia, he withdrew and joined Moscosco Tribe, No. 34, of which he is now a member. He was admitted to the Great Council of New Jersey in 1862, and at the same council was elected Great Chief of Records. He passed through the various chieftaincies of the Great Council, which at that time contained but four Tribes. During his term as Great Sachem, three Tribes were instituted respectively at Millville, Bridgeton, and Camden, in the latter of which he became a member by card. In 1865 he was admitted to the Great Council of the United States, and was elected Great Incohonee in 1868. During his chieftaincy, the Order was introduced in Alabama, Nevada, and Oregon, and Great Councils instituted in Texas, Tennessee, Indiana, and West Virginia. Brother Parsons took an active part in the civil affairs of the city of Camden, serving six years as a member of the Common Council, and was one of the committee on building the City Hall. He is prominent in other organizations, being Past Grand and Past Patriarch of the I. O. O. F., a member of the Masonic Fraternity, and Past Grand Chancellor of the Knights of Pythias of New Jersey.

Past Great Incohonee William B. Eckert. — William B. Eckert was admitted into the Great Council of the United States in 1861, and was elected Great Incohonee in 1870. He is not now connected with the Order. He is a resident of the city of Philadelphia, Pa.

Past Great Incohonee James P. Riely. — James P. Riely was born at Winchester, Va., in 1841. He was educated at the Winchester Academy and at Dickinson College, and studied law at Lexington University. In 1861 he entered the Confederate service, in which he served until the close of the war. He then resumed the practice of law, and soon won for himself a position of honor and distinction in his profession. He served as Clerk of the Court of Frederick County from 1871 until July 1, 1887, when his health became impaired, and his decline became rapid until death came January 1, 1888. Brother Riely was adopted in Shawnee Tribe, No. 2, of Winchester, Va., May 31, 1866, and passed through the various chieftaincies. He was elected Great Sachem of Virginia, April 13, 1869, and was admitted into the Great Council of the United States in September, 1870, in which body he at once took an active part in shaping the business and legislation. At the council held in Nashville, Tenn., September, 1872, he was elected Great Incohonee. After the expiration of his service as Great Incohonee, he served several great suns as Representative of the Great Council of Virginia. He was a man of fine physique, of marked ability, fine education, commanding person, and was an eloquent orator. By his early death the Order and community in which he lived lost a valuable member.

Past Great Incohonee George W. Lindsay. — George W. Lindsay was born in Baltimore, Md., May 10, 1826, his parents having moved to that city from Fintnaugh, Ireland, the previous year. He attended school until his 15th year, at which time he was apprenticed to learn the printing business with John Murphy, a well-known resident of Baltimore, with whom he served five years, and continued five years after his apprenticeship had expired. In 1857, by reason of ill-health, he abandoned the printing business and started a real estate and collection agency, and by industry, energy, and indomitable perseverance succeeded in establishing one of the most successful agencies of that kind. Brother Lindsay joined Ottawa Tribe, No. 16, of Baltimore, November, 1849. He was elected Great Sachem of Maryland in 1855, and was admitted into the Great Council of the United States in that same year. He was elected Great Incohonee at the council held at Indianapolis in September, 1874. Brother Lindsay may truthfully be designated an active member of the Order, as his membership for over 40 years will prove. He is also active in other organizations, being Past Grand of the I. O. O. F., having joined that Order in 1848, a member of the Masonic Fraternity since 1863, a member of the Knights of Pythias since 1869, and Past Supreme Chancellor of that Order, a member of the Improved Order of Red Men since 1849, and a member of the Knights of Honor since 1878. In 1871 Brother Lindsay was elected one of the Judges to the Orphan's Court of Baltimore, and has held that position by successive re-election down to the present time. No better indication could be given of the high regard in which he is held by his fellow-citizens. His decisions, as Judge of that Court, have been sound, wise, and considerate, and in the direction of avoiding rather than encouraging litigation. From the researches of Brother Lindsay have been obtained the data upon which was based the action of the G. C. U. S., concerning the first epoch in the History of our Order, tracing the origin to the Patriotic Societies previous to the Revolution, all of which has been fully treated in this History. He is a firm friend, positive in his convictions, of iron will, yet courteous and considerate towards those with whom he is compelled to differ. He is among the most prominent and efficient public men in his native city.

Past Great Incohonee Adam Smith.—Adam Smith was born in Sembach, Kingdom of Bavaria, March 14, 1824. At the age of ten he came to America, making his home in the city of Philadelphia, where his early life was passed, and where he obtained such education as was offered in the public schools of Philadelphia, further improved by private reading and study. Brother Smith became a member of Delaware Tribe, No. 10, the precise date of his admission we cannot give, but as early as 1855, he left Philadelphia and settled at Marysville, Cal., where he opened a hotel, and invested largely in mining enterprises as well as ranching and stock raising. Not meeting with the desired success he removed to San Francisco, at which place he has since lived, and where he has made for himself a handsome fortune. Very soon after his arrival in San Francisco, he assisted in the organization of California Tribe, No. 1, which was instituted in 1864. At that time, so far as is known, Brother Smith was the only Past Sachem on the Pacific coast. From the organization of California Tribe, until the Great Council of California was instituted, he held the position of

Vice Great Incohonee, and he devoted his time and money and energy to the establishment of the Order on the Pacific slope. He was elected Great Sachem of the Great Council at its organization in 1868, and was chosen its first Representative to the Great Council of the United States, into which body he was admitted the same year. At the Council of the G. C. U. S. in 1868, he was elected Great Junior Sagamore, and in 1870 was elected Great Senior Sagamore, in 1876, Great Incohonee, and in 1882, Great Prophet, thus having been honored with every administrative position in the Great Council. Besides the work done by Brother Smith in California and Oregon, he ably assisted in establishing the Order also in Utah and Nevada. On his return from the Council of the G. C. U. S., at which he had been elected Great Incohonee, he was given a reception by the Order in California. Over 500 men were in line, and the procession marched to Red Men's Hall where a formal reception was held. Large delegations from the different Tribes were in attendance, and the occasion was one worthy of the Order, and of the distinguished chief thus honored. To write the history of Adam Smith as a Red Man, would be to write the History of the Order west of the Rocky Mountains, for much of its success and prosperity in that section of the country is due largely to his zeal and unbounded generosity. As a token of the affectionate regard felt for him by all his associates in the Great Council of the United States, he is invariably referred to as "Uncle Adam" Smith, and his genial good-nature, his generous disposition, and his sterling worth as a man, bind him by the ties of strongest affection to all who know him. While he has passed the allotted threescore years and ten, every friend and brother of Adam Smith unite in the hope that he may be spared to our Order for many great suns.

Past Great Incohonee Morris H. Gorham. — Morris H. Gorham was born in the city of New York, May 17, 1823. In 1835, his parents removed to Catawissa, Pa. While here he improved the very limited facilities for getting an education. In 1840 the family removed to Minersville, Pa. When old enough to learn a trade he was apprenticed to learn the pattern-making business, in which he acquired a reputation for industry, care, and close attention to business. In 1853 he located permanently in the city of Philadelphia, for a short time working at his trade. In 1850 he commenced the business of manufacturing regalia for beneficial organizations, making a speciality of that for the Improved Order of Red Men. In the meantime, he had been adopted into Chattahoochee Tribe, No. 17, January 25, 1854, and he continued a member of this Tribe until his death. From the time of his adoption he took an earnest interest in the symbolism and mysteries of the organization, and to him, as much as to any other one man, is due the symmetry and beauty of our present ritualistic work. He was admitted into the Great Council of Pennsylvania in 1854, and subsequently passed through the various chieftaincies of that body, being elected Great Chief of Records in 1857, and serving until 1864, when he was elected Great Sachem. In 1865 he was admitted into the Great Council of the United States where he soon won the esteem and confidence of his colleagues. He was elected Great Prophet of the G. C. U. S. in 1862, and Great Chief of Records in 1866, serving for four great suns, when he was succeeded by P. G. I. Joshua Maris. In 1878 he was elected Great Incohonee. In the Great Council of the United States, Brother Gorham served on each of the important committees at different times, and the imprint of his work and ability is seen upon nearly every page of the records of the G. C. U. S. He was author of a History of the Order, to which reference has been made in these pages, and it is due to his researches that we have been able to treat so fully of the second epoch in the History of the Order. He died very suddenly March 15, 1883. Every possible mark of respect was shown to his memory by the Great Council of Pennsylvania, and the funeral ceremonies were attended by a large number of prominent members of the Order. At the grave, Past Great Incohonee Joseph Pyle officiated as Sachem, and Past Great Incohonee Charles H. Litchman as Prophet, in the beautiful ceremony of our Order.

Past Great Incohonee Charles H. Litchman. — Charles H. Litchman was born in Marblehead, Mass., April 8, 1849. He was educated in the public schools of his native town, and has held various offices therein by election and appointment, and has also represented the town in the Legislature of the State.

Brother Litchman became interested in the Improved Order of Red Men from a visit made to Providence, R.I., in April, 1872. On his return to Marblehead he induced eight others to accompany him to Providence, where on July 19, 1872, they were adopted in Miantonomah Tribe, No. 3, of that city. He became a charter member of Manataug Tribe, No. 1, of Marblehead, at its institution August 1, 1872, being elected the first Senior Sagamore of the Tribe. When the Great Council of Massachusetts was formed December 23, 1873, he was elected Great Sachem, and was re-elected to that position in August, 1874. He was admitted into the Great Council of the United States at the Council held at Indianapolis, September, 1874, was elected Great Junior Sagamore in 1876, Great Senior Sagamore in 1878, and Great Incohonee in 1880. He declined to be a candidate for Great Prophet in opposition to Past Great Incohonee Adam Smith, but was elected to that position subsequently in 1884. From his entrance into the Great Council of the United States, he served on important committees, the most recent of which is the Committee on Revision, by which the Constitution and Digest of the Order have been revised, and by which the ritual for the adoption ceremony has been perfected, and the degrees of the Order are now being also amended. Brother Litchman is a member of several fraternities, being a Past Grand and Past Chief Patriarch of the I. O. O. F., a member of the Knights of Pythias, a member of Amity Lodge of Danvers, and St. Andrew's Chapter of Boston, Mass., of the Masonic Fraternity, Past Regent of the Royal Arcanum, Past Noble Commander of the Golden Cross, and Past Grand Commander of the American Legion of Honor, etc.

Past Great Incohonee George B. Colflesh. — George B. Colflesh was born in Chester County, Pa., March 16, 1826. He received a common-school education in his native State, and in early manhood removed to Baltimore, where he obtained the position of foreman in a large carriage factory. In a few years he established a business for himself, and by close attention and strict integrity built up a large and profitable trade. Brother Colflesh joined the Improved Order of Red Men in Pocahontas Tribe, No. 3, in 1849, and passed through various chieftaincies of his Tribe, and in the Great Council of Maryland.

In the Great Council of his State he served on many important committees and was active in whatever would advance the interests and prosperity of the Order. He took an active part in the erection of Red Men's Hall, of which he was a trustee. Brother Colflesh was admitted to the Great Council of the United States in 1858, and passed successively through the chieftaincies until he became Great Incohonee in 1882, and Great Prophet of the G. C. U. S. in 1886. When the Chieftains' League was organized Brother Colflesh took an active part in the organization, and was elected Supreme Treasurer in 1890. Brother Colflesh was modest and unassuming in his manner, and endeared himself to those who knew him more by the sterling worth of his character than by any exploitation of his own personality.

P. S. Just as this History was going to press, intelligence was received of the death of Past Great Incohonee Colflesh, July 28, 1893. His funeral took place on the 29th of July, and was attended by Past Great Incohonees Pyle, Baker, Lindsay, and Conley, and by a large number of citizens and members of the Order, and of the fraternities and organizations to which he belonged in the city of Baltimore.

Past Great Incohonee William H. Hyronemus. — William H. Hyronemus was born in the city of Cincinnati, Ohio, April 6, 1842. In his infancy his parents removed to Nashville, Tenn., which has been since his home. He has identified himself with the interests of that city in every possible way, and holds a position of influence in the trust and confidence of his fellow-citizens. To the early education of the public schools, he supplemented a self-education gained in the experience of manhood and by a course of private reading, and the position of affluence which he enjoys is due entirely to his own energy and perseverance. He joined the Improved Order of Red Men in 1867, and has ever been an active worker in his Tribe and in the Order. He was Chief of Records of the Tribe for many years, and also served as Great Chief of Records of Tennessee, from the date of his admission, 1875, until 1876, when he was elected Great Sachem. After completing his service as Great Sachem, he was re-elected as Great Chief of Records, and continued in that chieftaincy until 1890, when he declined further to be a candidate for re-election.

In 1877 he was admitted to the Great Council of the United States, and was elected Great Junior Sagamore in 1880, Great Senior Sagamore in 1882, and Great Incohonee in 1884, and is at present chairman on the Committee on Finance of the G. C. U. S. He is a member of other organizations, and has served several terms as a member of the City Council in his city. He enjoys the esteem and respect of all who know him as a good man, a genial companion, a generous friend, and a stanch supporter of the Improved Order of Red Men.

Past Great Incohonee Ralph S. Gregory. — Ralph S. Gregory was born in Delaware County, Ind., February 28, 1846. He lived upon a farm until 15 years old, when he entered the High School at Muncie, Ind. He then entered the preparatory department of Wabash College, where he continued until 1862, when he entered the army as a private soldier in Company B., 84th Indiana Volunteer Infantry. He remained in the army about two years, when, on account of failing health, he was honorably discharged at Shell Mound, Tenn., having attained the rank of Orderly Sergeant. On returning home, having regained his health, he returned to College and remained through the junior year. He then entered Asbury University under the control of the M. E. Church. This university is now known as the De Pauw University. He graduated with honors in the class of 1867, and then took charge of the Huntington High School, where he continued as teacher and instructor for two years. He then studied law and was admitted to the bar in 1869, and has since won an enviable reputation in his chosen profession of the law. He has a pleasing address, and presents his arguments not only with logic but with rhetorical finish. He is a Knight Templar of the Masonic Fraternity, and a member of the Knights of Pythias. He is a charter member of De Ember Tribe, No. 30, of Muncie, Ind. He passed through the various chieftaincies of his Tribe, and in due time was elected Great Sachem of Indiana. He was admitted into the Great Council of the United States in 1879, was appointed Great Mishinewa in 1880, elected Great Junior Sagamore in 1882, Great Senior Sagamore in 1884, Great Incohonee in 1886, and Great Prophet in 1888. He is at the present time a Representative to the G. C. U. S. from Indiana. Brother Gregory, by his ability and genial good-nature, is one of the influential and highly respected members of the Great Council of the United States.

Past Great Incohonee Charles C. Conley. — Charles C. Conley enjoys the distinction of being the only brother of the Order upon whom was conferred the rank and honor of Past Great Incohonee, without having served as presiding chief of the Great Council of the United States. Brother Conley was born in the village of Milton, Sussex Co., Del., November 9, 1833. He is a descendant of old Revolutionary stock, his grandfather being Major in the Revolutionary Army, and his father in the coast service, and he himself, with honor in the late Civil War. In early life his parents removed to Philadelphia, which has since been his home. His education was received in the public schools of Philadelphia, but circumstances compelled him to engage in earning his own livelihood at an early age. Brother Conley was adopted in Shawnese Tribe, No. 8, of Philadelphia, July, 1856. He was admitted to the Great Council of Pennsylvania in 1858. November 9, 1858, he withdrew from Shawnese Tribe, and became a charter member of Chippewa Tribe, No. 51, in which he has since held active membership. He passed through the various chieftaincies of the Great Council of Pennsylvania, and was then elected Great Chief of Records in May, 1878, and filled that chieftaincy for ten consecutive years. Brother Conley was present at the Council of the G. C. U. S. for the first time, as Past Great Sachem, in 1870, and subsequently as a Representative from the Great Council of Pennsylvania at the Council held in 1877. In 1884 he was elected Great Chief of Records of the Great Council of the United States, which chieftaincy he now holds. At the Council held at Boston, Mass., September, 1890, by unanimous vote of the Great Council, the honors and title of Past Great Incohonee were conferred upon Brother Conley "for meritorious service." This is the only instance in the history of the Order, but follows the analogy of conferring the honor of Past Sachem upon the Chief of Records of a Tribe, after five consecutive years of faithful service. Brother Conley has been a prominent figure in the Order for the last 25 great suns, and holds this prominence by his merit as a Chief, his ability as a man, his fidelity as a friend, and his unswerving loyalty to the Order.

Past Great Incohonee Thomas J. Francis. — Thomas J. Francis is a resident of Camden, N.J., although he was born in Philadelphia, May 6, 1831. He resided in Philadelphia until 1850, when he made Camden his permanent home, with the exception of a few years that he lived at Wilmington, Del. After faithful service in his own reservation, he was admitted into the Great Council of the United States in 1866. He was elected Great Senior Sagamore of the G. C. U. S. in 1887, to fill a vacancy, and Great Incohonee in 1888. During his chieftaincy a remarkable prosperity was manifested in the Order, there having been a gain of 31,000 in the membership during the two years he held that chieftaincy. In 1890 he was elected Great Prophet, in which chieftaincy he served until the Council of Atlanta, Ga., in September, 1892. Brother Francis is a member of Leni Lenape Tribe, No. 2, of Camden, N.J., into which Tribe he was adopted in 1852, thus having been a member of the Order for more than forty years. He has ever taken a prominent part in all matters concerning the Order, both in the Tribe in which he is a member and in the Great Council of his reservation. He has represented his Great Council in the G. C. U. S. many times. In private life Brother Francis is a respected citizen, and has won the confidence and respect of his friends and neighbors. Brother Francis still takes an active and earnest interest in the Order, and is never weary of well-doing when he can advance its interests, or do anything to increase its prosperity.

Past Great Incohonee Thomas K. Donnalley. — Thomas K. Donnalley was born in Philadelphia, October 20, 1838. He received his education in the public schools of that city. On leaving school he learned the business of cutting, and followed this occupation until 1857, when he established the business of furnishing goods for fraternal societies, in which he has been actively engaged from that time. Brother Donnalley was adopted in Pequod Tribe, No. 18, on April 19, 1860, since which time he has held a chieftaincy of some kind in the Order, thus proving his active interest and zeal. He was admitted to the Great Council of Pennsylvania in January, 1864, and in the deliberations of that body has always taken an active and prominent part. His administration as Great Sachem of Pennsylvania was one of marked success. He was admitted to the Great Council of the United States in 1866, and at once took an active and prominent part in the legislation of that body. When Brother Conley declined further re-election as Great Chief of Records of Pennsylvania, Brother Donnalley was elected to the position, and has ably filled that chieftaincy from then until the present time. Brother Donnalley served with honor during the late Civil War. He is a member of nearly all the fraternal organizations of the United States, but to the Improved Order of Red Men gives the greater part of his energy and ability. Brother Donnalley was elected Great Junior Sagamore of the G. C. U. S. in 1886, Great Senior Sagamore in 1888, Great Incohonee in 1890, and Great Prophet in 1892, which latter position he now holds. He is also Chairman of the Committee on Revision, and has done efficient work in the latest revision of the Constitution and adoption ceremony of the Order. He has the appointment of Exemplifier from the present Great Incohonee, and in that capacity he has exemplified the work of the Order in many reservations. Brother Donnalley is an active worker, a stanch friend, a faithful member of society, and a true Red Man.

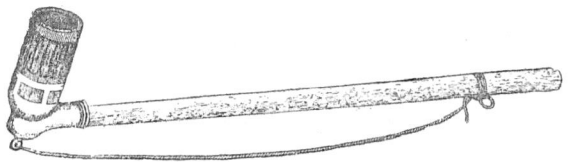

CHAPTER XI.

REVISED DIGEST OF THE DECISIONS, LAWS, ETC., OF THE GREAT COUNCIL OF THE UNITED STATES.

AMENDMENTS.

CONSTITUTION OF THE GREAT COUNCIL OF THE UNITED STATES.

1. This Constitution shall not be altered, amended, or repealed, unless the proposition for that purpose be presented in writing, signed by representatives of three Great Councils, and lie over for one great sun, and then receive the assent of two-thirds of those present and entitled to vote; provided, action upon a proposition to amend any of the laws may be taken at the same council at which it is submitted, if seven-eighths agree to the same.

BY-LAWS OF THE GREAT COUNCIL OF THE UNITED STATES.

2. No alteration or amendments to these By-Laws shall be made unless presented at a great sun's council, signed by representatives from three Great Councils, read upon three separate suns, and then adopted by two-thirds of the representatives present.

GENERAL LAWS FOR GREAT COUNCILS.

3. Any amendment, alteration, or addition to these General Laws shall be proposed in writing and acted upon as prescribed in Article XIX of the Constitution of the Great Council of the United States. — General Law.

4. Propositions to amend the laws must be signed by representatives from at least three Great Councils. — IX, 73.

APPEALS.

5. All appeals taken from the action of a State Great Council, or a Tribe working under the immediate jurisdiction of the Great Council of the United States, to the Great Council of the United States, as hereinafter provided for, shall be received and passed upon; but in all cases the action or decision of a State Great Council or the Tribe shall be final and conclusive until reversed by the Great Council of the United States, except where the sentence involves expulsion from the Order.

6. An appeal may be taken from the action or decision of a Tribe under the jurisdiction of the Great Council of the United States to the Great Council of the United States by any member or person who thinks his rights have been denied by such decision or action, upon giving written notice and

filing said appeal within one moon from the date of said action of appeal, and provided, that a copy of the appeal has been placed in the hands of the Great Incohonee, with proof that the Tribe has received due notice.

7. Members of Tribes may appeal from the action of a State Great Council, provided two copies of the appeal have been presented, mailed or sent to the Great Sachem, not less than twenty suns prior to the kindling of the council fire of the Great Council of the United States; and the Great Sachem shall certify, under seal of his Great Council (on each of the copies), the date that he received the appeal and forthwith send one to the appellant, who shall immediately send it to the Great Incohonee, who shall report its reception to the Great Council. All appeals from the action of a State Great Council must be made so that they can be acted upon at the council following the decision or action taken, and a failure to do so shall be a bar to all further proceedings; provided, the council of said State Great Council is not held within the time mentioned above. — Art. XVII, Constitution G. C. U. S.

8. Appeals that are made from the action of a State Great Council or a Tribe under the jurisdiction of the Great Council of the United States, which set forth that the grievance is a violation of law, and not brought about through informalities as laid down in the Code of Procedure, may be acted upon by the Great Incohonee, provided that copies of said appeals have been served upon the legal authorities. — IX, 23.

9. It is the imperative duty of every Great Sachem to certify that he has received an appeal; it is also the duty of Chiefs of Tribes to certify that an appeal has been received, provided said appeal is couched in respectful language. — IV, 198.

10. An appeal, not accompanied by evidence that the law has been complied with, shall be dismissed. — IV, 402.

11. Appeals from questions of law shall be referred to the Judiciary Committee. — IV, 63.

12. A Chief of Records has no authority to make out an appeal to the Great Council of the United States from the action of the Great Council of his State, without specific instructions from his Tribe in regular council, and no subsequent action of the Tribe can remedy the defect. — VI, 172.

13. The ruling of a Great Sachem can be challenged only by an appeal taken in regular form, and is in no particular affected by a protest. —V, 165.

14. Where there is a State Great Council, a brother cannot appeal from the action of his Tribe to the Great Council of the United States until the case has been heard and determined by the State Great Council. — II, 251.

15. Speaking of the character of the appellant is not in order during the consideration of an appeal. — III, 357.

16. In all reports of the Committee on Appeals and Grievances there shall be a clear and sufficient statement of the matters at issue, so as to obviate the necessity of reading all the papers in each case. — IV, 134.

17. A brother feeling that injustice has been done him by a Tribe shall appeal to the Great Sachem of the reservation within two moons from the date of the notice of the action of the Tribe, stating distinctly and specifically

the reason or reasons he may have for believing the wrong has been done him. He shall be required, however, first to serve a copy of the appeal upon the Tribe, of which service due proof shall be furnished the Great Sachem. As soon as the Great Sachem has received an appeal in proper form, he shall, within one seven suns, notify the Tribe, and the Chief of Records shall immediately deliver to the Great Sachem the journal of the committee by which the case was tried, together with the testimony taken before it and copies of the records of all the council sleeps containing matter relating thereto and all papers connected therewith, signed by the Sachem and Chief of Records, under seal. Should the Tribe neglect or refuse to comply herewith, it shall be sufficient cause for its suspension.

18. The Great Sachem shall refer all documents and papers to such committee as the laws of the State Great Council may designate. — Code of Procedure.

Appeals as Regards Benefits.

19. Should any person feel aggrieved at the action of a Tribe for failing to pay benefits that may be claimed to be due, such person shall appeal from said action by giving the Tribe notice thereof within twenty suns after said action, whereupon the Sachem shall, without delay, appoint a suitable member of the Order as a commissioner to take such testimony as either party may offer in relation to the case.

20. The commissioner shall, within twenty suns, proceed to take the testimony, giving each party ten suns' notice of the time and place of meeting for that purpose. The Sachem shall represent the Tribe, which may be represented also by counsel. The aggrieved party may appear in person and may also be represented by counsel. All testimony must be taken down fully by the commissioner and signed by the witnesses after being fully read to them, and should objections be made to the examination of any witness, or to any question, or to any testimony offered, he shall note the same, and he shall give ample time and opportunity to both parties to present witnesses, and for them to testify. All testimony shall be written in ink.

21. After taking all the testimony the parties may offer, the commissioner shall immediately report to the Tribe, whereupon the Chief of Records shall notify the aggrieved party that the subject will be considered at the next council of the Tribe, at which time the Tribe shall consider it, when all the evidence in the case shall be read and the claim finally determined.

22. After final action shall have been had by the Tribe, the Chief of Records shall immediately notify the aggrieved party of the action of the Tribe. If the Tribe should still refuse to pay the benefits claimed, then the aggrieved party shall appeal to the State Great Council at any time within twenty suns from the date of the notice, by filing an appeal with the Tribe; otherwise the action of the Tribe, at the expiration of the time, shall be final and conclusive.

23. When an appeal from the action of the Tribe has been filed, the Tribe, through the Chief of Records, shall, without delay, transmit the appeal to the Great Sachem, together with the testimony taken by the commissioner, ex-

tracts from the records of the Tribe of all proceedings, and all other papers and documents relating to the case which were offered in evidence in the case when before the Tribe, and which alone shall be examined by the parties authorized by the laws to hear appeals.

24. Should the Tribe neglect or refuse to appoint a commissioner within two seven suns after receiving notice of an appeal, or shall neglect to send the appeal and papers to the Great Sachem within one moon after the filing of the appeal, it shall be sufficient cause for the Great Sachem to reverse the action of the Tribe, and direct it to pay the benefits. Provided, that the Tribe shall have the right to appeal to the Great Council from the action of the Great Sachem. Provided, further, that the amount of wampum claimed shall be placed in the hands of the Great Keeper of Wampum until the case is finally settled.

25. An appeal of a Tribe from the action of a Board or Committee on Appeals shall not be entertained unless the Tribe has obeyed the mandate of the Great Sachem or Great Council, and the amount of wampun involved has been placed in the hands of the Great Keeper of Wampum to be held until the case has been finally settled under the laws of the Order. — Code of Procedure.

Duties of Commissioner.

26. A commissioner is only a ministerial officer. He has no power to make a ruling. His duty is to enter in his journal what is offered, and leave to the Tribe and to the authorized committee to pass upon the relevancy or irrelevancy of what is offered.

I. The commissioner must give the party presenting the appeal at least ten suns' notice in writing of the time and place of the meeting.

II. The party presenting the appeal shall, at the time and place appointed by the commissioner, present his witnesses. There shall be no one present at the time of the hearing except the parties and the one witness under examination while the testimony is being taken.

III. Counsel representing either party must be a member of the Order in good standing, and shall present a certificate to that effect.

IV. After the appellant is through with his witnesses, the witnesses for the Tribe shall be presented.

V. All objections made to the testimony of witnesses by either party shall be noted on the records by the commissioner, who shall then proceed to take down the testimony as if no objections had been made.

VI. New evidence may be introduced after the case has been closed on either side, if there be reasons for so doing. Such new evidence need not be confined to that which is merely rebuttal. The tribunal that decides the case finally must exercise its discretion as to the evidence thus presented. — Code of Procedure.

Appropriations.

27. The object for which Tribes are chartered is to raise wampum, from the fees for adoptions and degrees, and from dues from members, for mutual

REVISED DIGEST. 479

relief in cases of sickness or other disabilities for which the laws may provide. It is, therefore, improper to appropriate such wampum for any other purpose than relief, and the necessary expenses for conducting the legitimate business of the Tribe. — V, 373, 428.

28. A Tribe has no right to appropriate or donate in any way wampum toward paying the adoption fee of a paleface. — V, 423, 434.

29. Funds paid into the wampum belt of a Tribe are for the purpose of relieving the sick or distressed, the burial of the dead, the education of the orphan, and the assistance of the widow, and to pay the legitimate expenses of the Tribe, and cannot be appropriated from the belt to pay the expenses of balls, suppers, or collations, or any other social purposes. — VI, 165, 185.

ARREARS.

30. Unless by-laws otherwise provide, the mere fact that a member is in arrears to such an extent as to deprive him of the password does not of itself deprive him of his right to vote when in the council chamber. — V, 257, 329.

31. A member has the right to attend the councils of his Tribe, even though he may not be entitled to the password, and can do so until he is suspended for non-payment of dues. — III, 224.

32. Members in arrears may attend Tribal councils as long as they can communicate the universal password and explanation. — III, 190, 224, 245.

ASSESSMENTS.

33. A Tribe has not the right to make an assessment on the members except as laid down in the By-Laws. — V, 371, 428.

APPLICATION FOR AID.

34. No application for pecuniary aid can be circulated, unless permission is received from the proper authorities. — Vol. VII.

AUTHORITY.

35. The Great Council of the United States is the source of all true and legitimate authority over the Order wheresoever established; it possesses, as such, supreme and absolute power and jurisdiction : —

I. To establish, regulate, and control the forms, ceremonies, written and unwritten work of the Order, and to change, alter, and annul the same, and to provide for the safe keeping and uniform teaching and dissemination of the same.

II. To provide, publish, print, and furnish all rituals, forms, ceremonies, cards, odes, charters, charts, and certificates.

III. To prescribe the form, material, and color of all regalia, emblems, jewels, and such blanks as may be used by the Order.

IV. To provide for the emanation and distribution of all passwords, and to regulate the mode and manner of using the same; and generally to prescribe such regulations as may be necessary to secure the safe and easy intercourse and identification of members.

V. To establish the Order in States, Districts, Territories, Provinces, or countries where the same has not been established.

VI. To provide a revenue for the Great Council of the United States by means of a *per capita* tax upon the membership, either from Great Councils or Tribes under its immediate jurisdiction, and the sale of supplies furnished by it.

VII. To provide for returns from Great Councils, Tribes, and other branches under its jurisdiction.

VIII. To hear and determine all appeals from Great Councils and Tribes, when the same are legally brought before it, and to provide by legislation for the enforcement of all its decrees and decisions.

IX. To enact laws and regulations of general application to carry into effect the foregoing, and all other powers reserved by this Constitution to the Great Council of the United States or its Great Chiefs, and such as may be necessary to enforce its legitimate authority over the Order.

X. All power and authority in the Order not delegated to Great Councils, Tribes, and Councils of the Degree of Pocahontas, by their charters, or the general laws or rules and decisions of this Great Council, are reserved to the Great Council of the United States.

XI. All power and authority enjoyed, exercised, and possessed by the several State Great Councils exist only by virtue of their charters and the sanction and consent of the Great Council of the United States duly granted them. — Constitution G. C. U. S.

BENEFITS.

36. Tribes shall enact laws for the payment of seven suns and funeral benefits. — Constitution G. C. U. S. Art. 8.

37. The amount to be paid for funeral and other benefits is a matter for local jurisdiction, and can be adjudicated by the Great Council of the United States, only when introduced on an appeal. — IV, 289.

38. A fundamental principle of the Order is that a fund must be raised and maintained, by the equal contributions of *all* the members, from which all benefits are to be paid; and in order to sustain this fund, certain forfeitures and penalties are to be enforced against delinquent brothers who fail to keep their contributions promptly paid as required by the laws. Among these penalties is forfeiture of benefits. A brother, to avail himself of these benefits, or to qualify his relatives or friends to receive them, must keep his dues paid up as required by the Constitution and By-Laws of his Tribe. — V, 375.

39. A Tribe has the right to reduce the amount to be paid for benefits, in order to relieve itself from financial difficulties, without the consent of those unable to follow the hunt. — II, 207.

40. It is not necessary that a member should be so sick as to be unable to leave his bed or room, to entitle him to benefits; if he is really and truly

unable to follow the hunt, transact his accustomed business, or earn a living on account of bodily infirmity, he is entitled. — II, 245.

41. Any member of a Tribe unable to follow the hunt is entitled to the care of the relief chiefs thereof, although some law may render him ineligible to receive benefits. — III, 190, 225.

42. When a beneficial member becomes insane, and is confined in a public institution, the Tribe must pay the benefits. — VI, 13, 49, 64.

43. No member in good health is entitled to benefits, whether an inmate of a benevolent institution or not. — VI, 153, 178.

44. A State Great Council can prohibit Tribes under its jurisdiction from paying funeral expenses to the family of a brother who dies non-beneficial, and can prohibit Tribes from carrying into effect any measure it sees fit, subject to an appeal to the Great Council of the United States. — VI, 160, 185.

45. A member more than three moons in arrears for seven suns' dues or assessments, forfeits all claims upon the Tribe for benefits of any character. — VII, 9.

46. When a brother in good standing becomes unable to follow the hunt, and is reported to the Relief Chiefs, he cannot after that become in arrears to his Tribe, as it is the duty of the Sachem to pay to the Chief of Records from the wampum drawn for his benefits a sum sufficient to prevent the brother becoming in arrears to the Tribe.

47. A Tribe cannot refuse to grant benefits of a suicide, if they are otherwise due under the laws of the Tribe.— Vol. II.

48. A member more than three moons in arrears for seven suns' dues, and reported unable to follow the hunt, would not be entitled to benefits. — Vol. VII.

49. A member is entitled to benefits only when through sickness or disability he is unable to follow his usual business or some other occupation whereby he can earn a livelihood for himself and family. — Vol. VII.

BENEFICIAL DEGREE COUNCILS.

50. A member of a Beneficial Degree Council, more than three moons in arrears to the Tribe, but in good standing in the Degree Council, would be entitled to seven suns' benefits from the Degree Council if otherwise qualified. — IX, 22.

51. Degree Councils should be governed by the Constitution of Tribes in the reservation in which they are located. They shall be under the immediate control of the Great Council having jurisdiction in the reservation. — Vol. IV.

CARDS — WITHDRAWAL.

52. Application for a withdrawal card shall be made either personally or in writing, and the same shall be granted, provided the brother is clear upon the books of the Tribe, free from charges, and there be no valid objections.

53. Any withdrawal card may be revoked for cause by the Tribe granting the same, and when so revoked the person holding said card shall be subject

to the Tribe which issued the same. A withdrawal card may be renewed if lost or destroyed. — Art. VIII, Constitution G. C. U. S.

54. The power to provide and publish withdrawal cards belongs to the Great Council of the United States. — Art. I, Constitution G. C. U. S.

55. A brother taking a withdrawal card is entitled to the universal password and the right to visit for the balance of the term, and for that time alone. By the end of the term referred to the password will have run out, and he would not be entitled to another. — V, 609, 671.

56. When a member applies for a withdrawal card, he is compelled to take the card and is no more a member of the Tribe. — I, 135.

57. Where evidence of former membership is in possession of the Great Chiefs, after proving applicants in the private work, cards or certificates shall be issued to enable them to regain their former standing in the Order. — III, 35, 163, 165.

58. No such title or personage as Ancient Red Man is known to, or recognized by, the Order. A Red Man holding a withdrawal card which has run over one great sun, can be admitted at any time subject to the laws of the reservation wherein the card may be presented. When thus elected and restored to membership he assumes the rank and is entitled to the same privileges he held or was entitled to prior to his taking a withdrawal card. — IV, 157, 212.

59. A brother residing in one reservation has not the right to deposit his card in a Tribe in another, without getting permission so to do from the Great Sachem of the State in which he resides. — V, 178, 199.

60. The power of granting cards or certificates to members in good standing of extinct Tribes, is vested in the Great Chief of Records only of the Great Council to which said Tribe would be attached if working. — IV, 158, 190.

61. It is the duty of a Tribe upon the issuance of a withdrawal card to a brother who has served the proper time as Sachem, to rank him on said card as Past Sachem, regardless of the fact that said brother has not received the Past Sachem's or Great Council degree; and it is the further duty of a Tribe to furnish said brother with a certificate which will entitle him to claim his rights in the hunting-grounds to which he may remove. — IV, 157, 190.

62. The Sachem and Chief of Records have no right to grant a withdrawal card to a member in good standing of a Tribe that has failed to meet for several moons, but has not surrendered its charter, except on vote of the Tribe in regular council. — V, 141, 196.

63. When a brother presents his withdrawal card as an applicant for membership, the application must be referred to a committee of investigation, which must make a strict investigation of the health, character, and standing of the applicant, and on the report, whether favorable or unfavorable, a ballot must be had, as in case of a paleface, and the brother shall not become a member of the Tribe unless all these requirements have been fully carried out. — IX, 21.

64. If the applicant is rejected his card must be returned to him undefaced. — IX, 23.

65. A brother who has lost, or been dispossessed of a withdrawal card, from no cause which would impeach his conduct, may obtain a new card, bearing the same date, from the Tribe which granted the original one, the Tribe being the judge as to the propriety of issuing the new one. When issued, the card must certify on its face that it is a duplicate. — VII.

Cards — Travelling.

66. To the Great Council of the United States alone belongs the power of providing and publishing travelling cards. — Constitution G. C. U. S.

67. Travelling cards, for the use of members, may be used or recognized only when procured from the Great Council of the United States, and they are in accordance with the form adopted. They are for special use and must be obtained through State Great Councils. — Constitution G. C. U. S.

68. A travelling card shall be *prima facie* evidence of the good standing of the brother to whom issued. Upon the back thereof shall be placed the amount for seven suns, and funeral benefits allowed by the Tribe issuing it. — Constitution G. C. U. S.

69. No Tribe issuing a travelling card shall be held legally responsible for more wampum than may be allowed by the provisions thereof. — IV, 301.

70. It is the duty of a Tribe to grant a travelling card to any member who may request it, and who has complied with the laws relative to issuing the same. — V, 610, 673.

Ceremonies.

71. The ceremonies shall not be altered or amended unless the proposed change be submitted in writing and, after being twice read on different suns, be adopted by the votes of three-fourths of the members present entitled to vote. — Constitution G. C. U. S.

Certified Receipts.

72. Certified receipts for the use of members may be used or recognized only when procured from the Great Council of the United States, and they are in accordance with the form adopted. They are for special use and must be obtained through State Great Councils. — Constitution G. C. U. S.

73. A certified receipt shall be *prima facie* evidence of the payment of dues by the brother to whom issued. Upon the back thereof may be printed a request for communicating to the brother the Universal Password. — Constitution G. C. U. S.

74. Orders for the password must be upon the form adopted and issued by the Great Council of the United States, and must be accompanied by the official certified receipt for dues, as furnished by said body. — IX, 138.

Charters.

75. To the Great Council of the United States alone belongs the power to publish and provide Charters. — Constitution G. C. U. S.

76. Five or more Tribes in any State, District, Territory, or the Dominion

of Canada, having not less than fifteen Past Sachems, and a membership of not less than five hundred, may petition the Great Council or Great Incohonee praying for a charter for a Great Council therein. Should the majority of the representatives vote in favor of the same it shall be granted, and the Great Incohonee, or a Past Sachem deputized by him, shall kindle the council fire of said Great Council. The petition shall be in the following form : —

To the Great Council of the United States, Improved Order of Red Men :

The Past Sachems of the undersigned Tribes represent that they are working under charters granted by the Great Council of . . . . , that the Order has increased so that the membership is at present . . . . , and we have . . . . Past Sachems in good standing. We believe that it would be of advantage to the Order if a Great Council was established in our reservation. We therefore pray that you grant the prayer of our petition.

Witness our hands and the seal of the Tribes this . . . . Sun of . . . . Moon, G. S. D. . . . .

The same to be signed by the Sachem and Chief of Records of each Tribe, and the seal thereof to be attached.

Should the application as aforesaid be made to the Great Incohonee prior to the first sun of Sturgeon Moon, he may, by and with the consent of the elective Great Chiefs, grant a dispensation for the same, and institute the Great Council.

As soon as a Great Council has been organized, all Tribes located in its reservation shall thereafter be under the jurisdiction of said Great Council.

77. In reservations where there are no Great Councils, persons desirous of kindling a council fire of a Tribe therein shall present an application signed by not less than thirty brothers or palefaces, accompanied by the charter fee and the cards of the brothers. If the application is received by the Great Incohonee during the interim, the Great Incohonee may, by and with the advice of the Great Chiefs, grant a dispensation and institute the Tribe.

78. All travelling or other expenses of the Great Incohonee, or his deputy, incurred in lighting the council fire of a Great Council or Tribe shall be paid by such Great Council or Tribe.

(Sections 77 and 78 shall also apply to Councils of Degree of Pocahontas, except as to fee and number on petition. — Constitution G. C. U. S.)

79. The charter of a Tribe should be in the council chamber during the burning of the council fire. — III, 59, 60.

80. A Tribe cannot erase names of charter members and put others in their stead. — IV, 253, 297.

81. A State Great Council has authority to enact a law requiring new Tribes to work under a dispensation for a stated period of time before granting a charter. — IV, 254, 298.

82. A Tribe has a right to print a copy of its charter with its Constitution and By-Laws. — IV, 80, 106.

83. A charter remains open only until the Tribe is instituted, and neither the Great Incohonee, Great Sachem, or Great Chief of Records has the right to grant a dispensation to open the charter and adopt palefaces for less than the constitutional fees. — V, 424, 434.

84. Those whose names appear on the application and are admitted to membership are the charter members of a Tribe. — V, 423, 434.

85. When the names of any persons who are or have been members of the Order, appear on an application for a charter of a new Tribe, the withdrawal cards or dismissal certificates of said members from the Tribe or Tribes to which they formerly belonged must accompany the application, or be in possession of instituting Chiefs, before they can become members of the new Tribe. — V, 608.

86. Application for a Tribal charter must be signed by not less than twenty brothers or palefaces accompanied by a fee of not less than twenty fathoms. If the application be made during the interim of a State Great Council, the Great Sachem may, by and with the consent of the Great Chiefs, grant a dispensation to light the council brand, if deemed for the interest of the Order, the petition and a report of the action thereon to be submitted to the next council of said Great Council. — General Laws.

Form of Application for Charter.

To the Great Council of . . . . . . of the Improved Order of Red Men:

The undersigned, members of the Order (or palefaces), residing in . . . . respectfully petition your Great Council to grant them a charter to establish a Tribe of the Improved Order of Red Men, to be located in . . . . The said Tribe to be known as . . . . , Tribe No. . . of the Improved Order of Red Men, under your jurisdiction, and we pledge ourselves to be governed by the laws thereof.

Signed, ...

Enclosed is the charter fee.

Applications for charters for Degree Councils must be signed by at least ten brothers of the Chief's Degree. A Degree Council may be beneficial or otherwise, as may be set forth by the petitioners. It may admit brothers to membership residing anywhere within the jurisdiction of the Great Council by which it has been chartered. It shall not confer degrees upon any brother unless a certificate be presented from his Tribe authorizing the same.

87. Application for a Council of the Degree of Pocahontas shall be signed by not less than ten brothers of the Chief's Degree and ten females, and accompanied by a fee of not less than fifteen fathoms, and acted upon in the same manner as an application for a Tribal charter. Members of the Degree of Pocahontas, desirous of becoming applicants on a charter, must present their withdrawal cards with the application. — General Laws.

88. When Tribes are legally reinstated and acknowledged as such by the Great Chiefs (during the interim), the Past Sachems, if returned in good standing, would be entitled to a seat in the Great Council.

89. The law concerning applications for charters of Degree Councils relates only to the minimum number of names necessary on the application and their rank; the law of Great Councils concerning charter fees for Tribes would otherwise govern. — IX, 22.

CHARGES AGAINST MEMBERS — SEE TRIALS, ETC.

90. Charges against members of Tribes and Beneficial Degree Councils must be made in accordance with the Code of Procedure. — Constitution G. C. U. S.

CHIEFS.

91. The elective Chiefs of the Great Council of the United States shall be a Great Incohonee, Great Senior Sagamore, Great Junior Sagamore, Great Prophet, Great Chief of Records, and Great Keeper or Wampum. — Constitution G. C. U. S.

92. The appointed Chiefs shall be a Great Tocakon, a Great Minnewa, and a Great Guard of Forest. — Constitution G. C. U. S.

CHIEFS OF GREAT COUNCIL.

93. The elective Chiefs of a State Great Council shall be Great Sachem, Great Senior Sagamore, Great Junior Sagamore, Great Prophet, Great Chief of Records, and Great Keeper of Wampum.

94. The appointed Chiefs shall be Great Sannap, Great Mishinewa, Great Guard of Wigwam, and Great Guard of Forest. — General Laws.

CHIEFS OF TRIBE.

95. The elective Chiefs of a Tribe shall be Sachem, Senior Sagamore, Junior Sagamore, Prophet, Chief of Records, and Keeper of Wampum, all of whom must be members of the Chief's degree. Great Councils may provide for a Collector of Wampum, who also must be a member of the Chief's degree. The Prophet must be a Past Sachem. The appointed Chiefs shall be First and Second Sannap, Guard of the Wigwam, Guard of the Forest, four Warriors, and four Braves. — Constitution G. C. U. S.

CHIEFS OF A DEGREE COUNCIL.

96. The elective Chiefs of a Degree Council shall be Sachem, Senior Sagamore, Junior Sagamore, Chief of Records, Keeper of Wampum, and Prophet.

97. The appointed Chiefs shall be Sannap, Guard of Wigwam and Guard of Forest, and such others as the ceremonies define. — General Laws.

CHIEFS OF DEGREE OF POCAHONTAS.

98. The elective Chiefs of a Council shall consist of Pocahontas, Wenonah, Powhatan, Keeper of Records, and Keeper of Wampum. Councils may also elect a Collector of Wampum.

99. The appointed Chiefs shall be First and Second Scout, First and Sec-

ond Runner, two Counsellors, four Warriors, Guard of Wigwam, Guard of Forest, and such others as the ritual may define. — General Laws.

Eligibility of Chiefs.

100. To be eligible to the chieftaincy of Great Incohonee, a brother must be a Past Great Sachem, and have served one term in an elective chieftaincy.

101. No brother shall be eligible to the chieftaincy of Great Prophet unless he is a Past Great Incohonee.

102. To be eligible for Great Representatives, brothers must be Past Sachems in good standing.

103. After a Great Council shall have been instituted two great suns, no brother shall be eligible to the chieftaincy of Great Sachem unless he has served one term as an elective Chief of a Great Council; nor to the chieftaincy of Great Prophet unless he has served in the chieftaincy of Great Sachem.

104. The elective chiefs of a Tribe must be members of the Chief's degree. The Prophet must be a Past Sachem.

105. To be eligible to the chieftaincy of Prophetess in a Council of Pocahontas the member must have served a term as Pocahontas.

106. Great Representatives must be residents of the reservation they represent during the entire term for which they are elected, and removal of residence from their reservations shall operate as a forfeiture of their position.

107. No one shall be eligible to any chieftaincy unless he has been duly admitted to the Great Council and received the rank of Past Great Sachem.— General Laws.

108. The retiring Sachem, being a Past Sachem on the sleep of raising up of Chiefs, is eligible to be elected to the chieftaincy of Prophet. — VIII, 20.

109. Great Councils have the right to enact laws requiring other qualifications for brothers desirous of advancing to the chieftaincy of Sachem, than that of being exalted to the Chief's Degree. — IX, 85.

110. The Sachem is eligible for re-election. — IX, 22.

DUTIES OF CHIEFS.

Great Incohonee.

111. The Great Incohonee shall preside at all councils of the Great Council, preserve order and enforce the laws thereof; have a watchful supervision over all branches of the Order, and see that all constitutional enactments, rules, and regulations of the Great Council are observed.

Among his special prerogatives are the following: —

To call special councils of the Great Council.

To appoint all committees not otherwise provided for, to visit any Great Council, or branch of the Order, and to give such instruction as the good of the Order may require, always adhering to the usages of the Order.

He shall have general supervision of the Order, and grant such dispensations as he may deem for its interest, also grant dispensations for the kindling of council fires of Great Councils and other branches of the Order.

He shall appoint and commission Deputy Great Incohonees as may be required in States, Territories, or countries where Great Councils do not exist.

He may hear and decide such appeals and questions of law as may be submitted to him by Great Councils or their Great Chiefs, and Tribes under the immediate jurisdiction of the Great Council, or their Chiefs, and such decisions shall be binding until finally passed upon or reversed by the Great Council.

He shall, at every great sun council, present a printed report of all his official acts and decisions during the interim, with such recommendations as he may deem for the advancement of the Order.

He shall have exclusive right to create and promulgate all passwords, and to rescind and change the same if circumstances require. — Const. G. C. U. S.

112. In case of the temporary absence of any Chief, his position may be filled by the Great Incohonee. — II, 138.

113. The Great Incohonee has no authority to answer any questions, or make decisions, unless the same come from a Great Council or a Tribe under the jurisdiction of the Great Council of the United States. Tribes under a State Great Council desiring information upon any subject, must make the inquiry through the proper authorities in their reservation. — VII.

114. In all appeals not arising from charges and hearing under the Code of Procedure, the Great Incohonee has exclusive power to rule thereon, subject to approval by the Great Council of the United States. — IX, 23.

115. In case of the absence of all Chiefs qualified to preside, the senior Past Great Incohonee present shall preside, and, if none be present, the Great Council may select any member to preside. — VI, 88.

116. The Great Incohonee has the right to hear and decide such appeals and questions of law as may be submitted to him, and such decisions are binding until passed upon and reversed by the Great Council. — IX, 28, 140.

117. The Great Incohonee is hereby authorized and empowered to appoint one or more capable and efficient brothers, who shall have full power to exemplify and instruct Tribes in the written, unwritten, and floor work, whose construction shall be legal, and to be taken as correct, unless reversed by the Great Incohonee, or the Great Council of the United States, the brother or brothers so appointed to be known as "Exemplifier," or "Exemplifiers," and only to render such service when requested by a Tribe or Tribes, and all service rendered shall be paid therefor by the Tribe or Tribes desiring the same. — IX, 144.

118. The Great Senior Sagamore shall assist the Great Incohonee in kindling and quenching the council fire; advise, assist, and support him in preserving order, and preside in his absence. In case of the death, resignation, or disqualification of the Great Incohonee, he shall be invested with all his authority and power. — Constitution G. C. U. S.

119. The Great Junior Sagamore shall have charge of the wicket, and perform such other duties as the nature of his chieftaincy may require. In case of the death, resignation, or disqualification of the Great Senior Sagamore, he shall be invested with all his authority and power. — Constitution G. C. U. S.

120. In absence of the Chiefs authorized to preside, the senior Past Great Incohonee present (not a Great Chief), shall preside, and if none be present then the members shall by vote designate a member to preside. — By-Laws G. C. U. S.

121. The Great Prophet shall perform all the duties prescribed in the ceremonies. — Constitution G. C. U. S.

122. The Great Chief of Records shall keep a just and true record of all the proceedings of this Great Council. When the same have been printed he shall transmit to each Great Council as many copies as it may have Past Great Sachems, Great Chiefs and branches of the Order under its jurisdiction. Also one to each branch under the immediate control of this Great Council. Also one to each Great Chief, member, and Representative. He shall collect all the revenues of the Great Council and pay the same over to the Great Keeper of Wampum on or about the first of every moon, taking a receipt therefor. He shall preserve and keep the evidence of the unwritten work and such alterations as may from time to time be made therein, and all other records of secret councils. He shall prepare all charters for Great Councils and other branches that are granted by the Great Council, notify all Great Councils, Chiefs and members of the Great Council of the United States of all councils of this Great Council; carry on all the necessary correspondence, attest all official documents, and perform such other duties as this Great Council may from time to time direct. He shall make out and have printed an alphabetical roll of the Great Chiefs and Representatives and call the same at the kindling of each council fire, and the names of those present, including Past Great Incohonees and Past Great Sachems, who are not Representatives, shall be entered upon the record. He shall submit to the Great Council at each council a printed report of his accounts, together with the standing of the Order. He shall receive for his services such sum (not less than sixteen hundred fathoms per great sun) as the Great Council may fix at the time of his election. He shall give security, satisfactory to the Committee on Finance, in the sum of three thousand fathoms of wampum. — Constitution G. C. U. S.

123. The Great Chief of Records is strictly forbidden to deliver any supplies to any one unless the cash accompanies the order therefor. — V, 89.

124. The Great Chief of Records shall retain in the office twenty-five copies of the printed record of each council of the Great Council of the United States. — V, 89.

125. The Great Keeper of Wampum shall pay all orders drawn on him by the Great Incohonee, attested by the Great Chief of Records. He shall, at the great sun's council, present a printed report of his receipts and disbursements. For the faithful performance of his duties he shall give a bond,

satisfactory to the Committee on Finance, in the sum of not less than five thousand fathoms of wampum. — Constitution G. C. U. S.

126. The Great Tocakon, Great Minnewa and the Great Guard of Forest shall perform such duties as are defined in the charge books, and such as may be assigned them by the Great Council. — Constitution G. C. U. S.

127. A Past Great Sachem who is not a Representative can be appointed either Great Tocakon or Great Minnewa. — V, 465, 495, 543.

128. Representatives who are not Past Great Sachems can be appointed to and fill a sub-chieftaincy in the Great Council of the United States. — VII, 680, 696.

Chiefs of State Great Councils — Duties of.

129. The Chiefs of a Great Council shall perform such duties as are defined in the charge books, and such as may be assigned them under the By-Laws of said Great Council.

130. A Great Sachem has no authority to reinstate an expelled brother. — VII, 9.

131. A Great Sachem may decline to give his reasons for making a decision, if he thinks it for the interests of the Order to so refuse, being responsible only to his Great Council. — II, 185, 202.

132. A Great Sachem has general supervision of the Order in his reservation. If in a council chamber, in an official capacity, he should call the attention of the Tribe to any violation of law. The Tribe is the party to deal with individual members, and the Tribe is responsible to its Great Council for any violation of the laws of the Order. — IV, 353, 393.

133. A Great Sachem can appoint for his deputy a member of the Order who is serving in a Tribe as Prophet, if not forbidden by local laws. — V, 257, 329.

134. The Great Sachem of any reservation can hold the position of Great Representative at the same time. — V, 462, 541.

135. A Great Sachem is the representative of a Great Council during the interim between the councils of such Great Council, and also of the interests of the Order in his reservation, and his powers are such as are given him by the Ritual, Constitution, and By-Laws of the Great Council of the United States and its general laws for the government of State Great Councils, and the Constitution and By-Laws of the Great Council of the State of which he is Great Sachem, but of course he is not in fact the Great Council. A Great Council is necessary, notwithstanding the power of right given to the Great Sachem, that due and proper legislation may be had for the benefit of the Order under its immediate jurisdiction. — V, 683.

136. A Great Sachem while occupying that Chieftaincy is eligible to be voted for as Great Prophet for the ensuing term. — III, 191, 225.

137. No Chief in a Great Council can retain his Chieftaincy who is not in good standing in a Tribe. — V, 142, 196.

138. The first Great Prophet of a Great Council is the Senior Past Great Sachem. — VII, 694.

139. A brother is eligible for nomination and election to the Chieftaincy of Great Sachem who is not in possession of the Degree of Pocahontas. — VII, 626.

140. The first Prophet of a Great Council shall be entitled to the rank and honors of Past Great Sachem. — General Laws.

141. Any Great Chief of Records or Great Keeper of Wampum of a Great Council, having served five great suns in succession as such, shall be entitled to the rank and honors of Past Great Sachem. — General Laws.

142. The Great Mishinewa shall have command of processions or public demonstrations of Great Councils and act as assistant runner of the Great Sachem during the burning of the council fire, and perform such other duties as the Great Sachem or Great Council may direct. His position in the wigwam shall be at the left of the Great Sachem. — V, 60.

143. A Great Chief cannot retain his Chieftaincy and officiate therein if expelled from his Tribe. — VII, 18.

144. A Great Chief can retain his Chieftaincy pending an appeal to the Great Council of the State, or the Great Council of the United States. — VII, 18.

145. When a Great Sachem has been expelled from the Order, the Great Chief of Records is the proper Chief to declare the station vacant, and the Great Senior Sagamore is the proper Chief to assume the Chieftaincy. — VII, 18.

CHIEFS OF A TRIBE AND BENEFICIAL DEGREE COUNCIL — DUTIES OF.

146. The Chiefs of a Tribe (or Beneficial Degree Council) shall perform such duties as are defined in the charge books, and such as may be laid down in the laws for the government of Tribes.

147. The Senior Sagamore is the proper Chief to have charge of the wickets. — III, 293.

148. In absence of any local law, Tribes have the right to nominate Chiefs on the sleep of election. — IV, 395.

149. A Chief who has been tried and found guilty, and resigns, having been re-elected by the Tribe subsequently, is entitled to be raised up. — V, 373, 418.

150. A Junior Sagamore, never having been raised to the Senior Sagamore's stump, is not eligible to the Chieftaincy of Sachem, if the local law provides that he must fill the Chieftaincy of Senior Sagamore. — V, 171.

151. The First Prophet of a Tribe, neglecting to attend to his duty, either by failing to attend, or by deporting himself in a manner unbecoming a Red Man, and the station being declared vacant, the same can be filled by dispensation. — VII, 626.

152. Any Chief of Records, Collector of Wampum, or Keeper of Wampum, having served five great suns in succession as such, shall be entitled to the degree of Past Sachem. — General Laws.

153. The First Prophet of a Tribe shall be entitled to the honors of a Past Sachem. — General Laws.

154. The resignation of a Sachem and the raising up of his successor, does not create a vacancy in the position of sub-Chiefs who were appointed by the former Sachem. — VII, 183, 186.

155. An elective Chief can resign a Chieftaincy to which he has been raised at any time he may desire. — VI, 419.

156. The Chief of Records should announce the receipts of each council, and enter them on the records. — VII, 22.

157. The Chief of Records has no right to take the seal away from the wigwam, if the Tribe decides to the contrary. — VII, 22.

158. If the stump of Sachem is not declared vacant for absence, he is entitled to the rank and honors of a Past Sachem. — VII, 23.

Chiefs of Degree of Pocahontas.

159. The Chiefs of the Councils of the Degree of Pocahontas shall perform such duties as are laid down in the rules and ceremonies.

Committees.

160. Immediately after the raising up of the Great Incohonee, he shall appoint a Committee on Finance and a Committee on Laws, to consist of three members each and to serve during his Chieftaincy; and as soon as the council fire of each Great Council is kindled, he shall appoint a Committee on Credentials, to consist of three members, and immediately after the reading of the long talks, the following committees, to consist of seven members each, *viz.*: Distribution of Long Talks, State of the Order, Judiciary, Appeals and Grievances, Charters, Reports, Mileage and Per Diem, Beneficiary, and Degree of Pocahontas. — Constitution of G. C. U. S.

Committees — Duties of.

161. The Committee on Finance shall examine the books, vouchers, and accounts of the Great Chief of Records and the Great Keeper of Wampum, before each great sun council, and for that purpose shall meet at the office of the Great Chief of Records at least four suns prior to the council. They shall make estimates for and recommend appropriations of wampum, for general and special purposes during the interim of the councils, based on revenue likely to be received; and no expenditure of wampum shall be made over and above an appropriation, unless the same has received the approval of the Finance Committee. It shall be their duty to see that the necessary bonds have been entered by those required to do so by the laws, to place the same in the hands of the Great Incohonee, and submit their report at each great sun council.

I. The Committee on Constitution and Laws shall examine all laws that may be referred to them during the interim of the councils, and report as to their action on the same. It shall be their duty to see that the laws referred to them do not conflict with the laws and usages of the Order.

II. The Committee on Credentials shall examine and report on all credentials that may be referred to it.

REVISED DIGEST. 493

III. The Committee on Distribution shall have referred to it the long talks of the Great Chiefs, and shall examine and refer to the various committees the subjects treated in the talks.

IV. To the Committee on the State of the Order shall be referred that portion of the Great Chief's long talks that relates to the status of the Order, and in its report it shall embody the condition and progress that the Order has made, and shall recommend such measures as it may think advantageous to the whole Order.

V. The Committee on Judiciary shall consider all questions of a proper construction of the laws, and other judicial matters that may be referred to it by the Great Council.

VI. The Committee on Appeals and Grievances shall investigate all appeals and other matters of a like character that may be referred to it, and report to the Great Council its decision thereon, with such recommendations as it thinks the evidence warrants.

VII. The Committee on Charters shall examine and report on all petitions and dispensations issued by the Great Incohonee, for Tribes, Councils of the Degree of Pocahontas or Great Councils, and report as to the advisability of granting charters.

VIII. The Committee on Reports shall examine and report as to the correctness of all returns and reports presented by Great Councils and Tribes.

IX. The Committee on Mileage and Per Diem shall calculate the number of miles travelled by Great Chiefs, Representatives and members of the Committee on Finance present at each great sun council; also make out a complete and correct roll of the same and report the amount that each is entitled to, and no order shall be drawn until the report is approved by this Great Council.

X. The Committee on the Degree of Pocahontas shall have referred to it all matters appertaining to said branch of the Order, and it shall report to the Great Council such recommendations as it may deem beneficial.

XI. It shall be the duty of each committee or member of this Great Council to return to the Great Chief of Records at the final quenching of the council fire all books and papers belonging to this Great Council, unless otherwise ordered by this Great Council. — Constitution G. C. U. S.

Consolidation.

162. Great Councils of the respective States are permitted to consolidate the organizations now known by the various titles of "Red Men" with the Improved Order of Red Men, under such regulations as will not conflict with the laws and usages of our Order. Such bodies will be allowed to use their present regalia after attaching thereto the jewels adopted by this Great Council for its various Chiefs, provided that when the same is replaced it shall be with the regulation style adopted for Tribes of the Improved Order of Red Men. The past presiding officers of such bodies shall be entitled to the rank and honors of Past Sachems, and a dispensation is hereby granted for that purpose. Before these privileges herein mentioned shall be bestowed upon the said bodies, the members thereof shall be severally adopted and

instructed in the work of our Order and take our regular charters, as required by the laws of the Order in the case of palefaces. — VI, 170.

163. When a Tribe under the jurisdiction of the Great Council of the United States consolidates with another Tribe, the effect is the same as if the Tribe had become extinct. The Chiefs of the Tribe are compelled to deliver to the proper Chiefs all property, to be held in trust. — V, 608, 672.

164. Great Councils have the right to legislate relative to the consolidation of Tribes under their jurisdiction. — V, 608, 672.

Costumes.

165. Exposing a portion of our paraphernalia to the view of palefaces, and wearing of tribal costumes in public parade prohibited. — I, 83; III, 225.

166. The Great Sachem has not the power to grant a dispensation to Tribes to appear in public in the costumes worn in the Tribes. — IV, 254, 298.

167. A Tribe has the right to dispose of such portion of its paraphernalia as it does not need to a sister Tribe only; but in case of a surrender of its charter, all its property and paraphernalia must be turned over to the custody of the Great Council. — IV, 353, 393.

168. There is no law controlling the costumes. But the "colors of the Order" are clearly defined, and are not confined to any particular article, but designate "rank," and inferentially designate the colors of the costumes. — V, 371, 416.

169. It is improper to show certain of the costumes to palefaces, and it is also improper to allow palefaces to manufacture them. — VII, 25.

170. The costumes of the Order are not matters of public legislation or public law. Our laws, as published for the information of our membership generally, as well as the paleface world, provide a regalia, consisting of the ordinary sash, and the funeral sash and badge, to be worn in public. But the costume is created *by the secret work*, and is intended solely to embellish and illustrate it; and the members of the Order have no more right to expose to public view, or to speak of it in the presence of palefaces, than they have to exhibit the secret signs and passwords. Therefore, the costumes are a part and portion of the secret paraphernalia of the Order, and must not be worn outside of the wigwam, nor in any manner or for any other purpose than that prescribed in the Ritual. — III, 255.

Councils.

171. The great sun council fire shall be kindled on the second Tuesday of Corn moon, at the ninth run, rising of the sun, at such place as the Great Council may designate.

I. The place of kindling the council fire shall be determined at each great sun council by a majority of those entitled to vote; provided, that the resolution fixing the place shall have been read on two separate suns.

II. State Great Councils shall hold one council every great sun. — Constitution G. C. U. S.

Council Brand.

172. The principal feature of our organization is the carrying out of the habits and customs of the Red Men of the forest, and as the council brand was considered one of their most sacred emblems, its abolishment is deemed an innovation upon our ritual. — V, 160, 210.

Dating.

173. Prior to the year A.D. 1865, the Jewish style, namely, the year of the world, was observed by Red Men in dating their documents. At the council held in G. S. 5626, this system was discontinued, and G. S. D., or Great Sun of the Discovery, was adopted, the year 1492 being considered G. S. D. 1. For convenience, it was determined that the great sun should commence on the first of Cold moon, so as to conform to the common era. To find the date of the old style, add to the common era 3760; *e.g.* $1877+3760=5637$. To find the date by Red Men's style, subtract 1491 from the common era; *e.g.* $1877-1491=386$. — III, 59.

Degrees.

174. The degrees of the Order are the Adoption, Hunter's, Warrior's and Chief's; also the Degree of Pocahontas, of Beneficial Degree Councils, and of Past Sachem, each of which is separate from the others. The Adoption degree, Degree of Pocahontas, and Beneficial degree cannot be conferred upon a paleface except in the Tribe or Council to which said paleface has been elected.

I. No Tribe shall confer degrees upon a member of another Tribe, except by permission, under seal, of the Tribe to which said member belongs.

II. Brothers desirous of advancing shall make application for degrees in open council; the application shall be referred to the Tribe while working in the degree applied; a ballot shall be had, and if not more than three black twigs are cast it shall be granted. If rejected, the application cannot be renewed for three moons. — Constitution G. C. U. S.

175. Past Great Incohonees or Vice Great Incohonees have no power to confer the Past Sachem's degree upon brothers of Tribes in hunting grounds where no Great Council exists, unless by special authority of the Great Council of the United States. — I, 230; II, 57.

176. The Great Council of any reservation has the right to confer the Past Sachem's degree upon Past Sachems in good standing of another reservation, with the consent of the Great Sachem or Great Council thereof. Consent for Past Sachems to receive the Past Sachem's degree outside of their own jurisdiction shall be recognized only when said Past Sachems shall have proved themselves in good standing in the Order, and when their application for the same shall bear the seal and signatures of the Great Sachem and Great Chief of Records of their own reservation. — VI, 14, 49, 64.

177. The eligibility of members for degrees is a matter for local jurisdictions to determine. — III, 134, 164.

178. In case of change in the degree work, members in good standing who were in possession of the former degrees, are entitled to all changes without any additional requirements. — II, 138, 156.

179. To confer the degrees free of charge is in conflict with the laws fixing the fees. — IV, 160, 214.

180. All business of the Tribe shall be transacted in the Adoption degree. When a degree is to be conferred, if the regular business of the Tribe is not completed, the Sachem may declare a recess in the Adoption degree for that purpose, and proceed to kindle the council fire in the degree about to be conferred, and then proceed exactly in accordance with the ritual for said degree. Otherwise the council fire may be quenched in the Adoption degree and kindled in the degree to be conferred. Each degree is complete within itself. The council fire may not be kindled twice in the same degree on the same sleep, and it must be quenched in one degree before proceeding to kindle it in another degree. — IV, 5, 53.

181. When a single degree is to be conferred, the council fire may be kindled in that degree. — V, 258, 329.

182. A Sachem has the right, at his option, after giving proper notice, whenever requested in writing by five or more brothers, to convene the Tribe in special council for degree work, or other business proper to be transacted at a special council. — V, 258, 329.

183. The balloting for a degree shall take place in the council of the degree for which the application is made. — VI, 13, 49, 64.

184. A Degree Council has a right to confer degrees on a brother who is deaf, so much so that he cannot hear the different charges and obligations when read to him. The brother has his rights, and no Tribe or Degree Council can violate them. — VI, 119, 176.

Degree of Pocahontas.

185. Any member of the Improved Order of Red Men who has been exalted to the Chief's degree and is in good standing in his Tribe, and any woman over eighteen years of age and of good moral character, shall be eligible to membership in any Council of the Degree of Pocahontas. The fee for adoption into a Council shall not be less than one fathom. — VII, 99.

186. Past officers of organizations that were in existence prior to the promulgation of the Degree of Pocahontas, said ladies having accepted the provisions of the law, shall be entitled to the rank and honor of Past Chiefs. — VII, 553.

187. State Great Councils shall report every great sun to the Great Council of the United States the standing of the Councils of the Degree of Pocahontas under their jurisdiction. — VII, 553.

188. A Past Pocahontas of the Degree of Pocahontas may be appointed Deputy of a Council. — VII, 627.

189. Representatives to the Great Council of the United States cannot impart the secret work of the Degree of Pocahontas to their State Great Council. — VII, 628.

190. The elective Chiefs of a State Great Council who are not members of a Council of the Degree of Pocahontas have the right to visit Councils in an official capacity. — VIII, 214.

191. State Great Councils have the right to enact laws taxing Councils of the Degree of Pocahontas; they have also the right to provide for representation from said Councils, provided the representative is a Past Sachem in good standing in Tribe and Council. — VIII, 596.

192. Great Councils may establish rules by which a Great Sun Council of the members of the Degree of Pocahontas can be held at such time and place as they may deem proper, and regulations designating the business that may be transacted thereat. At such Councils, Past Chiefs, Past Sachems who are members, and those who may be selected as representatives from the various Councils, shall be entitled to a seat and a voice in the deliberations.

Deputy Great Sachems.

193. A State Great Council has the right to divide its reservation into districts, in which a representative of the Great Sachem can be appointed to be termed a Deputy, and the Deputy Great Sachems are accountable to the Great Sachem. — II, 184, 202.

194. It is the duty of Deputy Great Sachems to enforce obedience to the laws and customs, and also the correct working of the Order in their respective districts. — II, 184, 202.

195. It is imperative that a Deputy Great Sachem shall have received the Great Council degree. — V, 257, 329.

196. A Deputy Great Sachem can grant a dispensation to perform the dedicatory and raising-up ceremony in public. And palefaces, ladies and gentlemen, can be admitted to the wigwam during such service. — V, 493, 539.

Deputy Great Incohonees.

197. The Great Incohonee shall appoint and commission a Past Sachem in any State or Territory where there is no Great Council as a Deputy Great Incohonee, whose duty it will be to visit, instruct, and raise up the Chiefs of Tribes under his charge. Prior to first of Corn moon in each great sun he shall make a full report to the Great Incohonee of their condition, and such suggestions as he may deem for the advantage of the Order, and transmit to the Great Chief of Records such wampum as he may have received, and perform such other duties as the Great Incohonee may desire. — General Laws.

198. Any Past Sachem in good standing is eligible to be appointed as Deputy Great Incohonee. — VI, 12, 49, 64.

199. Deputy Great Incohonees have not the exclusive right to institute Tribes in their respective reservations. — IV, 227.

200. A Deputy Great Incohonee cannot declare a station vacant if the elected Chief fails to present himself for raising up. That is a power that can be exercised only by the Tribe. — VI, 15, 49.

201. A Past Deputy Great Incohonee does not rank as Past Great Sachem after the formation of a Great Council. — VI, 420.

202. It is not proper for a Deputy Great Incohonee to keep in his possession a copy of the work of the Order. — II, 57, 142.

203. A Tribe is not bound to pay the expenses of the Deputy Great Incohonee incurred by his visit to raise up its Chiefs, unless such visit is made by special invitation of the Tribe, as he has power to appoint a qualified Chief to perform that duty. — II, 183, 196, 202.

DISMISSAL CERTIFICATES.

204. A member suspended for non-payment of dues, desirous of joining a Tribe in the same reservation, after one great sun's suspension, shall be entitled to receive, and the Tribe shall grant, upon proper application, a dismissal certificate upon the payment of not less than one fathom nor more than one great sun's dues.

I. A member suspended for non-payment of dues, wishing to regain membership in another reservation, shall be entitled to receive, and the Tribe shall grant, upon proper application, a dismissal certificate upon the receipt of not less than one fathom nor more than one great sun's dues.

II. In all cases wherein a Tribe has refused to reinstate a member suspended for non-payment of dues, he shall be entitled to receive, and the Tribe, upon proper application, shall grant a dismissal certificate upon the receipt of one fathom. — Constitution G. C. U. S.

205. Where the books of an extinct Tribe have been lost or destroyed, the Great Chief of Records, upon being satisfied of the good standing of any member of such extinct Tribe, may issue to him a card of withdrawal. Where the books of an extinct Tribe are in possession of the Great Chief of Records, he may issue cards to former members of the extinct Tribe; cards shall have the same privilege as a card issued by an existing Tribe. — V, 201.

206. Dismissal certificates may be received upon deposit in any Tribe, but the privilege of visiting a Tribe shall not be awarded to the holder of a dismissal certificate. — V, 201.

207. They shall be in the form following, to wit: —

IMPROVED ORDER OF RED MEN.

To all whom it may concern, Fraternal Greeting:

This certifies that . . . . was admitted to membership in . . . . Tribe, No. . , under the jurisdiction of the Great Council of . . . . , on the . . sun, . . . moon, G.S.D. . . , by . . . . , and that he retained his membership in said Tribe until the . . sun, . . . moon, G.S.D. . . , when he was suspended for non-payment of dues, and is entirely dismissed from membership in said Tribe.

In witness whereof, we have hereunto subscribed our names and affixed the seal of our Tribe, this . . sun, . . . moon, G.S.D. . . . .

[SEAL]

. . . . Sachem.

, ... C. of R.

The certificate must have printed thereon the seal of the Great Council of the United States and signature of the Great Chief of Records thereof.

208. A Tribe is not compelled to grant a dismissal card to a suspended member liable to criminal charges, provided that charges have been preferred against him. — V, 423, 435.

209. A brother of an extinct Tribe, who has been suspended for non-payment of dues, upon proper application to the Great Chief of Records, is entitled to receive a dismissal certificate upon the payment of one fathom. — VI, 14, 64.

Diplomas
(or Certificates of Membership).

210. The only authorized Diploma, Red Men's Chart or Certificate of Membership, is the one issued by the Great Council of the United States, to be procured only through the Great Chief of Records of each State Great Council. — VIII, 357.

211. Tribal Chiefs have no right to sign and affix the seal of the Tribe to any Red Man's Chart, Diploma or Certificate of Membership, except those issued by the Great Council of the United States. — VIII, 357.

Dues.

212. A brother expelled from the Order cannot pay his dues to the Tribe pending an appeal. — IV, 303.

213. A brother suspended for non-payment of dues, forfeits all claims upon the Tribe. — IV, 5, 60.

214. A State Great Council has no right to make or approve of a law to allow a Tribe to suspend members from the Order for non-payment of dues after six moons. — V, 92.

215. A Tribe may deduct the seven suns' dues from the seven suns' benefits. — IV, 259.

Elections.

216. The election of Great Chiefs of the Great Council of the United States shall take place on the second sun of the great sun's council, at the third run, setting of the sun. A majority of votes polled shall be necessary to an election. If on the first ballot no one is elected, a second ballot shall immediately be had, and if no choice is then made, a third ballot shall be had, when only the two who received the highest number of votes on the second ballot shall be eligible. Blank votes shall not be counted. — Constitution G. C. U. S.

217. The Chiefs of a State Great Council shall be elected by ballot, at such time and in such manner as the By-Laws of the Great Council may prescribe.

218. Great Representatives must be elected at the same time and in the same manner as the Chiefs of a State Great Council. — General Laws.

219. In elections requiring a majority of the whole number cast to elect, all of the scattering votes must be counted. — I, 128.

220. A Chief of a State Great Council, when at his station or attending to his duties, cannot be deprived of his vote. — II, 44, 51, 55.

221. If there be only one nominee for a chieftaincy, and his name be found upon some of the ballots, he is elected, although such ballots are in number exceeded by blank ballots. — III, 60, 61.

222. A Representative may explain his vote on his name being called during the calling of yeas and nays after the main question has been ordered. — III, 355.

223. It is proper for a Representative who was present at the time of his nomination to a chieftaincy to offer his declination on the succeeding sun. — II, 49.

224. The nomination, election, and raising up of Chiefs of a Tribe should take place under "Rule 10, New Business," excepting always that the Great Chiefs shall be at liberty to exercise their discretion at visitations or institution of Tribes. — III, 191, 225.

225. It is not within the province of a Tribe on an election by ballot for Chiefs, to permit a brother who improperly voted to announce his vote in order to change the result; but if a disqualified brother has voted the ballot should be declared null and void and a new ballot be ordered. — III, 191, 226.

226. Failure to object to the voting of disqualified brothers, although objections to such voting may have been invited by the Sachem, avails nothing; and in the absence of local law governing such cases, the remedy for the result of an election at which disqualified voters have participated, is to hold another ballot. — III, 191, 224, 226.

227. A member on the sleep of his adoption has the same right to vote on any question as any other brother of the same degree. — III, 41.

228. No member can be required to divulge his reasons for casting a black twig. — III, 134, 162, 164.

229. The correct mode of voting in Great Councils is the usual show of the Order.

230. If an application receives favorable report, is balloted upon, and two or more black twigs appear, and a brother states that the twigs were put in through mistake, a new ballot may be ordered at once under the circumstances, and not lie over one seven suns. — IV, 159, 190.

231. The adoption of the report of the Committee on Elections and Returns settles all the incidental questions which it was required to pass upon as a Returning Board, and only by an appeal from the action of the Great Council adopting that report could its acts be brought in question. — V, 165.

232. The nomination and election of a qualified person would hold good whether he was present or absent at the election, if not forbidden by the By-Laws or Rules. — V, 258, 329.

233. In the case of a contested election, or a protest against the admission of a Representative, a committee of five shall be appointed, neither of whom shall be members of the State Great Council from which the contest or

protest originates. It shall without delay examine all evidence produced by either side, and report the facts to the Great Council, with such recommendation as may be deemed just; provided, that in all cases of a contest or a protest, the parties contesting or protesting shall file a copy of the same with the Great Sachem of the reservation from which the brothers hail, at least ten suns prior to the great sun's council of this Great Council. — By-Laws G. C. U. S.

Extinct Tribes.

234. All regalia, costumes, seal, books, and papers of the Order shall be surrendered to the Great Council of the United States on the extinction of a State Great Council or Tribe under the jurisdiction of the Great Council of the United States. — II, 83.

235. The numbers indicate the numerical positions of the Tribes in their respective reservations. To give the names and numbers of extinct Tribes to new petitioners is to falsify their places in the Order and to give seniority to junior Tribes. The effects of extinct Tribes are required to be surrendered to their Great Councils, in trust, to be restored whenever a legal number of its former members may apply for a restoration of its charter, under such laws as its Great Council has adopted. — IV, 91, 109.

236. A legal number of the members of an extinct Tribe who were in good standing when the Tribe ceased to exist, can, upon application to the proper authority, receive a dispensation to re-light the council brand of said Tribe, subject to the laws of the Great Council to which it may be subordinate, and all other members of said extinct Tribe must make application for admission in due form of law, subject to examination by a committee and to ballot. — IV, 353, 391.

237. When the charter of a Tribe has been surrendered and an application is made in due form for the reorganization of said Tribe, the Great Sachem may, at his discretion, grant a dispensation for the same, and at the next council fire of the State Great Council a new charter may be granted to the brothers making such application. — IV, 353, 391.

238. The Great Sachem has the right to demand the property of an extinct Tribe, to be held in trust for the future use of the members of such Tribe. — V, 142, 196.

Forms.

239. The forms written or unwritten shall not be altered or amended unless the proposed change be submitted in writing, after being twice read, on different suns, and be adopted by the votes of three-fourths of the members present entitled to vote.

Forms of Charges — See Code of Procedure.

Fees.

240. A State Great Council may establish its own fees for adoption and degrees.

Funds.

241. The funds of the Great Council of the United States must be deposited in such places as will allow interest on the daily balances, and the interest so accruing, and received must be added to the Permanent Fund. — VIII, 125.

State Great Council — How Composed.

242. A Great Council shall be composed of Past Sachems. It is the supreme tribunal of the Order in the State, district, territory, or country in which it is located, and no Tribe or branch of the Order can exist therein without its sanction. Every member shall receive the Great Council degree before he can take his seat. The Great Council shall always be opened in that degree for the introduction of Representatives, who shall be Past Sachems. The Great Council may establish regulations in regard to representation therein.

I. By virtue of authority from the Great Council of the United States, Great Councils may be established in States, districts, territories, or the Dominion of Canada. They shall be governed by their charters, the Constitution and By-Laws of this Great Council, the General Laws adopted for their government, and such laws as they may adopt in accordance with the same. — General Laws.

243. No one can institute a Great Council except the Great Incohonee, or a member of the Great Council of the United States, duly authorized by him. — V, 610, 677.

244. A Great Council has no power or right to legislate in regard to the status of the first Prophet of a Tribe created by the Great Incohonee. — IV, 181, 191.

245. A Past Great Sachem in good standing, who is not a Representative, and against whom no charge is pending, can fill any position he may be appointed or elected to. — V, 373, 428.

246. A Chief of a Great Council whose Tribe surrenders its charter must obtain a withdrawal card from the Great Chief of Records, and deposit it in another Tribe within three moons, or his chieftaincy shall be forfeited. — VI, 119, 176.

247. A Great Council has a right to adopt an amendment to its Constitution, permitting Tribes to hold councils once a moon. — IV, 253, 279, 299.

248. A Great Council may be reprimanded by the Great Council of the United States, for careless and unheeded infringement of laws. — I, 8, 9.

249. A Great Council is allowed to kindle its council fires at such places as it may from time to time determine upon. — I, 216.

250. Great Councils are required to hold a council in every great sun according to Article III, General Laws: "This Great Council shall hold at least one great sun council." — V, 529, 540.

251. The Chiefs forming a Great Council must be Past Sachems. — V, 609, 671.

252. A Great Council must keep its records in the English language. — III, 223; V, 610, 671.

253. In case of the division of a State, the Tribes of the newly formed State must establish a Great Council or put themselves under the jurisdiction of the Great Council of the United States. — II, 233, 251.

254. Great Councils have the right to fix the time at which the six moons terms of Tribes shall end, but they should so arrange that the terms shall commence and end uniformly. — IV, 196; VIII, 85.

255. Great Councils failing to pay per capita tax in accordance with Article V, By-Laws Great Council of the United States, shall be deprived of their vote, and the Representatives thereof shall forfeit all claims to mileage and per diem. — VII, 669, 670.

256. Great Councils shall have full authority and control over all Tribes and other branches of the Order in their reservations, subject to the laws of this Great Council. They shall enforce a strict adherence to the forms, ceremonies, style of regalia, jewels, charges, blanks, and other supplies furnished by this Great Council, and shall be responsible for any violation they may sanction or allow, and no Tribe or Council can legally exist within their reservations without their sanction and authority. — Constitution G. C. U. S.

257. Great Councils alone have the right to grant permission to Tribes to hold trading posts. — VIII, 563.

Honors.

258. A Great Council or Tribe does not possess authority to vary the period of a chief's term of office in a Tribe from that provided by the laws and ceremonies of the Great Council of the United States. — III, 134, 162, 164.

259. In all Tribes instituted under the immediate authority of the Great Council of the United States, more than two moons prior to the close of the term, the chiefs elected at the time of such institution, and who may serve until the end of the term, shall be entitled to the full honors of their several positions. — III, 232, 285.

260. If a Great Council changes the time of the election of Chiefs, the terms of the said Chiefs must cease, but such change in the term cannot work a forfeiture of the honors. — III, 116, 117.

261. The Chiefs of a Tribe which surrenders its charter previous to the end of a full elective term, forfeit the honors thereof. — III, 190, 225.

262. The first Prophet of a Tribe is entitled to rank as Senior Past Sachem. — IV, 82, 107.

263. A Sachem who has served a majority of the sleeps of his term, and is in good standing, and resigns, is not entitled to the honors of Past Sachem.

264. The brother elected to fill the unexpired term of the chieftaincy is entitled to the honors of the position. — IV, 254, 289.

265. When Great Chiefs announce themselves as such, and enter the council chamber, the Sachem must call up the Tribe. — V, 141, 196.

266. When Deputy Great Chiefs announce themselves as such for the

purpose of raising up the Chiefs of a Tribe, the Sachem shall call up the Tribe as soon as they enter the council chamber. — V, 141, 196.

267. Great Councils may adopt laws conferring the rank, title, rights, and privileges of a Past Sachem upon each of the Chiefs of a Tribe elected at the institution thereof; provided, such Chiefs serve to the end of the term for which they were elected. — General Laws.

INCORPORATION — ACT OF.

268. An act to incorporate the Great Council of the United States, of the Improved Order of Red Men.

WHEREAS, The Improved Order of Red Men is an Order instituted for the purpose of affording relief to such of its members as may be suffering from sickness or distress, or other causes, and for the furtherance of the general welfare of the members thereof.

AND WHEREAS, The Great Council of the United States of the Improved Order of Red Men, a body organized for the better government of the Order, desire for the more effectual accomplishment of its charitable objects, and as a means for the better execution of the purposes of its organization, to be constituted a body politic and corporate.

SECTION I. *Be it enacted by the Senate and House of Representatives of the Commonwealth of Pennsylvania, in General Assembly met, and it is hereby enacted of the same.*

That the Great Council of the United States, of the Improved Order of Red Men, is hereby constituted a body politic and corporate in deed and in law, by the name, style, and title of the Great Council of the United States of the Improved Order of Red Men, which corporation shall consist of Louis Muth, C. G. Bittorf, William M. Fields, R. F. Gardner, L. Vanfossen, William S. Quigley, S. Sullivan, John L. Boker, William G. Gorsuch, G. W. Lindsay, George H. M. Marriot, William Colton, Robert Sullivan, Richard Marley, and William H. Ford, of Maryland; Andrew J. Baker, Morris H. Gorham, E. F. Stewart, C. Weistenberg, William Adrain, L. C. Pierce, A. Gibbs, W. J. Goodwin, and A. Cameron, of Pennsylvania; Joshua Maris, William R. Mac-Farlane and S. Rianhard, of Delaware; J. A. Parsons, John D. Moore, B. F. Wood, and Charles F. Johnson, of New Jersey; J. A. Burch, Thomas Rich, Moses L. Merrill, and A. C. Prather, of the District of Columbia; George Berg, of Missouri; T. A. Bosley and David Baker, of Ohio; A. J. Francis and R. B. McCracken, of Kentucky; Hugh Latham, E. L. Lunsford, and J. B. Shaner, of Virginia; Theobald Gachter and August Roettger, of West Virginia; Alfred Shaw, of Louisiana, and all other persons who are now members, or who shall hereafter be admitted as such, agreeably to the Constitution and By-Laws of the said Great Council, and by the said corporate name shall have perpetual succession, and shall be forever capable in law to take, hold, and sell real estate, in fee simple or otherwise, and to mortgage and let the same, and to take and hold real or personal estate, by gift, grant, devise, or bequest, or other lawful means, and sell or dispose of the same; to have a common seal, and the same to break, alter, and renew at pleasure; to sue and be sued, and generally to do all such matters and things that may be lawful and necessary for them to do for the furtherance of the objects recited in the preamble of this act.

SECTION 2. The said Great Council may hold its annual or other sessions in this or any other State of the United States, and may locate its principal office at such place from time to time as it may elect within the said limits.

SECTION 3. That the said Great Council shall have power from time to time to establish, and make, and put into execution such Constitution, By-Laws, Rules, and Regulations, as may be passed from time to time by the Great Council, and the same to revoke, annul, alter, or amend at pleasure; *provided*, that the said Constitution, By-Laws, Rules, and Regulations be not repugnant to the Constitution and the laws of the United States, or of the Commonwealth of Pennsylvania, nor repugnant to the provisions of this act.

SECTION 4. The Legislature reserves the right to modify, alter, or annul the privileges hereby granted, in such manner, however, as to do no injustice to the corporator.

JAMES R. KELLEY,
Speaker of the House of Representatives.
DAVID FLEMING,
Speaker of the Senate.

Approved, the thirtieth day of March, one thousand eight hundred and sixty-six.

A. G. CURTIN.

269. There is no law of the Great Council of the United States which prohibits a Tribe in any reservation from applying to the proper authorities for an act of incorporation. — V, 179, 228.

INDIAN RELICS.

270. The Great Chief of Records of the United States is instructed to have a suitable case made for the protection and preservation of the Indian relics, or other matters that may be presented to the Great Council of the United States. — V, 233.

271. Great Councils are recommended to gather and preserve the literature, trophies, and antiquities of the Aborigines of America. — V, 233.

INSURANCE.

272. No corporation or association is permitted to use the name of the Improved Order of Red Men under which to conduct the business of insurance, without the consent of the Great Council of the United States.

LAWS.

273. By-Laws in conformity with the Constitution of the Great Council of the United States may be made. Also, General Laws for the government of Great Councils and laws for the government of Tribes under the immediate jurisdiction of this Great Council.

274. Great Councils shall have full power to enact general laws for the government of Tribes and Councils of Degree of Pocahontas within their jurisdiction. — Constitution G. C. U. S.

275. The laws of the Great Council of the United States are the supreme authority of the Order. Local laws which conflict with those of the Great Council of the United States are null and void, even if by some error they have been approved by the committee on Constitution and By-Laws of the Great Council of the United States. — V, 610, 671.

276. A law of a State Great Council to be valid must be endorsed by the Great Council of the United States. A Great Council of a State cannot make a law that vitiates a law of the Great Council of the United States, or violates any laws thereof. — V, 608, 671.

277. All constructions given to law points decided in appeal cases, decisions, and rulings of each council, shall be collected and published in an appendix attached to the records of the council at which the same shall have been made or determined, and it shall be the duty of the Great Chief of Records to prepare the same. — IV, 220.

278. The power to set aside a positive law of a State Great Council is not vested in the Great Incohonee. — IV, 4, 60.

279. Amendments admitted under the Constitution of the Great Council of the United States, relating to the amendment of the By-Laws, may be amended and the subject discussed after the third reading. — V, 304.

280. The Great Incohonee has not the power to render decisions to individual members of a State where a Great Council is in existence. — V, 436, 442.

281. WHEREAS, All power and authority enjoyed, exercised, and possessed by the several Great Councils exist only by virtue of their charters and sanction and consent of the Great Council of the United States duly granted them; Therefore, the Great Council of the United States doth adopt and establish a Constitution or General Law for their government. — General Laws.

282. The Great Council has full power to enact By-Laws for its government, and General Laws for the regulation of Tribes and Councils of Pocahontas under its jurisdiction; provided, they do not conflict with the Constitution and By-Laws of the Great Council of the United States and these General Laws. When said laws are adopted, three copies thereof, cer_ tified by the Great Sachem and Great Chief of Records, shall be transmitted to the Great Chief of Records of the Great Council of the United States, who shall immediately refer them to the Committee on Constitution and Laws, upon whose approval they shall be binding upon the Great Council. — General Laws.

283. Objections to the manner in which the laws of a Great Council have been adopted must be brought before the Great Council of the United States by way of an appeal; otherwise it is the duty of the committee to approve said Constitution, if in conformity with the laws of the Great Council of the United States. — III, 162.

284. A copy of all the Constitutions and By-Laws of Great Councils and Tribes, which shall have been submitted to the Great Council of the United States for approval, shall be filed among the archives of the State Great Council. — III, 373.

285. Great Councils have authority to promulgate a Constitution for Tribes under their jurisdiction, and all such Tribes must conform thereto and adopt By-Laws accordingly. — III, 191, 226.

286. A State Great Council is the proper body to construe its Constitution and Laws, and the Great Council of the United States can only consider the case after the action of the State Great Council shall have been had, and an appeal regularly taken to the Great Council of the United States. — IV, 21, 58.

287. Tribes under the immediate jurisdiction of the Great Council of the United States are obliged to conform to the Constitution adopted by that body for their government, and all By-Laws must be in conformity to said Constitution and receive the approval of the Great Council of the United States. — IV, 81, 101, 102.

288. All amendments to the By-Laws of Great Councils, or By-Laws of Tribes under the jurisdiction of this Great Council, must be attested by the seal, and signed by the Chiefs thereof, and all such proposed amendments not so attested shall not be received by the Great Council of the United States. — IV, 300.

289. Laws do not go into effect until promulgated by the Great Council, under seal, and the signatures of the Great Incohonee and Great Chief of Records. — Vol. VIII, 141.

290. Tribes have the right to enact a law compelling Chiefs to memorize the charges prior to being raised up. — IX, 85.

Lotteries or Gift Enterprises.

291. The giving, holding, getting up, and advertising any gift enterprise, lottery, or anything in the nature thereof, in which the name of the Order or of any Tribe thereof, is, or may be used, is prohibited. — III, 80, 100, 101.

Mark.

292. The dimensions of the mark or badge to be used as a pin shall be three-quarters of an inch long, and half an inch wide; and for a charm or totem, to suspend by a watch chain or otherwise, shall be one and a quarter inches in length, by seven-eighths of an inch wide. — IV, 22, 27.

293. The Great Council of the United States, in adopting the report on badge, did not intend to confer the exclusive right upon any member of the Order to manufacture said badge, but intended to be open to free competition. — IV, 139.

294. It is unlawful to wear the "mark" or "sign manual" in any other way than is specified in the private work. — III, 191, 224, 226.

295. Members of the Order will be entitled to wear inscribed upon their

mark or badge only the emblems of the degree to which they have attained. — IV, 22, 27.

296. The use of the motto or any of the words or emblems of the Order as an advertisement of any business is a gross violation of the laws of the Order, and is prohibited. — VI, 512.

MEMBERSHIP.

297. The Great Council of the United States shall be composed of: —

I. All Past Great Incohonees and Past Great Sachems.

II. The elective Chiefs of the Great Council.

III. The Representatives of State Great Councils.

IV. Great Representatives must be Past Sachems in good standing in their Great Councils. — Constitution G. C. U. S.

298. A State Great Council shall be composed of Past Sachems. — General Laws.

299. Degree Councils shall be composed of members of the Chief's Degree. — General Laws.

300. No person shall be adopted into a Tribe of the Order except a free white male, of good moral character and standing, of the full age of twenty-one great suns, who believes in the existence of a Great Spirit, the Creator and Preserver of the Universe, and who is possessed of some known reputable means of support. — Constitution G. C. U. S.

301. Any brother of the Order holding a withdrawal card desirous of becoming a member of a Tribe shall make application as in case of a paleface, accompanying his application with his withdrawal card, which shall be referred to a committee of three, whose duty it shall be to report as to his standing and qualifications at a stated Council. — Constitution G. C. U. S.

302. An application for adoption into a Tribe must be recommended by two brothers in good standing, and be accompanied by one-half the adoption fee. The application shall be referred to a committee of three, who shall make a strict investigation of the health, character, and qualifications of the applicant, and report at the next Council. — Constitution G. C. U. S.

303. Any member of the Improved Order of Red Men who has been exalted to the Chief's Degree, and is in good standing in his Tribe, and any woman over eighteen years of age and of good moral character, shall be eligible to membership in any Council of the Degree of Pocahontas. — General Rules D. P.

304. No brother of this Order shall be permitted to hold membership with the Order known as the Independent Order of Red Men, and any brother persisting in associating himself therewith may be expelled forthwith. — I, 48.

305. It is inconsistent with the established principles of the Improved Order of Red Men as a beneficial organization to admit any class of honorary or non-beneficial members. — III, 118.

306. All persons who are in anywise connected with other organizations which have appropriated any part of the name of the Improved Order of Red Men are disqualified for membership. — III, 191, 224, 225.

307. The Great Council of the United States has no power to grant dispensations to adopt minors under twenty-one great suns of age. — III, 263, 272.

308. This Order possesses no dominion over the conscience of its members. A brother may renounce the Order, but said renunciation cannot release the member from amenability for matters anterior to his renunciation. If a renunciation in due form comes to the knowledge of a Tribe, and the member is in good standing, and the renunciation is without disrespect to the Order, or the Tribe, it can but strike his name from the roll. With such renunciation, even verbal, all claims upon the Order for benefits or relief become void. — III, 266, 278.

309. A brother cannot hold membership in more than one Tribe at the same time. Any brother obtaining membership in a Tribe while still a member of another Tribe, would be subject to charges, and if proved guilty, to expulsion. — V, 142, 196.

310. The North American Indians are not eligible to membership. — IV, 36, 54.

311. Descendants of the Indian race are eligible to membership. — IV, 326.

312. A Tribe which becomes extinct and is reorganized, may refuse, after such reorganization, to reinstate a former member who was in arrears at the time the Tribe became extinct. — IV, 725.

313. Candidates who may be unable to give any of the signs, grips, or salutations by reason of the loss of an arm, are required and instructed to repeat verbally at the different stages of their progress, through the adoption degree, or other ceremonies of the Order, the manner in which they would be required to give the same, if in the full possession of all their members. — IV, 296.

314. A Tribe has not the right to debar a member from participating in any business, or at an election for Chiefs, as long as he is financially qualified. — IV, 4, 60.

315. A committee to which an application for adoption from a paleface has beeen referred cannot report leave to withdraw, but can only report as to his character and fitness. — IV, 159, 190.

316. The members to whom a charter may be restored shall have entire control of the subject of admitting or rejecting members, and the fact that the applicant was formerly a member of the Tribe, previous to the surrender of its charter, does not give him any rights as an applicant over any other petitioner. It is the duty of resuscitated Tribes to furnish all former members who may desire them with cards or dismissal certificates. — IV, 194.

317. A dispensation may be granted by the Great Incohonee to elect and adopt a paleface into a Tribe of an adjoining State where there is no Great Council, with a view of instituting a Tribe in that State. — IV, 353, 376.

318. Membership in an existing Tribe is necessary to good standing in a Great Council, either as a Chief or member. — V, 142, 196.

319. The loss of one leg will not disqualify a paleface for adoption into our Order. — VI, 14, 49, 64, 119, 176.

320. The consent to adopt a paleface of another jurisdiction may be asked by the Tribe directly of the proper authority of the reservation wherein the paleface resides. — VI, 49, 66.

321. Palefaces who have lost the sight of both eyes cannot be adopted into the Order. — Vol. VIII, 167.

322. Advanced age is not of itself a disqualification from membership. Tribes cannot enact a law prohibiting the adoption of a paleface after a certain age. Tribes may require an applicant at an advanced age to pay a fee so large that it would be considered an equivalent for guaranteeing the payment of benefits to him. — IX, 23.

Non-Resident.

323. No Tribe shall adopt a paleface resident of another State reservation unless by consent of the Great Sachem of such reservation; nor confer degrees upon a member of another Tribe, except by permission, under seal, of the Tribe to which said member belongs. — Constitution G. C. U. S.

Parliamentary Law.

324. An amendment to a motion may be accepted by the one who made the motion, without the consent of the one who seconded it. — III, 367, 368.

325. A measure or report adopted in portions or sections, a motion thereafter to adopt the entire report as a whole ruled out of order. — II, 256, 257.

326. A resolution similar to one just voted down cannot be renewed at the same council only through a motion to reconsider. — III, 343, 349.

327. A motion to strike from the record the names of those who made motions, not in order. — III, 159.

328. A member who, in debate, uses indecorous language and is declared out of order, does not thereby lose his right to the floor. — III, 173.

329. Matters indefinitely postponed cannot again be brought up before the Great Council of the United States before the next great sun council. — II, 80, 85.

330. A subject referred to a committee cannot be indefinitely postponed while it is still in the hands of the committee, the subject not being before the Great Council. — II, 83.

331. Cushing's Manual adopted by the Great Council of the United States as the guide when the Rules of Order do not provide. — III, 115.

332. When a substitute is offered for a resolution, an amendment can be offered to the original motion after the substitute has been rejected. — III, 251.

333. A motion to quench the council fire cannot be entertained in any Tribe until arriving at the order, as laid down in the Ritual, entitled "New Business." Should the motion prevail, the council fire must be quenched in due and regular form. — IV, 302.

334. It is not necessary to make a motion to receive and refer to a committee an application for adoption; nor to accept the report of the committee and proceed to ballot. — IV, 254, 298.

335. A Great Council has authority to amend their Rules of Order, provided such amendments do not conflict with any law of the Great Council of the United States. — IV, 254, 298.

336. A point of order that a Representative, having spoken once upon a question, is not in order to speak a second time until all desiring to speak have an opportunity to do so, not well taken unless raised as soon as the speaker commences. — IV, 379.

337. The adoption of the records of the previous council has no bearing upon the subject-matter under consideration at such council. — II, 39.

338. Under Rule 10 of the Ritual "New Business," any business may be considered that had not been introduced before. But when all the business submitted has been transacted under said rule, there is nothing to preclude other business being introduced and acted upon under the next rule. (Rule 11.) — III, 40, 54.

339. The effect of a protest is not to destroy the validity of any act done, but simply to enable members to place upon record the individual sentiments of the protestants. — V, 166.

340. When a resolution is referred to a committee it has the right to present a report expressing their views on the subject referred to it. — Vol. VIII, page 138.

341. A resolution which is mandatory and the same intended to make a change either in the regalia, forms, ceremonies, or other private work, written or unwritten, requires a three-fourths vote of the members present and entitled to vote. — Vol. VIII, page 530.

Parliamentary Law.

342. The Rules of Order adopted by the Great Council is its Parliamentary Law, and take precedence of any other code or manual. Any other law or rule applies only to cases not provided for in the Rules of Order.

Rules of Order.

I. The Great Incohonee may speak to points of order, rising for that purpose. Before putting a question he shall ask: "Is the Great Council ready for the question?" If no brother address him he shall rise and put the question, after which it will not be in order to address the Great Council upon the question.

II. No brother shall be permitted to vote or speak unless clothed in regalia according to his rank or station.

III. Every brother when he rises to speak shall address the Great Incohonee in a proper manner, and no brother shall pass out of the wigwam, or otherwise disturb the council, except to call to order.

IV. All personalities and indecorous language or reflection upon the Great Council, or its members, are positively prohibited.

V. No brother shall speak more than once upon the same question until all have had an opportunity so to do, nor more than twice without permission from the Great Council.

VI. If a brother, while speaking, be called to order by the Great Incohonee, he shall cease speaking and take his seat until the question of order is determined and permission given him to proceed.

VII. Every Chief or brother shall be designated by his proper title, according to his standing in the Order.

VIII. When a question is before the Great Council, no motion shall be received, except for the previous question, to lie on the table, to postpone indefinitely, or to a limited time; to divide, to commit, or to amend; and such motions shall severally have precedence in the order herein arranged. A motion to quench the council fire is always in order.

IX. The Great Council may resolve itself into a Committee of the Whole upon the following subjects and none other: For the consideration of the Constitution and Laws, and for the consideration of the work of the Order, written and unwritten.

X. Any brother who voted on the prevailing side can call for the reconsideration of a vote at the same great sun council in which it was passed, and if sustained by a majority of the votes the reconsideration shall be carried.

XI. If two or more brothers rise to speak at the same time, the Great Incohonee shall decide which is entitled to the floor.

XII. No motion shall be subject to debate until it has been seconded and stated by the Great Incohonee. It shall be reduced to writing at the request of any brother.

XIII. On the call of three brothers a majority may demand the previous question, which shall always be put in this form: "Shall the main question be now put?" and until it is decided, shall preclude all amendments and all further debate. If the main question be ordered, the amendments shall be voted upon in their order and then the original question.

XIV. The Great Incohonee shall pronounce the decision of the Great Council on all subjects; he may speak on points of order without debate, subject to an appeal to the Great Council by any two brothers — on which appeal no brother shall speak more than once.

XV. A motion to lie on the table shall be decided without debate.

XVI. When a question is postponed indefinitely it shall not be acted on until the next great sun council.

XVII. The yeas and nays may be demanded by any two members, and shall be entered upon the record; and every Representative must vote, unless excused by a majority of the Great Council.

XVIII. All questions shall be decided by a majority vote, except in cases otherwise provided for.

ORDER OF BUSINESS.

343. At the run fixed therefor the Great Incohonee shall take his station and command silence; have the wickets secured, the wigwam examined, and the council fire duly kindled.

REVISED DIGEST.

I. Roll of Chiefs.
II. Appointment of Committee on Credentials.
III. Credentials of Past Great Sachems and Representatives read and referred.
IV. Admission of Representatives and Past Great Sachems.
V. Roll of Representatives.
VI. The record of last council fire read and considered.
VII. Long Talks of Great Incohonee and other Chiefs.
VIII. The names of Great Councils and Tribes called in alphabetical order, for business or communications.
IX. Reports of committee.
X. Deferred business.
XI. New business.

These rules may be temporarily dispensed with by the Great Incohonee.

PASSWORDS.

344. Passwords for the various branches of the Order shall be promulgated by the Great Incohonee. — Ritual.

345. The Sachem has the right to communicate the password through the First Sannap to members in the wigwam who are qualified to receive it, but the Sannap requires express authority in each case to enable him so to act. — III, 134, 162, 164.

346. The Sachem alone possesses exclusive authority to communicate the password and explanation to members of his Tribe. — III, 190, 224, 245.

347. The Great Council password is designed exclusively for Great Councils, and all who are otherwise qualified for admission to Great Councils are entitled to a knowledge of this password.

348. The Past Sachem's password is not designed for working purposes, nor is any one except a Past Sachem entitled to its possession. — III, 190, 224, 225.

349. A member of a Tribe appearing at the wicket without the Universal password may be admitted without being instructed by the First Sannap in the forest. — III, 281, 343.

350. A brother who is not more than three moons in arrears is entitled to receive the Universal password. — IV, 193.

351. The law does not confer on any member the right to vouch for another who may be without the Universal password, whether in good standing or not. Every brother in good standing is entitled to the password, and its use is to enable such brother to visit any Tribe. A brother over three moons in arrears is not in good standing and is not entitled to the password, and consequently is not entitled to visit any Tribe but his own. — V, 490, 536.

352. The phrase "current term" shall be construed to mean during the currency of the certified receipt for dues paid to receive the Universal password. — V, 491, 536.

353. When a Sachem receives the official certified receipt and order thereon requesting that the Universal password be given to the bearer, he

shall first satisfy himself of the personal identity of the member, and he shall require him to prove himself in the unwritten work of the Order before he communicates the Universal password. — VIII, 525.

354. The Guard of the Forest is required to demand and receive the password of the sleep from a brother leaving the wigwam during the burning of the council fire. — VIII, 526.

355. The Guards cannot admit a brother on the retiring password. — VIII, 526.

356. Orders for the password must be upon the form adopted and issued by the Great Council of the United States and must be accompanied by the official receipt for dues as adopted by said body. — IX, 138.

Past Sachems.

357. Actual service in the Sachem's position entitles a member to take rank as a Past Sachem. — VIII, 130.

358. Service as first Prophet of a Tribe, as Chief of Records, Collector of Wampum, or Keeper of Wampum, for five successive great suns, shall entitle a member to the degree of Past Sachem. — General Laws.

359. Great Councils may adopt laws conferring the rank, title, rights, and privileges of a Past Sachem upon each of the Chiefs of a Tribe elected at the institution thereof; provided, such Chiefs serve to the end of the term for which they were elected. — General Laws.

360. A member is entitled to a Past Sachem's certificate immediately after his successor has been raised up as Sachem. — V, 257, 329.

361. A Tribe has not the right to withhold a certificate from a Past Sachem who has served a regular term as Sachem. — V, 528, 542.

362. The Great Incohonee and Great Sachem, respectively, alone have the power to issue dispensations exalting the first Prophets of new Tribes to the position of Past Sachem; the honors to be conferred only in the Great Council of a State, District, or Territory duly and regularly instituted. — IV, 290.

363. If a brother serves a term in a Tribe, that will entitle him to the honors of a Past Sachem, but before he receives the Past Sachem's degree he takes his withdrawal card from said Tribe as a Chief's degree member only, and deposits it in another Tribe as a brother of the Chief's degree, he must get his certificate as a Past Sachem from the first Tribe; and it is the duty of said Tribe to furnish said brother with a certificate which will entitle him to claim his rights in the hunting-grounds to which he may remove. — IV, 157, 190.

364. The first Prophet of a new Tribe is not entitled to the privileges and honors of a Past Sachem until a dispensation has been formally issued and received by him with the signature and seal of the proper authority. — IV, 157, 190.

365. Where the first Prophet takes a withdrawal card before the end of the term he loses the honors and the Great Incohonee or Great Sachem, as the

case may be, may appoint another Prophet and make him a Past Sachem by dispensation. — VI, 160, 214.

366. A State Great Council has the right to admit to its councils a brother who has been appointed a first Prophet of a Tribe and serves to the end of his term, provided, the brother produces a dispensation in regular form from the proper Chiefs creating him a Past Sachem. — IV, 207.

367. A member of the Order who has attained the rank of Past Sachem in one Great Council shall be entitled to admission into another upon a change of residence upon presenting a certificate in proper form from his Tribe. — IV, 403.

368. Great Councils cannot confer the Past Sachem's degree upon a brother for meritorious service. — Vol. VIII, 572.

369. The first Prophet of a Beneficial Degree Council is not entitled to the honors of Past Sachem. — VIII, 487.

370. When other associations make application for charters of our Order, their past officers would not be entitled to the rank and honors of a Past Sachem. The rule as regards consolidation only, refers to those organizations now known by the various titles of Red Men. — IX, 22.

371. A brother serving in the chieftaincy of Sachem of a Beneficial Degree Council is, at the end of his term, entitled to the rank and honor of a Past Sachem. — IX, 31.

372. A member who has received the honors of a Past Sachem illegally is not entitled to admission to a Great Council, and it would be the duty of the Great Sachem to debar the admission of any such brother. — IX, 32.

373. No Past Sachem is eligible to hold two elective chieftaincies in a Great Council. — IX, 136.

374. A Great Council would not have the right to confer the rank of Past Sachem upon any brother unless said brother had earned the honors as laid down in the ritual and laws.

375. Great Councils are composed of Past Sachems, who must have received the degree prior to their taking a seat, and when so admitted are entitled to all the rights and privileges guaranteed to them under the laws. While Great Councils have the right to establish regulations in regard to representation, yet said Representatives must be Past Sachems, and as Great Councils cannot exist without a certain number of Past Sachems, it naturally follows that said members are entitled to all the privileges therein, and cannot therefore be debarred from voting for Great Chiefs, where the law does not prescribe either the time or manner of holding an election for Great Chiefs.

PAST GREAT SACHEMS. — ADMISSION.

376. Before the admission of a Past Great Sachem a certificate must be received certifying that he has duly served as Great Sachem of a Great Council, or as the first Great Prophet, or five great suns as Great Chief of Records or Great Keeper of Wampum, and that he is in good standing in his Tribe. — By-Laws G. C. U. S.

377. All past Great Sachems whose credentials have been acknowledged by the Great Council shall be admitted to a seat, and entitled to all privileges, except that of voting and receiving mileage and per diem. — Constitution G. C. U. S.

378. Any Great Chief of Records or Great Keeper of Wampum, of any Great Council, having served five great suns in succession as such, shall be entitled to the degree of Past Great Sachem. — General Laws.

Past Great Representatives.

379. Past Representatives who are members of the Order in good standing, shall be entitled to admission as visitors, but shall not be allowed to participate in any business before the Great Council. — By-Laws G. C. U. S.

Permanent Fund.

380. The Permanent Fund shall consist of such sums as the Great Council may from time to time appropriate, donations and bequests made thereto, and accumulations of interest. The principal of said fund shall not be used, nor shall this article be amended or repealed, except seven-eighths of those entitled to vote agree thereto.

I. When in the judgment of the Great Council a sum sufficient for the purpose has been accumulated, the fund shall be invested in such a manner as the Great Council may then provide, in a Home forever dedicated to the widows and orphans of members of the Improved Order of Red Men.

II. The Great Incohonee, Great Prophet, Great Senior Sagamore, Great Junior Sagamore, Great Chief of Records, and Great Keeper of Wampum shall constitute the Board of Trustees of the Great Council of the United States. They shall have supervision of the Permanent Fund of the Great Council, and make such investments as they may deem for the best interests of said fund, until final investment in a Home, as above provided. They shall make a report thereon at each great sun council.

III. At each great sun council, the Finance Committee shall submit a resolution appropriating not less than one hundred fathoms, which sum shall be placed in the Permanent Fund already created. The wampum so appropriated, shall be invested by the Trustees, until the aggregate amount shall reach the sum needed for the purpose of the Home contemplated. — Constitution G. C. U. S.

381. Interest accruing from the Permanent Fund shall hereafter be carried to said account instead of to the General Fund account. — VII, 670, 671.

Penalties.

382. Any Great Council neglecting to forward its report and tax, on or before the first of Corn moon, shall forfeit its right to representation in the Great Council of the United States; provided, this penalty may be remitted by unanimous consent. — By-Laws G. C. U. S.

383. Any member guilty of the following offences, would be amenable to

the Tribe, and should be tried and punished by reprimand, fine, suspension, or expulsion : —

I. Violation of the obligations he has taken, either in the Adoption, or the degrees, or on assuming any chieftaincy, or the laws of the Order.

II. Revealing, or making known to a person or persons who are not at the time members of the Order, any of the secrets or the workings of the Tribe.

III. Making false statements in order to gain admission into the Order, knowing the same to be false ; or who shall knowingly conceal any infirmity or disease, either of body or mind.

IV. Using improper means to obtain benefits.

V. Misappropriating any of the funds, property or effects of a Tribe to his own use, or shall wrongfully divert or misappropriate the funds of the Tribe.

VI. Wilfully refusing to appear and testify or give his deposition, after being duly notified by the Tribe.

VII. Violating the criminal laws of his State.

VIII. Bringing suit in any of the civil courts of his State against his Tribe for the redress of any grievance, the adjudication of which is provided for within the Order by the laws thereof.

IX. Using any of the emblems, mottoes, titles, or initials of the Order, either as a Chief or member directly or indirectly, for the prosecution of any private business or enterprise. — Code of Procedure.

Forfeiture of Charters.

384. Any Great Council, Tribe, or Council of the Degree of Pocahontas may be suspended or dissolved, and its charter or dispensation forfeited to and reclaimed by the Great Council of the United States or the proper Great Council : —

I. For improper conduct.

II. For neglecting or refusing to conform to the Constitution, laws, and enactments of this Great Council, and of that to which it is subordinate, or to the general laws and regulations of the Order.

III. For neglecting or refusing to make its returns, or for non-payment of dues or taxes.

IV. For neglecting to hold regular councils as provided by law, unless prevented by unfortunate circumstances.

V. By its membership decreasing, so that it is left without a quorum.

385. But the charter or dispensation shall not be forfeited in either of the above cases until due notification of the offence by the proper Great Chiefs, under seal, and suitable opportunity has been given to answer the charges. — Constitution G. C. U. S.

Per Diem and Mileage.

386. The Great Council of the United States shall pay mileage and per diem to its Great Chiefs, Representatives, and members of the Finance Com-

mittee and Committee of Constitution and Laws. The mileage shall be at the rate of five inches per mile circular, to be computed by the nearest travelled route, and five fathoms per sun for each sun in attendance. — By-Laws G. C. U. S.

PHRASEOLOGY. — CALENDAR.

387.

Breath	A minute.
Run	An hour.
Sun	A day.
Sleep	A night.
Seven Suns	A week.
Moon	A month.
Cold Moon	January.
Snow Moon	February.
Worm Moon	March.
Plant Moon	April.
Flower Moon	May.
Hot Moon	June.
Buck Moon	July.
Sturgeon Moon	August.
Corn Moon	September.
Travelling Moon	October.
Beaver Moon	November.
Hunting Moon	December.
Great Sun	A year.
Rising of the Sun	Morning.
Setting of the Sun	Evening.
High Sun	Mid-day.
Low Sun	Midnight.
Paleface	One who is not a member of the Order.
Wampum Belt	Treasury.
Wigwam and Tepee	Place of Meeting.
Hunting Ground	Territory over which a Tribe has jurisdiction.
Reservation	Territory over which a Great Council has jurisdiction.
Records	The Minutes.
Talk or Long Talk	Speech or Report.
Kindling a council fire	Organizing a meeting.
Quenching a council fire	Closing a meeting.
Tribe and League	Branches of the Order.
Great Council	Head of the Order in a State, etc.
Following the hunt	Attending to business.
Crossing the path	Wronging another.
Wampum	Money.
Fathom	One dollar.
Foot	Ten cents.
Inch	One cent.

388. Initiation. The term is sometimes, but improperly used for adoption. — III, 192.

389. All Tribes shall have for titles Indian names, and they shall be local to the State or Territory. — III, 191, 531, 285.

390. The word "subordinate" in connection with a Tribe is superfluous, and should be stricken out wherever it occurs in the work of the Order. — I, 53.

391. It is not proper to use the term "scalped" for "suspended." — IV, 253, 298.

392. It is improper to use the word "tomahawked" for "expelled." — IV, 253, 298.

393. There is no list of terms or words in the phraseology of the Order, save those contained in the Calendar. — IV, 254, 298.

394. The use of the word "squaw" or "pappoose," as referring to wives and children of members of the Order is prohibited and condemned. — IX, 145.

395. The area to be determined as the hunting grounds of a Tribe is a question of local legislation. — IX, 22.

Printing of Records and Supplies of the Great Council.

396. The Great Chief of Records shall, at least two moons prior to the great sun's council, notify members of the Order who are practical printers that estimates will be received on or before the first of the Sturgeon moon for printing the records and all other printed matter needed for the great sun, and said bids shall be opened in the presence of the Finance Committee, who shall award the same to the lowest responsible bidder. — By-Laws G. C. U. S.

397. There shall be printed with the record of the proceedings of each great sun council of this Great Council, a directory of the Great Councils under its jurisdiction, with the names of the Great Sachems and Great Chiefs of Records thereof. — III, 315.

398. Great Councils have the right to print dispensations for their own use and reports for the use of Tribes under their jurisdiction. — III, 191, 226.

399. It is illegal for any Great Council, Tribe, or person to issue or print any supplies unless by order of the Great Council of the United States. — III, 136, 155, 167.

400. With the proceedings of each council of the Great Council of the United States, there shall be an appendix containing a digest of the decisions, amendments, and proposed amendments to the laws, together with such other business as may remain unacted upon. — IV, 181.

401. The Great Chief of Records of the United States is authorized to have printed in the record of every great sun council, a list of all Past Great Incohonees. — V, 660.

Quorum.

402. Representatives from a majority of Great Councils shall be necessary to constitute a quorum for the transaction of any business, except the admis-

sion of new members, and to kindle the council fire, and quench it from time to time, for which purposes alone, less than said majority may act. — Constitution G. C. U. S.

403. Five members or more, including one qualified to preside, shall constitute a quorum for the transaction of business in a Tribal council. — Constitution G. C. U. S.

Raising up of Chiefs.

404. The Chiefs of the Great Council of the United States shall be raised up, and enter upon their duties on the last sun of the great sun's council, immediately preceding the quenching of the council fire. — By-Laws G. C. U. S.

405. Should any of the Great Chiefs elect fail to be present at the run fixed for the raising up, the chieftaincy may be declared vacant, and the Great Council proceed to fill the vacancy; but should such absence be caused by sickness, or other cause, satisfactory to this Great Council, then he shall be raised up by any designated Great Chief, after the quenching of the council fire, and the fact shall be certified to, and entered upon the records of this Great Council. — By-Laws G. C. U. S.

406. The raising up of chiefs of a Tribe shall take place on the first council sleep of the term, unless a dispensation has been granted to postpone the same. Tribes may have their Chiefs raised up in public, provided a dispensation has been first obtained. — Constitution G. C. U. S.

Records.

407. The record (except that of the secret council) shall be published every great sun, and each Great Council shall be entitled to as many copies as it may have Past Great Sachems, Great Chiefs, and branches of the Order under its control. — Constitution G. C. U. S.

408. The Great Chief of Records of the United States, under the direction of the Great Council of the United States, may omit from the record any part of the proceedings — III, 280.

409. The Great Sachem of a Great Council, or the Sachem of a Tribe, has no legal right to ignore the records, and declare that they are not kept correctly after they have been read and approved by the Great Council or Tribe. — VI, 15, 49.

410. A Great Council or a Tribe is the sole judge of the correctness of the records thereof. — VI, 15, 49.

411. All resolutions presented to the Great Council of the United States must be submitted in writing, and in duplicate form, and unless so submitted, will not be considered. — III, 334.

412. Business transacted while the council fire of a Tribe is kindled in degree form, must be kept in a separate record book, and the approval of the same must be done while the council fire is burning in the degree. — IX, 83.

Regalia.

413. The regalia is adopted by the Great Council of the United States, and cannot be altered unless the proposed change be submitted in writing, and, after being read twice, on different suns, adopted by the votes of three-fourths of the members present entitled to vote. — Constitution G. C. U. S.

414. The regalia of the Order shall consist of a sash four and one-half inches wide, with pouch attached, of the pattern heretofore in use, and shall be trimmed and embellished for the several ranks, as hereinafter described, namely: —

For Adopted, a plain green sash, without embellishment or trimmings.

For Hunter's Degree, an orange sash, trimmed with white or silver lace, with a hunter's knife on the breast, of silver embroidery or white metal.

For Warrior's Degree, a blue sash, trimmed same as Hunter's, with knife and club crossed, of silver embroidery or white metal, on the breast.

For Chief's Degree, a scarlet sash, trimmed same as Warrior's, with knife, club and tomahawk crossed, of silver embroidery or white metal, on the breast.

For Prophet, a white sash, trimmed with gilt lace and fringe, with crossed calumets on the breast, in gilt embroidery or yellow metal.

For Sachem, a scarlet sash, trimmed with silver lace and fringe, with crossed tomahawks of silver embroidery or white metal, on the breast.

For Senior Sagamore, a scarlet sash, trimmed same as Sachem's, with crossed clubs, of silver embroidery or white metal, on the breast.

For Junior Sagamore, a scarlet sash, trimmed same as Senior Sagamore, with crossed knives of silver embroidery or white metal, on the breast.

For Chief of Records, a scarlet sash, trimmed same as Junior Sagamore, with a scroll in silver embroidery or white metal, on the breast.

For Keeper of Wampum, a scarlet sash, trimmed same as Chief of Records, with Wampum belt, in silver embroidery or white metal, on the breast.

For First Sannap, a scarlet sash, trimmed with plated or silver lace, with crossed arrows of silver embroidery or white metal, on the breast.

For Second Sannap, a scarlet sash, trimmed same as First Sannap, with single arrow, of silver embroidery or white metal, on the breast.

For Guard of the Wigwam, a scarlet sash, trimmed with plated or silver lace and crossed spears, of silver embroidery or white metal, on the breast.

For Guard of the Forest, a scarlet sash, trimmed same as Guard of Wigwam, with bow and arrow, in silver embroidery or white metal, on the breast.

For the appointed Warriors, blue sashes, trimmed with silver lace, with a single club in silver embroidery or white metal, on the breast, and the numerals 1, 2, 3, 4, indicating the special rank of the Warrior, above the emblem.

For the four Braves or Hunters, orange sashes, trimmed same as Warriors, with deer's head and antlers, in silver embroidery or white metal, on breast, and in addition thereto, the numerals 1, 2, 3, 4, to indicate the special rank of the Braves or Hunters.

The regalia for members of State Great Councils (except Great Prophet) shall consist of a scarlet sash, trimmed with gilt lace and fringe.

For Representatives of Tribes, or Degree Councils, a scarlet sash, with Indian shield, of yellow metal, bearing the initials and number of the Tribe, or Degree Council represented, stamped upon or engraved thereon, on the breast of the sash.

For Past Sachems, a scarlet sash, trimmed with gilt lace and fringe, with the knife, club, and tomahawk crossed, in gilt embroidery, or yellow metal, on the breast.

For Great Prophet, a white sash, trimmed with gilt lace and fringe, with calumets crossed upon a shield, of gilt embroidery, or yellow metal, to be worn or depending from the breast of sash.

For Great Sachem, a scarlet sash, trimmed with gilt lace and fringe, with tomahawks crossed upon a shield, of gilt embroidery or yellow metal, upon the breast of the sash or depending therefrom.

For Great Senior Sagamore, same style and trimmings, with crossed club on shield, as above described.

For Great Junior Sagamore, a sash, same style and trimmings as Senior Sagamore, with crossed knives on shield, in gilt embroidery, or yellow metal.

For Great Chief of Records, a sash, same style and trimmings as Great Junior Sagamore, with scroll on shield, in gilt embroidery, or yellow metal.

For Great Keeper of Wampum, a sash, same style and description as the Great Chief of Records, with wampum belt on shield, of gilt embroidery, or yellow metal.

For Great Sannap, a sash of the same style and trimming as the Great Keeper of Wampum, with single arrow on shield, in gilt embroidery, or yellow metal.

For Great Mishinewa, the usual official sash of the Great Council, with a quiver full of arrows on shield, in gilt embroidery on the breast thereof, or in gilt metal suspended therefrom.

For Great Guard of the Wigwam, a sash, same style and trimmings as Great Sannap, with crossed spears on shield, of gilt embroidery, or yellow metal.

For Great Guard of Forest, a sash, same style and trimmings as Great Sannap, with bow and arrow on shield, of gilt embroidery, or yellow metal.

The regalia for members of the Great Council of the United States, shall consist of a sash $4\frac{1}{2}$ inches wide, with pouch attached. The sash shall be composed of one stripe each of purple and scarlet material (except the Great Prophet's) running lengthwise of the sash, the purple stripe to be on the inside edge of the sash, to be trimmed with gilt lace and fringe.

For Great Prophet, the sash shall be of white and purple, of the same style and trimmings as already described, with an eagle of yellow metal, resting on crossed calumets, and upon the shield on the eagle's breast the letters G.C.U.S.

For Great Incohonee, a scarlet and purple sash, with eagle as above described, resting on crossed tomahawks.

For Great Senior Sagamore, sash as above, eagle resting on crossed clubs

For Great Junior Sagamore, a sash as above, eagle resting on crossed knives.

For Great Chief of Records, sash as above, eagle resting on scroll. On the scroll the date of institution of the Great Council of the United States.

For Great Keeper of Wampum, a sash as above, eagle resting on wampum belt.

For Great Tocakon, sash as above, eagle resting on crossed spears.

For Great Minewa, a sash as above, eagle resting on bow and arrow.

For Past Great Sachem, a sash as described, with eagle and shield on his breast, and the letters P.G.S. and initials of the wearer's jurisdiction on the shield.

For Representative of State or Territorial Great Councils, a sash as described, with eagle and shield. Upon the shield the letter "R," and the initials of the Great Jurisdiction represented.

415. The regalia of a Past Great Incohonee shall be a sash, four and a half inches wide, with pouch attached, composed of royal purple velvet, to be trimmed with gilt lace and fringe. At right angles with the length of the sash, a strip of gilt braid, one-quarter inch in width, may be attached for each great sun council the Past Great Incohonee has attended the Great Council of the United States. The jewel of a Past Great Incohonee shall be a gold or yellow metal cross-bar, composed of four links, containing the letters T.O.T.E., from which shall be pendant a gold or yellow metal eagle, with shield on his breast, on which shall be engraved the letters P.G.I.

416. For Vice Great Incohonees, Deputy Great Sachems, or Chiefs to raise up Chiefs, the jewel shall be a single tomahawk of yellow metal. The regalia shall conform to the title of the rank of the wearer.

Beneficial Degree Council.

417. Chiefs and members of Degree Councils shall wear a regalia in accordance with those used in the Tribes.

418. The emblems of the chieftaincy to be on the head-dress. — III, 134.

419. Members in Degree Councils are not properly clothed unless invested with regalia according to their rank and station therein. — III, 134, 164.

Degree of Pocahontas.

420. The regalia to be worn in a Tepee of the Degree of Pocahontas shall be as follows : —

The brothers shall wear the regalia to which they are entitled, in accordance with their rank in the Order; the sisters shall wear a collar of the Degree of Pocahontas, and, if elected or appointed to a position, the jewel thereof.

The regalia for sisters shall be a plain purple collar.

For Pocahontas, purple collar, trimmed with silver lace, with the emblem attached, white metal, consisting of crossed tomahawks.

For Prophetess, purple collar, trimmed with gold lace and fringe. Emblem, crossed tomahawks, inclosed in a circle of yellow metal.

For Wenonah, same as Pocahontas. Emblem, single tomahawk.

Keeper of Records, same as Pocahontas. Emblem, scroll.

Collector of Wampum, same as Pocahontas. Emblem, wampum belt on scroll.

Keeper of Wampum, same as Pocahontas. Emblem, wampum belt.

First Scout, same as Pocahontas. Emblem, crossed arrows.

Second Scout, same as Pocahontas. Emblem, single arrow.

Runners, same as Pocahontas. Emblem, single club.

Guard of Wigwam, same as Pocahontas. Emblem, single spear.

Guard of Forest, same as Pocahontas. Emblem, crossed spears.

Past Chiefs, the same as Prophetess.

Powhatan, same as Pocahontas. Emblem, crossed clubs, and tomahawk.

Councillor, same as Pocahontas. Emblem, quiver and arrow.

Warriors, same as Pocahontas. Emblem, bow and arrow with numerals 1, 2, 3, 4.

421. No change can be made in the regalia except by special action of the Great Council of the United States. — II, 135, 169, 171.

422. It is unlawful for a Tribe or State Great Council to dispense with any part of the regalia in parades. — III, 256, 277.

423. It is not in violation of the General Laws of the Great Council of the United States for a Tribe to have silver lace on the Chief's degree regalia, but in conformity with the law prescribing the regalia. — V, 528, 542.

424. Only brothers who have attained the rank of Past Great Sachem are entitled to wear a purple and scarlet regalia. — VI, 485.

425. Propositions to change the regalia or emblems must define what regalia or emblems are to be stricken out, and what is to be inserted in lieu thereof. — IX, 83.

REJECTIONS.

426. A paleface whose application for membership has been rejected shall not be adopted into any Tribe until at least six moons after his rejection. — Constitution G. C. U. S.

427. A brother whose application for advancement in the degrees has been rejected cannot again renew the application for three moons thereafter. — Constitution G. C. U. S.

RENUNCIATION AND RESIGNATION.

428. This Order possesses no authority over the conscience of its members. A brother may renounce the Order, but said renunciation cannot release the member from amenability for matters anterior to his renunciation. If a renunciation in due form comes to the knowledge of a Tribe, and the member is in good standing, and the renunciation is without disrespect to the Order or the Tribe, it can but strike his name from the roll. With such

renunciation, even verbal, all claims upon the Order for benefits or relief cease. — VIII, 266, 278.

429. A brother cannot resign from the Order. There are five ways by which his connection may be severed: 1st, non-payment of dues; 2d, expulsion, after trial; 3d, by withdrawal card; 4th, death; 5th, by renunciation. — VI, 119, 176.

REINSTATEMENT.

430. A member suspended or dropped from membership for non-payment of dues, may be reinstated in the Tribe from which he has been suspended or dropped, within one great sun after suspension, by paying one great sun's dues, and being reinstated in the manner prescribed by the local law. — V, 200.

431. After one great sun from the date of suspension, a member dropped or suspended for non-payment of dues may be reinstated upon the payment of the fee charged for adopted members of the same age, as prescribed by the By-Laws. — V, 200.

432. No action is necessary in reinstating a brother who has been suspended for cause after the termination of his suspension; he is then virtually a member in the same financial standing as at the time of suspension. — I, 12.

433. A member expelled from the Order cannot be restored to membership in the Tribe, except after application to the Tribe, and by permission of the Great Council Chiefs, during the interim; and the vote necessary to reinstate him is the same vote which expelled him from membership. — Code of Procedure.

REPRESENTATION.

434. A Great Council in hunting grounds containing less than one thousand members shall be entitled to one Representative; over one thousand and less than two thousand, two Representatives; over two thousand and less than three thousand, three Representatives; over three thousand and less than four thousand, four Representatives; over four thousand and less than five thousand, five Representatives; over five thousand and less than six thousand, six Representatives; over six thousand and less than seven thousand, seven Representatives; over seven thousand and less than eight thousand, eight Representatives; and all reservations having over eight thousand members, eight Representatives. — Constitution G. C. U. S.

435. A motion to admit Representatives without credentials cannot be entertained. — III, 313.

436. Only in case of the clearest and most palpable fraud should any reservation be deprived of its representation in the Great Council of the United States. — V, 165.

437. Past Great Incohonees possess all the rights of Representatives in the Great Council of the United States except that of mileage or per diem. — III, 333.

438. Great Councils may provide for a representative system, and may limit Tribes under their jurisdiction to one Representative. — General Rules.

439. Where a Great Council exists, no Past Sachem is eligible for Representative to the Great Council of the United States unless he has been admitted to a Great Council. — V, 13, 70, 80.

440. Credentials should be signed by the Chiefs of a Great Council who are in office at the time such credentials are made out. — V, 217.

441. Every newly admitted Representative is entitled to a copy of the Digest. — IV, 90.

442. In the matter of computing mileage for distance travelled by Representatives, the Committee on Mileage shall take the official guide for its government. — IV, 99.

443. The only way in which the validity of the election of Representatives could be tested would be by an appeal to the Great Council of the United States. — V, 165.

444. In no case can a brother act, or be considered as a competent Representative in this Great Council, unless he is in good standing in a Tribe of the jurisdiction he claims to represent. — V, 117.

445. Representatives to the Great Council of the United States have not the right to instruct the Tribes in their reservations in the amendments and decisions previous to their promulgation by the Great Council. They report to the body they represent, only. — IV, 417.

446. Great Councils entitled to more than one Representative should at all times have a portion of their Representatives entitled to a voice in the Great Council, and one-half of the number only should serve for two great suns. — VI, 52.

447. The Great Council of the United States does not admit or allow representation by proxy. When a Great Representative is unable to attend, he has not the right to hand his credentials over to *any* Chief. He *must* resign, and during the recess of the Great Council the Great Sachem can appoint, or the Great Council in council elect his successor. — VI, 120, 176.

448. Before a member can be acknowledged as a Representative, the following certificate must be received : —

Wigwam of Great Council of————, *Imp. O. R. M.*

This is to certify that an election held by the Great Council of . . . . . . , Brother . . . . . . was elected to represent the Great Council of . . . . . . in the Great Council of the United States for . . . . great suns, from the second Tuesday in Corn moon next.

Witness our hand and the Seal of Our Great Council, the . . . sun, . . . moon, G. S. D. . . .

                              . . . . Great Sachem.
[L.S.]   . . . . Great C. of R.

Each Representative shall be presented with a duplicate of the above credential, and either the original or duplicate shall be referred to the Committee on Credentials, who shall report thereon as soon as practicable. — By-Laws G. C. U. S.

449. A Representative to fill a vacancy must present a credential giving the name of the Representative in whose place he is appointed or elected, and stating the cause of such vacancy. — By-Laws G. C. U. S.

450. A Sachem is not eligible for election as Representative unless he is a Past Sachem. — IV, 13, 70, 81.

451. To entitle a Past Sachem to a seat in a Great Council he must be in good standing, and a member of a Tribe working under a legal and unforfeited charter, and the Tribe must have sent in its report, and paid the *per capita* tax due. — Vol. VIII, 596.

452. On the call of States, Representatives must not present their instructions, but if they involve a change in the laws they must present such amendments as they deem proper to carry out the instructions from their Great Council. — VIII, 527.

453. A protest or contest against the admission of a Representative or Representatives is not legal, unless a copy of said protest or contest has been filed by the protestants or contestants, with the Great Sachem of the Great Council from which the Representative or Representatives hail. — IX, 81.

Returns and Reports.

454. Each Great Council shall make out, and transmit to the Great Chief of Records on or before the first of Corn moon, a great sun's report of its work, in accordance with the form sent or delivered to it by the Great Chief of Records. This report shall be accompanied by the *per capita* tax due this Great Council. Any Great Council neglecting to forward its report and tax by the time specified herein, shall forfeit its right to representation; provided, this penalty may be remitted by unanimous consent. — By-Laws G. C. U. S.

455. Tribes under the immediate jurisdiction of the Great Council of the United States shall, within two seven suns after the last council sleep in Hot and Hunting moons, transmit to the Great Chiefs of Records of this Great Council, a correct report of the receipts and expenditures, together with the number of members, names, and number of adoptions, rejections, suspensions and cause, expulsions, admissions, and withdrawals by card, and death; also the *per capita* tax due. — By-Laws G. C. U. S.

Returns — Tax.

456. A Great Council owes *per capita tax* on the entire membership of Tribes under its jurisdiction. — III, 191, 224, 226.

457. The fiscal great sun shall commence on the 1st sun of Corn moon, and end on the 31st sun of Sturgeon moon of each great sun. All returns and reports intended for the Great Council of the United States shall be made out in accordance with the foregoing, and forwarded to the Great Chief of Records of the Great Council of the United States, on or before the 1st sun of the Corn moon of each and every great sun. — VI, 88, 433, 493.

458. It shall be the duty of the Great Chief of Records of the United

States to report the delinquency of each and every Great Chief of Records, and Chief of Records of every Tribe under the immediate jurisdiction of the Great Council of the United States. — IV, 506, 306.

459. A Tribe is required to make returns and pay tax to the Great Council of the United States for the six moons succeeding institution. — IV, 159, 218.

460. The *per capita tax* is to be paid upon all members on the books of the Tribe. — 14, 70, 81.

REVENUE.

461. The charter fee for the Great Councils shall be thirty fathoms. For Tribes and Councils of the Degree of Pocahontas, fifteen fathoms.

I. Each Great Council shall pay every great sun a *per capita tax* of ten inches for every member under its jurisdiction.

II. Each Tribe under the immediate jurisdiction of this Great Council shall pay a *per capita tax* of ten inches for every member on its books at the end of each term.

III. The revenue of the Great Council of the United States shall be the proceeds for the sale of charters, rituals, cards, odes, diplomas, and such other printed matter as the Great Council may reserve the authority to furnish; also fees for charters for Great Councils, Councils of Degree of Pocahontas and Tribes, and such tax as may be adopted by the Great Council.

IV.

	Fa.	Ft.	In.
Charters	1	5	0
Question Books, each	2	5	0
Adoption " "	1	0	0
Degree " "	1	2	5
Raising up Ceremonies, each		2	5
Funeral " "	1	0	0
Ceremonies D. of P.	1	2	5
Proposition Books D. P.	2	5	0
Beneficial D. C. Ceremonies	1	2	5
Ode Books, Music, each		3	5
Ode Cards, each			5
Travelling Cards, each		1	2
Withdrawal Cards, each		1	2
Dismissal Certificates		1	2
First Prophet's Dispensations			5
Digests		7	5

— By-Laws G. C. U. S.

REVENUE OF STATE GREAT COUNCIL.

462. The revenue of a State Great Council shall be derived as follows: —

I. For charter of a Tribe, including books, etc., not less than twenty fathoms; and such per cent of the Tribe's receipts or other tax as the Great Council may adopt.

II. For charter of a Council of Pocahontas, not less than fifteen fathoms. — General Rules.

463. Odes used by the various branches of the Order must be purchased through the regular channels. — VIII, 152.

Ritual — Care of.

464. The Rituals and other private work of the Order should be held by, and remain in charge of, the presiding Chief of each branch of the Order, to be kept by said Chief in some safe receptacle, under lock and key, within the wigwam. — VI, 421.

465. The Great Council deems it inexpedient to have the private work translated or printed in any language, other than the languages in which the same is now printed. — VIII, 569.

Sabbath.

466. Tribes or other branches of the Order are prohibited from using the name and seal of the Improved Order of Red Men for picnics and excursions on the sun commonly known as the Sabbath, or the first day of the week. — IV, 61 ; VI, 421.

Seal.

467. Each Tribe shall have a seal with appropriate device, which shall be affixed to all official documents emanating therefrom. — Constitution G. C. U. S.

468. All seals should date from the time of institution, with the standard of time then in use, but it is not imperative to have the date thereon. — III, 80, 100.

469. Great Councils and Tribes must procure and use the press-seal instead of the paper-seal; but the impression of the seal may be printed upon circulars, notices, or other printed communications. — III, 114; IV, 406.

470. The seal impressed on paper, and pasted upon a certificate, is not legal and proper. — IV, 119.

Standard or Flag.

471. The flag or standard of the Improved Order of Red Men, shall be in the form of an oblong square or parallelogram, in the proportion of seven long to five wide.

It shall consist of a white field, five wide and seven high. Attached to it shall be four horizontal bars, of equal width, the aggregate width of the four being equal to the height of the field.

The color of the bars, respectively, shall be green, orange, blue, and scarlet, the green bar being at the bottom, and the others placed above it in the order above enumerated.

A purple stripe, of one-half the width of one of the bars, shall enclose the entire circumference of the flag; the outer edge of the purple stripe (except where attached to the staff) shall be trimmed with fringe composed of the emblematic colors in the flag.

Upon the base or lower edge of the white field shall be delineated the upper section of the globe, showing portions of the eastern and western continents, the date G. S. D. 1, appearing immediately above the globe on the edge of the field next the staff, and the date of the common era, appearing in like manner and position on the opposite edge of the field.

Above the globe, and in the centre of the field, shall appear the American eagle, bearing the emblems of our Order in his talons, and in his beak a scroll or ribbon containing the legend or motto of our order, "Freedom, Friendship, and Charity," and upon his breast the shield or escutcheon, with the four emblematic bars, and a field upon which shall appear the four mystic characters, T. O. T. E.

Above the eagle shall appear the thirteen stars; upon the horizontal bars may appear the name of the Great Council of the United States, the Great Council of a State, or of the Tribe to be designated by it.

The staff shall be surmounted by the eagle of the Order, and shall be decorated with cord and tassels displaying the emblematic colors of the Order. — IV, 377, 380.

STRICKEN FROM THE ROLL.

472. The Great Council of the United States provides in the law that a paleface to be adopted into a Tribe, must be full twenty-one great suns of age. The body has also prepared a number of questions, among them is one relating to age. It is expected that each paleface will answer these questions correctly. A failure to do so would make him amenable to the penalties as laid down in the penal code. Where a paleface has answered these questions in accordance with his knowledge and belief, and sometime after his adoption it has come to his and the members' knowledge that he was not twenty-one great suns of age at the time of his adoption, and has not as yet attained the age, it follows that he is not legally a member of the Order, and it would be the duty of the Tribe to so notify him, and strike his name from the roll.

SUSPENSIONS.

473. A member of the Order who becomes in arrears for dues for the period of one great sun may be suspended or dropped from membership, but he cannot be expelled from the Order for being in arrears for dues. — V, 200.

474. A brother suspended for non-payment of dues must make application to be reinstated and a committee appointed as in case of a paleface, and upon the report of the committee, a ballot must be taken. — V, 14, 70, 81.

475. An elective Chief, who has been tried for any offence against the laws or usages of the Order, and sentenced to suspension for one moon or more, loses his chieftaincy. — V, 169, 198.

476. In the event of the Sachem's suspension, the Chief presiding at the time must declare the station vacant, and the proper Chief to assume the station and conduct an election is the Senior or Junior Sagamore, as the case

may be; in the event of their absence, a Past Sachem may be called to preside. — 169, 198.

477. The suspension of a member for non-payment of dues does not work absolute forfeiture of membership, nor does it relieve the person suspended from the operation of the penal provision of the laws. It simply annuls his claims to the benefits of the Tribe in case of sickness or other disability during the period of his suspension and from visiting his own or any other Tribe. In all other respects he is precisely on the same footing as any other member of the Tribe. — V, 374, 433.

478. A State Great Council cannot enact a law by which Tribes under its jurisdiction are enabled to "drop" members who are in arrears for dues for a less amount than one great sun's dues. — VI, 14, 49, 64.

479. The vote of a Tribe necessary to place in good standing a brother who has been suspended for non-payment of dues is a question for State Great Councils to decide. — VI, 302.

480. A Great Sachem or Deputy has no power to suspend a Sachem for gross violation of law. Punishment can be inflicted only after due trial. — V, 302.

481. A member suspended for non-payment of dues can regain membership in the Order only by reinstatement in accordance with the law or by a dismissal certificate granted by the Tribe of which he formerly was a member. A suspended member having been adopted into another Tribe must be excluded from membership upon full proof of his former suspension. He would also be liable under the law to have charges brought against him and a penalty imposed for a violation of his obligation, in falsely answering question No. 6, but this should be done in the Tribe from which he was suspended for non-payment of dues. — VIII, 489.

TAMMANY'S DAY.

482. The various Great Councils and Tribes are recommended to assemble in their wigwams, or at such other places as may be designated by dispensation, for the celebration of Tammany's Day, in commemoration of the Great Chief whose virtues have won for him an honorable place in history. — III, 143, 157, 163, 165.

483. Tammany's Day falls on the 12th of Flower Moon. — III, 374, 428.

TERMS OF CHIEFS.

484. The Chiefs of the Great Council of the United States shall be elected for two great suns. — Constitution G. C. U. S.

485. The Chiefs of State Great Councils shall be elected for one great sun. — General Laws.

486. Great Councils may enact a law that the term of the Great Chief of Records and the Great Keeper of Wampum may be two great suns. — General Laws.

487. Terms of Tribes and Councils of Pocahontas under the jurisdiction

of the Great Council of the United States shall be six moons. — By-Laws G. C. U. S.

488. Terms of Tribes and Councils of Pocahontas shall be six moons, but State Great Councils may provide that the term of these branches may be one great sun. — General Laws.

489. Representatives to the Great Council of the United States shall serve for two great suns from the first sun of Corn moon next succeeding their election, but at the first election by a Great Council entitled to more than one Representative, one-half the number to which it is entitled shall serve for one great sun only. — By-Laws G. C. U. S.

Trials.

490. Any Chief or member of this Great Council may be removed or expelled from membership in the body upon a charge being preferred against him; said charge to be confined to a violation of any of the obligations he may have taken, the laws of this body, or for any improper conduct tending to degrade his position or the Order.

I. Any member of the Great Council desiring to prefer charges against any of its members shall file said charge, with specifications in triplicate, with the Great Incohonee, who shall immediately submit the same to the Great Council. The Great Incohonee shall refer such charge to a special committee of five; if said charges are against the Great Incohonee, the same shall be filed with the Great Chief of Records, who shall submit the same to the Great Council, and the Great Senior Sagamore shall appoint the committee of five, and shall also preside during the time the charge is under consideration by the Great Council.

II. A copy of the charge or charges must be furnished by the accuser at least ten suns prior to the time of trial; provided, the alleged offence or offences were not committed during the councils of the Great Council, or within ten suns prior thereto. If within the time mentioned, then one sun's notice will be sufficient.

III. The committee shall fully investigate the charge or charges, report the result of such investigation to the Great Council, recommending such punishment as they may deem proper, and if the report is adopted by a vote of three-fourths of the Representatives present, it shall be recorded as the judgment of the Great Council.

IV. Suspension or expulsion from a Great Council or a Tribe to which a Chief or member of this Great Council belongs, shall operate as a suspension or expulsion from chieftaincy or membership in this Great Council, and the vacancy thereby created shall be filled in the manner prescribed by the laws. — By-Laws G. C. U. S.

491. A Great Council, in the absence of law, cannot prefer charges, try, convict, and punish a member thereof for violation of his obligation, or any improper conduct whereby the Order may be brought into contempt, but it

has the right and power to enact by-laws for its government, subject to approval by the Great Council of the United States. — III, 113, 115.

492. No member can be put on trial for an offence unless the charge or charges be reduced to writing, signed by the accuser and distinctly specify the cause or causes of complaint, and the time and place of occurrence, a copy of which shall be furnished to the accused by the Chief of Records before the next council sleep. At the first council sleep after the charge shall have been preferred, a committee of five shall be selected to investigate the charge, of whom one shall be appointed by the Sachem, one by the Senior Sagamore, and the remaining three shall be drawn by lot from among the members present (in good standing), in the manner following, to wit: The twig box shall be placed immediately in front of the Sachem, and a number of ballots equal to all the members present entitled to serve (less the two members of the committee previously appointed, such members as may be named as witnesses, and the accused and accuser), shall be placed therein. Three of said ballots shall have written on them the word "Committee," the rest shall be blank. The Chief of Records shall then call over the names of the members present (a list of whom shall be entered on the records, as also of those excused by reason of being witnesses), and each, as his name is called, shall draw a ballot from the twig box, and hand the same to the Sachem, who shall announce the nature of the ballot, whether blank or otherwise, retaining the ballots until the drawing is over. The three members drawing the ballot with the word "Committee" thereon shall, with the brothers before appointed, constitute the committee.

I. The committee shall organize on the sleep of its appointment, by the election of a chairman and secretary, after which, with as little delay as possible, the secretary shall notify the accused and the accuser or accusers, of the time and place appointed for investigating the charges. At the time so appointed the committee must proceed with the investigation, even though one of the parties be absent, unless a written notice be received stating his inability to attend by reason of sickness, no other reason being admissible. In the event of such notice being received, the committee shall adjourn to another fixed time, of which both parties shall have notice. This adjournment shall not extend beyond two seven suns, at which time the committee shall proceed with the investigation. Each side shall have the right to be represented before the committee by counsel, who must be members of the Order in good standing.

II. It shall be the duty of the committee to examine the parties, their proof and witnesses. The committee shall keep a correct record of the proceedings, and shall also reduce the testimony taken to writing, to be signed by the witness at the end of his or her examination, the same being first carefully read over to them. After having heard the evidence, the committee shall reduce its opinion as to the guilt or innocence of the accused, on each charge and specification, to writing (to be plainly written in ink), and report the same, together with the journal and the original testimony, to the Tribe at its earliest stated council after the work of the committee is completed.

III. When the committee submits its report, the accused must be notified thereof by the Chief of Records under seal, and directed to be present at the next stated council, at which time the report must be considered. If the report is approved by a majority of the members voting, it shall be recorded as the judgment of the Tribe. The Tribe must then prescribe the degree of punishment to be imposed in accordance with the law; the vote thereon must be by ballot, and a majority of the votes cast shall decide, except for expulsion, when the assent of two-thirds of the members voting shall be necessary.

IV. When a motion prescribing the punishment is before the Tribe, the same shall be considered as any other motion and be subject to the same rules; provided, that motions and amendments relative to the degree of punishment shall be treated as a blank, and the blank shall be filled by voting upon the most severe punishment first. If that be lost, a less severe punishment shall be voted upon until the judgment of the Tribe is declared. As soon as the Tribe has fixed the penalty, it shall be the duty of the Chief of Records to notify the brother.

V. When a member of one Tribe desires to prefer a charge or charges against a member or members of another Tribe, he shall present such charge or charges in the usual form to the Tribe of which he (the accuser) is a member. Said Tribe shall forthwith forward to the Tribe to which the accused belongs a certified copy of the charge or charges over the signatures of the Sachem and Chief of Records, and attested by the seal of the Tribe; and the Tribe to whom such charge or charges shall be sent shall proceed to hear and determine the same in like manner as if preferred by a member of its own body.

VI. A Tribe, upon due investigation and trial, having decided that a charge or charges made against a brother have not been sustained, its decision is final. The brother who preferred the charges cannot appeal from the decision of the Tribe. — Code of Procedure.

493. A member, while charges are pending against him, so long as he is a member of the Tribe, has a right to prefer charges against any brother. — IV, 159, 212.

494. A brother cannot be expelled until after due trial in accordance with the requirements of the laws governing the body of which he is a member. — IV, 82, 107.

495. A member who clandestinely leaves his former hunting grounds after incurring a large amount of indebtedness with his brother Red Men, and without providing any way to liquidate such indebtedness, and compelling brothers, members of said Tribe, to pay a large amount for him after he has left, may be expelled after due trial. — IV, 203.

496. If a By-Law of the Tribe says that a brother proved guilty shall be expelled, while the constitution states that a resolution to expel a brother can be adopted only by ballot, the Tribe must ballot, upon the resolution of expulsion. — IV, 404.

497. Members in good standing are competent to constitute a committee on charges without regard to the rank of the accused brother. — VI, 420.

498. When a brother is acquitted of charges that have been preferred against him, the decision is final, and irregularities not objected to at the time of trial, cannot be made the basis of an appeal. — IX, 26, 140.

Tribes.

499. Tribes exist by virtue of charters issued by the Great Council of the United States or those granted by the Great Councils of reservations wherein the Tribes are located. — Constitution G. C. U S.

500. If Tribes admit palefaces for less than the constitutional fees they violate the laws of their reservation and are amenable therefore to the Great Council. The Great Incohonee, or Great Council of the United States, cannot take cognizance of such matters until the resources of the local laws are exhausted, and then the matter should be brought to the attention of the Great Incohonee in the shape of formal charges. — V, 372, 428.

501. A Tribe working in the German language by consent of a State Great Council *and custom*, can change its mode of working and work in the English language; provided permission is received from the legal authorities. — IV, 158, 212.

502. It is contrary to the usage of the Order and subversive of its general welfare and harmony to permit a Tribe to work in both the German and English languages. — IV, 5, 60.

503. A dispensation permitting a Tribe to ask help financially from other Tribes and jurisdictions, should only be granted in extreme cases of hardship and want, and then permission must be had from the legal authorities of the reservations. — IV, 160, 214.

504. No business but that specified in the "call" for a special kindling of the council fire of any branch of the Order, or business incident to it, can be transacted thereat. — V, 374, 428.

505. A Tribe has the privilege to "vary the Order of Business," as may best suit its convenience, if there is no violation of any law on that subject, or anything destructive of the Ritual. — V, 178, 199.

506. Tribes in reservations where Great Councils exist must present business to its State Great Council. — VI, 149.

507. Tribal jurisdiction is a subject for local legislation. — VI, 304.

508. Tribes exist by virtue of charters issued by the Great Council of the United States, or those granted by the Great Councils of reservations wherein the tribes are located. When the Great Council of the United States places a reservation under a Great Council, and through the authority invested, said Great Council lights the council brands of several Tribes in said reservation, and legally issues to them charters, and the Tribes in said reservation having applied for and received a charter for a Great Council, and said body having been duly constituted, when so constituted has full authority and control over all Tribes in said reservation. No Tribe can legally exist within that reservation without its authority and consent. It is not necessary to renew the charters. The same is as much in force and makes the Tribe amenable to the Great Council as if said body had granted them. — IX, 32.

Twigging.

509. Upon the report of the committee a ballot shall be taken, and if two or more black twigs shall have been deposited, action on the application shall be deferred until the next stated council of the Tribe, when another ballot shall be had and if not more than three of the twigs then cast are black the candidate shall be declared elected. If rejected his application shall not be renewed in any Tribe of the Order for the space of six moons. — Constitution G. C. U. S.

510. When an applicant for membership has been twigged for, the box should be examined by the Senior Sagamore, and the result announced by the Sachem. — V, 198.

511. In all cases a ballot must be had upon the report of a committee on a candidate for admission by adoption or card, whether the report is favorable or unfavorable. — VIII, 487.

Vacancies.

512. If any of the Great Chiefs is temporarily absent his chieftaincy shall be filled by appointment of some member by the Great Incohonee. — Constitution G. C. U. S.

513. In case of a vacancy in the representation from a Great Council by death, removal, or other cause, the Great Sachem thereof may appoint a qualified Past Sachem to serve for one great sun. — By-Laws G. C. U. S.

514. All vacancies by removal, death, suspension, resignation, or otherwise, shall be filled by election or appointment as the case may be, and the brother who fills the unexpired term is entitled to the honors of the term. — Constitution G. C. U. S.

515. A Tribe has no right to declare the stump of a Chief vacant without first giving him an opportunity to submit an excuse for his absence. — IV, 203.

516. In case of a vacancy, the Tribe may fill it upon the same sleep it occurs if it has no law to the contrary. — IV, 82, 110.

517. If the Sachem resigns, the Senior Sagamore can be elected to fill the vacancy without resigning his chieftaincy. His elevation to the Sachem's stump will vacate his station. This rule governs the Junior Sagamore. — IV, 82, 110, 111.

518. The stump of an elective Chief can become vacant only by the resignation, expulsion, absence without excuse, or death; but a Tribe may impose a fine upon a Chief for neglect of duty. — 15, 82, 107.

519. If the Prophet's stump is vacant, and there is no Past Sachem present to fill it, a Chief or degree member may be appointed to occupy it temporarily. — 254, 298.

520. A vacancy in representation can exist only where a regularly elected Representative has resigned, or on the death of one or more of the Representatives; but if a regularly elected Representative *cannot*, or fails to, attend the councils of this Great Council, the Great Sachem of a State has no right to

appoint a substitute, under the law as it now exists, neither a substitute nor an alternate being recognized by the laws of this Great Council. — IV, 18, 55.

521. In case of the death, resignation, or disqualification of the Great Incohonee, the Great Senior Sagamore shall be invested with all his authority and powers, and be entitled to the rank of Past Great Incohonee at the expiration of his term of service. — Constitution G. C. U. S.

522. In case of the death, resignation, or disqualification of the Great Senior Sagamore of the Great Council of the United States, the Great Junior shall be invested with all his authority and power. — Constitution G. C. U. S.

VISITATIONS.

523. When a Tribe shall have arrived at the forest of the Tribe proposed to be visited, the Sannap of the visiting Tribe shall enter the wigwam and and announce the presence of his Tribe; then the Sachem shall direct his Sannap to proceed to the forest and ask the visiting Sachem or Chief in charge if he will vouch for all the members of his Tribe accompanying him; if an affirmative answer is returned, the Sannap of the Tribe to be visited shall then escort the visitors into the wigwam; the visiting Sachem shall give, at the two wickets, the words required by the regulations of the Order; and the respective Chiefs having been saluted, the Sannap shall formally introduce the visiting Chiefs and brothers to his Sachem and Tribe, when the honors of the Order shall be tendered, and the brothers seated. — IV, 352, 392.

524. A Deputy Great Sachem or Deputy Great Incohonee has not the power to introduce to a Tribe in his district a visiting brother from another jurisdiction, who does not have the universal password, or an order for the same. — IV, 253, 298.

525. A brother shall at all times be allowed to visit and attend the council of any Tribe under the jurisdiction of any Great Council, in conformity with the Ritual, provided he is legally in possession of the universal password. — Constitution G. C. U. S.

VOTING.

526. Representatives and Past Great Incohonees alone shall be entitled to vote upon any question before the Great Council of the United States. — Constitution G. C. U. S.

527. It is proper to use the word "twig" for "vote." — IV, 254, 298.

528. The presiding Chief has a right to vote on all applications for membership, for degrees, and on the election of Chiefs. — IV, 254, 208.

529. To constitute a legal vote for the admission of candidates, or the application for degrees, the number of twigs should be at least equal to the number of brothers required to make a quorum. — VII, 587.

530. If only a quorum is present at the council of a tribe, unanimous consent is requisite to adopt an appropriation of wampum for any other purpose than benefits. — IX, 23.

531. To expel a member the assent of two thirds of the members voting is necessary. — IX, 23.

532. A majority of the votes cast shall be necessary to suspend a member. — IX, 23.

Withdrawal of Applications.

533. No proposition for membership shall be withdrawn after it has been referred to a committee, except by unanimous consent. — Constitution G. C. U. S.

ERRATA.

Chieftaincies.

534. Neither Great Councils nor Great Sachems have the right to create an office or chieftaincy not provided for by any legislation of their bodies or the Great Council of the United States.

Councils.

535. When the council sleep of any Tribe, Council of the Degree of Pocahontas, or other body under the jurisdiction of this Great Council or the Great Council of any reservation, shall fall upon a legal holiday, said council may be dispensed with without dispensation; provided, that should the holiday fall upon the sleep of election, said election shall take place at the regular council preceding such holiday.

Membership.

536. Whenever a brother in good standing has lost his membership by reason of the dissolution of his Tribe, and he is refused membership in any Tribe by reason of age, then said member, upon payment of the indebtedness charged against him on the books of said defunct Tribe, shall be considered a member at large, under the jurisdiction of the Great Council wherein he resides, and under such regulations as to seven suns' dues and otherwise as said Great Council may adopt, and shall receive the universal password, which will admit him into any Tribe throughout the great reservation; and if a Past Sachem, he shall be entitled to attend the councils of the Great Council on presenting a certificate, signed by the Great Sachem and the Great Chief of Records, that he has paid the sum laid down in the laws governing cases of this kind.

Reinstatement.

537. A member expelled from the Order cannot be restored to membership in the Tribe, except after application to the Tribe, and by permission of the Great Council or the Board of Great Council Chiefs, during the interim, and the vote necessary to reinstate him is the same vote which expelled him from membership. — Code of Procedure.

Reorganization.

538. If the law of a Great Council fails to specify the number required to be present at the institution of a Tribe or its reinstitution, the instituting Chief should be the judge, provided that not less than the quorum necessary to kindle a council fire is present.

CHAPTER XII.

LEGISLATION. — CONSTITUTIONS.

THE practical management of an organization requires a certain theory of legislation, and the choice of officers needed to properly transact the business provided for in the laws thereof. While the titles differ, the duties of the chiefs, or officers, of this Order are relatively similar to those performed by kindred fraternal and benevolent societies.

The legislation, by which the Order is governed, provides for a Great Council of the United States, which is the supreme power. From this emanates all authority for the establishment of local branches in towns and cities, and Great Councils in the various States and Territories.

The Great Council of the United States has for its chiefs, or officers, the presiding officer who is known as Great Incohonee; the Great Senior Sagamore, second in authority; Great Junior Sagamore, third; Great Prophet, who is usually a Past Great Incohonee; the Great Chief of Records, who in other organizations would be known as the Supreme Secretary; the Great Keeper of Wampum, corresponding to Supreme Treasurer; the Great Tocakon, the runner of the Great Incohonee; the Great Minewa, who has charge of the inner wicket, and the Great Guard of the Forest, who has charge of the outer wicket. There is a standing Committee on Finance, composed of three members, which meets every great sun previous to the council of the Great Council of the United States, for the examination of the books and accounts of the Great Chief of Records and Great Keeper of Wampum, as well as for the purpose of making estimates concerning the appropriations for the ensuing term, and a Committee on Laws, of three members, whose duties are defined in the laws. At each council of the Great Council of the United States additional committees are appointed, consisting of seven members each, on Distribution of Longtalks, State of the Order, Judiciary, Appeals and Grievances, Charters, Mileage and Per Diem, and Degree of Pocahontas. Among these committees is divided the business upon various matters considered by the Great Council of the United States.

The State Great Council, under authority delegated to it by the Great Council of the United States, within the State exercises authority similar to that exercised by the Great Council of the United States over the entire Order. Where a State Great Council exists, Tribes within that reservation are organized by the authority and consent of said body. The presiding chief is called Great Sachem. The other chiefs are Great Senior Sagamore, Great Junior Sagamore, Great Chief of Records, Great Keeper of Wampum, Great Sannap, Great Mishinewa, Great Guard of Wigwam, and Great Guard of Forest. Their duties are similar to the corresponding chiefs of the Great Council of the United States. Each Great Council selects such committees as are necessary for the proper transaction of business.

The local branches of the Order are Tribes, Degree Councils, and Councils of the Degree of Pocahontas.

Tribes may be organized with not less than seven members, a quorum consisting of not less than five members, including one qualified to preside. The chiefs of a Tribe are Sachem, who presides, Senior Sagamore, Junior Sagamore, Chief of Records, Collector of Wampum, Keeper of Wampum, two Sannaps, four Warriors, four Braves, two Powwows, Guard of the Wigwam, and Guard of the Forest. To the Tribe is entrusted the beneficial features of the Order. Among the duties enjoined upon the Tribe, and practised by the Order, is the injunction to visit the sick, relieve the distressed, bury the dead, and educate the orphan. In addition to the chiefs above named, Tribes have committees on relief, on visitation of the sick, on entertainment, and for such other purposes as may be necessary for the proper transaction of Tribal business. A stipulated sum is paid during each seven suns' sickness which under the laws may not be less than one fathom per seven suns, or one dollar per week. Tribes usually adopt a law limiting the payment of the full benefit, which varies from four to twelve fathoms per seven suns, for a stated time, in some instances thirteen, in others twenty-six weeks. The funeral benefit is also a matter of local legislation, varying in the different Tribes.

The Councils of Pocahontas are organized for the admission of any woman of good moral character, and members of the Order who have attained the Chief's Degree. The chiefs of the Council, whose duties correspond with similar chiefs of the Tribe, consist of Pocahontas, who is the presiding chief, Wenonah, Prophetess, Keeper of Records, Collector of Wampum, Keeper of Wampum, Powhatan, two Scouts, two Runners, two Counsellors, four Warriors, Guard of Wigwam, and Guard of the Forest. Councils usually select a double set of Warriors, four men and four women. As a rule Councils are not beneficial. That is, do not pay seven suns' and funeral benefits. The Degree is intended more for social purposes, and for advancing the interests and prosperity of the Improved Order of Red Men. It is intended to be for the Order what the Rebekah Degree is for Odd Fellowship, the Eastern Star Degree for Masonry, and the Women's Relief Corps for the G. A. R.

In a few reservations Degree Councils have been organized. These were originally instituted for the purpose of perfecting the degree work, and conferring the degrees upon members adopted in Tribes. It facilitated the business of the Tribes, and the work of the Order was given in a very much more satisfactory manner. In some instances these Councils are beneficial, in others not. The chiefs governing them are almost exactly similar to those of the Tribe. They possess no legislative authority, all the local power being vested in the Tribe.

The Constitution of the Order is herewith appended, which will give in detail the laws and regulations now in force. In Chapters VII and VIII of this History, devoted to the printed records of the Great Council of the United States, frequent mention is made of the votes by which the laws of the Order have been evolved and perfected. While changes may be made from time to time, it is probable the Constitution which follows will remain substantially intact for many great suns, and fairly indicate the machinery of government by which the Order is managed, and its fraternal and benevolent work accomplished,

CONSTITUTION OF THE GREAT COUNCIL OF THE UNITED STATES.

ARTICLE I.

NAME, AUTHORITY AND POWER.

SEC. 1. This body shall be known by the name, style and title of the GREAT COUNCIL OF THE UNITED STATES OF THE IMPROVED ORDER OF RED MEN.

SEC. 2. The Great Council of the United States is the source of all true and legitimate authority over the Order wheresoever established; it possesses, as such, supreme and absolute power and jurisdiction: —

1. To establish, regulate and control the forms, ceremonies, written and unwritten work of the Order, and to change, alter and annul the same, and to provide for the safe keeping and uniform teaching and dissemination of the same.

2. To provide, publish, print and furnish all rituals, forms, ceremonies, cards, odes, charters, charts and certificates.

3. To prescribe the form, material and color of all regalia, emblem, jewels and such blanks as may be used by the Order.

4. To provide for the emanation and distribution of all passwords, and to regulate the mode and manner of using the same; and generally to prescribe such regulations as may be necessary to secure the safe and easy intercourse and identification of members.

5. To establish the Order in States, Districts, Territories, Provinces or countries where the same has not been established.

6. To provide a revenue for the Great Council of the United States by means of a *per capita* tax upon the membership, either from Great Councils or Tribes under its immediate jurisdiction, and the sale of supplies furnished by it.

7. To provide for returns from Great Councils, Tribes and other branches under its jurisdiction.

8. To hear and determine all appeals from Great Councils and Tribes, when the same are legally brought before it, and to provide for legislation for the enforcement of all its decrees and decisions.

9. To enact laws and regulations of general application to carry into effect the foregoing, and all other powers reserved by this Constitution to the Great Council of the United States or its Great Chiefs, and such as may be necessary to enforce its legitimate authority over the Order.

10. All power and authority in the Order not delegated to Great Councils, Tribes and Councils of the Degree of Pocahontas, by their charters, or the

general laws or rules and decisions of this Great Council, are reserved to the Great Council of the United States.

ARTICLE II.

How Composed.

SEC. 1. The Great Council of the United States shall be composed of: —
1. All Past Great Incohonees and Past Great Sachems.
2. The elective Chiefs of the Great Council.
3. The Representatives of State Great Councils.

SEC. 2. A Great Council in hunting grounds containing less than one thousand members shall be entitled to one representative; over one thousand and less than two thousand, two representatives; over two thousand and less than three thousand, three representatives; over three thousand and less than four thousand, four representatives; over four thousand, and less than five thousand, five representatives; over five thousand and less than six thousand, six representatives; over six thousand and less than seven thousand, seven representatives; over seven thousand and less than eight thousand, eight representatives; and all reservations having over eight thousand members, eight representatives.

SEC. 3. Great Representatives must be Past Sachems in good standing in their Great Councils. They shall be elected at the same time and in the same manner as the Chiefs of their Great Councils, and shall serve for two great suns from the first sun of the next succeeding Corn moon; but at the first election by a Great Council, entitled to more than one representative, one-half the number to which it is entitled shall serve for one great sun only.

SEC. 4. In case of a vacancy in the representation from a Great Council from death, removal or other cause, the Great Sachem thereof may appoint a qualified Past Sachem to serve for one great sun. Representatives must be residents of the reservation they represent during the entire term for which they are elected, and removal of residence from their reservations shall operate as a forfeiture of their position.

SEC. 5. Representatives and Past Great Incohonees alone shall be entitled to vote upon any question or resolution before the Great Council.

SEC. 6. All Past Great Sachems whose credentials have been acknowledged by the Great Council shall be admitted to a seat and entitled to all privileges, except that of voting and receiving mileage and per diem.

SEC. 7. No one shall be eligible to any chieftaincy unless he has been duly admitted to the Great Council and received the rank of Past Great Sachem.

ARTICLE III.

Chiefs of Great Council.

SEC. 1. The Elective Chiefs of this Great Council shall be a Great Incohonee, Great Senior Sagamore, Great Junior Sagamore, Great Prophet, Great

Chief of Records and Great Keeper of Wampum, all of whom shall be elected by ballot for two great suns, on the second sun of the great sun's council, at the third run, setting of the sun.

SEC. 2. The appointed Great Chiefs shall be a Great Tocakon, Great Minewa and a Great Guard of Forest, all of whom shall be appointed by the Great Incohonee at the time of his raising up.

ARTICLE IV.
ELIGIBILITY TO CHIEFTAINCIES.

No brother shall be eligible to the chieftaincy of Great Incohonee unless he shall have served one term in an elective chieftaincy. No one shall be eligible to the chieftaincy of Great Prophet unless he is a Past Great Incohonee.

ARTICLE V.
GREAT SUN COUNCIL.

SEC. 1. The great sun council fire shall be kindled on the second Tuesday of Corn moon, at the ninth run, rising of the sun, at such place as the Great Council may designate.

SEC. 2. The place of kindling the council fire shall be determined at each great sun council by a majority of those entitled to vote; provided that the resolution fixing the place shall have been read on two separate suns.

ARTICLE VI.
QUORUM.

Representatives from a majority of State Great Councils shall be necessary to constitute a quorum for the transaction of any business, except the admission of new members and to kindle the council fire and quench it from time to time, for which purposes alone less than said majority may act.

ARTICLE VII.
REVENUE.

The revenue of this Great Council shall be the proceeds from the sale of charters, rituals, cards, odes, diplomas, and such other printed matter as the Great Council may reserve the authority to furnish; also fees for charters for Great Councils, Councils of Degree of Pocahontas and Tribes, and such tax as may be adopted by this Great Council.

ARTICLE VIII.
TRIBES, MEMBERSHIP, PRIVILEGES.

SEC. 1. Tribes exist by virtue of charters issued by the Great Council of the United States, or those granted by the Great Councils of reservations wherein the Tribes are located.

Sec. 2. Great Councils shall have full power to enact general laws for the government of Tribes within their jurisdiction. The following rules shall be incorporated in said general laws : —

1. A Tribe shall never consist of less than seven members, and shall kindle its council fire at least twice a moon. Five members or more, including one qualified to preside, shall constitute a quorum for the transaction of business, and if a quorum only be present no wampum shall be appropriated (except for benefits) without unanimous consent.

2. The Elective Chiefs of a Tribe shall be a Sachem, Senior Sagamore, Junior Sagamore, Prophet, Chief of Records and Keeper of Wampum, all of whom must be members of the Chief's degree. Great Councils may provide for a Collector of Wampum, who also must be a member of the Chief's degree. The Prophet must be a Past Sachem. The appointed Chiefs shall be a First and Second Sannap, Guard of the Wigwam, Guard of the Forest, four Warriors and four Braves.

3. The raising up of Chiefs shall take place on the first council sleep of the term, unless a dispensation has been granted to postpone the same. Tribes may have their Chiefs raised up in public, provided a dispensation has been first obtained.

4. All vacancies by removal, death, suspension, resignation or otherwise, shall be filled by election or appointment as the case may be, to serve the residue of the term, and the Chiefs so serving shall be entitled to the honors of the term.

5. No person shall be adopted into a Tribe of the Order except a free white male, of good moral character and standing, of the full age of twenty-one great suns, who believes in the existence of a Great Spirit, the Creator and Preserver of the Universe, and who is possessed of some known reputable means of support.

6. An application for adoption must be recommended by two brothers in good standing, and accompanied by one-half the adoption fee. The application shall be referred to a committee of three, who shall make a strict investigation of the health, character and qualifications of the applicant, and report at the next council.

7. Upon the report of the committee a ballot shall be taken, and if two or more black twigs shall have been deposited, action on the application shall be deferred until the next stated council of the Tribe, when another ballot shall be had, and if not more than three of the twigs then cast are black, the candidate shall be declared elected. If rejected, his application shall not be renewed in any Tribe of the Order for the space of six moons thereafter.

8. Brothers desirous of advancing shall make application for degrees in open council; the application shall be referred to the Tribe while working in the degrees; a ballot shall be had and if not more than three black twigs are cast it shall be granted. If rejected the application cannot be renewed for three moons.

9. No proposition for membership shall be withdrawn after it has been

referred to a committee, except by unanimous consent, and in all cases a ballot shall be had whether the report be favorable or unfavorable.

10. No Tribe shall adopt a pale face resident of another State reservation unless by consent of the Great Sachem of such reservation; nor confer degrees upon a member of another Tribe, except by permission, under seal, of the Tribe, to which said member belongs.

11. Any brother of the Order holding a withdrawal card desirous of becoming a member of a Tribe, shall make application as in case of a pale face, accompanying his application with his withdrawal card, which shall be referred to a committee of three, whose duty it shall be to report as to his standing and qualifications at a stated council, when a ballot shall be had, as in case of a pale face.

12. Application for a withdrawal card shall be made either personally or in writing, and the same shall be granted, provided the brother is clear upon the books of the Tribe, free from charges, and there be no valid objections.

13. Any withdrawal card may be revoked for cause by the Tribe granting the same, and when so revoked the person holding said card shall be subject to the Tribe which issued the same. A withdrawal card may be renewed if lost or destroyed.

14. A member suspended for non-payment of dues, desirous of joining a Tribe in the same reservation, after one great sun's suspension, shall be entitled to receive, and the Tribe shall grant, upon proper application, a Dismissal Certificate upon the payment of not less than one fathom nor more than one great sun's dues.

15. A member suspended for non-payment of dues, wishing to regain membership in another reservation, shall be entitled to receive, and the Tribe shall grant, upon proper application, a Dismissal Certificate upon the receipt of not less than one fathom nor more than one great sun's dues.

16. In all cases wherein a Tribe has refused to reinstate a member suspended for non-payment of dues, he shall be entitled to receive, and the Tribe shall, upon proper application, grant a Dismissal Certificate upon the receipt of one fathom.

17. Dismissal Certificates may be received upon deposit in any Tribe, under the same laws as withdrawal cards, but the privilege of visiting shall not be awarded to the holder of a Dismissal Certificate.

18. Tribes shall provide for carrying into effect the beneficial character of the Order, by enacting laws for the payment of seven suns' and funeral benefits.

19. Trials, charges and penalties against Great Councils, Tribes and members of either of the said bodies, shall be governed by the code of procedure as adopted by the Great Council of the United States.

20. Each Tribe shall have a seal with appropriate device, which shall be affixed to all official documents emanating therefrom.

21. A brother shall at all times be allowed to visit and attend the council of any Tribe under the jurisdiction of any Great Council, in conformity with the Ritual, provided he is legally in possession of the Universal Password.

22. Whenever a brother in good standing has lost his membership by reason of the dissolution of his Tribe, and he is refused membership in any Tribe by reason of age, then said member, upon payment of the indebtedness charged against him on the books of said defunct Tribe, shall be considered a member at large, under the jurisdiction of the Great Council wherein he resides, and under such regulations as to seven suns' dues and otherwise as said Great Council may adopt, and shall receive the universal password; which will admit him into any Tribe throughout the great reservation; and if a Past Sachem he shall be entitled to attend the councils of the Great Council on presenting a certificate, signed by the Great Sachem and the Great Chief of Records, that he has paid the sum laid down in the laws governing cases of this kind.

23. When the council sleep of any Tribe, Council of the Degree of Pocahontas or other body under the jurisdiction of this Great Council or the Great Council of any reservation, shall fall upon a legal holiday, said council may be dispensed with without dispensation; provided, that should the holiday fall upon the sleep of election, said election shall take place at the regular council preceding such holiday.

ARTICLE IX.

Forfeiture of Charters.

Any Great Council, Tribe, or Council of the Degree of Pocahontas may be suspended or dissolved, and its charter or dispensation forfeited to and reclaimed by the Great Council of the United States or the proper Great Council: —

1. For improper conduct.
2. For neglecting or refusing to conform to the Constitution, laws and enactments of this Great Council or the Great Council to which it is subordinate, or the general laws and regulations of the Order.
3. For neglecting or refusing to make its returns, or for non-payment of dues or taxes.
4. For neglecting to hold regular councils as provided by law, unless prevented by unforeseen circumstances.
5. By its membership decreasing, so that it is left without a quorum.

But the charter or dispensation shall not be forfeited in either of the above cases until due notification of the offence by the proper Great Chiefs, under seal, and a suitable opportunity has been given to answer the charges.

ARTICLE X.

Duties of Great Chiefs.

Sec. 1. The Great Prophet shall perform all the duties prescribed in the ceremonies.

Sec. 2. The Great Incohonee shall preside at all councils of the Great Council, preserve order and enforce the laws thereof; have a watchful supervision over all branches of the Order, and see that all Constitutional enactments, rules and regulations of the Great Council are observed.

Among his special prerogatives are the following: —

To call special councils of the Great Council.

To appoint all committees not otherwise provided for, to visit any Great Council or branch of the Order, and to give such instruction as the good of the Order may require, always adhering to the usages of the Order.

He shall have general supervision of the Order, and grant such dispensations as he may deem for its interest, also grant dispensations for the kindling of council fires of Great Councils and other branches of the Order.

He shall appoint and commission Deputy Great Incohonees as may be required in States, Territories or Countries where Great Councils do not exist.

He may hear and decide such appeals and questions of law as may be submitted to him by Great Councils or their Great Chiefs, and Tribes under the immediate jurisdiction of the Great Council, or their chiefs, and such decisions shall be binding until fully passed upon or reversed by the Great Council.

He shall, at every great sun council, present a printed report of all his official acts and decisions during the interim, with such recommendations as he may deem for the advancement of the Order.

He shall have exclusive right to create and promulgate all passwords, and to rescind and change the same if circumstances require.

SEC. 3. The Great Senior Sagamore shall assist the Great Incohonee in kindling and quenching the council fire; advise, assist and support him in preserving order, and preside in his absence. In case of the death, resignation or disqualification of the Great Incohonee, he shall be invested with all his authority and power.

SEC. 4. The Great Junior Sagamore shall have charge of the wicket, and perform such other duties as the nature of his chieftaincy may require. In case of the death, resignation or disqualification of the Great Senior Sagamore, he shall be invested with all his authority and power.

SEC. 5. The Great Chief of Records shall keep a just and true record of all the proceedings of this Great Council. When the same have been printed he shall transmit to each Great Council as many copies as it may have Past Great Sachems, Great Chiefs and branches of the Order under its jurisdiction. Also one to each branch under the immediate control of this Great Council. Also one to each Great Chief, member and Representative. He shall collect all the revenues of the Great Council and pay the same over to the Great Keeper of Wampum on or about the first of every moon, taking a receipt therefor. He shall preserve and keep the evidence of the unwritten work and such alterations as may from time to time be made therein, and all other records of secret councils. He shall prepare all charters for Great Councils and other branches that are granted by the Great Council, notify all Great Councils, Chiefs and members of the Great Council of the United States of all councils of this Great Council; carry on all the necessary correspondence, attest all official documents, and perform such other duties as this Great Council may from time to time direct. He shall make out and have printed an alphabetical roll of the Great Chiefs and Representatives and call the same at the kindling of each council fire, and the names of those present, including Past Great Incohonees and Past Great Sachems who are not Representatives, shall be entered upon the record. He shall submit to the Great Council at each council a printed report of his accounts, together with the standing of the Order. He shall receive for his services such sum (not less than sixteen hundred fathoms per great sun) as the Great Council may fix at the time of his election. He shall give security, satisfactory to the Committee on Finance, in the sum of three thousand fathoms of wampum. He shall also have charge of the Beneficiary Fund of the Order, issue certificates and conduct all the correspondence.

SEC. 6. The Great Keeper of Wampum shall pay all orders drawn on him by the Great Incohonee, attested by the Great Chief of Records. He shall, at the great sun's council, present a printed report of his receipts and disbursements. For the faithful performance of his duties, he shall give a bond, satisfactory to the Committee on Finance, in the sum of not less than five thousand fathoms of wampum.

SEC. 7. The Great Tocakon, Great Minewa and the Great Guard of Forest shall perform such duties as are defined by the charge books, and such as may be assigned them by the Great Council.

ARTICLE XI.

COMMITTEES.

SEC. 1. Immediately after the raising up of the Great Incohonee he shall appoint a Committee on Finance and a Committee on Constitution and Laws, to consist of three members each, to serve during his chieftaincy.

As soon as the council fire of each Great Council is kindled he shall appoint a Committee on Credentials to consist of three members, and immediately after the reading of the long talks, the following committees, to consist of seven members each, viz. : —

Distribution of Long Talks, State of the Order, Judiciary, Appeals and Grievances, Charters, Reports, Mileage and Per Diem, Beneficiary, and Degree of Pocahontas.

ARTICLE XII.

GREAT COUNCILS.

SEC. 1. By virtue of authority from the Great Council of the United States, Great Councils may be established in States, Districts, Territories or the Dominion of Canada. They shall be governed by their charters, the Constitution and By-Laws of this Great Council, the General Laws adopted for their government and such laws as they may adopt in accordance with the same.

SEC. 2. Great Councils shall have full authority and control over all Tribes and other branches of the Order in their reservation, subject to the laws of this Great Council. They shall enforce a strict adherence to the forms, ceremonies, style of regalia, jewels, charges, blanks and other supplies furnished by this Great Council, and shall be responsible for any violation they may sanction or allow, and no Tribe or Council can legally exist within their reservations without their sanction and authority.

SEC. 3. Great Councils shall be composed of Past Sachems, but Great Councils may provide for a representative system, and may limit Tribes under their jurisdiction to one representative.

ARTICLE XIII.

GRANTING CHARTERS.

SEC. 1. Five or more Tribes in any State, District, Territory or the Dominion of Canada, having not less than fifteen Past Sachems and a membership of not less than five hundred, may petition the Great Council or Great Incohonee praying for a charter for a Great Council therein. Should the majority of the representatives vote in favor of the same it shall be granted, and the Great Incohonee, or a Past Sachem deputized by him, shall kindle the council fire of said Great Council. The petition shall be in the following form : —

To the Great Council of the United States, Improved Order of Red Men : —

The past Sachems of the undersigned Tribes represent that they are working under charters granted by the Great Council of   , that the Order has increased so that the membership is at present   , and we have   Past Sachems in good standing. We believe that it would be of advantage to the Order if a Great Council was established in our reservation. We, therefore, pray that you grant the prayer of our petition.

Witness our hands and the Seal of the Tribes this   Sun of   Moon, G. S. D.

The same is to be signed by the Sachem and Chief of Records of each Tribe, and the Seal thereof to be attached.

SEC. 2. Should the application as aforesaid be made to the Great Incohonee prior to the first sun of Sturgeon moon, he may, by and with the consent of the elective Great Chiefs, grant a dispensation for the same, and institute the Great Council.

As soon as a Great Council has been organized, all tribes located in its reservation shall thereafter be under the jurisdiction of said Great Council.

SEC. 3. In reservations where there are no Great Councils, persons desirous of kindling a council fire of a Tribe therein shall present an application signed by not less than thirty brothers or palefaces, accompanied by the charter fee and the cards of the brothers. If the application is received by the Incohonee during the interim, the Great Incohonee may, by and with the advice of the Great Chiefs, grant a dispensation and institute the Tribe.

SEC. 4. All traveling or other expenses of the Great Incohonee, or his deputy, incurred in lighting the council fire of a Great Council or Tribe, shall be paid by such Great Council or Tribe.

(Sections 3 and 4 shall also apply to Councils of D. of P., except as to fee and number on petition.)

ARTICLE XIV.
REGALIA, FORMS AND CEREMONIES, HOW ALTERED.

The regalia, jewels, forms, ceremonies or other private work, written or unwritten, shall not be altered or amended unless the proposed change be submitted in writing, and after being twice read, on different suns, be adopted by the vote of three-fourths of the members present entitled to vote.

ARTICLE XV.
TRAVELING CARD OR CERTIFIED RECEIPT.

Traveling cards, or certified receipts, for the use of members, may be used or recognized only when procured from the Great Council of the United States, and they are in accordance with the form adopted. They are for special use and must be obtained through State Great Councils.

A traveling card shall be *prima facie* evidence of the good standing of the brother to whom issued. Upon the back thereof shall be placed the amount for seven suns, and funeral benefits allowed by the Tribe issuing it.

A certified receipt shall be *prima facie* evidence of the payment of dues by the brother to whom issued. Upon the back thereof may be printed a request for communicating to the brother the Universal Password.

ARTICLE XVI.
TERMS.

A term of the Great Council of the United States shall be two great suns; of Tribes and Councils working under its immediate jurisdiction six moons; of Great Councils one great sun, and Tribes or Councils under their control six moons; but State Great Councils may provide that the term of its Tribes or Councils may be one great sun.

ARTICLE XVII.
APPEALS.

SEC. 1. All appeals taken from the action of a Great Council, or a Tribe working under the immediate jurisdiction of this Great Council, to the Great Council of the United States, as hereinafter provided for, shall be received and passed upon as a last resort; but in all cases the action or decision of a Great Council or the Tribe shall be final and conclusive until reversed by this Great Council, except where the sentence involves explusion from the Order.

SEC. 2. An appeal may be taken from the action or decision of a Tribe under the jurisdiction of this Great Council to this body by any member or person who thinks his rights have been denied by such decision or action, upon giving written notice and filing an appeal within one moon from the date of said action of appeal; and provided, that a copy of the appeal has been placed in the hands of the Great Incohonee, with proof that the Tribe has received due notice.

SEC. 3. Members or Tribes may appeal from the action of a Great Council provided two copies of the appeal have been presented, mailed or sent to the Great Sachem not less than twenty suns prior to the kindling of the council fire of the Great Council of the United States, and the great Sachem shall certify, under the seal of his Great Council (on each of the copies), the date that he received the appeal and forthwith send one to the appellant, who shall immediately send it to the Great Incohonee, whose duty it shall be to report its reception to the Great Council. All appeals from the action of a Great Council must be made so they can be acted upon at the council following the decision or action taken, and a failure to do so shall be a bar to all further proceedings; provided, the council of said State Great Council is not held within the time mentioned above.

ARTICLE XVIII.
Permanent Fund.

SEC. 1. The Permanent Fund shall consist of such sums as the Great Council may from time to time appropriate, donations and bequests made thereto, and accumulations of interest. The principal of said fund shall not be used, nor shall this article be amended or repealed, except seven-eighths of those entitled to vote agreed thereto.

SEC. 2. When in the judgment of the Great Council a sum sufficient for the purpose has been accumulated, the funds shall be invested in such a manner as the Great Council may then provide, in a Home forever dedicated to the widows and orphans of members of the Improved Order of Red Men.

SEC. 3. The Great Incohonee, Great Prophet, Great Senior Sagamore, Great Junior Sagamore, Great Chief of Records and Great Keeper of Wampum shall constitute the Board of Trustees of the Great Council of the United States. They shall have supervision of the Permanent Fund of the Great Council and make such investments as they may deem for the best interests of said fund until final investment in a Home as above provided. They shall make a report thereon at each great sun council.

SEC. 4. At each great sun council the Finance Committee shall submit a resolution appropriating not less than one hundred fathoms, which sum shall be placed in the Permanent Fund already created. The wampum so appropriated shall be invested by the Trustees until the aggregate amount shall reach the sum needed for the purpose of the Home contemplated.

ARTICLE XIX.
By-Laws, General Laws and Amendments.

By-Laws in conformity with this Constitution may be made. Also, General Laws for the government of Great Councils, and laws for the government of Tribes under the immediate jurisdiction of this Great Council.

This Constitution shall not be altered, amended or repealed, unless the proposition for that purpose be presented in writing, signed by representatives of three Great Councils, and lie over for one great sun and then receive the assent of two-thirds of those present and entitled to vote; provided, action upon a proposition to amend any of the laws may be taken at the same council at which it is submitted, if seven-eighths agree to the same.

BY-LAWS OF GREAT COUNCIL.
ARTICLE I.
Admission.

Sec. 1. Before the admission of a Past Great Sachem a certificate must be received, certifying that he has duly served as Great Sachem of a Great Council, or as the first Great Prophet, or five great suns as Great Chief of Records or Great Keeper of Wampum, and that he is in good standing in his Tribe.

Sec. 2. Before a member can be acknowledged as a representative the following certificate must be received:—

Wigwam of Great Council of —— Imp. O. R. M. This is to certify that at an election held by the Great Council of   Brother   was elected to represent the Great Council of   in the Great Council of the United States for   great suns, from the second Tuesday in Corn moon next.

Witness our hand and the Seal of our Great Council, the   sun moon, G. S. D.

[L.S.]

Great Sachem.
Great C. of R.

Each representative shall be presented with a duplicate of the above credential, and either the original or duplicate shall be referred to the Committee on Credentials, who shall report thereon as soon as practicable.

A representative to fill a vacancy must present a credential giving the name of the representative in whose place he is appointed or elected, and stating the cause of such vacancy.

Sec. 3. In the case of a contested election, or a protest against the admission of a representative, a committee of five shall be appointed, neither of whom shall be members of the Great Council from which the contest or protest originates. They shall, without delay, examine all evidence produced by either side, and report the facts to the Great Council, with such recommendation as they may deem just; provided, that in all cases of a contest or a protest, the parties contesting or protesting shall file a copy of the same with the Great Sachem of the reservation from which the brothers hail, at least ten suns prior to the great sun's council of this Great Council.

Sec. 4. Past Representatives who are members of the Order in good standing shall be entitled to admission as visitors, but shall not be allowed to participate in any business before the Great Council.

ARTICLE II.

Election and Raising up of Great Chiefs.

Sec. 1. In the election of Great Chiefs a majority of votes cast shall be necessary to a choice. If on the first ballot no one is elected, a second ballot shall immediately be had, and if no choice is then made a third ballot shall be had, when only the two who received the highest number of votes on the second ballot shall be eligible. Blank votes shall not be counted.

Sec. 2. The Great Chiefs shall be raised up, and enter upon their duties on the last sun of the great sun's council, immediately preceding the quenching of the council fire.

Sec. 3. Should any of the Great Chiefs elect fail to be present at the run fixed for the raising up, the chieftaincy may be declared vacant, and the Great Council proceed to fill the vacancy; but should such absence be caused by sickness or other cause satisfactory to this Great Council, then he shall be raised up by any designated Great Chief after the quenching of the council fire, and the fact shall be certified to, and entered upon the records of this Great Council.

ARTICLE III.

Councils.

Sec. 1. In absence of the Chiefs authorized to preside, the senior Past Great Incohonee present, (not a Great Chief), shall preside, and if none be present, then the members shall by vote designate a member to preside.

Sec. 2. If any of the Great Chiefs are temporarily absent, his chieftaincy shall be filled by appointment of some member by the Great Incohonee.

ARTICLE IV.

Duties of Committees.

Sec. 1. The Committee on Finance shall examine the books, vouchers, and accounts of the Great Chief of Records and the Great Keeper of Wampum before each great sun council, and for that purpose shall meet at the office of the Great Chief of Records at least four suns prior to the council. They shall make estimates for, and recommend appropriations of wampum, for general and special purposes during the interim of the councils, based on revenue likely to be received; and no expenditure of wampum shall be made over and above an appropriation, unless the same has received the approval of the Finance Committee. It shall be their duty to see that the necessary bonds have been entered by those required to do so by the laws, to place the same in the hands of the Great Incohonee, and submit their report at each great sun council.

Sec. 2. The Committee on Constitution and Laws shall examine all laws that may be referred to them during the interim of the councils, and report as to their action on the same. It shall be their duty to see that the laws referred to them do not conflict with the laws and usages of the Order.

SEC. 3. The Committee on Credentials shall examine and report on all credentials that may be referred to them.

SEC. 4. The Committee on Distribution shall have referred to them the long talks of the Great Chief and shall examine and refer the subjects treated in the talks to the various committees.

SEC. 5. To the Committee on the State of the Order shall be referred that portion of the Great Chiefs' longtalks that relates to the status of the Order, and in their report they shall embody the condition and progress that the Order has made, and shall recommend such measures as they may think advantageous to the whole Order.

SEC. 6. The Committee on Judiciary shall consider all questions of a proper construction of the laws, and other judicial matters that may be referred to them by the Great Council.

SEC. 7. The Committee on Appeals and Grievances shall investigate all appeals and other matters of a like character that may be referred to them, and report to the Great Council their decision thereon, with such recommendations as they think the evidence warrants.

SEC. 8. The Committee on Charters shall examine and report on all petitions and dispensations issued by the Great Incohonee, for Tribes, Councils of the Degree of Pocahontas or Great Councils, and report as to the advisability of granting charters.

SEC. 9. The Committee on Reports shall examine and report as to the correctness of all returns and reports presented by Great Councils and Tribes.

SEC. 10. The Committee on Mileage and Per Diem shall calculate the number of miles traveled by Great Chiefs, representatives and members of the Committee on Finance present at each great sun council; they shall also make out a complete and correct roll of the same and report the amount that each is entitled to, and no order shall be drawn until the report is approved by this Great Council.

SEC. 11. The Committee on Beneficiary shall examine and report to the Great Council all matters relating to the Beneficiary Fund and the laws governing the same, and such subjects relating to insurance as may be referred to them.

SEC. 12. The Committee on the Degree of Pocahontas shall have referred to them all matters appertaining to said branch of the Order, and they shall report to the Great Council such recommendations as they may deem beneficial.

SEC. 13. It shall be the duty of each committee or member of this Great Council to return to the Great Chief of Records at the final quenching of the council fire all books and papers belonging to this Great Council, unless otherwise ordered by this Great Council.

ARTICLE V.

GREAT SUN'S REPORT.

Each Great Council shall make out and transmit to the Great Chief of Records on or before the first of Corn moon a great sun's report of its work, in accordance with the form sent or delivered to it by the Great Chief of Records. This report shall be accompanied by the *per capita* tax due this Great Council. Any Great Council neglecting to forward its report and tax by the time specified herein shall forfeit its right to representation; provided this penalty may be remitted by unanimous consent.

ARTICLE VI.

SIX MOONS' REPORT.

Tribes under the immediate jurisdiction of this Great Council shall, within two seven suns after the last council sleep in Hot and Hunting moons, transmit to the Great Chief of Records of this Great Council a correct report of the receipts and expenditures, together with the number of members, names and number of adoptions, rejections, suspensions and cause, expulsions, admissions and withdrawals by card, and death; also the *per capita* tax due.

ARTICLE VII.

REVENUE.

SEC. 1. The charter fee for Great Councils shall be thirty fathoms. For Tribes and Councils of the Degree of Pocahontas, fifteen fathoms.

SEC. 2. Each Great Council shall pay every great sun a *per capita* tax of ten inches for every member under its jurisdiction.

SEC. 3. Each Tribe under the immediate jurisdiction of this Great Council shall pay a *per capita* tax of ten inches for every member on its books at the end of each term.

ARTICLE VIII.

DUTIES OF DEPUTY GREAT INCOHONEES.

It shall be the duty of the Deputy Great Incohonees to visit, instruct and raise up the Chiefs of the Tribes under their charge, and prior to the first of Corn moon report to the Great Incohonee their condition, and such suggestions as they may deem for the advantage of the Order, and at the same time, transmit to the Great Chief of Records such wampum as they may have received, and to perform such other duties as the Great Incohonee may desire.

ARTICLE IX.

MILEAGE AND PER DIEM.

The Great Council of the United States shall pay Mileage and Per Diem to its Great Chiefs, representatives, and members of the Finance Committee and Committee on Constitution and Laws. The mileage shall be at the rate of five inches per mile circular, to be computed by the nearest traveled route, and five fathoms per sun for each sun in attendance.

ARTICLE X.
Removal from Chieftaincy and Membership.

Sec. 1. Any Chief or member of this Great Council may be removed or expelled from membership in the body upon a charge being preferred against him; said charge to be confined to a violation of any of the obligations he may have taken, the laws of this body, or for any improper conduct tending to degrade his position or the Order.

Sec. 2. Any member of the Great Council desiring to prefer charges against any of its members shall file said charge, with specifications in triplicate, with the Great Incohonee, who shall immediately submit the same to the Great Council. The Great Incohonee shall refer such charge to a special committee of five; if said charges are against the Great Incohonee, the same shall be filed with the Great Chief of Records, who shall submit the same to the Great Council, and the Great Senior Sagamore shall appoint the Committee of five, and shall also preside during the time the charge is under consideration by the Great Council.

Sec. 3. A copy of the charge or charges must be furnished by the accuser at least ten suns prior to the time of trial; provided the alleged offense or offenses were not committed during the councils of the Great Council, or within ten suns prior thereto. If within the time mentioned, then one sun's notice will be sufficient.

Sec. 4. The Committee shall fully investigate the charge or charges, report the result of such investigation to the Great Council, recommending such punishment as they may deem proper, and if the report is adopted by a vote of three-fourths of the representatives present, it shall be recorded as the judgment of the Great Council.

Sec. 5. Suspension or expulsion from a Great Council or a Tribe to which a Chief or member of this Great Council belongs, shall operate as a suspension or expulsion from chieftaincy or membership in this Great Council, and the vacancy thereby created shall be filled in the manner prescribed by the laws.

ARTICLE XI.
Printing of Records and Supplies of the Great Council.

The Great Chief of Records shall, at least two moons prior to the great sun's council, notify members of the Order who are practical printers that estimates will be received on or before the first of Sturgeon moon for printing the records and all other printed matter needed for the great sun, and said bids shall be opened in the presence of the Finance Committee, who shall award the same to the lowest responsible bidder.

ARTICLE XII.
Amendments.

No alteration or amendments to these By-Laws shall be made unless presented at a great sun's council signed by representatives from three Great

Councils, read upon three separate suns, and then adopted by two-thirds of the representatives present.

ORDER OF BUSINESS.

1. At the run fixed therefor the Great Incohonee shall take his station and command silence; have the wickets secured, the wigwam examined, and the council fire duly kindled.
2. Roll of Chiefs.
3. Appointment of Committee on Credentials.
4. Credentials of Past Great Sachems and Representatives read and referred.
5. Admission of Representatives and Past Great Sachems.
6. Roll of Representatives.
7. The record of last council fire read and considered.
8. Long Talks of Great Incohonee and other Chiefs.
9. The names of Great Councils and Tribes called, in alphabetical order, for business or communications.
10. Reports of Committees.
11. Deferred business.
12. New business.

These Rules may be temporarily dispensed with by the Great Incohonee.

RULES OF ORDER.

1. The Great Incohonee may speak to points of order rising for that purpose. Before putting a question he shall ask: "Is the Great Council ready for the question?" If no brother address him he shall rise and put the question, after which it will not be in order to address the Great Council upon that question.
2. No brother shall be permitted to vote or speak unless clothed in regalia according to his rank or station.
3. Every brother when he rises to speak shall address the Great Incohonee in a proper manner, and no brother shall pass out of the wigwam, or otherwise disturb the council, except to call to order.
4. All personalities and indecorous language or reflection upon the Great Council or its members, are positively prohibited.
5. No brother shall speak more than once upon the same question until all have an opportunity so to do, nor more than twice without permission from the Great Council.
6. If a brother, while speaking, be called to order by the Great Incohonee, he shall cease speaking and take his seat until the question of order is determined and permission is given him to proceed.
7. Every Chief or brother shall be designated by his proper title, according to his standing in the Order.
8. When a question is before the Great Council, no motion shall be re-

ceived except for the previous question, to lie on the table, to postpone indefinitely, or to a limited time; to divide, to commit or to amend; and such motions shall severally have precedence in the order herein arranged. A motion to quench the council fire is always in order.

9. The Great Council may resolve itself into a Committee of the Whole upon the following subjects and none other: For the consideration of the Constitution and Laws, and for the consideration of the work of the Order, written and unwritten.

10. Any brother who voted on the prevailing side can call for the reconsideration of a vote at the same great sun council in which it was passed, and if sustained by a majority of the votes the reconsideration shall be carried.

11. If two or more brothers rise to speak at the same time, the Great Incohonee shall decide which is entitled to the floor.

12. No motion shall be subject to debate until it has been seconded and stated by the Great Incohonee. It shall be reduced to writing at the request of any brother.

13. On the call of three brothers a majority may demand the previous question, which shall always be put in this form: "Shall the main question be now put?" and until it is decided, shall preclude all amendments and all further debate. If the main question be ordered, the amendments shall be voted upon in their order and then the original question.

14. The Great Incohonee shall pronounce the decision of the Great Council on all subjects; he may speak on points of order in preference to other brothers; decide questions of order without debate, subject to an appeal to the Great Council by any two brothers — on which appeal no brother shall speak more than once.

15. A motion to lie on the table shall be decided without debate.

16. When a question is postponed indefinitely it shall not be acted on until the next great sun council.

17. The yeas and nays may be demanded by any two members, and shall be entered upon the record; and every representative must vote, unless excused by a majority of the Great Council.

18. All questions shall be decided by a majority vote, except in cases otherwise provided for.

GENERAL LAWS

FOR THE GOVERNMENT OF GREAT COUNCILS UNDER THE JURISDICTION OF THE GREAT COUNCIL OF THE UNITED STATES, IMPROVED ORDER OF RED MEN.

PREAMBLE.

WHEREAS, All power and authority enjoyed, exercised and possessed by the several Great Councils exist only by virtue of their charters and the sanction and consent of the Great Council of the United States duly granted them; Therefore, the Great Council of the United States doth adopt and establish the following Constitution or General Laws for their government: —

ARTICLE I.

NAME.

This body shall be known as the Great Council of —————— of the Improved Order of Red Men.

ARTICLE II.

HOW COMPOSED.

This Great Council shall be composed of Past Sachems. It is the supreme tribunal of the Order in the State, District, Territory or country in which it is located, and no Tribe or branch of the Order can exist therein without its sanction. Every member shall receive the Great Council degree before he can take his seat. The Great Council shall always be opened in that degree for the introduction of representatives, who shall be Past Sachems. The Great Council may establish regulations in regard to representation therein.

ARTICLE III.

COUNCILS.

This Great Council shall hold one council every great sun.

ARTICLE IV.

CHIEFS.

SEC. 1. The elective Chiefs shall be Great Sachem, Great Senior Sagamore, Great Junior Sagamore, Great Prophet, Great Chief of Records and Great Keeper of Wampum.

SEC. 2. The appointed Chiefs shall be Great Sannap, Great Mishinewa, Great Guard of Wigwam and Great Guard of Forest.

ARTICLE V.

ELIGIBILITY AND TERMS OF GREAT CHIEFS.

SEC. 1. After a Great Council shall have been instituted two great suns no brother shall be eligible to the chieftaincy of Great Sachem unless he has served one term as an elective Chief of a Great Council; nor to the chieftaincy of Great Prophet unless he has served in the chieftaincy of Great Sachem.

SEC. 2. The term of Great Chiefs shall be one great sun; provided that Great Councils may enact a law that the term of the Great Chief of Records and Great Keeper of Wampum may be two great suns.

ARTICLE VI.

HONORS.

SEC. 1. The first Prophet of a Tribe, or the first Great Prophet of a Great Council, shall be entitled to the honors of a Past Sachem or a Past Great Sachem, as the case may be; to entitle them to said honors they must receive a dispensation from the Great Incohonee or Great Sachem, setting forth that they have served in said chieftaincies.

SEC. 2. Any Chief of Records, Collector of Wampum or Keeper of Wampum of any Tribe, having served five great suns in succession as such, shall be entitled to the degree of Past Sachem.

SEC. 3. Any Great Chief of Records or Great Keeper of Wampum of any Great Council, having served five great suns in succession as such, shall be entitled to the degree of Past Great Sachem.

SEC. 4. Great Councils may adopt laws conferring the rank, title, rights and privileges of a Past Sachem upon each of the Chiefs of a Tribe elected at the institution thereof; provided such Chiefs serve to the end of the term for which they were elected.

ARTICLE VII.

ELECTION OF CHIEFS.

The Great Chiefs shall be elected by ballot, at such time and in such manner as the By-Laws of the Great Council may prescribe.

ARTICLE VIII.

FEES FOR ADOPTION AND DEGREES.

This Great Council may establish its own fees for Adoption and Degrees.

ARTICLE IX.

APPLICATION FOR CHARTERS.

SEC. 1. Application for a Tribal Charter must be signed by not less than twenty brothers or pale faces, accompanied by a fee of not less than twenty fathoms. If the application be made during the interim of a Great Council, the Great Sachem may, by and with the consent of the Great Chiefs, grant a dispensation to light the council brand, if deemed for the interest of the Order, the petition and report to be submitted to the next council of the Great Council.

FORM OF APPLICATION FOR CHARTER.

To the Great Council of   of the Improved Order of Red Men:—

The undersigned, members of the Order (or palefaces) residing in   respectfully petition your Great Council to grant them a charter to establish a Tribe of the Improved Order of Red Men, to be located in
The said Tribe to be known as   Tribe No.   of the Improved Order of Red Men, under your jurisdiction, and we pledge ourselves to be governed by the laws thereof.

    Signed,
Enclosed is the charter fee.

SEC. 2. Application for a charter for Council of the Degree of Pocahontas must be signed by not less than ten brothers of the Chief's Degree and ten females, and accompanied by a fee of not less than fifteen fathoms, and acted upon in the same manner as an application for a Tribal charter.

SEC. 3. Applications for charters for Degree Councils must be signed by at least ten brothers of the Chief's Degree. A Degree Council may be beneficial, or otherwise, as may be set forth by the petitioners. It may admit brothers to membership residing anywhere within the jurisdiction of the Great Council by which it has been chartered. It shall not confer degrees upon any brother unless a certificate be presented from his Tribe authorizing the same.

ARTICLE X.
BY-LAWS.

The Great Council has full power to enact By-Laws for its government, and General Laws for the regulation of Tribes and Councils of Pocahontas under its jurisdiction. Provided they do not conflict with the Constitution and By-Laws of the Great Council of the United States and these general laws. When said laws are adopted, three copies thereof, certified by the Great Sachem and Great Chief of Records, shall be transmitted to the Great Chief of Records of the Great Council of the United States, who shall immediately refer them to the Committee on Constitution and Laws, upon whose approval they shall be binding upon the Great Council.

ARTICLE XI.
AMENDMENTS.

Any amendment, alteration or addition to these General Laws must be proposed in writing and acted upon as prescribed in Article XIX of the Constitution of the Great Council of the United States.

CODE OF PROCEDURE.
CHARGES AGAINST MEMBERS.

SEC. 1. Any member guilty of the following offences would be amenable to the Tribe, and should be tried and punished by reprimand, fine, suspension or expulsion : —

1. Violation of the obligations he has taken either in the Adoption or the Degrees, or on assuming any chieftaincy, or the laws of the Order.

2. Revealing or making known to a person or persons who are not at the time members of the Order any of the secrets or the workings of the Tribe.

3. Making false statements in order to gain admission into the Order, knowing the same to be false; or who shall knowingly conceal any infirmity or disease, either of body or mind.

4. Using improper means to obtain benefits.

5. Misappropriating any of the funds, property or effects of a Tribe to his own use, or shall wrongfully divert or misappropriate the funds of the Tribe.

6. Wilfully refusing to appear and testify or give his deposition, after being duly notified by the Tribe.

7. Violating the criminal laws of his State.

8. Bringing suit in any of the civil courts of his State against his Tribe, for the redress of any grievance, the adjudication of which is provided for within the Order by the laws thereof.

9. Using any of the emblems, mottoes, titles or initials of the Order, either as a Chief or member directly or indirectly, for the prosecution of any private business or enterprise.

SEC. 2. No member can be put on trial for an offense unless the charge or charges be reduced to writing, signed by the accuser and distinctly specifying the cause or causes of complaint, and the time and place of occurrence, a copy of which shall be furnished by the Chief of Records before the next council sleep. At the first council sleep after the charge shall have been preferred, a committee of five shall be selected to investigate the charge, of whom one shall be appointed by the Sachem, one by the Senior Sagamore, and the remaining three shall be drawn by lot from among the members present (in good standing), in the manner following, to wit: The twig box shall be placed immediately in front of the Sachem, and a number of ballots equal to all the members present entitled to serve (less the two members of the committee previously appointed, such members as may be named as witnesses, and the accused and accuser), shall be placed therein. Three of said ballots shall have written on them the word "Committee," the rest shall be blank. The Chief of Records shall then call over the names of the members present (a list of whom shall be entered on the records, as also of those excused by reason of being witnesses), and each, as his name is called, shall draw a ballot from the twig box, and hand the same to the Sachem, who shall announce the nature of the ballot, whether blank or otherwise, retaining the ballots until the drawing is over. The three members drawing the ballot with the word "Committee" thereon shall, with the brothers before appointed, constitute the committee.

SEC. 3. The committee shall organize on the sleep of its appointment, by the election of a chairman and secretary, after which, with as little delay as possible, the secretary shall notify the accused and the accuser or accusers, of the time and place appointed for investigating the charges. At the time so appointed the committee must proceed with the investigation, even though one of the parties be absent, unless a written notice be received stating his inability to attend by reason of sickness, no other reason being admissible. In the event of such notice being received, the committee shall adjourn to another fixed time, of which both parties shall have notice. This adjournment shall not extend beyond two seven suns, at which time the committee shall proceed with the investigation. Each side shall have the right to be represented before the committee by counsel, who must be members of the Order in good standing.

SEC. 4. It shall be the duty of the committee to examine the parties, their proof and witnesses. The committee shall keep a correct record of the proceedings and shall also reduce the testimony taken to writing, to be signed by the witness at the end of his or her examination, the same being first carefully read over to them. After having heard the evidence, the committee shall reduce its opinion as to the guilt or innocence of the accused, on each charge and specification, to writing (to be plainly written in ink), and report the same, together with the journal and the original testimony, to the Tribe at its earliest stated council after the work of the committee is completed.

SEC. 5. When the committee submits its report, the accused must be notified thereof by the Chief of Records under seal, and direct him to be present at the next stated council, at which time the report must be considered. If the report is approved by a majority of the members voting, it shall be recorded as the judgment of the Tribe. The Tribe must then prescribe the degree of punishment to be imposed in accordance with the law; the vote thereon must be by ballot, and a majority of the votes cast shall decide, except for expulsion, when the assent of two-thirds of the members voting shall be necessary.

SEC. 6. When a motion prescribing the punishment is before the Tribe, the same shall be considered as any other motion and be subject to the same rules; provided, that motions and amendments relative to the degree of punishment shall be treated as a blank, and the blank shall be filled by voting upon the most severe punishment first. If that be lost, a less severe punishment shall be voted upon, until the judgment of the Tribe is declared. As soon as the Tribe has fixed the penalty, it shall be the duty of the Chief of Records to notify the brother.

SEC. 7. A brother feeling that injustice has been done him by the Tribe must appeal to the Great Sachem within two moons from the date of the notice of the action of the Tribe, stating distinctly and specifically the reason or reasons he may have for believing the wrong has been done him. He shall first, however, be required to serve a copy of the appeal upon the Tribe, of which service due proof shall be furnished the Great Sachem. As soon as the Great Sachem has received an appeal in proper form, he shall, within one seven suns, notify the Tribe, and the Chief of Records shall immediately deliver to the Great Sachem the journal of the committee by whom the case was tried, together with the testimony taken before it, and copies of the records of all the council sleeps containing matter relating thereto, and all papers connected therewith, signed by the Sachem and Chief of Records, under seal. Should the Tribe neglect or refuse to comply herewith, it shall be sufficient cause for its suspension.

SEC. 8. The Great Sachem shall refer all documents and papers to such committee as the laws of the Great Council may designate.

SEC. 9. When the member of one Tribe desires to prefer a charge or charges against a member or members of another Tribe, he shall present such charge or charges in the usual form to the Tribe of which he (the accuser) is a member. Said Tribe shall forthwith forward to the Tribe to which the accused belongs a certified copy of the charge or charges over the signatures of the Sachem and Chief of Records, and attested by the seal of the Tribe; and the Tribe to whom such charge or charges shall be sent shall proceed to hear and determine the same in like manner as if preferred by a member of its own body.

SEC. 10. A Tribe, upon due investigation and trial, having decided that a charge or charges made against a brother have not been sustained, its decision is final. The brother who preferred the charges cannot appeal from the decision of the Tribe.

SEC. 11. A member expelled from the Order cannot be restored to membership in the Tribe, except after application to the Tribe, and by permission of the Great Council or the Board of Great Council Chiefs, during the interim, and the vote necessary to reinstate him is the same vote which expelled him from membership.

SEC. 12. Should any person feel aggrieved at the action of a Tribe for failing to pay benefits that may be claimed to be due, such person must appeal from said action by giving the Tribe notice thereof within twenty suns after said action, whereupon the Sachem shall without delay appoint a suitable member of the Order as a commissioner to take such testimony as either party may offer in relation to the case.

SEC. 13. The commissioner shall, within twenty suns, proceed to take the testimony, giving each party ten suns' notice of the time and place of meeting for that purpose. The Sachem shall represent the Tribe, and may also be represented by counsel. The aggrieved party may appear in person and may also be represented by counsel. All testimony must be taken down fully by the commissoner and signed by the witnesses after being fully read to them, and should objections be made to the examination of any witness, or to any question, or to any testimony offered, he shall note the same, and he shall give ample time and opportunity to both parties to present their witnesses, and for them to testify. All testimony shall be written in ink.

SEC. 14. After taking all the testimony the parties may offer, the commissioner shall immediately report to the Tribe, whereupon the Chief of Records shall notify the aggrieved party that the subject will be considered at the next council of the Tribe, at which time the Tribe shall consider it, when all the evidence in the case shall be read and the claim finally determined.

SEC. 15. After final action shall have been had by the Tribe, the Chief of Records shall immediately notify the aggrieved party of the action of the Tribe. If the Tribe should still refuse to pay the benefits claimed, then the aggrieved party must appeal to the Great Council at any time within twenty suns from the date of the notice, by filing an appeal with the Tribe; otherwise the action of the Tribe, at the expiration of the time, will be final and conclusive.

SEC. 16. When an appeal has been filed from the action of the Tribe, the Tribe through the Chief of Records shall, without delay, transmit the appeal to the Great Sachem, together with the testimony taken by the commissioner, extracts from the records of the Tribe of all proceedings, and all other papers and documents relating to the case which were offered in evidence in the case when before the Tribe, and which alone shall be examined by the parties authorized by the laws to hear appeals.

SEC. 17. Should the Tribe neglect or refuse to appoint a commissioner within two seven suns after receiving notice of an appeal, or shall neglect to send the appeal and papers to the Great Sachem within one moon after the filing of the appeal, it shall be sufficient cause for the Great Sachem to reverse the action of the Tribe, and direct them to pay the benefits. Provided, that the Tribe would have the right to appeal to the Great Council from the action of the Great Sachem. Provided, further, that the amount of wampum claimed shall be placed in the hands of the Great Keeper of Wampum until the case is fully settled.

SEC. 18. An appeal of a Tribe from the action of a Board or Committee on Appeals cannot be entertained unless the Tribe has obeyed the mandate of the Great Sachem or Great Council, or the amount of wampum involved has been placed in the hands of the Great Keeper of Wampum, the same to be held until the case has been finally settled by the laws of the Order.

GENERAL INSTRUCTIONS

FOR COMMISSIONERS APPOINTED BY TRIBES TO TAKE TESTIMONY.

RULE 1. A commissioner is only a ministerial officer. He has no power to make a ruling. His duty is to enter in his journal what is offered, and leave to the Tribe and to the authorized committee to pass upon the relevancy or the irrelevancy of what is offered.

RULE 2. The commissioner must give the party presenting the appeal at least ten suns' notice in writing of the time and place of the meeting.

RULE 3. The party presenting the appeal shall, at the time and place appointed by the commissioner, present his witnesses. There shall be no one present at the time of the hearing except the parties and the one witness under examination while the testimony is being taken.

RULE 4. Counsel representing either party must be a member of the Order, in good standing, and shall present a certificate to that effect.

RULE 5. After the appellant is through with his witnesses, the witnesses for the Tribe shall be presented.

RULE 6. All objections made to the testimony of witnesses by either party must be noted on the records by the commissioner, and then proceed to take down the testimony as if no objections were made.

RULE 7. New evidence may be introduced after the case has been closed on either side, if there be reasons for so doing. Such new evidence need not be confined to that which is merely rebuttal. The tribunal that decides the case finally must exercise its discretion as to the evidence thus presented.

FORMS.

The following forms may be used, when circumstances require; but the form is not imperative, so that the substance is clearly set forth: —

No. 1.
CHARGES.

. . . . . . Sun . . . . Moon, G. S. D. . . .
To . . . .
. . . . . . Tribe No. . . . Imp. O. R. M. The undersigned, a member of . . . . Tribe, No. . . . Imp. O. R. M., under the jurisdiction of the Great Council of . . . . Imp. O. R. M., hereby charges . . . . a member of . . . . Tribe, No. . . . Imp. O. R. M., with having been guilty of conduct unbecoming a Red Man, as more fully appears in the following: —

SPECIFICATIONS.

First . . . .
Second . . . .
Third . . . .
Witnesses.

}

Signature of Accuser.

No. 2.

NOTICE TO ACCUSED.

. . . . Sun . . . . Moon, G. S. D. . . .
To . . . .
Brother:

You are hereby notified that at a stated council of . . . . Tribe, No. . . . Imp. O. R. M., held on the sleep of . . . . . . sun of . . . . . . moon, G. S. D. . . . . . . the following charges were preferred against you, to wit:

(Here insert copy of charges in full.)

This is therefore to summon you to be and appear before said Tribe on the sleep of . . . . sun . . . . moon, at the . . . . . . run, G. S. D. . . . . at which time the committee will be selected to try said charges.

Fraternally in F., F. and C.,

[SEAL.]

Chief of Records.

No. 3.
FORM OF SUBPŒNA TO ACCUSED.

. . . . Sun . . . . . . G. S. D. . . .
To . . . .
   Sir and Brother:
     You are hereby notified that on the . . . . , sun . . . . moon, G. S. D. . . . . . charges preferred against you were referred for trial to the undersigned committee.
     You are hereby required to appear before said committee at . . . . on the . . . . sun of . . . . moon, G. S. D. . . . . . at the . . . . run, to make answer to said charges, and proceed with the trial thereof.

                                       } Committee.

. . . . Secretary.

No. 4.
FORM OF SUBPŒNA TO ACCUSER OR WITNESS.
To . . . .
   Brother:
     You are hereby required to attend, under penalty of our laws, before a committee of . . . . Tribe, No. . . . Imp. O. R. M., selected to investigate charges against Bro. . . . . on the . . . . sun of . . . . moon, G. S. D. . . . . . to testify in said case.   Fraternally,

                                  Secretary of Committee.
. . . . Sun . . . . Moon, G. S. D. . . .

No. 5.
REPORT OF COMMITTEE.

. . . . Sun . . . . Moon, G. S. D. . . .
Sachem, Chiefs and members of . . . . . . Tribe, No. . . . Imp. O. R. M.
   Sirs and Brothers:
     Your committee selected to try charges preferred against Brother . . . . by Brother . . . . report that the accompanying documents contain the proceedings of and the evidence taken before said committee.
     That, from all that appeared to said committee in said case, they find Brother . . . . as to the . . . . specifications of the charge.

                                       } Committee.

No. 6.

NOTICE TO ACCUSED AS TO REPORT.

.... Tribe, No. ... Imp. O. R. M.
.... Sun .... Moon, G. S. D. ...
To ....
Sir and Brother:

Take notice that the committee selected to try the charges preferred against you by Brother .... have filed their report, and the report will be considered at the next stated council of the Tribe, on the sleep of the .... sun .... moon, G. S. D. ...

Yours in F., F. and C.,

[SEAL.] .... Chief of Records.

No. 7.

FORM OF APPEAL FROM THE ACTION OF A TRIBE.

.... Sun .... Moon, G. S. D. ...
To .... the Great Sachem of the Great Council of .... Imp. O. R. M.
Sir and Brother:

Your petitioner having been notified that he has been .... from .... Tribe, No. ... Imp. O. R. M., and feeling that injustice has been done, would respectfully appeal from the action of said .... Tribe, No. ... Imp. O. R. M., for the following reasons, to wit:

1st. That the decision of said .... Tribe, No. ... Imp. O. R. M., is contrary to the laws and the usages of the Order.

2d. That said decision is contrary to and against the evidence.

3d. Errors of law, and excepted to at the time of trial:

(The petitioner must state the errors committed.) Your petitioner would therefore ask that said decision of said .... Tribe, No. ... Imp. O. R. M., be reversed, and that he may be restored to all things he has lost thereby.
(Signed by petitioner.)

Two must be made out, and one filed with the Tribe, in accordance with the law.

TRIBAL CHARTERS.

HOW APPLIED FOR, ETC.

Extract from Article XIII, Constitution G. C. U. S.

Sec. 4. Application for a Charter for a Tribe must be made by at least thirty brothers or pale faces, accompanied by the charter fee and the cards of the brothers. If application be made during the interim of this Great Council, the Great Incohonee may, by and with the advice of the Great Chiefs, grant a dispensation and institute the Tribe.

Sec. 5. All traveling or other expenses of the Great Incohonee, or his Deputy, in lighting the Council brand of a Tribe, shall be paid by such Tribe.

FORM OF PETITION.

To the Great Council of the United States of the Improved Order of Red Men:

The undersigned pale faces, or members of the Order, residing in ———— ————, respectfully petition the Great Council to grant them a Charter to establish a Tribe of the Improved Order of Red Men, to be located in ————, County of ————, State of ————, and known as ———— Tribe, No. —, and under your jurisdiction. Should this, our petition, be granted, we hereby pledge ourselves, individually and collectively, to be governed by the Constitution, Laws and Usages of the Order.

Inclosed is the Charter fee, 15 fathoms.

(*The petition must be signed by the petitioners.*)

The name selected should be that of some aboriginal tribe, title, designation or word common to the locality. The number will be supplied by the Great Council. The petition and charter fee should be sent to the Great Chief of Records of United States. In due time the petitioners will receive notice of the disposition made of the petition. If not granted the fee will be returned. In the meantime the petitioners should arrange the necessary preliminary business, so as to have as little delay as possible on the arrival of the Great Chiefs to institute the Tribe. The chiefs may be selected at an informal meeting, so that they can be nominated and elected at once. The wigwam should be entirely private and secure from intrusion.

CONSTITUTION

FOR TRIBES UNDER THE IMMEDIATE JURISDICTION OF THE GREAT COUNCIL OF THE UNITED STATES.

NOTE. — The following is intended for the Constitution of all Tribes under the immediate jurisdiction of the Great Council United States. Such Tribes may make By-Laws in conformity therewith, but must not alter said Constitution or fail to work in accord thereto until a Great Council is established in their respective reservations. Said Constitution must not be changed in any way by interlineation, erasure, insertion, or otherwise, but must be taken and used intact by the Tribes, the Great Council of the United States alone having the right to change or modify it.

When By-Laws are adopted three copies thereof shall be transmitted to the Great Chief of Records of the Great Council of the United States, who shall immediately refer them to the Committee on Constitution and Laws, upon whose approval they shall be binding upon the Tribe.

ARTICLE I.
Name, Title, Composition, and Powers.

1. This Tribe shall be known by the name mentioned in its By-Laws.

2. It shall be composed of duly qualified and legally admitted brothers, and possess such power and authority as its Charter, the Constitution and Laws of the Order define as belonging to a Tribe.

ARTICLE II.
Chiefs.

1. The Elective Chiefs of this Tribe shall consist of a Sachem, Senior Sagamore, Junior Sagamore, Prophet, Chief of Records, and Keeper of Wampum — all of whom must be members of the Chief's Degree.

A Collector of Wampum may be elected, who must be a member of the Chief's Degree.

The Prophet must be a Past Sachem.

2. The appointed Chiefs shall consist of a First and Second Sannap, Guard of the Wigwam, Guard of the Forest, four Warriors and four Braves.

ARTICLE III.
Qualifications of Chiefs.

1. After the Tribe has been instituted two great suns, no brother shall be eligible for Senior Sagamore, unless he has served one term as Junior Sagamore; nor Sachem unless he has served one term as Senior Sagamore.

2. No brother resigning, or who may be removed from a position previous to the expiration of the term for which he has been elected, unless it be to fill a higher position, shall be entitled to the honors; but the incumbent who shall fill the residue of the term, shall be entitled to the full honors thereof.

ARTICLE IV.
Election of Chiefs.[1]

1. The election for Chiefs shall take place at the last stated council in the Hot and Hunting moons; and the nominations may be made two seven suns previous to the election.

2. The Chief of Records and Keeper of Wampum, shall be elected for one great sun; and, if the Tribe deem it expedient, a Collector of Wampum may

---

[1] The Chiefs elected (at the institution of a Tribe) more than two moons prior to the close of a term, shall be entitled to the full honors thereof.

be chosen for the same period, to perform such duties as the By-Laws may prescribe.

3. The election shall be by ballot, and a majority of the votes polled shall be necessary to a choice.

ARTICLE V.
Raising and Appointing of Chiefs.

1. The raising up of Chiefs shall take place on the first council sleep of the Cold and Buck moons, unless a dispensation has been granted to postpone the same. Tribes may have their Chiefs raised up in public, provided a dispensation has been first obtained.

2. The Sachem shall appoint the various appointive Chiefs named in the Constitution.

ARTICLE VI.
Duties of Sachem.

The Sachem shall act as presiding chief of the Tribe; enforce a rigid adherence to the Constitution, Laws and Ritual of the Order; give the casting vote whenever the Tribe may be equally divided upon any question before it, except when the yeas and nays are taken; sign all orders for wampum that may be ordered by the Tribe; appoint a majority of all committees not otherwise provided for; convene special councils of the Tribe whenever requested in writing by five brothers so to do, and perform such other duties as may be required of him by his chieftaincy, the By-Laws, or by a vote of the Tribe.

ARTICLE VII.
Duties of Senior Sagamore.

The Senior Sagamore shall see that the brothers demean themselves in an orderly manner; preside in the absence of the Sachem; appoint a minority of all committees not otherwise provided for, and perform such other duties as may be prescribed by the By-Laws, or required of him by a resolution of the Tribe.

ARTICLE VIII.
Duties of Junior Sagamore.

The Junior Sagamore shall aid the Senior in preserving order and decorum, and take his seat when he is absent. When the Sachem and Senior are absent, he shall preside.

ARTICLE IX.
Duties of Chief of Records.

1. The Chief of Records shall keep an accurate record of the proceedings of the Tribe, have charge of the seal, keep correct accounts between the Tribe and its members; receive all Wampum due the Tribe, and pay the same over to the Keeper of Wampum, taking his receipt for the same.

2. He shall, at the end of each six moons' term, furnish the Great Chief of Records of the Great Council of the United States, a report containing the whole number of members, those over three, six and nine moons in arrears; the amount of wampum received by the Tribe, the amount expended for benefits, funerals and other purposes; amount invested; the number and names of those adopted, admitted by card, reinstated, withdrawn, suspended, expelled, deceased and rejected, together with the names of the Chiefs elect, and a list of Past Sachems not more than three moons in arrears, and forward the same with a tax of ten inches for each member on the books at the close of each six moons' term, within seven suns after the first council sleep of the term.

3. At the expiration of his term he shall deliver to his successor all books, papers and other matters belonging to his Chieftaincy.

ARTICLE X.
Duties of Keeper of Wampum.

1. The Keeper of Wampum shall attend each council of the Tribe; receive all wampum due the Tribe, giving his receipt therefor; keep regular and correct accounts of all wampum received and paid by him, and report the condition of the belt at the end of each term; pay all orders authorized by a vote of the Tribe, attested by the Sachem and Chief of Records.

2. He shall have his accounts ready for settlement on the sleep succeeding the election, and attend the committee for that purpose whenever requested. He shall deliver to his successor (or to a committee appointed to receive the same), at the expiration of his term, resignation, or removal, all wampum remaining in the belt, and all books, papers, or other matter appertaining to his chieftaincy. He shall, before entering upon his duties, give such security as the Tribe may require.

ARTICLE XI.
Duties of Collector of Wampum.

The Collector of Wampum (if the Tribe elect one), shall assist the Chief of Records in the performance of his duties, act for him in his absence and perform such other duties as the Tribe may direct.

ARTICLE XII.
Appointed Chiefs.

The appointed chiefs shall perform such duties as may be required of them by the Tribe, Charge Books, and Laws of the Order.

ARTICLE XIII.
Removals and Vacancies.

1. Any Chief may be removed for inattention to the duties of his chieftaincy, or conduct unbecoming a member of the Order, after trial and con-

viction. Every Chief against whom charges are preferred shall fill his chieftaincy until the same has been determined, unless otherwise ordered by a two-thirds vote of the members present.

2. Any elective or appointed Chief absent for four consecutive council sleeps, or more than three moons in arrears for seven suns' dues, may be removed by a vote of the Tribe, provided he has had at least one seven suns' notice to show cause why he should not thus be dealt with.

3. All vacancies shall be filled by election or appointment according to the nature of the chieftaincy, and the Chief so elected and serving to the end of the term shall be entitled to the honors thereof.

ARTICLE XIV.

MEMBERSHIP.

1. No person shall be adopted into a Tribe of the Order except a free white male, of good moral character and standing, of the full age of twenty-one great suns, who believes in the existence of a Great Spirit, the Creator and Preserver of the Universe, and who is possessed of some known reputable means of support, and free from all infirmities that might render him burdensome to the Tribe.

2. An application for adoption must be recommended by two brothers in good standing, and accompanied by one-half the adoption fee. The application shall be referred to a committee of three, who shall make a strict investigation of the health, character and qualifications of the applicant, and report at the next council.

3. Upon the report of the committee a ballot shall be taken, and if two or more black twigs shall have been deposited, action on the application shall be deferred until the next stated council of the Tribe, when another ballot shall be had, and if not more than three of the twigs then cast are black, the candidate shall be declared elected. If rejected, his fee must be returned to him, and his application shall not be renewed in any Tribe of the Order for the space of six moons thereafter.

4. No pale face can be adopted for a less sum than three fathoms.

5. Any brother of the Order holding a withdrawal card, or dismissal certificate, desirous of becoming a member of a Tribe, shall make application as in case of a pale face, accompanying his application with his withdrawal card, or dismissal certificate, which shall be referred to a committee of three, whose duty it shall be to report as to his standing and qualifications at a stated council, when a ballot shall be had, as in case of a pale face.

6. Should a pale face neglect or refuse to present himself for adoption within six seven suns from the date of his election (unless a satisfactory excuse be given), the proposition fee shall be forfeited to the Tribe, and he cannot be admitted except by a new election.

7. No proposition for membership shall be withdrawn after it has been referred to a committee, except by unanimous consent, and in all cases a ballot shall be had whether the report be favorable or unfavorable.

8. No Tribe shall adopt a pale face resident of another State reservation unless by consent of the Great Sachem of such reservation; nor confer degrees upon a member of another Tribe, except by permission, under seal, of the Tribe to which said member belongs.

ARTICLE XV.
Reinstatement.

1. A member suspended for non-payment of dues, wishing to be reinstated, shall make application therefor to the Tribe, when a committee of three shall be appointed, who shall investigate his fitness for membership, and on the report of the committee a ballot shall be had, and if not more than three black twigs appear against him, he shall be declared elected.

2. A member applying for reinstatement within one great sun of his suspension, shall pay one great sun's dues; if after one great sun, he shall pay the same fee as a pale face of the same age.

3. A member suspended for improper conduct shall, at the expiration of the time for which he was suspended, be reinstated; and shall pay all dues and assessments accrued during his suspension. Should he be guilty of improper conduct during his suspension, he shall be liable to trial as provided for in the Code of Procedure.

ARTICLE XVI.
Cards and Dismissal Certificates.

1. A member may withdraw from his Tribe upon a personal or written application, by paying all dues and demands against him on the books, together with a fee for his card (which shall not be less than twenty-five inches), and provided there be no charges pending against him.

2. A member desirous of visiting a Tribe outside of his own reservation must pay all dues and demands against him for the current term, and receive a certified receipt signed by the Sachem and attested by the Chief of Records with the seal, which shall be the only evidence to prove him in good standing.

3. A member suspended for non-payment of dues, desirous of joining a Tribe in the same reservation, after one great sun's suspension, shall be entitled to receive, and the tribe shall grant, upon proper application, a Dismissal Certificate upon the payment of not less than one fathom nor more than one great sun's dues.

4. A member suspended for non-payment of dues, wishing to regain membership in another reservation, shall be entitled to receive, and the Tribe shall grant, upon proper application, a Dismissal Certificate upon the receipt of not less than one fathom nor more than one great sun's dues.

5. In all cases wherein a Tribe has refused to reinstate a member suspended for non-payment of dues, he shall be entitled to receive, and the Tribe shall, upon proper application, grant a Dismissal Certificate upon the receipt of one fathom.

6. Dismissal Certificates may be received upon deposit in any Tribe, under the same laws as withdrawal cards, but the privilege of visiting shall not be awarded to the holder of a Dismissal Certificate.

ARTICLE XVII.
Degrees.

1. Brothers desirous of advancing should make application for degrees in open council; the application shall be referred to the Tribe while working in the degrees; a ballot shall be had, and if not more than three black twigs are cast it shall be granted. If rejected, the application cannot be renewed for three moons.

2. Any brother in good standing who has been a member of his Tribe for one seven suns, may apply for the Hunter's Degree; and one seven suns after he shall have received that degree he may apply for the Warrior's Degree; and one seven suns after he shall have received that degree, he may apply for the Chief's Degree. In cases of necessity, on application with the requisite fee, the Great Incohonee, or his Deputy, may grant dispensations to confer degrees in less time than required by the foregoing clause.

3. The fees to be paid on application for the Hunter's, Warrior's or Chief's Degree, shall not be less than one fathom each.

4. The elective Chiefs shall see that the degrees are properly conferred.

5. This Tribe shall not confer degrees upon a brother of another Tribe, without its consent given under seal.

ARTICLE XVIII.
Dues.

Every member of this Tribe shall pay into the Wampum Belt thereof such sums as the By-Laws may prescribe, which shall not be less than ten inches per seven suns.

ARTICLE XIX.
Benefits.

1. Any brother qualified as required by this Constitution and the By-Laws of this Tribe, if unable to follow the hunt (his usual occupation), and to such an extent as to disqualify him from following some other occupation, shall be entitled to receive from the Wampum Belt such sum as the By-Laws may prescribe; *provided*, his disability does not result from his own improper conduct; and, *provided further*, that the Tribe may enact a By-Law that no benefits shall be allowed for the first seven suns' disability. They may also provide for a graded scale of benefits.

2. A member unable to follow the hunt and residing beyond the jurisdiction of the Relief Chiefs, desiring to receive seven suns' benefits, shall cause to be presented to his Tribe a written application, accompanied by his physician's certificate, stating the time in attendance and the nature of his sickness

or disability, with directions how the wampum shall be forwarded (at his risk), attested by the Sachem and Chief of Records under seal of a Tribe in his vicinity or a justice of the peace, and such other proof as may be required. He shall not be entitled to seven suns' benefits for more than four seven suns preceding such application.

3. In the event of the Great Spirit calling a beneficial member from the hunting grounds of his fathers, the Tribe shall appropriate the amount prescribed in the By-Laws (not less than twenty fathoms), toward defraying the funeral expenses, to be paid to such person as the brother may designate; *provided*, that should the Relief Chiefs be satisfied that said benefits would be diverted from that purpose, they may see that said expenses are paid, not exceeding the amount specified in the By-Laws.

4. A member shall not be entitled to benefits for any disease or infirmity with which he was afflicted previous to his admission into the Tribe, nor when so afflicted as to prevent him from following his usual occupation but able to pursue some other business, or for any sickness or disability originating from intemperance or immoral conduct; or while any charge is pending against him, but, when he has been acquitted, after due trial, he may claim for the time, if otherwise entitled. A member, if unable to follow the hunt, when in arrears to the Tribe to the amount of more than three moons' dues and fines, cannot by payment of such arrears become entitled to benefits during that sickness or disability; nor can a member while receiving benefits become in arrears so as to debar him therefrom, it being the duty of the Sachem to pay to the Chief of Records, from the wampum drawn for his benefits, a sum sufficient to prevent his becoming in arrears to the Tribe to the amount of more than three moons' dues. No member shall be entitled to seven suns' or funeral benefits unless he shall have been a member of the Tribe for at least six moons.

5. In case the wampum shall at any time be reduced to a less amount than five feet for each member, or to less than fifty fathoms, the Tribe may make application to the Great Incohonee for a dispensation to suspend the payment of benefits, or to reduce the same below the amount fixed in their By-Laws. The resolution to apply must be read at two councils, and be adopted by a vote of two-thirds of the members present. The Great Incohonee, upon being satisfied of the inability of the Tribe, may grant such dispensation.

ARTICLE XX.

CHARGES AGAINST MEMBERS.

(See pages 562, 563, 564, 565, and 566, substituting for "Great Sachem" the words "Great Incohonee.") On page 566 substitute for Section 18 the following sections numbered 18 and 19.

18. A member three moons in arrears for fines or dues shall not be entitled to the password, hold chieftaincy or vote.

19. Any brother who shall refuse or neglect to pay his fines or dues, as

prescribed by the by-laws, for one great sun, shall be suspended, unless otherwise ordered by the Tribe.

General Instructions for Commissioners appointed by Tribes to take testimony (see page 566).

ARTICLE XXI.

Public Displays.

No concert, festival, or other public assemblage except funerals, shall be allowed without permission, nor shall any brother appear in the regalia or costume of the Order at any concert, festival, public assemblage or procession, unless by permission of the Great Council, Great Incohonee, or Deputy Great Incohonee.

ARTICLE XXII.

Kindling the Council Fire.

The council fire of this Tribe shall be kindled on such sleeps, and at such time, as the By-Laws may designate; *provided* that Sunday shall not be selected for regular councils.

ARTICLE XXIII.

Quorum and Dissolution.

1. Five members or more, including one qualified to preside, shall constitute a quorum for the transaction of business; and if a quorum only be present no wampum shall be appropriated (except for benefits) without unanimous consent.

2. A Tribe should not be dissolved as long as seven members are willing to continue it.

3. Should a Tribe become extinct, all the books, wampum, papers, regalia and other private matters shall be forwarded to the Great C. of R. of U. S.

ARTICLE XXIV.

Interpretation of Laws.

The provisions of this Constitution shall be interpreted and construed according to their most plain and obvious meaning; and should any doubt arise as to the proper construction of any clause or article thereof, it shall be referred to the Great Incohonee, whose decision shall be final, until reversed by the Great Council of U. S.

ARTICLE XXV.

Regalia.

No brother shall be permitted to wear any regalia except that belonging to his rank or station in the Tribe.

ARTICLE XXVI.

By-Laws — Alterations and Amendments.

1. By-Laws may be made by each Tribe for its special government, provided they do not contravene this Constitution, and shall have received the approval of the Committee on Constitution and Laws of the Great Council of United States.

2. No alteration or amendment can be made to this Constitution for five great suns, and not then unless the same be offered in writing at a regular stated Council of the Great Council of United States, and receive the votes of two-thirds of the members present at the next stated council, whereupon it shall become a part of this Constitution.

RULES OF ORDER.

1. The Sachem having taken his seat, the chiefs and brothers shall clothe themselves with appropriate regalia, take their respective seats, and at the sound of the tomahawk observe general silence.

2. The business shall be proceeded with in the order prescribed in the Charge Book.

3. The Sachem shall preserve order and pronounce the decision of the Tribe on all subjects; he shall decide questions of order without debate, subject to an appeal to the Tribe by any three brothers — on which appeal no brother shall speak more than once, when the question before the Tribe shall be: "Shall the decision of the Sachem stand as the judgment of the Tribe?" which question shall be taken by the Senior Sagamore.

4. During the reading of the records, communications, and other papers, or when a brother is addressing the Sachem or Tribe, silence shall be observed in the wigwam.

5. Any brother who shall misbehave himself in the council of the Tribe, disturb the order or harmony thereof, either by abusive, disorderly, or profane talk, or refuse obedience to the Sachem, shall be admonished of his offense by the presiding chief; and if he offend again, he shall be excluded from the wigwam for the sleep, and afterwards dealt with as the By-Laws prescribe.

6. No brother shall be interrupted while speaking, except it be to call him to order, or for the purpose of explanation.

7. If a brother, while speaking, be called to order, he shall, at the request of the Sachem, take his seat until the question of order is determined, and permission given him to proceed.

8. Every brother, when he speaks or offers a motion, shall rise and respectfully address the Sachem. Brothers speaking shall confine themselves to the question under debate and avoid all personality and indecorous language.

9. If two or more brothers rise to speak at the same time, the Sachem shall decide which is entitled to the floor.

10. No brother shall speak more than once on the same question until all the brothers wishing to speak shall have had an opportunity to do so, nor more than twice without permission of the Sachem. Each brother, while speaking, shall designate the chief or brother spoken of by his proper rank or title, according to his standing in the Order.

11. No motion shall be subject to debate until it shall have been seconded and stated from the chair. It shall be reduced to writing at the request of any member.

12. When a question is before the Tribe no motion shall be in order except to quench the council fire; to lay on the table; the previous question; to postpone indefinitely; to postpone for a certain time; to divide; to commit, or to amend — which motions shall severally have precedence in the order herein arranged.

13. No brother of another Tribe, except a chief of the Great Council, shall be allowed to speak without permission of the Sachem.

14. On the call of five brothers a majority of the Tribe may demand the previous question, which shall always be put in this form: "Shall the main question be now put?" and until it is decided shall preclude all further amendments and debate.

15. When a blank is to be filled the question shall be first taken upon the highest sum or number, and the longest and latest time proposed.

16. Any brother may call for a division of the question when the sense will admit of it; but a motion to strike out and insert shall be indivisible, except at the option of the mover.

17. Before putting a motion the Sachem shall ask: "Is the Tribe ready for the question?" If no brother rise to speak the Sachem shall rise and put the question; and after he has on that subject risen, no brother shall be permitted to speak.

18. All communications, petitions and memorials shall be presented through a brother of the Tribe, or by the Sachem. A brief statement of their contents shall be entered on the records.

19. Any brother may excuse himself from serving on a committee, if at the time of his appointment he is a member of two other committees. No brother can be appointed on a committee when absent from the Tribe.

20. The brother first named on a committee shall act as chairman until another is chosen by the brothers of the committee. The mover of a resolution referred to a special committee is usually the first named thereon.

21. No committee can be finally discharged until all the debts contracted by it shall have been paid.

22. A motion to quench the council fire is always in order after the regular business has been gone through, which motion shall be decided without debate; but, if decided in the affirmative, the council is not closed until the council fire is quenched in due form.

23. A motion to lie on the table shall be decided without debate.

24. When a question is postponed indefinitely it shall not be acted on during that or the next succeeding stated council.

25. No motion to reconsider a vote shall be received unless made by a brother who voted with the prevailing side in the first instance.

26. No brother shall be permitted to speak or vote unless clothed in regalia according to his rank or station in the Tribe.

27. On the call of five brothers, the yeas and nays shall be taken; when every brother shall vote, and the names and manner of voting shall be entered on the records.

FORMS.

" Forms for Charges," " Notice to Accused," " Form of Subpœna to Accused," " Form of Subpœna to Accuser or Witness," " Report of Committee," " Notice to Accused as to Report," and " Form of Appeal from the action of a Tribe " will be found on pages 567, 568, and 569.

DEGREE OF POCAHONTAS.

CONSTITUTION.

RULE I.

TITLE.

This body shall be known as ———— Council No. —, of the DEGREE OF POCAHONTAS, IMPROVED ORDER OF RED MEN.

RULE II.

MEMBERSHIP.

Any member of the Improved Order of Red Men who has been exalted to the Chief's degree, free white, and is in good standing in his Tribe, and any white woman over 18 years of age, of good moral character, shall be eligible to membership in any Council of the Degree of Pocahontas.

RULE III.

OBJECTS.

Among the objects of this Degree shall be the moral advancement of the members of the Improved Order of Red Men, their families and lady friends, for the promotion of social enjoyment among the members of the Degree, and the general welfare and prosperity of the Order.

RULE IV.

CHARTERS.

Charters may be granted by Great Councils to establish Councils in their jurisdiction upon the application of not less than twenty persons, ten of whom shall be members of the Improved Order of Red Men, who have been exalted to the Chief's Degree. The charter fee shall not be less than fifteen fathoms, for which the Council shall receive the charter, rituals, proposition book, and unwritten work of the Degree.

Councils shall be under the control of the Great Council within whose jurisdiction they may be located.

In jurisdictions where no Great Councils exist, application must be made to, and charters granted by, the Great Council of the United States, in accordance with Article XIII, Constitution, Great Council of the United States.

RULE V.
Councils.

Councils shall kindle their council fires at least once a moon.

RULE VI.
Chiefs.

1. The Elective Chiefs shall be Pocahontas, Wenonah and Powhatan, who shall be chosen by ballot, to serve six moons, and the Keeper of Records and Keeper of Wampum, who shall be chosen for twelve moons. The Council may select a Collector of Wampum to keep the wampum accounts of the Council.

2. The retiring Pocahontas shall fill the stump of Prophetess. At the institution of the Council the sister selected as Prophetess shall receive the honors of a Past Chief.

3. Past officers of organizations that were in existence prior to the promulgation of the Degree of Pocahontas, said bodies having accepted the provisions of the law, shall be entitled to the rank and honors of Past Chiefs.

4. The appointed Chiefs shall be two Scouts, two Runners, two Guards, two Counsellors and four Warriors, to be appointed by the Pocahontas.

RULE VII.
Raising up of Chiefs.

The raising up of Chiefs shall take place on the first council sleep of the term, unless a dispensation has been granted to postpone the same. Councils may have their Chiefs raised up in public, provided a dispensation has been first obtained.

RULE VIII.
Vacancies.

All vacancies by removal, death, suspension, resignation or otherwise, shall be filled by election or appointment, as the case may be, to serve the residue of the term, and the Chiefs so serving shall be entitled to the honors of the term.

RULE IX.
Application for Membership.

1. An application for adoption must be recommended by two members in good standing, and accompanied by one-half the adoption fee. The application shall be referred to a committee of three, who shall make a strict investigation of the health, character and qualifications of the applicant, and report at the next council.

2. Upon the report of the committee, a ballot shall be taken, and if two or more black twigs shall have been deposited, action on the application shall be deferred until the next stated council of the Council, when another ballot shall be had, and if not more than three of the twigs then cast are black, the candidate shall be declared elected. If rejected, the application shall not be renewed in any Council of the Order for the space of six moons thereafter.

3. No proposition for membership shall be withdrawn after it has been referred to a committee, except by unanimous consent, and in all cases a ballot shall be had whether the report be favorable or unfavorable.

4. No Council shall adopt a pale face resident of another State reservation unless by consent of the Great Sachem of such reservation.

5. Any member of the Degree holding a withdrawal card, desirous of becoming a member of a Council, shall make application as in case of a pale face, accompanying the application with a withdrawal card, which shall be referred to a committee of three, whose duty it shall be to report as to his or her standing and qualifications at a stated council, when a ballot shall be had, as in case of a pale face.

6. Application for a withdrawal card shall be made either personally or in writing, and the same shall be granted, provided the member is clear upon the books of the Council, free from charges, and there be no valid objections.

7. Any withdrawal card may be revoked for cause by the Council granting the same, and when so revoked the person holding said card shall be subject to the Council which issued the same. A withdrawal card may be renewed if lost or destroyed.

8. A member suspended for non-payment of dues, desirous of joining a Council in the same reservation, after one great sun's suspension, shall be entitled to receive, and the Council shall grant, upon proper application, a Dismissal Certificate upon the payment of not less than one fathom nor more than one great sun's dues.

9. A member suspended for non-payment of dues, wishing to regain membership in another reservation, shall be entitled to receive, and the Council shall grant, upon proper application, a Dismissal Certificate upon the receipt of not less than one fathom nor more than one great sun's dues.

10. In all cases wherein a Council has refused to reinstate a member suspended for non-payment of dues, he or she shall be entitled to receive, and the Council shall, upon proper application, grant a Dismissal Certificate upon the receipt of one fathom.

11. Dismissal Certificates may be received upon deposit in any Council,

under the same laws as withdrawal cards, but the privilege of visiting shall not be awarded to the holder of a dismissal Certificate.

RULE X.
Fees.

The admission fee shall not be less than one fathom.

RULE XI.
Duties of Chiefs.

The Chiefs shall perform the duties of similar Chiefs as are laid down in the rules for government of the Tribes of the Improved Order of Red Men, as adopted and promulgated by the Great Council in whose reservation they may be located.

RULE XII.
Laws.

1. Councils may establish laws for the carrying into effect the beneficial feature of the Improved Order of Red Men, by the enactment of laws providing for the payment of seven suns and funeral benefits.
2. Councils must have a seal with an appropriate device, which shall be affixed to all official documents emanating therefrom.
3. A member shall at all times be allowed to visit and attend any Council of the Degree, in conformity with the ritual, provided he or she is legally in possession of the password.
4. Charges, trials and penalties against members of the Degree of Pocahontas, shall be governed by the Code of Procedure, as adopted by the Great Council of the United States.

RULE XIII.
By-Laws.

Councils may establish By-Laws for their own government, provided they do not contravene these rules, and the laws and usages of the Order, but the same shall not go into effect until they receive the approval of the proper authority under whose jurisdiction they are.

RULE XIV.
Report.

Great Councils shall make out and present to the G. C. of R. of G. C. of U. S. a report every great sun of the standing of the Councils of the Degree of Pocahontas under their jurisdiction.

RULE XV.

Districts — Tax — Great Sun Council.

1. Great Councils may establish Districts in their reservations, and they may provide that the Great Sachem may appoint a Deputy to act as the representative of the Great Sachem, who shall have charge of the Councils located in the District.
2. Past Chiefs shall be eligible to the chieftaincy of Deputy.
3. Great Councils may enact laws taxing Councils of this degree.
4. Great Councils may establish rules by which a Great Sun Council of the members of the Degree of Pocahontas can be held at such time and place as they may deem proper, and regulations designating the business that may be transacted thereat. At such councils, Past Chiefs, Past Sachems who are members, and those who may be selected as representatives from the various councils, shall be entitled to a seat and a voice in the deliberations.

RULES OF ORDER.

1. The Pocahontas having taken her seat, the chiefs and members will clothe themselves with appropriate regalia, take their respective seats, and at the sound of the tomahawk there shall be general silence.
2. The business shall be proceeded with in the manner prescribed in the Charge Book.
3. The Pocahontas shall preserve order and pronounce the decision of the Council on all subjects; she shall decide questions of order without debate, subject to an appeal to the Council by any three members — on which appeal no member shall speak more than once, when the question before the Council shall be: "Shall the decision of the Pocahontas stand as the judgment of the Council?" which question shall be taken by the Wenonah.
4. During the reading of the records, communications, and other papers, and when a member is addressing the Pocahontas or Council, silence shall be observed in the wigwam.
5. Any members who shall misbehave in the council, disturb the order or the harmony thereof, either by abusive, disorderly, or profane language, or shall refuse obedience to the Pocahontas, shall be admonished of their offense, and if they offend again, they shall be excluded from the teepee for the sleep, and afterwards dealt with as the By-Laws prescribe.
6. No member shall be interrupted while speaking, except it be to be called to order, or for the purpose of explanation.
7. If a member, while speaking, be called to order, he shall, at the request of the Pocahontas, take his seat until the question of order is determined, and permission given him to proceed.
8. Every member, when speaking or offering a motion, shall rise and respectfully address the Pocahontas. Members speaking shall confine them-

selves to the question under debate and avoid all personality and indecorous language.

9. If two or more members rise to speak at the same time, the Pocahontas shall decide which is entitled to the floor.

10. No member shall speak more than once on the same question until all the members wishing to speak shall have had an opportunity to do so, nor more than twice without permission of the Pocahontas. Each member, while speaking, shall designate the chief or member spoken of by their proper rank or title, according to their standing in the Order.

11. No motion shall be subject to debate until it shall have been seconded and stated from the chair. It shall be reduced to writing at the request of any member.

12. When a question is before the Council no motion shall be in order except to quench the council fire; to lay on the table; for the previous question; to postpone indefinitely; to postpone for a certain time; to divide; to commit, or to amend — which motions shall severally have precedence in the order herein arranged.

13. No member, except a chief of the Great Council, or a member of the Council, shall be allowed to speak without permission of the Pocahontas.

14. On the call of three members a majority of the Council may demand the previous question, which shall always be put in this form: "Shall the main question be now put?" and until it is decided shall preclude all further amendments and debate.

15. When a blank is to be filled the question shall be first taken upon the highest sum or number, and the longest and latest time proposed.

16. Any member may call for a division of the question when the sense will admit of it; but a motion to strike out and insert shall be indivisible, except at the option of the mover.

17. Before putting the question the Pocahontas shall ask: "Is the Council ready for the question?" If no member rises to speak the Pocahontas shall rise and put it; and after she has risen, no member shall be permitted to speak.

18. All communications, petitions and memorials shall be presented through a member of this Council or by the Pocahontas. A brief statement of their contents shall be entered on the records.

19. Any member may be excused from serving on a committee, if at the time of his appointment he is on two other committees. No member can be appointed on a committee when absent from the Council.

20. The member first named on a committee shall act as chairman until another is chosen by the members of the committee. The mover of a resolution referred to a special committee is usually the first named thereon.

21. No committee can be finally discharged until all the debts contracted by it shall have been paid.

22. A motion to quench the council fire is always in order after the regular business has been gone through, which motion shall be decided without debate. If decided in the affirmative, it is not quenched until the council is closed in due form.

23. A motion to lie on the table shall be decided without debate.

24. When a question is postponed indefinitely it shall not be acted on during that or the next succeeding stated council.

25. A motion to reconsider the vote upon any question in a Council must be made at the same Council, but its consideration may be postponed to a subsequent Council, but cannot be received unless made by a member who voted with the majority in the first instance.

26. No brother shall be permitted to speak or vote unless clothed in regalia.

27. On the call of three members, the yeas and nays shall be ordered; when every member shall vote, and the names and manner of voting shall be entered on the records.

CHAPTER XIII.

DEGREE OF POCAHONTAS.

IN all ages the poet has sung and the historian has written of the influence of woman upon the destinies of the world. Her assistance has made success possible where without it failure was inevitable. Her refining influence has lifted man from the base and sordid passions inherent to his nature and brought him, if not to perfection, yet a little nearer the divine ideal. What more appropriate, then, than that she should be called upon, and her influential co-operation secured in an organization like ours, whose mission is "to visit the sick, to relieve the distressed, bury the dead, and to educate the orphan." On woman falls the chief burden of sorrow which the trials and tribulations of the world visit, as a seemingly inevitable legacy, upon mankind. Like gold from the crucible, she emerges from the sorrow and becomes at once the guide and consolation of man, — guiding him to a better life and consoling him in misfortune and distress.

Nearly fifty years ago the first attempt was made to engraft upon the laws of the Order legislation which should provide for an auxiliary branch, or degree, into which might be admitted the female relatives of members of the Order. The various attempts in this direction are recorded in that chapter of this history devoted to the extracts from the written records of the Great Council of the United States. It will there be seen that the Great Council of the United States steadily refused to give heed to the appeals made in behalf of such a degree, and it was not until the council of the Great Council of the United States held at Elmira, N.Y., in G.S.D. 394 (September, 1885), that positive action was taken and legislation adopted which permitted the establishment of Councils of the Degree of Pocahontas. At this council rules and regulations were adopted

THE CAPTIVE'S RESCUE.

to go into effect on and after January 1, 1886, under which Councils of the degree could be organized. At the following council of the Great Council of the United States, held at Detroit in 1886, a ritual was presented and adopted.

This legislation was taken upon recommendation of the Great Council of Massachusetts in whose reservation an organization had been in existence for two years known as Pocahontas Council, No. 1, of Marblehead, Mass. Immediately after the promulgation of the rituals governing the degree, this organization was transformed into a Council of the Degree of Pocahontas.

The first Council of the Degree, instituted under the legal and recognized laws of the Great Council of the United States, was Wenonah Council, No. 1, of Philadelphia, Pa., whose council fire was lighted on the 28th sleep of Cold moon, G. S. D. 396 (February 28, 1887), at Red Men's wigwam, 928 Race Street, in that city.

The name of the degree is taken from the celebrated character in Indian history, Pocahontas, whose brief life presents a touching and beautiful picture of grace, beauty, and virtue, as well as of constant friendship to the palefaces, who repaid friendship and hospitality with ingratitude and treachery.

We present herewith the legend of her life.

In the winter of 1607-8 Captain John Smith proceeded up the Chickahominy River for the purpose of exploration. He fell into an ambush, and was captured by a band of Indians, two or three hundred in number, under the command of Opechancanough, Sachem of the Pamunkeys, a reputed brother of Powhatan. In trying to escape, Captain Smith fell into a swamp and was finally captured. He escaped immediate death by diverting the attention of his captors with a round ivory double compass-dial which he presented to Opechancanough. He was tied to a tree for the purpose of execution, but the chief in command interceded, his execution was postponed, and he was conducted to the camp of Powhatan. On his arrival, the women and children flocked around to gaze upon a being so different from any they had ever seen before. The warriors of the tribe immediately began a grand war dance, which Captain Smith describes in these words : " A good time they continued this exercise, and then cast themselves in a ring dancing in such severall postures, and singing and yelling out such hellish notes and screeches, being strangely paynted, every one his quiver of arrowes, and at his backe a club; on his arme a fox or an otter's skinne, or some such matter for a vambrace; their heads and shoulders paynted red, with oyle and pocones mingled together, which scarlet-like color made an exceeding handsome show; his bow in his hand, and the skinne of a bird with her wings abroad dryed, tyed of his head; a piece of copper, a white shell, a long feather, with a small rattle growing at the tayls of their snaks tyed, or some such like toy." The dance was three times renewed, Smith and the Sachem standing in the centre of the band of warriors.

For several days Captain Smith was kept by the Indians, and feasted with unbounded hospitality. On arriving at the village, he was detained until Powhatan could receive him in proper state. It was said that he was then introduced to the Chief, the multitude hailing him with a tremendous shout as he walked in. Powhatan — a majestic and finely-formed savage, with a marked countenance, and an air of haughtiness, sobered down into gravity by a life of sixty years — was seated before a fire, clothed in a robe of raccoon skins, with all the tails hanging over him. Around him sat the chiefs and other members of the tribe. All had their heads and shoulders painted red; many had their hair decked with the white down of birds. Some wore a great chain of white beads about their necks, but no one was without ornament of some kind. Then followed a long and solemn council to determine the fate of the captive. It was decided he must die. Two large stones were brought in before the Chief, and Smith was laid upon them, his head placed in position for beating out his brains with clubs. At the fatal moment when the weapons were raised and the blows about to be given, Pocahontas, the daughter of Powhatan, rushed forward, and earnestly entreated with tears that the captive might be saved. Her request was at first rejected, and the signal given to the executioners to complete their work. Pocahontas then knelt down, put her arms about Smith, laid her head over his, and declared he should not be killed, except she first perished. Powhatan relented; the decree was reversed, and the life of

Captain Smith was saved. The Captain was detained as a prisoner for two days longer, and then sent under guard to Jamestown.

This celebrated scene is preserved in a beautiful piece of sculpture over the western door of the Rotunda of the Capitol at Washington. The group consists of five figures, representing the precise moment when Pocahontas, by her interposition, saved Smith from being executed. Smith is attired in military dress, reclining on his elbow, his body extended ready to receive the death blow from the war mace of the Indian who stands near his head.

All the information which comes down to us describes Pocahontas as being a woman of remarkable grace, beauty, and kindness of heart. Frequently by her interposition and friendly warning the Colony at Jamestown was saved from destruction. She was married to Mr. John Rolfe, by whom she was taken to England. There she was received at Court by both the King and Queen with the most flattering marks of attention. Concerning her death it is thus written: "It is the last and saddest office of history to record the death of this incomparable woman, in about the 22d year of her age. This event took place at Gravesend where she was preparing to embark to Virginia with her husband and child." They were to have gone out in 1617, and suitable accommodations had been made on the ship of the Admiral. It was also recorded that she died as she had long lived, a most sincere and pious Christian. Her death was a happy mixture of Indian fortitude and Christian submission, affecting all those who saw her by her beauty and virtue which were marked characteristics of her life. Of the character of Pocahontas, it is remarked that considering all circumstances it is not surpassed by any in the whole range of history; and that for those qualities which more especially do honor to our nature — a humane and feeling heart, and unshaken constancy in her attachments — she stands almost without a rival. She gave evidence of possessing, in a high degree, every attribute of mind and heart which should be and has been the ornament and pride of civilized woman in all countries and times. Her unwearied kindness to the English was entirely disinterested; she encountered danger and suffering, and every kind of opposition and difficulty to bestow it; and her aid was given modestly and unostentatiously, and without wish for or hope of reward.

In 1892 the Bishop of Indiana visited England, and in an article written after his return he says: —

"This noble Indian Princess, Pocahontas, of Virginia, was buried in the chancel of St. George's Church, Gravesend, England. The knowledge gained is from the church register, dated March 27, 1617. There is no monument in the church, as it was destroyed by fire in 1727. She had been on a visit to England with her husband, where she had been received at court and was about to return to Virginia, when she was taken sick aboard ship at Gravesend and died, and her body was taken ashore and buried. The rector of St. George's Church is about undertaking the restoration of the church and extending the church. It would seem proper that some memorial of this distinguished Princess, and friend of the whites in the early settlement of Virginia, should be placed in this church where she was buried. Of course, Rebecca Rolfe, as she was known after her marriage, was converted and a church woman."

From the register of her burial the following is copied: —

"March 27, 1617.
"Rebecca Rolfe, the wife of John Rolfe gentleman, a Virginia lady born, is buried in this chancel."

From Pocahontas some of the proudest families of Virginia have been pleased to trace their lineage. The numerous descendants of her son have been noted for their integrity, ability, and culture, and have always ranked among the most distinguished Virginians. Of these John Randolph was a conspicuous example. It is related that an exciting debate took place in the House of Representatives at Washington, on one side of which was Mr. Randolph, and on the other, Mr. Jackson, also of Virginia. Mr. Randolph had spoken and Mr. Jackson arose to reply. He had not proceeded far when, having occasion to refer to some part of the speech of Mr. Randolph, he alluded to him as "My friend from Virginia." He had scarcely given utterance to the word "friend," when Mr. Randolph sprang to his feet, and looking first at Mr. Jackson and then at the Speaker, keeping his arm extended meantime, and his long bony finger pointed at Mr. Jackson, said in his peculiar voice: —

"Mr. Speaker! I am not that gentleman's friend, Sir. I have never been his friend, Sir, nor do I ever mean to be his friend, Sir!"

He then took his seat.

Mr. Jackson, meantime keeping his position on the floor, looking first at Mr. Randolph and then at the Speaker, replied:

"Mr. Speaker, I am at a loss to know by what title to address the honorable member from Virginia." Then pausing awhile with his finger beside his nose, he said: "I have it, Sir — I have it — it shall be " — looking Mr. Randolph full in the face — "The Right Honorable Descendant of Her Majesty, Queen Pocahontas!"

The entire countenance of Mr. Randolph changed instantly from a look of mingled aversion and contempt to a smile the most complaisant and gracious, and he bowed most courteously, giving evidence that of all the honors he ever coveted, that of having descended from Pocahontas was the one he most highly prized.

It seems fitting to conclude this chapter with the lines attributed to Miss F. N. Caulkins, of New Haven, Conn., based upon the following: —

"Pocahontas, having renounced the religion of her ancestors, was baptized in the small, rude church at Jamestown, by the name of Rebecca. In Captain Smith's account of her, she is called 'the first Christian ever of that nation — the first Virginian that ever spoke English.' Again he says — 'In London, divers courtiers, and others of my acquaintances, have gone with me to see her, that generally concluded God had a great hand in her conversion.'"

"Not thou, the red-browned heroine, whose breast
Screened the brave captive from the axe's gleam;
Not Pocahontas, lov'd, renown'd, caress'd,
But meek Rebecca, is my gentle theme.

"And yet she was a nut-brown maid, a child
Of tawny lineage — but of aspect bright —
A sunny gleam that through the woodlands wild,
Ran freely on, in her own path of light;

"A golden arrow darting from the bow;
A song-bird warbling in the lonely shade;
A mountain stream, in whose meand'ring flow,
The depth of Heaven, its own pure blue surveyed.

"Star of Virginia, in her darkest hour,
　Her joy, her theme of glory and of song;
　Her wild red rose, that in the Stuart's bower
　Shed grace — not took it — from the courtly throng.

"Her — her I sing not — and yet her I sing —
　Freed from earth-worship, cleansed from rites obscene;
　Who, from unnumber'd gods, to Zion's King
　Escaping, waves her palm of deathless green.

"She prays — celestial brightness gilds her face,
　And to resplendence fades her olive dye;
　She prays — the howling demons of her race,
　Bewilder'd, from the dazzling vision fly.

"With folded arms before the fount she stood —
　Encircled by the hush'd and rev'rent air;
　Her upward glance was a sweet hymn to God —
　Her downward look, a soul-suffusing prayer.

"The heavenly manna dropping from the shrine,
　She gathered in her heart, and, bending low,
　Bound her green leaf upon the living vine,
　And felt its fragrant shadow round her flow.

"First Convert of the West! The Indian child
　A matron stands — from whose sweet tongue
　Flows the pure stream of English, undefil'd —
　Flows the deep anthem, and eternal song.

"She died afar — no pilgrim finds her tomb —
　Unknown the spot, yet holy is the ground;
　The Saviour's breath there left its rich perfume,
　And angels keep their guardian watch around.

"As Pocahontas, while these skies remain,
　Still our Zodiac show the Virgin sign;
　But, as Rebecca, when yon stars shall wane,
　Yon Heavens roll by, she, as a star, shall shine."

THE PALEFACE FRIEND.

CHAPTER XIV.

CHIEFTAINS' LEAGUE.

THE desire for a uniformed rank in the Order became manifest when the tide of prosperity came in, and the permanence of the organization seemed assured. The success of similar side degrees in other organizations led men to suppose that the same influence would be exerted upon our Order, if a degree could be added, principally social in its nature, and whose members could adopt a uniform, appropriate and attractive, to be used on public occasions.

Attempts were made at various times to secure favorable action by the Great Council of the United States, but it was not until the council held at Elmira, N.Y., Corn moon, G. S. D. 394 (September, 1885), that the consent of the G. C. U. S. was obtained and legislation adopted laying the groundwork for the Chieftains' League.

At the above council Representative Henry Poole, of Michigan, presented a document relating to a uniformed rank to be known as the "Knights of Tammany," which was referred to the Committee on State of the Order. The Committee, after duly considering the subject, reported, "that there is a call in some jurisdictions for a Uniformed Degree, is beyond question, and it is time to accede to that call." The Committee also recommended that the Great Chiefs, assisted by a special committee of five, be appointed to report rules and rituals for said Uniformed Degree. The report was adopted, and the Great Chiefs, with Past Great Incohonee A. J. Baker, of Pennsylvania, and Charles H. Litchman, of Massachusetts, and Representatives Henry Poole, of Michigan, August Graf, of Missouri, and George T. Fowler, of Maryland, were appointed as the special committee recommended.

At the council of the Great Council of the United States, held in the city of Detroit, Mich., G. S. D. 395, this special committee submitted a report containing a code of laws for the government of the Uniformed Degree. The committee instead of recommending "Knights of Tammany," substituted the name "Chieftains' League," for the title of the new branch of the Order. It also recommended that the ceremony for the Beneficial Degree Councils be used as the ceremony for the Uniformed Degree. A new ritual, however, was adopted.

Immediately after the laws establishing the Uniformed Degree were promulgated, Beneficial Degree Councils were merged into Chieftains' Leagues, and new Leagues sprang up in every section of the great reservation. Two State Leagues were formed, Pennsylvania and New Jersey. At the next council of the Great Council of the United States, held at Wilmington, Del., G. S. D. 396, Representatives from State Leagues applied for admission, and the members of the Great Council of the United States realized that a mistake had been made in framing the laws governing the Uniformed Degree, which provided for representation from State Leagues in accordance with the laws governing representation for State Great Councils. The difficulty was compromised for the time by admitting one Representative from each State League.

The ritual which was adopted had at previous councils of the G. C. U. S. been presented by the advocates of a higher degree. The Chiefs were known as Bashaba, Senior Paniese, Junior Paniese, Mishinewa, Prophet, Keeper of Records, Keeper of Wampum, and Sannap.

From the first there seemed to be considerable friction between the League and the Order. This friction was due not to any desire on the part of the members of the League in any way to embarrass the Order. On the contrary, those whose influence was strongest in its establishment were among the most faithful members of the Order. But so much of the time of the Great Council of the United States was taken up in the consideration of legislation affecting the degree, that many of the members of the G. C. U. S. expressed regret that the Degree had been authorized. This feeling manifested itself strongly at the council held at Chicago, in G. S. D. 397, but culminated finally at the council held at Baltimore, G. S. D. 398, at which, by an almost unanimous vote, resolutions were adopted as follows: —

"*Resolved*, That all Leagues and Great Leagues of Red Men, in the jurisdiction of this Great Council, shall on and after the 1st sun of Sturgeon moon, G. S. D., 398, be an independent organization, and not subject to any laws or regulations of this Great Council, but are hereby authorized to form their own Great League of the United States from the Leagues and Great Leagues now existing.

"*Resolved*, That the Great Leagues or subordinate Leagues shall not transgress in any way upon the Constitutional Laws of the Improved Order of Red Men, and that present Chieftains of the various Leagues, be entitled to the same honors and privileges as though they had served to the full end of their term, and that Leagues shall not accept or retain members in the Chieftains' League, unless said members first be members in good standing of the Chief's Degree of the Improved Order of Red Men, and to retain membership in the League members must continue membership in their respective Tribes."

Immediately after the quenching of the council fire, a meeting of members of the Chieftains' League was held at which Past Great Incohonee Ralph S. Gregory, of Indiana, presided, and Past Great Sachem William J. Dinsmore, of Massachusetts, acted as Secretary. The Chairman and Secretary were directed to issue a call for a meeting of Representatives of all Leagues to be held in New York City on the 16th of Cold moon, G. S. D. 399.

This meeting was held and a large number of Representatives was present. Past Great Sachem William J. Dinsmore, of Massachusetts, was elected Chairman, and Past Great Sachem Thomas D. Tanner, of Pennsylvania, Secretary.

Resolutions were adopted asking the Great Council of the United States to reconsider its action and to give the League another hearing.

A resolution was adopted to form a permanent organization, to be known and styled "THE NATIONAL CHIEFTAINS' LEAGUE OF THE UNITED STATES."

Committees were appointed to draft a code of laws and to prepare a ritual, uniform, and a Manual of Arms and Drill.

Past Great Incohonee George B. Colflesh, of Maryland, was elected Treasurer.

The first regular meeting of the National League was held at Red Men's Hall, Philadelphia, 21st sun, Worm moon, G. S. D. 399 (March 21, 1890).

At this meeting a ritual was adopted, and a code of laws, uniform, and a Manual of Arms and Drill.

At this meeting, also, a declaration was made stating the causes leading to the organization of the League, and a Preamble adopted, as follows : —

HISTORICAL.

The Chieftains' League was created as a higher degree of the Improved Order of Red Men, by the Great Council of the United States, and that august body, in its wisdom, deeming it impracticable to properly legislate for an Order or Branch with whom many of its members had no connection, saw fit, on the 12th sun, Corn moon, G. S. D. 398, in Great Council assembled, in the city of Baltimore, Md., to grant the Chieftains' Leagues their independence, thus permitting only members of the Leagues to legislate for its advancement.

Delegates from the various Leagues in the United States assembled in the city of New York, on the 16th sun, Cold moon, G. S. D. 399, accepted the conditions expressed by the Great Council, and organized the "National Chieftains' League of the United States," and elected temporary Chieftains; adjourning to meet in Red Men's League Room, Philadelphia, on the 21st sun, Worm moon, where the permanent organization was perfected, and the following Constitution, General Laws, etc., adopted, the Supreme Chieftains being elected on the 21st sun of Worm moon, when adjournment was taken, the National League to be reconvened in Boston on Wednesday following the first Tuesday of Corn moon, G. S. D. 399.

PREAMBLE.

Objects of the Chieftains' League.

1st. The first great object of the Chieftains' League is, through its organization, to call especial attention to the unsurpassed benevolent, protective fraternity of the Improved Order of Red Men ; an Order conceived, born, and bred of true American patriotism, honor, benevolence, and charity, and one of the worthiest and most sublime stars in the constellation of secret fraternal institutions, shedding its effulgent lustre over humanity's pathway, dispelling the darkness and gloom of "man's inhumanity to man," easing the burdensome trials and vicissitudes of life, and making clear the divinely constructed and broad brotherhood of mankind.

2d. To unite in still stronger bonds of fraternal affection; to promote increased benevolence and charity, and to give all moral and material aid possible to members of the Improved Order of Red Men who may become associated with this branch of the Order.

3d. To establish a thorough, effective, uniformed rank, and well disciplined semi-military degree or adjunct to the Improved Order of Red Men.

In relation to conferring honors upon members of Chieftains' Leagues, already existing, the following was made a law : —

"All Leagues and State Leagues now in existence accepting the provisions of the Constitution and Laws of the National Chieftains' League shall be granted a charter free of expense, and be entitled to all privileges and emoluments prescribed therein, and all Past Sachems or present Sachems serving to the end of their term, and who are members of Chieftains' Leagues in good standing now, shall be recognized as Past Chieftains.

"Past Great Incohonees and the present Great Incohonee, if now members in good standing of Chieftains' Leagues, and Past Great Sachems and all present Great Sachems serving to the end of their term, now members in good standing of Chieftains' Leagues, shall be accorded the honors of Past Supreme and Past Superior Chieftains respectively. Also, duly accredited Representatives to the preliminary and Constitutional Convention for the formation of the National Chieftains' League of the United States shall be Past Supreme Representatives.

"The President of the preliminary and Constitutional Convention shall be entitled to the rank and honor of Past Supreme Chieftain, and all elected and appointed Chieftains of the National Chieftains' League, and serving to the end of the first term, shall be entitled to the full honors as though having served for one full great sun, and all Past Chieftains, as determined by this Article, participating in the formation of the National Chieftains' League of the United States, shall be eligible to any elective or appointed chieftaincy at the first election of the National Chieftains' League of the United States."

As a matter of historical interest and record, we give the Chieftains elected at the formation of the National League. They were as follows:—

Supreme Chieftain,	GEORGE E. GREEN,	New York.
1st Vice Supreme Chieftain,	Z. R. ROBBINS,	Connecticut.
2d Vice Supreme Chieftain,	PAOLA SALSBURY,	California.
Sitting Past Supreme Chieftain,	WILLIAM J. KAIN,	Pennsylvania.
Supreme Recorder,	T. D. TANNER,	Pennsylvania.
Supreme Treasurer,	GEORGE B. COLFLESH,	Maryland.
Supreme Messenger,	GEORGE H. MOSS,	New York.
Supreme Sentinel,	CHARLES BROWN,	New Jersey.
Major General,	J. F. HEFFERNAN,	Illinois.

It was arranged that the annual sessions of the National League should be held at the place where, and just previous to the time at which, the council fire of the G. C. U. S. is kindled. Accordingly, the next annual session was held at Cleveland, O., in Corn moon, G. S. D. 400, at which the uniform of the League was changed to that of the Continental army, a description of which is as follows:—

Hat. — *For Officers:* The three-cornered Continental hat of black felt, four-inch round crown, four-and-a-half-inch brim, trimmed as follows: *General Officers:* white plume, five inches in height above the cockade in which it is supported. Cockade made of blue cloth, of material of coat, cut circular, two-and-a-half inches in diameter, on a box-plaited bow, five inches long, of buff cloth, of material of pants. In centre of cockade, gilt or brass letters, "C. L.," inclosed in circle one-and-a-half inches in diameter, surmounted by spread eagle. Hat to be trimmed one-half inch from edge of brim with one-quarter-inch gold braid. *Line and Field Officers:* same hat as General Officers, with exception of plume of royal purple to within one inch of top, which shall be white, and one-eighth-inch gold braid for trimming. *Non-Commissioned Officers, Musicians, and Privates,* wear hat of same style and material as officers, four inch round crown, three-and-a-half-inch brim, with half-inch buff leather trimming on edge of brim, dark-blue plume, four inches high, above cockade of blue cloth in circle one-and-a-half inches in diameter, on circular ground of buff cloth two-and-a-half inches in diameter; on face of cockade to be placed brass or gilt letters, "C. L.," in monogram.

Uniform of General and Field Officers.

Coat. — *General and Field Officers:* Double-breasted Continental coat pattern of 1776, of dark-blue material, known as Middlesex broadcloth, with facings and linings of skirt of buff of same material (sample of shades and quality of material furnished by the Supreme Officers). Buttons on front of coat of plain brass or gilt, one inch in diameter; balance of buttons of same size covered with buff cloth same as facing. Patterns and details of coat in accompanying illustration. *Line Officers:* single-breasted Continental coat, pattern of 1776, of same color and material as that of Field Officers. Patterns and details in accompanying illustration. *Non-commissioned Officers, Musicians, and Privates:* same coat as Line Officers.

Vest. — The long cutaway Continental vest, cut high, as in

Uniform of Captain and Line Officers.   Uniform of Musicians and Privates.

illustration, of buff Middlesex broadcloth, as per sample, buttoned with nine small brass or gilt buttons of one-half inch diameter, military collar, four-inch square flap for pocket. This vest for all officers and privates.

Pants. — *For all Officers and Privates:* knee-pants of barndoor pattern, extending just below the knee, with ten-inch opening on side, buttoned with four small plain brass buttons, same as vest, fastened at extreme bottom with straps of material of pants, and nickel buckles, material buff, same as vest.

Leggins. — *For all Commissioned Officers:* Black enamelled leather boots, or top-boot leggins extending to top of knee in front, and sloping to top of calf of leg in rear.

Mounted officers wear spurs.

Non-commissioned Officers and Privates: White duck spring-bottom leggins (spring bottom extending to vamp of shoe), extending two inches above the knee, cut shapely to the leg, buttoned with plain brass or gilt buttons, same as on vest, fastened under instep with strap of same material, and nickel buckle.

Equipments. — *General Officers:* U.S. Regulation Epaulet, with appropriate insignia ; regulation straight sword, with white grip and nickel scabbard, suspended at left side by two-and-a-half inch white webbed cotton cross-belt over right shoulder, under vest, attached to sword with white leather thong.

Field and Line Officers. — U.S. regulation epaulet with proper insignia, regulation straight sword with black grip and scabbard suspended on left side in same manner as General Officers with black leather thong.

Non-commissioned Officers, Musicians, and Privates wear white-webbed cotton cross-belts, two and a quarter inches in width, suspending on the left side outside of coat the sword, and on the right a cartridge-box, belts to cross in front of centre of body, fastened there by polished brass plate or shield with silver letters, T. O. T. E. diagonally across the face thereof.

Sword. — Silver or nickel cross-hilt, straight sword, white grip, black scabbard, nickel trimmed, fastened to cross-belt by black enamelled leather thong.

Cartridge-box of black enamelled leather, six inches wide, four inches deep, with brass letters I. O. R. M. on centre of face thereof.

In cold or stormy weather capes may be worn as follows : —

For commissioned officers, dark-blue mackintosh, double cape, buff lined, cape to extend to within one foot of ground, outside cape, extending to tip of fingers, with arm at natural length.

Non-commissioned officers, musicians, and privates, dark-blue mackintosh, buff-lined cape extending to the knee, with four-inch collar.

Mounted officers may wear regulation gauntlet gloves; all others white cotton or lisle-thread.

Regulation chevrons for non-commissioned officers, of white material.

It is further ordered and directed that on all parades of the Chieftains' Leagues, in the uniform of the League, the national flag of the United States shall be carried.

There shall be at least two musicians detailed from each company, one of which shall be a fifer and the other a snare drummer.

At the council of the G. C. U. S., held immediately after, the good-will of the members thereof was expressed towards the League, by the adoption of a preamble, and resolutions which quoted the declaration of objects stated in the Preamble of the League, already given, and which concluded as follows, —

"*Whereas*, It is fitting that this Great Council shall manifest its appreciation of the effort being made, through the instrumentality of said body, to build up and strengthen the Order; therefore

"*Resolved*, That it is the sense of this Great Council that the Chieftains' League is a valuable auxiliary to the Improved Order of Red Men, and we earnestly commend it to the favorable consideration of the members at large, as deserving of their warmest support."

Leagues are now in existence in Alabama, Colorado, California, Connecticut, Illinois, Indiana, Iowa, Kansas, Maryland, New Hampshire, New Jersey, New York, Ohio, Pennsylvania, Rhode Island, Washington (State), and West Virginia.

The present Supreme Chieftains are: —

Supreme Chieftain,	THOMAS K. DONNALLEY,	Pennsylvania.
1st Vice Supreme Chieftain,	JOSEPH PYLE,	Delaware.
2d Vice Supreme Chieftain,	WILLIAM G. MOCK,	Pennsylvania.
Sitting Past Supreme Chieftain,	E. S. BORTEL,	Pennsylvania.
Supreme Recorder,	THOMAS D. TANNER,	Pennsylvania.
Supreme Treasurer,	GEORGE B. COLFLESH,	Maryland.
Supreme Messenger,	C. J. VAUGHAN,	Georgia.
Supreme Sentinel,	W. E. DAVIS,	Iowa.
Major General,	CHARLES F. TUPPER,	New York.

The information concerning the Chieftains' League herein presented, is furnished through the kindness of Supreme Recorder Thomas D. Tanner. He further reports the present condition of the League as very encouraging. Wherever public display has been made of the handsome uniform adopted, the result has been beneficial, both to the League and to the Order. With proper support on the part of the members of the Order, there is every reason to hope that the National Chieftains' League will prove itself a valuable adjunct to the Improved Order of Red Men.

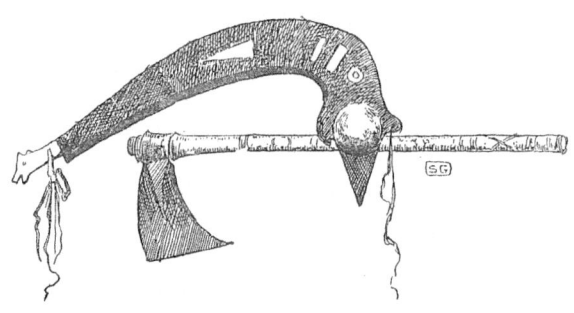

INVOKING THE GREAT SPIRIT

CHAPTER XV.

THE DEGREES OF THE ORDER. — THE THEORY OF THEIR CONSTRUCTION. — THE LESSONS TAUGHT.

NEARLY all fraternal and benevolent organizations have certain ceremonies, forms of initiation, or methods by which the uninformed are brought into full fellowship, and the society made secure from intrusion. These forms and ceremonies comprise the ritualistic work, and connected with them is usually a sign language by which the affiliated can be known to each other, even if speaking different languages.

Whether these ritualistic ceremonies symbolize the building of a temple, the valor, struggles, and martyrdom of the Crusaders, the friendship of Jonathan and David, the constancy of Damon and Pythias, or whatever may be the lesson they seek to teach, all claim to preach and secure the practice of the great principles of human brotherhood, and to bring about the realization, as far as possible by human agency, of the Fatherhood of God and the Brotherhood of Man.

While great age may be claimed for other organizations, and attempts made, with greater or less success, to trace their origin to the dim traditions of the past, to a time when the memory of man runneth not to the contrary, it seems sufficient for our claim to establish the fact that the ritualistic work of the Improved Order of Red Men, like its origin, is purely American. It stands, and must ever stand, original, unique, and distinct, growing more instead of less valuable and interesting with the lapse of time, and eventually giving to posterity its only realistic demonstration of those mystic ceremonies known only in the record of the past, and which must otherwise fade into oblivion. Founded, as has been said, on the manners, traditions, and customs of the Aborigines of the American continent, it portrays an existence more fascinating the more studied, the most interesting when most faithfully portrayed. It is a record which will give to future generations their only knowledge of the manners and customs of that race as practised in their sylvan home, and by which their people were bound together in the strong bonds of amity and love.

The work of the Order is divided into four sections or degrees, — Adoption, Hunter's, Warrior's, and Chief's, — each of which illustrates a phase of Indian character, custom, or ceremonies.

Commencing with the Adoption (or initiation) degree, the ceremony exemplifies the ancient form of adoption, or naturalization, used by the primitive Red Men. Concerning this, in his admirable work descriptive of the League of the Iroquois, Mr. Lewis H. Morgan says: —

"The Iroquois never exchanged prisoners with Indian nations, nor ever sought to reclaim their own people from captivity among them. Adoption or torture were the alternative chances of the captive. If adopted, the allegiance and affections of the captive were transferred to his adopted nation. When the Indian went forth to war, he emphatically took his life in his hand, knowing that if he was taken it would be forfeited by the laws of war; and if saved by adoption, his country, at least, was lost forever. From the foundation of the Confederacy, the custom of adoption has prevailed among the Iroquois, who carried this principle farther than any other Indian nations. It was not confined to captives alone, but was extended to fragments of dismembered tribes, and even to the admission of independent nations into the League. It was a leading feature of their policy to subdue adjacent nations by conquest, and having absorbed them by naturalization, to mould them into one common family with themselves. The fruit of this system of policy was their gradual elevation to a universal supremacy, — a supremacy which was spreading so rapidly at the epoch of their discovery as to threaten the subjugation of all the nations east of the Mississippi.

"A regular ceremony of adoption was performed in each case to complete the naturalization. With captives this ceremony was the gauntlet, after which new names were assigned to them; and at the next religious festival their names, together with the tribe and family into which they were respectively adopted, were publicly announced. Upon the return of a war party with captives, if they had lost any of their own number in the expedition, the families to which these belonged were first allowed an opportunity to supply from the captives the places made vacant in their households. Any family could then adopt out of the residue any who chanced to attract their favorable notice, or whom they wished to save. At the time appointed, which was usually three or four days after the return of the band, the women and children of the village arranged themselves in two parallel rows just without the place, each one having a whip with which to lash the captives as they passed between the lines. The male captives, who alone were required to undergo this test of their powers of endurance, were brought out, and each one was shown in turn the house in which he was to take refuge, and which was to be his future home, if he passed successfully through the ordeal. They were then taken to the head of this long avenue of whips, and were compelled, one after another, to run through it for their lives, and for the entertainment of the surrounding throng, exposed at every step, undefended, and with naked backs, to the merciless inflictions of the whip. Those who fell from exhaustion were immediately despatched as unworthy to be saved; but those who emerged in safety from this test of their physical energies were from that moment treated with the utmost affection and kindness.

"Not only so, but he was received into the family into which he was adopted with all the cordiality of affection, and into all the relations of the one whose place he was henceforth to fill. By these means all recollections of his distant kindred were gradually effaced, bound as he was by gratitude to those who had restored a life which was forfeited by the usages of war. If a captive, after adoption, became discontented, which is said to have been seldom the case, he was sometimes restored, with presents, to his nation, that they might know he had lost nothing by his captivity among them."

The ceremony of Adoption by the Improved Order of Red Men is typical of the form of naturalization or Adoption above described. The paleface nation is the great field from which recruits are obtained. After they have been adopted by the Tribe, they are supposed to be bound to the Order by the ties of gratitude, and to become active agents in the administration of its benevolence and charity.

The Hunter's Degree is intended to illustrate the manners and customs of the primitive Red Men governing the chase. The hunters provided sustenance for the tribe. They were skilful, and rarely returned from the hunt without an abundance of game, the result of the chase. In this connection Mr. Morgan says: "Hunting was a passion with the Red Man. He pursued it for the excitement and employment it afforded as well as for subsistence, frequently making long and toilsome expeditions."

By the Warrior's Degree is illustrated the manner of enlistments for war.

Mr. Morgan's description of the usages in the League of the Iroquois is very interesting in this connection. He says:—

"After war had been declared against any nation, either by the congress of sachems at Onondaga, or by an individual nation against a neighboring enemy, the existence of the war was indicated by a tomahawk painted red, ornamented with red feathers and with black wampum, struck in the war-post in each village of the League. Any person was then at liberty to organize a band and make an invasion. This was effected in a summary manner. Dressed in full costume, the war-chief who proposed to solicit volunteers and conduct the expedition went through the village sounding the war-whoop to announce his intentions; after which he went to the war-post, Ga-on-dote, and having struck into it his red tomahawk, he commenced the war-dance. A group gathered around him, and, as their martial ardor was aroused by the dance, they enlisted, one after the other, by joining in its performance. In this manner a company was soon formed; the matrons of the village prepared their subsistence while the dance was performing, and at its close, while they were yet filled with enthusiasm for the enterprise, they immediately left the village, and turned their footsteps towards the country of the enemy. If the movement was simultaneous in several villages, these parties joined each other on their march, but each band continued under the direction of its own war-chief. Their subsistence was usually charred corn, parched a second time, pounded into fine flour, and mixed with maple-sugar, thus reducing it in bulk and lightness to such a degree that the warrior could carry without inconvenience in his bear-skin pocket a sufficient supply for a long and perilous expedition. The band took the war-path in single file, and moved with such rapidity that it was but five days' journey to the country of the Cherokees, upon the southern banks of the Tennessee. At their night encampments they cut upon the trees certain devices to indicate their numbers and destination. On their return they did the same, showing also the number of captives and the number slain. When the returning party reached the outskirts of their village, they sounded the war-whoop to announce their approach, and to summon the people to assemble for their reception. Then leading their captives, they entered the village in a dancing procession, as they had shortly before gone out. After they had reached the war-post in the centre of the place, a wise-man addressed them in a speech of welcome and congratulation; in reply to which a speech was made by one of the band, descriptive of their adventures, after which the war-dance was again employed."

By the Chief's Degree is illustrated the religious forms and ceremonies of the Indians. The Indians believed in a multitude of spirits, good and evil. Over and above these, supreme in power and control, was the Great Spirit, who ruled the world through the agency of the inferior spirits of His own creation, to whom He entrusted the immediate supervision of the various works of nature. Their mythology abounds with beautiful legends, illustrative at once of their superstition and of their unbounded faith in the Great Spirit and the immortality of the soul. Among the Iroquois, at least, reverence for the aged was also one of the precepts of the ancient faith. "It is the will of the Great Spirit that you reverence the aged, even though they be as helpless as infants." The obedience of children, kindness to the orphan, hospitality to all, and a common brotherhood, were among the doctrines held up by their religious instructors. These precepts were taught as the will of the Great Spirit, and obedience to their requirements as acceptable in His sight. "If you tie up the clothes of an orphan child, the Great Spirit will notice it and reward you for it." "To adopt orphans and bring them up in virtuous ways, is pleasing to the Great Spirit." "If a stranger wander about your abode, welcome him to your home, be hospitable towards him, speak to him with kind words, and forget not always to mention the Great Spirit."

In making these quotations from the admirable work of Mr. Morgan, it is difficult to refrain from still further extracts; but in another part of this history, wherein is given an outline of the characteristics of the Indian race, and more especially the treatment, management, and discipline of the League of the Iroquois, we have not hesitated to avail ourselves to the fullest extent of the mine of wealth provided by his research and ability.

By the description thus given of the theory upon which the ritualistic work has been prepared, the reader will be convinced that for originality, beauty, and dramatic effect it is unequalled by the ritualistic work of any fraternal organization. In its exemplification it admits of a high order of dramatic talent, and when properly rendered cannot fail to make a pleasing and lasting impression upon the mind of the paleface adopted.

In the Degree of Pocahontas, of necessity the ideal Indian princess has been exemplified rather than the matter-of-fact, prosaic Indian squaw. The Indian regarded woman as an inferior being. She was for most purposes a beast of burden. It was regarded as beneath the dignity of a warrior to labor, and most of the drudgery of the camp fell to the lot of the women. The legend of Pocahontas and the virtues of her life have been taken as the basis for the ideal ceremony used by the Degree of Pocahontas. Iconoclasts would make us believe that such a being as Pocahontas never existed. One by one the legends of our childhood days are destroyed, and after awhile existence itself will be but a dream. Yet we love to linger over these beautiful traditions, and among them none is sweeter, purer, brighter, and better than that which gives us the history of Pocahontas, the Indian princess. The adventures of Captain Smith, who was one of the colonists that settled at Jamestown, Va., in 1607, are familiar to all. He had intelligence, tact, and indomitable courage, and yet these would not have availed to secure for the colonists a permanent footing "had it not been for the interposing humanity of the Princess Pocahontas, who, at the moment when the uplifted club was about to execute its commission of death, threw herself upon the bound victim, and by the eloquence of her looks, her tears, and her language softened her father's heart, arrested, and turned aside the blow."

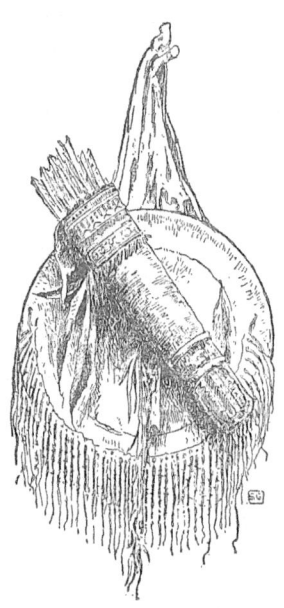

CHAPTER XVI.

NOMENCLATURE OF THE ORDER.

THE paleface adopted into our Order witnesses many things which to him seem strange and startling, until their meaning is explained and more clearly understood as he advances through the various degrees. Not only are the ceremonies original, in everything unlike those of any other organization, but he notices a peculiar nomenclature in the terms used to describe the transactions of the organization. He is a member of a *Tribe*, not a *Lodge;* he attends a *council*, not a *meeting;* time is marked by *suns, seven suns, moons,* and *great suns,* not by *days, weeks, months, years;* he assists in *kindling* and *quenching the council fire,* not in *opening* and *closing the meeting;* he uses *fathoms, feet,* and *inches* of *wampum* to pay his dues, not *dollars, dimes,* and *cents* of *money*. The use of these terms, he soon learns, has a meaning and significance which he desires to know. It is fitting, therefore, that the concluding chapter of our History should give brief attention to this interesting phase of our Order, and what here follows will show that in this, as in all else practicable, the Improved Order of Red Men follows closely its primitive prototypes, and thereby assists in perpetuating what might otherwise sink into oblivion.

We have already shown that, in those earlier societies from which we trace our origin, the personal identity of the members was concealed in the names given to them upon being adopted into the Order. This custom exists among the Red Men of the present time. The adopted name of "Split Log," assumed by Generalissimo Francis Shallus, in the Society of Red Men, is a counterpart of "Sitting Bull," "White Cloud," and other names among the Red Men of the plains familiar in contemporaneous history. Much of the difficulty in identifying the individuals composing the membership of the Society of Red Men results from the fact that almost invariably they are referred to on the Minute Book by the name given to them on the sleep of their adoption. Where these are names of persons admitted after 1822, the Minute Book gives the proper name of the newly admitted brother and the name assigned him at adoption. The same care was not observed in the Muster Rolls that have been preserved, covering the admissions for the period prior to 1821.

The proper names given to Indians were usually taken from animals of various kinds, and even fishes and reptiles, such as Beaver, Otter, Black Fish, Rattlesnake, etc. They had also other descriptive names suggested by personal qualities, and sometimes given from fancy or caprice. As we have said, they did not always preserve the names first given to them, but often assumed a new name after coming to maturity. These names expressed some meritorious act, or remarkable circumstance, in the life of the holder.

So in relation to localities, the name was eminently descriptive. The name they had for the place where Philadelphia now stands, and which was the name taken by Tribe No. 4, organized in that city, was *Kuequenaku*, which means the "Grove of the Long Pine Trees."

To the white men they met, they gave names derived from some remarkable quality which they observed in them, or from some circumstance which strikingly engaged their attention. When told the meaning of the name of William Penn, they translated it into their own language by *Miquon*, which means a feather or quill. The Iroquois called him *Onas*, which, in their idiom, meant the same thing. The first name given by the Indians to the Europeans who landed in Virginia, was *Wapsid Lenape*, meaning "White People." When the Europeans began to commit murders on the Red Men, whom they pierced with swords, they received the name of *Mechanschican*, "Long Knives," to distinguish them from others of the same color. The English settlers in New England were called *Yengees*, in the endeavor to imitate the sound of English. They were also called *Chanquanquock*, "Men of Knives," because of the presents of these instruments given to the natives. But after some of the Indians had been shipped to sea, and when the people of the middle colonies began to murder them, and call on the Iroquois to insult them, and assist in depriving them of their lands, they were called *Schwannack*, which signifies "salt beings," or "bitter beings," but they were very careful not to use that term of contempt and hatred against any white person whom they knew to be amicably disposed towards them, and honest and well-meaning. The Englishman, to distinguish him from the Yengees and the Mechanschican, was called *Saggenash*. Thus, could we understand the proper translation of each Indian word, we would find it an absolute and correct delineation of some peculiarity of action, motion, or deportment, or dress, of those whom it meant to designate or describe. Probably no more expressive illustration of Indian word-painting can be given than in the title by which the great Delaware nation was known, *Lenni Lenape*. Lenape signifies "man, nation, or people." In the name *Lenni Lenape*, the word Lenni means "original," hence *Lenni Lenape*, "Original People!"

"The words squaw, sachem, tomahawk, and wigwam," says Heckewelder, "are corruptions by the English from the words of Delaware stock." *Ochqueu* was the Delaware word for woman; *Sakima*, for chief; *Tamahican*, for hatchet; *Wickwam* (both syllables long as in English *weekwawm*), a house. *Calumet*, according to the same authority, is not an Indian word. The Delaware for tobacco pipe is *Poakan*, pronounced as two syllables. *Wampum* is an Iroquois word, and means marine shell. *Papoose* was used by the Indians of New England to designate a child.

The Indians generally, but their chiefs more particularly, had many figurative expressions, understood when one nation spoke to another, but needing explanation when an Indian spoke to the white people. For the purpose of a proper understanding, as we have already explained, the subject was "talked into" a wampum belt which, therefore, became a necessary adjunct to the communication.

The language of the Indian was eminently mystical. Each sentence, and sometimes each expression, was a word-picture. A runner sent with a message of importance of a private nature, was told to take it "under ground," that expression being made to indicate that no one, except the person for whom it was intended, should know of it. No chief paid attention to a mere report, even though it bore the evidence of truth. Not having come to him *officially*, he considered that he had not heard of it, and that it was to him as the "song of a bird which had flown by." When he was officially informed, through the wampum belt sent by some distant chief or leading man of the nation, whose position entitled him to credit, he then declared "I have heard it," and acted accordingly.

The expression in the preceding sentence recalls to our memory how often in childhood's days we wondered how our parents could have obtained knowledge of matters which we thought none knew but ourselves. The answer to our query as to the source of the information usually was, "I heard a bird sing!"

The Indian was fond of metaphor, and the samples of his eloquence which have come down to us abound in metaphorical expressions. We have already referred to that beautiful metaphor used to designate the close of the Revolutionary War, "The Great Spirit spoke and the whirlwind was still." Heckewelder, in his "Indian Nations," published at the beginning of the present century, gives many interesting examples from which we extract the following:—

"Two black clouds are drawing towards each other." — Two powerful foes are marching against each other.

"To bury the hatchet." — To make or conclude a peace.

"You have spoken with your lips, not from the heart." — You do not intend to do as you say.

"You keep me in the dark." — You wish to deceive me.

"Singing birds." — Tale-bearers.

"Don't listen to the singing of the birds." — Don't believe what stragglers tell you.

"What bird was it that sung that song?" — Who was it that told that lie?

"To kindle a council fire at such a place." — To appoint a place where national business is to be transacted or the seat of government established.

"To remove the council fire to another place." — To establish another place for the seat of government.

"The council fire has been extinguished." — Blood has been shed by the enemy at the seat of government which has put the fire out.

"Never suffer grass to grow on this warpath." — Be at perpetual war with the nation; this path leads to it.

"The path to that nation is again open." — We are again on friendly terms.

"I hear sighing and sobbing in yonder direction," indicates that a chief of a neighboring nation has died.

"I wipe the tears from your eyes, cleanse your ears, and place your aching heart which bears you down to one side, in its proper position." — Consolation in time of great sorrow, as when condoling with a nation on the death of a chief.

"I lift you up from this place and set you down again at my dwelling place." — I invite you to arise hence and come and live where I live.

"We have concluded a peace which shall last as long as the sun shall shine and the river flows with water." — The peace concluded is to continue as long as the world stands or to the end of time.

"To bury deep in the earth." — To consign to oblivion an injury done.

We are told that the Red Men divided the year into 13 periods, or moons, corresponding to the old Persian year, and that this was the greatest astronomical accuracy attained by the primitive Red Men. The Indian did not reckon as we do, by days, but by nights. Upon departing on a journey, he would say, "I will return home in so many nights." Sometimes, pointing to the heavens, he would say, "You will see me when the sun stands there," and unless prevented by something absolutely beyond his control, he invariably returned at the time set.

The Leni Lenape divided their year into four parts like ours, spring, summer, autumn, and winter. The different nations had different names for the moons, generally suited to the climate under which they respectively lived. The Lenape, when they owned the country bordering on the Atlantic, called the month of March the *Shad* moon, because the fish began to pass from the sea into the fresh-water rivers to lay its spawn at that time. But there being no fish in the country to which they afterwards removed, they changed the name of the month and called it the *Running sap*, or the *Sugar-making* moon, because at that time the sap of the maple tree, from which sugar is made, begins to run. December was called the *Hunting* moon, it being the time when the stags had all dropped their antlers or horns.

The Calendar published in Chapter XIII shows how the Order follows this custom, and the names assigned to the various months in the chronology of the Improved Order of Red Men. The careful and accurate member of the Order, desiring to preserve the individuality and originality of our literature, will always use the terms as given in the Calendar, all of which have a meaning and significance. Nor will he pervert significant words and expressions by using them improperly, or by substituting other words with an application entirely foreign to the use to which they are put. For instance, how often do some brothers say, "Our Tribe *scalped* several palefaces at its last council!" The primitive Red Man *scalped* an *enemy*, not a *friend*. Again, with proper care in acquiring the terms used in the Calendar, it is just as convenient and far more appropriate to say, "Our Tribe kindled its council fire on the sleep of the 17th of this moon," as to say (within the Order and at a council), "Our Lodge held a meeting on the 17th of this month!" The extracts we have given from the Minute Book of 1822–1827, and the references to the earlier Tammany Societies, show how careful our predecessors were in the proper use of these terms. Let us emulate them in accuracy in the proper use of the nomenclature of our Order.

Our rivers, mountains, lakes, and towns bear to all coming time, indelibly impressed upon them by their titles, the beautiful nomenclature of the primitive Red Man. Nothing escaped his keen vision and watchful observation. The Indian who in the solitude of the forest could identify the unseen animal, by a difference in footfall imperceptible to the untrained ear of the white man, could not fail to be duly impressed with the beauty and grandeur of the mighty works of nature by which he was surrounded. He gave them names which signified his reverence or fear, his pleasure or admiration, or which gave his idea of some prominent peculiarity for which the object named was notable. Wherever the hidden meaning of these names has been revealed, their remarkable aptness has been manifest, as the few examples mentioned in this chapter and history prove. They indicate a quality of mind that justifies an appreciation of the Indian (at least of former days) far above the plane usually accorded him in modern times. We should judge him as he *was*, not as he *is*. He *was* what he made himself, guided only by the light, as he saw it, that came from the Great Spirit. He *is* the result of three centuries of cruel wrong, treachery, and oppression which have decimated and degraded his race, but have been unable to tame or conquer his peculiarities and characteristics.

Let not the paleface arrogate to himself too much of credit for his superiority. He is but the evolution of the condition of barbarism from which he emerged, or the simian ancestry from which he ascended. Yet, with all his learning and boasted civilization, he has been unable to conceive a more sublime or beautiful image of the Divine Power than that reverently acknowledged and worshipped by the Indian as the Great Spirit.

> "We bow to Heaven's recorded laws,
> He turned to nature for a creed."

In the solitude of the forest, in the majesty of the mighty mountain ranges, and in the great lakes and rivers of our land, he saw evidence of the power of that Great Spirit, and the imagery of his spoken language translated the conception of his mind concerning the mysterious forces by which he was surrounded. The rivers and great waters of the deep, utilized by the palefaces for bearing upon their bosoms the burdens of men, were to him evidences of that mysterious power which spoke in the thunder and flashed in the lightning, and whose good-will he sought to gain by the council and dance that preceded every great undertaking. The vast forests, beneath whose protecting branches he found shelter from the elements, by the animal life which they contained, gave him sustenance for himself and his tribe. There was a sweet and rhythmic beauty in many of the names and terms he used, some of which have been sung in song and told in story until they have become household words with the people of the world. Longfellow has immortalized many of them in his beautiful poem of Hiawatha and the love story of Minnehaha. We acknowledge their aptness, their beauty, and their appropriateness by retaining them. But they expressed to the Indian a meaning and a significance impossible with us, and they were a part of the homage always rendered by him to the Great Spirit whose power they realized in the glory of the night, the foliage of the forest, and the splendor of the noon-day sun!

Throughout this History prominence has been given constantly to the thought that our Order is founded on the customs of the Aborigines of the American continent. To those who love the Order best, not the least of its attractions, not the least of the reasons why it should appeal to the sentiment and support of palefaces and its members, is that feature which preserves with historical accuracy the nomenclature and peculiarities of the Indian race. This chapter has shown something of that nomenclature, and other chapters have recorded some of those peculiarities.

The value of the ceremonies of our Order, therefore, is their historical accuracy. They seek not merely to imitate, but to preserve. When the time comes that the Indian race is extinct, our Order will occupy a place original and unique, growing more interesting as years pass on, and becoming at once the interpreter of Indian customs and the repository of Indian traditions.

Could a higher destiny await any organization? Could a higher ambition inspire its members, than to emulate the virtues, preserve the customs, and transmit to posterity the history of an extinct race? Such is our destiny. Let such be our ambition. That the destiny may be fulfilled and the ambition realized, is the sincere wish and belief of the compilers, publishers, and editor of this History of the Improved Order of Red Men, dedicated to the dissemination of the principles of Freedom, Friendship, and Charity throughout the Order to all its worthy members!

INDEX.

A.

Act of Incorporation, G. C. U. S., 323, 504, 505.
Adams, Samuel, 155.
Additional Contributors, 3.
Advent of the Pilgrims, 24.
Aged and Infirm Members, Report of Committee on, 382-384.
Alabama, 342, 345, 347, 353, 359, 394, 395, 404, 406, 407, 439.
AMERICAN INDIANS:
Description of, 25: wigwam of, 26; Medicine Man, 27; burial of dead, *ib.*; reverence for the aged, 28 ; division of time, *ib.*; belief in the Great Spirit, 29; marriage customs, 30; government of, *ib.*, 31, 32; League of the Iroquois, *ib.*, 33-37; laws of marriage, 38; Constitution of Sachems, 39; raising up of rulers, 40; powers of Sachems, 41; plan of succession and ceremonies, *ib.*, 42, 43; belief, 44-46; mythology, *ib.*; tobacco and its virtues, 47; their conception of heaven, 48; state after death, 49; *ib.*, 50; ceremonies of worship, 51; thanksgivings and prayers, *ib.*, 52, 53; dances of, 54-56; polygamy forbidden, 58; hospitality of, 59, 60; "New Religion" of, 62-81; Redjacket's immortal speeches, *ib.*-87; Red-jacket and William Penn, 86; Farmer's Brother before the Council of Genesee, 87, 88; Corn Planter to President Washington, 89, 90; Black Thunder and the American Commissioners, 91-93; Black Hawk's Lament, *ib.*-95; Captain Pipe to the British Commander at Detroit, 95-97; Logan's appeal, *ib.*, 98; anecdotes of, *ib.*-114; records of, *ib.*-119; story of Cunning Fox, the Huron Chief who visited the Delawares, 120-124; enlistment for the war-path and Aboriginal costume, 125-132; exploits of a Mandan Chief, *ib.* 132-138; legends and concluding *résumé* of Indian character, 140-148.
AMERICAN REVOLUTION:
Events leading up to, 150-172: Tammany Society's work, 172-174.
Ancestors, Worship of, 52, 53.
Ancient Red Men, 277, 302.
Arizona, 372, 447.
Arkansas, 388, 389, 393, 447.

B.

Bates, Frank A., 114.
Beneficial Degree Council, 317, 481, 523.
BENEFITS:
As regards appeals, 477; ordinary, 480, 481.
BIOGRAPHIES:
Of Past Great Incohonees, 449-474.
Birthday of Washington, 228.
Black Hawk's Lament, 93-95.
Burial of Dead, 27, 28, 47, 48, 68, 71.

C.

California, 293, 319, 339, 356, 367, 404, 436.
California Indian Relics, 380.
CARDS:
Withdrawal, 481, 482; Travelling, 483, 575.
Celebration of St. Tammany Day in 1783, 177, 178.
Charters, 483-486, 517.
Charleston, Tribe of, 207, 208.
Charter Members, 248, 250.
CHIEFS:
Of the Mountain, 288; titles changed, 338; Great Council, Tribe, Degree Council, Degree of Pocahontas, Great Incohonee, and State Great Council, 486-492; raising up, 520; terms of, 531-532; creation of, 538.
Chieftains' League, 22, 284, 394, 395, 404, 408, 416, 595-604.
Colorado, 369, 372, 382, 387-390, 447.
Connecticut, 169, 311, 382, 392, 395, 404, 435.
Constitution and By-laws, G. C. U. S., 281, 282, 309, 322, 360, 387, 389, 415, 421, 475, 539-587.
Contents, Table of, 7, 8.
Continental Uniform proposed, 366, 380.
Contributors, Additional, 3.
Council Brand, 495.
Council Brand, The, publication commenced, 357.

D.

DANCES:
War, 54; Feather, 55; For the Dead, *ib.*; collection of, *ib.*, 56.
Danish, Translation of Ritual, 389.
Daughters of Powhatan, 319, 320.
Declaration of Independence, 161.

620   INDEX.

Dedication of Wigwams, 294.
DEGREES:
Uniformed, 391, 392; Digest regulations, 495-497; theory of their constitution, and the lessons taught, 605-610.
Delaware, 169, 196, 202, 209, 286, 287, 297, 299, 304, 305, 312, 314, 318, 321, 337, 355, 428.
Demonstration, first public, 258.
DEPUTIES:
Great Sachems, Great Incohonees, 497, 498.
Digest, 347, 357, 408, 418, 421, 475-538.
Diploma, Members, 408, 409, 413, 415, 499.
District of Columbia, 260, 261, 282, 283, 289, 297, 299, 303, 305, 314, 318, 321, 337, 427.

E.

Early Initiation Ceremonies, 204-206.
Editors, List of, 1, 3.
Elections, 499-501.
Errata, 538.
Evil, The Abode of, 48, 75, 76, 78.
Exemplification of the Work, 413.

F.

Fac Simile of "General Orders," 234.
First Organization, 19, 247.
Five Nations, The, 24, 32, 35.
Flag, Official, 360, 361, 406, 529, 530.
Florida, 369, 372, 382, 387-389, 446.
Funeral Ceremony, 294.

G.

Georgia, 169, 353, 359, 365, 367, 369, 372, 377, 394, 395, 418, 438.
General Laws for Grand Councils, 475.
Gorham, Morris H., 17, 199.
Grand Sun of the Discovery, 320, 322.
Great Britain and the United States, Peace of, 34, 87.
GREAT COUNCIL OF THE UNITED STATES:
Date of organization and introduction to, 17, 18, 20, 22, 197, 199, 203, 210, 258, 262, 263, 269; Council fire kindled, 1847, at Baltimore, 281; Council fire kindled, 1848, at Washington, 285; Council fire kindled, 1849, at Baltimore, 287; Council fire kindled, 1850, 289; Special Council fire, 294; Council fire kindled, 1851, 295; Council fire kindled, 1852, 297; Council fire kindled, 1853, 299; Council fire kindled, 1854, 303; Council fire kindled, 1855, 305; Council fire kindled, 1856, 307; Council fire kindled, 1857, 309; Council fire kindled, 1858, 310; Council fire kindled, 1859, 312; Council fire kindled, 1860, 314; Council fire kindled, 1861, 315; Council fire *not* kindled, 1862, 317; Council fire kindled, 1863, 318; Council fire kindled, 1864, at Philadelphia, 319; Council fire kindled, 1865, at Baltimore, 321; Council fire kindled, 1866, 323; Council fire kindled, 1867, at Philadelphia, 337; Council fire kindled, 1868, at Cincinnati, 338; Council fire kindled, 1869, at St. Louis, 342; Council fire kindled, 1870, at Baltimore, 344; Council fire kindled, 1871, at Philadelphia, 347; Council fire kindled, 1872, at Nashville, 350; Council fire kindled, 1873, at Wilmington, 353; Council fire kindled, 1874, at Indianapolis, 355; Council fire kindled, 1875, at Richmond, 359; Council fire kindled, 1876, at Philadelphia, 362; Council fire kindled, 1877, at Columbus, 364; Council fire kindled, 1878, at Baltimore, 366; Council fire kindled, 1879, at New York, 369; Council fire kindled, 1880, at Boston, 372; Council fire kindled, 1881, at Annapolis, 378; Council fire kindled, 1882, at Easton, 381; Council fire kindled, 1883, at Atlantic City, 385; Council fire kindled, 1884, at Springfield, 387; Council fire kindled, 1885, at Elmira, 390; Council fire kindled, 1886, at Detroit, 392; Council fire kindled, 1887, at Wilmington, 394; Council fire kindled, 1888, at Chicago, 403; Council fire kindled, 1889, at Baltimore, 406; Council fire kindled, 1890, at Boston, 409; Council fire kindled, 1891, at Cleveland, 413; Council fire kindled, 1892, at Atlanta, 419.
Great Spirit, The, 29, 30, 44, 46-48, 62, *ib.*-81; *ib.*-84; 142, 144.

H.

Hascall, Lee Claflin, Proposal for an Official History, 405, 412, 415.
Hawaiian Islands, 364, 446.
Heaven, Indian conception of, 47, 48, 70.
HISTORY:
Theory of, 5; first proposed, 301, 302; report of committees of, 325-336, 403-420.
Homes proposed, 390, 394, 417, 418.
Horton, R. G., 166.

I.

Incohonees, Past Great, 1, 19, 211, 282, 407, 449-474.
Illinois, 293, 342, 353, 359, 363, 365, 367, 377, 396, 404, 406, 407, 432.
Iroquois, League of, 12, 24, 25, 32-40, 42, 43, 53, 57, 97, 606-610.
Independent Order of Red Men, 292-294.
Indiana, 309, 337, 342, 363, 366, 377, 404, 432.
INDIAN:
Pen picture of, 25; government of, 30, 31, 39-43; wit, 98; honor, *ib.*; recklessness, *ib.*; justice (1), 99; magnanimity, *ib.*; deception, 100; shrewdness, *ib.*; equality, 102; matrimony, *ib.*; toleration, *ib.*; justice (2) 103; preaching *vs.* practice, *ib.*; character contrasted, 104; torture, *ib.*; suffering, 105; notions of the whites, *ib.*; success among, 106; curiosity, 107; rules of conversation, *ib.*; loss of confidence, *ib.*; self-esteem, 108; signal barbarity, 108, 109; anecdotes, *ib.*, 110; captivity of

INDEX. 621

Hannah Duston, 111-114; records, *ib.*-139; legends, 140-148.
Indian Territory, 414, 448.
IMPROVED ORDER OF RED MEN:
Organization at Baltimore, 247; calendar adopted, 251, 252; charter from Legislature of Maryland, 253; public demonstration, 258; charter for Great Council of the District of Columbia, 260, 261, 262; organization of the Great Council of the United States, 263; charter of Logan Tribe, No. 1, 265, 266; loss of records, and discussion of dates of charters of Nos. 1, 2, and 3, 268; another version, 270-280.
Iowa, 310, 350, 385, 388, 389, 390, 408, 433.
Introduction, 11-15.

J.

Jones, William T. (first Great Sachem), 268, 274, 278.
Jubilee Celebration, 416-418.

K.

Kansas, 350, 362, 365, 385, 388, 389, 390, 442.
"Keepers of the Faith," 50, 67, 68, 72, 73.
Kentucky, 299, 300, 305, 312, 314, 318, 321, 337, 393, 406, 430.
King Philip of the Wampanoags, 25.

L.

Lafayette, General, visit of, 235-241.
Latham, Hugh, 199, 271, 286, 287, 295, 374, 381, 451.
LEGISLATION:
Constitutions, 539-587.
Logan Tribe, No. 1, charter of, 265, 266.
Louisiana, 181, 293, 307, 311, 321, 337, 342, 345, 347, 360, 369, 382, 426.

M.

Maine, 382, 404, 406, 410, 446.
Mandan Chief, Robe of, 130.
MANITTO:
The Great, 123; Ode to, 126.
Mark, 507, 508.
Marley, Richard, 19, 211, 228, 269, 271, 272, 295, 316, 342, 459.
Marriage customs, the, 30, 57, 58, 102.
Maryland, 20, 149, 156, 157, 169, 183, 247, 253, 260, 263, 264, 265, 267, 276, 278, 286, 287, 289, 290, 293, 297, 299, 303, 305, 312, 314, 318, 321, 337, 341, 404.
Massachusetts, 24, 31, 154, 156, 157, 169, 293, 350, 353, 355, 375, 392, 395, 404, 409, 413, 443.
Mather, Dr. Cotton, Account of the Captivity of Hannah Duston, 111-114.
Medicine Man, 27, 74, 141.
MEMBERSHIP:
Resident, 508; non-resident, 510; rejections, renunciation, and resignation, 524; reinstatement, 525; stricken from roll and suspensions, 530; twigging, vacancies, 536; visitation, voting, 537; withdrawals and applications, 538; errata, 538.
Metamora Tribe, No. 2, 266.
Michigan, 339, 342, 350, 438.
Minute Book, Philadelphia Society, 208, 209, 212, 214, 215, 216-246.
Mississippi, 345, 347, 350, 355, 359, 362, 425.
Minnesota, 359, 396, 445.
Missouri, 293, 307, 311, 314, 324, 337, 434.
Mitchell, Dr. Samuel L., 188.
Mock Adoption, 410, 412.
"Mohicans" (Mohegans), Last of, 118-139.
Montana, 390, 448.
Mothers, Land Titles descend in, 38.
Mythology, 44, 45, 46, 50.
Muirhead, William, 19, 211, 273.

N.

Names of Officers, 204, 206, 260, 282, 286, 288, 291, 296, 298, 302, 305, 306-307, 308, 310, 311, 313, 315, 317, 318-319, 320, 322, 337, 340, 345, 351, 357, 363-364, 369, 374, 384, 389, 393, 405, 412, 422.
Nebraska, 353, 359, 363, 366, 382, 408, 414, 443.
New Hampshire, 169, 363, 379, 382, 404, 445.
New Jersey, 169, 293, 295, 298, 299, 304, 312, 314, 318, 321, 337, 377, 392, 395, 429.
New Mexico, 448.
New Religion, The, by Ga-ne-o-di-yo, or Handsome Lake, the Seneca Sachem, 62-81.
Nevada, 345, 347, 350, 353, 404, 440.
New York, 20, 156, 166, 169, 174, 182, 196, 209, 211, 287, 290, 291, 293, 296, 300, 304, 305, 311, 347, 350, 377, 392, 404, 428.
NOMENCLATURE:
Of money, 252; of the Order, 611-618.
North American Indians ineligible to Membership, 349.
North Carolina, 169, 311, 314, 353, 355, 359, 385, 406, 410, 419, 430.

O.

Objects of the Order, 14.
Office for Great Chief of Records, 301.
Official Totem (illustrated), 348.
Ohio, 293, 297, 298, 299, 304, 305, 312, 314, 318, 321, 337, 377, 404, 406, 430.
ORDER OF RED MEN:
Perpetuates the original, 11; Hodenosaunee, 12; "Freedom, Friendship, and Charity," 13; Improved Order of, 19; Ho-de-no-sau-nee, 35.
Oregon, 345, 353, 404, 406, 419, 421, 439.
Origin of Motto, 13, 169, 170.

P.

Passwords, 513, 514.
PAST OFFICERS:
Sachems, 514; Great Sachems, 515; Great Representatives, 516; vacancies, 536.

Past Great Incohonees, Photographs of, 315, 316.
PATRIOTIC SOCIETIES:
Prefatory definition, 6; date of organization, 17, 18; Saint Tammany, 18; the New Religion, 62-81; origin of the Improved Order of Red Men, 149, 150; various English acts, like Stamp Act, etc., 151, 152; St. Tamina Society and Sons of Liberty, 153-162; Society of the Cincinnati, *ib.*-165; R. G. Horton's account of the formation of the Tammany Society of New York, 166-170; Tammany Society and contemporaneous history, *ib.*-184; origin of the St. Tamina Society, 185-187; Oldest Inhabitants' Association and certificate, 188; Dr. Samuel L. Mitchell's paper on Tammany's Patron Saint, *ib.*-194; variations in orthography, 195; the name, " Red Men " appears, 196, 197; connecting link between the St. Tamina Society of 1771, and the Improved Order of Red Men of 1834, 198.
Penalties of Infractions of Indian Rules, 31, 60.
Pennsylvania, 156, 169, 175, 177, 178, 196, 201, 210, 287, 288, 290, 291, 293, 297, 299, 304, 305, 312, 314, 318, 321, 337, 377, 392, 395, 404, 424.
Peter, G. A. (founder), 268, 280, 301, 320, 454.
Picture Writings (illustrated), 115, 116, 117, 119, 127, 128, 129, 130, 140.
POCAHONTAS:
Tribe, No. 3, 267; degree of, 22, 298, 303, 356, 368, 391, 394, 395, 396, 404, 406, 408, 410, 414, 421, 496-497, 523-524, 581-587; History of, 588-594.
Preamble, Red Men's Society of Pennsylvania, 201.
Preface, 5, 6, 7.
Proxy Representation, 289.

R.

Rainmakers, The, 140, 141.
Red-jacket, 62, 81-87.
REGALIA:
G. C. U. S., 286; full specifications of, 294, 295; distinctive, 341, 521-524.
Red Men, Primitive, 23-148.
Requiem, Indian Mother's, 48.
Representation, 525-527.
Returns, Tax and Revenue, 527-529.
REVISED DIGEST:
Constitution G. C. U. S., 475; by-laws G. C. U. S., *ib.*; general laws for Great Councils, *ib.*; appeals, *ib.*; appeals as regards benefits, 477; duties of Commissioner, 478; appropriations, *ib.*; arrears, 479; assessments, *ib.*; application for aid, *ib.*; authority, *ib.*; Beneficial Degree Councils, 481; cards, withdrawal, 481-483; travelling, *ib.*; ceremonies, 483; certified receipts, *ib.*; charters, *ib.*-486; charges (see trials), 486; Chiefs (of Great Council), (of Tribe), (of a Degree Council), (of Degree of Pocahontas), (eligibility),

(duties of), *ib.*-492; committees, *ib.*-493; consolidation, *ib.*; costumes, 494; Councils, *ib.*; Council Brand, 495; dating, *ib.*; Degrees, *ib.*-497; Deputy Great Sachems, and Deputy Great Incohonees, *ib.*; dismissal certificates, 498-499; diplomas, *ib.*; dues, *ib.*; elections, *ib.*-501; extinct Tribes, *ib.*; forms, *ib.*; fees, *ib.*; funds, 502; State Great Councils (how composed), *ib.*, 503; honors, *ib.*, 504; Act of incorporation, *ib.*, 505; Indian relics, *ib.*; insurance, *ib.*; laws, *ib.*-507; lotteries or gift enterprises, *ib.*; Mark, *ib.*; membership, 508-510; nonresidents, *ib.*; Parliamentary law, *ib.*-511; rules of order, *ib.*-513; past chiefs, 514-516; permanent fund, *ib.*; penalties, *ib.*; forfeiture of charters, 517; per diem and mileage, *ib.*, 518; phraseology (calendar), *ib.*; printing of records and supplies, 519; quorum, *ib.*; Raising of chiefs, 520; records, *ib.*; regalia, 521-524; rejections, renunciation, and resignation, reinstatement, *ib.*, 525; representation, *ib.*-527; returns, tax and revenue, *ib.*-529; stricken from the roll, and suspensions, 530; Tammany Day, 531: terms of chiefs, *ib.*; trials, 532-535; Tribes, *ib.*; twigging, 536; vacancies, *ib.*; visitation, 537; voting, *ib.*; withdrawals and errata, 538.
Rhode Island, 169, 293, 350, 375, 392, 393, 395, 404, 405, 441.

S.

Skinner, John S., 185, 187.
Shallus, Francis, 213, 215.
Six Nations, 32, 91.
SOCIETY:
Of the Cincinnati, 162, 163, 165; of Red Men, second epoch in history of, 199; the Fort Mifflin organization, *ib.*, 200; Preamble of the Red Men's Society of Pennsylvania, 201; first officers, 204; ceremonies of initiation, *ib.*-206; the Tribe at Charleston, S.C., 207, 208; early Minute Books, *ib.*-210; ancient Tribes of Reading, Pa., Albany, N.Y., Baltimore, Md., *ib.*, 211; records lost, 213, 214; list of white men adopted, 216; documentary evidence, 217-246.
Songs, the Red Men's " Free and Easy," 221, 222, 223, 224, 229; Pocahontas, 593-594.
Sons of Liberty, 18, 20, 118, 153, 154, 155, 156, 157, 158, 159, 160, 161, 162, 177, 184, 196.
South Carolina, 160, 169, 355, 388, 389, 394, 395, 412, 414, 444.
St. Tamina Day, 20, 177, 201, 531.
SPEECHES:
Of Handsome Lake, 62-81; of Red-jacket, *ib.*-87; of Ho-na-ya-wus, or Farmer's Brother, *ib.*-88; Corn Planter, 89-91; Black Thunder, *ib.*-93; Black Hawk's Lament, *ib.*-95; Captain Pipe, *ib.*-97; Logan, the Mingo Chief, *ib.*-98; Last of the Mohicans (Mohegans), 118-139.

INDEX.   623

STATE GREAT COUNCILS:
History of, and statistics, 423-448; how composed, 502, 503.
Statistics, 287, 289, 292, 297, 299, 301, 305, 307, 309, 311-312, 313-314, 315, 317, 319, 321, 322, 337, 338, 341-342, 344, 347, 348, 351, 354, 356, 363, 365, 367, 370, 373, 376, 379-380, 382, 386, 388, 390-391, 393, 395-396, 404, 408, 411, 414-415, 420, 423-448.

SUBJECT:
Outline of, 17; the evidence from Tradition, 18; Epochs, 19-22.

T.

Table of Contents, 7, 8.

TAMMANY:
Society of, 18, 20; Columbian Order, 162; account of, 166-170; Colonel Willet's report, *ib.*-174; Odes, 178, 180; Legend of Patron Saint, 188-194; various spellings, 195; various societies, 196; connecting links with the Improved Order of Red Men, 198.

Tennessee, 339, 342, 357, 437.
Texas, 339, 342, 360, 372, 385, 390, 436.
Thanksgivings, Indian Pæans, 51, 52, 53.
Thanks, Return of, 7.
The Calumet, First Paper published in Interest of the Order, 339-340, 357.
Theory of Government. 35-41.
Time, Indian Division of, 28, 49, 50, 251, 252, 495, 518.
Title Page, 1.
Toronto, Dominion of Canada, 395, 396, 448.
Totems of the North American Indians, 119.
Traits of Indian Character, 58-62, 140-148.
Trails, 532-535, 562-569.

U.

UNIFORM:
Degree, proposed and adopted, 391, 392; Chieftains' League, 595-604.

UNION:
Improved and Independent Orders, 346, 354, 356, 367, 370, 386.

Utah, 350, 355, 382, 419, 441.

V.

VARIOUS EARLY COUNCILS:
At Fort Mifflin, 18, 196, 199, 200, 201, 202, 203; at Charleston, 207; at New York, 208; Great Council of Pennsylvania, 210; at Philadelphia, 214, 215, 226; adjourned for social purposes, 220; at Philadelphia, 221-246.

Vermont, 392, 395, 448.
Veteran's Badge, 419, 421.
Virginia, 169, 283, 286, 289, 297, 299, 304, 305, 312, 314, 321, 337, 393, 404, 425.

W.

Wampum Belt, The, 384.
Washington, George, 77, 89, 108, 163, 164, 171, 179, 202.
Washington Monument, 356.
Washington (State of), 351, 355, 404, 406, 409, 414, 419, 442.
West Virginia, 293, 318, 321, 342, 343, 345, 404, 435.
Wigwam, Description of, 26, 27.
Wisconsin, 347, 350, 359, 390, 396, 440.
Work of the Order, Revision of, 283, 284, 286, 294, 295, 296, 298, 305, 306, 308, 309, 310, 311, 313, 314, 318, 322, 324, 341, 349, 352, 354, 358, 364, 368, 381, 421, 529, 605-610.
Wyoming, 419, 448.

www.ingramcontent.com/pod-product-compliance
Lightning Source LLC
Chambersburg PA
CBHW070904300426
44113CB00008B/932